GLOBAL MARKETING STRATEGIES

Sixth Edition

GLOBAL MARKETING STRATEGIES

Sixth Edition

Jean-Pierre Jeannet

F. W. Olin Distinguished Professor of Global Business
Babson College, Wellesley, Massachusetts

Professor of Global Marketing and Strategy
International Institute for Management Development (IMD)
Lausanne, Switzerland

H. David Hennessey

Associate Professor of Marketing and International Business
Babson College, Wellesley, Massachusetts

Associate, Ashridge Management College
Berkhamsted, United Kingdom

Houghton Mifflin Company   **Boston**   **New York**

V.P., Editor-in-Chief: George T. Hoffman
Technology Manager/Development Editor: Damaris Curran
Project Editor: Cecilia Molinari
Editorial Assistant: Celeste Ng
Senior Production/Design Coordinator: Jennifer Meyer Dare
Senior Manufacturing Coordinator: Priscilla Bailey
Senior Marketing Manager: Steve Mikels

Cover image: Jun Yamashita/Photonica

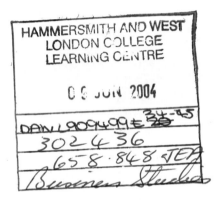
Printed in the U.S.A.

Library of Congress Control Number: 2002109489

ISBN: 0–618–310592

23456789-QUT-07 06 05 04 03

302 436

Brief Contents

Contents

Preface

As the sixth edition of *Global Marketing Strategies* goes to press, we face a new environment where the world of global business has undergone substantial changes. Since our last edition, many of the factors that drove globalization have receded. We have witnessed the rapid decline of Internet-based businesses, a substantial decline in the value of stock market-based assets, and signs that several emerging economies, such as Argentina and Brazil, are struggling with unlimited globalization. In addition, we have also experienced the tragic events of September 11, 2001, which have changed the political situation in many parts of the world. Combined with continued opposition to globalization forces by activists, this might make one believe that the forces of globalization are subject to challenge, if not in partial retreat.

However, for those observers who have remained close to business, it is apparent that the practice of globalization itself remains on a growth path, and that more and more companies, regardless of nationality, industry, or size, are adopting the principles of global marketing. We are thus living in a world where we can observe opposition to the impact of globalization on national economies, while at the same time the practice of global marketing finds an increasing number of adherents. This conflicting development is driven by the fact that globalization as an economic or political force is part of the public discourse, while global marketing is driven by underlying economic forces and imperatives that have not waned despite the dramatic events that have taken place over the past three years. We can therefore affirm our statement from the previous edition's preface that global marketing has become the norm and, as practiced by countless companies and managers all over the world, is here to stay regardless of setbacks to globalization on the geopolitical landscape.

As we look ahead, we are likely to see more challenges to the impact of globalization on the world and national economies, particularly in areas where the benefits to individuals and countries may not be apparent. Because the practice of global marketing is becoming ever more prevalent and sophisticated, this new edition strengthens several areas of the text that needed improvement, and reflects changes and new concepts in the field. We hope this will provide students and executives alike with the most modern version of global marketing as practiced by leading firms in all parts of the world.

MAJOR FEATURES RETAINED

Global Marketing Strategies continues to target the manager and student with a global marketing vision, regardless of nationality, industry, or location. We believe that success in global marketing today is not only a function of broad cultural understanding, but also modern global strategic thinking, which we refer to as a global mindset. As in previous editions, we look at the global marketing task through the eyes of the marketing manager and we maintain our strategic focus throughout this sixth edition. Structurally, we have maintained the same chapter sequence as in the previous edition, with the exception of the fifth edition's Chapter 18, which has been incorporated into Chapter 10. We have retained our emphasis on the practical aspects of global marketing by including numerous current examples from well-known companies in Europe, Asia, and the Americas. Finally, we continue to offer full-length cases in a separate soft-cover book that allow students and executives to explore global marketing issues in depth.

MAJOR CHANGES IN THE SIXTH EDITION

We have updated the text material in the sixth edition by using examples from the late 1990s and early 2000s, with a particular concentration on the years 2000 to 2002. Since our final completion of most revisions was in late summer 2002, most chapters have many sources dated in 2002, which makes the text more up-to-date than in the past.

Philosophically, we have moved more strongly in the direction of global marketing, having adopted a global mindset to the extent possible throughout the text. This is sometimes an issue of language only, but is often reflected in material and content. Some of the chapter headings have also been adjusted accordingly.

Structurally, the text has undergone some changes. The text design has been revised and enhanced. All chapters have been updated, and some have undergone substantial changes as detailed below. By moving all footnotes to the end of each chapter, we hope to reduce text clutter and add to the readability of the text. Wherever possible, we have also updated the suggested readings listed at the end of each chapter through the inclusion of new materials not previously available. Partly because of the prevalence of global marketing, the chapter on "Export and Trade Process" (Chapter 18 in previous editions) has been eliminated as a separate chapter. Parts of this chapter were incorporated in Chapter 10, "Pricing for Global Markets."

Chapter 1, "Introduction to Global Marketing," has been extensively updated with new, more current examples. Structurally, the chapter remains largely unchanged.

Part I, "Understanding the Global Marketing Environment," has not been structurally changed, but has been updated to reflect the realities of groups like the EU, NAFTA, ASEAN, and the World Trade Organization. Chapter 2, "The Global Economy," has been updated to include the latest available statistics on world trade and growth rates. The chapter also includes recent examples of the impact of the events surrounding September 11, 2001 and the global discussion about imposed steel tariffs, which were challenged by both the EU and the WTO. Chapter 3, "Cultural and Social Forces," was updated to include new statistics and additional insights on dealing with Hindu and Moslem cultures in the context of global business. Chapter 4,

"Political and Legal Forces," has been updated to show how countries such as China are using product standards to protect themselves from poor quality imports. The chapter also explains how some firms are preparing to deal with kidnappings of executives. The latest political risk statistics are included in this chapter.

Part II, "Analyzing Global Marketing Opportunities," includes a large volume of updated information. Chapter 5, "Global Markets and Buyers," includes the recent revisions to the regional trade groups as well as a review of these groups' importance relative to the WTO. New sources of information on buyers were also added to this chapter. Chapter 6, "Global Marketing Research," has been updated to contain many online sources of information. The chapter also identifies some of the practices companies use to get around cultural limitations of certain survey techniques.

In Part III, we have made several changes that reflect our own teaching experience with some of the global marketing concepts. The changes in Chapter 7, "Developing a Global Mindset," reflect the latest conceptual developments in this area and contain new visuals and examples. Chapter 8, "Global Marketing Strategies" has been substantially revised. The order of topics has been changed, and an enhanced discussion of global marketing strategies has been added, as well as many new references and examples. Chapter 9, "Global Market Entry Strategies," has been streamlined to better cover web-based global marketing strategies. The revision in Part IV, "Designing Global Marketing Programs," focused on updating examples and references and maximizing new company examples from 2000 to 2002. Chapter 10, "Pricing for Global Markets," has been updated with recent examples of how companies are managing transfer pricing to respond to governmental auditing of company practices. Chapter 11, "Global Communications Strategies," has been improved with a stronger focus on global communication practices and the elimination of some parts that dealt largely with country-specific promotions. Chapter 12, "Managing Global Advertising," has been streamlined to make it easier for the reader. It includes substantial updating in examples and references, as well as new visuals, graphics, and tables. Chapter 13, "Global Product and Service Strategies," includes an expanded discussion of pan-European products encouraged by the introduction of the euro as a currency. Chapter 14, "Developing New Products for Global Markets," has been revised with new examples to illustrate how companies are developing new products in a global context. Chapter 15, "Managing Global Distribution Channels," has been updated with many examples of how companies are using joint ventures and acquisitions to expand distribution.

Part V of the book, "Managing the Global Marketing Effort," has been substantially updated with new examples and newly formulated global concepts. Chapter 16, "Organizing for Global Marketing," reflects the strengthening of the role of the global marketing organization, with further enhanced discussions of concepts such as global mandates. Chapter 17, "Planning and Controlling Global Marketing," has seen a substantial revision and includes the latest forms of corporate and business strategies. Several new concepts from our previous work in global strategy have been introduced, making this chapter substantially different from previous editions.

The inside front and back covers now feature color charts reflecting world population growth, and trade and industry statistics. We have also updated the eight pages of color inserts in the text with new summaries of world statistics.

COMPLETE TEACHING PACKAGE

The teaching package for the sixth edition includes a variety of resources designed to facilitate instructor-led classes as well as online learning environments.

- The *Instructor's Resource Manual* contains suggestions on how to design a global marketing course, student projects, answers to text questions, brief chapter outlines, and a completely revised test bank.
- The *Case Teaching Guide*, downloadable from the instructor web site, contains complete case teaching notes.
- The PowerPoint slides, including over 25 slides per chapter plus additional slides for the cases, combine clear, concise text and art. These are downloadable from the instructor web site.
- Videos highlight well-known companies and up-to-date global issues. The video guide provides complete teaching notes to set the stage for each video and stimulate discussion.
- The student web site includes Internet exercises with hyperlinks to key web resources and companies, suggested applications of course content for projects and research papers, and recommended Internet sites for research on many global marketing topics.
- The instructor web site includes the *Case Teaching Guide*, lecture notes, PowerPoint slides, and comments on the Internet exercises, as well as additional mini-cases, scenarios, and critical thinking incidents that can be used for testing purposes or to provide additional examples of course concepts.

ACKNOWLEDGMENTS

Preparing a new edition of a textbook on global marketing remains a major undertaking that could not have been completed without the active support of a great many people.

We are indebted to our home institution, Babson College, for generously supporting us in the manuscript stage and allowing us the flexibility to spend time overseas to develop the material for this book. In particular, we have profited from research support from the William F. Glavin Center for Global Management and the F. W. Olin Foundation's support of the F. W. Olin Distinguished Chair in Global Business. We are indebted to the International Management Development Institute (IMD) for its support of our case research and for allowing us to publish IMD cases in the separate casebook. We are thankful to Ashridge Management College for providing access to its extensive database, which proved helpful in updating this new edition. And finally, we would like to express our gratitude to our colleagues at Babson, IMD, and Ashridge for their support and willingness to discuss global marketing issues, which has helped us clarify many of our concepts.

As we prepared our materials for this sixth edition, we relied on the research help of Yelena Zaharoff from the W. F. Glavin Center and William C. McCann, research assistant, who worked wonders with web-based searches to find interesting new examples to enrich our text.

For their assistance with the supplements package, we would like to thank Jacob Chacko (Clayton College & State University) and Milton Pressley (University of New Orleans).

Throughout the development of this edition and the previous editions, a number of reviewers have made important contributions. These reviews were extremely important in the revision and improvement of the text. We especially thank the following people:

B. G. Bizzell,
Stephen F. Austin University

Jean Boddewyn,
CUNY—Bernard M. Baruch College

Martin Bressler,
Houston Baptist University

Sharon Browning,
Northwest Missouri State University

Roger J. Calantone,
Michigan State University

Jacob Chacko,
Clayton College & State University

Alex Christofides,
Ohio State University

John Chyzyk,
Brandon University

William Cunningham,
Southwest Missouri State

Charles P. de Mortanges,
University of Limburg

Dharma deSilva,
Wichita State University

Susan P. Douglas,
New York University

Adel I. El-Ansary,
The George Washington University

John Eldred,
Kingston University

Jeffrey A. Fadiman,
San Jose State University

Ying Fan,
University of Lincolnshire

Kate Gillespie,
University of Texas at Austin

John L. Hazard,
Michigan State University

Joby John,
Bentley College

H. Ralph Jones,
Miami University

W. Wossen Kassaye,
Bentley College

A. H. Kizilbash,
Northern Illinois University

Saul Klein,
Northeastern University

G. P. Lauter,
The George Washington University

Monle Lee,
Indiana University South Bend

Sarah Maddock,
University of Birmingham

Joseph L. Massie,
University of Kentucky

Lisa McConnell,
Oklahoma State University

James McCullough,
The University of Arizona

Taylor W. Meloan,
University of Southern California

Aubrey Mendelow,
Duquesne University

Joseph C. Miller,
*Kelley School of Business,
Indiana University*

Avvari V. Mohan,
Universiti Telekom, Malaysia

Kadayam H. Padmanabham,
University of Michigan, Dearborn

Thomas Ponzurick,
West Virginia University

Zahir A. Quraeshi,
Western Michigan University

Samuel Rabino,
Northeastern University

Daniel Rajaratnam,
Baylor University

Pradeep Rau,
University of Delaware

F. J. Sarknas,
University of Pittsburgh

Jan N. Saykiewicz,
Duquesne University

Chris Simango,
University of Northumbria

J. Steenkamp,
University of Leuven

Michael Steiner,
University of Wisconsin—Eau Claire

Gordon P. Stiegler,
University of Southern California

Ruth Lesher Taylor,
Southwest Texas State University

L. Trankiem,
*California State University at
Los Angeles*

Arturo Vasquez,
Florida International University

Phillip D. White,
University of Colorado at Boulder

Van R. Wood,
Virginia Commonwealth University

Yoo S. Yang,
Chung Ang University, Seoul

Attila Yaprak,
Wayne State University

Poh-Lin Yeoh,
University of South Carolina, Columbia

We are grateful to our publisher, Houghton Mifflin Company. Throughout the revision, we have had the pleasure of working with a number of their editors who have seen this project through to its completion. We thank them for their patience, encouragement, and professionalism in supporting our writing efforts. The marketing, production, art, editorial, permissions, and manufacturing staffs have substantially added to the quality of this finished book. Houghton Mifflin has also accommodated the need to include the latest statistics, visuals, and references in this edition.

This edition has benefited from our work with numerous executives who face the challenges of global marketing daily. Our work on executive programs with Serono, Siemens, Deloitte Touche Tohmatsu, Bausch & Lomb, EMC, Medtronic, Jardine Matheson, DSM, Novartis, ICI, Zeneca, Sun Microsystems, and many others has helped shape our thinking for this revision.

We extend our greatest gratitude to our students at Babson College and IMD Institute for their constant help and inspiration. Their interest in global marketing issues inspired us to undertake and complete this project.

Finally, we thank our families for their support through the revisions, page proofs, artwork, and emails. We are pleased to dedicate this version to the memory of Patricia Jeannet.

Jean-Pierre Jeannet

H. David Hennessey

Introduction

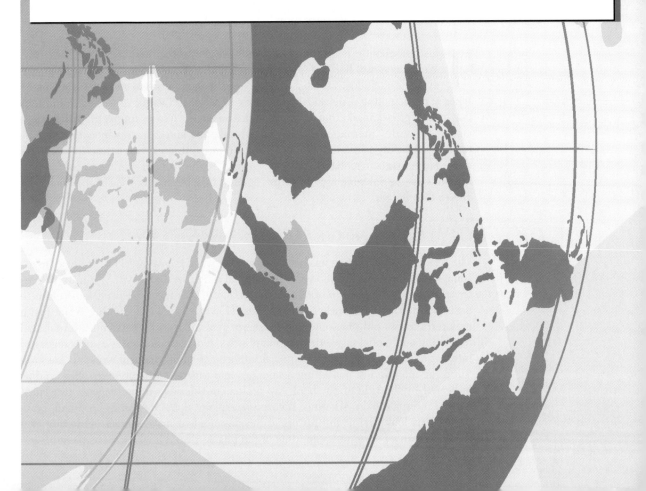

I n the first chapter of the text, we introduce the field of global marketing. An overview of the most important global marketing decisions is given, and the major problems likely to be encountered by international firms are highlighted. Chapter 1 of this text also explains the conceptual framework we used to develop the book. Understanding this underlying plan will help you to integrate these concepts quickly into an overall framework for global marketing. It should also make it easier for you to appreciate the complexities of global marketing.

CHAPTER 1
**Introduction to
Global Marketing**

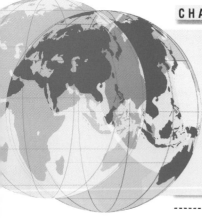

Chapter 1

Introduction to Global Marketing

CHAPTER OUTLINE

- The Development of Global Marketing
- The Scope of Global Marketing
- Exploring the Challenge of Global Marketing
- Factors Limiting Standardization of Global Marketing Strategies
- Participants in Global Marketing
- The Importance of Global Marketing
- Why Study Global Marketing?
- Organization of This Book

This first chapter is intended to introduce you to the field of global marketing. We concentrate here on the scope of global marketing, and we provide several examples to illustrate that it is a broad-based process encompassing many types of participating firms and a wide range of activities. We next present definitions that relate global marketing to other fields of study. We examine the differences among domestic, international, and global marketing and explain why companies often have difficulty marketing abroad. The chapter continues with a description of the major participants in global marketing. We also explain why mastering global marketing skills can be valuable to your future career. A conceptual outline of the book concludes the chapter.

THE DEVELOPMENT OF GLOBAL MARKETING

The term *global marketing* has been in use only since the early 1980s. It began to assume widespread use in 1983 with the seminal article by Ted Levitt.[1] Prior to that, *international marketing*, or *multinational marketing*, was the term used most often to describe international marketing activities. However, global marketing is not just a new term for an old phenomenon; there are real differences between international marketing and global marketing. In many ways, global marketing is a subcategory of international marketing and has special importance in our present world. It has captured the attention of marketing academics and business practitioners alike, and as indicated by the title of our book, we attach considerable importance to this latest type of international marketing. Before we explain global marketing in detail, however, let us look first at the historical development of international marketing as a field and gain a better understanding of the phases through which it has passed.

DOMESTIC MARKETING

Marketing that is aimed at a single market, the firm's domestic market, is referred to as domestic marketing. In domestic marketing, the firm faces only one set of competitive, economic, and market issues and essentially must deal with only one set of customers, although the company may serve several segments in this one market. The marketing concepts that apply to domestic, or single-country, marketing are those we expect our readers to be well versed in; they will not be covered further in this book.[2]

EXPORT MARKETING

The field of export marketing covers all marketing activities involved when a firm markets its products outside its main (domestic) base of operation and when products are physically shipped from one market or country to another. Although the domestic marketing operation remains of primary importance, the major challenges of export marketing are the selection of appropriate markets or countries through marketing research, the determination of appropriate product modifications to meet the demand requirements of export markets, and the development of export channels through which the company can market its products abroad. In this phase, the firm may concentrate mostly on the product modifications and run the export operations as a welcome and profitable by-product of its domestic strategy.

INTERNATIONAL MARKETING

When practicing international marketing, a company goes beyond exporting and becomes much more directly involved in the local marketing environment within a given country or market. The international marketer is likely to have its own sales subsidiaries and will participate in and develop entire marketing strategies for foreign markets. At this point, the necessary adaptations to the firm's domestic marketing strategies become a main concern. Companies going international now will have to find out how they must adjust an entire marketing strategy—including how they sell, advertise, and distribute—to fit new market demands.

An important challenge for the international marketing phase of a firm becomes the need to understand the different environments in which the company needs to operate. Understanding different cultural, economic, and political environments becomes necessary for success. This understanding is generally described as part of a company's internationalization process, whereby a firm becomes more experienced in operating in various foreign markets. It is typical to find considerable emphasis on the environmental component at this stage. Typically, much of the field of international marketing has been devoted to making the environment understandable and to assisting managers in navigating through the differences. The development of the cultural/environmental approach to international marketing is an expression of this particular phase.[3]

MULTINATIONAL MARKETING

The focus on multinational marketing came as a result of the development of the multinational corporation. These companies, characterized by extensive development of assets abroad, operate in several foreign countries or markets as if the firms were local companies. Such development led to the creation of many domestic strategies—thus, the name *multidomestic strategy*—whereby a multinational firm competes with many strategies, each one tailored to a particular local market. The major challenge of the multinational marketer is to find the best possible adaptation of a complete marketing strategy for an individual country. This approach to international marketing leads to the maximum amount of localization and to a large variety of marketing strategies. Often, the attempt of multinational corporations to appear "local" wherever they compete results in the duplication of some key resources. The major benefit is the ability to tailor a marketing strategy completely to the local requirements. Unilever, a European-based company with operations in 150 countries, markets food and personal care products globally. Its senior management describes its marketing as "multi-local multinational," to emphasize its focus on the individual tastes of consumers around the world. "There is no such thing as a global consumer. Every consumer is local," says its CEO, Niall Fitzgerald.[4]

PANREGIONAL MARKETING

Given the diseconomies of scale of individualized marketing strategies, each tailored to a specific local environment, companies have begun to emphasize strategies for larger regions. These regional strategies encompass numerous markets, such as pan-European strategies for Europe, and have developed as a result of regional economic and political integration. Such integration is also apparent in North America, where in 1993 the United States, Canada, and Mexico committed themselves to a far-reaching trade pact in the form of the North American Free Trade Agreement (NAFTA). In the Pacific Rim area, regional integration took a step forward with the first Pacific Rim country summit, held in Seattle in 1993. The summit followed a decade of rapid economic progress in that part of the world. Clearly, progress toward integration has been most pronounced in Europe, with the passing of the Maastricht Treaty to form the European Union (EU) and the implementation of the European Monetary Union (EMU) through the introduction of the euro.

Companies considering regional marketing strategies try to tie together operations in one region rather than around the globe, the aim being increased efficiency. Many firms are presently working on such solutions, moving from many multidomestic strategies toward selected panregional strategies.

GLOBAL MARKETING

Over the years, academics and international companies alike have become aware that opportunities for economies of scale and enhanced competitiveness are greater if they can manage to integrate and create marketing strategies on a global scale. A global marketing strategy involves the creation of a single strategy for a product, service, or company for the entire global market. Such a strategy encompasses many countries simultaneously and is aimed at leveraging the commonalities across many markets. Rather than tailor a strategy perfectly to an individual market, in global marketing the company settles on one general strategy that can be applied throughout the world market while at the same time maintaining flexibility to adapt that strategy to local market requirements where necessary. The challenge for management is to design marketing strategies that work well across multiple markets. Not only do markets appear increasingly similar in environmental and customer requirements, but also large investments in technology, logistics, or other key functions force companies to expand their market coverage.

Thus, global marketing is the last stage in the development of the field of international marketing. Although global marketers face their own unique challenges stemming from finding marketing strategies that fit many countries, the skills and concepts of the earlier stages continue to remain important and necessary. In fact, companies that take a global marketing approach will be good exporters because they will include some exporting in their strategies. Such firms will also have to be good at international marketing because designing one global strategy requires a sound understanding of the cultural, economic, and political environments of many countries. Furthermore, few global marketing strategies can exist without some local tailoring, which is the hallmark of multinational marketing. As a result, global marketing is but the last of a series of skills, all included under the umbrella of international marketing.

THE SCOPE OF GLOBAL MARKETING

A company such as Boeing, the world's largest commercial airline manufacturer and one of the leading exporters from the United States, obviously engages in global marketing when it sells its aircraft to airlines across the world. Likewise, Ford Motor Company, which operates automobile manufacturing plants in many countries, engages in international marketing, even though a major part of Ford's output is sold in the country where it is manufactured.[5]

Today, however, the scope of global marketing is broader and includes many other business activities. Those of large U.S. store chains, such as Kmart and Wal-Mart, include a substantial amount of importing. When these stores search for new products abroad to sell in the United States, they practice another form of global marketing. A whole range of service industries are involved in global marketing; major advertising agencies, banks, investment bankers, accounting firms, consulting companies, hotel chains, airlines, and even law firms now market their services worldwide.

Entertainment is another important product category with large global potential. The worldwide recorded music retail market was estimated at $36.96 billion in 2000. The United States accounted for 38 percent of the world market, followed by Japan, with 18 percent; the United Kingdom, 8 percent; Germany, 7 percent; and France, 5 percent.[6] This entire market was dominated by "the Big Five," a few large firms from the United States and Europe that claimed a large share of the world market. Vivendi Universal leads with 23 percent of the market, followed by Sony of Japan with 16 percent, EMI of the United Kingdom and Warner of the United States with 13 percent, and Bertelsmann of Germany with 12 percent.[7] All of these firms are heavily engaged in global marketing. Despite the global nature of the industry, domestic artists dominated sales. In the United States, domestic artists accounted for 92 percent of recorded music sales, compared to 40 percent for Germany, and 51 percent for France and the United Kingdom.[8]

Global marketing is even engulfing social causes. Global Legacy is a project created by a Canadian businessman who wants to eradicate urban deprivation worldwide. Started in London's Tower Hamlets, the project includes local companies, business schools, and foundations. The founder would like to replicate his projects in approximately twenty different cities worldwide, using global-marketing style concepts for market entry and market preparation.[9]

DEFINING GLOBAL MARKETING MANAGEMENT

Although much conceptual work has been accomplished in global marketing, the use of the word *global* remains unclear among many marketing academics and executives. For many, *global* is just a new or replacement term for *international*. Since we take it to mean something new and different, we plan to make use of the term in a judicious way. For us, global marketing is a subset, albeit different and distinct, of international marketing. In general, we still occasionally use the term *international* to describe factors that relate to the entire field and use *global* mainly when it refers to the specific new phenomenon of marketing globally. The term *global* was selected as the title for this book to indicate that a significant portion of this text will deal specifically with new concepts and strategies, without neglecting the standard conventions of export, international, or multinational marketing.

Having examined the scope of international and global marketing, we can now define it more accurately. Any definition has to be built, however, on basic definitions of marketing and marketing management, with an added explanation of the international dimension. We understand *marketing* as the performance of business activities directing the flow of products and services from producer to consumer. A successful performance of the marketing function by a firm is contingent on the adoption of the *marketing concept. Marketing management* is the execution of a company's marketing operation. Management responsibilities consist of planning, organizing, and controlling the marketing program of the firm.[10] To accomplish this job, marketing management is assigned decision-making authority over product strategy, communication strategy, distribution strategy, and pricing strategy. The combination of these four aspects of marketing is referred to as the *marketing mix*.

For global marketing management, the basic goals of marketing and the responsibilities described above remained unchanged. What is different is the execution of these activities in more than one country. Consequently, we define *global marketing management* as a process to craft a coherent, integrated, and unified marketing strategy for a product or service against the entire global market opportunity. For a marketing strategy to be global does not require complete standardization. Rather, it suffices if core elements are applied consistently across multiple markets and with varying degrees of customization, as the situation requires. By "global opportunity," we imply that the strategy is built around a full and complete understanding of all relevant markets but need not include all countries. A coherent strategy around several key markets suffices to meet the requirements for a global marketing strategy. Global marketing thus requires moving from a single-country to a multicountry focus. As you can see in Figure 1.1, many countries or markets are involved simultaneously when we speak of global marketing activities.

A U.S. firm exporting products to Korea is engaged in a marketing effort across two countries: the United States and Korea. Another U.S. firm operating a subsidiary in Korea that manufactures and markets locally under the direction of the head office in the United States is also engaged in global marketing if the head office staff directs and supervises this effort. Consequently, global marketing does not always require the physical movement of products across national borders. Global marketing occurs whenever marketing decisions that encompass many countries are made.

Figure 1.1: International and Global Marketing

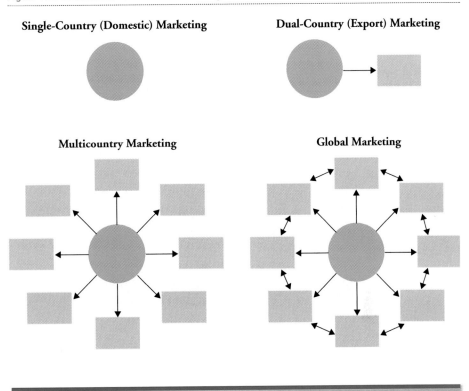

RELATIONSHIPS WITH OTHER FIELDS OF STUDY

The field of global marketing is related to other fields of study. In its broadest terms, global marketing is a subset of *international business*, which is defined as the performance of all business functions across national boundaries. International business includes all functional areas, such as international production, international financial management, and international marketing (see Figure 1.2).[11]

International trade theory, which explains why nations trade with each other, is a related concept. This theory is aimed at understanding product flows, in the form of either exports or imports, between countries. A U.S. corporation exporting medical equipment to Brazil would find its transactions recorded as an export in the United States, but the same transaction is treated as an import in Brazil. In this situation, global marketing and international trade are concerned with the same phenomenon.[12]

Should the U.S. company produce its machinery in Brazil and sell locally, however, there would be no exchange of goods between the two countries. Consequently, there would be no recognized trading activity. As we have seen earlier, however, the U.S. company's decision to build the equipment in Brazil and sell it there is still considered a global marketing decision. Therefore, we can conclude that global marketing goes beyond strict definitions of international trading and includes a wider range of activities.

Figure 1.2: International and Global Marketing and
Related Fields of Study

Global marketing should not be confused with *foreign marketing*, which consists of marketing activities carried out by foreign firms within their own countries. Marketing by Chinese firms in China is, therefore, defined as foreign marketing and is not the principal focus of this book. However, Chinese firms engaged in marketing their products in the United States are engaged in global marketing and are subject to the same concepts and principles that govern U.S. firms marketing in China.

EXPLORING THE CHALLENGE OF GLOBAL MARKETING

Companies that market products or services globally have always had to deal with a wider range of issues than those encountered by domestic firms. The following example gives some insight into the special difficulties encountered in the international market. When a company uses an initial marketing strategy abroad, success or failure depends greatly on the market where it is used. When Apple Computer Company began distribution of its personal computers in Japan, the company had to live for years with a very small market share. Japanese competitors and IBM had begun to market Japanese-language machines. Only Japanese who understood English very well could use the early Apple computers. It wasn't until years later that Apple adapted its products to the Japanese language and built a subsidiary staff around local managers. Eventually, Apple recalibrated its marketing strategy for Japan, targeting the school and home markets. Apple ranked fourth and market share in Japan stood at 9 percent in 2000, ahead of IBM and Toshiba.[13] Despite Apple's difficulties in the United States over the years, the company has been able to maintain its relatively high share in Japan and was reaping the benefit through high sales of its newer iMac and iBook computers.[14]

In marketing its computers abroad, Apple tried to duplicate a marketing strategy that had been successful in its home market. It failed initially in Japan, whereas in Europe it succeeded, with Apple achieving a higher market share than in its home market. The success in its European markets also caused the company to bring the lessons learned abroad back to the United States by transferring executives from abroad. Apple's example shows that success in international markets does not always require the complete transformation of a company's strategy, but that doesn't mean one will never have to change anything. The Apple situation supports a pattern in which managers have to evaluate situations and sometimes change, sometimes adapt, and at other times extend the same strategy abroad. The reasons for these patterns are explained in the next section.

FACTORS LIMITING STANDARDIZATION OF GLOBAL MARKETING STRATEGIES

From a global marketing manager's point of view, the most cost-effective method for marketing products or services worldwide is to use the same program in every country, provided environmental conditions favor such an approach. As we have seen in the previous section, however, local market characteristics may require some form of adaptation to local conditions. One of the challenges of global marketing is to be able to determine the extent to which a standardized approach may be used for any given local market. The global marketing manager must become aware of any factors that limit standardization. Such factors can be categorized into four major groups: market characteristics, competitive conditions, marketing infrastructure, and regulatory conditions.[15]

The debate over the amount or extent of standardization is one of the longest in the field of international marketing. Some, like Levitt,[16] see markets as becoming more similar and increasingly more global. Others point out the difficulties in using a standardized approach, as experienced by many companies and as illustrated by the research of many academics.[17]

MARKET CHARACTERISTICS

Market characteristics can have a profound effect on a global marketing strategy. The *physical environmental conditions* of any country—determined by climate, product use conditions, and population size—often force marketers to make adjustments to products to fit local conditions. Many cars in Canada come equipped with a built-in heating system that is connected to an electrical outlet to keep the engine from freezing when it is turned off. Cars manufactured for warmer climates are not equipped with such a heating unit but are likely to feature air conditioning.

The product use conditions for washing machines differ considerably between the United States and Europe. Most American machines are of the top leader type, requiring clothes to be loaded from the top. By contrast, most European machines are front loader types. Because the front-loading machines use a more gentle washing action mechanism (tumbling clothes versus back-and-forth agitation for U.S. machines), Whirlpool was planning to introduce the front-loading type in the U.S. market in 2002. To accommodate different U.S. washing practices, the firm decided to install a drawer in the bottom of the machine, thus raising it and avoiding the bending down that users would have to do during loading, as well as enlarging the tub and the opening for accommodating the larger U.S. loads. Despite these changes, front-loading machines are expected to take only a small percentage of the U.S. market due to their higher price.[18]

A country's *population* affects the market size in terms of volume, allowing for lower prices in larger markets. Market size, or expected sales volume, greatly affects channel strategy. Company-owned manufacturing and sales subsidiaries are often possible in larger markets, whereas independent distributors are often used in smaller countries.

Macroeconomic factors also greatly affect international marketing strategy. Income level, or gross national product (GNP) per capita, varies widely among nations—from below $100 per year for some of the world's poorest nations to above $25,000 per year for rich countries such as Denmark, the Netherlands, and the United States. As can be expected, marketing environments will differ considerably according to income level. If the population's level of technical skill is low, a marketer may be forced to simplify product design to suit the local market. Pricing may be affected to the extent that countries with lower income levels show a higher price elasticity for many products, compared with more developed countries. Furthermore, convenient access to credit is often required of buyers in developing countries. This has a negative impact on the sale of capital goods and consumer durables.

To accommodate the lower income level in China, McDonald's typically resorted to introductory pricing, which sometimes fails to cover the cost of the burger. Lower prices attract more customers, though, and a restaurant can then become profitable quickly. Half of China's seventy-three McDonald's restaurants were profitable by mid-1996, although at the country level the company was not yet profitable.[19] A Chinese family of three would pay about 10 percent of a typical monthly urban salary to eat one meal out at McDonald's. Despite these prices, eating habits quickly adjusted. By 1999, McDonald's operated thirty-four restaurants in Beijing alone.[20]

Cultural and social factors are less predictable influences on the marketing environment, and they have frustrated many international marketers. Customs and traditions have the greatest effect on product categories when a country's population has had prior experience with a given product category. Although Coca-Cola has been very successful transferring its Coke brand into many countries, it has also run into difficulties with other products. Its canned coffee drink, Georgia Coffee, which met with success in Japan, did not find acceptance elsewhere. And a soy drink that did very well in Hong Kong did not take off in the United States. Nestlé, which wanted to capitalize on the cold-coffee-drink opportunity in the United States, stopped marketing its Nescafé blended cold-coffee drinks because the size of the iced-coffee category in the United States had not met its expectation.[21]

Language can be another hurdle for international marketing, and international marketers are focusing their attention on this problem. Few areas have been as affected by language as the software industry. One of the most daunting tasks for western software companies was to enter the Asian markets with products using Chinese characters. A pair of Chinese-language characters in Microsoft's translation of its Windows 95 operating system resulted in unexpected difficulties. Among the large selection of available characters were two that could form the term "communist bandit," which was clearly unacceptable to the Chinese government. A seventy-thousand-phrase dictionary offered these characters. The problem stemmed in part from programs written for the more complex characters in Taiwan and Hong Kong that had also found their way onto the mainland. Eager to meet local market requirements, Microsoft had to promise to exchange all disks and to eliminate offensive terms.[22] Such a move is definitely worthwhile: currently ranked third, it is expected that the Chinese market for PCs will become the world's second largest market behind the United States.

Different language environments affect even the Internet. Although most people consider English to be the language of the Internet community, when it comes to online shopping, data show that the majority of consumers may browse the Web in more than one language. Examples of such consumers are speakers of English as a second language. Consumers also prefer to buy products and services in their native language. Less than half of all web users were native English speakers, and only a third were U.S. citizens. By 2003, it is expected that two-thirds of ecommerce spending will originate from outside the United States, and two-thirds of all Internet users will come from outside North America.[23]

INDUSTRY CONDITIONS

Industry conditions often vary by country because products are frequently in varying stages of the product life cycle in different markets. Also, a company may find that one country's limited awareness of or prior experience with a product requires a considerable missionary sales effort and primary demand stimulation, whereas in more mature markets, the promotional strategy is likely to concentrate on brand differentiation. The level of local competition can be expected to vary substantially by country. The higher the technological level of the competition, the more an international company must improve the quality level of its products. In countries where competitors control distribution channels and maintain a strong sales force, the strategy of a multinational company may differ significantly from that in a country where the company holds a competitive advantage.

The telecommunications industry is typical of widely differing industry conditions. Only a few years ago, the industry was fragmented, with operators and suppliers restricted to their domestic markets only. Today the industry in most countries is experiencing a major push toward liberalization. The process has unfolded differently from country to country, however, having reached the most advanced stage in the United States. In Japan, the market power is still concentrated in the hands of a single or a few companies, which is no longer the case in the United States or Europe. As in other countries, the wireless service providers in Japan have split off from the traditional fixed net providers. Japan's leading fixed net provider, NTT, spawned Japan's leading wireless company (DoCoMo), which has in turn begun to enter international markets with its innovative i-mode.[24] In Europe, competition has been heating up among the major players, spawning specialist wireless firms such as Vodafone, which claims approximately 100 million customers worldwide. Many of the European competitors have entered the U.S. market.[25]

To compete in such differently structured markets requires a substantial adjustment in the strategy of a firm like AT&T Wireless. To meet foreign competition head-on in the U.S. market, AT&T Wireless introduced mMode to compete directly against DoCoMo's i-mode. The company also had to change technology, moving away from complete reliance on older TDMA technology prevalent in the United

States and beginning to introduce GSM-3G, the prevalent technology used in most other countries which allows callers to use their phone anywhere in the world.[26]

MARKETING INFRASTRUCTURE

For historical and economic reasons, the marketing infrastructure assumes different forms in different countries. Practices in distribution systems often entail different margins for the same product, which requires a change in company pricing strategy. Availability of outlets is also likely to vary by country. Mass merchandisers such as supermarkets, discount stores, and department stores are widely available in the United States and other industrialized countries, but they are largely absent in less industrialized nations in southern Europe, Latin America, and other parts of the world. Such variations may lead to considerably different distribution strategies. Likewise, advertising agencies and the media are not equally accessible in all countries, and the absence of mass media channels in some countries makes a pull strategy less effective.

REGULATORY ENVIRONMENT

The regulatory environment must also be considered when developing a global marketing strategy. Product standards issued by local governments must be observed. To the extent that they differ from one country to another, unified product design often becomes a challenge. Tariffs and taxes may require adjustments in pricing, and such adjustments may mean that a product can no longer be sold on a high-volume basis. Specific restrictions may also be problematic. In Europe, restrictions on advertising prohibit the mention of a competitor's name, although such an approach may be an integral part of the advertising strategy in the United States.

Under the auspices of the World Trade Organization (WTO), the international trade body based in Geneva, efforts are under way to deal with the multitude of patent law interpretations. Indonesia and India were traditionally two countries that adhered to the rule of patenting processes for pharmaceutical drugs, rather than the products themselves. As a result, a local firm could copy the products of international pharmaceutical firms as long as it used a different manufacturing process to arrive at the final product. As a result of India joining the WTO, its old patent rules will have to change by the year 2005, and its local firms will also have to apply for product patents, a substantial change for India's twenty-four thousand local pharmaceutical firms.[27]

To carry out the international marketing task successfully, international managers have to be cognizant of all the factors that influence the local marketing environment. Frequently, they need to target special marketing programs for each country. With newly emerging institutions such as the WTO, however, the world is moving closer to a level playing field, with fewer differences in regulations and with increased opportunities for firms and governments to file lawsuits if they believe they have suffered from undue protection or unfair trade practices.

PARTICIPANTS IN GLOBAL MARKETING

Several types of companies participate in global marketing. Among the leaders are multinational corporations (MNCs), global corporations, exporters, importers, and many different service companies. These firms may be engaged in manufacturing consumer or industrial goods, in trading, or in the performance of a range of services.

What all participants have in common is a need to deal with the complexities of the global marketplace.

THE ROLE OF MULTINATIONAL CORPORATIONS IN GLOBAL MARKETING

Multinational corporations (MNCs) are companies that manufacture and market products or services in several countries. Typically, an MNC operates several plants abroad and markets products through a large network of fully owned subsidiaries. No clear definition exists, and MNCs are also referred to as global companies, transnational firms, or stateless corporations. For the purposes of this text, we have chosen the terms *international corporations*, *multinational corporations*, and *global corporations*. We use the term *international* to indicate a company with some international activities. The term *MNC* is reserved for a company with extensive overseas operations, including overseas manufacturing in several countries. We would call a company "global" if its operations span the globe and follow a coherent and integrated strategy for the entire world. Although *multinational (MNC)* and *global* tend to be more specific terms, we have chosen to use the term *global firm* most often because it is the preferred terminology of many researchers and executives.

The United Nations Conference on Trade and Development (UNCTAD) listed approximately sixty thousand active MNCs in 2000, with a total of 800,000 recorded affiliates worldwide. These figures were up from 53,600 MNCs and 449,000 affiliates three years earlier. These companies undertook about $1,000 billion in investments; some of these investments abroad served to overcome trade barriers, but increasingly the investment goal has been to locate operations in countries where they could operate most efficiently. Sales of foreign affiliates were estimated at $15.68 trillion.[28]

Fortune's list of the world's largest 500 companies (Global 500) shows how much international business has been developed outside the United States by huge, growing firms around the world. *Fortune*'s ranking includes service companies as well as industrial firms and is based on revenue. In 2001, 185 of the top 500 firms were U.S. based; 156 European firms were included in the list. Other countries were represented in smaller numbers, such as South Korea, and China (twelve firms), Sweden (five firms), Russia (five firms), and India (one firm).[29]

At the same time, foreign investment increased rapidly. Of the more than $1,270 billion in foreign direct investments (FDI) in 2000, the largest share was invested in Western Europe ($633 billion), followed by the United States ($281 billion). Only $8.2 billion was invested in Japan. Overall, the total FDI for Asia amounted to $143 billion.[30] In the aftermath of a global recession and the impact of the terrorist attacks on September 11, 2001, cross-border and direct foreign investment were expected to drop by about 40 percent in 2001.[31]

THE ROLE OF GLOBAL COMPANIES IN GLOBAL MARKETING

True global companies differ from MNCs because they pursue integrated strategies on a worldwide scale rather than separate strategies on a country-by-country basis. They tend to look at the whole world as one market and to move products, manufacturing, capital, or even personnel wherever they can gain an advantage. Global firms also tend to have a strong base in all of the major economic regions of North America,

Europe, and the Pacific Rim. Products are developed for the entire world market, and the organization has undergone changes to be able to move from regional to product line–based profit centers. Many of the senior executives come from foreign countries.

Bartlett and Ghoshal differentiate among several types of internationally active firms. In their view, global firms operate on a world scale and tend to be heavily centralized; strategies tend to be controlled closely from the head office. In the multinational firm, each country is treated as a separate market. Multinational firms develop fairly independent clones of the parent firm in each market and focus on mostly local business. International firms have a pattern of more decentralization than global firms do, but the source of their strength is the exploitation of developments from their home market.[32]

General Electric (GE), one of the largest U.S. corporations, is pursuing its own particular global strategy. Each of the company's business units is expected to reach the number 1 or number 2 positions worldwide in its respective area. From its beginnings, however, GE has been more of an international company. It is based in the United States, with most of its international business concentrated in Europe and Japan. In 1980, only two of its major divisions (plastics and jet engines) were true global players. In 2001, international revenues accounted for 40 percent, up from just 29 percent in 1987.[33]

Texas Instruments (TI) is pursing globalization to compete in the very tough market for memory chips. The company designated a single design center and factory worldwide for each type of memory chip. It built two of its four new memory chip plants in Taiwan and Japan to take advantage of lower capital costs. An alliance with Hitachi of Japan helps share research costs. The international side of TI's business has now grown to 72 percent of corporate revenue. It has operations in more than twenty-five countries, and the bulk of its revenue comes from Asia.[34]

FIRMS BASED IN EMERGING ECONOMIES PARTICIPATE IN GLOBAL MARKETING

A recent development in international business is the rise of international firms based in emerging countries or in smaller countries not typically hosts to global firms. This development has important implications for global marketing. As these firms enter the global markets, they begin to compete locally or regionally, and some have even achieved global status in their own right.

South Korea has spawned an increasing number of multinational and global firms. Leaders are the large conglomerates, or *chaebol*, that get involved in several different types of businesses. Names such as Hyundai Motor ($20.5 billion), Samsung Electronics ($26 billion), and LG Electronics ($15 billion) have become widely known in world markets.[35] Although economic developments in Korea have reduced the size of these firms, they remain among the most notable global competitors from emerging countries.

One of the most aggressive and successful Korean firms is Samsung Electronics, with sales of $38.5 billion in 2001. The vast majority of its sales are from exports. The company is active in semiconductors, telecommunications, personal computers (PCs), notebook computers, televisions, home appliances, fiber optics, and many other products.[36] The company started its first semiconductor operation in 1974, and it has held the number 1 position in dynamic random access memory chips

(DRAMs), the most common kind of PC memory chips, since 1993.[37] Samsung Electronics is the world leader in thirteen product categories and has gained recognition[38] as "best product."[39] It was listed as the leader by *Business Week* in its "World Information Technology 100" list of companies.

Other Asian countries have also spawned several global firms. Acer Inc., founded in 1976 in Taiwan, already ranks as an international firm with sales of $6.7 billion in 1998. Known for making PCs, monitors, fax machines, notebook computers, servers, and custom chips, the company has also become a major producer of key components for PCs. It supplies well-known PC firms in Japan and the United States. The company has developed a global distribution network and has 42 percent of its sales in North America, 24 percent in Europe, 4 percent in Latin America, and 24 percent in the Asia Pacific area. Domestic sales account for only 10 percent of volume. As part of its global expansion, Acer has bought out the stake of Texas Instruments in its joint venture producing memory chips in Taiwan.[40] Acer has intensified its cooperation with IBM of the United States. IBM accounts for more than one-third of Acer's computer equipment sales already.[41] And to expand its position in Europe, Acer has acquired plants from Siemens of Germany as that company began to exit the PC business. Acer plans to use the plants to supply its own brand of PCs as well as to continue supplying equipment for Siemens under the German company's brand name.[42] Since then, Acer has split its various businesses and separated the component business from the computer business. Both businesses are managed globally.

Thailand is the home base of another rapidly growing firm with regional impact and global ambitions. Charoen Pokphand, typically referred to as CP Group, has grown in just twenty-five years into a firm operating in twenty countries, and it had revenues of $12 billion in 2000.[43] The company's origins were in chicken farming, with a weekly output of approximately 25 million chickens. Later, CP branched out into motorcycles, telecommunications, and semiconductor manufacturing.[44] The firm has signed joint venture agreements with U.S. firms such as NYNEX and Wal-Mart. In China, CP is considered the largest foreign investor, with 170 ventures operating various types of agrobusinesses and animal-feed mills. The ventures are spread across most of China's thirty provinces and represent total assets of more than $4 billion. With more than sixty thousand employees, the ventures generate revenues of about $3.6 billion (1998).[45] Despite some recent setbacks due to the economic recession in Thailand, the company continues on its expansion course, focusing its agrobusiness on the countries of Thailand, Indonesia, India, and Vietnam and focusing on new ventures in retailing and telecommunications.

Asia Pulp & Paper (APP) is an Indonesia-based paper company associated with the Sinar Mas Group, majority-owned by the Widjaja family. The company has risen in a short period of time to become one of the world's largest players in its industry. The company leverages major timber assets in Indonesia and built several large mills there. Additional expansion took place in China, with the company reaching estimated sales of $3 billion in 1999. Although it is said to have over invested in plant and equipment, the company remains a major player and is a typical example of an Asian local business expanding internationally. It plans to expand globally, with sales in North America and Europe.[46]

Even from mainland China, firms have begun to expand overseas. By the end of 1999, about six thousand Chinese companies were estimated to have invested

$7.0 billion in about 160 countries.[47] Jinan Qingqi Motorcycle, a Chinese state-owned company, set up its first assembly plants in Pakistan and in Lithuania in 1995. Other ventures in Sri Lanka and Argentina followed, producing the 50–100 cc brand-name motorcycles. Konka Group, China's second-largest television producer, set up its first overseas plant in India in 1999. Konka holds a 51 percent ownership and plans to move production from an initial 300,000 sets to 1 million sets a year, with sales going to both India and Pakistan. A second venture in Mexico will ship to Canada, the United States, and Argentina, with a planned capacity of 1 million units.[48]

Latin America has also been the home of many newly emerging global firms. Vitro, a Mexico-based glass-making company with sales of $3.0 billion (2001), made its first large acquisition in the United States in 1989. The company has since grown its international business to $801 million in 2001. It exports to seventy countries and operates about fifteen international subsidiaries with 100 facilities.[49] About 80 percent of its exports go to the United States, where the firm employs 2,500 people.[50] Vitro has entered into several alliances with global firms, including Ford Motor, Solutia, Pilkington, Whirlpool, General Electric, Owens Corning, and Ashahi. These alliances account for almost 70 percent of its total volume. Other emerging international groups based in Latin America include PDVSA of Venezuela, in oil and refining; Petrobras, the Brazilian oil company; Cemex, a Mexican cement producer; and many family-owned firms not listed on the stock market but still important economically.

New entrants into the global marketplace also come from regions not seen previously among global marketers. South African Breweries, a large regional brewery with about $4.36 billion in sales, joined the ranks of global firms by acquiring Miller Brewery of the United States from Philip Morris. To be renamed SAB-Miller, the company will control 20 percent of the U.S. beer market. SAB gains a U.S. distribution platform for its successful Pilsner Urquell brand, while offering access to a fast growing emerging market to Miller's Miller Lite and Miller Genuine Draft.[51] SAB had shown its mettle by successfully operating in China. The South African brewer pursued a strategy of acquiring local brands and further developing them, instead of pushing its own international brands. SAB estimates that before long China will surpass the United States as the world's largest beer market, raising the importance of doing well in that huge market.[52]

New global firms are also born in traditional but small industrialized countries. Despite its small domestic market, Finland is home to Nokia, a company that had its origins in paper and forestry products but has now changed completely to telecommunications. Nokia reached sales of about $28 billion in 2001, with a total number of employees surpassing fifty-four thousand. Nokia operates eighteen factories in ten different countries, maintains R&D operations in fifteen countries, and markets its products in 130 countries. Its largest markets are the United States and China. The company concentrates on mobile telecommunications infrastructure systems and mobile phone handsets.[53] Nokia became the global leader in handsets, with a market share of 35 percent and a volume of more than 100 million handsets shipped in 2001.[54] Its success has also driven up the value of its brand name, which was ranked eleventh among a list of global firms led by names such as Coca-Cola, Microsoft, and Intel.[55]

The summaries of the strategies of these recently emerging global firms clearly demonstrate that global marketing is not only practiced by firms from the major industrial nations of Europe, the United States, and Japan. Companies from many different countries are entering the world of global marketing, making the need to understand global marketing practices universal.

SERVICE COMPANIES AS PARTICIPANTS IN GLOBAL MARKETING

Early global companies were largely manufacturers of industrial equipment and consumer products. Many of the newer global firms are service companies. Banks, investment bankers, and brokers have turned themselves into global service networks; airlines and hotel companies have gained global status. Less noticeable are the global networks of accounting and professional service firms, consulting companies, advertising agencies, and a host of other service-related industries. This globalization of the service sector has not been restricted to the United States but has been mirrored in other countries as well.

Retailers stand out among the service companies pursuing international marketing strategies. Although they have seen themselves in the past as domestic business, retailers have begun to globalize. In Europe alone, about fifty U.S. retailers have operations, compared with less than fifteen just a few years ago. The Gap, Pier 1, Foot Locker, and Toys "R" Us are but a few of the major stores. Other U.S.-based retailing chains have expanded in Latin America. The retailer with the most important foreign operations is Wal-Mart. The company opened its first foreign stores in Mexico in 1991 and operated 1,186 by 2002, with a total of $35 billion in sales. Wal-Mart had already become the number 1 retailer in the United States, Canada, and Mexico, with growing operations in Europe (Germany, the United Kingdom), the rest of Latin America, and Asia (China, Japan). China, with its huge potential, was viewed as the only other country where Wal-Mart might replicate its business model and logistics system, with possibly three thousand stores. By 2002, Wal-Mart operated just nineteen stores in China. The last major move was made into Japan where Wal-Mart took a minority ownership in a major Japanese retail chain.[56]

Non-U.S.-based retailers are globalizing as well. Carrefour of France, a major operator of hypermarkets, has become a leading competitor of Wal-Mart in several countries. It has store operations in thirty-one countries, with sales of $40 billion in 1999. Ahold, a Dutch supermarket chain, expanded into the United States through acquisitions of Stop & Shop, Bi-Lo, Finast, Giant-Carlisle, Tops Market, and Pathmark, and operates in seventeen different countries.[57] Ahold's U.S. sales represented 59 percent of total corporate revenue and amounted to $35 billion in 2001.[58] And finally, IKEA, a Swedish furniture retailer, has expanded, first throughout Europe and then into the United States. Now it is the world's largest furniture retailer. With 140 company-owned stores worldwide and another twenty franchised operations, IKEA had sales of $9.6 billion in 2001 and operated in more than twenty countries. IKEA'S sixteen U.S. stores had combined sales of $1.2 billion in 2001 and accounted for 13 percent of overall sales. The United States is the second most important market for IKEA after Germany.[59] All of these retailing stores demonstrate that global marketing has become important even for a traditional and formerly domestic industry. In 2001, the world's top retailers accounted for 16 percent of retail sales, but by 2009 it is predicted that this number will rise to 40 percent. With leading stores continuing to globalize, the concentration is expected to go hand in hand with further globalization across all markets.[60]

Financial service firms are also expanding globally. U.S.-based investment banks are leaders in raising capital for clients worldwide, not just in the United States. Merrill Lynch has made acquisitions in the United Kingdom and Canada and recently began retail brokerage operations in Japan, adding about 4,500 new staff in the process. Morgan Stanley Dean Witter expanded its European staff faster than its domestic staff, to 3,800, to tap a market that was viewed as becoming as large as the U.S. market for mergers and acquisitions.[61] Just as globally active are the professional accounting firms. Although affected by the well-known Enron debacle that dismantled Arthur Anderson's global network, the remaining four leading accounting firms remain committed to global expansion and maintaining large office networks around the globe.[62]

International financial services institutions have also undertaken a path of rapid globalization. HSBC started in Hong Kong as the Hong Kong and Shanghai Banking Corporation and turned itself into one of the world's largest financial groups operating around the globe. HSBC runs 427 offices in Hong Kong and another 170 offices across twenty other Asian countries. It has recently been one of the first banks to apply for a license to operate in China, where banking laws will be liberalized as a result of China's membership in the World Trade Organization (WTO). HSBC began its North American expansion by acquiring Marine Midland Bank New York in 1980, and followed up with the acquisition of Republic New York in 1999. In Europe, HSBC expanded through Midland Bank in the United Kingdom.[63] ING Group and ABN Amro, both Dutch-based firms, have expanded their networks in Europe and the United States. Banco Santander, the largest Spanish bank, has expanded its operations throughout Latin America. Deutsche Bank acquired Bankers Trust of the United States to become one of the world's largest banks. And Credit Suisse and UBS, two Swiss-based banks, have expanded asset management and investment banking around the world.[64] This drive to globalize service industries has led to the development of global marketing activities in many new sectors that previously had been viewed as domestic only.

EXPORTERS AS GLOBAL MARKETERS

Exporters are important participants in global marketing. In 2000, total U.S. merchandise exports amounted to $781 billion, up from $393 billion in 1990.[65] U.S. exports rose 82 percent between 1990 and 1998. As a contributor to the overall economy, the role of export trade has been growing. In 1990, exports and imports combined equaled 13 percent of the U.S. gross domestic product (GDP). In 1999, they amounted to well over 30 percent. It was estimated that more than 11 million jobs depended on exports in 1999.[66]

We find many global corporations among the leading U.S. exporters. Their exports from the United States alone add up to substantial amounts. Boeing, the world's largest aerospace company, had export sales in 1998 of $26.5 billion, or 47 percent of corporate revenue. Boeing exports are high because the company sells to customers in more than 145 countries from a largely U.S. manufacturing base.[67] Other major exporters include General Motors (cars, locomotives), Ford (cars and parts), Daimler-Chrysler (cars and parts), General Electric (jet engines, turbines, plastics, medical systems, and locomotives), and Motorola (communications equipment and semiconductors). Global companies with production sites located around the world naturally have a smaller percentage of exports. However, global firms, even those with extensive networks of manufacturing sites around the world, supply some of their markets on an export basis because few firms in today's competitive environment could supply each market from local sources only.

Small and medium-sized firms are also exporters, although the extent of their involvement differs by geographic region. About 51,000 U.S. firms export regularly, and about 87 percent of those employ fewer than five hundred. As a whole, exporting accounts for about 12 percent of U.S. GNP, up from 7.5 percent in 1987.[68] Small firms have a bigger chance today because of new communications technology. One such example is Cardiac Science Inc., a small manufacturer and distributor of cardiac medical devices. The company used some help from the U.S. Department of Commerce. Its most potent weapon, however, turned out to be the opening of its own web site. The company, with sales of under $1 million in 1997, began to open up international business and shipped to customers in forty-six countries in 1998. Sales for 2002 were estimated at $42 million and are expected to grow to $78 million in 2003.[69]

The record of European small to medium-sized exporters is quite different. In Germany, medium-sized firms are called *Mittelstände*. These firms, with sales of under U.S. $250 million, account for a large share of Germany's exports. These firms typically market industrial products, which means they are little known to the average consumer. In their chosen market niche, however, they have become worldwide leaders. They focus on a technical niche and a narrow product assortment but sell worldwide. Typically, they have about a dozen sales subsidiaries abroad. Most of them maintain their own presence in the U.S. market. Although less well known than large German firms such as BMW or Siemens, they have been able to do extremely well in the role of exporter.[70]

IMPORTERS AS PARTICIPANTS IN GLOBAL MARKETING

Importing is as much an international marketing activity as exporting. Companies that neither export nor have multinational status may well participate in global marketing through their importing operations. Many of the largest U.S. retail chains maintain import departments that are in contact with suppliers in many overseas countries. Other major importers are global firms that obtain products from their plants abroad or from other clients. Among the largest U.S. importers are oil companies and subsidiaries of foreign-based firms, particularly in Europe and Japan.

Few firms operate as importers only. Many firms, such as Home Depot, operate part of their business as importers. Home Depot practices global sourcing by buying about 6 percent of its merchandise abroad. Given its 1,200 stores in the United States, Home Depot must ship about 94,000 containers in a single year to the United States. This volume is expected to grow substantially in the near future. For the internationally sourced part of Home Depot's sales, the process of importing is the reverse of exporting, and thus part of the field of global marketing.

As we have seen from this section, global marketing includes many different types of players. Rather than specifying a particular type of participant in the global market each time, we will use *international company* or *global company* as umbrella terms that may include MNCs, global firms, exporters, importers, or global service companies.

START-UP FIRMS AND ENTREPRENEURIAL VENTURES IN GLOBAL MARKETING

There is growing evidence among new ventures, particularly in the high-technology field, that an early involvement in global marketing can actually be a requirement for later success. Traditionally, managers believed that expansion into international markets came as a logical extension of a domestic strategy, and that the domestic market had to be secured first. For many industries, however, not entering international markets can have substantial strategic risks: competitors elsewhere might occupy important segments first, thus preventing later international market expansion. Logitech, a maker of computer input devices, was founded with a global marketing approach at the outset. Located in both Europe and the United States from the start, the company never had a "domestic" market. It considered the global market as the only relevant one. Logitech grew to a company with US $943 million in sales in 2001 and expanded its product line to include speakers, cameras, and accessories for hand-held computers.[71] Similarly, many upstart companies in the United States, Europe, and Asia are intending to become immediate global marketers.

ECOMMERCE COMPANIES ENTER GLOBAL MARKETING

Few sectors of the economy have been growing faster than ecommerce. Web-based companies have achieved a global reach from the moment they first opened for business. Yahoo!, the U.S.-based portal company, has grown overseas even faster than in the United States. Nearly half of Yahoo!'s traffic comes from overseas, although just 16 percent of its revenue is international. Started only in 1994, Yahoo! maintains about twenty-four portals and offices in Europe, Asia, Australia, and Canada.[72] AOL concluded a joint venture with Bertelsmann of Germany in 1995 to tap into the European market and entered into another deal with Cisneros, a Venezuela-based group, to penetrate Latin America.[73] By 2001, the company had merged with Time Warner to create AOL Time Warner and was buying back its German partner's 50 percent stake for $6.75 billion.[74] AOL Europe had been able to grow to a membership of more than 4.6 million by focusing on the United Kingdom, Germany, and France alone.[75] Charles Schwab, the U.S.-based discount brokerage company, has seen its Asian business grow substantially, the result of a decision to enter the Japanese market with its online trading technology for individual investors, with Tokyo Marine Securities as a partner. Schwab and other ecommerce brokerage firms, such as DLJ*direct* and E*Trade, could enter the Japanese market with their new technology. Smaller firms without major international infrastructure are thus in a position to compete for markets far way.[76]

By 2002, close to half a billion people throughout the world had gained Internet access from their homes.[77] Although the United States still had the largest number of Internet users, growth in the United States had slipped below rates experienced in Europe and elsewhere. The average penetration rate for Europe is 34 percent coverage, of which 31 percent is dial up and the rest is broadband. Within Europe, the penetration rate was highest in Sweden, with 59 percent, followed by Norway (53 percent), Switzerland (53 percent) and Denmark (52 percent). France, Spain, Portugal, and Greece recorded the lowest penetration rates.[78] With this rapid expansion of access to the Internet by millions of people around the world, the Internet is expected to become a major driving force in global marketing that no company, large or small, domestic or foreign, can afford to neglect.

THE IMPORTANCE OF GLOBAL MARKETING

The globalization of markets is one of the major forces affecting companies worldwide. Although global marketing once meant forays abroad from a strong domestic market base, it has now assumed the meaning of open trade, in which a company can be attacked anywhere, including in its home markets. "Sanctuaries," or protected domestic markets, are rapidly disappearing. This change has increased the importance of global marketing to many firms and made it the widely practiced activity it is today.

Global marketing is expanding rapidly. The combined value of world exports (in the form of physical goods or merchandise) and services (also sometimes referred to as invisibles, such as financial services) exceeded $7.5 trillion in 2000. Merchandise exports amounted to $6,186 billion in 2000, and international trade in services reached $1,435 billion in the same year. For the years 1990 to 2000, world merchandise exports grew 6 percent annually and exceeded world GDP growth most of those years. This indicates that the global aspect of the world economy was growing faster than the domestic segments, further contributing to the rapid pace of the globalization of the economy.[79]

World services exports, or earnings, took many forms. The role of banks, insurance companies, accounting firms, and consulting companies has already been well documented. A recent effort in this field comes from medical institutions. Several leading U.S. medical centers have begun to market their services abroad. In 1997, an estimated 385,000 international patients were treated at U.S. hospitals on an outpatient basis, and another 66,000 received inpatient care. In the Philadelphia region, ten local hospitals formed a venture, Philadelphia International Medicine, with the goal of bringing six thousand foreign patients to those hospitals every year. Spending on medical services was believed to amount to $60 million, with another $140 million to be spent in the region for travel, hotels, and food for patients' families.[80] Johns Hopkins in Baltimore was estimated to treat seven thousand international patients annually, generating an annual $30 million in revenue. Other leading hospitals included the Cleveland Clinic and the Mayo Clinic in Rochester, Minnesota.[81] This is not solely a U.S. phenomenon: in Thailand, many privately held local clinics have started to attract Japanese patients. Thai medical costs are said to be among the lowest in the world, and they are only 25 percent of corresponding costs in Japan.[82]

A substantial portion of global marketing operations is not recorded in international trade statistics. In particular, overseas sales of locally manufactured and locally sold products made by foreign subsidiaries are not included in world trade figures because the products do not cross any borders. Consequently, total volume in global marketing far exceeds the volume for total world trade. Sales of overseas subsidiaries of U.S. companies are estimated at three times the value of these companies' exports. Although no detailed statistics are available, this pattern suggests that the overall volume of global marketing amounts to a multiple of recorded world trade volume.

As we pointed out earlier, the global marketing activities of firms go beyond mere exports of products and services. The volume of this trade, however, can be used to gauge the pervasiveness of global marketing activities. When Wal-Mart, the U.S.-based discount retail chain and the world's largest retailer, began to expand its operations abroad, it brought along its price-cutting culture of everyday low prices. This represents an export of a domestic marketing strategy and, as such, is part of the field of global marketing. However, since Wal-Mart exports an idea only and not any measurable goods or services, this part of global marketing is not registered in world trade statistics.[83] Likewise, Starbucks, the Seattle-based coffee retail chain, entered the Japanese market and brought its store concept to Japan, thus engaging in a form of global marketing even though it sources most of its products locally and even raised the capital for expanding its retail stores through a joint venture and local capital.[84] A considerable amount of global marketing takes the form of similar conceptual approaches. Data measuring the extent of these approaches are not available, however.

THE LOGIC FOR INVOLVEMENT IN GLOBAL MARKETING

Companies become involved in international markets for various reasons. Some firms simply respond to orders from abroad without any organized efforts of their own, but most companies take a more proactive role because they have determined that it is to their advantage to pursue export business on an incremental basis. The profitability of a company can increase when fixed manufacturing costs are already committed and additional economies of scale are achieved.

For some firms, the impetus to globalize comes from a domestic competitive shock. General Electric Lighting (a division of General Electric [GE]) was the traditional market leader in the United States and had been in the business since 1878. In 1983, Westinghouse, its largest U.S. competitor, sold its lighting division to Philips of the Netherlands. This brought a strong foreign competitor into GE's backyard, yet GE was not competing in Philips's territory in Europe. As a result, GE Lighting expanded by buying Tungsram, a Hungarian lighting company, in its first big move into eastern Europe. This expansion was followed by the acquisition of Thorn-EMI's lighting interest, a U.K.-based unit. And in Asia, GE Lighting concluded a joint venture with Hitachi of Japan. These acquisitions gave GE's international lighting sales a boost from just 20 percent in 1988 to more than 50 percent for 1996. In Europe alone, GE Lighting's share rose to 15 percent in just a few years.[85] GE Lighting also built plants in China that are being used as supply points for retail stores anywhere in the world. With an accumulated investment of more than $100 million, GE exported about $275 million of lighting products worldwide from its Chinese plants.[86] The nature of the GE lighting business thus changed from a predominantly domestic business into a global one.

Some companies pursue growth in other countries after their domestic market has reached maturity. Coca-Cola, a market leader worldwide in the soft-drink business, finds that on a per capita basis, foreign consumers drink only a fraction of the amount of soft drinks consumed by Americans. In the U.S. market, per capita consumption amounts to 419 servings (one serving equals 8 fl. oz.), whereas the corresponding amount for China is only nine servings. Growth in the U.S. market amounted to 5 percent annually over the past ten years, compared to 16 percent for China. However, the company, which still sees enormous additional potential in international markets, already generates 70 percent of its total revenue overseas.[87] Although the volume in China is still small compared to the company's overall sales, the market has been growing rapidly and Coca-Cola has invested about $1.1 billion in China since 1979, and operates twenty-eight plants there, with additional plants planned over the next few years.[88]

The Swiss-based food company Nestlé has five hundred factories in seventy-seven countries, employs 230,000 workers, and had sales of $50 billion in 2001. It is one of the world's oldest and most well-established global firms.[89] Facing maturing markets in Europe, Nestlé is considering Asia as a major source of growth and new revenue. Nestlé has targeted China as a key market and has opened joint ventures in China for marketing Nescafé, Coffee-Mate creamer, and milk powder. Since 1980, Nestlé has invested more than $500 million in the Chinese market, built fifteen modern factories there, and hired about five thousand employees.[90] The company has achieved several leading positions in key product lines in China; for example, it is number 1 in instant coffee and dehydrated foods, and is now the sixth largest food company in all of China. Although Nestlé had been trading in China since 1908, its first factory was not built there until 1990. Its Greater China region accounts for about $800 million in sales. Clearly, the company expects emerging markets such as China to play a much larger role in its strategy in the future, particularly with about 1 billion Asians expected to join the ranks of those who can afford packaged food over the next decade.[91]

Customers moving abroad provide reasons for many firms to follow. Major U.S. banks have shifted to serve their U.S. clients in key financial centers around the world by opening branches in these financial centers. Advertising agencies in the United States have created networks to serve the interests of their multinational clients. When some Japanese automobile manufacturers opened plants in the United States, many of their component suppliers followed and built operations nearby. Not following these clients would have meant a loss of business. For some firms, however, the reason to become involved in global marketing has its roots in pure economics. Producers of television shows in Hollywood spend about $1.5 million to produce a single show for a typical series. However, U.S. networks pay only about $1 million to air a single show. As a result, the series producers rely on international markets for the difference. Without the opportunity to market globally, they would not even be able to produce the shows for the U.S. market.[92] In Chapter 7 we revisit these reasons for becoming involved in global marketing, and we devote a section of Chapter 7 to global logics and the underlying causes of the global marketing "imperative."

WHY STUDY GLOBAL MARKETING?

You have probably asked yourself, Why study global marketing? You may also have wondered about the value of this knowledge to your future career. While it is not very likely that many university graduates can find an entry-level position in international or global marketing, it is nevertheless a fact that U.S.-based international companies hire large numbers of marketing professionals each year. Since many of these firms are becoming increasingly global, competence in global marketing will become even more important in the future—and many marketing executives will pursue global marketing as a career. Other career opportunities exist with a large number of exporters, and candidates will require international marketing skills. Furthermore, many university graduates are hired each year for the marketing efforts of foreign-based companies in the United States. These companies are also looking for international and global competence within their managerial ranks.

With the U.S. service sector becoming increasingly global, many graduates joining service industries have found themselves confronted with international opportunities at the early stages of their careers. Today, consulting engineers, bankers, brokers, public accountants, medical services executives, and ecommerce specialists are all in need of global marketing skills to compete in a rapidly changing environment. Consequently, a solid understanding and appreciation of global marketing will benefit the careers of most business students, regardless of the field or industry they choose to enter.

As we have seen from the many examples cited in this first chapter, however, global marketing concepts are not limited to U.S. firms expanding abroad. Companies from all countries are affected by the globalization of markets. Global firms can be headquartered just as easily in Japan, the United Kingdom, Germany, the Netherlands, India, China, or Canada. Consequently, the concepts described in this text are meant for any aspiring global marketer, whether the person intends to start a career in the United States or in emerging regions such as Asia, Latin America, and eastern Europe, where more and more global marketing executives will be needed to ensure the survival of firms based there.

A GROWING NEED FOR GLOBAL MARKETERS

Compared with other industrialized nations, the United States sorely lacks a sufficient number of global marketing professionals. As active participants in global marketing, global marketers play a key role in the success of international firms. In this competitive business, the United States has seen its share of world exports steadily decline. In 1953, the United States accounted for 19 percent of total world exports, more than twice the share of the second-ranked United Kingdom, which claimed about 8 percent. At that time, Japan accounted for only 2 percent of world exports. The U.S. share of world exports was down to 12.5 percent in 2000, still ahead of Japan (7.7 percent), the United Kingdom (4.5 percent), and China (4 percent). In 2000, the European countries that are part of the European Union accounted for 36 percent of world exports.[93]

There are additional indications that the United States is lagging behind other countries in global marketing. From 1870 to 1970, the United States almost always reported a positive trade balance, exporting more goods than it imported. This situation began to change in the 1970s, and despite the large increase in earnings of the service industry, the overall balance of trade has turned negative. It has been estimated that its large trade deficit has cost the United States several million jobs. Although many reasons for this lagging performance lie beyond the control of individual companies, company management can do much to redress the imbalance. Foreign companies fight much harder than U.S. firms to retain foreign markets. Because the domestic markets for foreign firms are usually smaller than the U.S. market, foreign firms are more motivated than U.S. firms to succeed abroad.

Despite the alarming imbalance of trade, foreign trade, or global marketing, is still not given sufficient attention by large sectors of U.S. society. Whereas university graduates in other countries have learned one or more foreign languages as a matter of course, U.S. graduates usually have limited foreign language competency. About fifty thousand Japanese business professionals work in the New York City area, and all possess a good understanding of English; only about one thousand U.S. business professionals working in Tokyo have a solid command of the Japanese language. Although it is too simplistic to associate foreign-language capabilities with effectiveness in global marketing, this comparison nevertheless serves as an indicator of interest in international business. Although the concepts introduced in this text are certainly important to anyone living overseas because of a global marketing assignment, the following section will demonstrate that these concepts have just as much validity for those of us who stay home.

A NEED FOR GLOBAL MINDSETS

Few of us can avoid the impact of global competition today. Many of our domestic industries have been greatly affected by foreign competition, which has made enormous inroads in the manufacture of apparel, textiles, shoes, electronic equipment, and steel. As a result, these industries have become global and have been pulled into the global economy.[94] Although foreign competition for many consumer goods has been evident for years, inroads by foreign firms in investment goods industries have been equally spectacular. The management of companies competing with foreign firms requires global minds: an ability to judge the next move of foreign competitors by observing them abroad and thus being better prepared to compete at home.

Import competition has been rising even in industries that were once reserved largely for domestic companies. Nissin, a Japanese maker of instant noodles, invented instant noodles, called "Cup Noodles," in 1971. Based on a strong 40 percent market share in the Japanese instant noodles segment, Nissin expanded its U.S. position to account for a 10 percent share of the instant noodle market. Its products are placed next to the leading soup company, Campbell Soup, in U.S. supermarkets. The company operates about twenty-five plants in eight countries. Although the initial results in the United States were not successful, Nissin stayed in for the long term and is now a successful competitor in the United States. Nissin also brought an entirely new product concept to the United States and eventually forced U.S. suppliers, such as Campbell and Lipton, to adapt to its strategy.[95]

Foreign competition has also reached U.S. retailers. Based in Sweden, IKEA, the world's largest furniture retailing chain, came to the United States in 1985. IKEA brought with it a concept new to the United States: large stores where consumers could browse, buy, and take furniture home in disassembled form at the end of their visit. Although successful and profitable now, IKEA had to struggle in the early years, and it made several changes to its retailing formula to adapt to U.S. requirements. From a base of fifteen stores in the United States and eight stores in Canada, the company hopes to expand by opening an average of five stores in North America over the next ten years.[96] This planned rollout is likely to have an impact on the U.S. domestic furniture retail scene. IKEA is but one example of an international global competitor entering a previously "safe" market with new ideas, thus bringing global competition to the doorstep of largely domestic companies.

The need to become more competitive in a global economy will force many changes on the typical company. Companies will have to become international and compete in global markets to defend their domestic markets and to keep up with global competitors based in other countries. These firms will need an increasing cadre of managers with a global perspective.[97] This perspective requires not only knowledge of other countries, economies, and cultures but also a clear understanding of how the global economy works. Managers with a global perspective will also have to integrate developments in one part of the world with actions in another. A U.S. executive will be required to use input, facts, or ideas from several other countries to make decisions in U.S. markets so that the best products may be marketed most efficiently and effectively.

Managers with a global perspective will also be challenged to deal with new strategies that were not part of the domestic or older international business scenes. These concepts have been included in our text and will become apparent to you on a chapter-by-chapter basis. As a result, you will come to appreciate that the term *global* is more than just a replacement for *international*. The meaning of the term is a combination of a new perspective on the world and a series of new strategic concepts that add to the competitiveness of global marketing strategies. Mastering both this new outlook and the new concepts will become a requirement for firms that aspire to the position of global player in their chosen industries or market segments. Because this global mindset is so important to marketers, we have devoted much of Chapter 7 to covering the concept in depth.

ORGANIZATION OF THIS BOOK

This text is structured around the basic requirements for making sound global marketing decisions. It takes into account the need to develop several types of competencies for analyzing global marketing issues. The global marketer must be able to deal with making decisions at various levels of complexity. We will discuss each of these dimensions of the global marketing task before we discuss the outline for this text.

COMPETENCIES

To compete successfully in today's global marketplace, companies and their managers must master certain areas. *Environmental competence* includes knowledge of the dynamics of the world economy; of major national markets; and of political, social, and cultural environments. *Analytic competence* is needed to pull together a vast array of information and data and to assemble relevant facts. *Strategic competence* helps executives focus on the strategic or long-term requirements of their firms, as opposed to short-term, opportunistic decisions. A global marketer must also possess *functional competence*, or a thorough background in all areas of marketing. Finally, *managerial competence* is the ability to implement programs and organize effectively on a global scale. Managers with domestic responsibility also need analytic, strategic, functional, and managerial competence, but they do not need global competence. Consequently, we will concentrate on those areas that set global marketing executives apart from their domestic counterparts.

DECISION AREAS

Successful global marketing requires the ability to make decisions not typically faced by single-country firms. These decision groupings include environmental analysis, global opportunity analysis, global marketing strategies, global marketing programs, and marketing management. Managers must continuously assess foreign environments and perform *environmental analyses* relevant to their businesses. In a second step, managers need to do an *opportunity analysis,* which will tell them which products to pursue in which markets. Once opportunities have been identified, *global marketing strategies* are designed to define the long-term efforts of the firm. The company may then design *global marketing programs* to determine the marketing mix. Finally, international marketing must *manage the global marketing effort*, which requires attention to planning, personnel, and organization.

Figure 1.3: International Marketing Management

Our five competence levels are closely related to the five major global marketing decision areas described above. Environmental competence is needed to perform an analysis of the global economic environment. Analytic competence is the basis for global opportunity analysis. Sound global marketing strategies are based on strategic competence. To design global marketing programs, one needs functional competence. Finally, managerial competence is needed for managing a global marketing effort.

CHAPTER ORGANIZATION

This text is organized around the flow of decisions, as depicted in Figure 1.3. The five decision areas are treated in several chapters that delineate the respective competence levels most appropriate for each decision area.

- Chapter 1 provided an introduction and overview of global marketing and its challenges today.
- Part 1, Chapters 2 through 4, is concerned with the global marketing environment. To build environmental competence, special emphasis is given to the economic, cultural, social, political, and legal forces companies must navigate to be successful.
- Part 2, Chapters 5 and 6, concentrates on the global market opportunity analysis. Chapters in this section highlight international markets or countries, international buyers, and the research or analysis necessary to pinpoint marketing opportunities globally.
- Chapters 7, 8, and 9, which make up Part 3, deal with strategic issues. Chapter 7 deals primarily with the mindset of the global marketer. Chapter 8 introduces the elements of global marketing strategy. Chapter 9 describes how companies can enter markets they have decided to target.
- Part 4, Chapters 10 through 15, develops the competence for designing global marketing programs consistent with a global strategy. The chapters in this section cover product strategies, product development, channel management, pricing, promotion and communications, and advertising.
- The text concludes with Part 5, Chapters 16 and 17. Here the emphasis is on building managerial competence in a global environment. Chapters 16 and 17 deal with organizational and controlling issues and also with the technical aspects of the export and import trade process.
- Finally, the cases included with this book address global marketing issues and give you an opportunity to practice the concepts developed in the text. These cases feature a range of complexity levels and address different decision areas of the global marketing process. They are all based on real situations, although the names of some of the companies are disguised.

CONCLUSIONS

As a separate activity of business, global marketing is of great importance to nations, to individual companies, and to prospective managers. With markets and industries becoming increasingly global, most companies must become active participants in global marketing. The competitive positions of most companies, both abroad and in their domestic markets, rest on their ability to succeed in global markets. At the same time, the economies of entire countries rest on the global marketing skills of managers. The standard of living of many people will depend on how well local industry does in the global marketplace. These forces will place a premium on executive talent that can direct marketing operations from a global perspective. Clearly, many business professionals will need to understand the global dimension as it pertains to the marketing function if they are to progress in their careers.

In assembling a trained cadre of professional global marketing executives, the United States has typically lagged behind other countries. The U.S. market is so large that domestic problems tend to overshadow global marketing opportunities. As a result, most U.S. executives develop their careers largely in a domestic setting and have little direct exposure to foreign markets. Executives in foreign countries are more apt to have traveled abroad and tend to speak one or two foreign languages. Thus, their ability to understand global complexities is more developed than that of U.S. executives. All of these facts give many foreign firms a considerable edge in competing for global dominance.

Although the need to develop a global competence may be clear, the circumstances that determine successful marketing practices for foreign markets are far less clear. The foreign marketing environment is characterized by a wide range of variables not typically encountered by domestic firms. This situation makes the job of global marketing extremely difficult. Despite the complexities involved, however, there are concepts and analytic tools that can help global marketers. By learning to use these concepts and tools, you can enhance your own global marketing competence. You will be able to contribute to the marketing operations of a wide range of firms, both domestic and foreign.

Questions for Discussion

1. Explain the scope of global marketing.
2. How and why does global marketing differ from domestic marketing?
3. Which do you think would be the most relevant factors that would limit the standardization of international marketing for products like yogurt, automobiles, and desktop personal computers?
4. How does global marketing, as a field, relate to your future career in business? How do you expect to come into contact with global marketing activities?
5. Why are so many U.S. industries facing import competition?
6. Investigate one or two U.S. firms that do well abroad and analyze why they are successful.
7. Explain the major roles of multinationals (MNCs) and global corporations, as well as other types of firms, in international marketing, and explain how they participate in this activity.
8. What do you think are the essential skills of a successful "global marketer"?
9. What are the important skills for successful global minds?
10. List ten items and/or activities that you hope to understand or accomplish after studying this book.

For Further Reading

Bartlett, Christopher, and Yves Doz. *Managing the Global Firm*. Stamford, Conn.: Thompson Business Press, 1990.

Bartlett, Christopher, and Sumantra Ghoshal. *Managing Across Borders*. Boston: Harvard Business School Press, 1989.

Buzzell, Robert D. "Can You Standardize Multinational Marketing?" *Harvard Business Review*, November–December 1968, pp. 102–113.

Drew, Martin, and Paul Herbig. "Marketing Implications of Japan's Social-Cultural Underpinnings." *Journal of Brand Management*, January 2002, vol. 9, pp. 171–179.

Friedman, Thomas L. *The Lexus and the Olive Tree*. New York: Anchor Books, 2000.

Gingrich, James A. "Five Rules for Winning Emerging Market Consumers." *Strategy & Business*, 2nd quarter 1999, no. 15, pp. 19–33.

Govindarajan, Vijay, and Anil K. Gupta. "Taking Wal-Mart Global: Lessons from Retailing's Giant." *Strategy & Business*, 4th quarter 1999, no. 17, pp. 14–25.

Jeannet, Jean-Pierre. *Managing with a Global Mindset*. London: Pitman, Financial Times Management, 2000.

Jolly, Vijay K., Matti Alahuhta, and Jean-Pierre Jeannet. "Challenging the Incumbents: How High Technology Start-Ups Compete Globally." *Journal of Strategic Change*, January 1992, vol. 1.00–00, pp. 11–1 to 11–12.

Kashani, Kamran. "Beware of Pitfalls in Global Marketing." *Harvard Business Review*, September–October 1989, pp. 91–98.

Levitt, Theodore. "The Globalization of Markets." *Harvard Business Review*, May–June 1983, pp. 92–102.

Ohmae, Kenichi. *The Borderless World*. New York: Harper & Row, 1990.

———. "Managing in a Borderless World." *Harvard Business Review*, May–June 1989, pp. 152–161.

———. *Triad Power*. New York: Free Press, 1985.

Porter, Michael E. "The Strategic Role of International Marketing." *Journal of Consumer Marketing*, Spring 1986, pp. 17–21.

Prahalad, C. K., and Yves L. Doz. *The Multinational Mission*. New York: Free Press, 1987.

Reich, Robert B. *The World of Nations*. New York: Knopf, 1991.

Taylor, William. "The Logic of Global Business: An Interview with ABB's Percy Barnevik." *Harvard Business Review*, March–April 1991, pp. 91–105.

UNCTAD World Investment Report 1998. New York: United Nations, 1998.

Endnotes

1. Theodore Levitt, "The Globalization of Markets," *Harvard Business Review*, May–June 1983, pp. 92–102.
2. Philip Kotler and Gary Armstrong, *Principles of Marketing*, 9th ed. (Englewood Cliffs, N.J.:Prentice Hall, 2000).
3. Gerald Albaum, *International Marketing and Export Management* , 3rd ed.(Reading, Mass.: Addison-Wesley, 1998).
4. "Everything from Soup to Soap," *The Asian Wall Street Journal*, February 1, 2002, p. 10.
5. "Remaking Ford," *Business Week*, October 11, 1999, p. 132.
6. "The World Music Market Thinks Globally, Acts Locally," *The Wall Street Journal Europe*, September 7, 2001, p. 4.
7. "Vivendi Holds the Lead in Market Share," *The Asian Wall Street Journal*, July 27, 2001, p. 10.
8. "The World Music Market Thinks Globally, Acts Locally," *The Wall Street Journal Europe*, September 7, 2001, p. 4.
9. "Inside Track—Selling a Strategy for Social Revolution," *Financial Times*, April 22, 2002, p. 18.
10. Philip Kotler, *Marketing Management*, 11th ed. (Englewood Cliffs, N.J.: Prentice-Hall, 2002).
11. Henry W. Lane, Joseph J. DiStefano, Martha L. Maznevski, *International Management Behavior* (Oxford, U.K.: Blackwell, 1996); Paul W. Beamish, Allen J. Morrison, and Philip M. Rosenzweig, International *Management: Text and Cases*, 4th ed. (New York: McGraw-Hill, 1999); David K. Eiteman, Arthur I. Stonehill, and Michael H. Moffet, *Multinational Business Finance*, 9th ed. (Reading, Mass.: Addison-Wesley, 2000); Alan C. Shapiro, *Multinational Financial Management*, 6th ed. (New York: Wiley, 1999).
12. Paul R. Krugman and Maurice Obstfeld, *International Economics: Theory and Policy*, 5th ed. (Reading, Mass.: Addison-Wesley, 2000); Francisco L. Rivera-Batiz and Luis A. Rivera-Batiz, *International Finance and Open Economy Macroeconomics*, 2nd ed. (New York: Macmillan, 1994); Jeffrey D. Sachs and B. Felipe Larrain, *Macroeconomics in the Global Economy* (Englewood Cliffs, N.J.: Prentice Hall, 1993); Beth V. Yarbrough and Robert M. Yarbrough, *The World Economy: Trade and Finance* (Chicago, Ill.: International Thomson, 2000).
13. "2000 PC Sales in Japan Dip 2.5 Percent in 3 Key Shopping Areas," *Jiji Press English News Service*, Tokyo, May 16, 2001.
14. "Apple Plans October Start for iBook Sales in Japan", *Asian Wall Street Journal*, September 8, 1999, p. 8.
15. This section draws heavily on Robert D. Buzzell's classic article "Can You Standardize Multinational Marketing?" See *Harvard Business Review*, November–December 1968, pp. 102–103.
16. Theodore Levitt, "The Globalization of Markets," *Harvard Business Review*, May–June 1983, pp. 92–102.
17. Kamran Kashani, "Beware of the Pitfalls of Global Marketing," *Harvard Business Review*, September–October 1989, pp. 91–98.
18. "In Doing Laundry, Americans Cling to Outmoded Ways," *The Wall Street Journal*, May 16, 2002, p. 1.
19. "Macworld," *Economist*, June 29, 1996, p. 61.
20. "Fast Food, Western Colas Highlight China Growth," *National Catholic Reporter*, January 29, 1999, p. 15.
21. "Soda Pop Shakes Awake Dozing Coffee Companies," *Wall Street Journal Europe*, June 9, 1999, p. 4.
22. "A Matter of Wording," *Far Eastern Economic Review*, October 10, 1996, p. 72.
23. "Global Village," *Line56*, San Francisco, September 2001, p. 24.
24. New Era for Japan," *Telecommunications*, September 2001, vol. 35, no. 9, pp. 84–88.
25. "Tale of A Bubble," *Business Week*, June 3, 2002, p. 48.
26. "Zeglis the Zealot," *Forbes*, May 27, 2002, p. 59
27. "Patents of EMR: The Choice Between Two Evils," *Statesman* (India), January 18, 1999.
28. *World Investment Report 2001* (Geneva: UNCTAD, 2001).
29. "The World's Largest 500 Corporations," *Fortune*, July 23, 2001, p. 144.
30. *World Investment Report 2001* (Geneva: UNCTAD, 2001, table 2, p. 3).
31. "Aftermath of Terror: Economic Ripple," *The Wall Street Journal*, September 24, 2001, p. A8.

32. Christopher Bartlett and Sumantra Ghoshal, *Managing Across Borders* (Boston: Harvard Business School Press, 1998).

33. General Electric, *Annual Report*, 2001.

34. Texas Instruments, *10-K Report*, 2001.

35. "The Asiaweek 1000, 2000," *Asiaweek* web site.

36. Samsung Electronics web site.

37. "Silicon Rush," *Far Eastern Economic Review*, February 14, 2002, p. 30.

38. "Information Technology 100," *Business Week*, June 24, 2002, p. 114.

39. Samsung Electronics, *Annual Report*, 2000.

40. "Taiwan's Acer Moves to Buy Out TI Stake in Chip Venture," *Dow Jones Online News*, March 4, 1998.

41. "IBM, Taiwan's Acer Will Announce Pact to Deepen Their Ties," *Wall Street Journal*, June 7, 1999, p. C17.

42. "Siemens to Quit PC Market, Sell Plants to Acer," *Wall Street Journal*, April 24, 1998, p. A13

43. "A Couple of Successful Joint Ventures Has Thailand's Largest Multinational Sitting atop the Heap," *Far Eastern Economic Review*, December 27, 2001, p. 82.

44. "From Chickens to Microchips," *Far Eastern Economic Review*, January 23, 1997, pp. 38–45.

45. "CP Committed to Business in China," *Bangkok Post*, July 1, 1999, p. 2.

46. "Pulp Fiction," *Far Eastern Economic Review*, February 14, 2002, p. 38.

47. "China: Investors to Looks Abroad," *Asiainfo Daily China News*, March 20, 2001, p. 1.

48. "China Encourages Manufacturers to Invest Overseas," *Far Eastern Economic Review*, April 15, 1999, p. 82.

49. Groupo Vitro, *Annual Report 1998, Annual Report 2001*.

50. "Vitro Plans Expansion in U.S.," *Mexico Business Monthly*, May 1, 1999.

51. "SAB Purchases $5.6 bn Miller Brewing," *Financial Times*, May 31, 2002, p. 19.

52. "The China Brew," *Far Eastern Economic Review*, June 13, 2002, p. 47.

53. *www.Nokia.com* (2002).

54. "Nokia Faces Big Hurdles to Stay Ahead of the Race," *Financial Times*, June 4, 2002, p. 23.

55. "Nokia Is Europe's Most Valuable Brand," *M2 Presswire*, July 13, 1999.

56. "Wal-Mart: Can the Arkansas Giant Export Its Price-Cutting Culture Around the World?" *Newsweek*, May 20, 2002, p. 59.

57. "The Top 200 Global Retailers," *Stores*, January 23, 2000 (www.stores.org/archives).

58. "Ahold Plans to Post 15 Percent Earnings Rise for 2001 and 2002," *The Wall Street Journal Europe*, January 9, 2002, p. 5

59. Corporate web site (www.Ikea-US.com).

60. "Circling the Globe," *The Grocer Yearbook 2002*, p. 16.

61. "The Deal Machine," *Business Week*, November 1, 1999, p. 70.

62. "Deloitte Restates Its Case," *Fortune*, April 29, 2002, p. 65.

63. "HSBC in Calif: De Novos Now, Deals Later," *American Banker*, May 13, 2002, p. 1.

64. "European Banks Rethink Globalization," *Wall Street Journal*, October 5, 1998, p. A23.

65. *World Trade in 2000–Overview* (Geneva: World Trade Organization, 2001).

66. "United States Trade," *Cambridge International Forecast Country Report*, April 1, 1999, p. 1.

67. Boeing Co., *Annual Report 1998*.

68. "Small Business and International Trade Going Global by Online Growth," *Los Angeles Times*, February 11, 1998, p. D1.

69. "Pounding Pulse at Cardiac Science," *Business Week*, April 22, 2002, p. 111.

70. Hermann Simon, "Lessons from Germany's Midsize Giants," *Harvard Business Review*, March–April 1992, pp. 115–123.

71. "Information Technology 100," *Business Week*, June 24, 2002, p. 114.

72. "Economy Hampering Yahoo!'s Goals," *Advertising Age*, March 12, 2001, p. 31.

73. "U.S. Service Firms Find the World's a Stage," *Knight-Ridder Business News*, July 9, 1999.

74. "Europe Could Be Silver Lining for AOL," *Broadband Networking News*, January 15, 2002, p. 1.

75. "AOL's Growth Is Continuing," *The Asian Wall Street Journal*, March 22, 2001, p. M6.

76. "Schwab to Go to Japan," *Financial Times*, October 21, 1999, p. 21.

77. "Internet Access Hits Half a Billion Worldwide," *Europmedia*, March 7, 2002.

78. "The Pope of Broadband," *The Wall Street Journal*, June 10, 2002, p. R11.

79. *World Trade in 2000–Overview, The* World Trade Organization (WTO), Geneva, 2001.

80. "Hospitals Seek Foreign Patients," *Philadelphia Business Journal*, November 13, 1998, p. 1.

81. "Medical Globe-Trotting," *Pittsburgh Business Times & Journal*, January 15, 1999, p. 1.

82. "Hospitals Seek Foreigners as Poor Economy Prices Locals Out," *South China Morning Post*, May 30, 1999, p. 4.

83. "Wal-Mart World," *Newsweek*, May 20, 2002, p. 50.

84. "Seattle Coffee Rivalries Percolate in Japan," *The Nikkei Weekly*, June 3, 2002, p. 12.

85. "Old World, New Investment," *Business Week*, October 7, 1996, pp. 50–51.

86. "GE Lighting Will Enlarge Procurement in China," *Asiainfo Daily China News*, January 31, 2002, p. 1.

87. Coca Cola Company, *Annual Report*, 2001.

88. "Coca Cola to Build Six More Plants in China," *Business Asia Today*, November 12, 2001.

89. Nestlé Company, *Annual Report*, 2001.

90. "Nestlé Operating Profitably in China," *Asia Pulse*, April 22, 1999.

91. Nestlé Company, *Annual Report*, 2001; and corporate web site (www.nestle.com).

92. "Think Globally, Script Locally," *Fortune*, November 8, 1999, p. 157.

93. *World Trade in 2000–Overview* WTO, 2001.

94. Thomas L. Friedman, *The Lexus and the Olive Tree* (New York: Anchor Books, 2000).

95. "Nissin, Japan's Instant Noodle Creator, Faces Global Challenges," *Dow Jones Business News*, February 12, 2001.

96. "IKEA plans aggressive growth," *Home Textiles Today*, February 4, 2002, p. 22.

97. Jean-Pierre Jeannet, *Managing with a Global Mindset* (London: Pitman, Financial Times Management, 2000).

Part I

Understanding the Global Marketing Environment

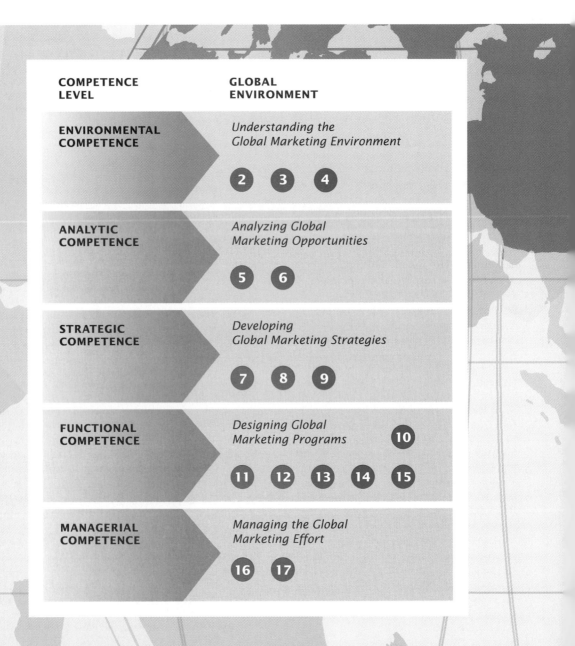

COMPETENCE LEVEL	GLOBAL ENVIRONMENT
ENVIRONMENTAL COMPETENCE	*Understanding the Global Marketing Environment* — 2 3 4
ANALYTIC COMPETENCE	*Analyzing Global Marketing Opportunities* — 5 6
STRATEGIC COMPETENCE	*Developing Global Marketing Strategies* — 7 8 9
FUNCTIONAL COMPETENCE	*Designing Global Marketing Programs* — 10 11 12 13 14 15
MANAGERIAL COMPETENCE	*Managing the Global Marketing Effort* — 16 17

This part of the book introduces you to the environmental factors that influence global marketing decisions. Throughout Part I, we maintain an analytical emphasis so that general concepts can be applied from country to country. Rather than describe a large number of environmental differences, we focus on several approaches that companies adopt to cope with these differences. Our aim is to maintain a managerial point of view throughout.

In Chapter 2, we explain the nature of the various global economic forces that shape developments within individual countries as well as within the global economy. In Chapter 3, we describe the social and cultural influences that shape the local marketing environment, and in Chapter 4, we discuss the political and legal forces that affect global firms, and we focus on how companies cope with these forces.

CHAPTER 2
The Global Economy

CHAPTER 3
Cultural and Social Forces

CHAPTER 4
Political and Legal Forces

Chapter 2

The Global Economy

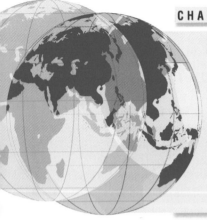

Billions of dollars in goods and services are traded between nations each day. Businesses establish operations and borrow funds in locations throughout the world. Financial investors expeditiously purchase stocks and bonds on U.S., European, and Asian markets. Banks lend and arbitrage currencies worldwide. The scope and significance of the international economy are appreciated only when these transactions are interrupted or threatened.

A multidimensional network of economic, social, cultural, and political ties links the nations of the world. As these connections become more important and complex, countries will find themselves richer but more vulnerable to foreign disturbances, and this vulnerability will move the issues surrounding international trade and finance increasingly into the political arena.

This chapter introduces the important aspects of world trade and finance. We begin by explaining comparative advantage, which is the basis for international trade. We then explain the international system for monitoring world trade, particularly the balance of payments measurement system. From this base, we describe the workings of the foreign exchange market and the cause of exchange rate movements. Finally, we discuss the international agencies that promote economic and monetary stability, as well as the strategies that countries use to protect their own economies.

To operate effectively in multiple countries, it is critical to have a global perspective of the world economic systems and how countries manage their own fiscal policies relative to their trading partners. Interest rates, inflation rates, and balance of payments are variables that will ultimately affect the exchange rates and company performance. A marketer with a global mindset will understand the interaction of these variables so that he or she can interpret how an improvement in the Japanese economy will affect the U.S. dollar and the resulting impact on exports and imports to Mexico.

INTERNATIONAL TRADE: AN OVERVIEW

Few individuals in the world are completely self-sufficient. Why should they be? Restricting consumption to self-made goods lowers living standards by narrowing the range and reducing the quality of the goods we consume. For this reason, few nations have economies independent from the rest of the world, and it would be difficult to find a national leader willing or able to impose such an economic hardship on a country.

Foreign goods are central to the living standards of all nations. Nevertheless, as you can see in Table 2.1, there is considerable variation among countries concerning their reliance on foreign trade. In 2000, imports were 15 percent or less of the gross domestic product (GDP) of Japan and the United States, whereas Mexico had an import-to-GDP ratio of 42 percent.

Even in countries that seemingly do not have a great reliance on imports, such as the United States (where imports were 15 percent of the 2000 GDP and exports were 9 percent), world trade in goods and services plays an important role. In 2000, the U.S. trade in imports and exports was $2.0 trillion, making it the largest trading country in the world. In addition, the volume of U.S. trade has increased, from 17 percent of GDP in 1985, to 27 percent in 1994, to 31.4 percent in 2001, down from 2000, at 34 percent. In addition, most U.S. *Fortune* 500 companies receive over 50 percent of their profits from overseas.[1]

Peter Johnson, a student, is awakened in the morning by his Sony clock radio. After showering, he puts on an Italian-made jacket while listening to the latest release by Tears for Fears, a British rock group. At breakfast, he has a cup of Brazilian coffee, a bowl of cereal made from U.S.-grown wheat, and a Colombian banana. A quick glance at his Swiss watch shows him that he will have to hurry if he wants to be on time for his first class. He drives to campus in a Toyota, stopping on the way to fill the tank with gas from Saudi Arabian oil. Once in class, he rushes to take a seat with the other students, 30 percent of whom hold non-U.S. passports.

The figures given in Table 2.1 are useful for identifying the international dependence of nations, but they should be viewed only as rough indicators. In a disruption of international trade, there is little doubt that the United States would be harmed much less than Canada or Norway. But this is not to say that a disruption of trade would not be harmful to the United States, or to Japan as well. Both the United States and Japan have large domestic markets but depend heavily on world trade for growth.

So far, the focus has been on world trade for goods. Services also are an important and growing part of the world's economy. Services make up approximately 25 percent of the world's trade, totaling $1,350 trillion in 2000.[2] Industries such as banking, telecommunications, insurance, construction, transportation, tourism, and consulting make up over half the national income of many rich economies. A country's invisible exports include export of services, transfers from workers abroad, and income earned

Table 2.1 Imports and Exports as a Percentage of GDP, 2000 Estimates (in Billions of Dollars)					
	GDP	Imports	Imports/GDP	Exports	Exports/GDP
INDUSTRIAL					
Australia	385	71	19%	64	17%
Canada	635	249	39	277	44
Japan	4,620	380	8	479	10
Norway	157	34	22	58	37
Switzerland	263	483	31	81	31
United States	8,241	1,258	15	782	9
DEVELOPING					
Brazil	782	59	7%	55	7%
China	1,062	225	21	249	23
India	491	50	10	42	9
Mexico	431	183	42	66	39
Russia	435	44	10	105	24
Saudi Arabia	152	33	22	84	55
South Korea	466	161	34	173	37

Source: "Imports and Exports as a Percentage of GDP, 1998 Estimates" adapted from WTO Report 2000, and the U.S. Embassy, Riyadh, Key Economic Data.

on overseas investments. In volume, the top five countries in service exports were the United States ($253.36 billion), the United Kingdom ($101.52 billion), France ($82.58 billion), Germany ($79.31 billion), and Italy ($61.18 billion).[3]

THE GROWTH IN WORLD TRADE

World trade has grown sixteenfold since 1950, far outstripping the growth in GDP.[4] The opening of world markets has fueled this growth. The Bretton Woods conference of world leaders in 1944 led to the establishment of the General Agreement on Tariffs and Trade (GATT) in 1948, which will be discussed in detail later. The original group of twenty-three countries expanded to almost one hundred. GATT, and now the World Trade Organization (WTO), has helped to reduce tariffs from 40 percent in 1947 to an estimated 4 percent in 2000.[5] A recent study showed that open economies with limited duties and government restrictions grew 1.2 percent faster per year than closed economies.[6] The WTO reports that tariffs are down to an average of 3.8 percent in developed countries. The WTO has 144 members, and another thirty-one countries, including Kazakhstan, Saudi Arabia, Vietnam, and the Russian Federation, have petitioned to join.[7] The principle of free trade has led to the building of market interdependencies. As shown in Figure 2.1, international trade has grown much faster than world GDP output. Thus, national economies are becoming much more closely linked and interdependent by means of their exports and imports. Foreign direct investment, another indication of global integration, grew by 100 percent between 1990 and 1997.[8]

Because of the lengthy (seven years) Uruguay Round of GATT talks and agreements that ended in 1993, world trade has grown 6 percent per year since 1993, ver-

Figure 2.1: Growth of World Trade and GNP

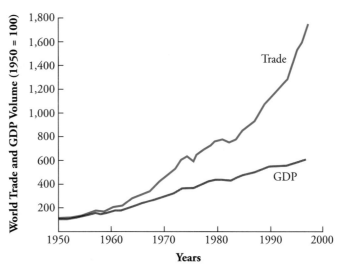

sus 4 percent for the 1980s.[9] In fact, in 1997, the WTO estimated that world trade of goods grew by 10 percent, three times the world GDP growth. In 1998, world trade grew by only 3.5 percent because of the economic contraction in Asia.[10] As the WTO replaced GATT in 1996, the major challenge was to assure compliance and to assert its authority over powerful regional trade agreements like the European Union (EU), the North American Free Trade Agreement (NAFTA), the Common Market of the South (MERCOSUR), and the Asian-Pacific Economic Cooperation (APEC). There are over one hundred regional agreements between countries granting preferential access to each other's markets. All but three of the 144 members of the WTO belong to at least one of these regional pacts.[11] Understanding the economics of trade is critical to understanding that the need for free trade flows from country to country.

The growth in world trade was negatively affected in several ways by the terrorist attacks of September 11, 2001. The increased cost of risk insurance has burdened exporters. The enhanced border protection and the increased security for containers, which account for 60 percent of world trade, will all increase the cost of exports and imports. Therefore, all these factors will slow the growth in world trade.[12]

THE BASIS FOR TRADE: ABSOLUTE VERSUS COMPARATIVE ADVANTAGE

Internationally traded goods and services are important to most countries, as you saw in Table 2.1. Because jobs and the standard of living are closely tied to these inflows and outflows, there is much debate about why particular countries find their comparative advantages in certain goods and services and not in others. And there is debate about why other countries have different advantages and disadvantages.

Over the past twenty years, there has been a dramatic rise in the volume of trade, and numerous changes have occurred in the patterns of trade as well. Countries that once exported vast amounts of steel, such as the United States, are now net importers of the metal. Japan, once known for inexpensive, handmade products, now competes globally in high-tech products. What caused these trade pattern changes? Why do countries that can produce almost any product choose to specialize in only certain goods? Where do international cost advantages originate? In the twenty-first century, will we still think of Indonesia and China as having the greatest advantage in hand-made goods, or in the future, will they compete in the world economy as Japan and Taiwan do today?

The early work of Adam Smith provides the foundation for understanding trade today. Smith saw trade as a way to promote efficiency because it fostered competition, led to specialization, and resulted in economies of scale. Specialization supports the concept of absolute advantages—that is, sell to other countries the goods that utilize your special skills and resources, and buy the rest from those who have some advantage. This theory of selling what you are best at producing is known as *absolute advantage*. But what if you have no advantages? Will all your manufacturers be driven out of business? David Ricardo, in his 1817 publication, *Principles of Political Economy*, offered his theory of comparative advantage.[13] This theory maintains that it is still possible to produce profitably what one is best at even if someone else is better. The following sections develop further the concepts of absolute and comparative advantage—the economic basis of free trade and hence all global trade.

ABSOLUTE ADVANTAGE

Although many variables may be listed as the primary determinants of international trade, productivity differences rank high on the list. Take, for example, two countries—Vietnam and Germany. Suppose the average Vietnamese worker can produce either 400 machines or 1,600 pounds of tomatoes in one year. Over the same period, the average German worker can produce either 500 machines or 500 pounds of tomatoes. (See example 1 in Table 2.2.) In this case, German workers can produce more machinery, *absolutely*, than Vietnamese workers can; whereas Vietnamese workers can produce more tomatoes, *absolutely*, than can their German counterparts. Given these figures, Vietnam is the obvious low-cost producer of tomatoes and should export them to Germany. Similarly, Germany is the low-cost producer of machines and should export them to Vietnam.[14]

COMPARATIVE ADVANTAGE

We should not conclude from the previous example that absolute differences in production capabilities are necessary for trade to occur. Consider the same two countries—Vietnam and Germany. Now assume that the average Vietnamese worker can produce either 200 machines or 800 pounds of tomatoes each year, whereas the average German worker can produce either 500 machines or 1,000 pounds of tomatoes. (See example 2 in Table 2.2.) Germany has an absolute advantage in both goods, and it appears as though Vietnam will benefit from trade because it can buy cheaper

Table 2.2 Absolute Versus Comparative Advantage: Worker Productivity Examples

	Vietnam	Germany
EXAMPLE 1		
Yearly output per worker		
Machinery	400	500
Tomatoes	1,600	500
Absolute advantage	Tomatoes	Machinery
EXAMPLE 2		
Yearly output per worker		
Machinery	200	500
Tomatoes	800	1,000
Opportunity costs of production	1 machine costs 4 lb tomatoes	1 machine costs 2 lb tomatoes
	or	*or*
	1 lb tomatoes costs 0.25 machines	1 lb tomatoes costs 0.50 machines
Absolute advantage	None	Tomatoes
		Machinery
Comparative advantage	Tomatoes	Machinery

goods from Germany than Vietnam can make for itself. However, the basis for mutually advantageous trade is present, even here. The reason lies in the concept of comparative advantage.

Comparative advantage measures a product's cost of production, not in monetary
terms but in terms of the forgone opportunity of producing something else. It focuses
on tradeoffs. To illustrate, the production of machines means that resources cannot
be devoted to the production of tomatoes. In Germany, the worker who produces 500
machines will not be able to grow 1,000 pounds of tomatoes. If we standardize, the
cost can be stated as follows: each pound of tomatoes costs 0.5 machines, or 1 machine costs 2 pounds of tomatoes. In Vietnam, producing 200 machines forces the
sacrifice of 800 pounds of tomatoes. Alternatively, 1 pound of tomatoes costs 0.25 machines, or 1 machine costs 4 pounds of tomatoes.[15]

From the example above, we see that, even though Vietnam has an absolute disadvantage in both commodities, it still has a comparative advantage in tomatoes. For
Vietnam, the cost of producing a pound of tomatoes is 0.25 machines, whereas for
Germany, the cost is 0.5 machines. Similarly, even though Germany has an absolute
advantage in both products, it has a comparative cost advantage only in machines. It
costs Germany only 2 pounds of tomatoes to produce a single machine, whereas in
Vietnam, the cost is 4 pounds of tomatoes.

The last step in the discussion of the concept of comparative advantage is
to choose a mutually advantageous trading ratio and show how it can benefit both

Table 2.3 Mutually Advantageous Trading Ratios	
Tomatoes	**Machines**
Germany, 1 pound tomatoes = 0.50 machines	Vietnam, 1 machine = 4 pounds tomatoes
Vietnam, 1 pound tomatoes = 0.20 machines	Germany, 1 machine = 2 pounds tomatoes

countries. Any trading ratio between 1 machine = 2 pounds of tomatoes (Germany's domestic trading ratio) and 1 machine = 4 pounds of tomatoes (Vietnam's domestic trading ratio) will benefit both nations (see Table 2.3). Suppose we choose 1 machine = 3 pounds of tomatoes. Since Germany will be exporting machinery, it gains by obtaining 3 pounds of tomatoes rather than the 2 pounds it would have produced domestically. Likewise, because Vietnam will be exporting tomatoes, it gains because 1 machine can be imported for the sacrifice of only 3 pounds of tomatoes, rather than the 4 pounds of tomatoes if Vietnam made the machine itself.

Another way to think of comparative advantage is in terms of the value of labor. If workers are paid relative to their output, at the end of one year a German worker could have 500 machines or 1,000 pounds of tomatoes, and a Vietnamese worker could have 200 machines or 800 pounds of tomatoes. Given the relative output of each, a German worker could trade 1 machine for 2 pounds of tomatoes in Germany or 4 pounds of tomatoes in Vietnam. The Vietnamese worker could trade 1 pound of tomatoes for 0.25 machines in Vietnam or 0.5 machines in Germany. In the end, the Vietnamese worker will have fewer goods because productivity is less, which means he or she will be paid less. Thus, the goods will be cheaper than in Germany, where the output per worker is higher and therefore more expensive.

The discussion of comparative advantage illustrates that relative rather than absolute differences in productivity can form a determining basis for international trade. Although the concept of comparative advantage provides a powerful tool for explaining the rationale for mutually advantageous trade, it gives little insight into the source of the relative productivity differences. Specifically, why does a country find its comparative advantage in one particular good or service rather than in another? Is it by chance that the United States is a net exporter of aircraft, machinery, and chemicals but a net importer of steel, textiles, and consumer electronic products? Can we find some systematic explanations for this pattern?

The answers to these questions are more than just academic concerns; they have an impact on the standards of living and the livelihoods of millions of people. The importance of understanding productivity differences is especially apparent in countries where trade barriers (for example, tariffs and quotas) are about to be either erected or dismantled. For instance, during the formative years of the European Common Market, discussions centered on the economic disruptions that would occur when Germany, Italy, and France dropped their tariff barriers and permitted free trade among themselves. These issues have resurfaced each time a new country (such as Greece, Spain, or Portugal) has applied for membership in the European Community (now the European Union). They were hotly debated in 1982, when the U.S. government proposed trade liberalization measures for Latin American countries in the Caribbean Basin Initiative. These same issues were at the center of discussions during the Uruguay Round of GATT trade talks, which ran into difficulty over the elimination of farm subsidies by member countries.

The notion of comparative advantage requires that nations make intensive use of those factors they possess in abundance. They export *these* goods and import *those* goods for which they have a comparative disadvantage. So Hungary, with its low labor cost of one dollar per hour, will export labor-intensive goods, such as unsophisticated chest freezers and table linen, while Sweden, with its high-quality iron ore deposits, will export high-grade steel. In essence, the theory of comparative advantage states that countries engage in international trade exporting in those areas in which they are efficient and that they import goods that they are relatively inefficient at producing.[16]

Michael Porter argues that, although the theory of comparative advantage has appeal, it is limited just to the factors of production, which include land, labor, natural resources, and capital. Porter's study of ten trading nations that account for 50 percent of world exports and one hundred industries resulted in a new theory. This theory postulates that a country will have a significant impact on the competitive advantage of an industry depending on the following factors:

1. The elements of production
2. The nature of domestic demand
3. The presence of appropriate suppliers or related industry
4. The conditions in the country that govern how companies are created, organized, and managed, as well as the nature of domestic rivalry[17]

This view of competitive advantage does not refute the theory of comparative advantage; rather, it helps explain why industries have a comparative advantage.

BALANCE OF PAYMENTS

Newspapers, magazines, and nightly television news programs are filled with stories relating to aspects of international business. Media coverage often centers on the implications of a nation's trade deficit or surplus or on the economic consequences of an undervalued or overvalued currency. What are trade deficits? What factors will cause a currency's international value to change? The first step in answering these questions is to gain a clear understanding of the contents and meaning of a nation's balance of payments.

The balance of payments is an accounting record of the transactions between the residents of one country and the residents of the rest of the world over a given period.[18] It resembles a company's statement of sources and uses of funds. Transactions in which domestic residents either purchase assets (goods and services) from abroad or reduce foreign liabilities are considered uses (outflows) of funds because payments abroad must be made. Similarly, transactions in which domestic residents either sell assets to foreign residents or increase their liabilities to foreigners are sources (inflows) of funds because payments from abroad are received.

Table 2.4 lists the principal parts of the balance of payments statement: the current account, the capital account, and the official transactions account. Three items are listed under the current account. The goods category states the monetary values of a nation's international transactions in physical goods. The services category shows

Table 2.4 Balance of Payments

	Uses of Funds	Sources of Funds
CURRENT ACCOUNT		
1. Goods	Imports	Exports
2. Services	Imports	Exports
3. Unilateral transfers	Paid abroad	From abroad
CAPITAL ACCOUNT		
1. Short-term investment	Made abroad	From abroad
2. Long-term investments	Made abroad	From abroad
a. Portfolio investment		
b. Direct investment		
OFFICIAL TRANSACTIONS ACCOUNT		
Official reserve changes	Gained	Lost

the values of a wide variety of transactions, such as transportation services, consulting, travel, passenger fares, fees, royalties, rent, and investment income. Finally, the unilateral transfers category includes all transactions for which there is no quid pro quo (that is, gifts). Private remittances, personal gifts, philanthropic donations, relief, and aid are included in this account.

The capital account category is divided into two parts based on time. Short-term investments refer to maturities less than or equal to one year, and long-term investments refer to maturities longer than one year. Purchases of treasury bills, certificates of deposit, foreign exchange, and commercial paper are typical short-term investments. Long-term investments are separated into portfolio investments and direct investments.

In general, portfolio investments imply that the purchaser holds no ownership rights over the foreign investment. Debt securities such as notes and bonds would be included under this heading. Direct investments are long-term ownership interests, such as business capital outlays in foreign subsidiaries and branches. Stock purchases are also included, but only if such ownership entails substantial control over the foreign company. Countries differ in the percentage of total outstanding stock an individual must hold for an investment to be considered a direct investment in the balance of payments statements. The International Monetary Fund reports that these values range from 10 percent for widely dispersed holdings to 20 percent, depending on the country.[19]

Because it is recorded in double-entry bookkeeping form, the balance of payments, as a whole, must always have its inflows (sources of funds) equal to its outflows (uses of funds). Therefore, the concept of a deficit or surplus refers only to selected parts of the entire statement. A deficit occurs when the particular outflows (uses of funds) exceed the particular inflows (sources of funds). A surplus occurs when the inflows considered exceed the corresponding outflows. In this sense, a nation's surplus or deficit is similar to that of individuals or businesses. If we spend more than we earn, we are running a deficit. If we earn more than we spend, we are running a surplus.

BALANCE OF PAYMENTS MEASURES

Three balance of payments measures are considered important by many business-people, government officials, and economists: the balance on merchandise trade, the balance on goods and services, and the balance on current account.[20] The balance on merchandise trade is the narrowest measure because it considers only internationally traded goods. For this reason, critics feel that it is of the least practical value. They argue that the balance on merchandise trade is a vestigial remnant of the seventeenth-century mercantilist conviction that if one country gained from trade, the other lost.[21] In the seventeenth century, domestic economic policies were geared toward ensuring that exports exceeded imports. In so doing, domestic jobs were provided, and the excess funds (usually precious metals) earned through the surpluses could be used to support armies and navies for imperialist expansions—or to defend against them. If jobs are the goal, however, there seems to be little point in separating goods from services. Both activities give jobs to willing workers.

Defenders of the balance on merchandise trade measure feel that jobs connected to physical goods are more important than service-oriented jobs, and therefore the balance on merchandise trade is a useful economic indicator. They contend that if an international disruption occurred, it would be better to live in a country with textile factories, steel mills, farms, and electronics firms rather than to live in a country with a labor force of insurance clerks, computer consultants, and tourist guides.

The balance on goods and services is linked directly to most national income accounting systems. It is reported in the national income and national product statements as "net exports." If this figure is positive, a net transfer of resources is taking place from the surplus nation to the debtor nations. Many analysts feel that a negative balance is an indication that a country is not living within its means. To have such a deficit position, the country would have to be a net borrower of foreign funds or a net recipient of foreign aid.

The most widely used measure of a nation's international payments position is the statement of balance on current account. As with the balance on goods and services statement, it shows whether a country is living within or beyond its means. Because it includes unilateral transfers, deficits (in the absence of government intervention) must be financed by international borrowing or by selling foreign investments. Therefore, the measure is considered a reflection of a country's financial claims on other countries.

EXCHANGE RATES

The purchase of a foreign good or service can be thought of as involving two sequential transactions: the purchase of the foreign currency, followed by the purchase of the foreign item itself. If the cost of buying either the foreign currency or the foreign item rises, the price to the importer increases. A ratio that measures the value of one currency in terms of another currency is called an *exchange rate*. With it, one can compare domestic and foreign prices.

When a currency rises in value, it is said to *appreciate*. If it falls in value, it is said to *depreciate*. Therefore, a change in the value of the U.S. dollar exchange rate from

1.17 euros to 1.00 euros is an appreciation of the euro and a depreciation of the dollar. After all, the euro now commands more dollars.

The strength of a domestic currency against the currency of your trading partners can have a negative effect. For example, the euro rose almost 15 percent in the first half of 2002, which made U.S. exports to Europe less expensive; however, exports from Europe to the United States become more expensive. Also, any profits made by European companies in their U.S. operations automatically lessened in value when they were converted back into euros to report earnings.[22]

As the yen dropped in value from 110 yen per dollar in 1997 to 145 yen to the dollar in mid-1998, Japanese car companies earned more yen for every car sold overseas. Every yen that the dollar rises against the Japanese currency adds about 6 billion yen ($41.9 million) to Honda's profits and about 10 billion yen ($69.8 million) to Toyota's.[23] The falling yen created the opposite problem for U.S. manufacturers exporting to Japan. For example, Eddie Bauer had to lower dollar prices on clothes in its twenty-six Japanese stores to keep the yen prices down. Recreational Equipment Inc., which sells outdoor clothing in Japan via catalogues and the Internet, saw the yen price of a $375 North Face mountaineering jacket go from 42,000 yen in 1997 to 55,000 yen in mid-1998. Needless to say, this increase in price reduced the number of jackets sold.[24]

THE FOREIGN EXCHANGE MARKET. Unlike major stock markets, where trading is done on central exchanges (for example, the New York Stock Exchange and the London Stock Exchange), foreign exchange transactions are handled on an over-the-counter market, largely by phone, fax, and email. Private and commercial customers, as well as banks, brokers, and central banks, conduct millions of transactions on this worldwide market daily.

Figure 2.2 shows that the foreign exchange market has a hierarchical structure. Private customers deal mainly with banks in the retail market, and banks stand ready to either buy or sell foreign exchange as long as a free and active market for the currency exists. Not all banks participate directly in the foreign exchange market. In the United States, a bank must have a substantial volume of international business to justify setting up a foreign exchange department. Thus, most small financial intermediaries handle customers' business through correspondent banks.

Banks that have foreign exchange departments trade with private commercial customers on the retail market, but they also deal with other banks (domestic or foreign) and brokers on the wholesale market. Generally, these wholesale transactions are for amounts of $1 million or more. Many of these trades are based on verbal agreements, and written documentation is formally exchanged some days later.

The foreign exchange market is probably as close as one can get to the economist's proverbial ideal of pure competition. There are many buyers and sellers, no one buyer or seller can influence the price, the product is homogeneous, there is relatively free entry into and exit from the market, and there is almost perfect worldwide information. If prices among banks differed by even a fraction of a cent, arbitrageurs would immediately step in for the profits they could earn risk-free. Through telex machines, telephone calls, and voice boxes that lead directly into the trading rooms of other banks and brokers, participants keep abreast of the market. Positions are opened and closed minute by minute, and the pace of activity in a foreign exchange dealing room can be quite frantic.

Figure 2.2: Structure of the Foreign Exchange Market

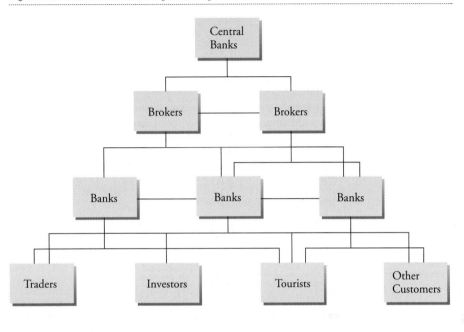

Central banks play a key role in the foreign exchange markets because they are the ultimate controllers of domestic money supplies. When central banks enter the market to influence the exchange rate value directly, they deal mainly with brokers and large money market banks. Their trading is not done to make a profit but to attain some macroeconomic goal, such as altering the exchange rate value, reducing inflation, or changing domestic interest rates. In general, even if central banks do not intervene in the foreign exchange markets, their actions influence exchange rate values because large increases in a country's money supply will increase its inflation rate and lower the international value of its currency.

CAUSES OF EXCHANGE RATE MOVEMENTS.   Exchange rates are among the most closely watched and politically sensitive economic variables. Regardless of which way the rates move, some groups lose while other groups gain. If a currency's value rises, domestic businesses will find it more difficult to compete internationally, and the domestic unemployment rate may rise. For example, the weakening of the yen in 1998, to 130 yen to the dollar, meant that Ford was losing money on every car it made in the United States and sold in Japan. Ford therefore expanded its production in Japan by using the excess capacity at Mazda Motor Corp., of which Ford owns 33.4 percent.[25]

If the value of the currency falls, foreign goods become more expensive, the cost of living increases, and goods become cheaper to foreign buyers. What are the causes of these exchange rate movements, and to what extent can governments influence them? The forces of supply and demand determine market exchange rates. The greater the supply of a currency to the foreign exchange market or the less the demand, the lower will be its international value. Similarly, the greater the demand for a currency in the foreign exchange market or the lower its supply, the higher will be its international value. Therefore, to predict movements in a currency's international value, one must identify the participants whose transactions affect these supply and demand forces and determine which factors will cause them to change their behavior.

Identifying the international participants is a relatively easy matter because they have already been implicitly mentioned in the discussion of the balance of payments. Recall that the balance of payments is nothing more than a summary of a nation's international transactions. In the current account and the capital account, traders, speculators, and investors are the major players. To this list, we will add government participants. The following sections will show how these groups act and react to overlapping market signals.

Traders. International trade in goods and services is influenced mainly by changes in relative international prices and relative income levels. For example, if the U.S. inflation rate exceeds the inflation rate of Brazil, then U.S. goods will become progressively more expensive than Brazilian goods. Consequently, U.S. consumers will begin to demand more of these foreign goods, thereby increasing the supply of dollars to the foreign exchange market (that is, increasing the demand for Brazilian reals). For the same reason, Brazilian consumers will reduce their demand for dollars (that is, reduce their supply of reals) as they purchase fewer U.S. goods. Therefore, relatively high inflation in the United States will cause the international value of the dollar to fall and the value of other currencies to rise.

Consumption is constrained by income, the ability to borrow, and the availability of credit. These constraints hold true for both individuals and nations. When speaking of a country's income, however, gross domestic product (GDP) is the most widely used measure. An increase in GDP will give the citizens of a nation the wherewithal to purchase more goods and services. Since many of the newly purchased goods are likely to be foreign, increases in GDP will raise the demand for foreign products and therefore raise the demand for foreign currencies. For example, if the U.S. growth rate exceeds that of Brazil, there will be a net increase in the demand for Brazilian reals and a lowering of the dollar's international value.[26] A daily volume of $500 billion in foreign exchange trading is done between companies and banks. The companies are constantly exchanging currencies to reduce the risk of having funds in a weak currency.[27]

Speculators. Speculators buy and sell currencies in anticipation of changing future values. If the Japanese yen were expected to rise in relative value to the dollar, speculators would try to purchase yen (that is, sell dollars) in anticipation of that change. As the demand for yen increased in the spot market and the supply of yen for dollars fell, the yen's exchange rate value would rise. (A spot market exists for the immediate delivery of currency within two days of the transaction.) Similarly, as the supply of dollars increased and the demand for them decreased, the international value of the dollar relative to the yen would fall. Consequently, spot market rates are strongly influenced by future expectations.

Investors. One of the main factors influencing investors' decisions is the differential between international interest rates. For example, if Italian interest rates were greater than U.S. interest rates (adjusted for factors such as risk, taxability, and maturity), then investors would have an incentive to place their funds where they earned the highest return—in Italy. The supply of dollars in the foreign exchange market would rise (as U.S. investors purchased Italian securities), and the demand for dollars would fall (as Italians purchased domestic rather than U.S. securities). The effect of these investments would be to lower the value of the dollar relative to the Italian lira.

As important as relative interest rates are to the international investment decision, expected changes in exchange rates are equally important. A substantial difference can exist between the interest rate at which funds are placed in foreign investments and the net return after repatriation. The gains made on higher foreign interest rates can be partially or fully offset by changes in a currency's value. Contracting on the forward exchange market may eliminate this risk, but in general, the forward rates are arbitraged to the point where these rates completely offset the interest rate advantage, which is why relative inflation rates reappear as an important determinant of international transactions. A relatively high domestic inflation rate is one of the major causes of depreciation in the exchange value of a currency.[28] Therefore, a high inflation rate implies that the currency carries high nominal interest rates, an expensive spot exchange value, and a relatively cheap forward exchange rate value.

Governments. Governments enter foreign exchange markets in various ways, ranging from the international purchase of goods and services to the granting of foreign aid. Perhaps the most pronounced impact of governments is as discretionary interveners in foreign exchange markets. Suppose that the United States and Japan agreed to lower the dollar's value relative to the yen. To do so, dollars would have to be supplied—and yen demanded—in the foreign exchange markets.

For the United States, this would mean putting upward pressure on the domestic money supply as newly created dollars are exchanged for circulating Japanese yen. For Japan, this type of intervention would mean putting downward pressure on its money supply as dollar reserves are used to take yen off the market. Because governments have such strong and direct controls over domestic money supplies, subsequent changes in other economic variables (for example, inflation rates or interest rates) will also result from this activity.

INTERNATIONAL AGENCIES FOR PROMOTING ECONOMIC AND MONETARY STABILITY

Stability in the international economy is a prerequisite for worldwide peace and prosperity. For this reason, at the end of World War II, representatives from several countries met at Bretton Woods, a small ski resort in New Hampshire, and formed both the International Monetary Fund and the World Bank (the International Bank for Reconstruction and Development). With headquarters in Washington, D.C., these two agencies continue to play major roles in the international scene. Although they have many notable achievements, perhaps their most important contribution has been to initiate forums for summit discussions of controversial financial topics.

INTERNATIONAL MONETARY FUND

The major goals of the International Monetary Fund (IMF) are to promote orderly and stable foreign exchange markets, maintain free convertibility among the currencies of member nations, reduce international impediments to trade, and provide liquidity to counteract temporary imbalances in international payments. Although the IMF has no legal powers to enforce its decisions, strong and subtle pressures can be applied to noncomplying nations.

In the early years following its creation, the IMF focused its attention on restoring currency convertibility among members and ensuring that adequate liquidity existed for countries experiencing balance of payments difficulties. Free convertibility was regained by 1958, but the liquidity issue was a much more difficult problem to solve. International trade expanded rapidly in the postwar period, but international reserves in both dollars and gold grew less rapidly. To increase the amount of international liquidity and to take some of the pressure off these reserve assets, the IMF began issuing special drawing rights (SDRs) to member nations in 1970. These SDRs (mutual book credits) gave nations the right to purchase foreign currencies, and with these currencies, they could finance temporary balance of payments deficits.

In 1973, major trading nations abandoned the fixed exchange rate system set up at Bretton Woods in 1944. As a result, the need for increases in world liquidity to finance balance of payments deficits was reduced substantially. Prior to the 1970s, the agency funded operations with contributions from member nations, but this changed as the IMF began selling some of its gold reserves and banking part of the capital gain.

The IMF's core mission is to help stabilize an increasingly global economy. The IMF has shifted its focus over the years from exchange rate relations among industrialized countries to the prevention and rescue of economic instability in developing countries and countries in transition. For example, in 1998 and 1999, the IMF led a $17.2 billion rescue for Thailand, provided a $42 billion package for Indonesia, and brokered a $41.5 billion deal for Brazil. South Korea got a whopping $58.4 billion when it was on the verge of bankruptcy.[29] Such rescue packages stabilize the world economy and avoid the total economic collapse of developing countries.

Over the past decade, the IMF has begun to extend longer-term credits to developing nations, rather than only short-term balance of payments aid. To qualify for such loans, countries may have to take drastic economic steps, such as reducing tariff barriers, privatizing government-owned businesses, curbing domestic inflation, and cutting government expenditures. For example, in 2002, the International Monetary Fund demanded that Argentina implement tough reforms before it could qualify for an IMF rescue package.[30] Although many nations have resented such intervention, banks worldwide have used the IMF as a screening device for their private loans to many developing countries. If countries qualify for IMF loans, they are considered for private credit.

WORLD BANK (INTERNATIONAL BANK FOR RECONSTRUCTION AND DEVELOPMENT)

The World Bank gives long-term loans mainly to developing nations. In this sense, it functions like a merchant banker (that is, supplier of capital) for developing nations. The World Bank acts as an intermediary between the private capital markets and developing nations. It makes long-term loans (usually for fifteen or twenty-five years), carrying rates that reflect prevailing market conditions. By virtue of its AAA credit rating, the bank can borrow private funds at relatively low market rates and pass the savings to developing nations. Because it must borrow to obtain capital and is not funded by members' contributions, however, the World Bank must raise lending rates when its costs (that is, market interest rates) rise.

In 1997, when private funds were pouring into developing economies, some critics questioned the future role of the World Bank. With the Asian crisis, however, the flow of private funds to developing countries dropped by more than $100 billion in 1998. The World Bank has expanded its role from mostly loans to partial guarantees of government bonds for investment projects. In Thailand, the World Bank partially guaranteed the Electricity Generating Authority of Thailand. The guarantee attracted investors and spawned interest for similar programs in South Korea and the Philippines.[31] The World Bank and four regional development banks in the Americas, Africa, Asia, and Europe have been encouraged to focus more on people development and environmental projects in addition to traditional infrastructure projects. The development banks are being encouraged by the Group of Seven (see below) to sharply reduce funding to those countries that do not demonstrate commitment to poverty reduction. In addition, the banks are focusing more on trying to get governments to improve financial supervision, strengthen bankruptcy laws, and reduce red tape.[32]

GROUP OF SEVEN

The world's leading industrial nations have established a Group of Seven (G7), which meets regularly to discuss the world economy. Finance ministers and central bank governors from the United States, Japan, Germany, France, Britain, Italy, and Canada make up this group. The group works together informally to help stabilize the world economy and reduce extreme disruptions. For example, the G7 met in June 1999 and developed proposals to reduce the debt of thirty-three impoverished nations, mostly in Africa, by 70 percent. Occasionally, Russia is represented at the meeting, at which times the group is called the G8. The G7 worked together in 2002 to assemble a unified list of terrorist organizations so that is could freeze their assets.[33]

EUROPEAN MONETARY SYSTEM

In the early 1970s, a group of European countries established the European Joint Float agreement. The values of the currencies were fixed against one another in a narrow range of plus or minus 2.25 percent. The movement of these currencies back and forth within this range became known as the snake. This early system was later replaced by the European Monetary System (EMS), which included the fifteen members of the European Union (EU). Britain was the last to join, in late 1990. The EMS includes a set of features to force member countries to regulate their economies so that their currency stays within 2.25 percent of the central rates. If a currency slips out of this percentage band, it may be required to increase or lower interest rates to stay in line with the other currencies. The EU countries had all contributed to the European Monetary Cooperation Fund, which had a pool of over $30 billion to buy or sell currency and thus keep all currencies within their acceptable percentage band. The EMS also developed a new currency called the European Currency Unit (ECU), made up of a weighted average of fifteen currencies from the EU countries. The EMS tended to produce abnormal results because of the dominance of the German mark and therefore the German Bundesbank. This led the French and German finance ministers to recommend a monetary union for Europe. With the support of German chancellor Helmut Kohl and French president François Mitterrand, a proposal was made for a European currency area and a European central bank. After study, the European leaders produced the Maastricht Treaty in 1991.[34]

The Maastricht Treaty established the European Monetary Institute (EMI) in 1993 as a precursor to a European central bank. The EMI worked with the European central banks to evaluate each country's performance on the convergence criteria agreed to at Maastricht.[35] To be part of the new European Monetary System, countries had to have a budget deficit of less than 3 percent of GDP and a total government debt of less than 60 percent of GDP by 1997. The United Kingdom, Sweden, and Denmark opted out of the European Monetary Union (EMU). Greece joined when it met the convergence criteria in January 2001. The twelve EU countries of Austria, Belgium, Finland, France, Germany, Greece, Ireland, Italy, Luxembourg, the Netherlands, Portugal, and Spain all became part of the EMU. Beginning in January 1999, the new European Union single currency, the euro, replaced these twelve countries' national currencies. From 1999 until 2002, these EMU countries used national currencies for notes and coins, but most prices were also to be quoted in euros. On January 1, 2002, the euro bank notes and coins where introduced to replace the national currencies of the twelve participating countries. By February 28, 2002, all national currencies of twelve participating countries where fully replaced by the euro. The European Central Bank (ECB), established in 1998, has complete control over the euro and is obliged to maintain price stability and avoid inflation or deflation.[36] The national central bank governors from the eleven EMU countries sit on the ECB council and use interest rates to control inflation at less than 2 percent.

The supporters of the euro think it will reduce transaction costs and foreign exchange risk within Europe and provide a strong viable currency alternative to the dollar. The dollar accounts for over 50 percent of official reserves around the globe, which is more than twice its share of global output. The euro may also unite European capital markets and improve the liquidity of Europe's financial markets as private investors switch dollar assets into euros. Critics argue that the ECB must deal with eleven economies that may not be going in the same direction. For example, in 1999, the German and Italian economies slowed down, the French economy was flat, and the other EMU economies were expanding. In addition, local politicians may favor local over regional concerns. Wim Duisenberg, the president of the ECB, blamed the weakness of the euro in 1999 on Oskar Lafontaine, Germany's finance minister, who had pressed local banks to reduce interest rates.[37] At the same time, the ECB did not reduce interest rates because IG Metall, Germany's largest trade union, won a 4 percent pay raise, while Germany's inflation rate was only 0.2 percent. Finally, critics say that the future of the euro is unclear because it is uncertain when and how the United Kingdom and Sweden, as well as the other potential new members of the European Community, will join the EMU.[38]

INTERNATIONAL TRADE: DOES IT DESERVE SPECIAL TREATMENT?

The principles of comparative advantage can be applied to any type of trade—international, intranational, or interpersonal. But if this is true, why is there so much concern about the international sector? Few residents of Massachusetts complain about the jobs that Pennsylvania, California, or Michigan factories take away from the New England area. Do people perceive international trade as an "us against them" situation, whereas they perceive domestic trade as "us against us"? Are there legitimate differences when one goes beyond national borders?[39]

One can point to some obvious factors in differentiating international from intranational trade. Varying currencies, languages, traditions, and cultures are just a few examples. But how significant are they? Switzerland, a developed but relatively small European country, has four official languages (German, French, Italian, and Romansch) and an assortment of widely differing dialects. The country is divided into twenty-six cantons and, in most respects, each canton wields more authority than does the national government. The result is a nation in which rules and regulations vary canton by canton. Germany, France, Austria, Italy, and Liechtenstein border Switzerland. Although the Swiss franc is the national currency, many merchants throughout the country accept payment in any of the neighboring countries' currencies. What factors distinguish foreign from domestic trade in Switzerland? It seems that there are few, if any, distinguishing characteristics. Certainly, the ones listed above are more apparent than real. If this is true, then international trade becomes nothing more than a simple subset of broader trade issues.

PROTECTIONISM AND TRADE RESTRICTIONS

Economists have spent considerable time identifying and quantifying the net gains from international free trade. In large part, the benefits are obvious. After all, by its very nature, trade involves a voluntary exchange of assets between two parties. In the absence of coercion, the motives behind this exchange must be for mutual benefit. The controversy surfaces when domestic producers are considered. Foreign imports seem to take business away from domestic firms and to increase the domestic unemployment rate.[40]

Like all competitive or technological changes, free trade creates and destroys; it gives and it takes away. By increasing competition, free trade lowers the price of the imported goods and raises the demand for efficiently produced domestic goods. In these newly stimulated export industries, sales will increase, profits will rise, and stock prices will climb. Clearly, consumers of the imported goods and producers of the exported goods benefit by these new conditions. It is equally clear, however, that groups are harmed as well. Domestic producers of the import-competing goods are one of the most visible groups. They experience noticeable declines in market share, falling profits, and deteriorating stock prices.

Free trade has its beneficiaries and victims, which is true when any change is made. For instance, if someone were to discover a way for people to grow three or four sets of teeth in a lifetime, most people would benefit from this discovery. Nevertheless, some people—dentists, oral surgeons, and periodontists—would be hurt. Should this invention be withheld from the market because this group of people would be hurt? The true test of a discovery is not whether victims exist but whether the benefits outweigh the inevitable losses.

Herein lies the major reason for protectionist legislation. The victims of free trade are highly visible and their losses quantifiable; governments use protectionism as a means of lessening the harm done to this easily identified group. Conversely, the individuals who are helped by free trade tend to be dispersed throughout the nation rather than concentrated in one particular region. Their monetary gain is only a fraction of the total purchase price of the commodity.

A study by Australia's Center for International Economies (CIE) prepared a detailed model of the international trading system to measure the impact of reduced protectionism on world trade. If the countries in GATT reduced their tariff and non-tariff barriers by 50 percent, CIE estimates that trade would increase $750 billion: $208 billion in the United States, $245 billion in Europe, and $287 billion in Asia and the Pacific.[41] The GATT agreements reached in 1993 reduced the prices for U.S. consumers by $32.8 billion per year. For example, $17 billion came from the reduction of tarriffs and opening of the textile and apparel industry, and $1.2 billion came from reduced agricultural production.[42]

Protectionist legislation tends to be in the form of tariffs, quotas, and/or qualitative trade restrictions. This rest of this section describes these barriers and their economic effects.

TARIFFS

Tariffs are taxes on goods moving across an economic or political boundary. They can be imposed on imports, exports, or goods in transit through a country and on their way to another destination. In the United States, export tariffs are constitutionally prohibited, but in other parts of the world, they are quite common. Of course, the most common type of tariff is the import tariff, and we will focus our attention on this tariff.

Import tariffs have a dual economic effect. First, they tend to raise the price of imported goods and thereby protect domestic industries from foreign competition. Second, they generate tax revenues for the governments imposing them. It is important to recognize this duality because the situations resulting from the tariffs are often quite different from what was originally intended. Regardless of what the goals are (for example, increasing tax revenue or raising employment), tariffs may not be the most direct or effective means of attaining them.

Today, most nations impose import duties for protecting domestic manufacturers. In some cases (for example, when these import duties are imposed on agricultural products that are expensive to store), foreign sellers will lower their prices to offset any tariff increase. The net effect is for the consumer-paid price to differ only slightly, if at all, from the pretariff level. Consequently, the nation has greater tariff revenues but little additional protection for the domestic producers.

When tariffs do raise the price of the imported good, consumers of the imported good are at a disadvantage, whereas the import-competing industries are helped. After the United States imposed steel tariffs in March 2002, the European Union and

Malaysia implemented protective steel tariffs of their own, and Brazil and Canada threatened to follow. The EU, China, Japan, and South Korea complained to the World Trade Organization, and Russia was considering tariffs of its own to shield Ukraine and Kazakhstan steel producers. Countries reacted to the U.S. steel tariffs to protect local steel producers from steel imports around the world that would otherwise have gone to the U.S. market.[43] U.S. buyers of steel for automobile seats reported price increases for steel of 30 to 50 percent after the U.S. steel tariffs were instituted. These increased costs of steel will be passed on to the end consumers.[44] In yet another case, the U.S. government put a 33 percent tariff on Mexican brooms imported into the United States, owing to alleged dumping of the brooms below market prices; however, critics argue the tariff is to protect U.S. broom manufacturers, who have a strong lobby in Illinois.[45]

QUOTAS

Quotas are physical limits on the *amount* of goods that can be imported into a country. Unlike tariffs, which restrict trade by directly increasing prices, quotas increase prices by directly restricting trade. Naturally, to have such an effect, imports must be restricted to levels below the free trade level.

For domestic producers, quotas are a better means of protection. Once the limit has been reached, imports cease to enter the domestic market, regardless of whether foreign exporters lower their prices. Consumers have the most to lose with the imposition of quotas. Not only are their product choices limited and the prices increased, but the goods that are imported also carry the highest profit margins. Restrictions on imported automobiles, for instance, will bring in more luxury models with high-cost accessories.

Like tariffs, quotas have both revenue and protection effects. The protection effects are the most apparent because trade is unequivocally curtailed. The revenue effects are less obvious. When a government imposes arbitrary restrictions on imported goods, companies vie for the right to conduct this limited trade. The net effect is that consumers pay more for the goods in terms of higher prices.

ORDERLY MARKETING ARRANGEMENTS AND VOLUNTARY EXPORT RESTRICTIONS

The word *quota* has come to be associated with the most selfish of protectionist legislation. There can be strong political and economic repercussions associated with such unilateral, beggar-thy-neighbor policies. To avoid these problems, the new terms *orderly marketing arrangement* and *voluntary export restriction* have been introduced.[46] In general, an orderly marketing arrangement is an agreement between countries to share markets by limiting foreign export sales. Usually these arrangements have a set duration and provide some annual increase in foreign sales to the domestic market. In 1999, the U.S. Department of Commerce reached a voluntary agreement with Russia to limit Russian steel imports into the United States to 750,000 tons per year, compared with 3,500,000 tons imported in 1998. If Russia had not agreed to the limits, the U.S. Commerce Department was prepared to announce duties of 71 to 218 percent on Russian steel as a retaliation for Russia's allegedly selling steel in the United States below market prices.[47] Voluntary restraints can also take a funny twist. Mazak, a Japanese toolmaker with a factory in Kentucky, has used the voluntary restraint agreement to limit Japanese imports into the United States. In fact, Mazak prepared a video of Japanese screwdriver assembly factories to show how his Tokyo competitors were circumventing the agreement.[48]

The euphemistic terms described in the previous paragraph are intended to give the impression of fairness. After all, who can be against anything that is orderly or voluntary? When one scratches beneath the surface of these so-called negotiated settlements, however, a different image appears. First, the negotiations are initiated by the importing country with the implicit threat that, unless concessions are made, stronger unilateral sanctions will be imposed. In fact, these terms are neither orderly nor voluntary; they are quotas in the guise of negotiated agreements.

The Omnibus Trade and Competitiveness Act of 1988 gave the president of the United States the right to negotiate orderly marketing arrangements and set countervailing duties to deal with the problems of trade deficits, protected markets, and dumping. The use of these voluntary export restraints (VERs) has spread to textiles, clothing, steel, cars, shoes, machinery, and consumer electronics. There are approximately three hundred VERs worldwide, most protecting the United States and Europe. Over fifty agreements affect exports from Japan, and another thirty-five affect South Korea.[49] A study conducted by the Institute for International Economics in Washington, D.C., found that the import restrictions, tariffs, and voluntary restraints in Europe cost the European consumer dearly. For example, banana import restrictions cost European consumers $2.0 billion, or $0.55 per kilo; beef tariffs, local subsidies, and bans on hormone-treated beef cost consumers $14.6 billion, or $1.60 per kilo. The total cost of all this protection in Europe on fruits, cars, steel, textiles, video recorders, beef, milk, cheese, telephones, airlines, and more is estimated to be $43 billion. According to the research by the Institute for International Economics, these restrictions save approximately 200,000 jobs in Europe, at a cost of $215,000 per job saved—enough to buy each lucky worker a new Rolls Royce each year.[50]

The use of quotas and voluntary export restrictions is declining with the strengthening of the WTO and increased compliance by the 135 member countries. In its first three years (1995–1998), the WTO dealt with 132 complaints, with the dispute panels having complete power to force countries found in the wrong to change their ways, offer compensation, and/or face sanctions by all 135 member countries. The WTO has not been used by the big countries to control the smaller ones, as some feared. For example, Costa Rica asked the WTO to rule against U.S. barriers to its export of men's underwear and won the case, forcing the United States to change its import rules.[51]

The United Nations Conference on Trade and Development (UNCTAD), which represents the interests of the 48 percent poorest nations, is working with the WTO to bring the nations into the mainstream of world trade.[52]

FORMAL AND ADMINISTRATIVE NONTARIFF TRADE BARRIERS

The final category of trade restrictions is perhaps the most problematic and certainly the least quantifiable. Nontariff barriers include a wide range of charges, requirements, and restrictions, such as surcharges at border crossings, licensing regulations, performance requirements, government subsidies, health and safety regulations, packaging and labeling regulations, and size and weight requirements. Not all of these barriers are discriminatory and protectionist. Restrictions dealing with public health and safety are certainly legitimate, but the line between social well-being and protection is a fine one.

At what point do consular fees, import restrictions, packaging regulations, performance requirements, licensing rules, and government procurement procedures discriminate against foreign producers? Is a French tax on automobile horsepower targeted against powerful U.S. cars, or is it simply a tax on inefficiency and pollution? Are U.S. automobile safety standards unfair to German, Japanese, and other foreign car manufacturers? Does a French ban on the advertising of bourbon and Scotch (but not cognac) serve the public's best interest? Are chickens slaughtered in the United States not fit to grace the tables of Europeans, as claimed by EU officials, because U.S. producers use a different process to clean their fowl?[53]

Sometimes, nontariff barriers can have considerable impact on foreign competition. For decades, West German authorities forbade the sale of beer in Germany unless it was brewed from barley malt, hops, yeast, and water. If any other additives were used—a common practice elsewhere—German authorities denied foreign brewers the right to label their products as beer. In 1987, the European Court of Justice struck down the law.[54] Japanese officials used the "voluntary limits" on food exports when the Japanese market was flooded with Chinese mushrooms and leeks. Rather than go to the WTO and take action against China, the Japanese government chose to try to convince the Chinese government of the need for "voluntary restraints."[55]

GENERAL AGREEMENT ON TARIFFS AND TRADE (GATT)

Because of the harmful effects of protectionism, which were most painfully felt during the Great Depression of the 1930s, twenty-three nations banded together in 1948 to form the General Agreement on Tariffs and Trade (GATT). Through periodic trade rounds, or negotiations, GATT served as a major forum for the liberalization and promotion of nondiscriminatory international trade between participating nations.

The principles of a world economy embodied in the articles of GATT were *reciprocity, nondiscrimination,* and *transparency.* The idea of reciprocity is simple. If one country lowers its tariffs against another's exports, then it can expect the other country to do the same. This practice of reciprocity has been important in the bargaining process to reduce tariffs. Nondiscrimination means that one country should not give one member or group of members preferential treatment over other members of the group. Referred to as the "most favored nation" (MFN) status, the designation does not mean that one nation is the *most* favored but rather that the nation is favored to the same degree as other nations. Transparency refers to the GATT policy that nations replace nontariff barriers (such as quotas) with tariffs and then bind the tariff, which means to agree not to raise it. Nontariff barriers do much more harm to trade than tariffs, especially bound tariffs. Tariffs reduce uncertainty and are out in the open, so they are easier to negotiate to lower levels in the future. Through these principles, GATT effectively reduced trade restrictions and minimized price distortions.

Although its most notable gains were in reducing tariff and quota barriers on certain goods, GATT also helped to simplify and homogenize trade documentation procedures, reduce qualitative trade barriers, curtail dumping (that is, selling abroad at a cost lower than the cost of production),[56] and discourage government subsidies. GATT reduced tariffs from 40 percent in 1947 to fewer than 5 percent in 1990. The

Uruguay Round of GATT talks, which lasted from 1986 to 1994, ended in agreements covering the following areas:

- *Agriculture:* Europe will gradually reduce farm subsidies. Japan and Korea will start to import rice. The United States will reduce subsidies to growers of sugar, citrus fruit, and peanuts.
- *Entertainment, pharmaceuticals, and software:* New rules will protect copyrights, patents, and trademarks. Developing nations will have a decade to implement patent protection for drugs. France refused to liberalize access for the U.S. film industry.
- *Financial, legal, and accounting services:* For the first time, these services come under the rules of international trade.
- *Textiles and apparel:* The strict quotas limiting imports into the United States will be phased out over ten years.[57]

The final act of GATT was to replace itself with the World Trade Organization.

WORLD TRADE ORGANIZATION

The World Trade Organization (WTO), which replaced GATT in 1995, continues to pursue reductions in tariffs on manufactured goods as well as liberalization of trade in agriculture and services. The major benefit of the WTO over GATT is the resolution of disputes. Under GATT, any member could veto the outcome of a panel ruling on a dispute. WTO panels are more rigid. They must report their decisions in nine months and can be overturned only by consensus. Countries that break the rules must pay compensation, mend their ways, or face trade sanctions.

With 144 member countries as of 2002 and thirty more that want to join, the WTO is the global watchdog for free trade. The major role of the WTO is completing the unfinished business of GATT. WTO's efforts are in four areas. First, WTO will continue to push for liberalization for the trade of goods and services, especially in the areas of agricultural trade and services. Agriculture is always a difficult topic because every country wants to protect its farmers. Information technology is another item on the liberalization agenda for the WTO; the United States wants reduced tariffs on computers, semiconductors, and software.

Second, the WTO must decide how to integrate China. As the world's second largest economy and tenth biggest exporter, China became part of the WTO in December 2001. In addition, Chinese emigration policy and human rights policies have strained the U.S.-Chinese relationship, which may in turn restrict its admittance to the WTO.

The third challenge facing the WTO comprises the "new issues" of trade policy concerning foreign investment, competition, and labor standards. Although most countries want foreign investment, developing countries such as India, Malaysia, and Tanzania still want to set the terms of entry for foreigners. The United States and Europe insist on some core labor standards, such as a ban on child labor and trade union freedom. Although many countries are in favor of labor standards, the developing countries argue that low labor costs are the basis of most of their exports.

The fourth issue facing the WTO is the spread of regional trading agreements. The WTO acknowledges eighty regional agreements. Given the seven years it took to resolve many of the issues in the Uruguay Round of trade talks, it seems many governments are favoring regional agreements to establish some collective trade power. Also, the ratification of NAFTA in the 1990s along with the strengthening of the EU may prompt other countries to form similar alliances. Because these regional groups tend to favor regional trade over global trade, the WTO will need to address potential conflicts between regional and global needs.[58]

ECONOMIC INTEGRATION AS A MEANS OF PROMOTING TRADE

For years public policymakers, economists, and academics have argued over the linkage between economic freedom and economic growth. Through a study of 102 countries from 1975 to 1995, economists James Gwartney, Robert Lawson, and Walter Block classified countries based on concrete measures of economic liberty and compared these ratings with GDP per person and GDP growth per person. Countries with high levels of economic freedom, like Hong Kong, Singapore, New Zealand, the United States, and Switzerland, had a GDP of $16,000 per person and GDP growth per person of over 3 percent per year; whereas countries with low levels of economic freedom, like Zaire, Algeria, Iran, Syria, Haiti, and Romania, had a GDP of less than $2,000 per person and GDP growth per person of 11 percent per year.[59]

There is little argument that free trade bestows net gains on trading nations—especially in the long run. The problem is that with so many entrenched vested interest groups, it is difficult to update existing trading rules. A reduction of protectionist legislation causes considerable short-term dislocations and puts economic and political pressure on a nation's power structure.

As a partial step in the trade liberalization process, countries have begun to move toward limited forms of economic integration. Although the degree of economic integration can vary considerably from one organization to another, four major types of integration can be identified: free trade areas, customs unions, common markets, and monetary unions. Some of these concepts will be covered in detail in Chapter 5.

FREE TRADE AREAS

The simplest form of integration is a free trade area. Within a free trade area, nations agree to drop trade barriers among themselves, but each nation is permitted to maintain independent trade relations with nongroup countries. There is little attempt at this level to coordinate issues such as domestic tax rates, environmental regulations, and commercial codes, and generally, such areas do not permit resources (that is, labor and capital) to flow freely across national borders. Because each country has autonomy over its money supply, exchange rates can fluctuate relative to both member and nonmember countries. Examples of free trade areas are the Latin American Free Trade Area and the European Free Trade Area.

CUSTOMS UNIONS

Customs unions are a more advanced form of economic integration. They possess the characteristics of a free trade area but with the added feature of a common external tariff/trade barrier for the member nations. Individual countries relinquish the right to set their nongroup trade agreements independently. Rather, a supranational policy-making committee makes these decisions.

COMMON MARKETS

The third level of economic integration is the common market. Here, countries have all the characteristics of a customs union, but the organization also encourages resources (labor and capital) to flow freely among the member nations. For example, if jobs are plentiful in Germany but scarce in Italy, workers can move from Italy to Germany without having to worry about severe immigration restrictions. In a common market, there is usually an attempt to coordinate tax codes, social welfare systems, and other legislation that influence resource allocation. Finally, although each nation still has the right to print and coin its own money, exchange rates among nations are often fixed or permitted to fluctuate only within a narrow range. The most notable example of a common market is the European Union (EU). It was established in 1958 as the European Economic Community; in 1968, it became the European Community and finally the European Union in 1992. The EU has been an active organization for trade liberalization and continues to increase its membership.

MONETARY UNIONS

The highest form of economic integration is a monetary union. A monetary union is a common market in which member countries no longer regulate their own currencies. Rather, member-country currencies are replaced by a common currency regulated by a supranational central bank. With the ratification of the Maastricht Treaty by EU members, the European Union became the first monetary union in January 1999.[60]

THE GLOBAL ECONOMY

The global economy is in a state of transition from a set of strong national economies to a set of interlinked trading groups. This transition has accelerated over the past few years with the fall of the Berlin Wall, the collapse of communism, and the coalescing of the European trading nations into a single market. The investment by Europeans, the Japanese, and Americans in one another's economies is unprecedented. U.S. companies create and sell over $80 billion per year in goods and services in Japan. The flow of British direct investment abroad was $58.2 billion in 1997, of which 30 percent went to the United States. Britain is thus the biggest foreign owner of business in the United States, followed by the Dutch and the Japanese.[61] Foreign direct investment of private funds into emerging economies peaked in 1996 at $212 billion, and is estimated to be $145 billion in 2000. China is one of the largest beneficiaries, receiving $20 billion in 1998.[62] As companies globalize, manufacturing becomes more flexible, and engineers have instant access to the latest technology; microchips designed in California are sent to Scotland to be fabricated, shipped to the Far East to be tested and assembled, and returned to the United States to be sold.[63]

The physical shipment of goods is increasingly being replaced by local manufacturing as global companies bypass trade business and take advantage of local labor and market knowledge. While world trade of goods and services was $4.8 trillion, sales of foreign affiliates of transnational companies was $5.2 trillion. Foreign direct investment comes from industrial countries, especially the United States, Japan, Germany, France, and the United Kingdom, with approximately 60 percent of the funds going to developed economies. The growth of foreign investment, especially in China, will boost sales by foreign affiliates over the next ten years.[64]

There is no doubt the world is moving toward a single global economy. Of course, there are major difficulties on the horizon, such as the development of a market-based economy in eastern Europe, a reduction of hostilities and the establishment of political stability in the Middle East and parts of eastern Europe, and stabilization and growth in the former Soviet Union. The global marketer needs to understand the interdependencies that form the world economy to understand how a drop in the U.S. discount rate will affect business in Stockholm or how Britain's entry into the European Monetary System will affect sales in London.

Clearly, the economies of the world are becoming increasingly interlinked, with small changes in markets being felt in many places around the world. For example, the world equity markets rose in Europe, China, and Tokyo in June 1999 as traders around the world anticipated that U.S. Federal Reserve chairman Alan Greenspan would raise interest rates on June 30, 1999, by 0.25 percent.[65] Information technology, telecommunications, and the Internet have made worldwide information on prices, products, and profits available globally and instantaneously. With markets thus more transparent, buyers, sellers, and investors can learn about the best opportunities, thus lowering costs and ensuring that resources are used most efficiently. The focus of monetary policy, from Britain to Brazil, has been to control inflation, with great success—only 1 percent in the G7 economies, the lowest in half a century.[66] These changes are fundamentally changing national, regional, and global economic systems.[67] As the speed of change accelerates, successful companies will be able to anticipate the trends and either take advantage of them or respond to them quickly. Other companies will watch the changes going on around them and wake up one day to a different marketplace with new rules.

CONCLUSIONS

We learn from the study of economics that changes in rules or in financial circumstances help some groups and hurt others. Therefore, it is important to understand that papers and speeches have particular points of view. Exchange rate movements, tariffs, quotas, and customs unions can be viewed as alternative ways to achieve economic goals. The issue is not whether a change will take place; rather, *which* change will provide the most benefit to the greatest number with the least cost. Even though the global economy receives significant media and political attention, it is still in its infancy. A significant amount of international trade, 43 percent, is still realized through regional trade agreements between two or more countries. These agreements usually benefit participating countries but hurt nonparticipating ones.[68] There are also plenty of trade barriers to overcome, even by countries that advocate open markets, especially in terms of agriculture, industry, and services. In 2001 the World Bank estimated that the complete elimination of trade barriers could boost the global economy by as much as $2,800 billion by 2015.[69] The global economy's growing pains are felt throughout the world and the international financial institutions and regulators still have a long way to go before being able to confront them fully. The economic instability of Turkey and Argentina in 2001 and 2002 proved to have global repercussions, and the shift from crisis management to crisis prevention will have to be made by international financial institutions.[70] The global economy will mature, through both growth and contraction, over the next decades and the successful global marketer will be able to seize the opportunities through comprehension of global trade and the basics of international finance.

This chapter has described the fundamentals of international trade and finance. An understanding of the fundamentals will enable you to comprehend the technical issues raised by the media and to formulate your own views. It is particularly important to understand how actions or events in one part of the world can influence a business in another part of the world.

Questions for Discussion

1. If a nation has a balance on merchandise trade deficit, can you say that the nation also has a weak currency in the international markets?

2. Refer again to Question 1. Examine both the balance of payments statistics and the foreign exchange rate statistics presented in the International Monetary Fund's *International Financial Statistics*. What link, if any, do you see between Switzerland's balance on merchandise trade and the value of the Swiss franc over the past five years?

3. Calculate your individual balance of payments over the past month. What were your balance on merchandise trade, balance on goods and services, and current account balance?

4. Exchange rate changes have been called a "double-edged sword" because they hurt some sectors of the nation while helping other sectors. Explain why this is true.

5. If interest rates in the United Kingdom rise while those in Switzerland remain unchanged, what pressure will this situation put on the British pound versus the Swiss franc exchange rate?

6. Suppose the U.S. Federal Reserve reduces the rate of growth of the money supply, causing the U.S. inflation rate to fall, interest rates to rise, and economic growth to decline. What impact will these economic changes have on the actions of participants in the foreign exchange market?

7. The concept of *comparative advantage* is one of the most powerful in economic theory (both at the domestic level and the international level). Explain why this is true. What does the concept show?

What are its implications for international and intra-national trade?

8. Suppose Brazil can produce either 100 units of steel or 10 computers with an equal amount of resources. At the same time, Germany can produce either 150 units of steel or 10 computers. Explain which nation has a comparative advantage in the production of computers. Choose a mutually advantageous trading ratio and explain why this ratio increases the welfare of both nations.

9. In 2002, President Bush imposed a duty on many grades of foreign steel imported into the United States. Explain which groups in the United States were helped by this action and which groups were hurt by it. Do you believe this action is evidence of good economic thinking? Why?

10. Explain the similarities and differences between tariffs and quotas in terms of their economic effects on a nation's economy.

11. For each of the following distinct and separate cases, explain which trade theory best describes the trading pattern cited. Briefly explain why you chose the theory you did.
    (a) The opening of trade between the United States and China has resulted in U.S. importation of textiles and other handmade crafts from China and the exportation of machinery and steel from the United States to China.
    (b) Currently, the United States is a major importer of televisions from Japan. It once was a major exporter of televisions to Japan.

For Further Reading

Adelman, M. A. "Globalization of the World Economy." *Energy Policy*, December 1996, pp. 1021–1024.

Baldwin, Richard, et al., *Market Integration, Regionalism and the Global Economy.* Cambridge, U.K.: Cambridge University Press, 1999.

Brenner, Robert. *The Boom and the Bubble: The US in the World Economy.* New York: Verso Books, 2002.

"Getting a Grip on the GATT." *Financial Times,* February 5, 1991, p. 18.

Hufbauer, Gary. "U.S. Trade Policy and Global Growth: New Directions in International Economy." *Journal of Economic Literature*, March 1997, pp. 138–140.

Irwin, Douglas A. "The United States in a New Global Economy? A Century's Perspective." *American Economic Review*, May 1996, pp. 41–46.

Maddison, Andus, and Donald Johnston. *The World Economy: A Millennial Perspective*. Washington, D.C.: OECD, 2001.

Marriott, Cherie. "How Companies Fare in a Really Liberated Economy." *Global Finance*, January 1997, pp. 22–26.

Ohmae, Kenichi. *The Borderless World: Power and Strategy in the Interlinked Economy*. New York: Harper Business, 1999.

Pomeranz, Kenneth. *The Great Divergence: China, Europe, and the Making of the Modern World Economy*. Princeton, N.J.: Princeton University Press, 2002.

Porter, Michael E. *The Competitive Advantage of Nations.* New York: Macmillan, 1990.

Root, Franklin R. *International Trade and Investment*, 6th ed. Cincinnati, Ill.: Southwestern, 1990.

Rostow, W. W. *The Stages of Economic Growth*, 2d ed. Cambridge, U.K.: Cambridge University Press, 1971.

Schuknecht, Ludger, "A Trade Policy Perspective on Capital Controls." *IMF Publications Services*, March 1999, vol. 36, no. 1, p. 1.

Tolchin, Martin. *Buying into America: How Foreign Money Is Changing the Face of Our Nation.* New York: Times Books, 1988.

"World Industrial Survey." *Financial Times*, January 15, 1991, sec. 3, pp. 1–4.

Endnotes

1. *http://www.ustr.gov/reports/2002/ Annex%20I,U.S.%20Trade%20in%202001.pdf*, p. 2.

2. Frances Williams, "International Economy: WTO Sees Strong Surge in World Trade Economic Expansion," *Financial Times*, December 1, 2000, p. 16.

3. *The World Competitive Yearbook 2001* (Washington, D.C.: IMD, 2001).

4. "The World's Current Economic Troubles Strengthen the Case for a New Round of Trade Talks," *Economist*, March 10, 1998, Survey, p. 3.

5. "Border Battles," *Economist*, October 3, 1998, Survey, p. 6.

6. Jeffrey Sachs, "The Limits of Convergence," *Economist*, June 14, 1997, p. 20.

7. *www.wto.og; http://www.wto.org/english/thewto_e/whatis_e/tif_e/ org6_e.htm*.

8. "Does the WTO Need Rules for Foreign Direct Investment?" *Economist*, March 10, 1998, Survey, p. 10.

9. "Spoiling World Trade," *Economist*, December 7, 1996, p. 15.

10. "World Trade Growth Slower in 1998 After Unusually Strong Growth in 1997," WTO press release, April 16, 1999 (*www.wto.org/intltrade/ internet*).

11. *http://www.wto.org/english/thewto_e/whatis_e/tif_e/bey3_e.htm*; accessed May 6, 2002.

12. Christopher Rhoads, "World Economy Faces Drain from Sept. 11," *Wall Street Journal*, June 7–9, 2002, p. A3.

13. David Ricardo, *On the Principles of Political Economy and Taxation* (London: John Murray, 1821). Available from *http://www.econlib.org/ library/Ricardo/ricP1.html*; accessed April 30, 2002.

14. The concept of absolute advantage can be found in Adam Smith, *The Wealth of Nations* (New York: Prometheus Books, 1999; originally published 1776).

15. Ricardo, *On the Principles of Political Economy and Taxation*, Chapter 7.

16. "A Short Tour of Economic Theory: Why Trade Is Good for You," *Economist*, March 10, 1998, Survey, p. 4.

17. Michael E. Porter, *The Competitive Advantage of Nations* (New York: Macmillan, 1990), pp. 69–175.

18. An excellent source of historical and internationally comparable data can be found in the IMF Committee on Balance of Payment Statistics, *Annual Report*, published yearly by the International Monetary Fund (Washington, D.C.).

19. *http://www.unctad.org/en/subsites/dite/fdistats_files/ sources_definitions.htm*; accessed on October 22, 2002.

20. The classic discussion of balance of payments is found in James Meade, *The Balance of Payments* (London: Oxford University Press, 1951).

21. Examples of mercantilist thought can be found in Thomas Mun, "England's Treasure by Foreign Trade," in *Early English Tracts in Commerce*, ed. John McCullock (Norwich, England: Jarrold and Sons, 1952). See also Joseph Schumpeter, *History of Economic Analysis* (New York: Oxford University Press, 1954).

22. Christopher Rhoads, "European Companies, Policy Makers Welcome Strong Euro—Up to a Point," *Wall Street Journal*, June 7-9, 2002, p. A3.

23. Lisa Shuchman and Gregory White, "Japanese Car Makers to Hold U.S. Prices," *Wall Street Journal*, June 18, 1998, p. A15.

24. Khanh T. L. Tran, "Falling Yen Creates Painful Dilemma for U.S. Marketers in Japan," *Wall Street Journal*, June 30, 1998, p. A13.

25. Valerie Reitman, "Ford Might Build Its Vehicles in Japan," *Wall Street Journal*, January 7, 1998, p. A1.

26. For an alternative point of view, see Jacob A. Frenkel and Harry Johnson, "The Monetary Approach to the Balance of Payments: Essential Concepts and Historical Origins," in *The Monetary Approach to the Balance of Payments*, ed. J. A. Frenkel and H. G. Johnson (Toronto: University of Toronto Press, 1976).

27. Geoffrey Nairn, "Internet Fails to Transform the Foreign Exchange World," *Financial Times*, June 5, 2002, IT Review Section, p. 2.

28. "In Brief," *Wall Street Journal Europe*, May 28, 2002, p. M6.

29. Michael Phillips, "A Look at How the Global Finance Crisis Began and How It Spread," *Wall Street Journal*, April 4, 1999, p. R4.

30. "IMF Insists on Argentine Reform before Fresh Loan," *Financial Times*, April 22, 2002, p.1.

31. "The World Bank: Back in the Driving Seat," *Economist*, February 13, 1999, p. 71.

32. "Europe's Bank Rethinks Development," *Economist*, April 17, 1999, p. 76.

33. "International Economy and the Americas: Harmony for Once as G7 and IMF Delegates Set Agenda," *Financial Times*, April 22, 2002.

34. "Euro Brief: Eleven into One May Go," *Economist*, October 17, 1998, p. 81.

35. Andrew Fisher, "EMI: Technicians Look to 1999," *Financial Times*, September 27, 1996, World Economy and Finance section, p. 27.

36. "Euro Brief: Eleven into One May Go," *Economist*, October 17, 1998, p. 81.

37. "The Euro: Neurosis," *Economist*, February 27, 1999, p. 73.

38. "Ins and Outs," *Economist*, January 2, 1999, p. 21.

39. See Lester Thurow, *The Zero Sum Society: Distribution and the Possibilities for Economic Change* (New York: Basic Books, 1980).

40. For details on the arguments against protectionism, see Robert Z. Lawrence and Robert E. Litan, "Why Protectionism Doesn't Pay," *Harvard Business Review*, May–June 1987, pp. 60–67.

41. "Once and Future GATT," *Economist*, September 22, 1990, p. 39.

42. "GATT's Payoff," *Fortune*, February 7, 1994, p. 28.

43. "Bush's Bet on Steel Tariffs Isn't Paying Off So Far," *Asian Wall Street Journal*, March 28, 2002.

44. Edward Alden, "U.S. Steel Users Seek End to Import Tariffs," *Financial Times*, February 5, 2003, p. 2.

45. "One Bad Apple Agreement," *Wall Street Journal*, March 30, 1998, p. 18.

46. See Kent Jones, *Politics Versus Economics in World Steel Trade* (London: George Allen & Unwin, 1986).

47. Helene Cooper, "Russia Agrees to Limit Steel Shipments," *Wall Street Journal*, February 23, 1999, p. A8.

48. "Look Who's Taking Japan to Task," *Business Week*, June 4, 1990, p. 26.

49. "A Survey of World Trade," *Economist*, September 22, 1990, p. 8.

50. "Trade: Europe's Burden," *Economist*, May 22, 1999, p. 12.

51. "Fifty Years On," *Economist*, May 16, 1998, p. 21.

52. William Barnes, "Poor Nations Assert Place in Global Trade," *Financial Times*, February 21, 2000, p. 6.

53. "Trade: Standard Fare," *Economist*, May 24, 1997, p. 72.

54. "EC Claims Victory as Court Overturns Germany's Age-Old Ban on Beer Imports," *Wall Street Journal*, March 13, 1987, p. 29.

55. "Japan, Hoping to Avert Trade Restriction, Asks China to Limit Its Vegetable Exports," *Wall Street Journal*, March 6, 2001, p. B11A.

56. Economists prefer to define *dumping* as selling below the variable cost per unit because only in such cases is the decision uneconomical.

57. "What's Next After GATT's Victory?" *Fortune*, January 10, 1994, pp. 66–70.

58. "World Trade: All Free Traders Now," *Economist*, December 7, 1996, pp. 21–23.

59. "Economic Freedom: Of Liberty and Prosperity," *Economist*, January 13, 1996, pp. 21–23.

60. "The Euro: Neurosis," *Economist*, February 27, 1999, p. 73.

61. "Foreign Investment: Ruling the Merger Wave," *Economist*, January 23, 1999, p. 53.

62. "Uncertain Prospects," *Economist*, April 24, 1999, p. 23.

63. William Van Dusen Wishard, "The 21st Century Economy," *Futurist*, May–June 1987, p. 23.

64. "FDI Shifts with Global Growth," *Crossborder Monitor, Economist Intelligence Unit*, June 12, 1996, p. 12.

65. "Mood Lifts on Likelihood of U.S. Rate Rise," *Financial Times*, June 29, 1999, p. 36.

66. "The New Danger," *Economist*, February 20, 1999, p. 15.

67. "Stop the World, I Want to Get Off," *Economist*, September 18, 1996, Survey of the World Economy, p. 46.

68. Guy de Jonquieres, "Popular Trend Is at Odds with Global Free Trade," *Financial Times*, November 28, 2001. p. 10.

69. Guy de Jonquieres, "A Deal That Had to Be Done," *Financial Times*, November 28, 2001, p. 12.

70. Alan Beattie, "Architecture May Be Put to Test," *Financial Times*, November 28, 2001. p. 2

Chapter 3

Cultural and Social Forces

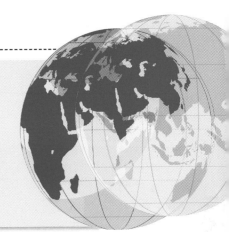

In Chapter 1, we explained that the complexities of global marketing are partially caused by societal and cultural forces. In Chapter 3, we describe some of these cultural and societal influences in more detail. It is not possible to list all of them—or even to describe all the major cultures of the world—only the more salient forces are highlighted. Figure 3.1 shows the components of culture that are described in this chapter. We also provide an analytical framework that suggests to the global marketing practitioner what to look for. Thus, rather than suggesting all the possible cultural or societal factors that may affect global marketers, we concentrate on the analytical processes marketers can use to identify and monitor any of the numerous cultural influences they will encounter around the globe.

A global marketer needs to be sensitive to different cultures, first, because it is critical to understand consumers before marketing to them, and second, because most marketing will be implemented by local managers, with whom the global marketer must interact. If you intend to market a product to a consumer, but the product offends him or her in some way, the consumer will not buy it. If you interact with a local manager in a way that shows no understanding of his or her culture, your plans may not be implemented as you want them to be.

A DEFINITION OF CULTURE

Culture is a learned set of ideals, values, and standards that is shared by members of a society. When this learned set is acted upon, it produces nonrandom and systematic behavior, within a range, that is recognizable and acceptable within that society. Cultures exist as a medium for societies to deal systematically with problems and matters that concern them. All cultures contain basic characteristics. First, a culture is shared

Figure 3.1: Cultural Analysis

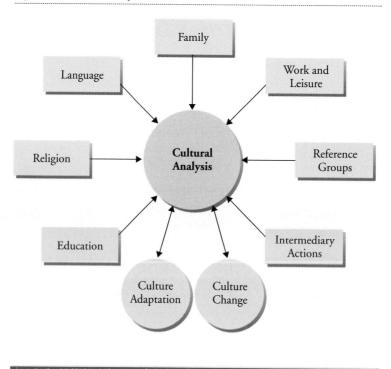

within a society, a defined group of people who depend on each other for survival. Second, culture is learned. Third, culture is based on symbols, the most important symbol being language. Finally, culture is integrated; all aspects of a culture function as a coordinated whole. Individual cultures do not produce uniform behavior for all members. For example, gender-based behavioral expectations exist in every culture. There are also subcultures, groups within a larger culture, that function with their own distinctive set of standards and behaviors.[1]

CULTURAL INFLUENCES ON MARKETING

The function of marketing is to earn profits from the satisfaction of human wants and needs. To understand and influence the consumer's wants and needs, marketers must understand the culture, especially in an international environment. Figure 3.2 illustrates how culture affects buyer behavior. As the figure shows, culture is embedded in elements of the society such as religion, language, history, and education. These elements send direct and indirect messages to consumers regarding the selection of goods and services. Culture provides a framework with which a society's members can appropriately satisfy basic human biological needs. The need for food is one of the basic biological needs that are infused with cultural meaning when humans seek to satisfy that need. Food consumption is heavily influenced by culture, and significant cultural variation regarding food consumption exists around the world. This variation can greatly influence the marketing of food products. For example,

Figure 3.2: Cultural Influences on Buyer Behavior

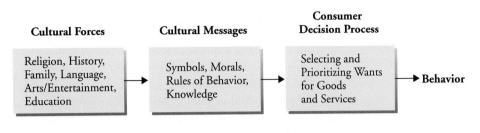

McDonald's, the fast-food chain, offers no beef or pork in its restaurants in India, a marked contrast to its operations elsewhere, to avoid offending the local Hindu and Muslim culture.[2]

ISOLATING CULTURAL INFLUENCES
One of the most difficult tasks for global marketers is assessing the cultural influences that affect their operations. Isolating cultural influences is difficult because culture cannot be observed directly. Because culture is an intangible set of ideals, values, and standards, the only way to analyze and understand it is to observe the behaviors of a culture's members. To achieve a realistic picture of a culture, data should be obtained in three different ways: first, by investigating the members' understanding of the ideals, values, and standards they share; second, by examining the extent to which a culture's members believe they are observing the shared ideals, values, and standards; and third, by looking at members' behaviors that can be directly observed. After a careful evaluation of these elements, it is then possible to portray a set of rules that may clarify the behavior within a culture. In the actual marketplace, there are always several factors working simultaneously, and it is extremely difficult to isolate any one factor.

Frequently, *cultural differences* have been held accountable for any noticeable differences between countries. However, when environmental factors differ, what is thought to be *cultural* may in fact be attributable to other factors. Quite often, when countries with both economic and cultural differences are compared, the differences are credited solely to the varying cultural systems. The analyst should be aware that although many of the differences are culturally based, other environmental factors, such as level of economic development, the political system, or the legal system, might be responsible for these differences. (These other aspects of the environment are discussed in Chapters 2 and 4.)

LANGUAGE

Language is a key component of culture because most of a society's culture finds its way into the spoken language. Thus, in many ways, language embodies the culture of the society. Knowing the language of a society can become the key to understanding its culture. Language is not merely a collection of words or terms. Language expresses the thinking pattern of a culture—and to some extent can even form the thinking. Linguists have found that cultures with a limited range of expression are more likely to be limited in their thought patterns. Many languages cannot accommodate modern technological or business concepts, a situation that forces the cultural elite to work in a different language. The French are particularly sensitive about their language and culture, so much so that the French government has proposed legal action to limit further incursions of other languages, especially English. For example, *airbag* is called *coussin gonflable de protection,* and *fast food* is *restauration rapide.* In Germany, there is growing pressure to protect the German language from incorporating too many foreign idioms. The main concern is the escalating use of *Denglisch,* a hybrid of the English and German languages.[3]

FORMS OF ADDRESS

The English language has one form of address: all persons are addressed with the pronoun *you.* This is not the case in many other languages. The Germanic, Romance, and Slavic languages always have two forms of address, the personal and the formal. Japanese has three forms. Depending on status, a Japanese person will speak differently to a superior, to a colleague, or to a subordinate, and there are different forms for male and female in many expressions. These differences in language represent different ways of interacting. English, particularly as it is spoken in the United States, is much less formal than Japanese. Japanese traveling to the United States will sometimes adopt Americanized nicknames. Most Japanese prefer to be called a combination of their last name and *san*—for example, *Endo-san* for Mr. Endo. Knowing the Japanese language gives a foreigner a better understanding of the cultural mores regarding social status and authority. Forms of address can be found to vary even within the same language. For example, in Australia, English immigrants are referred to as *poms,* short for "pomegranate," referring to their ruddy complexion.[4] Because Australians often use *pom* along with other derogatory words like *bloody, bastard,* or *whingeing,* it may be in poor taste to use *pom* in a business meeting.

OVERCOMING THE LANGUAGE BARRIER

Global marketing communications are heavily affected by the existence of different languages. Advertising has to be adjusted to each language, and personal contacts are made difficult by language barriers. To overcome these language barriers, businesspeople all over the world have relied on three approaches: the direct translation of written material, interpreters, and the acquisition of foreign language skills.

Translations are made for a wide range of documents, including sales literature, catalogs, advertising, and contracts. Although translation increases the initial costs of entering a market, few companies can conduct their business over the long run without translating material into the language of their customers. If a company does not have a local subsidiary, competent translation agencies are available in most countries. Some companies even route their foreign correspondence through a translation firm, thus communicating with foreign clients on all matters in the client's own language. This often increases the likelihood of concluding a deal. It is important when traveling in Asia not to use your senior management, who are usually bilingual, as translators. Translators are considered low-level staff positions in Asia, and Asian business contacts would therefore look down on your senior manager after his or her departure.

The use of translators is usually restricted to higher-level executives because of the high cost. Traveling with executives and attending meetings, translators perform a very useful function when a complete language barrier exists. They are best used for a limited time only, however, and realistically they cannot overcome long-term communication problems. The largest translation staff in the world belongs to the European Community (EC), which has 1,500 people translating 1.2 million pages of text per year into the three working languages of English, French, and German. EC bureaucrats also use machine translation to get a rough approximation that can be used for email and other less official communications.[5]

Both translation services and translators translate one language into another. In many situations, it is almost impossible to translate a given meaning into a second language. When the original idea or thought is not part of the second culture, the translation may be meaningless. Brand names have been particularly affected by this problem because they are not normally translated. Consequently, a company may get into difficulty with the use of a product name in a foreign country, even though its advertising message is fully translated. For example, General Motors' Chevy Nova translates in Spanish as "does not go"—certainly not the right name for a car. Coca-Cola translated into Chinese means "bite the wax tadpole."[6]

In contrast, a soft drink was launched in Japan with the brand name Pocari Sweat. To Japanese consumers, this name conveyed a positive, healthy, thirst-quenching image, and the drink became a market leader. Japanese consumers reacted to the brand name strictly because of its modern- and foreign-sounding name, not because of its content or meaning. This success of the brand name was credited to a local firm.[7]

Today, companies tend to choose product names carefully and test them in advance to ensure that the meaning in all major languages is neutral or positive. They also want to make sure that the name can be easily pronounced. Language differences may have caused many blunders, but careful translations have now reduced the number of international marketing mistakes. The language barrier still remains, however, and companies that do more to overcome this barrier frequently achieve better results. If one considers the value of developing cultural empathy through learning a foreign language, an argument can be made that learning any language will help a person to develop cross-cultural skills. Looking at foreign languages from that point of view allows the student to approach learning as a developmental skill that can be applied in many ways. In a sense, by learning one foreign language, the student can learn to appreciate many different cultures.

Whenever two executives get together and speak their respective languages, to some extent, the language they choose to conduct their business is frequently the one that is better spoken. For example, if a U.S. executive meets an Italian executive, and the Italian speaks better English than the American speaks Italian, it would be normal for the two to speak in English. There is strong evidence that English is becoming the global business language. According to a study by the Organization for Economic Cooperation and Development (OECD) in Paris, 78 percent of all web sites and 91 percent of secure web sites are in English.[8] Although English is becoming the language of commerce and electronic communications, personal relationships will often benefit from language skill in a customer's native tongue.

Even when executives understand each other's language, there can still be plenty of room for misunderstanding. When an American executive says yes in a negotiation, this usually means, "Yes, I accept the terms." However, *yes* may mean four different things in Asian countries. First, it may mean that the other side recognizes that you are talking to them but not necessarily that they understand what is said. Second, it could mean that what was said was understood and was clear but not that it was agreed to. Third, it may mean that the other party has understood the proposal and will consult with others about it. Finally, *yes* may mean total agreement. It takes skill to understand just what *yes* means in any type of negotiation.[9]

However, achieving some fluency in a foreign language is not the only cultural barrier to cross. At least as important is the use of nonverbal communication, or *body language.* Sometimes referred to as the "silent language," this includes elements such as touching, the distance between speakers, facial expressions, and speech inflection, as well as arm and hand gestures. During a visit to Australia, former U.S. president George Bush gave the V for "victory" sign with his palm turned inward, not realizing that this gesture was equivalent to the middle finger salute in the United States.[10] Mexicans come within a half-meter of a stranger for a business discussion, whereas Asians, Nordics, Anglo-Saxons, and Germanic peoples consider space within one meter as personal space. So when a Mexican moves closer than 16 to 18 inches to an English person, the English person feels invaded and steps back, giving the Mexican the message that he or she does not want to do business. For Latins, Arabs, and Africans, proximity is a sign of confidence. Obviously, understanding cultural space differences is important to overall communication.[11]

One can draw two major conclusions about the impact of language on global marketing. First, a firm must adjust its communication program and design communications to include the languages used by its customers. Second, the firm must be aware that a foreign language may contain different thinking patterns or indicate varying motivations on the part of prospective clients. These nuances are much more difficult to grasp. Depending on the extent to which such differences occur, the simple mechanical translation of messages will not suffice. Instead, the company may have to change the entire marketing message to reflect different cultural patterns.

RELIGION

Many businesspeople ignore the influence that religion may have on the marketing environment. Even in the United States, religion has had a profound impact, although people are not aware of it on a daily basis. Historically, the religious tradition in the United States, based on Christianity and Judaism, emphasizes hard work, thriftiness, and a simple lifestyle. These religious values have certainly altered over time; many of our modern marketing activities would not exist if these older values persisted. Thrift, for instance, presumes that a person will save hard-earned wages and use these savings for purchases later on. Today, ample credit facilities supplement or even supplant savings.

CHRISTIAN TRADITIONS
Still, however, religious customs remain a major factor in global marketing today. Christmas is one Christian tradition that, at least in respect to consumption, remains

an important event for many consumer goods industries. Retailers traditionally have their largest sales around that time. Christmas can also be used as an illustration of the substantial differences in customs among even largely Christian societies. A large U.S.-based retailer of consumer electronics learned about these differences the hard way when it opened its first retail outlet in the Netherlands. The company planned the opening to coincide with the start of the Christmas selling season with the hope that this tactic would allow the firm to show a profit in the first year. Advertising space was bought accordingly in late November and December. The results were less than satisfactory, however, because major gift giving in Holland takes place not on December 25, Christmas Day, but on St. Nicholas Day, December 6, the Dutch traditional day of gift giving. Thus, the opening of the company's retail operation in the Netherlands was late and missed the major buying season in that country.

Many other variations surrounding Christmas gift giving can be found. In France, it is traditional to exchange gifts on January 6, often called "Little Christmas." In the United States, Santa Claus brings Christmas gifts, but in the United Kingdom, Father Christmas brings them. In German-speaking countries, gifts are brought by an angel representing the Christ child, and Santa Claus or St. Nicholas comes on December 6 to bring small gifts and food to children who have behaved well. All of these examples show that local variations of religious traditions can have a substantial impact on global marketing activities.

ISLAM

The impact of religion on global marketing becomes more apparent when the observer compares one religion to another. It is beyond the scope of this text to give a complete description of all world religions, with specific implications for marketing. However, by using one non-Christian religion, Islam, we can document some of the potential impact. We chose Islam in view of its growing influence in many countries.

Islam is the religion of 20 percent of the world's population.[12] The 1.3 billion Islamic peoples are concentrated in the Middle East, North Africa, Malaysia, and Indonesia, and there are large populations in North America and Europe. To do business in Islamic countries, it is important to understand how the Islamic religion and law are intertwined and permeate all aspects of the culture and commerce.[13] The prophet Mohammed established Islam in A.D. 610 in Mecca. Thirteen years later, when Mohammed had to flee to nearby Medina, he established the first Islamic city-state.[14] By his death in 632, the holy book of Islam, the Koran, had been completely revealed. Muslims believe that it contains God's own words. The Koran was supplemented by the Hadith and the Sunna, which contain the reported words and actions of the prophet Mohammed. These works are the primary sources of guidance for all Muslims on all aspects of life.

With the expansion of the Islamic state, additional guidance was needed; as a result, the *shari'a*, or legal system, emerged. Based on the Koran, the *shari'a* gives details of required duties and outlines all types of human interactions. It constitutes what elsewhere would be considered criminal, personal, and commercial law. These Islamic guidelines cover all aspects of human life and categorize human behavior as obligatory, merely desirable, neutral, merely undesirable, or forbidden. The principal goal is to guide human beings in their quest for salvation because the basic purpose of human existence is to serve God. Divine guidance is to be accepted as given, and it is believed to meet both the spiritual and psychological needs of individuals, making them better social beings. The nonritual divine guidance covers, among other areas, the economic activities of society. This latter guidance offers people a wide range of choices while protecting them from evil. A set of basic values restricts economic action and should not be violated or transgressed.

The Islamic value system, as it relates to economic activities, requires a commitment to God and a constant awareness of God's presence, even while the person is engaged in material work. Wealth is considered a favor of God to be appreciated; it cannot be regarded as a final goal. Wealth is to be used to satisfy basic needs in moderation. Because the real ownership of wealth belongs to God, man is considered only a temporary trustee. Thus, material advancement does not entail higher status or merit. In Islam, all people are created equal and have the right of life, the right of liberty, the right of ownership, the right of dignity, and the right of education. For the true Muslim, the achievement of goals is both a result of individual efforts and a blessing from God. A Muslim should therefore not neglect the duty of working hard to earn a living.

In their work, Muslims are required to uphold the Islamic virtues of truth, honesty, respect for the rights of others, pursuit of moderation, sacrifice, and hard work. Moderation applies to almost all situations. The resulting Islamic welfare economy is based on the bond of universal brotherhood, in which the individuals, while pursuing their own good, avoid committing wrongdoing toward others. In their economic pursuits, true Muslims not only have their own material needs in mind but also accept their social obligations, thereby improving their own position with God. The Islamic culture has many specific implications for global marketers. A summary of these implications is given in Table 3.1.

The prohibition of usury has led to quite different practices with respect to lending in Arab societies.[15] Since this law prohibits interest payments, special Islamic banks were formed. These banks maintain three types of accounts: nonprofit accounts with a very small minimum deposit and the right of immediate withdrawal without notice, profit-sharing deposit accounts, and social services funds. These banks do not charge a fixed rate of interest on loans. Instead, the "interest payment" is levied according to the profits derived from the funds employed. Thus, the depositors receive earnings on their deposits, depending on the amount of profits earned by the bank. Such Islamic banks now exist in many countries, particularly Egypt, Saudi Arabia, Kuwait, Sudan, Dubai, and Jordan. One way that Islamic financial institutions stay viable is through a transaction process called *murabaha*. This financial transaction process works in place of western style interest payments. Suppose that an individual wants to buy a car. That individual asks an Islamic financial institution to buy it from the car dealer under the agreement that the individual will immediately buy it from the financial institution for a slight premium. The transactions are carried out simultaneously. Because the Islamic financial institution technically had brief ownership of the vehicle, the individual buyer did not break Islamic convention.[16]

The influence of Islam is also felt in Southeast Asia. Indonesia is a country of 210 million people, 85 percent of whom are Muslims.[17] Greater awareness of Islamic traditions also creates new business opportunities. Mr. Bambang, owner of eighty-five McDonald's restaurants in Indonesia, has tailored his menu and advertising to his

Table 3.1 Marketing in an Islamic Framework

Elements	Implications for Marketing
FUNDAMENTAL ISLAMIC CONCEPTS	
A. *Unity*—Concept of centrality, oneness of God, harmony in life.	Product standardization, mass media techniques, central balance, unity in advertising copy and layout, strong brand loyalties, a smaller evoked size set, loyalty to company, opportunities for brand extension strategies.
B. *Legitimacy*—Fair dealings, reasonable level of profits.	Less formal product warranties, need for institutional advertising and/or advocacy advertising, especially by foreign firms, and a switch from profit-maximizing to a profit-satisficing strategy.
C. *Zakat*—2.5 percent per annum compulsory tax binding on all classified as "not poor."	Use of "excessive" profits, if any, for charitable acts: corporate donations for charity, institutional advertising.
D. *Usury*—Cannot charge interest on loans. A general interpretation of this law defines "excessive interest" charged on loans as not permissible.	Avoid direct use of credit as a marketing tool; establish a consumer policy of paying cash for low-value products; for high-value products, offer discounts for cash payments and raise prices of products on an installment basis; sometimes possible to conduct interest transactions between local/foreign firm in other non-Islamic countries; banks in some Islamic countries take equity in financing ventures, sharing resultant profits (and losses).
E. *Supremacy of human life*—Compared with other forms of life, objects, human life is of supreme importance.	Pet food and/or products less important; avoid use of statues, busts—interpreted as forms of idolatry; symbols in advertising and/or promotion should reflect high human values; use floral designs and artwork in advertising as representation of aesthetic values.
F. *Community*—All Muslims should strive to achieve universal brotherhood—with allegiance to the "one God." One way of expressing community is the required pilgrimage to Mecca for all Muslims at least once in their lifetime, if able to do so.	Formation of an Islamic economic community—development of an "Islamic consumer" served with Islamic-oriented products and services ("kosher" meat packages, gifts exchanged at Muslim festivals, and so forth); development of community services—need for marketing or nonprofit organizations and skills.
G. *Equality of peoples*	Participative communication systems; roles and authority structures may be rigidly defined, but accessibility at any level is relatively easy.
H. *Abstinence*—During the month of Ramadan, Muslims are required to fast without food or drink from the first streak of dawn to sunset—a reminder to those who are more fortunate to be kind to the less fortunate and as an exercise in self-control.	Products that are nutritious, cool, and digested easily can be formulated for Sehr and Iftar (beginning and end of the fast).

(continued)

Table 3.1 Marketing in an Islamic Framework (cont.)

Elements	Implications for Marketing
Consumption of alcohol and pork is forbidden; so is gambling.	Opportunities for developing nonalcoholic items and beverages (for example, soft drinks, ice cream, milk shakes, fruit juices) and nonchance social games, such as Scrabble; food products should use vegetable or beef shortening.
I. *Environmentalism*—The universe created by God was pure. Consequently, the land, air, and water should be held as sacred elements.	Anticipate environmental, antipollution acts; opportunities for companies involved in maintaining a clean environment; easier acceptance of pollution control devices in the community (for example, recent efforts in Turkey have been well received by the local communities).
J. *Worship*—Five times a day; timing of prayers varies.	Need to take into account the variability and shift in prayer timings in planning sales calls, work schedules, business hours, customer traffic, and so forth.
ISLAMIC CULTURE	
A. *Obligation to family and tribal traditions*	Importance of respected members in the family or tribe as opinion leaders; word-of-mouth communication, customer referrals may be critical; social or clan allegiances, affiliations, and associations may be possible surrogates for reference groups; advertising home-oriented products stressing family roles may be highly effective—for example, electronic games.
B. *Obligations toward parents are sacred*	The image of functional products should be enhanced with advertisements that stress parental advice or approval; even with children's products, there should be less emphasis on children as decision makers.
C. *Obligation to extend hospitality to both insiders and outsiders*	Product designs that are symbols of hospitality, outwardly open in expression; rate of new product acceptance may be accelerated and eased by appeals based on community.
D. *Obligation to conform to codes of sexual conduct and social interaction*—These may include the following:	
1. Modest dress for women in public.	More colorful clothing and accessories are worn by women at home; so promotion of products for use in private homes could be more intimate—such audiences could be reached efffectively through women's magazines; avoid use of immodest exposure and sexual implications in public settings.
2. Separation of male and female audiences (in some cases).	Access to female consumers can often be gained only through women as selling agents, salespersons, catalogs, home demonstrations, and women's specialty shops.

(continued)

Table 3.1 Marketing in an Islamic Framework (cont.)	
Elements	**Implications for Marketing**
E. *Obligations to religious occasions*—For example, two major religious observances are celebrated: Eid-ul-Fitr, Eid-ul-Adha.	Tied to purchase of new shoes, clothing, and sweets and preparation of food items for family reunions, Muslim gatherings. There has been a practice of giving money in place of gifts. Increasingly, however, a shift is taking place to more gift giving; due to lunar calendar, dates are not fixed.

Source: "Marketing in Islamic Countries: A Viewpoint," by Mushtaq Luqmani, Zahir A. Quraeshi, and Linda Delene, *MSU Business Topics,* Summer 1980, pp. 20–21. Reprinted by permission.

Muslim customers. Arabic signs tell customers all food is certified *halal,* prepared according to Muslim laws. His staff is encouraged to wear Islamic dress and headwear. His restaurants are covered with green banners (green is the color of Islam). Pictures of Mr. Bambang and his wife in Islamic dress hang on the walls.[18]

Gillette faced another marketing challenge related to Islam when it wanted to introduce its shaving products in Iran. Islam discourages its followers from shaving, which made it difficult for Gillette's local distributor to secure advertising space. In the end, the distributor visited one local newspaper after another until he finally met an advertising manager without a beard. The distributor convinced the advertising manager that shaving sometimes was unavoidable, such as when a person had a head injury because of an accident, and that Gillette blades would be best. The advertising manager consulted with his clergyman and, having obtained the latter's permission, accepted the ad. As a result, other newspapers followed, and Gillette Blue was launched. The company is now working on television advertising, which currently is permitted only for domestically made products.[19]

Coca-Cola developed a global advertisement for Ramadhan (the Muslim fasting month), which was run in twenty countries. Developed by McCann-Erickson Malaysia, the commercial included a small boy and his mother carrying gifts to an orphanage. The mother had a rug and a basket of food; the boy had his cherished bottle of Coca-Cola. After sunset, the little boy leaves his house to return to the orphanage to break fast and share the Coca-Cola with his new friends. The ad ends with "Always in good spirit. Always Coca-Cola."[20]

The events of September 11, 2001, as well as the war in Afghanistan, raised the tensions between many westerners and Muslims. The views of many Muslim extremists do not represent the views of all Muslims. The entry of the Gulf countries, especially Saudi Arabia, into the WTO will have a big impact on the relationships between Muslims and other cultures. The advice of Professor Samuel Hayes III, an expert on Islamic law and finance, is to avoid mention of "the Palestinian-Israeli situation."[21] Certainly, global marketers require a keen awareness of how religion can influence business. They need to search actively for any such possible influences, even when the influences are not very apparent. Developing an initial awareness of the impact that religion has on one's own culture is often very helpful in developing cultural sensitivity.

EDUCATION

Though the educational system of a country largely reflects its own culture and heritage, education can have a major impact on how receptive consumers are to foreign marketing techniques. Education shapes people's outlooks, desires, and motivation. To the extent that educational systems differ by country, we can expect differences among consumers. Education not only affects potential consumers, however; it also shapes potential employees for foreign companies and for the business community overall. This will influence business practices and competitive behavior. Executives who have been educated in one country are frequently poorly informed about educational systems elsewhere. In this section, we will indicate some of the major differences in educational systems throughout the world and explain their impact on global marketing.

LEVELS OF PARTICIPATION

The level of education and participation of young people in educational systems drives a country's level of literacy and knowledge. Table 3.2 shows the participation of the population of various countries in secondary and higher education. In the United States, where education is compulsory until age sixteen, 96 percent of the relevant population attends school. Not all countries share this pattern. The large majority of students in Europe go to school only until age sixteen; then they join an apprenticeship program. In Germany, formal apprenticeship programs exist for about 450 job categories. These programs are under tight government supervision and typically last three years. They include on-the-job training, with one day a week of full-time school. About 70 percent of young Germans enter such a program after compulsory full-time education.[22] During the first year, they can expect to earn about 25 percent of the wages earned by a fully trained artisan in their field. Only about 30 percent of young Germans finish university education. In Great Britain, most young people take a job directly in industry and receive only informal on-the-job training. In the United States, about 56 percent of the work force stops at a high school education (or earlier). However, in a study of employees who have direct contact with customers in German, Japanese, and U.S. companies, the U.S. employees received the least training once employed.[23]

Participation in secondary education affects literacy levels and economic development. Even with similar levels of participation in secondary education, the attitudes of some countries about the quantity and quality of education differ. For example, Japanese high school students attend class more days per school year than students in the United States, where the school year is only 180 days long. Students in other countries also spend a higher percentage of their school day on core academic subjects. The differences in mathematics, science, and history are 1,460 total hours for high school students in the United States, 3,170 hours in Japan, 3,280 hours in France, and 3,528 hours in Germany.[24] Therefore, it is not surprising that in a 1998 study, high school seniors in the United States ranked near the bottom of the twenty-one countries surveyed, behind all their European counterparts and 6 percent below the international average.[25] These differences may explain why an OECD study of reading comprehension in eight countries found that the United States outperformed only Poland. One out of five Americans surveyed did not understand the

Table 3.2 Educational Statistics of Selected Countries (in Percentages)

Country	Participation in Secondary Education[a]	Participation in Higher Education[b]	Illiteracy Rates[c]
Argentina	77	11.0	3.5
Australia	96	28.0	1.0
Austria	97	12.0	2.0
Belgium	100	34.0	1.0
Brazil	66	70.0	16.0
Canada	95	46.0	1.0
Chile	85	9.0	4.8
Denmark	95	27.0	1.0
Finland	95	36.0	1.0
France	99	30.0	1.0
Germany	95	22.0	1.0
Greece	91	22.0	3.4
Hungary	97	14.0	0.8
Indonesia	56	3.0	15.0
Ireland	86	29.0	1.0
Japan	100	45.0	1.0
Malaysia	64	11.0	12.5
Mexico	66	17.0	9.9
Netherlands	100	27.0	1.0
New Zealand	93	26.0	1.0
Norway	98	30.0	1.0
Philippines	78	26.0	5.4
Poland	87	12.0	1.0
Portugal	90	11.0	9.2
South Africa	59	0.0	15.6
South Korea	100	34.0	2.8
Spain	92	32.0	2.8
Sweden	100	31.0	1.0
Switzerland	99	25.0	1.0
Turkey	51	7.0	13.0
United Kingdom	92	26.0	1.0
United States	96	36.0	1.0
Venezuela	49	NA	8.0

a. Percentage of relevant age group receiving full-time education.
b. Percentage of population twenty-five to thirty-four years old who have completed tertiary education equivalent to a bachelor's degree.
c. Adult (over fifteen years) illiteracy rate as a percentage of population.
Source: The World Competitiveness Yearbook 2001 (Lausanne: IMD, 1996). Copyright © 2001 IMD. Used by permission.

directions on an aspirin bottle. Why then is the United States economy so much more productive? A study by McKinsey Consulting found that differences in basic skills were not a large factor in productivity. Management talent, labor rules, and regulatory environment were more important—all areas in which the United States does well![26]

LITERACY AND ECONOMIC DEVELOPMENT

The extent of education affects marketing on two levels. First, there is the problem of literacy. In societies in which the average level of participation in the educational process is low, one typically finds a low level of literacy (see Table 3.2). A low literacy level not only affects earning potential and thus the level of consumption; it also determines the communication options for marketing programs, as we will see in Chapters 11 and 12. Second, education affects young people's earning potential. In countries such as Germany, where many of the youth have considerable earnings by age twenty, the value, or potential, of the youth market is quite different from that in the United States, where a substantial number of youths do not enter the job market until age twenty-one or twenty-two.

Recent studies by the OECD have found a definite link between the percentage of sixteen-year-olds staying in school beyond the minimum leaving age and a country's economic well-being. Countries such as Japan, Holland, Germany, Austria, and the United States get a high return on their educational expenses because so many young people stay in school, either in traditional or vocational schools. Portugal, Spain, Britain, and New Zealand get a poor return on their educational expenses because so few young people continue their education. On average, each additional year of formal schooling results in a return of 5 to 15 percent per year in additional earnings.[27]

The educational system also affects the type of employees and executive talent. The typical career path of a U.S. executive involves a four-year college program and, in many cases, a master's degree in business administration (M.B.A.) program. This type of executive education is becoming more popular in Europe and Asia. Top management talent may have university degrees in other fields. For example, a law degree is among the more popular. In many areas of the world, it may be impossible to hire university graduates. In the United States, the sales organizations of many large companies are staffed strictly with university graduates, but in many other countries, sales as a profession has a lower status, and it can be difficult to attract university graduates.

Different countries have substantially different ideas about education in general, and management education in particular. Although differences exist between countries, traditional European education emphasizes the mastery of a subject through acquisition of knowledge. In contrast, the U.S. approach emphasizes analytic ability and an understanding of concepts. Students passing through these two different educational systems will probably develop different thinking patterns and attitudes. It requires a considerable amount of cultural sensitivity for a global manager to understand these differences and to make the best use of the human resources that are available.

THE FAMILY

The role of the family varies greatly between cultures, as do the roles that the various family members play. Across cultures, we find differences in family size, in the employment of women, and in many other factors of great interest to marketers. The family is a primary reference group and has always been considered an important determinant of purchasing behavior, so these differences across cultures are of interest. Companies familiar with family interactions in western society cannot assume that they will find the same patterns elsewhere. For example, the Chinese value family above individuals or even country. People have strong ties with family members. In China, 67 percent of parents with children live with one of their children, and 80 percent of parents have contact with their children at least once a week. Within a family, an individual has no rights or property—expenses are shared.[28] Therefore, product advertising appeals must focus on benefits to the family, not on benefits to the individual.

Another factor to be taken into consideration in global marketing is family structure. The term *nuclear family* is used to refer to the immediate family group: father, mother, and children living together As a result of an increasing divorce rate, the "typical" family of father, mother, and children living in one dwelling is rapidly becoming a thing of the past, or "atypical." Furthermore, families are smaller than they used to be because of a drop in fertility rates. The current fertility rate of births per woman in the EU has dropped to 1.5, which is below the replacement rate and therefore results in an aging population. Italy and Spain have the lowest fertility rates in the EU: only 1.2 births per woman. These countries are increasing day care and tax benefits to encourage larger families.[29] In addition, an increasing number of women are working outside the home (see Table 3.3). These circumstances have substantially changed purchasing patterns, especially among U.S. families.

Marketers who have dealt only with U.S. consumers should not expect to find the same type of family structure elsewhere. In many societies, the role of the male as head of household is more pronounced, and in some cultures (as in Asia or Latin America) the differences tend to be substantial. Some cultures still encourage male versus female children. In most cultures, there are 105 boys born per every 100 girls, but in China the figure is 118.5 boys, and in South Korea, it is 116. In some areas of South Korea, male births outnumber female births 125 to 100, indicating that female fetuses may be aborted.[30] This male dominance coincides with a lower rate of participation by women in the labor force outside the home. This situation results in a lower family income because double wage earners increase the average family income. The number of children per family also shows substantial variations by country or culture. In many eastern European countries and in Germany, one child per family is fast becoming the rule, whereas families in many developing countries are still large by western standards.

So far, we have discussed only the nuclear family. However, for many cultures, the extended family—including grandparents, in-laws, aunts, uncles, and so on—is of considerable importance. In the United States, older parents usually live alone, either in individually owned housing, in special housing for the elderly, or in nursing

Table 3.3 Family Statistics of Selected Countries (in Percentages)

Country	Infant Mortality Rates[a]	Female Participation in Labor Force[b]
Afghanistan	163	36
Australia	5	44
Austria	5	40
Belgium	5	41
Brazil	32	36
Canada	5	46
Chile	10	34
China	32	45
Denmark	4	46
Finland	4	48
France	4	45
Germany	4	42
Greece	5	38
Hungary	9	45
India	69	32
Indonesia	41	41
Ireland	6	35
Italy	5	39
Japan	4	41
Malaysia	8	38
Mexico	29	33
Netherlands	5	41
New Zealand	6	45
Norway	4	46
Pakistan	83	29
Portugal	6	44
Singapore	3	39
South Africa	63	38
Spain	4	37
Sweden	3	48
Switzerland	4	41
Thailand	28	46
Turkey	34	38

(continued)

Table 3.3 Family Statistics of Selected Countries (in Percentages) (cont.)		
Country	Infant Mortality Rates[a]	Female Participation in Labor Force[b]
United Kingdom	6	44
United States	7	46
Venezuela	19	35

a. Infant mortality per 1,000 live births, 2000.
b. Percentage of total labor force, 2000.
Source: World Bank Atlas 2002. Copyright © 2002 The International Bank for Reconstruction and Development/The World Bank. Reprinted by permission.

homes (for those who can no longer care for themselves). In countries with lower income levels and in rural areas, the extended family still plays a major role, further increasing the size of the average household.

Because the family plays such an important role as a consumption unit, marketers need to understand family roles and composition from country to country. At this point, we are not so much concerned with the demographic aspects, although they will concern us as we discuss the various market opportunities in Chapters 5 and 6. Here, the primary emphasis is on the roles that individual family members play, their respective influences on each other, and the society's expectation about what role each family member ought to play. Such an understanding is crucial for the marketing of consumer products and tends to affect both communication policy and product policy.

Families are especially important in Asia, where expatriate Chinese families make up a phenomenal Chinese business network. Driven by poverty and political upheaval, waves of families fled China to other countries in Asia. They developed dense networks of thrifty, self-reliant, business groups that distrusted outsiders. The groups were driven by insecurity to accumulate assets. These Chinese networks have flourished. For example, ethnic Chinese make up 1 percent of the population and 20 percent of the economy in Vietnam. Comparable figures for other countries are 1 percent and 40 percent in the Philippines, 4 percent and 50 percent in Indonesia, and 32 percent and 60 percent in Malaysia.[31] Many of these families, now in their third generation, are large and complex, and some question whether they will be able to maintain tight family ownership and control of their business assets.[32]

WORK AND LEISURE

The attitudes a society holds toward work have a substantial impact on that society's or its culture's economic performance. David McClelland has maintained that it is not a country's external resources that determine its economic rise but its level of entrepreneurial spirit in exploiting existing resources.[33] What was found to be crucial was the orientation, or attitudes, toward achievement and work. Cultures with a high level of achievement motivation were found to show a faster rise in economic development than those with low achievement motivation.

Well-known German sociologist Max Weber investigated the relationship between attitudes toward work and those toward religion. In his famous work, *The Protestant Ethic and the Spirit of Capitalism,* published in 1904, Weber was one of the first to speculate on the influence of religion on the work ethic by demonstrating differences between Protestant and Catholic attitudes toward work. McClelland later expanded Weber's theory to cover all religions and found that economies with a more Protestant orientation exceeded economies with a Catholic orientation in per capita

Figure 3.3: Time Out: Statutory Holiday Allowances, Working Days 1994

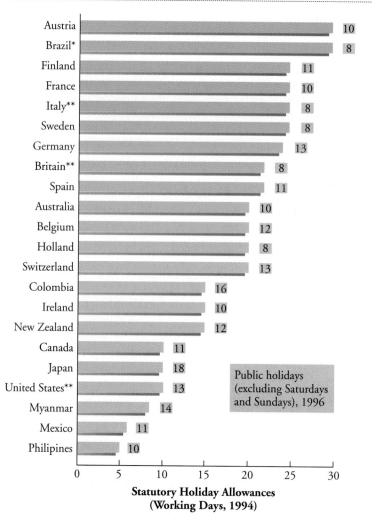

**Statutory Holiday Allowances
(Working Days, 1994)**

*Based on seven-day work week.
**Typical allowance (no statutory minimum).

Source: "Time Out: Statutory Holiday Allowances," *The Economist,* December 23, 1995-January 5, 1996. Copyright © 1995 The Economist Newspaper Ltd. Reprinted with permission, further reproduction prohibited. www.economist.com.

income. McClelland ascribed this difference to the Protestant (particularly Calvinist) belief that man did not necessarily receive salvation from God through work but that success in work could be viewed as an indication of God's grace. Consequently, accumulating wealth was not viewed as a shameful activity that needed to be hidden. Traditional Catholic doctrine viewed moneymaking in more negative terms. Weber theorized that this difference in attitude toward wealth caused Protestant societies to outperform Catholic societies in economic terms.

A discussion on work will usually lead to a discussion of its opposite—leisure. Different societies have different views about the amount of leisure time that is acceptable. In most economically developed countries, particularly where work has become a routine activity, leisure has become a major aspect of life. In such countries, the development of leisure industries is an indication that leisure can be as intensely consumed as any other product. Society significantly influences work and leisure through legalized holiday allowances and public holidays. As shown in Figure 3.3, European statutes require companies to give employees twenty-five to forty days of vacation annually, whereas the United States, Japan, Mexico, and the Philippines require only five to ten vacation days.[34] These differences are reflected in Table 3.4, which shows fewer working hours per year in Europe than in the United States, Japan, or Mexico. In the United States, vacations are shorter, so people tend to use up their allotted time off. These differences in the use of leisure time reflect, to some degree, differences in attitudes toward work (see Table 3.4). A study of 25,000 people from twenty-three countries found a wide variance in the attitudes toward self-employment. People from Poland (80 percent), Portugal (73 percent), and the United States (71 percent) preferred to be self-employed.[35]

REFERENCE GROUPS

Reference groups are people such as family, friends, and experts that consumers turn to for advice on product purchases. Many writers in marketing have documented the impact of reference groups on buying behavior.[36] Experience clearly indicates that the concept of reference group influence applies to many cultures. Differences can be found in the types of relevant reference groups and in the nature of their influence on individual consumers.

ROLE MODELS

Famous sports celebrities traditionally have been used to exploit the reference group concept. The idea is to tap the prestige of accomplished athletes to promote certain products. Not all sports are equally popular, however, in all parts of the world. The enormous interest in baseball in the United States is shared only by certain Latin American and Asian nations and not at all by Europeans. On the other hand, soccer dominates in Europe and Latin America and not in the United States. Some sports, such as tennis or golf, have an international following, but these sports do not attract large segments of the population. Consequently, finding an athlete whom people around the world will recognize equally is difficult.

There are some reference groups of U.S. origin that appear to have substantial universal appeal. The "American way of life" is one phenomenon that may explain the

Table 3.4 Values of Selected Countries			
Country	Average Number of Working Hours per Year[a]	Value of Society to Support Hard Work[b]	Managers' Sense of Entrepreneurship[c]
Australia	1,749	7.81	6.28
Austria	1,699	7.52	6.56
Belgium	1,712	6.42	6.66
Brazil	1,931	6.79	6.36
Canada	1,891	7.56	6.71
Chile	2,244	9.86	6.70
China	1,983	7.41	5.93
Denmark	1,687	6.39	5.61
Finland	1,723	8.27	6.91
France	1,587	5.36	5.37
Germany	1,688	6.80	5.87
Greece	1,780	5.90	6.15
Hong Kong	2,181	8.20	7.43
Hungary	1,988	6.12	6.67
India	2,097	5.12	4.78
Indonesia	2,065	5.00	5.00
Ireland	1,798	7.43	6.93
Italy	1,732	5.41	6.15
Japan	1,894	5.62	3.94
Malaysia	2,217	6.23	5.35
Mexico	2,150	5.48	4.88
Netherlands	1,696	7.39	6.92
New Zealand	1,873	5.89	6.04
Norway	1,730	6.24	5.19
Philippines	2,164	4.92	5.30
Portugal	1,738	5.78	5.33
Singapore	1,988	8.51	5.97
South Africa	1,929	5.07	5.07
South Korea	2,073	7.32	5.80
Spain	1,724	7.07	5.80
Sweden	1,860	6.88	7.27
Switzerland	1,855	7.39	6.60
Taiwan	2,167	7.44	6.86
Thailand	2,092	5.82	4.98
Turkey	2,074	6.46	6.61

(continued)

Country	Average Number of Working Hours per Year[a]	Value of Society to Support Hard Work[b]	Managers' Sense of Entrepreneurship[c]
United Kingdom	1,833	6.38	5.23
United States	1,918	8.38	7.11
Venezuela	1,956	3.84	4.62

Table 3.4 Values of Selected Countries (cont.)

a. Average number of working hours per year.
b. Values of the Society Support Competitiveness, where 0 equals "do not support competitiveness" and 10 equals "supports competitiveness." Average reported from 3,678 executives from 49 countries.
c. Managers' Sense of Entrepreneurship, where 0 equals "a lack of entrepreneurship" and 10 equals "a sense of entrepreneurship." Average reported from 3,678 executives from 49 countries.
Source: The World Competitiveness Yearbook 2001 (IMD, Switzerland), pp. 514, 470, 453.

success of many U.S. consumer products elsewhere. Though not always clearly defined, the American way of life does represent an attraction to large groups of people in most countries. What is considered American may in fact only be a cover for a modern or high-income lifestyle. Consequently, foreign consumers aspire to a high level of economic status as exemplified by the U.S. lifestyle or the commonly held image of such a life. In any case, some companies have successfully capitalized on this lifestyle, and Americans have become a reference group for numerous products in markets abroad.

Another U.S. symbol with international appeal is the American cowboy of the Wild West. The image of a cowboy on horseback triggers substantially similar reactions in most countries, even where the cultural background is otherwise diverse. The cowboy may very well be one of the few commonly shared symbols around the world, and this may account for the success of Philip Morris's well-known Marlboro campaign featuring rugged western scenes.

COUNTRY IMAGE

The success of the U.S. company Levi Strauss in foreign markets can be partially credited to the penchant of foreign consumers for western-style clothing. Several U.S. manufacturers of shoes, such as the Timberland and Sperry brands, have enjoyed strong sales in Europe. Other U.S. firms have had more difficulty, partially because of the image foreign consumers have of shoes manufactured in the United States. Market research revealed that French manufacturers were viewed as leading in high-fashion women's shoes, whereas Italian companies dominated the market for lightweight men's shoes. Europeans viewed shoes manufactured in the United States as stiff, heavy, boxy, and lacking variety in style; manufacturers in the United States took the lead only with western boots. Once a strong image exists in consumers' minds, it is extremely difficult to change that image.

On an international level, countries can assume the position of a reference group. Over time, various countries, or the residents of various countries, have become known for achievements in some aspects of life, culture, or industry. Other countries may therefore attach a special quality to the behavior of these consumers or to products that originate in these countries. When the German beer Beck was touted in the United States as "the German beer that is number 1 in Germany," the idea was to capitalize on the image of German beer drinkers as being the most discriminating. BSN Gervais-Danone, the French company that brewed Kronenbourg, attempted to take on Heineken, the leading exporter to the United States, by claiming "Europeans like Heineken, but they love Kronenbourg." This campaign tried to take advantage of the fact that Kronenbourg was the best-selling bottled beer in Europe. BSN decided not to emphasize French Alsace as the origin of the beer. Since the brand name Kronenbourg sounded German to most U.S. consumers, the company was relying on the positive image of German beers in general.[37]

A large number of studies indicate that the country of origin does influence consumer purchasing, although the impact may vary depending on the nationality of the consumer. In a study of U.S. and Thai consumers, both preferred Japanese, Korean, Chinese, and Taiwanese products; however, for the U.S. consumers, Malaysia and Indonesia were rated last and the Thai consumers rated Mexico and Brazil last.[38] The perfume industry, for decades dominated by French firms, has been greatly affected by the "made in Paris" phenomenon. Consumers all over the world have come to admire and expect more of perfumes made by French companies. U.S. firms have tried to overcome this handicap with aggressive marketing policies and the creation of new products based on market research and new insights into perfume-making chemistry. Still, it is very difficult to enter this high-prestige market, and some U.S. cosmetic leaders have not been able to duplicate their domestic success in other countries. To overcome the "made in Paris" mystique, foreign companies have acquired French cosmetic firms.

The impact of product origin has interested researchers for years. Numerous studies have been conducted, and the general agreement is that a strong correlation exists between country of origin and perceived product quality.[39] For reasons of tradition, consumers tend to attach some expertise to a certain country. For products originating in that particular country, the product image tends to be higher. A study in China about country of origin found that perceived product quality may be high for products coming from certain countries, but that perception would not counterbalance high animosity toward a country.[40] The study was done using Japan as the subject. Japan occupied China in the 1930s and massacred thousands of Chinese citizens during the occupation. The U.S. bombing of the Chinese embassy in Belgrade in 1999 could cause similar negative animosity. This strongly suggests that marketing managers must carefully consider the "made in . . ." implications of their products. If the country has a positive image, the origin of the product or company can be exploited. In other cases, the global firm may be advised to select a strategy that plays down the origin of the product. As global cosmetic firms have demonstrated in France, a positive country label can be obtained by opening operations in a country known for its achievements in a certain industry.

THE CHALLENGE OF CULTURAL CHANGE

What may appear to be a cultural difference may in fact be due to other influences, particularly economic factors. These other influences or factors are subject to considerable change over short time periods. For example, although Kellogg has sold

Kellogg's Corn Flakes in France since 1935, it has penetrated the breakfast market in only the last fifteen years. The slow growth of demand for corn flakes was related to two aspects of French culinary habits. First, the French did not eat corn; 80 percent of the corn harvested in France was fed to pigs and chickens.[41] Second, of those who ate cereal for breakfast, 40 percent poured on warm milk, which did not do much for the crunchiness or taste of corn flakes. To overcome these cultural factors, Kellogg put instructions on its cereal boxes and radically boosted television advertising with "Tony le Tigre." The average French person ate ten ounces of cereal in 1985, and Kellogg expected consumption to increase by 25 percent each year until 1990. However, the consumption of corn flakes in France has a long way to go to reach the average consumption of nine pounds in the United States, twelve pounds in England, and thirteen pounds in Australia.[42]

Kao, Japan's largest consumer marketing company, dominates the bleach, laundry detergent, household cleaning, and shampoo markets in Japan. Although Kao has expanded outside Japan, it has had difficulty in many markets. Kao's brand of facial care products, Biore, does well in Hong Kong, Taiwan, China, Singapore, Malaysia, and Indonesia, but is second place to Unilever's Pond brand in Thailand. After an extensive consumer research study, Kao found Thai women age eighteen to twenty-nine years did not understand proper face cleaning methods. Based on this research, Kao plans to expand its product line and change its marketing techniques. It expects to double its market share in Thailand in two years.[43]

The influence of culture on marketing is most prevalent with food products. However, quite a few firms have overcome cultural barriers. One such celebrated case is McDonald's, the U.S. fast-food franchise operator. The first year that McDonald's opened more restaurants abroad than in the United States was 1991. All of its top ten restaurants, measured in terms of sales and profits, are located overseas. Leading stores are in Moscow, Paris, and Rome, hardly places where one would expect a typical fare of U.S.-style hamburgers to do well. In general, however, McDonald's restaurants overseas have sales about 25 percent higher than the average U.S. outlet.[44] In fact, one of the company's stores in Poland holds the world record for first-day sales: it served 33,000 customers on its opening day.[45] Still, there are some countries where McDonald's, with its hamburger menu, does not do well or is not represented. One of them is India, where many people avoid eating beef for religious reasons.[46]

Campbell Soup has experienced more difficulties with marketing food globally. The company's overseas sales are only about 25 percent of total volume; its brands are not easily transplanted. Italians are not interested in buying canned pasta, which makes Franco-American SpaghettiOs a poor performer in Italy. In Argentina, where rival CPC's Knorr brand of dehydrated soup has dominated the market with an 80 percent share, Campbell is the outsider with its wet or canned soup. The challenge is even greater in Asia, where Campbell and other western food companies must find ways to sell food in exotic markets.[47]

Few companies have recently struggled as much with cultural differences as Disney. The U.S.-based entertainment company owns 49 percent of Euro Disney, a large theme park built outside Paris with a $4 billion investment. The park, designed as a carbon copy of Disney World in Orlando, Florida, opened in 1992 to much fanfare and a $10 million advertising campaign aimed at approximately thirty European countries.[48] Euro Disney was rescued by its bankers, who restructured the debt and negotiated a five-year moratorium on royalties and management fees to the U.S. parent. In 1998, Euro Disney made 290 million francs, with 12 million visitors. The difficulty in Europe is that people visit theme parks 0.23 times per person per year, compared with 0.60 times per person per year in the United States and Japan.[49] This experience contrasts sharply with Disney's success in Japan. Its theme park there was expected to attract 10 million visitors a year but achieved 17 million in 2001, more than 90 percent of them repeat visitors. One observer indicated that the Japanese have a strong affinity for fantasy and were not intimidated by the U.S.-manufactured icons. In fact, they wanted the undiluted American Disney. Coming to the Disney Park was linked to the Japanese tea ceremony, with its rules, roles, and symbolism. Japanese attending the Disney Park knew that they were "in" the United States and played that role during their visit.[50] Disney opened DisneySea park in Tokyo in 2002, plans a second park near Paris in 2003, and is developing a park in Hong Kong that is scheduled to open in 2005 or 2006.[51]

CULTURAL CHALLENGES TO MARKETING IN EASTERN EUROPE

The opening of eastern Europe to western businesses has created many cultural challenges. In the years following World War II, eastern European countries had little exposure to western-style marketing. As a result, consumption habits remained at levels more typical of western Europe thirty-five years ago. Several U.S. companies have now made their first entry into Poland, where consumers have to learn how to deal with western-style consumer goods. Gerber, a U.S.-based baby-food maker, moved into Poland by acquiring a local company in 1991. The company needed to educate consumers in the value and use of prepared baby foods. In the United States, about 630 jars of baby food are sold for each birth; the corresponding figure is 116 in Mexico and 624 in France. In Poland, it reached just 12 in 1993. Tradition in Poland calls for the mother to cook the baby's food. Although some mothers are now aware of the convenience of Gerber's product, only a few can yet afford it. The company is certain, however, that the market will grow substantially in the next few years.[52]

Retailers and franchise store operators have also had experience in eastern Europe. Kmart purchased thirteen stores in the Czech Republic and Slovakia. Its largest store in Bratislava, the capital of Slovakia, had sales of $40 million in the first year, surpassing all of the company's 2,400 stores in the United States. Despite this volume, the store was unprofitable because of inefficiencies, high costs, and low margins. Kmart found changing the relationship between sales clerk and consumer particularly challenging. Although the company's sales staff understands the customer concept, after forty years of communist rule, its implementation is still not natural to them.[53] According to a study of five hundred business executives traveling to eastern Europe, the cultural challenges are numerous. For example, Poles often expect on-the-spot decisions; in Kazakhstan, canceling a meeting at the last minute is common; punctuality is strictly observed in Romania; and to a Bulgarian, a nod of the head means no and a shake of the head means yes![54] Kmart exited the Czech Republic in 1996 because of low profitability.

The few examples reviewed in this section provide a glimpse of the challenges faced by global marketers. As is evident from global marketers' experiences, it is not easy to predict a product's future success or failure. Chapters 5 and 6 will provide some models for analyzing different strategies for countering cultural differences.

However, these examples also show that, with economic development, many traits or habits will disappear and other, more advanced habits will emerge. A marketer who faces differences between two countries must decide whether these differences are cultural or simply influenced by economic development. True cultural differences are likely to survive economic development, whereas differences driven by different income levels and living standards will rapidly disappear once economic development takes off.

ADAPTING TO CULTURAL DIFFERENCES

Some companies have made special efforts to adapt their products or services to various cultural environments. These strategies are most apparent in Japan, where foreign companies have to compete in an economically developed market with greatly differing cultural patterns. Japan has long been known for its thrifty, credit-adverse consumers. However, Visa and MasterCard have benefited from Japan's flourishing travel industry by promoting the use of credit cards for travel. Long before the 2000 Olympic games in Sydney, Australia, Visa offered Japanese consumers special travel and entertainment deals to attend the Olympics.[55] In addition, Japanese consumers have quickly taken to cards cobranded with groups, associations, and clubs because the typical Japanese is proud to belong to groups or associations.[56]

After years of marketing attempts, Japanese appear finally to be accepting credit cards. Younger Japanese consumers are now becoming frequent users of credit cards. Nippon Telegraph & Telephone (NTT) has developed a "smart card" containing a microchip that allows consumers to load funds from their bank account onto their card via the Internet, telephone, or vending machines and then use the card as electronic cash for retail transactions. NTT thinks the smart card will be preferred over credit cards. MasterCard International Japan is converting its entire portfolio of credit cards to multiapplication smart cards. MYCAL, the fourth largest retailer in Japan, owns supermarkets, department stores, clothing outlets, cinemas, and restaurants. The MYCAL Card Company was established in 1982 as a credit business for MYCAL. They issued 2.5 million cards by 2001.[57] It is projected that consumers will have one or two smart cards that will include loyalty programs, stored funds, credit access, and health information. Japan is expected to lead the world in smart cards.[58]

Even McDonald's, which started out in Japan decades ago with what is essentially a U.S.-style menu, concluded that it had to adapt its menu to the Japanese culture if it wanted to earn additional profits. It introduced McChao, a Chinese fried rice. Rice was an obvious first try in a country where 90 percent of the people eat rice daily. The results have been astounding. Sales have climbed 30 percent during the time McChao has been served. Even more important is the fact that 70 percent of McChao sales have been in the form of take-out food bought by single businesspeople. McDonald's continues to experiment in Japan with the Teriyaki McBurger and Chicken Tatsuta. Also in 1998, as Japan experienced its eighth year of recession, McDonald's cut the price of its hamburgers to 57 cents and increased sales by 30 percent during its summer promotion.[59]

Similar adjustments were needed for Domino's Pizza, one of the many pizza franchises selling in Japan. The types of pizza favored by Japanese consumers are quite different from those favored in the United States. Although Domino's advertises its pizza as "from the U.S.A.," it offers toppings such as teriyaki gourmet, consisting of Japanese-style grilled chicken, spinach, onion, and corn. In addition, Domino offers squid and tuna toppings, as well as corn salad.[60]

CULTURAL ANALYSIS FOR INTERNATIONAL MARKETING

It is not sufficient to describe cultural differences by citing only past experiences of companies. One could never cover all of the possible mistakes or cultural differences that international firms may experience abroad. Consequently, this text is restricted to a few examples indicating the kinds of problems international firms face. Because it is impossible to predict all the possible problems that can be encountered abroad, it becomes necessary to provide some analytical framework to deal with cultural differences.

In a classic article, James E. Lee exposed the natural tendency among executives to fall prey to a *self-reference criterion*. Lee defines the self-reference criterion as an "unconscious reference to one's own cultural values."[61] How does this self-reference criterion work? Within each culture, we have come to accept certain "truths," or basic facts. These facts, which have become part of our experience, are rarely challenged. As we continue our experience in one culture only, there are few occasions when such inherent beliefs can be exposed. The self-reference criterion also helps us understand new circumstances. Whenever we face an unknown situation, we have an inherent tendency to fall back on prior experience to solve the new problem. There is one substantial handicap to this automatic reflex: if the new situation takes place in a different cultural environment, then the self-reference criterion may invoke a past experience that is not applicable.

Lee suggests that, to avoid the trap of the self-reference criterion habit, executives approach problems using a four-step analysis. In the first step, the problem should be defined in terms of the executive's home cultural traits, habits, or norms. Here the analyst *can* invoke the self-reference criterion. In the second step, the problem should be defined in terms of the foreign cultural traits, habits, or norms. Value judgments should be avoided at this step. In the third step, the executive should isolate the personal biases relating to the problem and determine if or how they complicate the problem. Finally, in the fourth step, the problem should be redefined without the self-reference criterion influence so that the optimum solution can be found. Consequently, the four-step approach is designed to avoid culture-bound thinking on the part of executives or companies. (We will develop this approach in more detail in Chapter 6, where we present a model for analyzing the entire international environment.)

CULTURAL DIMENSIONS

Detailed studies of IBM managers around the world by Geert Hofstede identified four basic cultural dimensions. The first dimension is individualism versus collectivism. In a collectivist society, the identity or worth of persons as part of a social system outweighs their value as individuals. The second dimension is small versus large power distance. Large power distance cultures are more authoritarian, with subordinates dependent upon bosses. The third dimension is masculinity versus femininity, which reflects cultures dominated by males versus females. The last cultural dimension is weak versus strong uncertainty avoidance, which is a measure of risk tolerance versus risk aversion.

As shown in Figure 3.4, Venezuelans and Singaporeans are collective and authoritarian, so behavior tends to be for the good of society and to follow the authority of superiors. This situation is the diametric opposite for Americans or Australians, who are individualistic with a small power distance, or more democratic. In the uncertainty avoidance and male/female dimensions in Figure 3.5, notice that Americans (USA), Australians (AUL), and Venezuelans (VEN) are all members of masculine

Figure 3.4: The Position of 50 Countries and 3 Regions on the Power Distance and Individualism–Collectivism Dimensions[a]

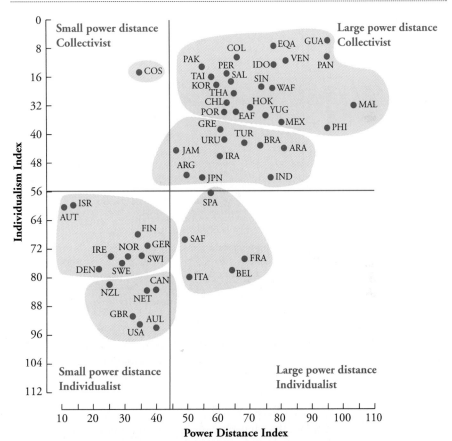

a. ARA, Arabic-speaking countries (Egypt, Iraq, Kuwait, Lebanon, Libya, Saudi Arabia, United Arab Emirates); ARG, Argentina; AUL, Australia; AUT, Austria; BEL, Belgium; BRA, Brazil; CAN, Canada; CHL, Chile; COL, Colombia; COS, Costa Rica; DEN, Denmark; EAF, East Africa (Ethiopia, Kenya, Tanzania, Zambia); EQA, Ecuador; FIN, Finland; FRA, France; GBR, Great Britain; GER, Germany F.R.; GRE, Greece; GUA, Guatemala; HOK, Hong Kong; IDO, Indonesia; IND, India; IRA, Iran; IRE, Ireland (Republic of); ISR, Israel; ITA, Italy; JAM, Jamaica; JPN, Japan; KOR, South Korea; MAL, Malaysia; MEX, Mexico; NET, Netherlands; NOR, Norway; NZL, New Zealand; PAK, Pakistan; PAN, Panama; PER, Peru; PHI, Philippines; POR, Portugal; SAF, South Africa; SAL, Salvador; SIN, Singapore; SPA, Spain; SWE, Sweden; SWI, Switzerland; TAI, Taiwan; THA, Thailand; TUR, Turkey; URU, Uruguay; USA, United States; VEN, Venezuela; WAF, West Africa (Ghana, Nigeria, Sierra Leone); YUG, Yugoslavia.
Source: Geert Hofstede, *Cultures and Organizations*, McGraw-Hill, 1991, pp. 23, 51, 83, and 111. Reprinted with permission of the McGraw-Hill Companies.

Figure 3.5: The Position of 50 Countries and 3 Regions on the Masculinity/Femininity and Uncertainty Avoidance Dimensions[a]

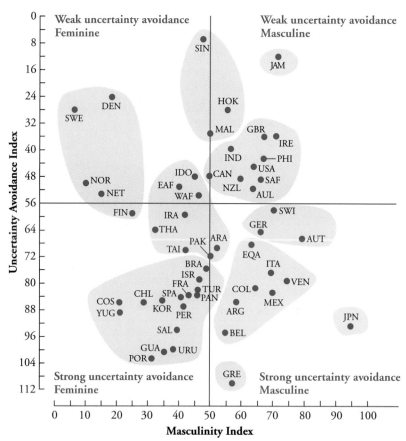

a. For country name abbreviations, see note a for Figure 3.4.
Source: Geert Hofstede, *Cultures and Organizations*, McGraw-Hill, 1991, pp. 23, 51, 83, and 111. Reprinted with permission of the McGraw-Hill Companies.

cultures, whereas the Singaporeans (SIN) are members of more feminine cultures. In addition, the Singaporeans are much more risk-tolerant than are Americans or Australians, and much more so than are the Venezuelans. The Hofstede analysis provides an overview of cultural differences that helps illustrate national consumer and managerial differences.[62]

Businesspeople moving to another culture will experience stress and tension, an experience often called culture shock. An individual who enters a different culture must learn to cope with a vast array of new cultural cues and expectations, as well as to identify which old ones no longer work. The authors of *Managing Cultural Differences* offer the following ten tips to deflate the stress and tension of cultural shock:

• Be culturally prepared.
• Learn local communication complexities.

- Mix with the host and nationals.
- Be creative and experimental.
- Be culturally sensitive.
- Recognize complexities in host cultures.
- Perceive oneself as a culture bearer.
- Be patient, understanding, and accepting of oneself and one's hosts.
- Be most realistic in expectations.
- Accept the challenge of intercultural experiences.[63]

The deregulation of telecommunications and air travel and the proliferation of digital commerce ensure that different people from around the global will experience increasing contact with one another. The amount of cultural mixing that has taken place in the last several decades is unprecedented in history and will only continue. In the United States 21 percent of marriages will be intercultural (combinations of black, Hispanic, white, and Asian). Local, national, and global business will become increasingly dependent on multicultural and polyglot customers and employees. To succeed, many global companies will have to pursue two apparently contradictory strategies. These companies must respond to global market demand with products and services of wide appeal but also tailor their offerings to markets organized around distinct identities. This situation could result, for example, in the simultaneous appearance of more English-language advertisements and media in China, Germany, and Mexico and more foreign-language advertisements and media in the United States.[64] Understanding these new and ever-changing cultural dimensions will be imperative to the success of global marketing strategies.

CONCLUSIONS

In this chapter, we introduced you to the wide variety of possible cultural and social influences present in global marketing operations. What we have presented here represents only a small sample of all the potential factors.

Culture is a learned set of ideals, values, and standards that are shared by members of a society and produce recognizable and acceptable patterns of behavior within that society. As economic globalization matures, the opportunities for cultural misunderstandings and conflict increase, which means understanding and recognizing the role of culture in marketing will become increasingly important. Culture produces meaning and substance for individuals and societies. Global marketers who understand and recognize the meaning and substance of cultures other than their own and the associated behaviors in those cultures will have a significant global advantage.

It is essential for global marketers to avoid a cultural bias, or the self-reference criterion, when dealing with business operations in more than one culture. As the president of a large industrial company in Osaka, Japan, once explained, our cultures are 80 percent identical and 20 percent different. The successful business person can identify the differences and deal with them. Of course, this task is very difficult, and few executives ever reach the stage where they can claim to be completely sensitive to cultural differences. The analytical concepts presented at the end of the chapter will help you to deal with cultural differences. These concepts will be refined further in Chapter 6.

Questions for Discussion

1. Explain the difference between wants and needs you may be born with, and culturally derived wants and needs.

2. What process can a marketer use to ensure that an advertisement or brochure gives the desired message in an unfamiliar language?

3. How would marketing automobiles to a predominantly Islamic population differ from marketing to a predominantly Christian population?

4. How do the educational systems of the United States, Japan, England, and Germany affect the marketing of banking services to young adults age sixteen to twenty-two?

5. What aspects of culture influence the marketing of women's designer blue jeans in different countries? How do these cultural influences affect magazine advertising?

6. A product's country of origin is said to influence consumer demand. Why do we prefer specific products from certain countries—for example, perfume from France, electronics from Japan, and beer from Germany?

7. What effect will the Internet have on cultural differences between France and India?

8. You have been asked to attend a meeting with Belgian, Turkish, and Japanese colleagues to develop a global plan for a new aftershave. Using Figures 3.4 and 3.5, what challenges would you face in the meeting? Assume that you represent your native culture.

9. When entering a new foreign market, how can one learn the culture?

For Further Reading

Bradley, T. L. "Cultural Dimensions of Russia: Implications for International Companies in a Changing Economy." *Thunderbird International Business Review,* January-February 1999, vol. 41, no. 1, pp. 49–98.

Chao, Paul. "Partitioning Country of Origin Effects: Consumer Evaluations of a Hybrid Product." *Journal of International Business Studies,* 2nd quarter 1993, p. 291.

Cordell, Victor V. "Effects of Consumer Preferences for Foreign Sourced Products." *Journal of International Business Studies,* 2nd quarter 1992, pp. 251–269.

David, Kenneth, and Vern Terpstra. *Cultural Environment of International Business.* Independence, Ken.: Southwestern, 2002.

Digh, Patricia. "Shades of Gray in the Global Marketplace." *HRMagazine,* April 1997, pp. 90–98.

Elashmawi, Farid, and Phillip R. Harris. *Multicultural Management 2000: Essential Cultural Insights for Global Business Success.* Houston, Tex.: Gulf, 1998.

Francis, June, Janet Lam, and Jan Wells. "Executive Insights: The Impact of Linguistic Differences on International Brand Name Standardization: A Comparison of English and Chinese Brand Names of Fortune-500 Companies." *Journal of International Marketing,* 2002, vol. 10, no. 1, pp. 98–117.

Goodyear, Mary. "Divided by a Common Language: Diversity and Deception in the World of Global Marketing." *Journal of the Market Research Society,* April 1996, pp. 105–122.

Gulbro, Robert, and Paul Herbig. "Differences in Cross-Cultural Negotiations Behavior Between Manufacturing and Service Firms." *Journal of Professional Services Marketing,* November 1995, vol. 13, no. 1, pp. 23–28.

Harris, Philip R., and Robert T. Moran. *Managing Cultural Differences,* 4th ed. Houston, Tex.: Gulf, 1996.

Harris, R., and R. Davidson. "Anxiety and Involvement: Cultural Dimensions of Attitudes Towards Computers in Developing Societies." *Journal of Global Information Management,* January-March 1999, vol. 7, no. 1, pp. 26–39.

Hasan, H., and G. Ditas. "The Impact of Culture on the Adoption of IT: An Interpretive Study." *Journal of Global Information Management,* January-March 1999, vol. 7, no. 1, pp. 5–16.

Hitt, Michael A., M. Tina Dacin, Beverly B. Tyler, and Daewoo Park. "Understanding the Differences in Korean and U.S. Executives' Strategic Orientations." *Strategic Management Journal,* February 1997, pp. 159–167.

Hofstede, Geert. *Cultures and Organizations.* London: McGraw-Hill, 1991.

Holden, Nigel. *The Clash of Civilizations and the Remaking of World Order.* New York: Simon & Schuster, 1996.

———. "Viewpoint: International Marketing Studies—Time to Break the English Strangle-hold." *International Marketing Review,* 1998, vol. 15. no. 2, pp. 86–100.

Iyer, Gopalkrishnan. "Cultures and Societies in a Changing World." *Journal of Global Marketing,* 1996, vol. 9, no. 3, pp. 95–96.

Marshall, R. Scott, and David M. Marshall. "Dynamic Decision-Making: A Cross-Cultural Comparison of U.S. and Peruvian Export Managers." *Journal of International Business Studies,* 4th Quarter 2001, vol. 32, no. 4, pp. 873–894.

McCarthy, Dennis M. P. "International Economic Integration and Business Cultures: Comparative Historical

Perspectives." *Business & Economic History,* Fall 1996, pp. 72–80.

Usunier, Jean Claude. *Marketing Across Cultures.* London: Prentice Hall, 1996.

Weiss, Stephen E. "Negotiating with 'Romans,'" Part 1. *Sloan Management Review,* Winter 1994, pp. 51–61.

———. "Negotiating with 'Romans,'" Part 2. *Sloan Management Review,* Spring 1994, pp. 85–99.

Williams, J. D., S. L. Han, and W. J. Qualls. "A Conceptual Model and Study of Cross-Cultural Business Relationships." *Journal of Business Research,* June 1998, vol. 42, no. 2, pp. 135–144.

Zacharakis, Andrew. "The Double Whammy of Globalization: Differing Country and Foreign Partner Cultures." *Academy of Management Executive,* November 1996, pp. 109–110.

Endnotes

1. William Haviland, *Anthropology* (New York: Holt, Rinehart and Winston, 1991).

2. Amrit Dhillon, "India Has No Beef with Fast-Food Chains," *Financial Times,* March 23, 2002.

3. "You Have Ways of Making Us Talk: Denglisch Ousts German: Sprechen Sie Denglisch?" *Economist,* February 24, 2001.

4. "Those Whingeing Poms," *Economist,* May 24, 1997, p. 40.

5. "Europe's Languages: Service Compris," *Economist,* August 29, 1998, p. 47.

6. Sherrie E. Zhan, "Marketing Across Cultures," *World Trade,* February 1999, vol. 12, no. 2, p. 80.

7. Allyson L. Stewart-Allen, "Cultural Quandaries Can Lead to Misnomers," *Marketing News,* November 23, 1998, p. 9.

8. "English and Electronic Commerce: The Default Language," *Economist,* May 15, 1999, p. 67.

9. Iris Kapustein, "Selling and Exhibiting Across the Globe," *Doors and Hardware,* September 1, 1998, p. 34.

10. James L. Grayson, "Gestures: The DO's and TABOOs of Body Language Around the World," *Security Management,* March 1999, p. 122.

11. Judith Bowman, "Before Going Overseas, Be Ready: Know the Protocol," *Mass High Tech,* April 26, 1999, p. 31.

12. Mushtaq Luqmani, Zahir Quraeshi, and Linda Delene, "Marketing in Islamic Countries: A Viewpoint," *MSU Business Topics,* Summer 1980, p. 17.

13. "How to do Business in Islamic Countries," *Harvard Business School Working Knowledge,* February 4, 2002, p. 1.

14. Muhammad Abdul-Rauf, "The Ten Commandments of Islamic Economics," *Across the Board,* August 1979, p. 7.

15. Ibid., pp. 15–16.

16. Jerry Useem, "Banking on Allah," *Fortune Magazine,* June 10, 2002, p. 154.

17. "Malaysia: Country Profile," *Asia & Pacific Review World of Information* (London: Walden Publishing, 1998), p. 1.

18. Jay Solomon, "How Mr. Bamband Markets Big Macs in Muslim Indonesia," *Wall Street Journal,* October 26, 2001, p. A1.

19. "Smooth Talk Wins Gillette Ad Space in Iran," *Advertising Age International,* April 27, 1992, pp. 1–40.

20. Kang Siew Li, "Coca-Cola's Global Ramadhan Commercial," *Business Times, New Straits Times Press,* January 14, 1998, p. 17.

21. "How to Do Business in Islamic Countries," *Harvard Business School Working Knowledge,* February 4, 2002, p. 1.

22. "Teaching Business How to Train," *Business Week/Reinvesting America,* 1992, p. 90.

23. Paul Osterman, "Reforming Employment and Training Programs," *USA Today,* January 1, 1999, p. 90.

24. "U.S. Pupils Short on Basics, Study Finds," *International Herald Tribune,* May 6, 1994, p. 3.

25. "Math, Physics Scores in U.S. Come Up Short," *Pittsburgh Post-Gazette,* February 25, 1998, p. A-1.

26. "Baffled: Reading Comprehension," *Economist,* December 9, 1995, p. 27.

27. Joop Hartog, "Behind the Veil of Human Capital," *OECD Observer,* January 1999, p. 38.

28. Fuqin Bian, John R. Logan, and Yanjie Bian, "Intergenerational Relations in Urban China," *Demography,* February 1998, pp. 119–122.

29. Leslie Crawford, "Spanish and Italian Mothers to Front a New Baby Boom," *Financial Times,* June 6, 2002, p.16

30. Sheryl Wu Dunn, "Korean Women Still Feel Demands to Bear a Son," *New York Times International,* January 14, 1997, p. A3.

31. Simon Saulkin, "Chinese Walls," *Management Today,* September 1996, pp. 62–68.

32. "Fissiparous Fortunes and Family Feuds," *Economist,* November 30, 1996, pp. 63–64.

33. David C. McClelland and David G. Winter, *Motivating Economic Achievement* (New York: Free Press, 1969).

34. "Why Jack Is a Dull Boy," *Economist*, January 5, 1996, p. 112.

35. "Countries with the Spirit of Enterprise," *Financial Times*, February 17, 2000, p. 27.

36. Leon G. Schiffman and Leslie Lazar Kanuk, *Consumer Behavior*, 3rd ed. (Englewood Cliffs, N.J.: Prentice Hall, 1987), p. 374.

37. "Big Battle Is Brewing as French Beer Aims to Topple Heineken," *Wall Street Journal*, February 22, 1980, p. 24.

38. Lyn S. Amine and Sang-Heun Shin, "A Comparison of Consumer Nationality as a Determinant of COO Preferences," *Multinational Business Review*, Spring 2002, vol. 10, no. 1, pp. 50–52.

39. M. Thakor, V. Katsanis, and Lea Prevel, "A Model of Brand and Country Effects on Quality Dimensions: Issues and Implications," *Journal of International Consumer Marketing*, 1997, vol. 9, no. 3, pp. 79–100.

40. Jill Gabrielle Klien, Richard Ettenson, and Marlene D. Morris, "The Animosity Model of Foreign Product Purchase: An Empirical Test in the People's Republic of China," *Journal of Marketing*, January 1, 1998, p. 89.

41. "While Americans Take to Croissants, Kellogg Pushes Corn Flakes on France," *Wall Street Journal*, November 11, 1986, p. 40.

42. Ibid.

43. "Kao Sets Bold Steps for Leadership in Facial-Care," *Nation*, June 24, 1999, p. 1.

44. "Overseas Sizzle for McDonald's," *New York Times*, April 17, 1993, p. D1.

45. "Big Mac's Counter Attack," *Economist*, November 13, 1993, p. 71.

46. "Overseas Sizzle," p. D1.

47. "Campbell: Now It's M-M-Global," *Business Week*, March 15, 1993, p. 15.

48. "Mr. Grumpy at the Door," *Financial Times*, September 1, 1993, p. 15.

49. Charles Fleming, "Euro Disney Reports 34% Profit Surge," *Wall Street Journal*, November 19, 1998, p. A19.

50. "Japan Enters the World of Fantasy," *Financial Times*, May 6, 1993, p. 8.

51. "Tokyo Theme Park a Small Risk for Disney," *Asian Wall Street Journal*, September 3, 2001, p. N1.

52. "In Poland, Gerber Learns Lessons of Tradition," *New York Times*, November 8, 1993, p. 1.

53. "In East Europe, Kmart Faces an Attitude Problem," *New York Times*, July 7, 1993, p. D1.

54. Scheherazade Daneshkhu, "Poor Communication and Bureaucracy Make Eastern Europe Frustrating," *Financial Times*, September 9, 1996, p. 12.

55. "Global Tie-Ins," *Credit Card Management*, January 1, 1999, p. 56.

56. "Japan's Growing Credit Card Culture," *Credit Card Management*, September 1998, p. 140.

57. "Mycal to launch Joint Credit Card with Aeon Group," *Jiji Press English News Service*, Tokyo, April 8, 2002, p.1.

58. "Japanese MYCAL Program on Track for Five Million Multi-Application MULTOS Cards," *Business Wire—Singapore*, May 11, 1999, p. 1.

59. Elizabeth Brent, "Japan's Deep Recession Spells Big Changes for Branches of U.S. Brands," *Nation's Restaurant News*, February 15, 1999, pp. 1–5.

60. Prasanna Raman, "Ang Works Hard to Build Domino's," *New Straits Times Press*, March 8, 1999, p. 30.

61. James E. Lee, "Cultural Analysis in Overseas Operations," *Harvard Business Review*, March–April 1966, pp. 106–114.

62. Geert Hofstede, *Cultures and Organizations* (London: McGraw-Hill, 1991), pp. 23, 51, 83, 111.

63. Philip R. Harris and Robert T. Moran, *Managing Cultural Differences*, 4th ed. (Houston, Tex.: Gulf, 1996), pp. 218–223.

64. G. Pascal Zachary, "A Mixed Future: Despite the Increased Blending of Races, Nationalities and Culture, Differences Will Continue to Flourish," *Wall Street Journal*, January 31, 1999, p. A1.

Chapter 4

Political and Legal Forces

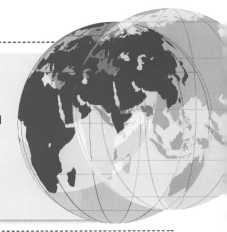

The purpose of this chapter is to identify the political and legal forces that influence global marketing operations. The first part of this chapter is concerned primarily with political factors; the second is devoted to the legal aspects of global marketing. The emphasis is on the regulations or laws that affect global marketing business transactions. Because many laws are politically inspired or motivated, it is difficult to separate political from legal forces. Nevertheless, some separation of the two areas is made here to allow for a better organization of the subject matter. Figure 4.1 illustrates the elements covered in the chapter and shows the relationships among them.

Dealing simultaneously with several political and legal systems complicates the job of the global marketing executive. These factors often precipitate problems that increase the level of risk in the global marketplace. To limit a firm's risk, global marketers need to be constantly aware of the world political situation; they need to see potential opportunities like the opening of China, Vietnam, or possibly Cuba. They must also predict the possible loss of opportunity in Argentina, Pakistan, or India due to political or economic events. Global companies have learned to cope with such complexities by developing risk reduction strategies. These strategies are explained toward the end of the chapter.

HOST COUNTRY POLITICAL FORCES

The rapidly changing nature of the global political scene is evident to anyone who regularly reads, listens to, or watches the various news media. Political upheavals, revolutions, and changes in government policy occur daily and can have an enormous impact on global business. As governments change, opportunities for new business

Figure 4.1: Relationship of Elements Covered in the Chapter

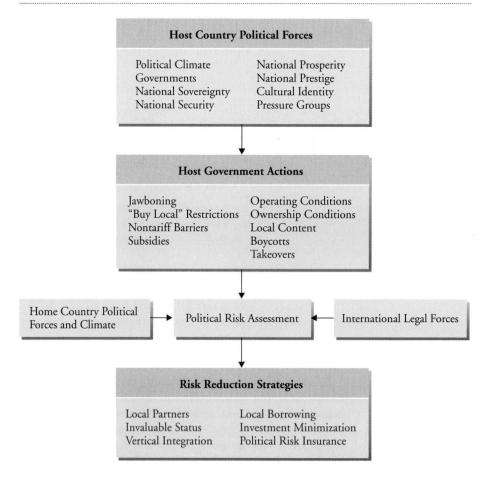

may be lost or gained. For the executive, these changes mean constant adjustments to maximize new opportunities and minimize losses.

Besides the global company, the principal players in the political arena are the host country governments, the home country governments, and the transnational bodies or agencies. Although we use the term *host country* extensively in the following sections, political actions take place increasingly in an environment of *regions*. One such regional example is the European Union (EU). Political actions of host countries can therefore apply to an entire region, or a grouping of countries. Although we do not make an explicit distinction each time, we have decided to apply the term *host country* interchangeably, to both single countries and country groupings.

The respective interactions of these groups result in a given political climate that may positively or negatively affect the operations of a global business. The difficulty for the global company stems from the fact that the firm is simultaneously subject to all these forces, which often have conflicting influences, whereas a strictly domestic corporation has to deal with only one, namely, the home country political climate. The situation is further complicated by the fact that companies maintain operations in scores of countries—meaning that companies must be able to manage many sets of political relationships simultaneously. In the following sections of this chapter, we discuss the host country political climate, the home country political climate, and transnational legal forces that regulate international trade. We also focus on political risk assessment and analyze the types of risk reduction strategies that may be employed to manage risk in such a complex world.

POLITICAL CLIMATE

Any country that contains an operational unit (manufacturing, finance, sales, and so on) of a global company can be defined as a host country. By definition, global companies deal with many different host countries, each with its own political climate. In each country, the political climate is largely determined by the way the various participants interact with each other. It is influenced by the actions of the host country government and local special interest groups, as well as by the prevailing political philosophy.

Stable political climates are those in which existing relationships among the key players are not expected to change. Conversely, political climates are unstable when the nature of the interactions or their outcomes is unpredictable. Though the political climate of a country can be analyzed with respect to various segments of a society, for the purpose of this text we restrict ourselves to those aspects of the political climate that relate to the business sectors.

Political instability can arise in any country. For example, in early 2000, the Freedom Party in Austria gained 27 percent of the electorate, enough to establish a coalition government with the People's Party. Jörg Haider, chairman of the Freedom Party, was a xenophobe who recommended that Austria close its borders to all immigrants. The rise of the Freedom Party led to mass demonstrations and contributed to foreign investors' fears. On February 29, 2000, Haider resigned as party chairman, but he will still be a political influence.[1]

There is a great deal of uncertainty about China's future, though it does not stem from the present direction of the economic course. With China's entry into the World Trade Organization (WTO) in November 2001, China's markets will continue to open. The import market into China is expected to be $150 billion in 2002 and will grow further as tariffs decline. For example, many goods have tariffs as high as 100 percent, but these tariffs are expected to decline to 25 percent by 2006, therefore reducing the price to Chinese consumers and the barriers to imports.[2]

GOVERNMENTS

Businesses operate in a country at the discretion of its government, which can encourage or discourage foreign businesses through various measures. The government plays the principal role in host countries by initiating and implementing policies regarding the operation, conduct, and ownership of businesses. In 2003, about 191 nations have been accepted as full members at the United Nations, giving some indication as to the large number of independent countries that exist at this time.

Although each government may give the impression of acting as a single and homogeneous force, governments in most countries represent a collection of various, and at times conflicting, interests. Governments are sharply influenced by the prevailing political philosophy, existing local pressure groups or special interest groups, and the government's own self-interest. All of these factors lead to government actions that global companies must not only recognize but also actively incorporate into their marketing strategies. Of prime importance, then, is the marketer's ability to understand the rationale behind government actions.

To evaluate the political risk in a country and understand how decisions are made, examining the political structure is useful. Is it a democracy, dictatorship, monarchy, or socialist government? Knowing the nature of the political system aids understanding of the relationship between business and government. One way to classify governments is by the degree of representation of the population in government. Parliamentary governments hold regular elections so that government policies reflect the will of the people. All democracies are classified as parliamentary. Over the past decade, the world has seen a considerable shift toward democratic government. This was most apparent in eastern Europe, where communist governments were swept away in the 1989 political upheaval. However, changes in Latin America are equally significant. In the early 1980s, true democracies existed in only a few countries, Venezuela and Costa Rica among them. Now, most military dictatorships in that region have ceased, and democratic governments have been installed in almost all Latin American countries.

Trying to understand governmental behavior makes sense only if there is a rational basis for leaders' actions and decisions. As many political scientists have pointed out, these actions usually flow from the government's interpretation of its own self-interest. This self-interest, often called national interest, may be expected to differ from nation to nation, but it typically includes the following goals:[3]

1. *Self-preservation.* This is the primary goal of any entity, including states and governments.
2. *Security.* To the extent possible, each entity seeks to maximize the opportunity for continued existence and to minimize threats from the outside.
3. *Prosperity.* Improving the living conditions for a country's citizens is an important and constant concern.
4. *Prestige.* Most governments or countries seek prestige either as an end in itself or to help reach other objectives.
5. *Ideology.* Governments frequently protect or promote an ideology in combination with other goals
6. *Cultural identity.* Governments often intervene to protect their country's cultural identity.[4]

The interaction of governments with foreign business interests can be understood through a basic appreciation of their national interest. The goals cited above are frequently the source of governmental actions either encouraging or limiting the business activities of global companies. Many executives erroneously believe that such limiting actions occur mostly in developing countries. On the contrary, there are many examples of restrictive government actions in the most developed countries, and these numerous examples indicate the universal nature of this type of governmental behavior. Such restrictive behavior most often occurs when a government perceives the attainment of its own goals to be threatened by the activities or existence of a body beyond its total control, namely, the foreign subsidiary of a company.

NATIONAL SOVEREIGNTY AND THE GOAL OF SELF-PRESERVATION

A country's self-preservation is most threatened when its national sovereignty is at stake. Sovereignty gives a nation complete control within a given geographic area, including the ability to pass laws and regulations and the power to enforce those laws and regulations. Governments or countries frequently view the existence of sovereignty as a key to reaching the goal of self-preservation. Though sovereignty may be threatened by several factors, the relationship between a government's attempt to protect its sovereignty and a company's policies to achieve its own goals is of primary interest to us.

Because subsidiaries, or branch offices, of global companies are substantially controlled or influenced by decisions made in headquarters, beyond the physical or legal control of the host government, such foreign companies are frequently viewed as a danger to the host country's national sovereignty. (It is important to recognize in this context that *perceptions* on the part of host countries are typically more important than facts.)

Many countries limit foreign ownership of newspapers, television stations, and radio stations for reasons of national sovereignty. Countries fear that if a foreign company controlled these media, it could influence public opinion and limit national sovereignty. The Australian-born Rupert Murdoch controls 70 percent of the major newspapers in Australia. He traded his Australian passport for an American passport to evade ownership restrictions in the United States. Kerry Packer, owner of Australia's largest magazine publishing company and television network, unsuccessfully tried to convince the Australian government that Murdoch was a foreigner and should reduce his holdings in Australia.[5] CADE, the Brazilian antitrust authority, suspended Nestlé's purchase of Chocolates Garoto because the combined company would gain control of more than half the Brazilian chocolate market.[6]

Over the past few years, globalization of the world economy has created many interdependencies among the economies of countries. This increase in interdependency has led to a decrease in the expression of national sovereignty issues, such as requiring local content and limiting foreign investment. In fact, the tendency at this time is for a loosening of trade restrictions. A worldwide trend toward reducing rules to limit foreign investment and privatization of many formerly government owned industries is opening up many opportunities previously closed to global firms. We will therefore devote a special section later in this chapter to these issues.

Many attempts at restricting foreign firms have been curtailed by the worldwide General Agreement on Tariffs and Trade (GATT), which was superseded by the World Trade Organization (WTO). The WTO agreements still exclude several areas that governments, for their own interest, do not want to liberalize. One such area is the airline industry; governments remain heavily involved in setting policy, restricting access to airspace, and limiting landing rights. It is therefore not surprising that the takeoff and landing slots at European airports are dominated by the major domestic airlines. For example, Alitalia has 70 percent of the slots in Rome;

Lufthansa, 60 percent at Frankfurt; SAS, 55 percent at Copenhagen; KLM, 50 percent at Amsterdam; Swiss Air, 50 percent at Zurich; Air France, 45 percent at Paris; and British Airways, 40 percent at London's Heathrow Airport.[7]

THE NEED FOR NATIONAL SECURITY

It is natural for a government to strive to protect its country's borders from outside forces. The military establishment typically becomes a country's principal tool to prevent foreign encroachment. Consequently, many concerns about national security involve a country's armed forces or related agencies. Other areas sensitive to national security are aspects of a country's infrastructure and its essential resources, utilities, and the supply of crucial raw materials, particularly oil. To ensure the security of all these sensitive areas, host governments tend to strive for control and to resist any influence foreign firms may gain over companies or agencies involved in these areas.

Examples of such government influence abound. The U.S. government, for one, does not typically purchase military material from foreign-controlled firms, even if they have subsidiaries in the United States. For example, the U.S. government continues to control the sale of high-speed computers. In early 2000, President Clinton required a license on the sale of all computers capable of 12.3 billion or more operations per second. This executive order allows export of all but extremely high-speed computers, which can be used for military purposes.[8]

The protection of national security interests such as defense and telecommunications through regulations requiring local sourcing is declining. This trend has been influenced by two factors. First, it is not economical for each country to have its own defense and telecommunications industry. The high cost of research and development means that in many cases the small local defense supplier will have inferior technologies. Second, the European Union has agreed to open up public spending to all EU companies. This opening of European public spending has caused many U.S. and Japanese firms to form alliances with European partners and has encouraged the U.S. and Japanese governments to open up their public spending markets so their industries are not excluded from European markets. Mongolia has opened all public projects to foreign suppliers and has eliminated all taxes on trade to stimulate foreign trade. Since Mongolia is now an independent country, trade and investment have become more important than defense. According to Prime Minister Narantsatsralt, this new policy, along with global support, helped Mongolia's gross national product (GNP) to grow by 3.4 percent from 1994 to 1998.[9]

FOSTERING NATIONAL PROSPERITY

A key goal for government is to ensure the material prosperity of its citizens. Prosperity is usually expressed in national income or gross national product (GNP), and comparisons between countries are frequently made with respect to per capita income or GNP per capita figures. Comparisons are also done on gross domestic product (GDP), and both GNP and GDP are adjusted by purchasing power parity to reflect a comparable standard of living. However prosperity is measured, most governments strive to provide full employment and an increasing standard of living. Part of this goal is to enact an economic policy that will stimulate the economic output of businesses active within the nation's borders. Global companies can assume an important role when they add to a host country's GNP and thus enhance its income.

However, any action that runs contrary to the host government's goals, though it may be in the best interest of the company, will likely cause a conflict between the foreign company and the host country government. A host country may also take actions that unilaterally favor local industry over foreign competitors to protect its own standard of living and prosperity. Europe protects its agricultural industries with high tariffs. For example, in 1997, the average EU tariff on beef was 87.7 percent; on cereals, it was 67.8 percent; on dairy products, it was 57.7 percent; and on sugar, it was 61.8 percent.[10]

For many countries, a high level of imports represents a drain on their monetary resources. It also represents lost opportunities for expanding their own industrial base. Under such circumstances, a host country may move toward a restriction of imports beyond the imposition of tariffs or customs duties. Such measures are called nontariff barriers. Both the Italian and French governments have protected their local automobile industries from Japanese competition by using nontariff barriers. The Italian government has restricted for many years the import of Japanese automobiles to 2,000 units annually. The French government, through selective use of import licenses, has limited Japanese producers to only 3 percent of the market.

For years, the German government has supported local employment. However, the rules of the EU open employment to any member of the EU. Given the high cost of German labor and the lack of flexibility of German trade unions, it is not surprising that 400,000 German construction workers are out of work, while over 190,000 other EU workers are employed on German construction sites.[11] In 1999, unemployment in Germany was at 11 percent, down from 12 percent in 1997. The high unemployment rate in Germany is often blamed on the social security cost of 42 percent of gross wages.[12]

Most host governments try to enhance a nation's prosperity by increasing its exports. To do this, some governments have sponsored export credit arrangements combined with some form of political risk insurance. Particularly in Europe, heads of governments often engage in state visits to encourage major export transactions. Political observers often have pointed out that both the French president and the German chancellor spend a substantial amount of their state visits on business and trade affairs, more so than is typically the case for the president of the United States. Attracting global companies with a high export potential to open operations in their countries is of critical interest to host governments. Frequently, such companies can expect special treatment or subsidies.

In many countries, regional or local governments can also influence decisions that affect global firms. For the U.S. location of new BMW and Daimler-Benz assembly plants, the relevant government was not a national one but state governments. Various local governments lobbied intensively for the plant. The winning state government for the Daimler-Benz plant, Alabama, had to offer a $253 million commitment in infrastructure improvements to attract the project. A year earlier, the state government of South Carolina committed $150 million to attract a BMW plant.[13]

The host government's export and import policies are of interest to companies considering locating operations in a particular country. By collecting information on a government's policies or orientation, a company can make an optimal choice that may give it access to benefits not available in other countries.

ENHANCING PRESTIGE

The pursuit of prestige has many faces; it does not always take the form of industrial achievement. Whereas the governments of some countries choose to support team sports or individual athletes to enhance national prestige, other host governments choose to influence the business climate for the same reason. Having a national airline enhances national prestige. Other developed countries may prefer to see their industries achieve leadership in certain technologies such as telecommunications, electronics, robotics, or aerospace.

A host government trying to enhance its country's prestige will frequently encourage local or national companies at the expense of a foreign company. The French government suspended the sale of Thomson to the Lagardere Group because of the latter's plans to sell the multimedia division of Thomson to Daewoo Electronics, a South Korean firm. The French government was sensitive to the French workers' fear of working for Korean owners.[14] The U.S. sensitivity to foreign investors seemed to have diminished in 1999, with the Japanese owning many of Hollywood's entertainment companies; the Germans buying Chrysler, Bankers Trust, and Random House; and the British purchasing New England Electric and Amoco.[15]

In the future, companies will need to develop a keen sense for what constitutes national prestige as perceived by host governments. Businesspeople cannot expect host governments to have an explicit policy on such issues. Instead, companies will have to derive, from observing overt or covert government actions over time, some notions about national prestige. Once a company has a clear definition or idea of what constitutes prestige for a host government, it can avoid policies that are in direct conflict with government intentions or aspirations and can emphasize those actions that tend to enhance the host country's prestige.

PROTECTING CULTURAL IDENTITY

With the global village becoming a reality, one of the major impacts felt by countries is in the area of culture. The breaking down of communications barriers has led to an increase in the activities of global, mostly U.S., media firms. These firms are most visible in entertainment: in the production and distribution of movies, television programs, videos, and music recordings. Even more important has been the role of satellite transmission in television programming. Most countries were able to determine broadcast policy on their own, but control over broadcasting, and therefore culture, is perceived to be in the hands now of a few large, mostly U.S., firms.

MTV has over twenty international channels, including MTV Latin America, MTV Nordic, MTV India, MTV Germany, MTV Italy, MTV Russia, MTV Southeast Asia, MTV UK, and others. MTV estimates it reaches 300 million households, or about one-third of the world.[16] In Europe, where MTV reaches 85 million households, there are five local channels for the United Kingdom, Germany, Scandinavia, Italy, and the rest of Europe. In 2000 through 2001, MTV Europe will add four additional channels to serve local market tastes and will still maintain the global MTV brand.[17] The European Parliament advocates curbs on foreign television to keep out U.S. sitcoms and game shows. France, Ireland, Portugal, and Belgium have quotas on their airwaves. In addition, through lottery and cinema taxes, European films receive subsidies of $600 million per year.[18]

Increasing globalization—in business, in media, and in general—is likely to produce more of such moves by host governments. Global firms will therefore be well advised to understand the cultural content, or significance, of their products or services. Insensitivity to cultural ideals in any aspect of global marketing operations can lead to unwanted reactions.

HOST COUNTRY PRESSURE GROUPS

Host country governments are not the only forces influencing the political climate and thus affecting the operations of foreign companies. Other groups have a stake in the treatment of companies or in political and economic decisions that indirectly affect foreign businesses. In most instances, they cannot act unilaterally. Thus, they try to pressure either the host government or the foreign businesses to conform to their views. Such pressure groups exist in most countries and may be composed of ad hoc groups or permanently structured associations. Political parties are common pressure groups, although they frequently cannot exert much influence outside the country of their home government. Parties generally associated with a nationalist point of view frequently advocate policies restricting foreign companies. Environmental groups have had a major influence on consumers around the world by raising concerns about nuclear energy, the transport of oil, waste disposal, rain forest destruction, fishing techniques, global warming, and so on. For example, scientists report that 1990 was the earth's warmest year on record since 1850, when people started recording the planet's temperature. The increased temperature is thought to be caused by human activities related to the escape of carbon dioxide, chlorofluorocarbons, and methane. There is fear that this warming will have a drastic effect on climate, agriculture, and sea levels. In a French study, researchers reported that heat-trapping greenhouse gases are at their highest levels in 420,000 years, and U.S. researchers found that fifty-seven species of butterflies are altering their migratory patterns in response to heat changes.[19] DuPont, one of the world's largest producers of chlorofluorocarbons (CFCs), stopped making CFCs by 2000, investing $500 million in CFC alternatives.[20] Environmental groups also forced McDonald's to replace Styrofoam packing with cardboard. Although McDonald's internal market research showed that environmental issues have neither a positive nor a negative impact on sales, the company has agreed to work with the Environmental Defense Fund, an environmental pressure group, to reduce unnecessary and harmful waste.[21] In another case, the British-based Global Witness human rights group forced DeBeers, the world's largest gem supplier, to guarantee that none of its diamonds were from rebel groups in Angola, Guinea, and other war-torn nations.[22]

Some of the most potent pressure groups are found within the local business community itself. These include local industry associations and occasionally local unions. When local companies are threatened by foreign competition, they frequently petition the government to intervene by placing restrictions on the foreign competitors. In China, the state-owned newsprint factories were being hurt by cheap newsprint from the United States, Canada, and South Korea. The China Ministry of Foreign Trade and Economic Cooperation found that the foreign suppliers were dumping on the Chinese market. In 1999, the Chinese therefore assessed a tax of 55 to 78 percent on U.S., Canadian, and South Korean newsprint.[23]

HOST GOVERNMENT ACTIONS

In the previous section, we focused on various governmental concerns and the underlying motivation for certain political actions. In this section, we analyze some of the typical policies that host governments may choose to control foreign-based businesses. The relationships between the underlying motivations and the chosen policies are also discussed. The host governments' policies are presented in order of their severity, from the least to the most severe.

JAWBONING

The informal intervention of governments in the business process, often without a legal basis, is called *jawboning*. Governments use this form of intervention to prevent an act that, though legal, is perceived to be contrary to their own interests or goals. The effectiveness of jawboning lies in the possibility of a stronger subsequent action should the "culprit" not fall into line. The leverage of host governments comes from the fact that foreign companies depend on permits and approvals issued by the host governments. Such favored treatment may be at risk if a company proceeds against the expressed wished of the host government, despite the fact that no laws were violated.

Microsoft had difficulty gaining acceptance in China because the powerful Ministry of Electronics Industries (MEI) withheld endorsement of Microsoft Windows (specially adapted with Chinese characters). Microsoft had not cultivated this important local contact, so Compaq and AST, China's biggest PC suppliers, did not install Microsoft software in their PCs. Microsoft sales improved, however, after Bill Gates visited China's president Jiang Zemin and signed an agreement with MEI to cooperate on software development.[24]

"BUY LOCAL" RESTRICTIONS

Since governments are important customers of industry in almost every country, they can use this purchasing power to favor certain suppliers. Frequently, local companies are favored over foreign companies. An industry particularly subject to such local favoritism is the telecommunications industry because telephone companies are state-run in most countries. For foreign companies, the case of Japan's Nippon Telegraph & Telephone Public Corporation (NTT) was particularly problematic. For years, NTT granted contracts exclusively to a few local suppliers, almost completely shutting out foreign-based companies. Pressures from foreign governments led to global agreements under the umbrella of GATT, and other global organizations have established new rules that tend to prevent direct government intervention except for cases of national security and a few other exemptions. Opportunities for foreign firms to contract with NTT opened up with an accord signed with the United States in 1980 and renewed in 1997; this accord was continued even after NTT was divided into smaller carriers in 1999.[25]

Few areas have recently received as much attention as the local buying preference in public sector contracts. Different from import and export transactions, these contracts frequently deal with local construction. Access to such contracts has been opened up in the EU through the "Europe 1992" initiative, whereby all public sector contracts now require open bidding. The EU has instituted a requirement to report contracts above a threshold of 5 million euros (about $5 million).

Supplies contracts have a lower limit of 200,000 euros; service contracts have the same limit. The 1992 Open Procurement rules were expected to generate annual public savings of 8 to 19 billion euros. According to a study done for the European Commission, however, the public procurement policy failed because most countries have not incorporated it into their national laws and therefore it is not being enforced.[26]

U.S. construction companies are trying to get access to the $278 billion Japanese public construction market with the help of the U.S. government. The 1988 Major Projects Agreement and the 1994 New Construction Market Access Pact between the Japanese and U.S. governments attempted to open the Japanese construction market.[27] However, the 560,000 construction companies in Japan exert significant influence in Japan through campaign contributions to politicians and the provision of numerous campaign workers.[28] A renewed effort to open the Japanese construction industry can be expected following Japan's bribery scandals involving public construction firms and politicians. Several construction firms were reported to follow *dango*, a system whereby contracts are shared among competing firms and a portion of the contract is regularly used as a payoff to politicians. According to a report by the Japanese Fair Trade Commission, 156 contractors were suspected of *dango*, or bid rigging, on 872 contracts on the new Kansai airport in 1996.[29] Although this scheme was not sanctioned by the Japanese government, its existence blocked global firms from gaining contracts based on level competition.

NONTARIFF BARRIERS

Under the category of nontariff barriers, we include any government action that is not an official custom tariff but that inhibits the free flow of products between countries. These barriers may not necessarily add to landed costs but are more likely to result in a limitation on product flows. Nontariff barriers are used by governments mostly to keep imports from freely entering the home market. Many types of measures may be taken. A common one is import restrictions, or quotas.

Nontariff barriers also affect the service industries. For example, limits on employing foreigners may prevent a consulting firm from using its critical human expertise, or restrictions on licensing professionals may hinder a supplier's ability to operate in a country.[30]

The use of nontariff barriers is growing. For example, China uses a large amount of silicon sealant during construction to prevent cracking and damage to concrete. To reduce the import of poor quality sealant, the China State Economic and Trade Commission requires all sealant to be imported through China Yuanwang Corp. China Yuanwang controls product specifications, pricing, and warehousing, so this requirement has resulted in a new tariff of up to 100 percent on imported sealants.[31]

SUBSIDIES

Government subsidies represent gifts that host governments dispense with the intention that the overall benefits to the economy by far exceed such grants. They are popular instruments, used both to encourage exports and to attract global companies to a certain country.

Governments may also use direct or indirect subsidies to encourage industries that will be major exporters. Exporters bring multiple benefits because they provide employment and bring increased revenue into the country through export sales. An example of a direct subsidy is a government paying a local shoe producer $1 for each pair of shoes to help it compete more effectively in foreign markets. GATT (now WTO) agreements outlaw direct export subsidies but usually do not prohibit indirect subsidies. An indirect subsidy is the result of a subsidy on a component of the exported product. For example, a government may provide a subsidy on the canvas used to manufacture tents, which are then exported.

Subsidies are one way for governments to support local industries. In most countries, subsidies amount to 2 to 3.5 percent of the value of industrial output. The rate of subsidy in the United States is estimated to be 0.5 percent; it is 1.0 percent in Japan. In Europe, subsidies range from 0.9 percent of industrial output in Britain, to 3.1 percent in Germany, 5.3 percent in Italy, and a high of 5.6 percent in Greece.[32] The logic of the subsidies is that they improve global competitiveness and create or protect jobs. The European Union has tightened its policy on state aid to industry. However, European governments continue to support manufacturing industries, especially the automobile industry. There are 300 automobile assembly plants in Europe, with approximately 30 percent excess capacity.[33]

The treatment of local aircraft makers has been an issue between the United States and Europe for the past ten years. The French government points to favorable treatment of Boeing by NASA and Pentagon contracts as another form of hidden subsidies. Boeing considered the 30 percent French ownership of Airbus to encourage local preference. An agreement in 1992 reduced tension between Airbus and Boeing, although in 1999, the U.S. Federal Trade Commission investigated both companies for price fixing. In addition, the Airbus consortium was supposed to be converted into the European Aerospace and Defense Company in January 1999, but the French have delayed the conversion. Critics argue that Boeing has lost market share to Airbus not because of subsidies, but because of Boeing's low productivity—216 workers per plane at Boeing versus 143 for Airbus.[34]

OPERATING CONDITIONS

Host governments have a direct influence on the operations of a foreign subsidiary by imposing specific conditions on the company's operations. The rules of conducting business may challenge the global company. For example, the requirement of *Mitbestimmung* (codetermination) in Germany necessitates the participation of labor on the management committee.[35] In Germany, there is a ban on bakers working between 10:00 P.M. and 4:00 A.M. The ban dates back to World War I, when supplies were short and authorities noticed that people ate less day-old bread than fresh bread. The law was repealed in November 1996, resulting in employment of 5,000 new bakery workers in six months.[36]

Operating conditions for global firms are of particular importance when they affect the freedom to run marketing programs. Host countries may restrict global firms in the area of pricing, advertising, promoting, selling, distributing, and many other marketing functions. Some of those restrictions, and the strategies to deal with them, are included in Chapters 10–15, which deal directly with marketing mix elements. When such operating restrictions apply to all firms, domestic and global, the competitive threat is lessened; however, companies might still find such restrictions a problem when they conflict with what they are accustomed to. When operating restrictions apply to foreign firms only, the result will be a lessening of competitiveness, and companies should seriously consider these constraints before entering a market.

Kidnappings pose an extremely difficult operating condition. Economic kidnapping is one of the fastest growing criminal practices in the world, with an estimated $500 million each year in ransom payments. Colombia had the highest kidnapping rate in the world in 2000; the Colombian National Police recorded 3,162 cases. Latin America has the most reported kidnappings, but it is not a problem unique to Latin America. Kidnapping has been on the rise in parts of Africa, Eastern Europe, and Southeast Asia. In 1999, Colombia, Mexico, Brazil, the Philippines, Venezuela, Ecuador, the former Soviet Union, Nigeria, India, and South Africa were the countries with the most kidnappings, from greatest to least. This phenomenon can be traced to the expansion of global companies into these regions over the last decade.[37] Worldwide kidnapping for ransom increased 6 percent in 1999, to 1,786 cases. Ninety-two percent of the kidnappings took place in ten countries, with Latin America having 75 percent of the kidnappings for ransom.[38]

LOCAL CONTENT

Many host governments impose a local-content regulation that requires global firms to demonstrate that the value added for their products or services meets these limitations. For product-based companies, local-content laws mean that some part of the manufacturing must be done in the host country. Such restrictions are often used to encourage local value-added activities. Occasionally, the regulations can also lead to the elimination of global competitors if the local market is not big enough to justify the manufacturing operation.

A constant point of discussion is the cars produced by Japanese transplant operations in the United States. Honda Motor Company assembled as much as two-thirds of its total U.S. sales volume in its two U.S. assembly plants and claimed a 50 percent local content. With that figure, Honda could not take advantage of a U.S.-Canadian free trade agreement, as it could have with 100 percent local content.[39] In 2002, General Motors opened a factory in Rayong, Thailand, where it manufactures the Zafira van for export to Asia, Europe, and Latin America. Initially the Thai government wanted 54 percent local content; however, the requirement was dropped to 30 percent local content because the local Thai work force did not have sufficient skills for complex manufacturing.[40]

Enforcing local content can also result in the elimination of global competitors. The European Commission issued The Television without Frontiers Directive 1989, which specified for member states that a majority proportion of broadcast content be of European origin "where practicable and by appropriate means." The directive allowed member states to apply stricter rules when it was deemed necessary for national and cultural reasons. France introduced the directive into legislation in 1992 by specifying that 60 percent of prime time be allocated to original EC works and 40 percent of time be allocated to original French language works. A similar law in France required all public and private radio stations to broadcast French songs 40 percent of the time.[41] Germany, Italy, and Spain also introduced legislation that applied stricter broadcasting quotas than the directive. This issue was a source of trade conflict between the United States and the EC because the United States sees it as hindering the free flow of some programming.[42]

Regulations imposed by host governments dealing with local content are most often found for products that are purchased by local government institutions or for groups that are in need of local government help, as through export financing. The recent trend in global trade negotiations has tended to reduce the restrictive character of some of these regulations. The local-content issue remains an important aspect for global marketers, however, and they should be aware of it.

OWNERSHIP CONDITIONS

Host governments sometimes require that local nationals become part owners of the foreign company. These governments believe that this policy guarantees fair contributions to the local economy. The restrictions can range from an outright prohibition of full foreign ownership to selective policies aimed at key industries. For example, China has local ownership requirements in many industries. Carrefour, the second largest global retailer after Wal-Mart, had to sell 35 percent of its share in its two wholly-owned stores in China to local partners.[43]

One country that has used ownership conditions extensively is India. India's Foreign Exchange Regulation Act of 1973 stipulated that foreign ownership may not exceed 40 percent unless the foreign firm or Indian company belongs to a key industry or manufactures materials such as chemicals, turbines, machinery, tractors, or fertilizers. International Business Machines Corporation (IBM) decided to leave rather than give up control. Later changes in the government have brought a softening of India's stance, however, and the country is again courting firms that can contribute new technologies.

India's Bharatiya Janata Party (BJP) was elected in 1998 on a platform of protectionism, threatening to throw out foreign companies. Once in power, however, the BJP opened markets to outsiders and is expected to continue reforms mandated by the WTO.[44] The BJP's open-market policies did not extend to Reader's Digest, however, which had left India in 1979, selling its business and the license to publish to Titan Industries and the Tata Group companies. In 1998, the Indian Foreign Investment Board deferred a proposal for Reader's Digest to repurchase Reader's Digest India.[45] In fact, in some industries such as ports and toll roads, the Indian government is allowing 100 percent foreign ownership to boost infrastructure investments.[46]

This situation demonstrates an important aspect in the control of foreign ownership. The 1960s and 1970s saw a tightening of the control over foreign ownership in many countries. During the late 1980s and 1990s, the trend has been toward trade liberalization because countries recognized the catalytic nature of foreign investment. This new trend has brought the elimination of many restrictions. As a result, we will devote a special section later in this chapter to this new development, which is of crucial importance to global marketers.

BOYCOTTS

The previously discussed policies are aimed at restricting or limiting the freedom of action of foreign firms. Boycotts, however, bar some companies completely from a given market. Typically, politically motivated boycotts tend to be directed at companies of certain origin or companies that have engaged in transactions with political enemies.

One of the most publicized boycott campaigns was the one waged by some Arab countries against firms that had engaged in business beyond simple export transactions with Israel. The boycott was administered by the twenty-two member countries of the Arab League. For example, one U.S. company on the Arab boycott list was Ford Motor Company, which supplied an Israeli car assembler with flat-packed cars for local assembly. Xerox was placed on the list after financing a documentary on Israel, and the Coca-Cola Company was added to the boycott list for having licensed an Israeli bottler.

The Arab League boycott became considerably less relevant with the changed political situation in the Middle East in the 1980s and 1990s. By the end of the 1990s, many countries enforced the boycott only selectively. For example, Coca-Cola returned to the Gulf soft-drink market in 1994 because it traded with Israel. Coca-Cola sales have grown at a rate of 25 percent per year and now comprise 33 percent of the $1.2 billion market in the Gulf.[47]

In Egypt, Coca-Cola employs 10,000 people, has thirteen factories, and sponsors the Palestinian National football (soccer) team.[48] After the attacks by Israel on Palestine, and because of the support of Israel by the U.S. government, many Arab leaders promoted boycotts of U.S. goods, such as Kentucky Fried Chicken.[49]

TAKEOVERS

No action taken by a host government is more drastic than a takeover. Broadly defined, takeovers are any host government–initiated actions that result in a loss of ownership or a loss of direct control by the foreign company. There are several types of takeovers. *Expropriation* is a formal, or legal, taking over of an operation with or without the payment of compensation. Even when compensation is paid, there are often concerns about the adequacy of the amount, the timeliness of the payment, and the form of payment. *Confiscation* is expropriation without any compensation. The term *domestication* is used to describe the limiting of certain economic activities to local citizens. Domestication can be done through expropriation, confiscation, or forced sales. Governments may domesticate an industry by imposing one of the following requirements: transfer of partial ownership to nationals, promotion of nationals to higher levels of management, or purchase of raw materials or components produced locally. If the foreign company cannot meet these requirements, it may be forced to sell its operations in the host country.

At one time, studies suggested that takeovers were becoming more frequent and were a major threat to companies operating abroad. Hawkins, Mintz, and Provissiero in 1975 found 170 foreign takeovers of U.S. subsidiaries registered for the period 1946 to 1973. Comparing these findings with the 23,282 U.S. subsidiaries operating outside the United States yielded a takeover rate of about 0.7 percent.[50] These statistics were supported by a broader survey of all countries by the United Nations. The U.N. survey identified 875 takeovers for the 1960–1974 period.[51] Ten countries had accounted for two-thirds of all takeovers, and fifty countries registered none at all. As many as eighty global firms were affected during the mid-1970s, when nationalization was at its peak. By 1985, expropriations had declined, and almost no takeovers were recorded. Instead of nationalizations, countries engaged in the massive process of privatization.[52] In general, global marketers may have to fear nationalization, and the resulting total loss of an asset, far less in the future. The loss of operating control

	Goal					
Action	**Self-Preservation**	**Security**	**Prosperity**	**Prestige**	**Ideology**	**Cultural Identity**
Jawboning	X	X	X	X	X	X
"Buy local" restrictions	X	X	X			
Nontariff barriers	X		X			
Subsidies	X		X			
Operating restrictions	X	X	X			X
Local content			X			
Ownership conditions		X				X
Boycotts					X	
Takeovers	X	X	X		X	

Table 4.1 Host Government Goal and Policy Actions

X = likelihood of using given action to accomplish that goal.

or freedom may prove to be a far greater political risk. Although takeovers seem less likely, in 1996, Hong Kong retailer Giordano had eleven stores in Shanghai closed and twenty-five stores in China closed temporarily because of an investigation of possible tax violations. However, the Chinese government was at odds with Mr. Lai, Giordano's founder and publishing tycoon, for an article in his *Next* magazine criticizing then premier Li Peng. The Chinese stores were reopened in 1999 after Mr. Lai sold his interest in the Giordano Company.[53]

This section has illustrated how host governments can influence the local operations of global companies. The previous section concentrated more on the motivations behind these governmental actions. Table 4.1 identifies certain policy actions and relates them to the underlying goals discussed in this chapter. Though any combination of goal and action is possible, history suggests that certain actions are more often associated with specific goals.

HOME COUNTRY POLITICAL FORCES

Managers of global companies must be concerned about other issues besides political developments abroad. Many developments that take place at home can have a great impact on what a company does globally. The political development in a company's home country tends to affect either the role of the company in general or, more often, some particular aspects of its operations. Consequently, restrictions can be placed on companies not only by host countries but also by home countries. Therefore, an astute global manager must be able to monitor political developments both at home and abroad.

This section of the chapter explores home country policies and actions directed at global companies. Some of these actions are unique and have only recently come into existence.

HOME COUNTRY ACTIONS

Home countries are essentially guided by the same six interests described earlier in this chapter: self-preservation, national security, prosperity, prestige, ideology, and cultural identity. In general, a home country government wishes to have its country's foreign companies accept its national priorities. As a result, home country governments at times look toward foreign companies to help them achieve political goals. They may engage in any or all the actions outlined earlier: jawboning, nontariff barriers, subsidies, operating restrictions, and so on.

How then do home country policies differ? In the past, home country governments have tried to prevent foreign companies from doing business on ideological, political, or national security grounds. In the extreme, this can result in an embargo on trade with a certain country. The U.S. government has taken unilateral actions in the past. Its embargo on trade with Cuba dates back to 1961, following the assumption of power by Fidel Castro. Since that time, U.S. businesses have been allowed neither to purchase from nor to sell to Cuba. Any U.S. company that wants to do business with Cuba must apply for a special license, but no such applications were granted until 1993. In 2001, Cuba purchased the first American goods since 1963 because the United States Congress passed legislation exempting food and medicine from the embargo.[54]

Unilateral embargoes, those imposed by one country only, expose businesses from that country to competitive disadvantage and thus are often fought by business interests. In Cuba, only the United States applied a trade embargo. In 1998, the Clinton administration resumed direct flights to Cuba, mail delivery, and cash contributions to independent charities and reduced restrictions on travel for academic, cultural, and athletic groups.

Because there is a risk to the competitiveness of its business if a country takes unilateral actions restricting the business community, the emphasis has shifted toward taking multilateral actions in combination with many other countries. Such action may come from a group of nations or, increasingly, from the United Nations. The trade embargo by the global community against South Africa was one of the first such actions. Because of consumer group pressures, many companies had already left South Africa to protest its apartheid regime, but the embargo became applicable to a wider group of firms in the late 1980s when it was imposed by most countries. When the political situation in South Africa changed and apartheid was abolished, the United States, together with other nations, lifted the embargo in July 1991. Since 1994, the United States has been the largest foreign investor in South Africa, with some of the largest firms being Dow Chemical, Ford, General Motors, Coca-Cola, Hyatt, and Electronic Data Systems (EDS).[55]

Other multilateral actions by the global community are the trade sanctions enforced by the United Nations against Iraq because of the Gulf War in 1991. This embargo substantially restricts the type of trade that companies can conduct.

HOME COUNTRY PRESSURE GROUPS

The kinds of pressures that international companies are subject to in their home countries are frequently different from the types of pressures brought to bear on them abroad. In many ways, international companies have had to deal with special interest groups abroad for a long time. But the types of special interest groups found domestically have only come into existence over the last ten to fifteen years. Such groups are usually well organized, tend to receive extensive media coverage, and have succeeded in catching many companies unprepared. Some of their actions have always been geared toward mobilizing support for pressuring the home country government to sponsor specific regulations favorable to their point of view, but special interest groups have also managed to place companies under direct pressure.

International companies can come under pressure for two major reasons: (1) for their choice of markets and (2) for their methods of business. A constant source of controversy involves global companies' business practices in three areas: product strategies, promotional practices, and pricing practices. Product strategies include the decision to cease marketing a certain product (such as pesticides or pharmaceuticals), usually for safety reasons. Promotional practices include the way the products are advertised or pushed through distribution channels. Pricing practices include the policy of charging higher or unfair prices.

The infant formula controversy of the early 1980s involved participants from many countries, and it serves as a good example of the type of pressure sometimes placed on international companies. Infant formula was being sold all over the world as a substitute or supplement for breast-feeding. Though even the producers of infant formula agreed that breast-feeding was superior to bottle-feeding, changes had started to take place in western society decades ago that brought about the decline of infant breast-feeding. Following World War II, several companies expanded their infant formula productions in Third World countries, where birth rates were much higher than in developed countries. Companies that had intended their products to be helpful found themselves embroiled in controversy. Critics blasted the product as unsafe under Third World conditions. Because the formula had to be mixed with water, the critics charged that the sanitary conditions and contaminated water in developing countries led to many deaths. As a result, they urged an immediate stop to all promotional activities, such as nurses visiting new mothers and the distribution of free samples.

As one of the leading infant formula manufacturers, Nestlé Company became the target of a boycott by consumer action groups in the United States and elsewhere. Under the leadership of the Infant Formula Action Coalition (INFACT), a consumer boycott of all Nestlé products was organized to force the company to change its marketing practices. The boycott ended in the passage of the World Health Organization's International Code of Marketing for Breast Milk Substitutes. INFACT has continued to support boycotts. For example, the General Electric boycott helped push General Electric (GE) out of the nuclear weapons business.[56]

Boycotts can have very visible effects. The 1990 boycott against tuna caught in nets that also trap and kill dolphins caused Heinz, owner of Star-Kist, to switch to dolphin-safe tuna. The other tuna manufacturers quickly followed suit.[57] Surprisingly, local home country pressure groups can affect trade. A Massachusetts state law denies state contracts to companies that do business in Myanmar (formerly Burma) because of that country's brutal dictatorship; Massachusetts is considering a similar law for Indonesia (over the repression in East Timor). Apple, Motorola, and Hewlett-Packard all cited the Massachusetts law when pulling out of Myanmar. The law probably violates the WTO Procurement Agreement of 1995, which requires open, nondiscriminatory government contracts. In addition, a U.S. District Court judge ruled that the Massachusetts law interferes with the U.S. federal government's right to set foreign policy; however, it is expected the dispute will be appealed by Massachusetts to the U.S. Supreme Court.[58]

Global marketers must continue to account for the influences of home country pressure groups or governments. Global trade sanctions imposed unilaterally are likely to occur again, but they typically affect only marginal markets. Pressure groups with specific interests, such as animal protection groups, environmentalists, or other such focus organizations, are likely to be of greater importance as global marketing develops.

SUDDEN CHANGES IN THE POLITICAL CLIMATE

The presence of political risk means that a foreign company can lose all or part of its investment in another country because of some political actions from either the host country government or other pressure groups. The previous sections have detailed the various elements of political risk by describing the participants, their motivations, and their available options to participate in and determine the political climate of a country. As we emphasized in the section on takeovers, the political climate of a country is hardly ever static. Instead, key decisions are often made during sudden and radical changes in the political climate of a host country. Sudden changes of power, especially when the new leadership is committed to a leftist economic and political philosophy, have frequently led to hostile political climates and takeovers. Such changes in government can happen because of open elections or unexpected coups d'état or revolutions.

Israel's attack on Palestine resulted in several boycotts in Egypt against American companies such as McDonald's and Coca-Cola. The Egyptians are sympathetic to the Palestinians and therefore boycott the United States as a sympathizer of Israel.[59]

For decades, sudden political change in a country meant sudden change in its economic policy, often resulting in damage to global firms. As a result of the sweeping political change in eastern Europe since 1989, the former Soviet Union has broken up into more than a dozen independent nations. Yugoslavia itself has disintegrated into several separate countries. Czechoslovakia ceased to exist as of January 1, 1993, and its breakup resulted in two independent countries: the Czech Republic and Slovakia.[60] GTECH (based in the United States), the world's largest lottery company, negotiated with Czechoslovakia in 1991, following a successful negotiation for a computerized lottery contract with Poland. Talks with Czechoslovakia concluded in 1992, but implementation was delayed because of the daunting infrastructure problems with telecommunications. The sudden border cutting the country in half meant that even transporting simple personal computers across a city suddenly became an issue. GTECH had to renegotiate the contract and establish two systems with two different currencies. The backup center in Bratislava, the city that was the capital of Slovakia, also became the operations point for the new system for Slovakia. Both systems, now up and running, reached approximately two thousand terminals in the Czech Republic and one thousand terminals in Slovakia.[61]

Faced with such a changing political climate, what can companies do? Global companies have reacted on two fronts. First, they have started to perfect their own intelligence systems to prevent being caught unaware when changes disrupt operations. Second, they have developed several risk-reducing business strategies that help to limit the exposure, or losses, should a sudden change occur. The following sections will concentrate on these two solutions.

POLITICAL RISK ASSESSMENT

Because more than 60 percent of U.S.-based companies suffered some type of politically motivated damage between 1975 and 1980, many companies established systems to analyze political risk systematically.[62] To establish an effective political risk assessment (PRA) system, a company has to decide first on the objectives of the system. Another aspect concerns the internal organization, or the assignment of responsibility within the company. Finally, some agreement has to be reached on how the analysis is to be done.

OBJECTIVES OF POLITICAL RISK ASSESSMENT

Potential risks have been described in detail in earlier sections of this chapter. Of course, companies everywhere would like to know about impending governmental instabilities so that no new investments will be made in those countries. But even more important is the monitoring of existing operations and their political environment. Particularly with existing operations, not much is gained by knowing in advance the potential changes in the political climate unless such advanced knowledge can also be used for future action. As a result, political risk assessment is slowly moving from predicting events to developing strategies to help companies cope with changes. But first, political risk assessment has to deal with the potential political changes. Examples of questions that must be answered include: Should we enter a particular country? Should we stay in a particular country? What can we do with our operations in country X if development Y can occur?

ORGANIZATION OF POLITICAL RISK ASSESSMENT

In a study conducted by the Conference Board, a U.S. research organization, more than half of the large U.S.-based global companies surveyed indicated that company internal groups were reviewing the political climate of both newly proposed and current operations. In companies that did not have any formalized systems for political risk assessment, top executives often obtained firsthand information through direct contact by traveling and talking with other businesspeople.[63]

Since the 1980s, several organizations have developed risk assessment measurement systems. For example, *Institutional Investor* magazine surveys global financial advisors and rates every country on their creditworthiness on a scale of 0 to 100. These data are available to all subscribers.[64] The way Gulf Oil was able to make use of its political risk assessment serves as an example of the power of correct information. Gulf's small team of analysts warned of the Iranian shah's probable fall several months before it was generally anticipated. The same group supported an exploration venture in Pakistan despite the Soviet invasion of Afghanistan that had just taken place. More risky was Gulf's decision to proceed with its operations in Angola. Before the civil war in Angola, Gulf's analyst foresaw that a Marxist group would emerge as the most powerful force among the three factions vying for control of the country. Gulf managers felt, however, that the Marxist government would provide both a stable and a reasonable government, so they decided to invest. Angola became one of Gulf's most important overseas production sources.[65]

Rather than rely on a centralized corporate staff, some companies prefer to delegate political risk assessment responsibility to executives or analysts located in the particular region. Exxon and Xerox both use their subsidiary and regional managers as major sources of information. Others use distinguished foreign policy advisors. Bechtel, the large California-based engineering company, used the services of Richard Helms, a former CIA director and U.S. ambassador to Iran. Henry Kissinger, a former U.S. secretary of state, has advised Merck, Goldman Sachs, and the Chase Manhattan Bank. General Motors and Caterpillar have also maintained outside advisory panels.[66]

INFORMATION NEEDS

Though expropriations and takeovers were a problem for companies in the past, companies now view other political actions as more dangerous. Some have seen delayed payments or restrictions on profit repatriation as major problems.[67] Political stability, the foreign investment climate, profit remittance, and taxation can all be more important than the fear of expropriation. In political risk assessment, international companies can look for answers to six broad key questions:

1. How stable is the host country's political system?
2. How strong is the host government's commitment to specific rules of the game, such as ownership or contractual rights, given its ideology and power position?
3. How long is the government likely to remain in power?
4. If the present government is succeeded, how would the specific rules of the game change?
5. What would be the effects of any expected changes in the specific rules of the game?
6. In light of those effects, what decisions and actions should be taken now?[68]

Another approach, used by an independent consultant on political risk, concentrated on viewing each country in terms of its political issues and the major political actors. The analysis determined which one of these actors would have the greatest influence with respect to important decisions.[69]

Several public or semipublic sources regularly monitor political risk. The Economist Intelligence Unit (EIU), a sister company of the *Economist,* monitors approximately sixty countries based on multiple factors. For 2000–2004, the top-ranked countries in terms of business environment and low risk are the Netherlands, the United Kingdom, the United States, and Canada. The bottom-ranked countries are Iraq, Iran, Nigeria, and the Ukraine.[70] The *International Country Risk Guide,* published monthly by Political Risk Services of East Syracuse, New York, includes financial, economic, and political risk forecasts and ratings for 130 countries.[71] The ratings vary from 100 for minimum risk to 0 points for maximum risk. The indicators used include economic expectations versus reality, economic planning failures, political leadership, external-conflict risk, corruption in government, law-and-order tradition, political terrorism, and the quality of bureaucracy. The results of these rankings are shown in Table 4.2. From May 2001 to May 2002, several countries have had large

Table 4.2 Country Risk, Ranked by Composite Risk Rating: *May 2002 Versus June 2001*[a]

Rank in May 2002	Country	Composite Risk Rating as of May 2002	Composite Risk Rating as of June 2001	May 2002 Versus June 2001	Rank in June 2001
1	Switzerland	91.8	90.3	1.5	4
2	Luxembourg	91.5	91.0	0.5	3
3	Norway	91.0	92.0	−1.0	2
3	Singapore	91.0	92.5	−1.5	1
5	Finland	89.0	89.5	−0.5	5
5	Ireland	89.0	88.8	0.3	6
7	Brunei	88.3	88.3	0.0	9
8	Denmark	88.0	88.8	−0.8	6
9	Austria	86.0	86.3	−0.3	12
10	Canada	85.5	86.5	−1.0	10
10	Netherlands	85.5	88.5	−3.0	8
12	Sweden	85.0	86.5	−1.5	10
13	Hong Kong	84.5	85.8	−1.3	13
14	Belgium	84.0	84.5	−0.5	18
15	United Kingdom	83.8	84.8	−1.0	16
16	Japan	83.5	85.8	−2.3	13
17	Germany	82.8	83.8	−1.0	19
18	Australia	82.5	79.8	2.8	29
18	Kuwait	82.5	84.8	−2.3	16
18	Taiwan	82.5	82.5	0.0	20
21	United Arab Emirates	82.3	85.3	−3.0	15
22	Cyprus	81.8	79.5	2.3	32
23	Spain	80.8	80.3	0.5	26
24	Italy	80.5	82.3	−1.8	22
25	France	80.3	80.8	−0.5	24
26	Bahrain	79.8	77.5	2.3	36
26	Qatar	79.8	72.8	7.0	59
28	Iceland	79.5	79.8	−0.3	29
28	South Korea	79.5	79.0	0.5	33
28	Portugal	79.5	79.8	−0.3	29
31	New Zealand	78.8	80.3	−1.5	26
31	Slovenia	78.8	78.3	0.5	34
31	United States	78.8	82.5	−3.8	20
34	Botswana	78.3	80.8	−2.5	24
35	Malta	77.8	78.3	−0.5	34
36	Oman	77.3	81.0	−3.8	23

(continued)

Table 4.2 Country Risk, Ranked by Composite Risk Rating: *May 2002 Versus June 2001*[a] (cont.)

Rank in May 2002	Country	Composite Risk Rating as of May 2002	Composite Risk Rating as of June 2001	May 2002 Versus June 2001	Rank in June 2001
37	Hungary	77.0	75.8	1.3	47
38	Bahamas	76.0	75.5	0.5	49
38	Poland	76.0	75.8	0.3	47
40	Chile	75.8	76.8	−1.0	39
40	Czech Republic	75.8	76.8	−1.0	39
40	Malaysia	75.8	76.5	−0.8	41
40	Namibia	75.8	77.3	−1.5	37
44	Latvia	75.5	75.3	0.3	50
45	Thailand	75.3	75.3	0.0	50
46	Greece	75.0	76.0	−1.0	45
47	People's Republic of China	74.8	72.5	2.3	62
47	Estonia	74.8	76.3	−1.5	43
49	Lithuania	74.3	76.3	−2.0	43
50	Croatia	73.5	75.3	−1.8	50
50	Slovak Republic	73.5	73.5	0.0	55
52	Saudi Arabia	73.3	80.0	−6.8	28
53	Costa Rica	72.8	77.3	−4.5	37
54	Kazakhstan	72.5	73.0	−0.5	57
55	Bulgaria	72.3	71.5	0.8	67
56	El Salvador	72.0	76.0	−4.0	45
57	Morocco	71.8	72.5	−0.8	62
57	Panama	71.8	73.3	−1.5	56
57	Trinidad and Tobago	71.8	74.8	−3.0	53
57	Tunisia	71.8	73.0	−1.3	57
61	Jordan	71.3	72.8	−1.5	59
62	Uruguay	70.8	76.5	−5.8	41
63	Philippines	70.5	71.0	−0.5	71
64	Mexico	70.3	74.0	−3.8	54
64	Syria	70.3	71.5	−1.3	67
66	Dominican Republic	69.8	72.5	−2.8	62
67	Russian Federation	69.5	68.0	1.5	79
68	Libya	69.3	71.3	−2.0	69
68	Peru	69.3	69.8	−0.5	75
68	Vietnam	69.3	68.0	1.3	79
71	Jamaica	68.8	72.5	−3.8	62
72	Iran	68.0	69.8	−1.8	75

(continued)

Table 4.2 Country Risk, Ranked by Composite Risk Rating: *May 2002 Versus June 2001*[a] (cont.)

Rank in May 2002	Country	Composite Risk Rating as of May 2002	Composite Risk Rating as of June 2001	May 2002 Versus June 2001	Rank in June 2001
72	Israel	68.0	70.5	−2.5	73
74	Azerbaijan	67.8	63.3	4.5	99
74	Romania	67.8	65.0	2.8	91
76	Gambia	67.5	67.5	0.0	83
77	Bolivia	67.3	68.0	−0.8	79
77	South Africa	67.3	72.8	−5.5	59
77	Yemen	67.3	66.5	0.8	85
80	Guatemala	67.0	72.0	−5.0	66
81	Egypt	66.8	70.0	−3.3	74
82	Gabon	66.3	68.3	−2.0	77
82	Ukraine	66.3	66.0	0.3	87
84	Senegal	66.0	65.8	0.3	89
85	Honduras	65.5	66.0	−0.5	87
86	India	65.3	65.8	−0.5	89
87	Cuba	65.0	64.8	0.3	92
87	Moldova	65.0	64.3	0.8	93
89	Mongolia	64.0	68.3	−4.3	77
89	Sri Lanka	64.0	60.0	4.0	114
91	Brazil	63.8	63.8	0.0	96
91	Guyana	63.8	64.3	−0.5	93
93	Cameroon	63.0	63.0	0.0	100
93	Suriname	63.0	63.0	0.0	100
95	Albania	62.8	63.5	−0.8	98
95	Uganda	62.8	66.5	−3.8	85
97	Guinea	62.3	60.0	2.3	114
97	Paraguay	62.3	67.5	−5.3	83
99	Belarus	62.0	60.8	1.3	110
100	Algeria	61.5	64.3	−2.8	93
100	Papua New Guinea	61.5	63.8	−2.3	96
102	Ghana	61.3	59.5	1.8	118
102	Kenya	61.3	61.5	−0.3	107
102	Myanmar	61.3	60.8	0.5	110
105	Bangladesh	61.0	62.5	−1.5	104
106	Mozambique	60.5	59.8	0.8	116
107	Armenia	60.3	60.8	−0.5	110
107	Colombia	60.3	62.8	−2.5	102

(continued)

Table 4.2 Country Risk, Ranked by Composite Risk Rating: *May 2002 Versus June 2001*[a] (cont.)

Rank in May 2002	Country	Composite Risk Rating as of May 2002	Composite Risk Rating as of June 2001	May 2002 Versus June 2001	Rank in June 2001
107	Togo	60.3	59.8	0.5	116
110	Ethiopia	60.0	61.5	−1.5	107
111	Burkina Faso	59.8	62.8	−3.0	102
111	Congo, Republic	59.8	60.5	−0.8	113
113	Ecuador	59.8	61.5	−1.8	107
113	Turkey	58.8	50.3	8.5	132
115	Madagascar	58.5	67.8	−9.3	82
116	Côte D'Ivoire	58.3	57.0	1.3	126
117	Indonesia	58.0	53.3	4.8	128
117	Nicaragua	58.0	58.5	−0.5	123
117	Niger	58.0	59.5	−1.5	118
120	Tanzania	57.5	59.3	−1.8	121
120	Venezuela	57.5	71.3	−13.8	69
122	Mali	57.3	62.5	−5.3	104
122	Pakistan	57.3	57.0	0.3	126
124	Malawi	57.0	59.5	−2.5	118
125	Haiti	55.8	58.3	−2.5	124
126	Lebanon	55.5	59.3	−3.8	121
127	Sudan	54.0	55.3	−1.3	128
128	Angola	52.0	52.5	−0.5	130
129	Argentina	51.8	71.0	−19.3	71
130	Nigeria	51.0	62.0	−11.0	106
130	Zambia	51.0	58.3	−7.3	124
132	Yugoslavia	50.0	48.0	2.0	136
133	Guinea-Bissau	48.3	48.3	0.0	135
134	Sierra Leone	47.8	42.3	5.5	139
135	Iraq	46.8	49.0	−2.3	134
135	North Korea	46.8	47.0	−0.3	137
137	Liberia	46.3	49.8	−3.5	133
138	Congo, Dem. Republic	43.0	51.8	−8.8	131
138	Somalia	43.0	46.5	−3.5	138
140	Zimbabwe	37.8	38.0	−0.3	140

a. The *International Country Risk Guide,* published monthly by Political Risk Services of East Syracuse, New York, includes financial, economic, and political risk forecasts and ratings for 130 countries. The ratings vary from 100 points for minimum risk to 0 points for maximum risk. The indicators used include economic expectations versus reality, economic planning failures, political leadership, external-conflict risk, corruption in government, law-and-order tradition, political terrorism, and the quality of the bureaucracy.
Source: International Country Risk Guide, (May 2002). Copyright © The PRS Group, L.L.C., East Syracuse, NY, USA.

changes in their risk rating. The United States, Saudi Arabia, and Oman have become more risky because of terrorism threats. Countries such as Argentina and Venezuela have become more risky because of both economic and political difficulties.

What companies do with their assessments depends on the data they collect. Exxon, for example, integrated its political assessment with its financial plans; in cases where Exxon expects a higher political risk, the company may add 1 to 5 percent to its required return on investment.[72] Political risk assessment should also help the company stay out of a certain country when necessary. The collected data should be carefully differentiated, however, so that the best decision can be made.

RISK REDUCTION STRATEGIES

Determining or assessing political risk should not be a goal in itself. The value of political risk assessment is in the integration of risk-reducing strategies that eventually enable companies to enter a market or remain in business. Many companies have experimented with different forms of ownership arrangements, production, and financing that were geared toward reducing political risks to an acceptable minimum. We will discuss the tools that managers can use to deal with political risk rather than leave a market or refuse to enter one.[73]

LOCAL PARTNERS

Relying on local partners with excellent contacts among the host country governing elite is a strategy that many companies have used effectively. This strategy can include placing local nationals on the boards of foreign subsidiaries or accepting a substantial capital participation from local investors. For example, General Motors joined forces with Shanghai Automotive Industry Corporation (a state-owned firm) in a 50-50 joint venture to make Buicks, minivans, and compact cars. China's current tariffs on imported cars range from 80 to 100 percent, but they are expected to decline to 25 percent by 2005 as part of China's entry into the WTO. Though many host countries require some form of local participation as a condition for entering their markets, many foreign firms enlist local firms voluntarily. Diamond Shamrock, a U.S.-based company, built its chemical plant in South Korea with the help of a local partner to get more favorable operating conditions.[74]

INVALUABLE STATUS

Achieving a status of indispensability is an effective strategy for firms that have exclusive access to high technology or specific products. Such companies keep research and development out of the reach of their politically vulnerable subsidiaries and, at the same time, enhance their bargaining power with host governments by emphasizing their contributions to the economy. When Texas Instruments wanted to open an operation in Japan more than a decade ago, the company was able to resist pressures to take on a local partner because of its unique advanced technology. This situation occurred at a time when many other foreign companies were forced to accept local partners.[75] The appearance of being irreplaceable obviously helps reduce political risk.

VERTICAL INTEGRATION

Companies that maintain specialized plants, each dependent on the others in various countries, are expected to incur fewer political risks than firms with fully integrated and independent plants in each country. A firm practicing this form of distributed sourcing can offer economies of scale to a local operation. This strategy can become crucial for success in many industries. If a host government were to take over such a plant, its output level would be spread over too many units, products, or components, thus rendering the local company uncompetitive because of a cost disadvantage. Further risk can be reduced by having at least two units engage in the same operation, thus preventing the company itself from becoming hostage to overspecialization. Unless multiple sourcing exists, a company could be shut down almost completely if only one of its plants were affected negatively.

LOCAL BORROWING

One of the reasons why Cabot Corporation prefers local partners is that it can then borrow locally instead of adding an additional level of risk with the investment funds being in a currency which is different from the currency of all the sales and costs of the venture.[76] Financing local operations from indigenous banks and maintaining a high level of local accounts payable maximize the negative effect on the local economy if adverse political actions were taken. Typically, host governments do not expropriate themselves, and they are reluctant to cause problems for their local financial institutions. Local borrowing is not always possible, however, because of restrictions placed on foreign companies, which otherwise crowd local companies out of the credit markets.

MINIMIZING FIXED INVESTMENTS

Political risk, of course, is always related to the amount of capital at risk. Given equal political risk, an alternative with comparably lower exposed capital amounts is preferable. A company can decide to lease facilities instead of buying them, or it can rely more on outside suppliers, provided they exist. In any case, companies should keep exposed assets to a minimum to limit the damage posed by political risk.

POLITICAL RISK INSURANCE

As a final recourse, global companies can purchase insurance to cover their political risk. With the political developments in Iran and Nicaragua and the assassinations of President Park of Korea and President Sadat of Egypt all taking place between 1979 and 1981, many companies began to change their attitudes on risk insurance. Political risk insurance can offset large potential losses. For example, as a result of the U.N. Security Council's worldwide embargo on Iraq until it withdrew from Kuwait, companies collected $100–$200 million from private insurers and billions from government-owned insurers.[77]

Companies based in the United States have two sources for such protection: government insurance and private insurance. The Overseas Private Investment Corporation (OPIC) was formed in 1969 by the U.S. government to facilitate the participation of private U.S. firms in the development of less developed countries. OPIC offers three kinds of political risk insurance in one hundred developing countries. The agency covers losses caused by currency inconvertibility, expropriation, and bellicose actions such as war and revolution.

INTERNATIONAL AND GLOBAL LEGAL FORCES

In many ways, the legal framework of a nation reflects a particular political philosophy or ideology. Just as each country has its own political climate, so does the legal system change from country to country. The legal systems of the world are based on one of four sources—(1) common law derived from English law, found in the United Kingdom, the United States, Canada, and countries previously part of the English Commonwealth; (2) civil, or code, law based on the Roman law of written rules, found in non-Islamic and non-Marxist countries; (3) socialist law derived from the Marxist-socialist system, found in China and other socialist nations; and (4) Islamic law derived from the Koran, found in Iran, Iraq, Pakistan, and other Islamic nations. Thus, globally active companies find themselves in a situation in which they have to conform to more than one legal system if they are conducting business in more than one foreign country. Although this situation is complicated enough, the difficulty in some cases of determining whose laws apply adds further to an already complex environment. Here we discuss some of the current major legal challenges that require adjustment and consideration at the corporate level. Of particular interest to us in this chapter are the laws pertaining to commercial behavior, such as laws against bribery and laws regulating competition and product liability. We also discuss the emergence of global courts. In later chapters, we present the specific legal requirements covering certain aspects of the global marketing program. Such material appears in the chapters on pricing, advertising, and products, among others.

LAWS AGAINST BRIBERY AND CORRUPT PRACTICES

Though bribery in international business has existed for years, the publicity surrounding some bribery scandals in the early 1970s caused a public furor in the United States about the practice. The Foreign Corrupt Practices Act (FCPA) of 1977 was intended to stop the payments of bribes. Though the act covers the whole range of record-keeping and control activities of a company both in the United States and abroad, its best-known section specifically prohibits U.S. companies, their subsidiaries, and representatives from making payments to high-ranking foreign government officials or political parties. The penalties for violation can be very stiff: an executive who violates the FCPA may be imprisoned for up to five years and fined up to $10,000. The company involved may be fined up to $1 million. The law prohibits outright bribery, but small facilitating payments are not outlawed as long as they are made to government clerks without any policy-making responsibility.

Bribery exists in both developed and less developed countries. In the United States, Salt Lake City officials used special funding to influence the Olympic site selection committee to pick their city for the 2002 Winter Olympics. The governments of Indonesia, Italy, Brazil, Pakistan, Zaire, and others have fallen partly because the people they governed could no longer stand having corrupt politicians.[78] The bribery scandals involving the construction industry in Japan and Italy are well known and have even led to enormous political change in those countries. In Italy, where bribing government officials by transferring large sums of money through their political parties was common, many leading politicians and business executives were jailed for the offense. One year later, bids for public works projects were reported to come in up to 40 percent below earlier cost estimates, and the Italian government is estimated to have saved up to $4.4 billion in 1994.[79] Other parts of the world in which bribery is common are China and Russia. In both countries, the changes toward more liberalization in trade have created opportunities for local officials to approve foreign investment. One source estimated that the "connection" payments in China amounted to 3 to 5 percent of the operating costs of a project.[80] The Chinese government is aggressively fighting corruption. For example, two government officials found using public funds for personal use were found guilty and executed. In another case, the government found eighteen officials who were helping to smuggle goods into China without paying the customs duty; seven of the eighteen were executed.[81]

IBM officials in Argentina allegedly paid $37 million in kickbacks for a $250 million contract with the state-owned Banco de la Nación. The officials involved have left IBM. This event followed charges in Mexico that IBM and city officials conducted an unlawful bidding process for the sale of a computer for the city's prosecutor's office. IBM settled the claim for $37 million, but the charges have not been dropped.[82] The two cases have cost IBM more than a loss of image. IBM lost the Banco de la Nación contract for $250 million, as well as two contracts from the Argentina's tax authority worth $500 million. In July 1998, IBM said that it would no longer bid on government contracts in Argentina or state contracts in other Latin American countries where it was the sole bidder. IBM headquarters has never admitted knowledge or responsibility for these events.[83]

As a result of the difficulties in deciding which law applies, global companies have resorted to developing their own codes of ethics, particularly concerning bribes. When developing such a code, companies have to decide if they will apply one code worldwide or differentiate their standards by country or region. Experience over the past decade has shown that the level of ethical behavior is rising over time, and what was acceptable behavior at one time may suddenly be cause for prosecution under local laws. As a result, it makes sense for companies to adopt the highest available standard, even if it would not yet be the norm in a given country.

Several studies have shown that corruption is closely linked to economic malpractice and that countries with high levels of corruption have lower economic investment and therefore lower economic growth rates. Higher corruption levels are also linked to lower investment in education, which pays smaller economic dividends because educational achievement is compromised. Shang-Jin Wei, a Harvard economist, argues that corruption acts as a tax on foreign investment. "An increase in the corruption level from that of Singapore to that of Mexico is equivalent to raising the tax rate by over 20 percentage points."[84]

A 1996 survey by the Hong Kong–based Political and Economic Risk Consultancy found that China, Vietnam, and Indonesia were the most corrupt. The lowest levels of corruption were reported for Switzerland, Australia, Singapore, the United States, and Britain. While most countries have laws aimed at fighting corruption, few apply them as strictly and consistently as does Singapore.[85]

The thirty-four signatory nations of the Organization for Economic Cooperation and Development (OECD), which represents the world's largest economies except

China, agreed to adopt common rules to punish companies and individuals who bribe. Twelve countries have already changed their domestic laws to comply with the treaty, including Germany, Japan, the United States, the United Kingdom, and South Korea. It is too early to tell if the treaty and new laws will be effective, although the OECD will monitor the countries' antibribery laws and conduct audits to see if the laws are followed.[86]

Transparency International, an independent organization, tracks how public and global businesses view corruption in eighty-five countries. As of 2001, the eleven least corrupt countries were Finland, Denmark, New Zealand, Iceland, Singapore, Sweden, Canada, the Netherlands, Luxembourg, and Norway. At the bottom of the list were Pakistan, Russia, Tanzania, Ukraine, Azerbaijan, Bolivia, Cameroon, Kenya, Indonesia, Uganda, Nigeria, and Bangladesh. The United States was tied with Israel for sixteenth place from the top.[87]

LAWS REGULATING COMPETITIVE BEHAVIOR

Many countries have enacted laws that govern the competitive behavior of their firms. In some cases, like the European Union, supranational bodies enforce their own laws. Unfortunately for global companies, these antitrust laws are frequently contradictory or enforced erratically, adding great complexity to the job of the global executive. These bodies, such as the EU Competition Commission, have stopped a number of acquisitions like GE's purchase of Honeywell, which was approved by U.S. officials. The United States, with its long-standing tradition of antitrust enforcement, has had considerable impact on the multinational operations of U.S. companies and is increasingly influencing those of foreign-based companies operating in the United States.

For example, Coca-Cola's proposed $1.75 billion takeover of Cadbury Schweppes PLC was reviewed by each of the European countries in which the company has operations, as well as by the European Commission.[88] Competitors of Microsoft went to Mario Monti, the head of the EU Competition Commission, to protest that Microsoft's Windows 2000 was designed to extend its dominance in PC-operating systems, servers, and electronic commerce. If found guilty of breaking the EU competition laws, Microsoft can be forced to alter Windows 2000 or can be prohibited from selling in Europe, as well as fined up to 10 percent of its total worldwide revenue, $2.5 billion, or the company could be forced to hand over access to the source code of the Windows operating system.[89] In February 2001, the EU Competition Commission blocked General Electric's $45 billion takeover bid for Honeywell because both companies are leaders in the jet engine and aircraft equipment markets and their combination would reduce competition in an industry with few suppliers to choose from and long, expensive contracts. Almost a year later, in January 2002, the commission approved Hewlett-Packard's $25 billion takeover bid for Compaq because the information technology hardware market had low barriers to entry and many suppliers, making it difficult for the combined companies to harm competition.[90] The European Competition Commission has proposed legislation to govern corporate mergers, acquisitions, and takeovers. DaimlerChrysler was fined $65 million by the European Competition Commission after a multiyear investigation into the company's antitrust practices.[91]

Sometimes international firms can be caught between competing legal systems.[92] The recently proposed affiliation of British Airways and American Airlines has shown the potential need for a two-track approval process that would include both national and regional approval. The British authorities want the AA/BA alliance to sell 168 prime-time slots at Heathrow as a condition of approval, but Karel Van Miert, the head of the European Competition Commission, wants AA/BA to give up 230 Heathrow slots and reduce the number of flights to cities like New York. The U.S. Department of Transportation is expected to approve the deal if Britain and the United States can agree on an open-skies air treaty that allows any carrier to fly between the two countries. The obstacle has been the U.S. reluctance to allow foreign companies to offer domestic flights in the United States. Richard Branson, the owner of Virgin Atlantic Airways, wants to offer a low-cost airline in the United States, and the AA/BA alliance may need to accommodate Branson's wishes.[93]

PRODUCT LIABILITY

Regulations or laws directly affect all aspects of global marketing, but regulations on product liability are included here because of their enormous impact on all firms. Specific regulatory acts, or laws, pertaining to other aspects of the marketing mix—namely, pricing, distribution, and promotion—have been included in other chapters.

Regulations on product liability are relatively recent in the United States. Other countries also have laws on product liability; a major problem for global marketers is the differences in laws in different countries or regions. In the United States, product liability is viewed in the broadest sense, or along the lines of strict liability. For a product sold in a defective condition that becomes unreasonably dangerous for the user, both producer and distributor can be held accountable.

Product liability laws have changed in Europe as well. In the mid-1970s, the European Commission (EC) proposed a set of regulations that was to supersede each member country's laws. Traditionally, the individual country laws had been rather lax by U.S. standards. In the United States, the plaintiff must prove that the product was defective at the time it left the producer's hand, whereas under the EC guidelines, manufacturers must prove that the product was not defective when it left their control. Nevertheless, there are differences due to the different legal and social systems. In the EU, trials are decided by judges and not common jurors. And the existing extensive welfare systems will automatically absorb many of the medical costs that are subject to litigation in the United States. Furthermore, it is typical for the loser in a court judgment in Europe to bear the legal costs. In the case of product liability cases, if a company is found to owe damages to a plaintiff, then it will also have to pay the plaintiff's legal costs according to typical fee standards. This stipulation differs substantially from the U.S. system, in which a winning plaintiff's lawyer typically is compensated through a predetermined percentage of the awarded damages, a practice that in the eyes of many experts has raised award damages and, as a result, liability insurance costs.

The rapid spread of product liability litigation, however, forces companies with global operations to review their potential liabilities carefully and to acquire appropriate insurance policies. Although a global marketing manager cannot be expected to know all the respective rules and regulations, executives must nevertheless anticipate potential exposure and, by asking themselves the appropriate questions, make sure that their firms consider all possible scenarios.

BANKRUPTCY LAWS

Bankruptcy laws vary from country to country. In the United Kingdom, Canada, and France, the laws of bankruptcy favor the creditors. When a firm enters bankruptcy, an administrator is appointed, and the appointee's job is to recover the creditors' money. In the United States, bankruptcy tends to protect the business from the creditors. Under Chapter 11 of the Federal Bankruptcy Code, the management prepares a reorganization plan, which is voted on by the creditors. In Germany and Japan, bankruptcies are often handled by the banks behind closed doors. The national bankruptcy systems have a wide variety of standards of openness to others. In addition, creditor preference varies from country to country. For example, Swiss law gives preference to Swiss creditors. There is a need for a global bankruptcy law, but until world accountancy standards are established, there is little chance of a global bankruptcy code.[94]

PATENTS, TRADEMARKS, AND COPYRIGHTS

Patents and trademarks are used to protect products, processes, and symbols. Patents and trademarks are issued by each individual country, so marketers must register every product in every country in which they intend to trade. The International Convention for the Protection of Industrial Property, honored by forty-five countries, gives all nationals the same privileges when applying for patents and trademarks. In addition, the agreement gives patent coverage for one year after application of the trademark or patent in one country, thus limiting piracy of the product in other countries.

The United States has an extensive patent system open to anyone. The top ten companies receiving U.S. patents in 2001, in order of number received were IBM, NEC, Canon, Micron Technology, Samsung, Matsushita, Sony, Hitachi, Mitsubishi, and Fujitsu. Note that, of the top ten patenting companies, only two were U.S. firms—seven were Japanese and one was Korean.[95]

It does not seem, however, that all countries have open and accessible patent systems. It took AlliedSignal eleven years to get a patent on amorphous metal alloys approved in Japan. AlliedSignal alleges that the Japanese patent office dragged its feet while the Ministry for Trade and Industry (MITI) launched a catch-up program with thirty-four Japanese companies.[96] The patent system in Japan is slow and tends to pressure companies to reach agreements rather than assign penalties, so it is not surprising to see many of the Japanese firms using the United States to protect their intellectual knowledge. For example, Fujitsu is suing South Korea's Samsung over semiconductor patents before the U.S. International Trade Commission.[97] Patent officials from Japan, the United States, Europe, and Canada met in Tokyo in May 1999 to discuss a global patent system whereby patents would be recognized in other countries. The global patent system was discussed at the 1999 WTO talks in Seattle.[98]

Piracy of products became a significant problem in the 1980s, affecting computers, watches, designer clothes, and industrial products. The sale of counterfeit goods ranging from Louis Vuitton bags and Rolex watches to car parts and medicines was estimated to be a hefty $150 billion a year. Patents, trademarks, and piracy will be discussed in more detail in Chapter 13.

The worldwide cost of software piracy is estimated to be $11.4 billion, with 96 percent of Chinese software being pirated, compared with 77 percent in eastern Europe and 27 percent in the United States.[99] Microsoft won $100,000 in a lawsuit against two companies in China—a small amount compared with the $1.0 billion the company estimates it has lost to pirated software in China. However, Microsoft believes that the Chinese government is serious about stopping piracy in China, having raided seventy to eighty factories in 1997 and confiscated their CD presses.[100]

U.S. businesses report that they lose almost $2 billion to Chinese piracy of motion pictures, books, records, music, software, and video games.[101] Although the information superhighway offers numerous opportunities for information exchange, the role of software patents, royalties, and encryption technology must be resolved. In 2000, China required that all Internet content providers have secure systems before they could receive licenses. The new rules were imposed to reduce leakage of state secrets, but the same rules were expected to slow the growth of the Internet in China.[102]

The importance of the copyright law for software became part of the international trade discussion when the Japanese government began considering a change in the law that would allow Japanese companies to reengineer all software to make compatible products, even when the U.S. supplier would not authorize it.[103] Because of its importance to firms that depend on copyright protection, such as in the music, video, publishing, and software industries, international firms will have to pay increased attention to the enforcement of copyright law.

With counterfeiting and related infringements on the rise, companies must develop strategies to reduce their damaging effects. Possible responses are to (1) do nothing if the effect is minimal; (2) co-opt the distributors through acquisition or licensing; (3) educate customers about the value of the original product through advertising; (4) investigate and bring legal action; (5) join coalitions like the International Anti-Counterfeiting Coalition, which brings pressure on governments and perpetrators; (6) use advanced technology, such as special ink or raised letters that are difficult to copy; and (7) continue to enhance the brand with new products, making it difficult for pirates to keep up.[104]

REGULATORY TRENDS AFFECTING GLOBAL MARKETING

In the past, international firms had to expend a large amount of energy to protect themselves from negative political decisions. Political risk consisted largely of losing operating freedom or, in the worst case, losing the asset in a country. The tremendous political change that has swept through the world over the past few years has actually brought an opening of trade and led to many more opportunities than in any five-year period since World War II. The key political events of total change in eastern Europe and the opening of countries such as China have significantly broadened the geographic boundaries within which international firms are allowed to participate.

Three major trends have emerged, each present to different degrees in some parts of the world. The first such trend, *trade liberalization,* is the opening of many countries to international trade, and it has swept many formerly "locked" countries.

Although trade liberalization has clearly been the case in the formerly socialist countries of eastern Europe, it and the corresponding opening of borders to imports and exports have also been of great importance in the emerging and developing economies. The second trend of importance is *deregulation.* This trend covers the various government actions aimed at allowing market forces more influence; it has resulted in a reduction of regulatory activities primarily in the western economies but also elsewhere in the world. Finally, *privatization,* a third major trend, is today engulfing mostly the countries of eastern Europe. Governments in many countries are turning over ownership of companies, services, and agencies to private investors. We now look at each of these trends in detail in an effort to understand how they have affected global marketing strategies.

TRADE LIBERALIZATION.   In the early 1980s, international trade with large parts of the world was very restricted. The governments of eastern Europe, most of Latin America, and many Asian countries such as China and India tightly controlled what could be imported and thus severely restricted business opportunities for global firms. As countries reduce local manufacturing requirements and reduce the tariffs on imports, two results occur. First, foreign companies increase direct investment because they see both local and regional opportunities. Second, the amount of trade in both imports and exports increases. For example, when Thailand and its neighbors reduced duties on cars from 70 to 5 percent, GM, Ford, and BMW invested in those countries and began selling cars throughout Southeast Asia from factories in Thailand, Indonesia, and the Philippines. Malaysia has refused to open its auto market of 400,000 cars per year because it wants to protect the government-owned auto company. If free trade continues to expand and includes China, experts expect interregional trade could grow by 40 percent by 2020.[105]

India has turned to international trade liberalization. Following the initial trade liberalization in 1991, several steps were taken to make India a more attractive place for global firms to invest, including much less regulation of foreign exchange, permission to use foreign brand names (which was not permitted previously), and the right to raise equity stakes to 51 percent in many sectors.[106] Because of the opening of India, many global firms entered or reentered the Indian market. Similar developments have led to trade liberalization between China and the rest of the world following China's entry into the WTO.

DEREGULATION.   A second trend affecting global marketing is the rapid deregulation of business everywhere. The United States is generally considered to have taken the lead with its deregulation of several industries, particularly transportation, airlines, banking, and telecommunications. The general ideas of deregulation were readily absorbed by some other governments, the United Kingdom among them. As part of the European integration drive, culminating in the Europe 1992 initiative, deregulation also became an important issue in Europe. Typically, deregulation not only prevents government intervention but also helps in opening doors to international competition.

The European Union is slowly opening its telecommunications market. The long-standing monopolies of the national telephone companies in most European countries are giving way to more open competition along the U.S. and U.K. models. Although data communication has already been deregulated, the trend now is to include regular voice communications as well. Sprint and France Telecom are working together, and MCI WorldCom and Qwest International are setting up high-speed networks in Europe.[107] Deregulation will bring more competition because the local phone companies can no longer count on their monopolies. It will also create opportunities for other carriers, such as AT&T from the United States and the various regional operating companies. In mobile communications, these U.S. firms have already penetrated the market, usually linking with local partners that were not previously active in telecommunications.

Similar efforts are under way in Asia, where telecommunications markets are growing rapidly. AT&T and British Telecom have taken a 30 percent ownership in Japan Telecom, the third largest player in Japan.[108] Other efforts have taken place in financial markets, where substantial deregulation is under way in banking and insurance. The opening of Japanese financial markets, particularly with respect to financial derivatives, is of importance to international banks.[109] Deregulation is typically accompanied by liberalization and the opening of markets for foreign competitors. This trend, therefore, adds to the set of opportunities encountered by international firms.

PRIVATIZATION. The third trend affecting global marketing is the current rush toward privatization. Under privatization, countries sell government-owned agencies, organizations, and companies to private stockholders or other acquiring firms. Starting in the late 1970s and early 1980s, acts of privatization overtook nationalizations, and for the period 1990–1992, the United Nations counted more than 150 privatizations.[110] Some of the earliest examples of privatization came from the United Kingdom, where the government privatized airlines (British Airways), telecommunications companies (British Telecom), and many utilities (British Airport Authority).

Privatization has swept through over one hundred countries, which have privatized 75,000 state-owned companies. The results have been good in central and eastern Europe as well as the Baltic states. The results have been poor in Russia, Armenia, Georgia, Kazakhstan, Moldova, Mongolia, and Ukraine. The International Monetary Fund (IMF) reports that much of the failures of privatization came from the turning over of mediocre assets to a large number of people who had neither the skills nor the financial resources to use them well. Privatization gained momentum as the formerly socialist countries of eastern Europe began to convert to a market economy.[111] The drive toward privatization was particularly strong in Poland, the Czech Republic, and Hungary. Philip Morris, the U.S.-based food and tobacco company, was able to acquire a stake in the Czech Republic's Tabak, a company with a tobacco monopoly. The Czech government indicated that the monopoly would eventually end; however, Philip Morris expected to get a head start through the acquisition. Many privatizations in Poland and the Czech Republic occurred through the distribution of shares, or coupons, to the local population. Nevertheless, the effort to privatize state industry in many parts of eastern Europe has resulted in significant opportunities for foreign firms to acquire the privatized companies.

Privatization has also become more common in other parts of the world. Argentina privatized almost its entire state holdings in a period of three years ending in 1993. This change resulted in a net inflow of $19.1 billion for the sale of airlines, oil companies, gas companies, and other industrial firms.[112] Privatization is also coming to western governments, where some countries have held industrial stakes for a long time. France and Italy, with long traditions for industrial holdings, privatized some of their state-controlled industrial firms.[113] For example, the French sold 49 percent of France Telecom for FFR 150–200 billion! [114]

The trend toward privatization is expected to continue, with approximately 1,300 separate deals anticipated worldwide, not including any activity in eastern Europe. Whenever privatization occurs, it is typically related to a decreasing involvement of the local government in that particular industry or sector. This change invariably leads to further trade liberalizations and deregulations. Both phenomena generate increased opportunities for global companies.

CONCLUSIONS

In this chapter, we have outlined the major political and regulatory forces facing global companies. Our approach was not so much to identify and list all possible influences or actions that may have an impact on global marketing operations. Instead, we have provided only a sample of these potential political and regulatory forces. It is up to executives with global responsibility to devise structures and systems that deal with these environmental influences. What is important to our discussion is the recognition that companies can adopt risk reduction strategies to compensate for some of these risks, but certainly not for all of them. For effective global marketing management, executives must be forward looking, anticipate potentially adversarial *or* positive changes in the environment, and not wait until changes occur. To accomplish these goals, systematic monitoring procedures that encompass both political and legal developments must be implemented.

The necessity of such monitoring for global firms has been demonstrated throughout this chapter. The past ten years have brought enormous political changes to the world, changes that are affecting the global marketing operations of global firms. The entry of China into the WTO and the desire of Russia to enter the WTO will continue to open markets and reduce trade tariffs. In many parts of the world, however, the existing trend toward open-market economies is still questionable; substantial political and regulatory risks remain for some countries. The War on Terrorism by the United States will continue to result in political and regulatory risks for western firms in Iran, Iraq, Saudi Arabia, and other markets. Past experience has shown, however, that the traditional purpose of assessing political risk—to ensure that assets of firms will not be lost through takeovers or other arbitrary host government decisions—will have to give way to finding the true opportunities that might exist. As a result, the approaches and processes traditionally used by global firms to assess political risk will have to be redirected at political opportunity assessment.[115]

Questions for Discussions

1. The construction industry in Japan has traditionally been dominated by domestic suppliers, with few foreign construction companies winning projects in Japan. What aspects of Japan's political forces may have influenced this control over the Japanese construction market? What political or legal forces may lead to the opening of this market for foreign firms?

2. Has the opening of public procurement markets in Europe been successful? Why?

3. How could a country develop its own expertise in a product that is primarily imported—for example, automobiles in Egypt?

4. Develop a political risk analysis for a country of your choice. In which direction is the country going and what effects would that direction have on global firms operating there?

5. What are the different methods that a company can use to obtain and/or develop political risk assessment information?

6. John Deere has decided to enter the tractor market in Central America. What strategies could the company use to reduce the possible effects of political risk?

7. While you are attempting to deliver a large computer system (selling price $1.4 million) to a foreign government, the minister of transportation advises you that a fee of $20,000 is required to ensure proper coordination of the customs clearance delivery process. What would you do?

For Further Reading

Akhter, Humayum, and Robert F. Lusch. "Political Risk and the Evolution of the Control of Foreign Business: Equity, Earnings, and the Marketing Mix." *Journal of Global Marketing,* Spring 1988, pp. 109–127.

Arend, Anthony Clark. *Legal Rules and International Society.* New York: Oxford University Press, 1999.

Brouthers, K. D., L. E. Brouthers, and G. Nakos. "Entering Central and Eastern Europe: Risk and Cultural Barriers." *Thunderbird International Business Review,* September–October 1998, vol. 40, no. 5, pp. 482–505.

Clougherty, Joseph A. "Globalization and the Autonomy of Domestic Competition Policy: An Empirical Test on the World Airline Industry." *Journal of International Business Studies,* 3d quarter 2001, vol. 32, no. 3, pp. 459–479.

Encarnation, Dennis J., and Sushil Vachani. "Foreign Ownership: When Hosts Change the Rules." *Harvard Business Review,* September–October 1985, pp. 152–160.

Erb, Claude B., Campbell R. Harvey, and Tadas E. Viskanta. "Political Risk, Economic Risk, and Financial Risk." *Financial Analysts Journal,* November-December 1996, pp. 29–46.

Filatotchev, Igor, "Effects of Post-Privatization Governance and Strategies on Export Intensity in the Former Soviet Union." *Journal of International Business Studies,* 4th quarter 2001, vol. 32, no. 4, pp. 853–872.

Fukuyama, Francis. "Managing Global Chaos: Sources of and Responses to Global Conflict." *Foreign Affairs,* March-April 1997, pp. 175–185.

Hadjikhani, Amjad, "The Behavior of International Firms in Socio-Political Environments in the European Union." *Journal of Business Research,* June 2001, vol. 52, no. 3, p. 263.

Harvey, Michael G., and Ilkka A. Ronkainen. "International Counterfeiters: Marketing Success Without the Cost and the Risk." *Columbia Journal of World Business,* Fall 1985, pp. 37–45.

Hauptman, Gunter. "Intellectual Property Rights." *International Marketing Review,* Spring 1987, pp. 61–64.

Huntington, Samuel P. "The Clash of Civilizations?" *Foreign Affairs,* 1993, vol. 72, no. 3, pp. 22–49.

Marwick, Sandy. "The Outlook for Global Risk in 1997." *Risk Management,* November 1996, pp. 48–55.

May, Christopher. *A Global Political Economy of Intellectual Property Rights: The New Enclosures?* Lincolnwood, Ill.: Routledge, 2000.

Moran, Therdore H., ed. *International Political Risk Management: Exploring New Frontiers.* Working Papers Series on Contemporary Challenges for Investors, Washington D.C., January 2001.

O'Byrne, Shannon Kathleen. "Economic Justice and Global Trade: An Analysis of the Libertarian Foundations of the Free Trade Paradigm." *American Journal of Economics & Sociology,* January 1996, pp. 1–15.

Raddock, David M. *Assessing Corporate Political Risk,* Totowa, N.J.: Roowman & Littlefield, 1986.

Vernon, Raymond. "Big Business and National Governments: Reshaping the Compact in a Globalizing Economy." *Journal of International Business Studies,* 3d quarter 2001, vol. 32, no. 3, pp. 509–519.

Vogl, Frank. "Supply Side of Global Bribery." *IMF Publications Series,* June 1998, vol. 35, no. 2, pp. 14–17.

Whitcomb, L. L., C. B. Erdener, and C. Li. "Business Ethical Values in China and the U.S." *Journal of Business Ethics* (Netherlands), June 1998, vol. 17, no. 8, pp. 839–853.

Endnotes

1. Eric Frey, "Haider Resigns as Chairman of Austria's Far-Right Party," *Financial Times,* February 29, 2000, p. 2.

2. Sean Silverthorne, "Promises and Problems for China in the WTO," *Harvard Business School Working Knowledge,* February 25, 2002, p. 1.

3. "Under Construction: Survey of Latin America," *Economist,* November 13, 1993, p. 5.

4. Kenneth David and Vern Terpstra, *Cultural Environment of International Business* (Independence, Ken.: Southwestern, 2002), p 241.

5. "Australian Media: Let Battle Commence," *Economist,* April 26, 1997, pp. 60–63.

6. *Latin Trade Newsletter,* April 3, 2002, published by LatinTrade.com, Miami, Florida.

7. "Let the Market Take Off," *Economist,* January 18, 1997, p. 74.

8. Nancy Dunne, "White House Cuts Computer Export Curbs," *Financial Times,* February 2, 2000, p. 5.

9. "Mongolian Premier Presents Paper on Country's Development Strategy," *Daily News Ulaanbaatar, BBC Worldwide Monitoring,* June 22, 1999, p. 1.

10. "Europe's Burden," *Economist,* May 22, 1999, p. 84.

11. "German Jobs: Odd Men In," *Economist,* June 14, 1997, p. 71.

12. John Grimond, "Survey: Germany: Wealth, but Not Work," *Economist,* February 6, 1999, p. G6.

13. Peter S. Canellos, "German Auto Plant Revs up in Alabama," *Boston Globe,* June 30, 1997, p. A1.

14. "Keep It French," *Economist,* December 7, 1996, p. 5.

15. "The British Are Coming: Foreign Investors Are Going on a Spending Spree in America, and That's Just Fine with Us," *Los Angeles Daily News,* December 16, 1998, p. N26.

16. Mimi Whitefield, "MTV Networks Global," *Miami Herald,* June 28, 1999, p. 9.

17. Katja Hoffman, "Youth TV's Old Hand Prepares for the Digital Challenge," *Financial Times,* February 18, 2000, p. 8.

18. Peter Cook, "Opposing the U.S. Culture," *Globe,* February 3, 1999, p. B2.

19. Dick Thompson, "What Global Warming?" *Time,* June 21, 1999, p. 62.

20. Natalie Noor-Drugan, "DuPont Hikes Prices: A Silver Lining for HFCs?" *Chemical Week,* May 13, 1998, p. 20.

21. Holman W. Jenkins Jr., "How to Save McDonalds," *Wall Street Journal Europe,* March 19, 1998, p. 12.

22. "DeBeers to Avoid Selling Dirty Diamonds," *Financial Times,* March 1, 2000, p. 22.

23. "China Starts New Antidumping Tax on Newsprint," *Dow Jones News Service,* June 3, 1999, p. 1.

24. "Tony Walker, Chinese Lesson," *Financial Times,* February 23, 1995, p. 14.

25. "Japan, U.S. to Hold NTT, Computer Talks in Tokyo," *World News Connection,* May 25, 1999, p. 1.

26. Joe Sanderson, "The EU Green Paper on Public Procurement," *European Business Journal,* 1998, vol. 10, no. 2, pp. 64–66.

27. Jon Choy, "Japan's Construction Industry: The Economic Engine That Can't," *Japanese Economic Institute,* September 4, 1998, p. 6.

28. Sandra Sugawara, "Japanese Construction Trade Built on Cronyism," *Washington Post,* January 31, 1998, p. A1.

29. "KIX Highlights Construction Project Bidding Ills," *Mainichi Daily News,* June 24, 1998, p. 1.

30. Douglas L. Fugate and Alan Zimmerman, "Global Services Marketing: A Review of Structural Barriers, Regulatory Limitations and Marketing Responses," *Journal of Professional Services Marketing,* 1996, vol. 13, no. 2, pp. 33–58.

31. Ian Johnson, "China Continues to Hobble Foreign Firms," *Asian Wall Street Journal,* March 23, 2000, p. 1.

32. "Subsidies to Industry," *Economist,* April 10, 1999, p. 105.

33. "A Handbrake on Subsidies: Governments Should Not Obstruct a Long Overdue Restructuring of the European Car Industry," *Economist,* February 13, 1999, p. 19.

34. "Aerospace: Hubris at Airbus, Boeing Rebuilds," *Economist,* November 28, 1998, p. 64.

35. Janine Brewis, "Corporate Germany Starts to Listen to Its Shareholders," *Corporate Finance,* February 1, 1999, p. 18.

36. "German Jobs: Odd Men In," *Economist,* June 14, 1997, p. 72.

37. Rachel Briggs, "The Kidnapping Business," *Guild of Security Controllers Newsletter, http://fpc.org.uk/hotnews/full?activeid=115&tableid=writes;* accessed November 2002.

38. Andrew Bolger, "Increase in Kidnapping for Ransom," *Financial Times,* April 24, 2000, p. 4.

39. "Honda: Is It an American Car?" *Business Week,* November 18, 1991, p. 81.

40. Julian Gearing, "Skill Deficit; Thailand's Poorly Trained Workforce Costs the Country Business," *Asiaweek,* December 1, 2000, p. 1.

41. Productivity Commission 2000, *Broadcasting,* no. 11, AusInfo, Canberra, *http://www.pc.gov.au/inquiry/broadcst/finalreport/appendixf.pdf.*

42. Office of the United States Trade Representative, *The 2002 National Trade Estimate Report on Foreign Trade Barriers (NTE), http://www.ustr.gov/reports/nte/2002/europeanunion.pdf.*

43. James Kynge, "Carrefour Told to Sell Stakes in Stores," *Financial Times,* June 12, 2002, p. 17.

44. Mark Drajem, "India BJP Government Showed Reforms to Continue Despite Rhetoric," *Dow Jones International News,* May 7, 1999, pp. 1–2.

45. James Mathew and Anjan Mitra, "Readers Digest Re-entry Put on Ice," *Business Standard,* December 1, 1998, p. 9.

46. "India Opens Trade Doors," *International Business Asia,* January 18, 1999, p. 4.

47. "Coke Opens Saudi Bottling Plant in Cola War," *Agence France-Presse,* May 5, 1999, p. 1.

48. James Cox, "Firms Say Arab Boycott Sinking," *USA Today,* June 4, 2001, p. B5.

49. Neil MacFarquhar, "An Anti-American Boycott Is Growing in the Arab World," *New York Times,* May 10, 2002, p. A.1.

50. Robert G. Hawkins, Norman Mintz, and Michael Provissiero, "Government Takeovers of U.S. Foreign Affiliates," *Journal of International Business Studies,* Spring 1976, pp. 3–16.

51. Ibid.

52. "Multinationals," Survey, *Economist*, March 27, 1993, p. 19.

53. Kristi Hastings, "Giordano's Return to China Sends Shares Higher," *Asian Wall Street Journal*, June 10, 1999, p. 4.

54. David Gonzalez, "Cuba Receives U.S. Shipment, First Purchase Since Embargo," *New York Times*, December 17, 2001, p. 10.

55. Christopher Ogden, "Special Report South Africa, Less Aid More Trade," *Time*, May 24, 1999, p. 57.

56. "History of INFACT," *www.infact.org.homepage;* accessed on June 23, 2002.

57. "P&G Can Get Mad, but Does It Have to Get Even?" *Business Week*, June 4, 1990, p. 27.

58. "U.S. Court Hears Appeal of Massachusetts' Burma Law," *Dow Jones News Service*, May 4, 1999, p. 2.

59. "International: Cairene Shoppers' Intifada," *Economist*, November 2, 2000, p. 50.

60. Jean-Pierre Jeannet, "The Marketing Challenge in Eastern Europe," teaching note (European Case Clearing House), 1993.

61. "Two for One Split," *Providence Sunday Journal*, May 2, 1993, sec. F, p. 1.

62. "More Firms Are Hiring Own Political Analysts to Limit Risks Abroad," *Wall Street Journal*, March 30, 1981, p. 17.

63. Franklin Root, "U.S. Business Abroad and Political Risks," *MSU Business Topics*, Winter 1968, pp. 73–80; Stephen I. Kobrin et al., "The Assessment and Evaluation of Noneconomic Environments by American Firms: A Preliminary Report," *Journal of International Business Studies*, Spring–Summer 1980, pp. 32–47.

64. Harvey D. Shapiro, "The World's a Dangerous Place," *Institutional Investor*, March 1999, vol. 33, no. 3, pp. 153–157.

65. "Multinationals Get Smarter About Political Risks," *Fortune*, March 24, 1980, p. 87.

66. Ibid.

67. "More Firms Are Hiring Own Political Analysts to Limit Risks Abroad," *Wall Street Journal*, May 2, 1981, p. 1.

68. Bob Donath, "Handicapping and Hedging the Foreign Investment," *Industrial Marketing Management*, February 1981, p. 57.

69. "Multinationals Get Smarter About Political Risks," *Fortune*, March 24, 1980, p. 98.

70. *Country Monitor*, Economic Intelligence Unit Limited, December 15, 1999, p. 12.

71. *International Country Risk Guide* (East Syracuse, N.Y.: Political Risk Services, May 2002). For detailed description of the methodology see *http://www.icrgonline.com/icrgMethods.asp.*

72. "Multinationals Get Smarter About Political Risks," *Fortune*, March 24, 1980, p. 88.

73. The following sections are adapted from *Insurance Decisions*, published by the CIGNA companies, Philadelphia, 1996. Reprinted by permission.

74. "More Firms Are Hiring Own Political Analysts to Limit Risks Abroad," *Wall Street Journal*, May 2, 1981, p. 17.

75. Yves L. Doz and C. K. Prahalad, "How MNCs Cope with Host Government Intervention," *Harvard Business Review*, March–April 1980, p. 52.

76. "Multinationals Get Smarter About Political Risks," *Fortune*, March 24, 1980, p. 98.

77. "Political Risk Insurers Fear Crisis Escalation," *Business Insurance*, 1990, vol. 24, no. 33a, p. 1.

78. "A Global War Against Bribery," *Economist*, January 1, 1999, p. 22.

79. "The Destructive Costs of Greasing Palms," *Business Week*, December 6, 1993, p. 133.

80. Ibid.

81. Hugo Restall, "Examining Asia: Corrupt Money on the Move?" *Asian Wall Street Journal*, March 27, 2002, p. A9.

82. "IBM's Last Tangle in Argentina," *Economist*, August 1, 1998, p. 31.

83. Ibid.

84. "A Global War Against Bribery," *Economist*, January 1, 1999, p. 22.

85. "Singapore Remains a Graft-Free Haven," *Straits Times*, April 9, 1996, p. 3.

86. G. Pascal Zachary, "Industrial Countries to Adopt Rules to Curb Bribery," *Wall Street Journal*, February 16, 1999, p. A18.

87. "Corruption Perceptions Index 2001," Transparency International e.V., *http://www.transparency.org/cpi/2001/cpi2001.html.* The Corruption Perceptions Index can be found at *www.transparency.org.*

88. "Coke's Proposed Deal for Cadbury Brands Draws Probe by EC," *Wall Street Journal*, April 23, 1999, p. B10.

89. Stephen Baker, "The World According to Monti Europe's Competition Czar Isn't Afraid to Take on U.S. Giants Like Microsoft—or the Justice Dept.," *Business Week*, March 25, 2002, p. 48.

90. Francesco Guerrera, "Companies & Finance—What a difference a Year Makes," *Financial Times*, February 1, 2002.

91. Stephen Baker, "The World According to Monti Europe's Competition Czar Isn't Afraid to Take on U.S. Giants Like Microsoft—or the Justice Dept.," *Business Week*, March 25, 2002, p. 48.

92. "Mergers and Acquisitions: Blessed Are the Litigators," *Economist*, January 11, 1997, p. 68.

93. "Come Fly with Me: European and American Regulators Seem About to Approve Yet More Airline Alliances," *Economist*, June 20, 1998, p. 69.

94. "Bankruptcy Laws," *Economist*, February 24, 1990, pp. 93–94.

95. "Preliminary List of Top Patenting Organizations," *U.S. Patent and Trademark Office, www.uspto.gov;* accessed February 7, 2003.

96. "American-Japanese Trade—Low Tricks in High Tech," *Economist*, September 29, 1990, p. 90.

97. Jim Landers, "Many Japanese Firms Protect Patents in the United States," *Dallas Morning News*, September 23, 1998, p. 2.

98. "Patents Officials See Need for Global Patent System," *Dow Jones International News*, May 20, 1999, p. 1.

99. "Software Piracy," *Economist*, June 27, 1998, p. 108.

100. "The Politics of Piracy," *Economist*, February 20, 1999, p. 64.

101. Ben Dolven, "Intellectual Property—Navigating in a Sea of Pirates," *Far Eastern Economic Review*, April 11, 2002.

102. James Kynge, "China Threatens Internet Operators with Secrecy Code," *Financial Times*, January 27, 2000, p. 1.

103. "Decompilation: A Divisive Issue," *Nikkei Weekly*, December 20, 1993, p. 8.

104. Clifford J. Shultz and Bill Saporito, "Protecting Intellectual Property: Strategies and Recommendations to Deter Counterfeiting and Brand Piracy in Global Markets," *Columbia Journal of World Business*, Spring 1996, pp. 18–28.

105. "A New Front in the Free-Trade Wars," *Businessweek*, June 3, 2002, p. 30.

106. "Back in Charge," *Far Eastern Economic Review*, July 8, 1993, p. 8.

107. "European Telecoms in a Tangle," *Economist*, April 24, 1999, p. 61.

108. "AT&T and BT Negotiate for 30% Joint Stake in Japan Telecom," *Wall Street Journal*, March 22, 1999, p. A4.

109. "Battle to Open Tokyo Markets Heats Up," *Wall Street Journal*, June 2, 1993, p. C1.

110. *World Investment Report 1993: TNCs and Integrated Production* (New York: United Nations Conference on Trade and Development, 1993), p. 17.

111. John Nellis, "Time to Rethink Privatization in Transition Economies," *Finance and Development*, June 1999, vol. 36, no. 2, pp. 16–18.

112. "Buying into Argentina Was the Easy Bit," *Financial Times*, December 7, 1993, p. 5.

113. "State-Run Groups Get Used to New Identity," *Financial Times*, January 24, 1994, p. 13.

114. "Privatisation Takes French Leave," *Economist*, December 9, 1995, p. 59.

115. Ideas expressed to authors by Clifton Clarke, retired vice president for global trade at Digital and now an independent consultant, April, 2002.

Part II

Analyzing Global Marketing Opportunities

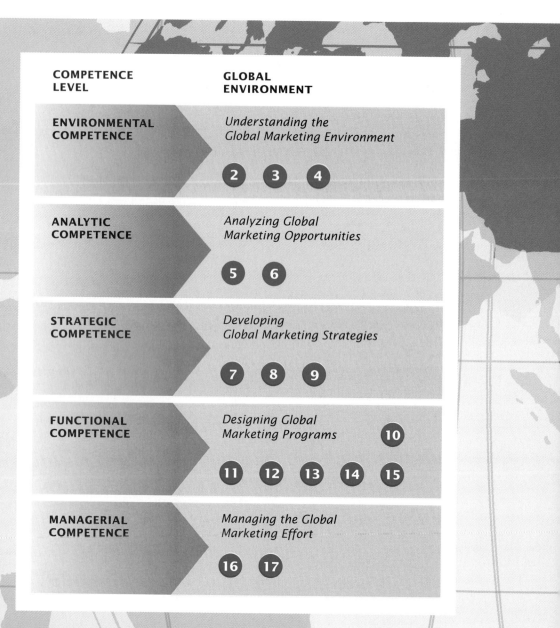

COMPETENCE LEVEL	GLOBAL ENVIRONMENT
ENVIRONMENTAL COMPETENCE	*Understanding the Global Marketing Environment* 2 3 4
ANALYTIC COMPETENCE	*Analyzing Global Marketing Opportunities* 5 6
STRATEGIC COMPETENCE	*Developing Global Marketing Strategies* 7 8 9
FUNCTIONAL COMPETENCE	*Designing Global Marketing Programs* 10 11 12 13 14 15
MANAGERIAL COMPETENCE	*Managing the Global Marketing Effort* 16 17

The global marketplace includes 207 countries or territories. Global companies are constantly searching for the most appropriate markets and the best opportunities for their firms. Analyzing, classifying, and selecting opportunities for future business is an important aspect of global marketing management. In Part II, we concentrate on the skills necessary to analyze, classify, and select global opportunities. We have given this part an analytic focus because we want to encourage analytic competence, a necessary component for success in global marketing.

Chapter 5 provides concepts for analyzing opportunities within countries and groups of countries. We discuss the major market segments within each country's consumer, industrial, and government sectors and analyze the differences in these segments from market to market. The second chapter of this part, Chapter 6, covers the methods by which global companies collect market data and discusses ways to analyze this market research data for decision making.

CHAPTER 5
Global Markets and Buyers

CHAPTER 6
Global Marketing Research

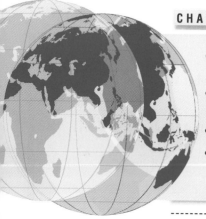

Chapter 5

Global Markets and Buyers

A ssessment of market opportunities is an important aspect of global marketing. Every time a company decides to expand into foreign markets, it must systematically evaluate possible markets to identify the country or group of countries with the greatest opportunities. This process of evaluating worldwide opportunities is complicated for several reasons. First, there are 207 countries and territories in the world; obviously, it is difficult to examine all these opportunities. Second, given the number of countries and the resource limitations, the initial screening process is usually limited to the analysis of published data. Third, many possible markets are small, with little data available about specific consumer, business, or government needs.

Potential buyers often vary from country to country. The buyer can be a consumer, a business, or a government. The challenge for the global marketer is to recognize the differences while looking for the similarities that cut across markets. This chapter will identify the characteristics of different buyers.

Figure 5.1 provides a chapter outline. First, we discuss the process for selecting markets, including the selection techniques and the selection criteria. Then, to illustrate the screening process, we present a detailed case study of how this process can be used to select a market for dialysis equipment. In the final sections of the chapter, we discuss the rationale for grouping countries together and present the market groups in existence around the world today. Last, we discuss the variables influencing the different types of buyer: consumer, business, and government.

Global marketers need to identify quickly where a firm should invest time and resources. It is difficult to know and understand the demand, competitive situation, and market entry requirements in every country. Therefore, the global marketer must be able to assimilate a large volume of information and make recommendations

Figure 5.1: International Market Selection

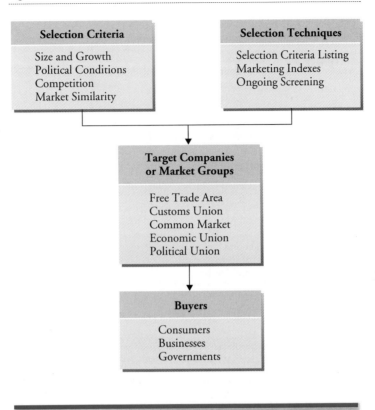

quickly. Also, as economic situations change, opportunities will change. Therefore, the global marketer needs to observe market changes constantly to identify new opportunities.

SCREENING GLOBAL MARKETING OPPORTUNITIES

SELECTION STAGES

The assessment of global marketing opportunities usually begins with a screening process that involves gathering relevant information on each country and filtering out the less desirable countries. A model for selecting foreign markets is shown in Figure 5.2. The model includes a series of four filters for screening out countries. The overwhelming number of market opportunities makes it necessary to break the process down into a series of steps. Although a firm does not want to miss a potential opportunity, it cannot conduct extensive market research studies in every country of the world. (The *World Bank Atlas* includes 207 countries and territories.[1]) The screening process is used to identify good prospects. Two common errors of country screening

Figure 5.2: A Model for Selecting Foreign Markets

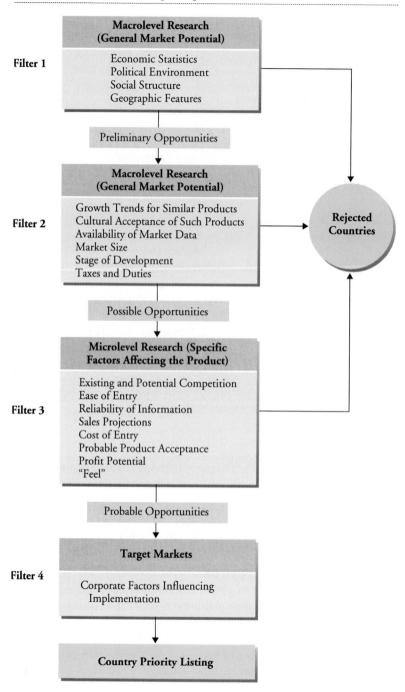

Source: R. Wayne Walvoord, "Export Market Research," *Global Trade Magazine,* May 1980, p. 83.
Reprinted by permission.

are (1) ignoring countries that offer good potential for the company's products and (2) spending too much time investigating countries that are poor prospects.[2] Thus, the screening process allows a global company to focus efforts quickly on the most promising market opportunities by using published secondary sources available through online databases and web sites.[3]

The first stage of the selection process uses macrovariables to discriminate between countries that represent basic opportunities and countries with little or no opportunity or with excessive risk. Macrovariables describe the total market in terms of economic, social, geographic, and political information. Often macroeconomic statistics indicate that the country is too small, as described by the gross national (or domestic) product. The gross national product may seem large enough, but the personal disposable income per household may be too low. Political instability can also be used to remove a country from the set of possible opportunities.

In the second stage of the selection process, variables that indicate the potential market size and acceptance of the product or similar products are used. Proxy variables are often used in this screening process. A *proxy variable* is a similar or related product that indicates a demand for your product. For example, if you are attempting to measure the potential market size and receptivity for a palm-held communication device, possible proxy variables may be the number of telephone lines per person, the number of personal computers per person, or the amount or frequency of cellular telephone usage. The number of telephone lines and cellular phones indicates communication needs, and the number of personal computers indicates a propensity to use advanced technologies. For example, the number of fixed and mobile phone lines per one thousand people is 1,316 in the United States, 1,073 in France, 1,271 in Finland, and 674 in Hungary. The number of personal computers per one thousand people is 585 in the United States, 301 in France, 396 in Finland, and 85 in Hungary. These numbers indicate that Finland may be more receptive to advanced technology than France.[4] The year-to-year growth rates and the total sales of similar or proxy products are good predictors of market size and growth. Other factors in the second stage of the selection process can also be used to screen out countries. Such factors include the stage of economic development, taxes, and duty requirements. If you do not plan to manufacture locally, a high import duty may eliminate a country from consideration in the second stage of the screening process.

The third stage of the screening process focuses on microlevel considerations such as competitors, ease of entry, cost of entry, and profit potential. Microlevel factors influence the success or failure of a specific product in a specific market. At this stage of the process, marketers may consider only a small number of countries, so it is feasible to get more detailed, up-to-date information from the U.S. Department of Commerce, the U.S. State Department, and companies currently operating in that country. The International Trade Administration of the Department of Commerce has an office in most major cities of the world and can provide information and contacts for many markets. Customs brokers and freight forwarders can also help at this stage of the process.

The focus of the screening process at the third stage switches from total market size to profitability. For example, based on the current and potential competitors, how much would you need to invest to gain a particular market share? Given the prices currently charged in the market, what margin can your company expect?

Given the cost of entry and the expected sales, what is the expected profit? This stage of the analysis focuses on the quantitative profit expected, but many subjective judgments are made to arrive at the expected profit. For example, an Israeli manufacturer of pipe insulation found that the market price in the United Kingdom was $10 per kilo versus $6 per kilo in the United States, but its cost was $5 per kilo. These numbers indicated profit potential in the United Kingdom if the company could gain access to the market.

The fourth stage of the screening process is an evaluation and rank ordering of the potential target countries based on corporate resources, objectives, and strategies. For example, although South Africa may have the same expected potential as Venezuela, Venezuela may be given a higher priority because successful entry into Venezuela can later be followed by entry into Colombia and Bolivia.

CRITERIA FOR SELECTING TARGET COUNTRIES

The process of selecting target countries through the screening process requires that the companies identify the criteria to be used to differentiate desirable countries from less desirable ones. Research on global investment decisions has shown that the four critical factors affecting market selection are market size and growth, political conditions, competition, and market similarity. In this section, we explain each of these factors and their relevance to the market selection process.

MARKET SIZE AND GROWTH. It is obvious that potential market size and growth are important factors in selecting markets. The larger the potential demand for a product in a country, the more attractive that market will be to a company. Measures of market size and growth can be on both a macro and a micro basis. On a macro basis, it may be determined that the country needs a minimum set of potential resources to be worth further consideration. Table 5.1 summarizes the potential macroindicators of market size. Several sources of readily available statistics serve as macroindicators of market size. If you are screening countries for a firm that sells microwave ovens, you may decide not to consider any country with a personal disposable income per household of less than $10,000 per year. The logic of this criterion is that if the average household has less than $10,000, the potential market for a luxury item such as a microwave oven will not be great. However, a single statistic can sometimes be deceptive. For example, a country may have an average household income of $8,000, but there may be 1 million households with an income of over $10,000. These 1 million households will be potential buyers of microwave ovens. One commercially available report on the attractiveness of different countries for business is the *World Competitiveness Report.* This annual report analyzes three hundred criteria for determining the overall competitiveness of the country and its strength by industry.[5]

The macroindicators of market potential and growth are usually used in the first stage of the screening process because the data are readily available and can be used to eliminate quickly those countries with little or no potential demand. The macroindicators focus on the total potential demand (population) and ability to afford a product (per capita income). Because the macroindicators of market size are general and crude, however, they do not necessarily indicate a perceived need for the

Table 5.1 Macroindicators of Market Size

Geographic Indicators

Size of the country in terms of geographical area

Climatic conditions

Topographical characteristics

Demographic Characteristics

Total population

Population growth rate

Age distribution of the population

Degree of population density

Economic Characteristics

Total gross national product

Per capita gross national product

Per capita income (also income growth rate)

Personal or household disposable income

Income distribution

---

product. For example, a country such as Iraq may have the population and income for a large potential market for razors, but the consumers, many of whom are Muslims, may not feel a perceived need for the product.

In the third stage of the screening process, it is recommended that microindicators of market potential be used. Microindicators usually indicate actual consumption of a company's product or a similar product, therefore indicating a perceived need. Table 5.2 lists several examples of microindicators of market size. These

Table 5.2 Microindicators of Market Size	
Radios	Hotel beds
Televisions	Telephones
Cinema seats	Tourist arrivals
Scientists and engineers	Passenger cars
Hospitals	Civil airline passengers
Hospital beds	Steel production
Physicians	Rice production
Alcohol consumption	Number of farms
Coffee consumption	Land under cultivation
Gasoline consumption	Electricity consumption

microindicators can be used to estimate market size. The number of households with televisions indicates the potential market size for televisions if every household purchased a new one. Depending on the life of the average television in use, one can estimate the annual demand. Although the actual consumption statistics may not be available for a certain product category, the consumption of similar or substitute products is often used as a proxy variable. For example, in determining the market size for surgical sutures, marketers may use the number of hospital beds or doctors as a proxy variable. The number of farms may indicate the potential demand for tractors, just as the number of cars is likely to indicate the number of tires needed.

The macro- and microindicators of market size allow the marketer to determine or infer the potential market size. Next, the marketer needs to evaluate the risk associated with each market opportunity.

POLITICAL CONDITIONS. The influence of the host country's political environment was described in detail in Chapter 4. Though political risk tends to be more subjective than the quantitative indicators of market size, it is an equally important variable. For example, the terrorist attacks on New York's World Trade Center and the Pentagon in Virginia, and the subsequent U.S. attacks on terrorists in Afghanistan, resulted in millions of dollars of U.S. assets being exposed to risk around the world. The threat of war between Pakistan and India in 2002 put both employees and assets at risk in the affected area.

Any company can be hurt by political risk, from limitations on the number of foreign company officials and the amount of profits paid to the parent company, to refusal to issue a business license. Marketers can use several indicators to assess political risk; some are listed in Table 5.3. Industrial disputes (strikes) can be a major disruption to business, and incidences vary greatly from country to country. The most strike-prone countries in the Organization for Economic Cooperation and Development (OECD) are Spain, Ireland, and Canada.[6]

Historically, extractive industries such as oil and mining have been susceptible to the political risk of expropriation. More recently, the financial, insurance, communications, and transportation industries have also been targets of expropriation. As shown in Table 5.3, many aspects of political risk assessment can be analyzed based on historical data. Note, however, that historical indicators are not always accurate

Table 5.3 Indicators of Political Risk

Probability of nationalization	Percentage of the voters who are communist
Bureaucratic delays	Restrictions on capital movement
Number of expropriations	Government intervention
Number of riots or assassinations	Limits on foreign ownership
Political executions	Soldier/civilian ratio
Number of socialist seats in the legislative	

because political conditions can change radically with a new government. Some of the syndicated services that rate political risk are the Business Environment Risk Index, the Political Risk Index of the Economist Intelligence Unit, and the International Country Risk Guide. For example, if you are considering opportunities in South America, you can consult the Economist Intelligence Unit Country Risk Service, which estimates the country risk to be 75 in Venezuela, 70 in Mexico, 65 in Argentina, and 50 in Brazil, whereas in Colombia, it is 40, and in Chile, it is 20. Other things being equal, Chile and Colombia would be less risky.[7] The Economist Intelligence Unit launched a new electronic-only information services called RiskWire in 2002. This new service tracks risk in sixty of the world's emerging and highly indebted countries.[8]

In addition to the major sources of information cited above, global companies often consult banks, accounting firms, and domestic government agencies for political risk information. The risk assessment services provided by Business International, Frost & Sullivan, Political Risk Services, and others are all useful long-term measures of risk. These sources do not preclude the need to keep attuned to current events, be they the collapse of the Berlin Wall, the invasion of Kuwait, the crushed student uprising in Tiananmen Square, the invasion of Kosovo by the Serbs, or the September 11, 2001, terrorist attacks in the United States. These critical events may not have been predicted by the risk assessment services, yet each had a profound effect on business in the respective areas.

COMPETITION. The number, size, and quality of the competition in a particular country affect a firm's ability to enter and compete profitably. In general, it is more difficult to determine the competitive structure of foreign countries than to determine the market size or political risk. Because of the difficulty of obtaining information, competitive analysis is usually done in the last stages of the screening process, when a small number of countries are being considered.

Some secondary sources describe the competitive nature of a marketplace. The International Market Research Mall (ecnext.imrmall.com) publishes an online listing of available research reports. These reports tend to concentrate on North America and Europe, but some reports can be obtained on Japan, the Middle East, and South America. Such research reports usually cost between $500 and $5,000, with the average fee being about $1,200. In some cases, there may be no research report covering a specific country or product category, or it may be too expensive. Another reliable source of information is the U.S. government. The U.S. Department of Commerce and the State Department (or the equivalent in other countries) may be able to provide information on the competitive situation. Also, in almost every country, embassies employ commercial attachés whose main function is to assist home companies entering that foreign marketplace. Embassies of the foreign country being investigated may also be able to help marketers in their analysis. For example, in investigating the competition for farm implements in Spain, you can call or write the Spanish embassy in Washington, D.C., and secure a list of manufacturers of farm implements in Spain. In developing countries, the United States Agency for International Development (U.S. AID) is a very good source of information.

The World Wide Web has opened up several sources of global market information, such as:

Stat-USA	www.stat-usa.gov
	National Trade Data Bank
	Global Business Procurement
	Opportunities
I-Trade	www.i-trade.com
	Index of Free Services
	Market Your Company
	Index of Fee-Based Services
International Trade Administration	www.ita.doc.gov
	International Trade
	Administration Assistance Centers
	Information Directory
Information Directories	www.pangaea.net
	http://.gats-info.eu.int
	www.sice.oas.org
	www.ustr.gov
UK Department of Trade and Industry	www.dti.gov.uk
Worldwide Market Reports	www.market-reports.co.uk

Other sources of competitive information vary widely, depending on the size of the country and the product. Many larger countries have chambers of commerce or other in-country organizations that may be able to assist potential investors. For example, if you want to investigate the Japanese market for electronic measuring devices, the following groups might be able to assist you in determining the competitive structure of the market in Japan:

- U.S. Chamber of Commerce in Japan
- Japan External Trade Organization (JETRO)
- American Electronics Association in Japan
- Japan Electronic Industry Development Association
- Electronic Industries Association of Japan
- Japan Electronic Measuring Instrument Manufacturers Association

The final and usually most expensive way to assess the market is to go to the country and interview potential customers and competitors to determine the size and strength of the competition. A trip to a potential market is always required before a final decision is made, so a country visit should not be overlooked as an important part of the screening process. If you are well prepared in advance, two to three days in a country talking to distributors, large buyers, and trade officials can be extremely valuable in assessing the competitiveness of the market and the potential profitability.

TECHNIQUES OF MAKING
MARKET SELECTION DECISIONS

The framework for making market selection decisions usually follows the systematic screening process shown in Figure 5.2. Different techniques can be used to accomplish the screening processes. These techniques vary from simple lists of selection criteria to complex combinations of different criteria in an index. These techniques will be discussed individually.

LIST OF SELECTION CRITERIA

The simplest way to screen countries is to develop a set of criteria that are required as a minimum for a country to move through the stages of the screening process. To illustrate the screening methodology, we have outlined the screening process that could be used by a manufacturer of kidney dialysis equipment as an example. This screening process is shown in Table 5.4.

The minimum cutoff number for each criterion will be established by management. As we move through the screening process, the criteria become more specific. The following sections give the rationale for each of the screening criteria and cutoff points.

MACROLEVEL GROSS NATIONAL PRODUCT. Introduction of dialysis equipment in a new market requires significant support functions, including salespeople; service people; replacement parts inventory; and an ensured continuous supply of dialysate fluid, needles, tubing, and so on. Some countries lack the technical infrastructure to

Table 5.4 Screening Process Example: Targeting Countries for Kidney Dialysis Equipment

Filter Number	Type of Screening	Specific Criterion
1	Macrolevel research	GDP over $1.5 billion
		GDP per capita over $1,500
2	General market factors relating to the product	Less than 200 people per hospital bed
		Less than 1,000 people per doctor
		Government expenditures over $100 million for health care
		Government expenditures over $20 per capita for health care
3	Microlevel factors specific to the product	Kidney-related deaths over 1,000
		Patient use of dialysis equipment—over 40 percent annual growth in treated population
4	Final screening of target markets	Numbers of competitors
		Political stability

support such high-level technology. Therefore, management may decide to consider only countries having a minimum size of $15 billion gross domestic product (GDP) or gross national product (GNP), thus excluding many of the developing economies of the world from consideration. (Note that the dialysis screening was done with 1985 data.) Also, dialysis requires substantial government support. A tradeoff then develops between acceptable expenditures for dialysis and acceptable kidney-related death rates. GDP per capita is an indicator of the level at which this tradeoff will occur. The lower the GDP per capita, the lower the expected government expenditure for dialysis equipment, given other pressing societal needs such as food and shelter. Therefore, the GDP per capita of over $1,500 would have been set as a minimum. These economic factors would have limited the market to the following countries plus the eighteen countries of Europe, excluding North America:

All of Europe (except Hungary)	Venezuela
Iceland	Australia
Russia	Iran
New Zealand	Argentina
South Africa	Iraq
Brazil	

GENERAL MARKET FACTORS RELATED TO THE PRODUCT: MEDICAL CONCENTRATION. Hemodialysis is a sophisticated procedure that requires medical personnel with advanced training. For a country to support advanced medical equipment, it requires a high level of medical specialization. Higher levels of medical concentration allow doctors the luxury of specialization in a field such as nephrology (the study of kidneys).

Management may determine that a population of less than one thousand per doctor and a population of less than two hundred per hospital bed indicate that medical personnel will be able to achieve the level of specialization needed to support a hemodialysis program. This second step of the screening process would eliminate Iran, Iraq, Brazil, and Venezuela. As can be expected, the majority of countries with high GNP and GDP per capita have a high level of medical concentration.

Public health expenditures show the government's contribution to the medical care of its citizens—a factor of obvious importance in hemodialysis. Management may believe that countries that do not invest substantially in the health care of their population generally are not interested in making an even more substantial investment in a hemodialysis program. Thus, countries that do not have a minimum of $20 expenditure per capita, or $100 million in total expenditures, for health care would be eliminated from consideration. This step thus would screen out Austria, Portugal, Yugoslavia, Russia, and South Africa. Thus, eighteen countries have the ability to purchase and satisfactorily support dialysis equipment. Dialysis programs were already under way in most of these countries.

The third stage of the screening process will be described next. This stage will identify which countries will provide the best opportunities for the sale of kidney dialysis machines.

MICROLEVEL FACTORS SPECIFIC TO THE PRODUCT. Management may decide that there are two microlevel factors to consider: (1) the number of kidney-related deaths and (2) the growth rate of the treated patient population.

1. *Kidney-related deaths.* The number of deaths due to kidney failure is a good indicator of the number of people in each country who could use dialysis equipment. The company will be interested only in countries with a minimum of one thousand deaths per year due to kidney-related causes. A lower death rate indicates that the country has little need for dialysis equipment or that the market is currently being well served by competitive equipment. The Netherlands, Argentina, Norway, Switzerland, and Sweden would have been eliminated from analysis on these grounds.

2. *Growth rate of the treated patient population.* Analysis of the growth rate of the kidney treatment population demonstrates a growth in potential demand. Newly opened markets with the greatest growth potential are the best targets for a new supplier of dialysis equipment. These are the countries in which the treated patient population continues to grow at a minimum of 40 percent per year. This criterion would have excluded all but the following: Italy, with 75.1 percent; Greece, with 63.4 percent; and Spain, with 60.1 percent. Competition in all three of these markets is substantially less than in the United States, Japan, and the remainder of western Europe.

FINAL SCREENING OF TARGET MARKETS. The screening process identified three target countries. To select one of these countries, an analysis of the competition and political stability is conducted. Discussions with the five major suppliers of dialysis equipment may indicate that Italy already has two local suppliers. Greece is being served by the four major European suppliers. Spain has a strong preference for U.S. equipment and is served by only one supplier. An evaluation of the political environment in each country indicates that Greece has a stable government, Italy's government is stable but is not increasing its medical expenditures, and Spain has a stable democracy.

After evaluating the data, management would most likely select Spain for the initial market entry. The final decision would be based on the following review of each market. Greece would be discounted as a potential market for the following reasons:

1. There is significant competition from other companies.
2. The corporate income tax is higher than that of Spain.
3. Products are subject to a "turnover" tax.
4. The inflation rate is high.

Italy would have been discounted for these reasons:

1. There is extensive foreign as well as local competition.
2. The projected growth for dialysis equipment is slower than it is in Spain.
3. Products are subject to a 14 percent value-added tax.
4. The inflation rate is extremely high.

Spain would be chosen for the following reasons:

1. The political outlook is stable; it appears that the current stable democracy will continue.
2. There is aggressive government support for health care.
3. A very high growth rate is predicted for kidney equipment (23 percent).
4. Competition at this time is minimal.
5. Spain imposes no value-added tax.
6. Government subsidies for home use of dialysis equipment will stimulate demand.
7. The inflation rate is lower than in Italy or Greece.
8. U.S. products and firms have a favorable reputation in the country.

The screening of markets for dialysis equipment is an example of how to analyze the world market and select a few countries for entry. The screening process must be tailored to the specific product or service.

MARKET INDEXES FOR COUNTRY SELECTION

Another technique for analyzing country selection criteria is to develop indexes that combine statistical data and allow the marketer to look at a large number of variables quickly. For example, for the past thirty-four years, Business International (now the Economic Intelligence Unit [EIU]), has published market indicators that allow managers to compare country opportunities quickly. The EIU publishes three indexes: market size, market growth, and market intensity.

Market size is the measure of total potential based on the total population (double-weighted); urban population; private consumption expenditures; steel consumption; cement and electricity production; and ownership of telephones, cars, and televisions. *Market growth* is an indicator of the rate of increase in the size of the market. The growth is determined based on an average of several indicators over five years: population; steel consumption; cement and electricity production; and ownership of passenger cars, trucks, buses, televisions, and telephones. The *market intensity* index measures the richness of a market, or the concentration of purchasing power. The average world intensity is designated as 1.0, and each country is calculated in proportion to the average world intensity. Intensity is calculated for each market by averaging the per capita consumption of steel, the ownership of telephones and televisions, the production of cement and electricity levels, private consumption expenditures (double-weighted), the ownership of passenger cars (double-weighted), and the proportion of urban population (double-weighted).

The EIU market indexes allow a quick visual review of the world's major markets. The United States, much of Europe, and Japan are big markets with low growth and high intensity. China, Brazil, and Indonesia offer higher growth rates and lower levels of market intensity.[9]

ONGOING MARKET SCREENING

The market screening process requires a significant amount of effort. After the target country is selected, there is a tendency to focus on the selected markets and ignore the rejected countries. The world market is continually changing, however, and countries that were rejected last year may provide significant opportunities just one year later. For example, Finland has long favored domestic banks, making it very difficult for foreign banks to operate. The move toward a single European market has caused Finland to become concerned about the limited access it provides to its banking market. So Finland's financial markets are suddenly much more accessible. The events in eastern Europe have also made countries such as Poland more attractive. For example, in Poland, the German Metro has 23 hypermarkets and 18 cash and carry stores, and plans to add 30 more stores by 2003. The French supermarket chains, Casino, Leclerc, Intermarche, and Carrefour are investing heavily followed by Ahold from Holland, Tesco from the U.K., and Jeronimo Martins from Portugal. Experts expect Poland will have 200 hypermarkets by 2005, as consumers move from shopping daily to weekly at the one-stop hypermarket shop.[10]

Political and economic events can also make an attractive market suddenly undesirable. The business costs, deferred spending, delayed shipments, cancelled business arrangements, insurance claims, and rehabilitation costs arising from the September 11, 2001, terrorist attacks changed the attractiveness of investing in U.S. markets.[11] For most companies, it is necessary to have an ongoing monitoring and screening of world markets to spot new emerging opportunities and to identify new potential risks.

GROUPING GLOBAL MARKETS

There are many ways to group international markets. The chapters on political, economic, and cultural environments demonstrate that the interaction among these variables causes each country to be unique, therefore making it difficult to group countries together. Despite these difficulties, it is often necessary still to group countries together so they can be considered as a single market or as a group of similar markets. In this section of the chapter, we explore the rationale for grouping markets and the various ways that marketers can group countries together.

RATIONALE FOR GROUPING MARKETS

The two principles that often drive the need for larger market groupings are critical mass and economies of scale. *Critical mass,* a term also used in physics and military strategy, indicates that a minimum amount of effort is necessary before any impact will be achieved. *Economies of scale* is a term used in production situations; it means that greater levels of production result in lower costs per unit, a situation that obviously increases profitability.

The costs of marketing products within a group of countries are lower for four reasons. First, the potential volume to be sold in a group of countries is sufficient to support a full marketing effort. Second, geographic proximity makes it easy to travel from one country to another, often in two hours or less. Third, the barriers to entry are often the same in countries within an economic grouping, for example, the European Union. Finally, in pursuing countries with similar markets, a company gains leverage with marketing programs. There is some debate over the long-term role of market groupings. Although the European Union has become a strong grouping with a single currency, many economic groupings may become subordinate to the World Trade Organization (WTO). Also, given the broad membership of the WTO and its strong enforcement powers, the regional market groupings will generally need to conform to the rules and practices of the WTO when dealing with any of the 144 WTO countries.

MARKETING ACTIVITIES INFLUENCED BY COUNTRY GROUPINGS

The major activities conducted before entering a new market are market research, product development or modification, distribution, and promotion. Each of these activities can be influenced by economies of scale and critical mass. In this section, we show how each of these four activities relates to country groupings.

MARKET RESEARCH. In the screening process, marketers use many readily available secondary sources of market information. As stated previously, these secondary sources are acceptable for selecting target countries, but they are not sufficient for developing a marketing strategy to penetrate a specific market. Before entering a new market, the company will need to invest in the acquisition of knowledge about the specific aspects of marketing the product in each country. Normally, the following questions must be answered:

1. Who makes the purchase decisions?
2. What decision criteria do consumers use to select the product?
3. How must the product be modified?
4. What are the channels of distribution?
5. What are the competitive price levels?

These and many other questions must be answered before the first product can be shipped. The cost of acquiring this knowledge will often be higher than domestic market research because of the travel distances, cultural differences, and language differences. Given the sizable investment required to obtain this firsthand market knowledge, a company can achieve economies of scale if two or more countries can be included in the same market research study.

PRODUCT DEVELOPMENT AND MODIFICATION. Development of new products and modifications of current products require a large investment. Given the cost, there are obvious economies of scale when these costs are spread over several markets. This is particularly true if the markets are similar and the same modified product can thus be sold in several markets. For example, supplying shampoo to Asia used to be a major headache for Procter and Gamble (P&G) because of the region's trade barriers. Every time P&G wanted to launch a "New and Improved" Pantene or Head and Shoulders, it had to refit its plants in Thailand, Indonesia, and the Philippines. With the ASEAN group of 10 countries that have formed the ASEAN Free Trade Area, P&G has cut product rollout costs by 70 percent.[12]

DISTRIBUTION. The distribution aspect of marketing is particularly important in serving international markets. In the case of exporting, the marketer is faced with all the mechanics of getting the product from the domestic market to the foreign market, which includes documentation, insurance, and financial arrangements. Also, the shipping rates will vary, depending on the size of the shipment. Less than carload- or container-size orders will be calculated at a higher price per pound than full carloads or containers. The mechanics and shipping aspects of exporting are influenced by economies of scale and critical mass. If one plans to ship only a small amount each month to a South American country, it may not be worth the effort and cost. Without a critical mass of business, it does not pay to learn the mechanics and process the paperwork. Also, if you do not have sufficient volumes to ship, transportation costs will escalate.

The distribution systems within foreign markets also are influenced by the number of markets served. Many distributors and dealers in foreign markets handle numerous markets. For example, Caps Gemini, a large software development and distribution firm, has operations in every European country. Given the multicountry nature of many distributors, it can be beneficial to enter a group of similar markets through the same distribution channels.

PROMOTION. A major task of the global company is promotion, which includes advertising and personal selling. Advertising is used as a communication device to give customers a message about a product via television, radio, or print media. In many parts of the world, these three forms of communication cross country boundaries. For example, Belgium has a population of about 10 million that is split between the Flemish-speaking north, with about 60 percent, and the Francophone south, with the remaining 40 percent. Thus, it is important to advertise in both languages: Flemish and French. In addition, both the French and Flemish speakers in Belgium are used to hearing versions of their languages from television and radio stations in neighboring France and the Netherlands.[13] So there may be economies of scale in grouping two or more markets together when entering a new area.

Selling is a very important part of the promotional process, which usually requires a local sales force. Establishing and managing a sales force is a large fixed expense that lends itself to economies of scale. Spreading the cost of a sales office, rent, secretarial staff, sales support, sales managers, and sometimes the salesperson over two or three countries can be cost effective.

GROWTH OF FORMAL MARKET GROUPS

Countries have used the concept of market groupings for centuries. The British Commonwealth preference system linked the markets of the United Kingdom, Canada, Australia, New Zealand, India, and former colonies in Africa, Asia, and the Middle East. The growth of market groups since World War II was encouraged by the success of the European Economic Community, now called the European Union (EU). The EU expanded in 1994 and 1995 to include the former European Free Trade Association (EFTA) members: Sweden, Austria, and Finland.

As we discussed in Chapter 2, a market group is created when two or more countries agree to reduce trade and tariff barriers among themselves, therefore creating a trade unit. Successful trade units or market groups are based on favorable economic, political, or geographic factors. A country will agree to join a trade unit based on one or more of these factors, if the expected benefits of becoming part of the trade unit exceed the disadvantages and loss of sovereignty caused by joining the group.

ECONOMIC FACTORS

The major benefit of every market group is usually economic. Member countries of the group experience reduced or eliminated tariffs and duties that stimulate trade between member countries. They also have common tariff barriers against firms from nonmember countries. Joining together with other countries gives members greater economic security, thus reducing the impact of competition from member countries and increasing the group's strength against foreign competitors. For example, the United States imposed tariffs of 8 to 30 percent on imported steel. Many countries have complained to the World Trade Organization about the American tariffs. The European Union is threatening to retaliate by imposing additional duties on imports from the United States, duties worth about $300 million a year.[14]

Consumers benefit from the reduced trade barriers through lower prices. Economies that are complementary rather than directly competitive tend to make better members of a market group. Most of the problems within the European Union have revolved around agricultural products; member countries are threatened by the importation of products such as eggs, milk, meat, and chicken from other member countries, which would lower prices, but hurt local farmers.

POLITICAL FACTORS

In most countries, the political system and its ideology are dominant forces. The political system usually reflects the aspirations of the nation. It's easy to see, then, why market groups are made up of countries with similar political aspirations. A major impetus for the original formation of the European Community was the need for a unified entity to protect against the political threat of the former U.S.S.R.

GEOGRAPHIC FACTORS

Countries that share common borders tend to function better in a market group for the simple fact that it is easier to move goods back and forth across the borders using the common truck and railroad systems. Also, countries that share boundaries are more likely to have experienced each other's cultures and are likely to have a history of trade.

TYPES OF MARKET GROUPS

There are five different types of market groups: free trade area, customs union, common market, economic union, and political union. When a country enters an agreement with another country or group of countries, the resulting association falls into one of these five categories. The level of integration and cooperation between countries depends on the type of group they form. Figure 5.3 shows which aspects of global integration are included in each type of agreement.

MAJOR MARKET GROUPS

Market agreements that formed the major market groups are shown in Table 5.5. The next sections describe most of these market groups and the agreements that brought them together. The sections are divided according to geographic area.

EUROPE. Europe has four major market groups: the European Economic Area (EEA), the European Union (EU), the European Free Trade Area (EFTA), and the Commonwealth of Independent States (CIS).

Figure 5.3: Forms of International Integration

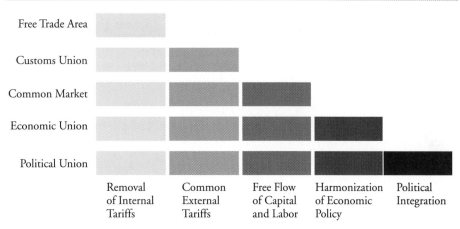

Source: Ruel K. Kahler and Roland L. Kramer, *International Marketing*, 5th ed., p. 343. Reprinted by permission of Southwestern Publishing Company.

The European Economic Area. The European Economic Area (EEA) consists of the fifteen members of the EU, plus the three members of the European Free Trade Association (EFTA): Norway, Iceland, and Liechtenstein. It enables the latter group to participate in most aspects of the single market, with the notable exceptions of agriculture and primary energy. Switzerland, which is also a member of EFTA, rejected participation in the EEA through a referendum in December 1992; however, close economic relations are maintained through various special agreements. Seven new bilateral trade accords between Switzerland and the EU were agreed upon in December 1998 and, after a lengthy ratification process, came into effect during the first half of 2002.

The EU has association agreements in force with Algeria, Morocco, Tunisia, and Israel, as well as an interim agreement with the Palestinian Authority. Association agreements with Egypt and Jordan have been signed but neither agreement has yet been ratified. These political and economic treaties are far-ranging, similar in some respects to association agreements with the Central and East European Countries except that they do not envisage full membership as a future possibility. They could be extended to other Mediterranean countries, and the EU plans to create a Mediterranean free-trade area by 2010. Algeria, Lebanon, the Palestinian Authority, and Syria are also part of the EU's Mediterranean policy initiative, and Libya may join soon.[15]

The European Union. The European Union was established in 1993 as a result of the drive toward a single market by the twelve members of the European Community (EC) in 1992. With the removal of all internal tariffs and common external tariffs and

Table 5.5 Summary of Market Agreements

European Agreements

EUROPEAN ECONOMIC AREA (EEA)

Austria	Italy
Belgium	Liechtenstein
Denmark	Luxembourg
Finland	Netherlands
France	Norway
Germany	Portugal
Greece	Spain
Iceland	Sweden
Ireland	United Kingdom

EUROPEAN UNION (EU) (Customs union)

Austria	Italy
Belgium	Luxembourg
Denmark	Netherlands
Finland	Portugal
France	Spain
Germany	Sweden
Greece	United Kingdom
Ireland	

EUROPEAN FREE TRADE ASSOCIATION (EFTA) (Free trade area)

Austria	Norway
Finland	Sweden
Iceland	Switzerland
Liechtenstein	

EUROPEAN MONETARY UNION (EMU)

Austria	Netherlands	Luxembourg
Belgium	France	Portugal
Finland	Germany	Spain
Ireland	Italy	(Economic Union)

COMMONWEALTH OF INDEPENDENT STATES (CIS)
  (Ad hoc group)

Armenia	Kazakhstan	Russia
Azerbaijan	Kyrgyzstan	Tajikistan
Belarus	Latvia	Turkmenistan
Estonia	Lithuania	Ukraine
Georgia	Moldova	Uzbekistan

African Agreements

EAST AFRICA COOPERATION (Customs union)

Ethiopia	Tanzania
Kenya	Uganda
Sudan	Zambia

FRENCH AFRICAN COMMUNITY

Berlin	Gabon
Burkina Faso	Guinea Bissau
Cameroon	Ivory Coast
Central African Republic	Mali
Chad	Niger
Congo	Senegal
Equatorial Guinea	Togo

ARAB MAGHREB UNION (Common market)

Algeria	Morocco
Libya	Tunisia
Mauritania	

ECONOMIC COMMUNITY OF WEST AFRICAN STATES (ECOWAS)
  (Customs union)

Benin	Liberia
Burkina Faso	Malli
Cape Verde	Mauritania
Gambia	Niger
Ghana	Nigeria
Guinea	Senegal
Guinea-Bissau	Sierra Leone
Ivory Coast	Togo

American Agreements

MERCOSUR (SOUTHERN COMMON MARKET)
  (Common market)

Argentina	Paraguay
Brazil	Uruguay

ANDEAN COMMON MARKET (ANCOM) (Common market)

Bolivia	Peru
Colombia	Venezuela
Ecuador	

(continued)

Table 5.5 Summary of Market Agreements (cont.)

CENTRAL AMERICAN INTEGRATION SYSTEM (Common Market)

Costa Rica	Honduras
El Salvador	Nicaragua
Guatemala	Panama

CARIBBEAN COMMUNITY AND COMMON MARKET (CARICOM)
(Common market)

Antigua and Barbuda	Jamaica
Bahamas	Montserrat
Barbados	Saint Kitts-Nevis
Belize	Saint Lucia
Dominica	Saint Vincent and the Grenadines
Grenada	Suriname
Guyana	Trinidad and Tobago
Haiti	

U.S.-CANADA FREE TRADE AGREEMENT (Free trade area)

Canada	United States

NORTH AMERICAN FREE TRADE AGREEMENT (NAFTA)
(Free trade area)

Canada	United States
Mexico	

Asian Agreements

ARAB COMMON MARKET (ACM) (Common market)

Egypt	Syria
Iraq	Kuwait
Jordan	

ECONOMIC COOPERATION ORGANIZATION (ECO)
(Ad hoc arrangement)

Afghanistan	Pakistan
Azerbaijan	Tajikistan
Iran	Turkey
Kazakhstan	Turkmenistan
Kyrgyzstan	Uzbekistan

ASSOCIATION OF SOUTH EAST ASIAN NATIONS (ASEAN)
(Free Trade Area)

Brunei	Myanmar
Cambodia	Singapore
Indonesia	Philippines
Laos	Thailand
Malaysia	Vietnam

ASIA PACIFIC ECONOMIC COOPERATIVE (APEC)

Australia	New Zealand
Brunei	Papua New Guinea
Canada	Peru
Chile	Philippines
China	Russia
Hong Kong	Singapore
Indonesia	South KoreanTaiwan
Japan	Thailand
Korea	United States
Malaysia	Vietnam
Mexico	

Source: Data from *1997 World Bank Atlas.* Adapted with permission from The World Bank.

the free flow of goods, capital, and people, the EU is a true common market. The members of the EU have agreed to the Maastricht Treaty, which established the European Monetary Union (EMU) in 1999, although the United Kingdom, Denmark, and Sweden did not join the EMU. The EMU united the currencies of the EMU members, with the European Central Bank dictating economic policy to the member country banks. The outlook for EMU is still mixed. No date has been set for the United Kingdom, Denmark, or Sweden to join the EMU. There are also twelve additional countries that have applied to the EU, with Hungary and Poland hoping to become members in 2004. All EU members can apply for EMU membership.[16]

The EU was referred to as the European Community until 1993 and was called the European Common Market when it was established in 1958. The EU has grown from the original six countries to fifteen countries, increasing its role over time through the establishment of the European Parliament, the Court of Justice, and the European Currency Unit (ECU).

The relaunch of the EU and the creation of the single European market, often referred to as "1992," were initiated by Lord Cockfield, the British commissioner of the EU and author of the internal market white paper published on June 14, 1985.[17] The white paper explained the logic for a single market and divided the obstacles to its formation into three areas: physical barriers at frontiers, technical barriers within different countries, and barriers designed to protect fiscal regimes. It took two years for the white paper to be approved by EU members and become the Single European Act. There was a compelling logic for the single market. Although bigger than the United States and Japan in population, Europe was underperforming its two largest competitors on almost every economic measure.

The EU commissioned several studies to measure the potential impact of a single market. Paolo Cecchini, a senior official of the EU, coordinated thirty different studies on the expected economic outcome of the 1992 initiative.[18] This report, known as the Cecchini report, documented the costs of continuing in a divided market and the benefits of building an integrated one.[19] The report summarized the economic gains if the EU implemented the single market as follows:

- A rejuvenation of the EU economy, adding 4.5 percent to GDP
- A reduction in inflation, with a fall in consumer prices of 6.1 percent
- A reduction in the cost of public programs through open bidding
- The creation of 1.8 million new jobs in the EU, reducing unemployment[20]

To illustrate the potential impact of The Europe 1992 Initiative, consider the pharmaceutical industry. The drug industry has a separate regulatory body, applying its own criteria for approving medicines, and mutual approval of licenses is nonexistent. Each country has a different system for pricing and paying for drugs. Also, rules regarding drug advertising vary from country to country. Within the spirit of the single market, the European Union is moving on several fronts to harmonize the EU drug industry. The European Medicines Agency opened its offices in 1996 and began reviewing drugs for use throughout the EU, thereby eliminating the need for pharmaceutical manufacturers to get drugs approved individually in all fifteen EU countries. The EU is expected to add several new members over the next ten years. The thirteen countries that have applied for membership are Estonia, Latvia, Lithuania, Poland, the Czech Republic, Slovakia, Hungary, Slovenia, Romania, Bulgaria, Malta, Cyprus, and Turkey.[21]

The European Free Trade Association. Countries that did not join the EU created the European Free Trade Association in 1959. The EFTA consisted of Austria, Finland, Iceland, Liechtenstein, Norway, Sweden, and Switzerland and operated as a free trade area. As the EU single market became a reality in 1992, the EFTA countries of Sweden, Austria, and Finland applied and were admitted as EU members. Switzerland voted not to be part of the EEA. Eventually, the EFTA will disappear as an independent market group.

The Commonwealth of Independent States. The collapse of the Berlin Wall in 1989, the breakup of the fifteen republics of the Soviet Union (e.g., Estonia, Latvia, Lithuania), and the opening of eastern Europe to free elections in 1990 resulted in the creation of the Commonwealth of Independent States. The CIS is really a very loose collection of nations that replaces the Council for Mutual Economic Assistance (COMECON). COMECON was formed in 1949 as a political union of eight eastern European communist countries, later joined by Cuba and Vietnam. Until 1990, these ten countries were tightly controlled by the Soviet Union, and COMECON operated as an enforced political group. COMECON countries depended on the Soviet Union as a major customer. In exchange, the Soviet Union provided oil and defenses against NATO forces.

The future of CIS as a single market group is doubtful. The eastern European countries of Poland, Hungary, and the Czech Republic have agreed to cooperate with the EU on trade, economic, industrial, and scientific issues; tourism; transport; communications; and environmental pollution. Given the economic and political difficulties in Russia, the former republics are more likely to cooperate with the western European groups than with Russia.

With 150 million citizens hungry for consumer goods, Russia is the largest single market in the CIS. Although the risks are high, the potential is great. The financial crisis and devaluation of the ruble in 1998 caused the price of imports to quadruple. Nestlé, a Swiss food company and one of the top foreign investors in Russia, opened a new production line in its factory in Rossiya. Andreas Schlaepfer, head of Nestlé in Russia, said, "Unlike [its] competitors, who build sweets factories from scratch, Nestlé took over an existing plant making existing Russian brands. Cost cutting is easier as we use less expensive Russian sugar and less expensive cocoa." Nestlé was expected to make $500 million in Russia in 1999.[22] The collapse of Russian currency has given local producers like Svoboda, a Moscow-based shampoo company, a big boost. Svoboda has taken share from Procter & Gamble, Unilever, and Colgate.[23]

NORTH AMERICA. *The North Atlantic Treaty Organization.* Although primarily a political organization, the North Atlantic Treaty Organization (NATO) has taken on more of an economic role with the demise of the Soviet military power. NATO was originally established to protect western Europe from the Soviet Union. NATO admitted the former Soviet bloc countries of Poland, Hungary, and the Czech Republic in 1998.[24] The Russian government opposes the expansion of NATO but accepted the creation of the NATO-Russian Consultative Council in 1997.[25] This organization allowed Russia to participate in discussions of NATO issues such as terrorism, crime, nuclear proliferation, and regional defense but did not allow it to vote or to exercise veto power. China is also concerned about the growth of NATO. China had not opposed NATO in the past because it helped enforce the U.S.-Japanese Security Agreement, which limits Japanese military investments. In May 2002, Russia joined the nineteen member countries of NATO to establish the NATO-Russia Council, which replaced the NATO-Russian Consultative Council. Work under the NATO-Russia Council focuses on several key areas, which include the struggle against terrorism, crisis management, nonproliferation of nuclear weapons, arms control and confidence-building measures, theater missile defense, search and rescue at sea, military-to-military cooperation and civil emergencies.[26]

AFRICA. Africa has seven major market agreements in force: the Afro-Malagasy Economic Union, the East Africa Customs Union, the Maghreb Economic Community, the Casablanca Group, the Economic Community of West African States, the West African Economic Community, and the French African Community. The success of the EU has prompted African countries to form these groups. The groups have had little success in promoting trade and economic progress, however, because most African nations are small and have limited economic infrastructure for producing goods.

The French African Community (CFA) was established in 1985 as a monetary union. The member countries have fixed their currencies to the French franc. After the French franc was replaced in January 2002 with the euro, the Cfa franc was pegged to the euro. Each euro is valued at 650 Cfa francs. The linking of many African currencies to the euro via the Cfa franc helps facilitate trade with Europe because there is little or no currency risk.[27]

The European disengagement from Africa is nearly complete, with only France continuing to provide significant military and financial aid. The United States has no current serious military or geostrategic interest in Africa. There has been a trend toward democratic elections throughout Africa. Democracy, along with the rebirth of South Africa, should halt the decline of living standards throughout Africa.[28] South Africa reached a free trade agreement with the EU in March 1999. This agreement will allow approximately $20 billion of free trade between South Africa and the EU members.[29]

LATIN AMERICA. There are five major market agreements in Latin America: MERCOSUR, the Andean Common Market, the Central American Common Market, the Caribbean Community and Common Market, and the Latin American Integration Association. Latin America is facing several problems that make it difficult to achieve significant economic integration and cooperation among the countries before 2005. Political turmoil, the low level of economic activity, and extreme differences in economic development from country to country are stumbling blocks to the success of regional market agreements.

MERCOSUR, the Southern Common Market, was formed in 1991 and inaugurated in 1995 with the following member states: Argentina, Brazil, Paraguay, and Uruguay, with Chile and Bolivia joining later as associate members. MERCOSUR's objective is to strengthen the economies of member countries by making them more efficient, unifying their markets to create scale economies, advancing more efficient use of resources, and improving macroeconomic policy coordination. It is the fourth largest economic bloc in the world, with a GNP of more than $1 trillion and a population of over 250 million. Eighty percent of the major companies in Latin America have operations in member countries. Trade among MERCOSUR members grew almost 300 percent between 1991 and 1999, totaling $18 billion at the end of 2000. In 2001, trade among MERCOSUR members, which makes up 18 percent of the group's total exports, fell 10 percent. MERCOSUR also coordinates the foreign policy of its members and benefits from the bloc's collective action in international negotiations.[30] Latin American and EU leaders held a two-day summit in June 1999 to explore the possibility of a Latin America–Europe free trade zone.[31]

The Andean Community is a subregional organization consisting of Bolivia, Colombia, Ecuador, Peru, and Venezuela and the bodies and institutions comprising the Andean Integration System (AIS). The five Andean countries together have over 113 million inhabitants living in an area of 4,700,000 square kilometers, with a combined 2000 GDP of $270 billion. The Andean Community has an agreement to enforce a four-tier common external tariff by December 31, 2003; to consolidate and sharpen the free trade area; to adopt a common agricultural policy; to strengthen the common foreign policy; and to continue improvements on macroeconomic policy harmonization.[32]

The Caribbean Community and Common Market (CARICOM) group of fourteen Caribbean island nations represents 13 million people. CARICOM has been trying to create a common market for twelve years, but the group has run into problems because it is made up of small, fragile economies that depend on commodity exports and tourism, industries that are threatened by international deregulation. Through CARICOM, trade barriers have been dismantled among member countries and a customs union has been created with common tariffs from nonmember countries. Differing levels of development present a challenge to the full integration of CARICOM regional economies. Special arrangements have been made to help the least developed countries, and the regional and economic sectors that are considered vulnerable.[33]

A conference of the leaders of the thirty-four Western Hemisphere countries (except Cuba) met in 1994. The group agreed to negotiate a Free Trade Area of the Americas (FTAA) by 2005. In 2001, the members of NAFTA, MERCOSUR, the Andean group, and the Caribbean Community and Common Market met to speed up the negotiations. The FTAA will support increased trade within the Western Hemisphere.[34]

NORTH AMERICA. The U.S.-Canada Free Trade Agreement, which became effective in 1989, removes barriers to trade and investment for most agricultural, industrial, and service businesses. The agreement eliminates tariffs for products manufactured in either country and then exported to the other. If less than 50 percent of the manufacturing cost takes place in the United States or Canada, then the goods are subject to the normal tariff. Because two-thirds of Canada's imports from the United States were already duty free, the agreement has not had much economic significance.

The North American Free Trade Agreement (NAFTA) was signed by the heads of state of Canada, Mexico, and the United States in October 1992 and was passed by the Canadian, Mexican, and U.S. governments in late 1993. NAFTA provides for the gradual ending of tariffs and trade barriers: over ten years for most goods and services and over fifteen years for some agricultural products. NAFTA, with a free trade area of 410 million people and a $10.7 trillion output,[35] has reduced trade barriers and increased trade among the three NAFTA countries 209 percent, from $297 billion in 1993 to $622 billion in 2001.[36]

MIDDLE EAST. There are two market agreements in the Middle East: the Arab Common Market and the Economic Cooperation Organization. The Arab Common

Market was formed in 1964 by Egypt, Iraq, Kuwait, Jordan, and Syria. Progress has been achieved toward the development of free trade and the elimination of tariffs among member countries. Its membership now includes Libya, Mauritania, Palestine, Somalia, Sudan, the United Arab Emirates, and Yemen.[37] The Arab Common Market is run by the Arab Economic Council, which is planning to increase pan-Arab commerce from 8 percent to 20 percent in the next five years.[38] Equalization of external tariffs is expected in the future. The Economic Cooperation Organization (ECO) was originally established by Pakistan, Iran, and Turkey to expand mutual trade and business ventures. In late 1992, the countries of Afghanistan, Azerbaijan, Kyrgyzstan, Turkmenistan, Uzbekistan, Kazakhstan, and Tajikistan joined the ECO. Linking primarily Islamic countries, the ECO is sizable enough, with 300 million people, to support economic initiatives. At meetings held in 1999, the ECO members agreed to cooperate on customs documentation, reducing the narcotics and arms trade, and improving trade in the region.[39]

ASIA. The Association of South East Asian Nations (ASEAN) includes Brunei, Cambodia, Indonesia, Laos, Malaysia, Myanmar (formerly Burma), Singapore, the Philippines, Thailand, and Vietnam. All ASEAN countries, with the exception of Singapore, have an abundance of labor and developing economies. Seeking closer economic integration and cooperation among themselves, ASEAN members began cutting intra-ASEAN tariffs in 1993. In 2002, the ASEAN countries of Indonesia, Malaysia, the Philippines, Singapore, Thailand, and Brunei established the ASEAN Free Trade Area (AFTA), which has agreed to limit tariffs on 93 percent of goods to 5 percent or less. ASEAN is also conducting talks with China about its entry into the trade group.[40] In a U.S.-ASEAN Business Council meeting held in June 1999, United Parcel Service (UPS) announced a commitment of $500 million in Asia, with a major logistics center in Singapore to support the ASEAN markets and the rest of Asia.[41] With its present membership of ten countries, ASEAN is not wealthy but has a population of 500 million, more than Europe or North America. Japan has suggested a summit with its ASEAN neighbors, but because of either Southeast Asians' long-standing suspicions of Japan or ASEAN's fear of antagonizing China, ASEAN's relationship with Japan has remained neutral.[42]

The Asia Pacific Economic Cooperation (APEC) initiative includes twenty-one members: seven nations from ASEAN and the United States, Australia, Canada, New Zealand, Japan, Papua New Guinea, Taiwan, Peru, Russia, Korea, Chile, Mexico, China, and Hong Kong. APEC was started by the United States and Australia to promote the multilateral interests of the member countries. The APEC trade group has been supported by former U.S. president Bill Clinton as his part of his vision of the "new Pacific community."

The future of country groupings in Asia is unclear. ASEAN is a large group in terms of population, but it is not an economic power. APEC is a weak collection of countries that want to promote trade, but it is not a formal union; no agreements have been formalized. APEC depends on the relationship between East Asia and the United States. As the Japanese economy recovers, China absorbs Hong Kong and Macau, the China-Taiwan issue is resolved, and the Korean tension is settled, Asia will face uncertainty. No matter what happens, China will undoubtedly be the focal point of the economic development of Asia.[43]

In an increasingly global trade environment, with 144 members in the WTO, there is considerable discussion of the role of the eighty regional trade groups that grant preferential access to each other's markets. With all of the WTO members, except Japan and South Korea, belonging to one or more regional trade groups, there is concern about the real value of trade groups. The preferential treatment of the members of trade groups creates trade diversion and ignores the principle of comparative advantage discussed in Chapter 2. Jagdish Bhagwati, an economics professor at Columbia University, argues that the regional trade groups act as stumbling blocks to rather than as building blocks for freeing world trade.[44]

Asia-Pacific Economic Co-Operation (APEC) was founded in 1989 initially as an informal dialog group, in response to the growing interdependence among Asia-Pacific economies. APEC has since become a regional force for promoting trade and economic cooperation in the region. The members of APEC include Australia, Brunei, Canada, Chile, China, Hong Kong, Indonesia, Japan, the Republic of Korea, Malaysia, New Zealand, Papua New Guinea, Peru, the Philippines, Russia, Singapore, Taiwan, Thailand, the United States, and Vietnam.[45]

GLOBAL BUYERS

All buyers go through a similar process for selecting a product or service for purchase. Although the process will be similar from country to country, the final purchase decisions will vary because of the differences in the social, economic, and cultural systems. Who actually makes the decision to buy, what they buy, why they buy, how they buy, when they buy, and where they buy are the factors that differentiate international buyers. To assume that buyers in different countries use the same buying processes and the same selection criteria can be disastrous. When launching disposable diapers worldwide, Procter & Gamble established a global marketing team in Cincinnati, believing that the diaper needs of babies should be the same around the globe. It later found out that although mothers in most countries are concerned about keeping their babies' bottoms dry, Japanese mothers had different needs. In Japan, babies are changed so frequently that thick, absorbent diapers were not necessary and could be replaced by thin diapers that take up less space in the small Japanese home.[46]

In every marketing situation, it is important to understand the potential buyers and the process they use to select one product over another. Most elements of a marketing program are designed to influence the buyer to choose one product over competitors' products. Figure 5.4 summarizes a process that can be used to analyze the global buyer.

Figure 5.4: Global Buyer Analysis Process

In the case of each type of buyer—consumer, business, and government—the marketer must be able to identify who the buyers are, the size of the potential market, and how they make a purchase decision. For example, who usually makes the decision to buy an automobile in Italy, the husband or the wife? When a Japanese company purchases a computer system, what type of people are involved? Is price more important than the reputation of the computer manufacturer? When a young man in Germany decides to open a savings account, what information sources does he use to select a bank? Having established a framework for understanding global buyers, we now examine each type of buyer—consumers, businesses, and governments—in the final sections of this chapter.

THE CONSUMER MARKET

Consumers around the world have many similar needs. All people must eat, drink, and be sheltered from the elements. Once these basic needs are met, consumers will seek to improve their standard of living with a more comfortable environment, more leisure time, and an increased social status. Although basic needs and the desire for an improved standard of living are universal throughout the world, people's ability to achieve these objectives is not universal. The economic, political, and social structure of countries affects the ability of consumers to fulfill their needs and the methods they use to achieve these goals. To understand a consumer market, we must examine the following four aspects of consumer behavior:

1. The ability of people to buy
2. Consumer needs
3. Buying motives
4. The buying process

THE ABILITY OF PEOPLE TO BUY

To purchase a product, a consumer must have the ability to buy. The medium of exchange in most societies is currency. The ability to buy a product is affected by the amount of wealth a country possesses and the distribution of its wealth. A country accumulates wealth by the sale of goods to other countries (exports) and the sale of goods within the country. These inflows of money are offset by the outflows of money to pay for necessary imports.

An important indicator of total consumer potential is gross national product (GNP) because it indicates the value of the production of goods and services in a country, which is an indicator of market size. The gross national income (GNI) is the GNP plus the net primary income from nonresident sources. The GNI per capita shows the value of production per consumer, which is a crude indicator of potential per consumer. GNI and GNI per capita can vary significantly from country to country. The total wealth in a country is an important indicator of market potential. With a GNI per capita of $35,620 in Japan and $27,146 in Sweden, it is expected the demand for automobiles will be greater in those countries than in Niger, with a GNI per capita of $180, or in India, with a GNI per capita of $450.[47]

The accumulated income (GNP) is divided among the members of a society. The government has a major influence on the distribution of wealth. A large government will take a large share of the wealth through taxes or ownership of industries. The government also sets policies and laws to regulate the distribution of wealth. For example, a graduated income tax, with a 60 to 90 percent tax on high levels of income and no tax on low levels of income, will help to distribute income evenly. The revenue that remains in the private sector will be distributed among workers, managers, and owners of industries. Low wages and unemployment tend to increase the size of the lower-income class. Concentration of business ownership in a few families will decrease the size of the upper class. Income distribution across the population of a country can distort the market potential in that country. For example, if a few people have all the wealth and almost all the remainder are poor, few people are left in the middle. Countries such as Sierra Leone, Guatemala, Guinea-Bissau, Paraguay, and Panama have the largest disparity between the income held by the top 20 percent and the bottom 20 percent of the population. The countries of Slovakia, the Czech Republic, Austria, Norway, and Finland have the lowest inequity between the top 20 percent and bottom 20 percent of the population.[48]

CONSUMER NEEDS

Money is spent to fulfill basic human needs. Abraham Maslow developed one framework to describe these basic human needs. Maslow's hierarchy of needs explains that humans tend to satisfy lower-level needs, such as the physiological needs for food, clothing, and shelter, before attempting to satisfy higher-level needs, such as safety, belongingness, or esteem. In Figure 5.5, the consumption patterns within different

Figure 5.5: Consumer Expenditure Patterns of Selected Countries (Percentage of Total Spending)

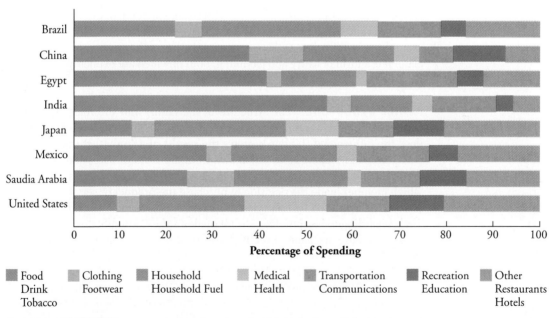

Source: Euromonitor Plc, 2002.

countries illustrate Maslow's theory. The figure shows that the structure of consumption for each country varies depending on the income per capita. A developing country, such as China, spends over 50 percent on food, whereas developed countries, such as the United States, spend less than 20 percent on food. Although it is possible to generalize about the order of consumer purchases based on Maslow's hierarchy of needs, the patterns may vary from one country to another.

BUYING MOTIVES

The ability to buy is influenced by various economic elements that are much easier to identify and quantify than elements in the motivation to buy. As mentioned earlier, all consumers have some similarities as members of the human race. However, buyer behavior is not uniform among all humans. Buyer behavior is learned, primarily from the culture. As a marketer moves from culture to culture (within and between countries), he or she will see that buyer behavior differs.

As we discussed in Chapter 3, culture refers to widely shared norms or patterns of behavior within a large group of people. These norms can directly affect product usage. For example, most mothers in Brazil feel that only they can properly prepare foods for their babies, and therefore they are reluctant to buy processed foods. This cultural norm in Brazil caused difficulty for Gerber, despite the fact that its products were selling well in other Latin American countries.[49]

Social class is a grouping of consumers based on income, education, and occupation. Consumers in the same social class tend to have similar purchase patterns. The perceived class structure and the distribution of income affects purchase behavior. Culture not only influences consumer behavior, it also affects the conduct of businesses. Harris and Moran suggest that cross-cultural training is very important for managers to be successful in dealing with businesspeople of different cultures.[50]

Consumers belong to different groups that also influence purchase behavior. For example, it is difficult to sell insurance in Muslim countries because religious leaders claim it is a form of usury and gambling, both of which are explicitly prohibited in the Koran.

FAMILY STRUCTURE. The structure of the family and the roles assigned to each family member play an important part in determining who makes a decision and who does the influencing. Table 5.6 shows the results of a study that examined and compared decision-making roles in families from the United States and Venezuela. Nine products and services were picked, and each family surveyed was asked to identify which member made the decision to purchase the product or service. The overriding contrast between the two samples involved the role of the husband. More joint decisions regarding major purchases were made in the United States than in Venezuela. In all purchase decisions except groceries and savings, the Venezuelan husband made more decisions than did the U.S. husband. Families in the United States make more joint decisions than do Venezuelan families.

Global marketers must be aware that variations in family purchasing roles may exist in foreign markets because of social and cultural differences. Marketing strategy may change based on the respective role of family members. For example, a U.S. manufacturer of appliances or furniture may find it advisable to incorporate the husband into a Venezuelan marketing strategy to a larger extent than in the United States.

Table 5.6 Mean Number of Purchase Decisions by Product Type

Product/Service	United States	Venezuela	Product/Service	United States	Venezuela
Groceries			Vacations		
Husband	.23	.23	Husband	1.00	1.51
Joint	.60	.69	Joint	3.68	3.18
Wife	3.20	3.08	Wife	.40	.41
Furniture			Savings		
Husband	.41	1.16	Husband	1.00	1.07
Joint	3.41	2.71	Joint	1.61	1.60
Wife	2.23	2.16	Wife	.44	.34
Major appliances			Housing		
Husband	.98	1.97	Husband	.34	.87
Joint	3.21	2.10	Joint	2.47	1.82
Wife	.85	.93	Wife	.34	.39
Life Insurance			Doctor		
Husband	2.65	3.38	Husband	.03	.10
Joint	1.23	.55	Joint	.35	.42
Wife	.15	.05	Wife	.62	.49
Automobiles					
Husband	2.59	4.16			
Joint	3.06	1.42			
Wife	.41	.40			

Source: Robert T. Green and Isabella Cunningham, "Family Purchasing Roles in Two Countries," *Journal of International Business Studies,* Spring–Summer 1980, p. 95. Reprinted by permission.

Family structure, particularly the number of two-parent families versus single-parent families, will affect the level of household income. Also, families with two working parents will have a higher level of pooled income than single-parent or one-working-parent families. The pooling of incomes will positively influence the demand for consumer durables and luxury goods.

RELIGION. As we noted in Chapter 3, religion affects behavior patterns by establishing moral codes and taboos. What, when, and how consumers buy can sometimes be a function of their religion. Traditional Catholics do not eat meat on Fridays during Lent, and Orthodox Jews are forbidden ever to eat pork. The Christian Sabbath is on Sunday, the Jewish Sabbath is on Saturday, and the Muslim Sabbath is on Friday. Religion influences the attitudes and beliefs of people with regard to interests, work, leisure, family size, family relationships, and so on. Many of these religious influences affect the type of products people purchase, why they buy them, and even which newspapers they read. For example, in some countries, if too much attention is given to the body in advertisements, the product in the advertisements may be rejected as immoral.

EDUCATIONAL SYSTEMS. Formal education involves public or private institutions where learning takes place in a structured environment. The literacy rate is the standard measurement used to assess the extent and success of educational systems, and it normally varies directly with economic development. In Europe and Japan, the literacy rate exceeds 90 percent (see Table 3.2), whereas in some developing countries, it is below 50 percent. A low level of literacy affects marketers in two ways: first, it reduces the market for products that require reading, such as books and magazines; second, it reduces the effectiveness of advertising.

Education includes the process of transmitting skills, ideas, attitudes, and knowledge. In effect, the educational process transmits the existing culture and traditions to the next generation. The goals of an educational system will often include broader political goals, such as India's programs to improve agriculture and reduce the birthrate.

THE BUYING PROCESS

It is difficult to generalize about consumer behavior in each country of the world and for every product category because consumption patterns vary considerably. The differences are caused by consumers' ability to buy and their motivation to buy. For example, consumption patterns for alcohol vary tremendously from country to country. As shown in Figure 5.6, the average consumption for alcohol in France is 70 liters per person, versus 20 liters in South Korea or 72 liters in the United States.

The high consumption of wine in Europe versus the United States is offset by the high U.S. consumption of soft drinks. The average American annual soft drink consumption is 861 8-oz. servings. For the average French consumer, it is 160 servings, and for the average German consumer, it is 358.[51]

Patterns of consumption also vary with services. For example, about 15 percent of the world's countries have 95 percent of all telephones. Studies by the Brookings Institution, the University of Texas, Stanford University, the University of Cairo, and the Massachusetts Institute of Technology indicate that telephones have significant economic benefits to the consumer in excess of the cost and contribute to a rise in per capita income. For example, the World Bank reported that when Sri Lankan farmers received telephones, prices of produce increased from 55 percent of Colombian prices to 85 percent, a result of buyers having access to better information.[52] The United Nations has established a fund to speed up the adoption of telephones around the world.

BUSINESS MARKETS

Business buyers around the world are much more predictable than consumers because they are more influenced by the economic considerations of cost and less by social or cultural factors. For example, a purchasing agent in Japan who is buying specialty steel for his or her company will attempt to get the best possible product at the lowest cost, which is similar to how a purchasing agent in the United States or Germany would act. The criteria that business buyers use will be much the

Figure 5.6: Alcohol Consumption for Selected Countries (in Litres per Person, 1998)

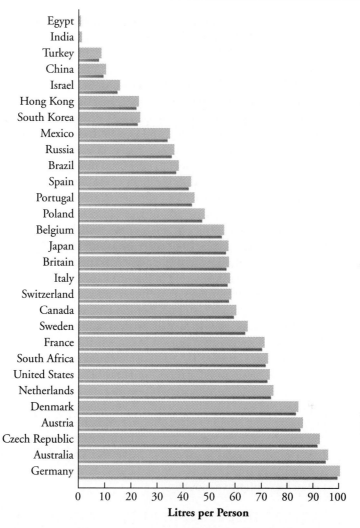

Source: Economist, December 16, 1999. Copyright © 1999 The Economist Newspaper Group, Inc. Reprinted with permission. Further reproduction prohibited. www.economist.com.

same around the world. However, the buying process used by business buyers and the negotiation process are influenced by local culture and vary from country to country. The terms *business buyer* and *industrial buyer* are used interchangeably in this chapter, although business buyers normally include all types of businesses, whereas industrial buyers are limited to manufacturing businesses.

BUYING MOTIVES

Industrial buying is less affected by cultural factors such as social roles, religion, and language than is consumer buying. Regardless of their background, purchasing agents will be primarily influenced by the use of the product, its cost, and the terms of delivery. Industrial products, such as raw materials or machinery, are sold to businesses for use in a manufacturing process to produce other goods. Because the objective of the manufacturer is to maximize profit, the critical buying criterion will focus on the performance of the product purchased versus its cost. This buying criterion is called the *cost-performance criterion*, and it is used along with other buying criteria such as service, dependability, and knowledge of the selling company.

Because the cost-performance criterion is critical, the economic situation in the purchasing country will affect the decision process. Cost-performance is a function of the local cost of labor and the scale of operation. As you can see in Figure 5.7, which lists manufacturing labor cost averages in selected countries, wage levels vary from country to country. Thus, selling an industrial robot that replaces three workers in the manufacturing of a certain product will be more easily justified in Japan or Germany, where average labor costs are 10–20 percent more than in the United States, than it will be in Italy, where labor cost is 25 percent less than in the United States.

Labor costs play a key role in the level and type of manufacturing. Countries with a surplus of labor normally have lower labor costs because supply exceeds demand. These lower pay rates result in a certain type of manufacturing that is labor-intensive. Therefore, these countries will be less apt to purchase sophisticated automated machinery because the same job can be done with cheaper labor. China's main objective, for example, is to import technology that optimizes its vast population. Companies wishing to export to labor-intensive countries must be aware that labor-saving measures may not be appreciated or readily applied. On the other hand, highly developed countries with a high labor rate are prime targets for automated manufacturing equipment. Countries with high labor rates have begun to see an emergence of service industries, which require human labor instead of machines. Labor in these areas is expensive because a great deal of expertise is needed. Thus, a country normally moves from labor-intensive to capital-intensive and then to technology-intensive industry.

FACTORS INFLUENCING GLOBAL PURCHASING

In many situations, a buyer will have the choice of purchasing a domestic product and/or service or a foreign product and/or service. The buyer's perceptions of product quality may be influenced by feelings of national loyalty, the product's country of origin, and the firm's competence in conducting global transactions. Although it is assumed that industrial buyers will be completely rational and will purchase products based on concrete decision criteria such as price, quality, and performance, research has shown that the country of origin influences professional purchases, even when all other variables are held constant.[53]

The global company must recognize country-of-origin images and use this information when developing a marketing strategy. Highly nationalistic countries tend to encourage economic self-sufficiency even at the expense of economic efficiency, which will have a negative effect on the global company. A study of purchasing behavior by Swedish companies found that buyers preferred to deal with domestic

Figure 5.7: Labor Costs per Worker-Hour for Selected Countries

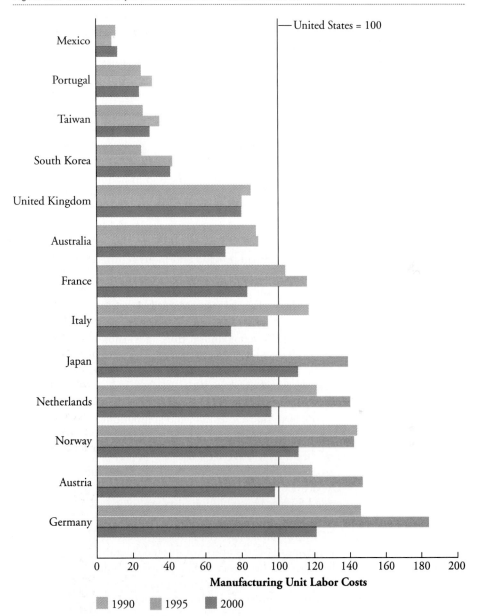

Source: U.S. Bureau of Labor Statistics, News Release USDL 01-311, September 25, 2001.

suppliers but would use foreign suppliers when necessary.[54] The study also found that the purchasing firm's competence for global business is positively related to the use of global suppliers. International purchasers generally have broad market knowledge, an ability to handle foreign cultural patterns, and a knowledge of international trade techniques.[55] Given the results of this analysis, the global company should pay close attention to the level of nationalism in a country, country-of-origin images, and the competence level of the purchasing function when dealing with global suppliers.

GOVERNMENT MARKETS

Numerous international business transactions involve governments. For example, governments handle 80 percent of all international trade of agricultural products. The U.S. government buys more goods and services than any other government, business, industry, or organization in the world.[56] Selling to governments can be both time consuming and frustrating. Governments are large purchasers, however, and selling to them can provide enormous returns.

The size of government purchases depends on the economic or political orientation of the country. In highly developed, free-market countries, the government has less of a role than in state-controlled markets, where most buying is under direct control of the state. Less developed countries lack the economic infrastructure to facilitate private companies; thus, governments play a major role in overseeing the purchase of foreign products. The amount of government purchases is also a function of state-owned operations. For example, in the United States, the only quasi-government-owned operation is the postal system, whereas in India, the government owns not only the postal system, but also the telecommunications, electric, gas, oil, coal, railway, airline, and shipbuilding industries.

THE BUYING PROCESS

Governmental buying processes tend to be highly bureaucratic. To sell to the U.S. Department of Defense, a firm has to get on a bidding list for each branch of the armed forces. These bidding lists are issued annually; thus, a firm that cannot get on the list must wait a full year to try again.

Governments make it harder for a foreign firm to sell to them; many place their own domestic firms ahead of foreign operations. Also, negotiating with foreign governments can be a very formal process. Understanding cultural differences is essential to avoid overstepping boundaries. Government procurement processes vary from country to country. The following section describes purchasing processes in Belgium.

MARKETING TO THE BELGIAN GOVERNMENT.[57] In Belgium, 90 percent of all public contracts are awarded to the lowest bidder. The remaining 10 percent are granted through "invitation to tender," with factors other than price coming into play. These other factors may include the company's financial viability, technical competence, and postsale service. Central government supplies, excluding data processing and telecommunications, must be bought through the Central Supplies Office.

Regional, local, and quasi-governmental bodies, such as Sabena Airlines, purchase supplies independently. Here are several recommendations to companies that wish to sell to the Belgian government:

- Manufacture in Belgium. Preference is given to a local supplier, other things being equal.
- Develop a European image. A strong EU image has favored companies such as Siemens and Philips.
- Use the appropriate language. Although both Flemish and French are official languages, ask which is preferred in the department that is accepting the bid.
- Emphasize the recruitment of labor following the winning of a contract. Companies are favored if they will employ Belgian people.
- When new technology is involved, get in at the beginning. It is often difficult and expensive for the government to change to a different technology later.
- Whenever possible, use local contractors. The Belgian government likes a bidder to use as many local contractors as possible.

Obviously, bidding for Belgian government work is particularly difficult for suppliers with no local participation of subcontractors or manufacturing in Belgium or the EU. However, every government market has some limitations.

ECONOMIC AND POLITICAL NEEDS OF GOVERNMENTS

Firms involved in selling to foreign governments must have not only an understanding of the political and economic structures, but also an ability to evaluate a country's industrial trends vis-à-vis the national system. Factors to be considered are the government's responsibility to industry, government priorities, national defense, high-tech industrial efficiency, and financial self-sufficiency. The level of economic development involves not only the GNP but the state of production. China, for example, is pushing for modernization but does not want production techniques at the expense of its large labor pool. The desire to reduce unemployment is of major interest to most countries. Governments are also confronted with balance of payments problems. Trade deficits—importing more than exporting—will affect the position of a country's currency with respect to foreign currencies. The more the government imports, the more expensive the products become because the government must use more foreign exchange.

Governments tend to protect their domestic industry to shrink high unemployment and GNP deficits. Whether products are for consumer, industrial, or government use, protection in the form of tariffs, subsidiaries, and quotas is levied if domestic industries are threatened. Because governments want to protect their domestic companies, they will avoid those products and services on which restrictions are imposed.

Protection of domestic products and services extends beyond that imposed by foreign governments. The threat of reducing national security has prompted governments to institute restrictions on various domestic products. The transfer of technology such as nuclear plants, computers, telecommunications, and military weapons is usually restricted so that these critical technologies do not get into the wrong hands.

CONCLUSIONS

The world marketplace is large and complex. A global company needs to evaluate the entire world market systematically and regularly to be sure that company assets are directed toward the countries with the best opportunities. The basis for an evaluation of countries should be a comparative analysis of different countries. Some may be unsuitable because of their unstable political situation, and others may have little potential because their population is small or the per capita income is low. The screening process gives the firm information about market size, competition, trade regulations, and distribution systems that will form the basis for the development of a market strategy. As global firms evaluate different consumer, business, and government market opportunities, they must be aware of the nature of the differences between countries.

The nature of the world marketplace has changed as a result of the development of major regional market groups. The economic integration of several countries offers great opportunities to companies. Many national markets that are small individually become significant when they are combined with other countries. The national markets in Europe are good examples. By locating production facilities in one country of a market group, the global company has access to the other countries with little or no trade restrictions. The market groups also increase competition. Local producers that completely dominated their national markets for years thanks to tariff protection now face competition from many other member countries.

The development of these market groups can also have negative effects on global companies. If a company is unable or unwilling to build a manufacturing plant in a certain market group, it may be unprofitable to export to that market. There are often more regulations between market groups, making it more complicated and expensive to move goods from one group to another. Also, the market group does not necessarily reduce the complexity of the consumer and cultural differences. For example, Germany and Spain are both in the EU, but the marketing programs, products, and strategies for success in each market will differ.

The success of market groups formed after World War II, particularly the EU, indicates that such groups will continue to grow. The potential entry of some eastern European countries into the EU, as well as the expansion of NAFTA to include other Central or South American countries, supports the growth of market groups and the growing interdependence of trading partners. Global companies need to monitor the development of new groups and any changes in the structure of current groups because changes within market groups will result in changes in market size and competition.

The largest business markets for U.S. goods are in countries that have a sophisticated industrial infrastructure, such as Canada, Japan, Germany, and England. These countries have a large industrial base, a financial basis, and a transportation network. These countries are also large importers and exporters of goods and services.

Developing countries offer a different type of market opportunity. They have specific economic needs that must be met with their limited financial resources. In these situations, the government is likely to get involved in the purchase process, offering concessions to get the best possible product or agreement. In many cases, the government will be the decision maker.

Questions for Discussion

1. Searching for the best global opportunity often requires an analysis of all the countries in the world. How will the initial screening differ from the final screening of possible countries for market entry?

2. If you were evaluating opportunities for exporting caviar but found that no countries had data on caviar consumption, what other indicators could you use to evaluate the size of each country's market?

3. Refer again to Figure 5.3. If the United States, Mexico, and Canada wanted to move from NAFTA, a free trade area, to an economic union, what steps would they need to take?

4. Imagine that you want to export hair shampoo. What are the advantages of grouping countries together rather than marketing to each country individually?

5. What are the differences among a free trade area, a customs union, and a common market? If you were marketing to a grouping of countries but had a manufacturing plant in only one of the countries, which of the three types of agreements would you prefer? Why?

6. How does establishing trade agreements between countries influence economic growth?

7. What critical factors influence a consumer's ability to purchase a product such as a stereo system?

8. Given the data on family decision making in the United States and Venezuela in Table 5.6, how will the marketing of automobiles be different in the two countries?

9. Will the buying process be more similar from country to country for deodorant or for delivery vans? Why?

10. If you were selling a product such as a nuclear power plant, which is purchased mostly by governments, how would you prepare to sell to Belgium, Egypt, and Mexico? What process would you use to understand the government buying process in each country?

For Further Reading

Acemogul, Daron, and Jaume Ventura. "The World Income Distribution." National Bureau of Economic Research Working Paper 8083, January 2001.

Belk, Russell W. "Unpacking My Library: The Marketing Professor in the Age of Electronic Reproduction." *Journal of Marketing*, January 2002, vol. 66, no. 1, pp. 120–127.

Craig, C. Samuel. "Conducting International Marketing Research in the Twenty-First Century." *International Marketing Review*, 2001, vol. 18, no. 1, pp. 80–90.

Craig, C. Samuel, and Susan P. Douglas. *International Marketing Research.* New York: Wiley, 2000.

Craig, C. Samuel, and Susan P. Douglas. "Responding to the Challenges of Global Markets: Change, Complexity, Completion and Conscience." *Columbia Journal of World Business,* Winter 1996, pp. 6–18.

Ganesh, Jaishankar. "Converging Trends Within the European Union: Insights from an Analysis of Diffusion Patterns." *Journal of Global Marketing,* November 1998, vol. 6, no. 4, pp. 32–49.

Kotabe, Masaaki. "Using Euromonitor Database in International Marketing Research."*Academy of Marketing Science Journal,* Spring 2002, vol. 30, no. 2, p. 172.

Levy, Brian. "Korean and Taiwanese Firms as International Competitors: The Challenges Ahead." *Columbia Journal of World Business,* Spring 1998, pp. 43–52.

Malhotra, Naresh K., James Agarwal, and Imad Baalbaki. "Heterogeneity of Regional Trading Blocs and Global Marketing Strategies: A Multicultural Perspective." *International Marketing Review,* 1998, vol. 15, no. 6, pp. 476–506.

Mejias, Roberto J. "Emerging Mexican and Canadian Strategic Trade Alliances Under NAFTA." *Journal of Global Marketing,* 2001, vol. 14, no. 4, p. 89.

Mitchell, Vincent W., and Michael Grentorex. "Consumer Purchasing in Foreign Countries: A Perceived Risk Perspective." *International Journal of Advertising,* 1990, vol. 9, no. 4, pp. 295–307.

Pinkerton, Richard L. "The European Community—'EC '92': Implications for Purchasing Managers."

International Journal of Purchasing and Materials Management, Spring 1993, pp. 19–26.

Russow, Lloyd C., and Andrew Solocha. "A Review of the Screening Process Within the Context of the Global Assessment Process." *Journal of Global Marketing,* 1993, vol. 7, no. 1, pp. 65–85.

Tam, Jackie L. M., and Susan H. C. Tai. "The Psychographic Segmentation of the Female Market in Greater China." *International Marketing Review,* 1998, vol. 15, no. 1, pp. 61–77.

van Rij, Jeanne Binstock. "Trends, Symbols and Brand Power in Global Markets: The Business Anthropology Approach." *Strategy & Leadership,* November-December 1996, pp. 18–24.

Endnotes

1. *World Bank Atlas 2002* (Washington, D.C.: World Bank, 2002), p.19.
2. Franklin R. Root, *Entry Strategies for Global Market* (New York: Jossey-Bass, 1998), p. 33.
3. See C. Samuel Craig and Susan P. Douglas, *International Marketing Research* (New York: Wiley, 2000), pp. 66–67 and 100–102, for a detailed listing of secondary sources of information.
4. *World Bank Atlas 2002,* pp. 54–55.
5. World Competitiveness Report 2001 (Lausanne, Switz: IMD, 2001).
6. *Society at a Glance: OECD Social Indicators,* (Paris, France: OECD, 2001), p. 99.
7. "Country-Risk Ratings," *Economist,* June 22, 1996, p. 100.
8. "Economist Intelligence Unit Launches New Electronic-Only Risk Service," *Information World Review,* February 2002, p. 4.
9. "EIU Market Indexes," *Crossborder Monitor,* August 28, 1996, p. 12.
10. "Taking the Long View," *Grocer,* May 26, 2001 vol. 224, no. 7505, pp. 46–48.
11. "India: Stock Market: Has It Bottomed Out?" *Businessline,* September 20, 2001.
12. "A New Front in the Free-Trade Wars," *Businessweek,* June 3, 2002, p. 30.
13. Edward Harris, "About Advertising: Ad Firms Can Find Themselves Tongue-Tied in Belgian Spots," *Wall Street Journal Europe,* July 19, 2000, p. A24.
14. "Tariffs Won, Steel Sings New Tune," *New York Times,* May 5, 2002, p. 7.
15. "Appendices: The European Union," *Economist Intelligence Unit,* April 25, 2002.
16. Michael Smith and Stefan Wagstyl, "Late Starters Strain to Catch Favourites for EU," *Financial Times,* February 15, 2000, p. 2.
17. Lord Cockfield, "Completing the Internal Market," white paper to the European Council (Luxembourg: Office of Publications of the European Communities, 1985).
18. Nicholas Colchester and David Buchan, *Europe Relaunched* (London: Economist Books, 1990), pp. 32–33.
19. Paolo Cecchini, *The European Challenge 1992: The Benefits of a Single Market* (London: Wildwood House, 1988).
20. James W. Dudley, *1992 Strategies for the Single Market* (London: Kogan Page, 1989), pp. 34–35.
21. Presentation by Dr. Nicolas Dahan, Professor Université de Marne-la-Vallée, Paris, France, June 4, 2002.
22. "Russia: Sweet Flows the Volga," *Economist,* June 5, 1999, p. 29.
23. "Russian Consumer Goods: The Joys of Devaluation," *Economist,* November 28, 1998, p. 66.
24. Carla Anne Robbins, "Senate Ratifies Treaty to Add 3 Nations from Former Warsaw Pact to NATO," *Wall Street Journal,* May 1, 1998, p. B2.
25. Ibid.
26. Press Release from NATO, "Rome Summit 28 May 2002," *http://www.nato.int / docu/ comm/2002/0205-rome/b020528e.htm;* accessed on October 28, 2002.
27. "The Euro Is Good for Business-Cfa Zone," *African Business,* March 2002, pp. 22–23.
28. "Africa for the Africans," *Economist,* September 7, 1996, Sub-Saharan African section, pp. 3–18.
29. Clive Sawyer, "EU Leaders Approve Trade Deal with South Africa," *Cape Argus,* March 25, 1999, p. 1.
30. Jerry Haar, "Bring Back Competitiveness: MERCOSUR Has Provided a Powerful Stimulus to Regional Trade," *LatinFinance,* March 1, 2002, p. S39.
31. Robert Wielaard, "EU, Latin America Use Regional Changes to Chart a New Course," *Associated Press Newswires,* June 30, 1999.
32. *http://www.comunidadandina.org/ingles/who.htm;* accessed on May 7, 2002.
33. Canute James, "LATIN AMERICA & CARIBBEAN—Single market for Caribbean 'by Year-End,'" *Financial Times,* July 13, 2001, p. xxx.
34. Claudio Katz, "Free Trade Area of the Americas: NAFTA Marches South," *NACLA Report on the Americas,* January-February 2002, pp. 27–31.
35. *World Bank Atlas 2002,* pp. 29, 46, 47.
36. "NAFTA at Eight Years," May 2002, *http://www.ustr.gov/regions/whemisphere/nafta.shtml;* accessed on October 28, 2002.
37. "Council of Arab Economic Unity," *Europa Year Book* (London: Publications Limited, 1999).
38. "Plan to Expand Pan-Arab Commerce to 20 Percent," *IPR Stratigic Business Information Database,* April 16, 2002.
39. "Economic Cooperation Organization Ends Session in Uzbek Capital," *Narodnoye Slovo,* June 15, 1999, p. 1.
40. "A New Front in the Free-Trade Wars," *Business Week,* June 3, 2002, p. 30.
41. Matthew C. Quinn, "International Business: UPS Betting on Southeast Asia," *Atlantic Constitution,* June 17, 1999, p. E2.
42. "Japan and Asia: Not So Fast," *Economist,* January 18, 1997, p. 37.
43. Barry Wain, "Two Takes on Asians' Future," *Asian Wall Street Journal,* April 12–13, 1996, p. 8.

44. "A Question of Preference: Do Regional Trade Agreements Encourage Free Trade?" *Economist,* August 22, 1998, p. 62.

45. "Asia-Pacific Economic Co-Operation (APEC)," *The Statesman's Yearbook* (New York: St. Martin's Press, 2002).

46. Brian Dumaine, "P&G Rewrites the Rules of Marketing," *Fortune,* November 6, 1989, p. 48.

47. *World Bank Atlas 2002* (Washington, D.C.: World Bank, 2002).

48. "High Inequality Countries," *Economist,* June 12, 1999, p. 98.

49. Ann Helmings, "Culture Shocks," *Advertising Age,* May 17, 1982, p. M-9.

50. Philip R. Harris and Robert T. Moran, *Managing Cultural Differences,* 4th ed. (Houston, Tex.: Gulf, 1996) pp. 5–29.

51. "Soft Drink Bottlers: Evolution of the Fittest. Global Top 11 Countries Ranked by Per Capita Soft Drink Consumption in 8-Ounce Servings," *Institutional Investor Americas,* March 2000.

52. "Third World Telephones," *Economist,* December 17, 1983, pp. 82–85.

53. Phillip D. White and Edward W. Cundiff, "Assessing the Quality of Industrial Products," *Journal of Marketing,* January 1978, pp. 80–86.

54. Lars Hallen, "International Purchasing in a Small Country: An Exploratory Study of Five Swedish Firms," *Journal of International Business Studies,* Winter 1982, pp. 99–111.

55. Ibid.

56. *Selling to the Government Markets: Local, State, Federal* (Cleveland, Ohio: Government Product News, 1975), p. 2.

57. The information in this section has been drawn from Business Global, "How to Sell to Belgium's Public Sector," *Business Europe,* October 2, 1981, pp. 314–315.

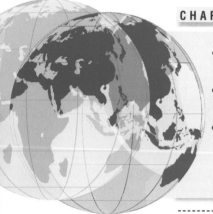

Chapter 6

Global Marketing Research

In Chapter 5, we introduced you to various consumers, markets, and environments. Our main purpose in Chapter 6 is to provide you with a method for collecting the appropriate data and a framework in which to analyze the environment, the market, and the consumers for your product. Figure 6.1 presents an overview of global market research and analysis.

Although this chapter is written around the market research issues in a global environment, our emphasis is managerial rather than technical. Throughout the chapter, we focus on how companies can obtain useful, accurate information that will help them to make more informed strategic and marketing decisions described in later chapters. As globalization continues, timely and precise marketing research becomes increasingly important. Market research has evolved over the last four decades and must continue to evolve to support global business.[1] Global marketers are able to use the power of the Internet to access current research from around the world. The volume of information available electronically makes it much easier for the global marketer to make informed decisions.

THE SCOPE OF GLOBAL MARKETING RESEARCH

Global marketing research is meant to provide adequate data and cogent analysis for effective decision-making on a global scale. In contrast to marketing research, which has a domestic focus, global research covers a multitude of environments, and there is a scarcity of comparable, relevant data. Because of this limitation, flexibility, resourcefulness, and ingenuity on the part of the researcher are often required to overcome the numerous obstacles in carrying out the research task.

Figure 6.1: International Marketing Research and Analysis

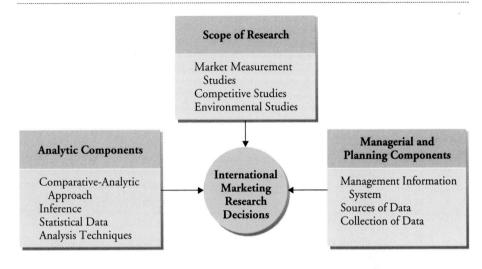

The analytical research techniques practiced by domestic businesses also apply to global marketing projects. The key difference is in the complexity of assignments because of the additional variables involved. Global marketers have to judge the comparability of their data across several markets; they frequently make decisions based on limited data. Traditionally, marketing research has been charged with the following three broad areas of responsibility:

1. *Market studies.* One of the most frequent tasks of researchers is to determine the size of a market and the needs of potential customers. From this data, it is possible to estimate expected sales for a product in a country or set of countries, which is an important factor in the development of a global marketing program.
2. *Competitive studies.* Providing insights about competitors, both domestic and foreign, is an important assignment for the global marketing researcher. The researcher must study the general competitive behavior of industries in the various markets within which the firm will compete.
3. *Environmental studies.* Given the added environmental complexity of global marketing, managers need factual and timely input on the international environment—particularly relating to the economic, political, and legal elements of the potential markets.

Global marketing research is used to make both strategic and tactical decisions. Strategic decisions include the selection of what markets to enter, how to enter them (exporting licensing, joint venture), and where to locate production facilities. Tactical decisions are decisions about the specific marketing mix to be used in a country. Table 6.1 shows the various types of tactical marketing decisions and the kinds of research used to collect the necessary data.

New-product development or product adaptation will require product benefit research and product testing to meet environmental conditions, customer tastes, and

Table 6.1 Global Marketing Decisions Requiring Marketing Research	
Marketing Mix Decision	**Type of Research**
Product policy	Focus groups and qualitative research to generate ideas for new products
	Survey research to evaluate new product ideas
	Concept testing, test marketing
	Product benefit and attitude research
	Product formulation and feature testing
Pricing	Price sensitivity studies
Distribution	Survey of shopping patterns and behavior
	Consumer attitudes toward different store types
	Survey of distributor attitudes and policies
Advertising	Advertising pretesting
	Advertising posttesting, recall scores
	Surveys of media habits
Sales promotion	Surveys of response to alternative types of promotion
Sales force	Tests of alternative sales presentations

Source: C. Samuel Craig and Susan P. Douglas, *International Marketing Research,* © 1983, p. 32. Reprinted by permission of Prentice-Hall, Inc., Englewood Cliffs, N.J.

competitive constraints. For example, the maker of Coach handbags used market research from department stores, boutiques, and factory outlets to revamp the manufacturing and marketing of its products and reported a 48 percent rise in net income in 2001. They also discovered that the quality of their Coach handbags was almost too good and consumers would not have to replace it.[2]

Advertising, sales promotion, and sales force decisions all require data from the local market in the form of testing. The type of information required is often the same as that required in domestic marketing research, but the process is made more complex by the variety of cultures and environments.

THE IMPORTANCE OF GLOBAL MARKETING RESEARCH

The complexity of the global marketplace, the extreme differences that can exist from country to country, and the frequent lack of familiarity with foreign markets accentuate the importance of global marketing research. Before making market entry, product position, or market mix decisions, a marketer must have accurate information about the market size, customer needs, competition, and so on. Marketing research provides the necessary information to avoid the costly mistakes of poor strategies or lost opportunities.

Marketing research can guide product development for a foreign market. Based on a research study conducted in the United States, one U.S. firm introduced a new cake mix in England. Believing that homemakers wanted to feel that they participated in the preparation of the cake, the U.S. marketers devised a mix that required homemakers to add an egg. Given its success in the U.S. market, the marketers were confident about introducing the product in England. The product failed, however, because the British did not like the fancy American cakes. They preferred cakes that were tough and spongy and could accompany afternoon tea. The step of adding an egg to the mix did not eliminate basic taste and stylistic differences.[3]

Companies are spending more on in-company research to keep up with volatile market segments. PepsiCo's research found that the European youth market was ready for a new cola that did not contain sugar. However, Pepsi also found that the youth market, especially males, was adverse to a diet soda; therefore, the soft drink giant launched Pepsi Max as a trendy, cool, sugar-free cola. The television campaign showed Pepsi Max drinkers "Living Life to the Max" and performing death-defying stunts.[4] Microsoft conducted global marketing studies through McCann-Erickson Worldwide to determine its target audience and brand positioning for its video game system, XBox. The result of the global marketing studies helped Microsoft speed its market entry for XBox by having the brand position and target market strategically aligned before the product was launched.[5]

CHALLENGES IN PLANNING GLOBAL RESEARCH

Global marketing researchers face five principal challenges:

1. Complexity of research design
2. Lack of secondary data
3. Costs of collecting primary data
4. Coordination of research and data collection across countries
5. Establishing comparability and equivalence[6]

Domestic research is limited to one country, but global research includes many countries. The research design is made more complex because the researcher defining the possible target market must choose which countries or segments should be researched. This initial step in the research process is further complicated by limited secondary information. Even if the appropriate secondary information exists, it may be difficult to locate and acquire. Thus, researchers are forced either to spend considerable resources finding such data or to accept the limited secondary data that are available. In many countries, the cost of collecting primary data is substantially higher than in the domestic market. This situation is particularly true for developing countries. Consequently, researchers have to accept tradeoffs between the need for more accurate data and the limited resources available to accomplish the tasks.

Even gathering demographics from country to country is not an easy task. There are various problems with using national census data. For example, the U.S. census is taken every ten years. Canada and Japan take a census every five years. Germany did one in 1987, twenty-seven years after its previous census in 1960. Although the United States, Canada, Australia, New Zealand, Mexico, Sweden, and Finland collect income data, many countries do not. Educational levels can be used to determine socioeconomic status, but educational systems vary widely from country to country, making comparisons very crude. Switzerland and Germany publish data on noncitizens. Ireland collects data on religion. Both these categories are excluded from the U.S. census. The measurement of marital status and household structure varies among countries. In Japan, household status is measured as single, married, married with children, single parent, or other, and marital status is measured as married and unmarried.[7] Great Britain measures marital status as married, cohabiting, single, widowed, divorced, and separated.[8] Ireland measures marital status as single, married, separated, or widowed.[9]

Because companies cannot afford to have each subsidiary obtain its own expensive primary data, coordination of research and data collection across countries becomes necessary. The borrowing of research results from another country is hindered by the general difficulty of establishing comparability and equivalence among various research data. Definitions of homemaker, socioeconomic status, incomes, and customers vary widely in Europe, even where the research is measuring the same thing. Full comparability can be achieved only when identical procedures are used. One study of consumers from eleven EU countries found that, even with the same scales, they were biased by the scale style. For example, in some countries, reverse-scored items and the amount of deviation from the midpoint influenced respondents differently, depending on their country of origin.[10] With research capabilities differing from country to country, global marketing research administration becomes a challenge. Companies that can manage this task successfully will be in a situation to avoid costly duplication of research. Research capabilities can also vary significantly in emerging markets where consumer habits and tastes change rapidly and conventional methods of research do not work. For example, the advertising agency Leo Burnett handed out notebooks, disposable cameras, and Post-it Notes to fashion-conscious Chinese youth. The agency asked them to record their fashion decisions and hand in the notebooks and content in two weeks because the participants were too timid for focus groups.[11]

CONCEPTUAL FRAMEWORK: THE COMPARATIVE ANALYTIC APPROACH

We have discussed the scope of marketing research situations and the difficulties encountered in conducting research. Although an understanding of the difficulties of collecting information for foreign markets helps to increase the quality of the information obtained, an overall conceptual framework is necessary to provide the analyst with the relevant questions to ask. Consequently, this section of the chapter focuses on building a framework that can guide global marketing managers in the formulation of market research studies.

Pioneered by T. A. Hagler in the late 1950s, comparative research actually led to the establishment of global marketing as a discipline.[12] Comparative marketing focuses on the entire marketing system, but this macro approach becomes less important when specific problems at the company level need to be analyzed. However, the comparative approach can be adapted to specific micro marketing problems.

MARKETING AS A FUNCTION OF THE ENVIRONMENT

Comparative marketing analysis emphasizes the study of the marketing process in its relationship to the environment. The marketing process is viewed as a direct function of the environment. Under changed environmental conditions, the existing marketing processes are also expected to change. In a dual-country analysis employing the comparative approach, the marketing environment in one country is investigated with respect to its effect on the marketing process. The resulting functional relationship is transferred to a second country, whose environment may be known but whose marketing process will be assessed based on the earlier analysis of the relationship between the marketing process and the environment in another country. This situation is illustrated in Figure 6.2.[13] The comparative marketing analysis allows the researcher to understand the relationship between the environment and the marketing process in one country and then to transfer that knowledge to another country while *adjusting* for differences in the environment.

EXAMPLE: MCDONALD'S. In the United States (the home country), McDonald's achieved its success through an aggressive, well-structured marketing mix. The elements may be described as follows:

- *Product/service design:* A standardized product of high and consistent quality emphasizing speed of service and long opening hours
- *Price:* A low-price policy
- *Distribution:* Placing restaurants primarily in areas where customers live—suburban and urban locations
- *Promotion:* A strong advertising campaign that focuses on consumers, particularly young people, via heavy use of television promotion

In the early 1970s, several other countries were targeted for possible expansion, and an assessment had to be made about the best approach for McDonald's to pursue. The traditional approach views success in the United States as a function of McDonald's effective marketing strategy, or as a direct result of the company's own efforts. The comparative analytic approach advanced here, however, views McDonald's success as a function of a given set of marketing mix variables that are

Figure 6.2: Managerial Approach to Comparative Analysis

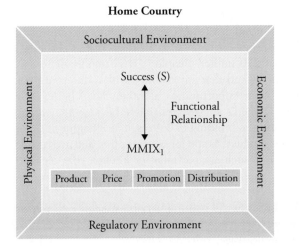
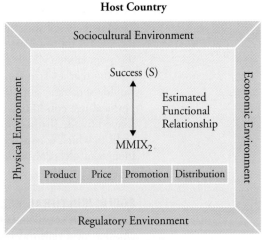

effective because of the country's environment. The main emphasis falls on the domestic environmental variables that allowed McDonald's marketing mix to be successful. The difference between the two approaches is important. The comparative analytic view sees McDonald's primarily as having been able to take advantage of an existing opportunity, whereas the traditional approach views McDonald's success primarily as a direct result of its own efforts.

VIEWING THE MARKETING MIX AS A FUNCTION OF THE ENVIRONMENT. Viewing a successful marketing mix as a function of the existing environment emphasizes an environmental view of the marketing process. This view is of great importance. Success is no longer defined as unilateral or as solely a function of the marketing mix. Thus, the company is viewed as taking advantage of a given opportunity rather than creating one by its own actions.

UNDERSTANDING THE MARKETING ENVIRONMENT

The first step in the comparative analytic approach is to look at the environmental factors. The critical environmental variables may be grouped into four major categories: physical, social/cultural, economic, and regulatory.

PHYSICAL VARIABLES. Included in physical variables are constraints with respect to the conditions of the product's use or the physical properties of the particular market: population, population density, geographic area, climate, and the physical conditions of the product's use (surroundings, space and size requirements, and so on). Variables such as population have an effect on the absolute size of any target market and, similar to climate, tend to be subject to little change over time. The physical-use conditions relate to a product's function in any given environment. As a result, we view the consumption of the product or service as a *physical event* directly influenced by physical environmental variables that have to be recognized to determine a marketing mix.

Several variables from the physical environment have contributed to McDonald's success in the United States. An important influence on McDonald's distribution or location policies was the concentration of the U.S. population in suburbia. Opening 11,368 units in the United States was possible because of the absolute size of the population, which is about 270 million people.[14] It is important to recognize that the market size is often finite and that any country with a different population would, of course, not offer the same opportunities, all other things being equal. The physical-use conditions of McDonald's are less restrictive because they are directly shaped by the firm's policies and the building of outlets. The situation is different in cases in which consumers take products home for consumption and are restricted by their own physical environments, such as apartment or kitchen size, electrical systems, and so on.

SOCIAL/CULTURAL VARIABLES. Social/cultural variables include all relevant factors from the social and cultural background of any given marketing environment, including local cultural background (race, religion, customs, habits, and languages), educational system, and social structure (individual roles, family structure, social classes, and reference groups).

As we have mentioned before, the social/cultural environment is a primary influence on the role expectations of buyers and sellers, regardless of the differences in the physical environment. Since the social/cultural environment does not change rapidly over time, many domestic marketers can lose sight of the fact that they have subconsciously chosen a marketing mix that incorporates many social/cultural values. Defining the social forces that affect a marketing mix is the first step in shedding the cultural bias that affects many managers without their realizing it.

In the case of McDonald's, several social and cultural forces greatly affected its success. For one, the value that U.S. society placed on time favored the consumption of meals with minimum effort. Saving time, in fact, created the desire for meals purchased outside the home on an unplanned or impulse basis. The result was a burgeoning demand for low-priced food that was available any time and that could be purchased with minimum shopping effort. Another important factor was the prevailing family structure in the United States and the trend toward a youth-oriented culture. Beginning in the 1970s, the decision-making role in families changed to such an extent that children often made the selection of a place to eat. McDonald's special emphasis on children and teenagers as advertising targets was successful largely because the strategy capitalized on these existing social trends.

The changing role of the wife in the typical U.S. household resulted in an ever-increasing number of women accepting employment outside the home. Whether this trend resulted in a lower valuation of the home-cooked meal in a social sense is debatable; nevertheless, it greatly increased the acceptability of eating meals outside the home.

Not to be underestimated is the habit or heritage of the hamburger itself. The hamburger represents a long-standing tradition of the U.S. food and restaurant scene, and hamburger made up the daily meal of many Americans before McDonald's arrived. It is fair to state, then, that the company's success stemmed greatly from the selection of an already existing and widely popular product. Aside from the type of service, the product did not represent an innovation. Of course, there are other reasons for dining out, and U.S. customers often make other choices, but the social and cultural influences paved the way for the success of an operation such as McDonald's.

Adjusting a marketing mix to consumer needs and tastes is very important, as McDonald's discovered in the Philippines. Whereas McDonald's used its standard menu in the Philippines, Jollibee, a local family-owned hamburger chain, tailored its menu to Philippine tastes. Jollibee offered a slice of pineapple on its Aloha Burger, as well as thin noodles, tofu, fish, and squid, and rice instead of French fries. Consequently, Jollibee enjoys 57 percent of the Philippine hamburger market, while McDonald's has only captured 36 percent.[15] Jollibee has 325 stores in the Philippines compared with McDonald's less than 200 stores.[16] McDonald's also found that it needed to adapt its menu in India, where the Maharaja Mac is made from lamb, not beef or pork, because of the Hindus' reverence of cows and the Muslims' abstinence from pork.[17]

What is important, then, is to isolate the salient social and cultural variables that affect the success of a company's products or services. The combined sociocultural variables create the *sociocultural event* that becomes an essential part of the consumption and use of any product or service. Understanding the nature of the sociocultural event in one country as the starting point for analyzing the respective variables in another country is the basis of the comparative analytic model.

ECONOMIC VARIABLES. Under the economic category, we include all aspects of the economic environment, on both a macro and micro level, such as gross national product (GNP), GNP per capita, price levels, income distribution, and the prices of competitive products and services. Economic considerations affect most consumption or buying decisions. To the extent that income levels of consumers differ from country to country, the tradeoffs consumers make to maximize economic satisfaction are different. Different price levels for products also cause changes in buying behavior, even under a constant income level. The global marketer must isolate the specific income and price variables to arrive at a given combination, termed the *economic event,* that affects the success of a given product or service. The comparative analytic model suggests that the elements and nature of the economic event with regard to another market can be found by first investigating the relevant factors in a company's home market.

For McDonald's, a significant variable of the economic environment was the income level of the U.S. population and the resulting disposable income available for frequent visits to fast-food restaurants. It is still more expensive to frequent a fast-food outlet than to prepare an equivalent meal at home; consequently, the success of fast-food outlets does not stem from their price advantage over food purchased in stores. Instead, it was the *relative price advantage* of fast-food restaurants over the more traditional, simple diner-type restaurants that ensured the tremendous success of fast-food outlets. Consuming a meal at a restaurant such as McDonald's becomes an economic event to the extent that economic variables are introduced into the consumer's decision-making process about the particular product or service choice.

REGULATORY VARIABLES. The regulatory environment includes all actions of governments or agencies influencing business transactions, such as commercial law or codes, consumer protection laws, product liability laws, regulatory agencies (for example, the U.S. Food and Drug Administration, the U.S. Department of Commerce, and the International Chamber of Commerce), local regulations, and zoning laws. Regulations do not tend to stimulate needs or demands for services and products. Instead, they act in an *enabling manner* (or disabling manner, depending on the point of view) by restricting choices for the international corporation or by prescribing the nature of its marketing effort. Companies have to be aware of the particular regulations that make an existing marketing program effective because such an approach may not be duplicated in other countries, even if it were desirable from a business point of view.

The possible effect of the regulatory environment can be illustrated by returning to our McDonald's example. Certainly, the use of television advertising to reach children was one of the reasons for McDonald's success in the United States. However, in many other countries, particularly those in Europe, such advertising is banned outright. On an operational level, it may be difficult to get teenage help in some countries or impossible to keep operating during hours customary in the United States. In many ways, the United States has a more liberal regulatory environment, so U.S. companies often face situations in which operations cannot be carried out in their accustomed fashion. This is true even when the target customers in other countries would respond positively to U.S. methods or practices and even when the relevant physical, economic, and social events indicate that their use would be beneficial.

ANALYZING ENVIRONMENTAL VARIABLES

Previous writers have emphasized the importance of environmental variables to international marketing. Robert Bartels highlighted physical, social, and economic variables in his environmental marketing concept. Robert Buzzell included a similar set of variables in his analysis of elements that may prevent a standardization of marketing programs across several countries.[18] Furthermore, Warren Keegan concentrated on the same variables as influencing extension versus adaptation decisions for product design or communications strategy.[19] The comparative analytic approach is different because it focuses on the situational variables and selects the salient environmental variables that may affect the product's or service's success in any country. Because the selected environmental variables are most clearly related to the success of a product or service in the home country, they can be referred to as *success factors*.

Traditionally, marketers have viewed success factors as variables under the control of marketing management. With the comparative analytic approach, success factors are treated as a function of the environment, which means that success is recognized as a function of outside factors not always subject to management's control. Typically, marketing programs succeed because management takes advantage of opportunities or positive constellations of success factors. Therefore, we are "allowed" to be successful provided we spot the opportunity. This view results in a greater appreciation of the role that environmental variables play in marketing and tends to avoid traditional interpretations that overestimate the impact of management's own actions in the marketplace.

The comparative analytical approach provides a methodology for marketers to analyze their success in current markets as a function of the marketing mix and the environment. It also provides an approach for isolating the critical environmental variables. These variables become the focus of the international market research process. In the McDonald's example, the variables we analyzed were population size, population density, family structure, the role of the mother, income levels, and the availability of advertising media to reach children. As we look at other countries, we must examine these environmental variables and adjust the McDonald's marketing mix appropriately. Starbucks had four thousand locations in North America in 2002. It entered Japan in 1996 with three stores, a number that grew to 368 stores in 2002. While Starbucks plans to grow to one thousand stores by 2007, analysts predict that the growth in stores will reduce overall productivity, which may require Starbucks to modify its marketing in Japan.[20]

THE RESEARCH PROCESS

Although conducting marketing research globally usually adds to the complexity of the research task, the basic approach remains the same for domestic and international assignments. Either type of research is a four-step process:

1. Problem definition and development of research objectives
2. Determination of the sources of information

3. Collection of the data from primary and secondary sources
4. Analysis of the data and presentation of the results

Although these four steps may be the same for both global and domestic research, problems in implementation may occur because of cultural and economic differences from country to country.

PROBLEM DEFINITION AND DEVELOPMENT OF RESEARCH OBJECTIVES

In any market research project, the most important task is to define what information you need. This process, which can take weeks or months, determines the choice of methodologies, the types of people you survey, and the appropriate period in which to conduct your research. The comparative analytic approach can be used to isolate the critical environmental variables in the home market. These variables should be included in the problem definition and research objectives.

Problems may not be the same in different countries or cultures because of differences in socioeconomic conditions, levels of economic development, cultural forces, or the competitive market structure.[21] For example, bicycles in a developed country may be competing with other recreational goods such as skis, baseball gloves, or exercise equipment, whereas in a developing country, they may be a form of basic transportation competing with small cars, mopeds, and scooters.

DETERMINATION OF DATA SOURCES

For each assignment, researchers may choose to base their analyses on primary data (data collected specifically for this assignment) or on secondary data (already collected and available data). Costs tend to be higher for research based on primary data, so researchers usually exhaust secondary data first. Often called desk research or library research, this approach depends on the availability of material and its reliability. Secondary sources may include government publications, trade journals, and data from international agencies or service establishments such as banks or advertisement agencies.

The quality of marketing statistics gathered from the Internet is definitely variable. For example, Polaroid Corporation conducted an email survey that asked 1,700 people about their use of Polaroid and image scanners. About one-quarter responded, saying that they had scanned a Polaroid picture. If this statistic is extrapolated across the entire population, then more Polaroid pictures were scanned than were taken in 1999. Polaroid Corporation did not find these statistics believable. One of the major problems with Internet market research is that the respondents do not represent the general population. They tend to be wealthier, more sophisticated technologically, and less racially diverse than the general population.[22] According to a report by the U.S. and Foreign Commercial Service in Beijing, Chinese government statistics are often collected by individual ministries or reported by state-owned enterprises and are riddled with *shuifen* ("water content"). China has begun to crack down on fraudulent statistics, using new laws to discipline local officials who exaggerate their success.[23] The Chinese government has taken the reliability and accuracy issues surrounding its statistical system seriously and has moved toward a more transparent system.[24]

Although a substantial body of data exists from the most advanced industrial nations, secondary data are not as readily available for developing countries. Not every country publishes a census, and some published data are not considered reliable. In Nigeria, for example, the population total is of such political importance that published census data are generally believed to be highly suspect. For these reasons, companies sometimes have to proceed with the collection of primary data in developing countries at a much earlier stage than they would for the most industrialized nations.

DATA COLLECTION

COLLECTING SECONDARY DATA. For any marketing research problem, the analysis of secondary data should be a first step. Although not available for all variables, data are often available from public and private sources at a fraction of the cost of obtaining primary data. Collection of data includes the task of calling, writing, or visiting the potential secondary sources. Often, one source will lead to another source until you find the desired information or determine that it does not exist. A good approach for locating secondary sources is to look for market or industry specific information. For example, if you wanted to locate secondary information on fibers used for tires in Europe, you may consider asking the editor of a trade magazine about the tire industry, the executive director of the tire manufacturing association, or the company librarian for Akzo, a Dutch company that manufacturers fibers. Web-based databases, microfilm, and compact disks are excellent sources of information, and these sources are available in most business libraries. Searches on these systems can quickly identify articles, books, and financial information on most business topics, marketing, and companies. Some of these web-based and commercial sources are:

Web Sites

www.country.data.com

www.developmentgateway.org

www.eiu.com

www.esomar.nl

www.euromonitor.com

www.europa.eu.int

www.ffas.usda.gov

www.greenbook.org

www.oecd.org

www.ita.doc.gov

www.prsgroup.com

www.stat-usa.gov

www.unctad.org

www.un.org

www.worldbank.org

Commercial Organizations

Advertising Age international issues (www.adage.com)

Country Forecasts, Political Risk Yearbook, Political Risk Group, East Syracuse, New York (www.icrgonline.com)

Dun and Bradstreet (annual) *Exporters Encyclopedia,* Dun and Bradstreet, New York

Economist Intelligence Unit, London (www.eiu.com)

Euromonitor, London (www.euromonitor.com)

Europa Publications, *World Yearbook* (www.europe.eu.int)

Gale Country and World Rankings Reporter

IMD (annual) *The World Competitiveness Yearbook,* IMD, Lausanne, Switzerland

JETRO (annual) *Economic Yearbook,* Jetro, Tokyo, Japan

OECD Society at a Glance, OECD Social Indicators, OECD, 2001, Paris

Media Guide International, Directories International, New York

Political Risk Group, *Political Risk Yearbook* (www.prsgroup.com)

Pricewaterhouse Coopers Information Guides—*Doing Business in …* Pricewaterhouse Coopers, New York

The Nikkei Weekly, *Japan Economic Almanac,* Nikon Keizai Shimbun, Tokyo

UN *Human Development Report,* United Nations Development Programme, New York: Oxford University Press

It would be impractical to list all the secondary data sources available on international markets. A partial list of such sources would be banks, consulates, embassies, foreign chambers of commerce, libraries with foreign information sections, foreign magazines, public accounting firms, security brokers, and state development offices in foreign countries. A good business library and the local U.S. Department of Commerce are always helpful places to start a search for secondary data. Table 6.2 lists some of the major sources of published secondary data.

Some of the problems associated with the use of secondary data are (1) lack of necessary data, (2) level of accuracy of the data, (3) lack of comparability of the data, and (4) timeliness of the data. In some cases, no data have been collected. For example, many countries have little data on the number of retailers, wholesalers, and distributors.

The accuracy of data varies from country to country, with data from highly industrialized nations likely to be more accurate than data from developing countries.[25] This variability is a result of the mechanism for collecting data. In industrialized nations, relatively reliable procedures are used for national accounting and for collecting population and industry statistics. In developing countries, where a major portion of the population is illiterate, the data may be based on estimates or rudimentary procedures. In addition, statistics could be manipulated for political reasons. For example, a study by the International Labor Organization found the actual unemployment in Russia to be over 14.2 percent, or 10.4 million people, compared with the official figure of 1.7 million people.[26] The growth of global market opportunities is causing companies to demand cross-border standards for audience measurement.

Table 6.2 Major Sources of Secondary Data

U.S. Department of Commerce

Foreign Trade Report: U.S. exports by commodity and by country

Global Market Surveys: Global market research on targeted industries

Country Market Surveys: Detailed reports on promising countries covering fifteen industries

Business America: Magazine presenting domestic and international business news

Overseas Marketing Report: Trade forecasts, regulations, and market profiles prepared for all countries

International Monetary Fund

International Financial Statistics: Monthly report on exchange rates, inflation, deflation, country liquidity, etc.

National Technical Information Services

Market Share Reports: Reports the size of eighty-eight markets and identifies export opportunities

United Nations

Yearbook of Industrial Statistics: Statistics of minerals, manufactured goods, electricity, and gas

Statistical Yearbook: Population, production, education, trade, wages

Demographic Yearbook: Population, income, marriages, deaths, literacy

World Bank

Country Economic Reports: Macroeconomic and industry trends

World Development Report: Population, investment, balance of reports, defense expenditures

Euromonitor Publications

European Marketing Data and Statistics: Population, employment, production, trade, standard of living, consumption, housing, communication

Predicasts

Worldcasts: Economics, production, utilities

The Economist

E.I.U. World Outlook: Forecasts of trends for 160 countries

Marketing in Europe: Product markets in Europe—food, clothing, furniture, household, goods, appliances

Business International Data Base: Economic indicators, GNP, wages, foreign trades, production, and consumption

Current differences in critical variables like household size cause country-to-country differences. Even within a market, these differences can be a problem. For example, in Argentina, the three ratings companies—IPSA Nielsen, IBOPE of Brazil, and Mercados y Tendencias—have conflicting results for video viewing, which was approximately 50 percent of the market.[27]

Data may not be directly comparable from country to country. The population statistics in the United States are collected every ten years, whereas population statistics in Bolivia are collected every twenty-five years. In addition, countries may calculate the same statistic but in different ways. For example, there are several indicators of national wealth. Gross national product (GNP) is the gross value of production in a country. Gross domestic product (GDP) is the value of all goods and services produced within a country and is often used in place of GNP. GDP per capita, suggesting the economic wealth of a country per person, is one of the most common measures of market size. Recently, the International Monetary Fund (IMF) decided that the normal practice of converting the local currency of GDP into dollars at market exchange rates understates the true size of developing economies relative to rich ones. Therefore, the IMF has decided to use purchasing power parities, which take into account the differences in international prices. As you can see in Table 6.3, GDP per capita is much higher based on purchasing power. For example, the GDP per capita in China jumped from $840 at market exchange rates to $3,920 on a purchasing parity basis, an increase of 466 percent.[28]

Another problem with GDP statistics is the hidden economy not shown in government statistics. This hidden economy, sometimes called the underground economy, includes unrecorded cash transactions, barter transactions, and illegal transactions, all of which are not reported to the government to avoid taxes or criminal charges. For example, in Greece, Spain, and Italy, the hidden economy is 20 to 30 percent of GDP, while in Japan and Switzerland, it is less than 4 percent of GDP. When using official GDP statistics, it is important to remember that they do not reflect the true size of the economy.

The reliability of government statistics varies from country to country. In the United Kingdom, inaccurate GDP growth data, which was sharply revised upward in

Table 6.3 Market Exchange Rates and Purchasing Power Parity in Developing Countries, 1988		
	GNP per Capita $	
Country	Market Exchange Rates	Purchasing Power Parity
Argentina	7,460	12,050
Brazil	3,580	7,300
China	840	3,920
Egypt	1,490	3,670
India	450	2,340
Indonesia	570	2,830
Malaysia	3,380	8,330
Mexico	5,070	8,790
Nigeria	260	800
Pakistan	440	1,860
Philippines	1,040	4,220
South Korea	8,910	17,300
Thailand	2,000	6,320
Turkey	3,100	7,030

Source: 2000 World Bank Atlas, Washington, D.C., 2000, pp. 42–43.

the early 1980s, is blamed for inflationary economic policies. Tim Holt, who now runs the Central Statistics Office in the United Kingdom, advises that changes to GDP figures have been less than 0.1 percent since 1995.[29] Even government statistics are faulty; a recent U.S. study showed the Consumer Price Index is overstated by 1 to 2 percent per year. The traditional methods of measuring are based on units of physical goods like cotton, steel, corn, and gloves, which were accurate indicators in the 1940s when farming, mining, and manufacturing made up over 50 percent of the country's output. Now these sectors account for less than 30 percent. The bulk of U.S. output consists of services, like electronic banking, that benefit consumers and create value difficult to measure. Leonard Nakamura, an economist at the Federal Reserve, argues that GDP in the United States is understated by 2 to 3 percent per year because the full value of new services, new goods, and product improvements is not taken into account.[30]

Finally, age of the data is a constant problem. Population statistics are usually two to five years old. Industrial production statistics can be one to two years old. With different growth rates, it is difficult to use older data to make decisions.

To test the quality of secondary data, marketers should try to answer the following questions:

1. When were the data collected?
2. How were the data collected?
3. What is the expected level of accuracy?
4. Who collected the data, and for what purpose?

COLLECTING PRIMARY DATA. If secondary data are not available or usable, the marketer will need to collect primary data. Experienced global researchers indicate that although secondary data may be available, going directly to potential consumers, distributors, and retailers may sometimes be less expensive in the long run than spending considerable time in libraries, embassies, and trade associations. Once a marketer has exhausted the supply of secondary sources or determined that they are not usable, the next step is to collect primary data that will meet the specific information requirements for making a specific management decision. Often primary sources will reveal data not available from secondary sources. For example, Vietnamese Health Ministry surveys show that about 50 percent of Vietnamese men smoke and 3.4 percent of women smoke. Even more specific, 60 percent of people with university degrees smoke.[31]

Sources of primary data are those in the target country who will purchase or influence the purchase of products. These sources are consumers, businesses, or governments. Collecting the appropriate data requires the development of a data-collecting process. The primary data collection process involves developing a research instrument, selecting a sample, collecting the data, and analyzing the results. These steps are the same in domestic and international environments. The process of collecting data in different cultures creates several challenges for the global marketer. These challenges include the comparability of data, the willingness of the potential respondent to participate, and the ability of the respondent to understand and communicate.

Comparability of data is important whether research is conducted in a single-country or multicountry context. Research conducted in a single country may be used later to compare with the results of research in another country.[32] For example, if a product is tested in France and is successful, the company may decide to test the Italian market. The test used for the Italian market must be comparable with the test in the French market to assess the possible outcome in Italy. Significant differences exist from country to country. For example, American teenagers give celebrity endorsements more credibility than do teenagers in the rest of the world; they are twice as likely to trust a celebrity when buying clothes than are their peers from Europe and Asia.[33] Obviously, that research would have a big impact on how a new product is marketed in the United States.

A second challenge in research is the willingness of the potential respondent to participate. For example, in many cultures a man will consider it inappropriate to discuss his shaving habits with anyone, especially with a female interviewer. Respondents in the Netherlands or Germany are notoriously reluctant to divulge information on their personal financial habits; the Dutch are generally more willing to discuss sex than money. Through careful planning, researchers can design instruments and techniques to overcome or avoid cultural limitations.[34] For example, in some cultures, it may be necessary to enlist the aid of a local person to obtain respondents' cooperation.

Another challenge in survey research involves translation from one language to another. Translation equivalence is important, first to ensure that the respondents understand the question and second to ensure that the researcher understands the response. Idiomatic expressions and colloquialisms are often translated incorrectly. For example, the French translation of a "full" airplane became a "pregnant" airplane; in German, "body by Fisher" became a "corpse by Fisher."[35] An automobile manufacturer used the line "topped them all" when promoting its product in an English-speaking market. When the product was introduced in French-speaking markets, the phrase was translated to "topped by all of them." The promotional slogan used by the Parker Pen Company, "Avoid embarrassment—use Parker Pens," translated in Spanish as "Avoid pregnancy—use Parker Pens."[36] To avoid these translation errors, experts suggest the technique of back-translation in the local dialect, so that *ji xuan ji*, which means "computers" to Chinese and Taiwanese, does not become "calculators" to Singaporeans or Malaysians through mistranslation.[37] First, the question is translated by someone who is bilingual and a native speaker of the foreign country. This person translates from the home language into the language of the country where it will be used. Then someone who is bilingual and who is a native speaker of the home language translates this version back to the home language. Another translation technique is parallel translation, in which two or more translators translate the question. The results are compared, and differences are discussed and resolved.

Data can be collected by mail, telephone, or face-to-face interview. The technique will vary by country. The European Society for Opinion and Market Research (ESOMAR) recently reported on interviewing techniques used in Europe. As shown in Table 6.4, face-to-face interviews at home or work are very popular in Switzerland and the United Kingdom, whereas interviews in shopping areas are popular in France and the Netherlands. Telephone interviewing dominates Swedish data collection.[38]

Data collection and privacy concerns being raised in the European Union (EU) may affect market research globally. The EU Data Privacy Directive passed in 1995

Table 6.4 Comparison of European Data Collection Methods

	France	Netherlands	Sweden	Switzerland	United Kingdom
Mail	4%	33%	23%	8%	9%
Telephone	15	18	44	21	16
Central location/streets	—	52	37	—	—
Home/work	—	—	8	44	54
Groups	13	—	5	6	11
Depth Interviews	12	12	2	8	—
Secondary	4	—	4	8	—

Source: Emanual H. Demby, "ESOMAR Urges Changes in Reporting Demographics, Issues Worldwide Report," *Marketing News,* January 8, 1990, p. 24. Reprinted by permission of the American Marketing Association.

requires unambiguous consent from a person for each use of his or her personal data.[39] This regulation could seriously limit the use of telephone interviews that ask questions related to health problems, political beliefs, sex habits, and so on. All fifteen EU nations have data privacy legislation and a government privacy commission to enforce the EU policy. This legislation stipulates that data cannot be sent to a non-EU country unless that country has an adequate level of privacy protection. The U.S. Department of Commerce is working with EU officials to develop the International Safe Harbor Privacy Principles for non-EU countries.[40]

Global market research requires sensitivity to local culture to provide meaningful results. In China, telephone and web interviews can be difficult to achieve with business respondents because managers often will not discuss issues without the assurance of face-to-face contact. Telephone surveys in Japan can lead to valuable information, provided the surveyor follows Japanese etiquette and allows for adequate introduction time before any discussion of the respondent's personal and business background. In southern Europe, telephone interviews and surveys of business respondents may require additional upfront reassurance regarding confidentiality and security of research methods and results. It is possible to have standard methods and tactics for a global survey or questionnaire, as long as the person conducting the survey or questionnaire understands and observes local etiquette.[41]

Another technique for collecting marketing research data is conducting focus groups. The researcher assembles a set of six to twelve carefully selected respondents to discuss a product. The focus group is often used at the early stage of a new product concept to gain valuable insights from potential consumers. The research company assembles the participants and leads the discussion, but it must avoid the potential bias from a company representative. Of course, the discussion leader must speak in the language of the participants. Representatives of the company can observe the focus group via video- or audiotaping, through a one-way mirror, or sitting in the room. In some countries, such as Japan, it may be difficult to get participants to criticize a potential product. Experienced focus group companies are resourceful at using questioning techniques and interpreting body language to get the full value from this research technique.

SAMPLE SELECTION. After developing the instrument and converting it to the appropriate language, the researcher will determine the appropriate sample design. Because of its advantage of predicting the margin of error, researchers generally prefer to use probability sampling. The great power of a probability sample lies in the possibility of predicting the corresponding errors: (1) sampling errors, or the chance of not receiving a true sample of the group investigated; (2) response errors, or the deviation of responses from the facts due to either incorrect recall or unwillingness to tell the truth; and (3) nonresponse errors, or uncertainty of the views held by members of the sample who were never reached. For these reasons, researchers generally prefer probability samples.[42]

In many foreign countries, however, the existing market infrastructure and the lack of available data or information substantially interfere with attempts to use probability samples of subsets of the population. Sampling of larger populations requires the availability of detailed census data, called *census tracks*, and maps from which probability samples can be drawn. When such data are available, they are often out of date. Thus, taking samples of subsets of data is not possible.[43] Further difficulties arise from inadequate transportation that may prevent fieldworkers from actually reaching selected census tracks in some areas of the country. Sampling is particularly difficult in countries whose citizens speak several languages because carrying out a nationwide survey is impractical.

RESEARCH TECHNIQUES

Various analytic techniques can be used in international marketing research. Although these techniques may be used in domestic marketing research, they are often modified to deal with the complexities of international markets.

DEMAND ANALYSIS

Demand for products or services can be measured at two levels: aggregate demand, for an entire market or country, and company demand, as represented by actual sales. The former is generally termed *market potential,* whereas the latter is referred to as *sales potential.* A very useful concept developed by Richard D. Robinson views both market and sales potential as a filtering process (see Figure 6.3). According to Robinson, demand or potential demand can be measured at six successive levels, the last and final level representing actual sales by the firm.[44] The six levels of demand are explained as follows.

POTENTIAL NEED. Of course, the country's consumers will not purchase the product if there is no need. Therefore, the researcher has to pose the question: Is there a potential need, either now or in the future? Potential need for a product or service is determined primarily by the demographic and physical characteristics of a country. The determinants are a country's population, climate, geography, natural resources, land use, life expectancy, and other factors termed part of the physical environment. The potential need could be realized only if all consumers in a country used a product fully, regardless of social, cultural, or economic barriers. This represents the ideal case that actually may never be reached.

Figure 6.3: Market Potential and Sales Potential Filter

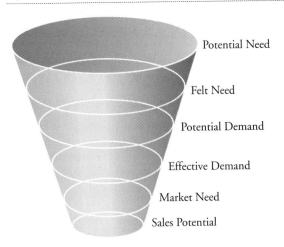

Potential Need

Felt Need

Potential Demand

Effective Demand

Market Need

Sales Potential

Source: Reprinted from *Internationalization of Business,* 2nd ed., by Richard D. Robinson, p. 36. Copyright © 1984 with permission of the author.

FELT NEED. Although a potential need, as defined above, may exist to the uninvolved observer, one should not assume that everyone in a market actually feels a need for the product or service under investigation. Because of different lifestyles, some consumers may not feel a need for a product. For instance, a farmer in a developing country who drives his produce to a local market in an animal-drawn cart potentially has a use for a pickup truck, but he actually may not feel the need for one. Thus, felt need is substantially influenced by the cultural and social environment, including the amount of exposure of consumers or buyers to modern communications. The key task for the researcher is to evaluate the extent to which the potential need is culturally and socially appropriate among the target customers.

POTENTIAL DEMAND. The felt need represents the aggregate desire of a target population toward purchasing a product. However, lack of sufficient income may prevent some customers from actually purchasing the product or service. The result is the potential demand, or the total amount the market would be ready to absorb. Economic variables preventing the realization of sales are generally beyond the control of any individual company. For example, the average income per household may seem to indicate a large demand for washing machines, but the distribution of income is skewed so that 10 percent of the population has 90 percent of the wealth.

EFFECTIVE DEMAND. Although potential demand might exist, regulatory factors might prevent prospective customers from satisfying their demand. Such regulatory factors include regulations on imports, tariffs, and foreign exchange; specific regulations on product standards with respect to safety, health, and pollution; legal restrictions such as patents, copyrights, and trademarks; fiscal controls such as taxes, subsidies, or rationing and allocations; economic regulations, including price and wage controls; and political regulations, including restrictions on buying foreign goods, the role of the government in the economy, and the power of the government to impose controls. The presence of any of these factors can cause the potential demand to be reduced to a lower level—in other words, to effective demand. Therefore, marketing research needs to uncover the extent to which regulatory factors are present and to determine the possible actions a firm may take to avoid some of the impact on demand.

MARKET DEMAND. The extent to which the effective demand can be realized depends substantially on the marketing infrastructure available to competing firms in a country. The degree to which a country's transportation system has been developed is important, as well as its efficiency in terms of cost to users. Additional services that marketers use regularly are storage facilities, banking facilities (particularly for consumer credit), the wholesale and retail structure, and the advertising infrastructure. The absence of a fully developed marketing infrastructure will cause market demand to be substantially below effective demand. Marketing research will determine the effectiveness of the present marketing system and locate the presence of any inhibiting factors.

SALES POTENTIAL. The actual sales volume that a company will realize in any country is essentially determined by its competitive offering vis-à-vis other firms that also compete for a share of the same market. The resulting market share is determined by the relative effectiveness of the company's marketing mix. In determining sales potential, the researcher will have to assess whether the company can meet the competition in terms of product quality and features, price, distribution, and promotion. The assessment should yield an estimate of the company's market share, given the assumptions about the company's mode of entry (see Chapter 9) and marketing strategy (see Chapter 8).[45]

The difficulty lies in collecting the facts that can be used to determine potential sales. Consider a situation in which a company is investigating a market that already has had experience with the product to be introduced. In such a case, the research effort is aimed at uncovering the data on present sales, usage, or production to arrive at the market demand (see Figure 6.3). Consequently, this effort is primarily in collecting data from secondary information sources or commissioning professional marketing research through independent agencies when necessary.

ANALYSIS BY INFERENCE

Available data from secondary sources are frequently aggregate and do not satisfy the specific needs of a firm focusing on just one product and a given period. A company must usually assess market size based on very limited data on foreign markets. In such cases, market *assessment by inference* becomes a necessity. This technique uses available facts about related products or other foreign markets as a basis for inferring the necessary information for the market under analysis. Market assessment by inference, a low-cost method that is analysis based, should take place before a company engages in any primary data collection at a substantial cost. Inferences can be made based on related products, sales in related markets, and related environmental factors.

RELATED PRODUCTS. Few products are consumed or used without any ties to other prior purchases or products in use. Relationships exist, for example, between replacement tires and automobiles on the road and between electricity consumption and the use of appliances. In some situations, it may be possible to obtain data on related products and their uses to form a basis for inferred usage of the particular product to be marketed. From experience in other, similar markets, the analyst can apply usage ratios that can provide low-cost estimates. For example, the analyst can determine the number of replacement tires needed per X automobiles on the road. A clear understanding of usage patterns can be gained from performing a comparative analysis as described earlier.

THE SIZE OF RELATED MARKETS. If market size data are available for other countries, this information can often be used to derive estimates for the particular country under investigation. For example, the market size is known for the United States and suppose that estimates are required for Canada, a country with a comparable economic system and comparable consumption patterns. Statistics for the United States can be scaled down by the relative size of GNP, population, or other factors to about one-tenth of U.S. figures. Similar relationships exist in Europe, where the known market size of one country can provide a basis for an inference about a related country. Of course, the results are not exact, but they provide a basis for further analysis. The cost and time lag for collecting primary market data often force the analyst to use the inference approach.

RELATED ENVIRONMENTAL FACTORS. A more comprehensive analysis can be provided after a full comparative analysis as outlined previously. After data are collected on the relevant environmental variables for a given product, an inference may be made on the market potential. The estimate's reliability depends on the type of data available on the success factors. Actual data on success factors are preferable, of course, to inferences based on the demand structure in a related market.

ANALYSIS OF DEMAND PATTERNS. By analyzing industrial growth patterns for various countries, researchers can gain insights into the relationship of consumption patterns to industrial growth. Relationships can be plotted between GDP per capita and the percentage of total manufacturing production by major industries. During earlier growth stages with corresponding low per capita incomes, manufacturing tends to center on necessities such as food, beverages, textiles, and light manufacturing. With increasing incomes, the role of these industries tends to decline, and heavy industry assumes greater importance. With analysis of such manufacturing patterns, forecasts for various product groups can be made for countries at lower income levels because they often repeat the growth patterns of more developed economies.

Similar trends can be observed for a country's import composition. With increasing industrialization, countries develop similar patterns, modified only by each country's natural resources. Energy-poor countries must import increasing quantities of energy as industrialization proceeds, whereas energy-rich countries can embark on an industrialization path without significant energy imports. Industrialized countries import relatively more food products and industrial materials than manufactured goods, which are more important for the less industrialized countries. These relationships can help the analyst determine future trends for a country's economy and may help determine future market potential and sales prospects.

MULTIPLE-FACTOR INDEXES

This technique has already been used successfully by domestic marketers. It entails the use of proxies to estimate demand if the situation should prevent the direct computation of a product's market potential. A multiple factor measures potential indirectly, using proxy variables that intuition or statistical analysis reveals to be closely correlated to the potential for the product under review.

A good example for such an approach is Ford Motor's analysis for its overseas tractor business.[46] To evaluate the attractiveness of its various overseas markets, the company developed a scale and rated each country on attractiveness and competitive strength. These two dimensions were measured based on the following criteria:

Country attractiveness	*Competitive strength*
Market size	Market share
Market growth rate	Product fit
Government regulations	Contribution margin
Price controls	Profit per unit
Nontariff barriers	Profit percentage, net of dealer cost
Local content	Market support
Economic and political stability	Quality of distribution system
Inflation	Advertising versus competition
Trade balance	
Political stability	

These items were evaluated by Ford's executives and rated on a ten-point scale. The items were combined based on the relative weight of each item to determine the coordinates of the X and Y axes. Figure 6.4 illustrates Ford's use of the market evaluation system for Ford's key countries. The weights are indicative of the firm's effort to rank markets via multiple-factor indexes.

COMPETITIVE STUDIES

As every marketer knows, results in the marketplace depend on other factors besides buyer characteristics and meeting buyer needs. To a considerable extent, success in the marketplace is influenced by a firm's competition. Companies competing on an international level have to be particularly careful about monitoring competition because some of the competing firms will be located abroad, thus creating additional difficulties in keeping abreast of the latest developments.

When Honda first entered the U.S. motorcycle industry in 1959, the British and U.S. motorcycle firms that dominated the industry did not pay much attention. Honda's entry with a 50 cc motorcycle posed little threat to the motorcycles of Harley Davidson and Triumph. But thirty years later, 80 percent of the motorcycles are Japanese, and they compete in categories from 50 cc to 1,400 cc. Many companies fail

Figure 6.4: Key-Country Matrix

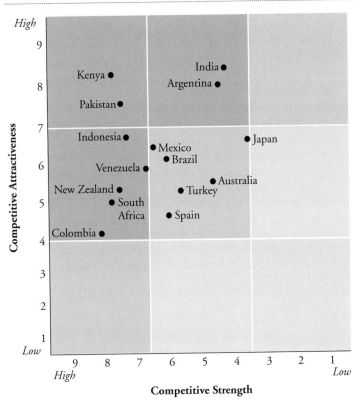

Source: Gilbert D. Harrell and Richard O. Kiefer, "Multinational Strategic Market Portfolios," *MSU Business Topics,* Winter 1981, p. 13. Reprinted by permission.

to spot competitors until it is too late. Swiss watchmakers were blindsided by competitors not even in the same business. While the Swiss were making increasingly more complex mechanized watches, Casio launched basic digital watches that sold at half the price of cheap mechanical watches. Only with the launch of the fashionable electronic Swatch watch in 1985 were the Swiss able to regain some of their lost market. The $2.8 billion Swatch Group plans to expand in India with an assembly operation targeting the middle and low-end price range with the Swatch and Tissot brands.[47]

First, a company must determine who its competitors are. The domestic market will certainly provide some input. It is of great importance, however, to include any foreign company that either presently is a competitor or may become one in the future. For many firms, the constellation of competitors will most likely change over time. The U.S. company Caterpillar once considered other domestic competitors its major competitors both domestically and abroad. However, the Japanese firm Komatsu has now established itself as the second largest firm for earthmoving equipment, forcing Caterpillar to concentrate more resources on tracking Komatsu. Only 15 percent of Komatsu's revenue is in the United States and Europe, but given the economic slowdown in Asia, Komatsu is focusing on the United States with its backhoe loader.[48] Therefore, a company's monitoring system should include *all* major competitors, both domestic and foreign. Monitoring should not be restricted to activity in the competitors' domestic market but must include competitors' moves anywhere in the world. Many foreign firms innovate first in their home markets, and expand abroad only when the initial debugging of the product has been completed. Therefore, a U.S. firm would lose valuable time if, say, a Japanese competitor's action would be picked up only on entry into the U.S. market. Any monitoring system needs to be structured to ensure that competitors' actions will be spotted wherever they occur first. Komatsu, Caterpillar's major competitor worldwide, subscribed to the *Journal Star*, the major daily newspaper in Caterpillar's hometown, Peoria, Illinois. Also important are the actions taken by subsidiaries; they may signal future moves elsewhere in a company's global network of subsidiaries.

Table 6.5 contains a list of the type of information a company may wish to collect about its competitors. Aside from the general business statistics, a competitor's prof-

Table 6.5 Monitoring Competition: Facts to Be Collected

Overall Company Statistics

Sales and market share profits

Balance sheet

Capital expenditures

Number of employees

Production capacity

Research and development capability

Marketing Operations

Types of products (quality, performance, features)

Service and/or warranty granted

Prices and pricing strategy

Advertising strategy and budgets

Size and type of sales force

Distribution system (includes entry strategy)

Delivery schedules (also spare parts)

Sales territory (geographic)

Future Intentions

New product developments

Current test markets

Scheduled plant capacity expansions

Planned capital expenditures

Planned entry into new markets/countries

Competitive Behavior

Pricing behavior

Reaction to competitive moves, past and expected

itability may shed some light on its capacity to pursue new business in the future. Learning about others' marketing operations will allow the investigating company to assess, among other things, the market share to be gained in any given market. Whenever major actions are planned, it is extremely helpful to know what the likely reaction of competitive firms will be and to include them in a company's contingency planning. In addition, of course, monitoring a competitor's new products or expansion programs may give early hints on future competitive threats.

Analysis that focuses on studying the products of key competitors can often miss the real strength of the competitor. Studying the core competencies in an industry is important for understanding an industry and where it is headed over the next five years. For example, Chaparral Steel, a profitable U.S. steel maker, sends its managers and engineers to competitors, customers, and suppliers' factories to identify the trends and skills that will lead steel making in the future. Chaparral also attends trade shows and visits university research departments to spot new competencies that may offer an opportunity or pose a threat.[49]

There are numerous ways to monitor competitors' activities. Thorough study of trade or industry journals is an obvious starting point. Also, frequent visits to major trade fairs where competitors exhibit their products can help a company monitor its competitors. At one such fair in Texas, Caterpillar engineers were seen measuring Komatsu equipment.[50] Other important information can be gathered from foreign subsidiaries located in the home markets of major competitors. The Italian office equipment manufacturer, Olivetti, assigned a major intelligence function to its U.S. subsidiary because of that unit's direct access to competitive products in the U.S. marketplace. A different approach was adopted by the Japanese pharmaceutical company Esei, which opened a liaison office in Switzerland, home base to several of the world's leading pharmaceutical companies.

There is a widespread impression that U.S. and European firms are much less vigilant than their Asian counterparts about monitoring competition. For example, Mitsubishi has between 650 and 800 employees in New York to gather intelligence information about their U.S. competitors. The South Koreans are not far behind; the intelligence systems of their three largest trading companies were developed by an ex-colonel of the South Korean military intelligence. The systems require real-time reporting to a central processing unit by every branch manager around the world.[51] The examples from Japan and Korea suggest that a business intelligence system requires a coordinated effort that draws on the knowledge of the entire organization. Keeping track of a firm's competitors is an important international research function. Kodak learned through competitive intelligence that Fuji was planning a new camera for the U.S. market. Kodak launched a competing model just one day before Fuji. Motorola discovered through a member of its intelligence staff who was fluent in Japanese that the Japanese electronics firms planned to build new semiconductor plants in Europe. Motorola changed its strategy to build market share in Europe before the new capacity was built. This type of intelligence can be critical to a firm.[52]

ENVIRONMENTAL STUDIES

Frequently it becomes necessary to study the international environment beyond the customary monitoring function that most global executives perform. Of particular interest are the economic, physical, sociocultural, and political environments.

In any focus on the economic environment, primary interest will be on the economic activity in target countries. Major economic indicators are GNP growth, interest levels, industrial output, employment levels, and the monetary policy of the country under investigation. Studies focusing on a country are frequently undertaken when a major decision regarding that country has to be made. Examples of these major decisions are a move to enter the country or a significant increase in the firm's presence in that market through large new investments.

Also frequently studied are the international economy and the role of the various supranational organizations as they affect the business climate for global companies. For example, it is important for companies active in Europe to learn about the possible impact of new regulations or decisions of the European Union. Frequently, reviews of such agencies or groups are ordered when a major move is imminent and information is needed on the potential impact of these decisions.

Since the physical environment tends to be the most stable aspect of the foreign marketing environment, such studies are frequently made for major market entry decisions or when the introduction of a new product requires a special analysis of that particular aspect of the environment. Included in the physical environment are population and related statistics on growth, age composition, birthrates, and life expectancy, as well as data on the climate and geography of a country.

Of particular interest is the sociocultural environment, which was already described in some detail in Chapter 3. The salient factors include social classes, family life, lifestyles, role expectations of the sexes, reference groups, religion, education, language, customs, and traditions. Market researchers have classified these statistics as *psychographics*. Of primary interest to the global company is the potential effect of these variables on the sale of its products. Since the sociocultural environment is also unlikely to change over the short run and changes that do occur tend to be of a more gradual nature, such studies are most likely ordered when a major marketing decision in the local market is contemplated. As a company gains experience in any given country, its staff and local organization accumulate considerable data on the social and cultural situation, and data can be tapped whenever needed. Therefore, a full study of these environmental variables is most useful when the company does not already have a base in that country and experience is limited.

Management will often investigate the regulatory environment of a given country because those influences can substantially affect marketing operations anywhere. Today, regulatory influences can originate with both national and supranational organizations. National bodies tend to influence the marketing scene within the borders of one country only, whereas supranational agencies reach beyond any individual country. National regulations may include particular rulings affecting all businesses, such as product liability laws, or rulings targeted at individual industries only. In the United States, the latter type would include regulations issued by the U.S. Food and Drug Administration (FDA) and the U.S. Department of Commerce. Examples of supranational regulations are those issued by the European Union with respect to business conducted among the member nations, and the United Nations' Center for Transnational Corporations' nonbinding code of conduct for international companies.

Regulatory trends can be of great importance to global companies and may even lead to new opportunities. It is generally accepted by most observers that U.S. safety and emission control regulations for passenger automobiles are the world's most stringent. Recognizing this fact, the French company Peugeot has maintained a small beachhead in the U.S. market, even with a small and insignificant sales volume, primarily to gain the experience of engineering cars under these stringent conditions. The company feels that this experience can be applied elsewhere when other countries adopt similar regulations. Consequently, a company will monitor the regulatory environment to adopt products and marketing operations for other reasons besides achieving local success. Firms may also find it useful to keep informed about the latest regulations regarding their business in countries that have led the way with pertinent legislation, even if they may not conduct any business there.

DEVELOPING A GLOBAL INFORMATION SYSTEM

Companies that are already or are planning to become global marketers must look at the world marketplace to identify global opportunities. Evaluating the full range of opportunities requires a global perspective for market research. Although many global players started in the triad of North America, Japan, and Europe, these areas represent only 15 percent of the planet's population. Eastern Europe offers opportunities, with a combined GNP from Hungary, Czechoslovakia, and the former East Germany. This region has relatively well-trained and low-paid workers. Indonesia, the fifth most populated country in the world, has cut government paperwork by 67 percent in an effort to stimulate growth and attract foreign investors. China, with the second largest economy and the largest population, offers significant opportunities. India, the second largest country, with 800 million people, has been eliminating regulations to open its markets. For example, in 1988, Indians bought 6 million televisions, up from only 150,000 sets a decade earlier. In approaching the marketplace from a global perspective, companies need to look not only at countries but also at industries and segments.

The forces that affect industry should be analyzed to determine the competitiveness of the industry and the role of the major forces, such as buyers, suppliers, new entrants, substitutes, and competitors.[53] In addition, companies need to look for global industry shifts and position themselves to take advantage of them. For example, a retailer examining the do-it-yourself market may notice that the car-servicing industry is shifting because of changes in automotive technology. Given the mechanical reliability of today's cars, the maintenance needs of owners of secondhand cars beyond the warranty do not require skilled labor on complex equipment. These repairs can be done in specialty workshops at a lower cost and can thus be done more conveniently than by the authorized dealer.[54] Predicting this type of industry shift opens opportunities for the vigilant company.

Globalization also means that companies are looking for new ways to segment markets, especially when demographics fail. There is a trend toward classifying consumers based on lifestyles, attitudes, and preferences rather than nationalities. If you plan to build a global brand, you need segments that are similar regardless of nationality.[55] Building a global brand does require having the same brand image and meaning in each country that optimizes brand effectiveness in local, regional, and international markets.[56]

Table 6.6 Top Twenty-Five Global Research Organizations

Rank 2000	Rank 1999	Organization	Research Company Headquarters	Parent Country	No. of Countries with Subsidiaries/ Branch Offices[1]	Full-time Employees	Global Research Revenues[2] (US$ millions)	Percent Change from 1999[3]	Revenues from Outside Home Country (US$ in millions)	Percent of Global Revenues from Outside Home Country
1	1	ACNielsen Corp.	Stamford, Conn.	USA	80	21,000	$1,577.0	2.1%	$1,056.6	67.0%
2	2	IMS Health Inc.	Westport, Conn.	USA	74	8,000	1,131.2	9.1	707.0	62.5
3	3	The Kantar Group	Fairfield, Conn.	U.K.	59	5,800	928.6	17.6**	662.8	71.4
4	4	Taylor Nelson Sofres Plc.	London	U.K.	41	7,125	709.6	8.5	533.9	75.2
5	5	Information Resources Inc.	Chicago, Ill.	USA	17	4,000	531.9	2.8	133.0	25.0
6	–	VNU Inc.	New York, N.Y.	USA	21	2,916	526.9	15.5	13.8	2.6
7	6	NFO WorldGroup Inc.	Greenwich, Conn.	USA	38	3,500	470.5	2.9	293.6	62.4
8	8	GFK Group	Nuremberg	Germany	34	4,212	444.0	9.1	277.1	62.4
9	10	Ipsos Group S.A.	Paris	France	24	2,437	304.2	13.0	238.1	78.3
10	11	Westat Inc.	Rockville, Md.	USA	1	1,430	264.4	9.3	0.0	0.0
11	9	NOP World	New York, N.Y. & London	U.K.	6	1,302	246.1	8.0	147.7	60.0
12	14	Aegis Research	Arlington Heights, Ill. & Hong Kong	U.K.	12	1,980	232.2	11.2	74.8	32.2
13	12	Arbitron Inc.	New York, N.Y.	USA	2	700	205.8	8.8	8.0	3.4
14	15	Video Research Ltd.	Tokyo	Japan	2	347*	174.3*	7.7*	0.0	0.0
15	13	Maritz Research	St. Louis, Mo.	USA	4	608	172.0	1.3	54.2	31.6
16	16	The NPD Group Inc.	Port Washington, N.Y.	USA	13	880	164.3	14.6	28.0	17.0

(continued)

17	18	Opinion Research Corp.	Princeton, N.J.	USA	8	1,900	123.9	10.6	35.8	28.9
18	17	INTAGE Inc.	Tokyo	Japan	2	370*	119.3*	6.8*	2.2*	1.8*
19	19	J.D. Power and Associates	Agoura Hills, Calif.	USA	5	550	104.0	11.9	16.0	15.4
20	20	Roper Starch Worldwide Inc.	Harrison, N.Y.	USA	2	448	73.9	12.0	10.6	14.3
21	–	Jupiter Media Metrix Inc.	New York, N.Y.	USA	15	850	69.1	152.6	10.4	15.0
22	21	Dentsu Research Inc.	Tokyo	Japan	1	96	67.6	8.0	0.2	0.3
23	25	IBOPE Group	Rio de Janeiro	Brazil	12	1,268	60.7	30.8	19.3	31.8
24	–	Harris Interactive Inc.	Rochester, N.Y.	USA	3	568	56.0	50.8	3.0	5.4
25	–	MORPACE International Inc.	Farmington Hills, Mich.	USA	3	345	54.3	22.3	14.2	26.1
Total						72,632	**$8,812.7**	**8.7%**	**$4,340.3**	**49.3%**

[1] Includes countries which have subsidiaries with an equity interest or branch offices, or both.

[2] Total revenues that include non-research activities for some companies are significantly higher. This information is given in the individual company profiles.

[3] Rate of growth from year to year has been adjusted so as not to include revenue gains or losses from acquisitions or divestitures. See company profiles for explanation. Rate of growth is based on home country currency.

* For fiscal year ending March 31, 2001.

** Constant currency basis.

Source: Marketing News, August 19, 2002. Copyright © 2002 American Marketing Association. Used with permission.

The demand for quality multicountry research has spurred the market research industry to expand beyond traditional national boundaries. In 2000, the world market for global market research was worth about $15 billion. The North American market was worth approximately $6,356 million; Europe was worth $5,944 million, with the United Kingdom, Germany, and France making up about 25 percent of the world market. Asia Pacific was worth $2,130 million, Central and South America was worth about $697 million, and the rest of the world was worth $136 million.[57]

In 1999, Nielsen introduced its first pan-European research service, called Quartz, which provides simulated market tests based on consumer reactions in five European countries. Twenty-five multinationals, including Nestlé, Procter & Gamble, and Danone Group, have already signed up for the service. Europanel, a consortium of Europe's leading consumer panel companies, has developed a pan-European service called the European Market Measurement Database. It tracks the movement of consumer goods throughout western Europe, based on information from fifty-five thousand households. ACNielsen, the leading global market research firm, offers services in over one hundred countries and had 2000 revenues of $1,577 million.[58] The global research companies have purchased several national market research companies.

Global market research companies have experienced rapid growth in recent years because of expanding research services, new research measuring devices, and innovative techniques. The largest industrial market research companies are shown in Table 6.6. The top twenty-five global research firms made up 58 percent of the total market in 2000. The larger firms have been acquiring smaller firms to expand their global abilities. Two firms, ACNielsen and IMS Health, account for one-third of the revenue of the top twenty-five global research companies.[59] Electronic scanner data are now available in many markets and offer very fast retail consumer data for marketers.[60] As a revolutionary communication tool, the Internet is also pushing research horizons, and revenues, as companies measure consumer response.

To assist decision making about marketing on a global scale, researchers must provide more than data on strictly local factors within each country. All firms that market their products in overseas markets require information that allows analysis across several countries or markets. However, leaving each local subsidiary or market to develop its own database does not usually result in an integrated marketing information system (MIS). Instead, authority to develop a centrally managed MIS must be assigned to a central location, with reports given directly to the firm's chief international marketing officer. Jagdish Sheth made an effective case for a centralized marketing research staff that would monitor buyer needs on a worldwide basis.[61] Sheth favors the establishment of a longitudinal panel in selected geographical areas encompassing all major markets, present and potential. By assessing client needs on a worldwide basis, the company ensures that products and services are designed with all buyers in mind. This approach avoids the traditional pattern of initially designing products for the company's home market and looking at export or foreign opportunities only after a product has been designed. A principal requirement for a worldwide MIS is a standardized set of data to be collected from each market or country. Though the actual data collection can be left to a firm's local units, they will do so according to central and uniform specifications.

Companies are analyzing only a small percentage of the data currently available, and in the case of retail, data available are doubling every year. A new technique of data mining has been developed to extract previously unknown yet comprehensive and useful information from large databases and to use this information to make critical business decisions. Coca-Cola is linking with its bottler's partners around the world to share information and best practice. In a planned seven-year rollout, Coca-Cola anticipates boosting revenue by sharing sales information and communicating more effectively with its partners. The new system will upgrade and expand data warehouses, decision support systems, and a worldwide Intranet to improve communications.[62]

CONCLUSIONS

In this chapter, we discussed the major challenges and difficulties in securing necessary data for global marketing. We have shown that effective marketing research is based on a conceptual framework combined with a thorough but flexible use of conventional marketing research practices. The amount of online secondary data from around the world has made it much easier for global marketers to assess global opportunities. There are many challenges when collecting primary data in multiple countries. Often research methods will have to be adapted to local environments. The final challenge of global marketing research is to provide managers with a uniform database covering all the firm's present and potential markets. Such a database will allow for cross-country comparisons and analysis as well as the incorporation of worldwide consumer needs into the initial product design process. Given the volume of secondary data and the difficulties in primary data collection, maintaining a global database is indeed a challenge for even the most experienced professionals.

The value of market research cannot be understated, especially in new developing markets. The use of properly conducted market research can reduce or eliminate most global marketing mistakes. Market research can uncover local adaptation needs, potential name problems, promotion requirements, and appropriate market strategies.[63] Sound global marketing research techniques uncover potentially costly and often embarrassing situations.

The world has changed greatly since the first edition of this text in 1987. At that time, market information around the world was sparse and unreliable, especially in developing and undeveloped countries. Now, through the efforts of the United Nations, global market research companies, and online data sources, information is available for every market in the world, from Canada and Mexico to Uzbekistan and Mongolia. For example, a recent report from the United Nations included in-depth analysis of the investment opportunities in Ethiopia, Tanzania, Egypt, Uzbekistan, Uganda, Peru, Mauritius, and Ecuador. This report includes information on the economy and specific opportunities in various industries, along with the availability of human resources, science and technology resources, and government support.[64] Global marketers can use the widely available information to make better market decisions and marketing strategies.

Questions for Discussion

1. Why is it so difficult to conduct marketing research in multicountry settings?

2. What role does the Internet play in global marketing research?

3. Comparative marketing analysis is a powerful technique that provides the basis for the study of global marketing. What is the comparative approach, and how is it applied to multicountry environments?

4. What are the advantages and disadvantages of secondary and primary data in global marketing?

5. What are the challenges of using a market research questionnaire developed in one country and used in several other countries?

6. If you were estimating the demand for vacuum cleaners, what type of inference analysis would you use? Give a specific example.

7. If you were the president of Kodak, how would you monitor reactions around the world to a major competitor such as Fuji Film?

For Further Reading

Asay, Sylvia, and Charles B. Hennon. "The Challenge of Conducting Qualitative Family Research in International Settings." *Family and Consumer Sciences Research Journal,* June 1, 1999, pp. 409–420.

Craig, C. Samuel, and Susan Douglas, "Conducting International Market Research in the Twenty-First Century," *International Marketing Review,* vol. 18, no. 1, 2001, pp. 80–90.

Craig, C. Samuel, and Susan P. Douglas. *International Marketing Research: Concepts and Methods.* New York: Wiley, 1999.

Douglas, Susan, Craig C. Samuel, and Edwin J. Nijssen. "Integrating Branding Strategy Across Markets." *Journal of International Marketing,* 2001, vol. 9, no. 2, pp. 97–114.

Greenbaum, Thomas L. "Understanding Focus Group Research Abroad." *Marketing News,* June 3, 1996, pp. H14, H36.

Helgeson, Neil. "Research Isn't Linear When Done Globally." *Marketing News,* July 19, 1999, p. 13.

Keillor, Bruce D., and G. T. M. Hult. "A Five-Country Study of National Identity Implications for International Marketing Research and Practice." *International Marketing Review,* 1999, vol. 16, no. 1, pp. 65–84.

Kumar, V. *International Marketing Research.* Upper Saddle River, N.J.: Prentice Hall, 2000.

McGorry, Susan Y. "Measurement in a Cross-Cultural Environment." *Qualitative Market Research,* vol. 3, no. 2, pp. 74–81.

Medina, Jose F., Sharon E. Beatty, and Joel Saegert. "Consumer Acquisition Patterns in an Industrializing Country: A Study of Global Convergence of Demand." *Journal of Global Marketing,* 1996, vol. 10, no. 2, pp. 5–25.

Mundorf, Norbert, Rudy Roy Dholakia, Nikhilesh Dholakia, and Stuart Westin. "German and American Consumer Orientations to Information Technologies: Implications for Marketing and Public Policy." *Journal of International Consumer Marketing,* 1996, vol. 8, no. 3, pp. 125–143.

"Research Companies Push Global Expansion." *Advertising Age,* March 8, 1993, p. 31.

Sheth, Jagdish N. "The Antecedents and Consequences of Integrated Global Marketing." *International Marketing Review,* vol. 18, no. 1, p. 16.

Steenkamp, Jan-Benedict. "The Role of National Culture in International Research." *International Marketing Review,* vol. 18, no. 1, pp. 30–44.

Winters, Lewis C. "International Psychographics." *Marketing Research: A Magazine of Management and Application,* September 1992, pp. 48–49.

Endnotes

1. Samual Craig and Susan Douglas, "Conducting International Market Research in the Twenty-First Century," *International Marketing Review*, 2001, vol. 18, no. 1, pp. 80–90.

2. "How Stodgy Turned Stylish," *The Wall Street Journal*, May 3, 2002, p. B1.

3. David A. Ricks, *Blunders in International Business*, 3d ed. (New York: Blackwell, 1999), pp. 130–136.

4. Juliana Koranteng, "Tracking What's Trendy, Hot Before It's Old News," *Advertising Age International*, May 1996, p. 130.

5. Tobi Elkin, "Gearning Up for Xbox Launch," *Advertising Age*, November 20, 2000, p.16.

6. C. Samuel Craig and Susan P. Douglas, *International Marketing Research* (New York: Wiley, 2000), pp. 16–9.

7. *http://www.stat.go.jp/english/data/kokusei/2000/kihon1/00/mokuji.htm*; accessed on May 24, 2002.

8. *http://www.statistics.gov.uk/statbase/ssdataset.asp?vlnk=5375&B4.x=74&B4.y=9*; accessed on May 24, 2002.

9. *http://eirestat.cso.ie/CNBLdesc.html*; accessed on May 24, 2002.

10. Hans Baumbartner, and Jan-Benedict E.M. Steenkamp, "Response Styles in Marketing Research: A Cross-National Investigation," *Journal of Marketing Research*, vol. 38, no. 2, pp. 143–156.

11. Gabriel Kahn, "Keeping in Touch with China's Taste Requires Creativity," *The Wall Street Journal Europe*, April 25, 2002, p. A6.

12. Jean Boddeyn, "A Framework for Comparative Marketing Research," *Journal of Marketing Research*, May 1966, pp. 149–153; Jean Boddeyn, *Comparative Management and Marketing* (Glenview, Ill.: Scott, Foresman, 1969).

13. Jean-Pierre Jeannet, "International Marketing Analysis: A Comparative-Analytic Approach," working paper, 1981.

14. Robert F. Hartley, "McDonald's: Could There Be Storms on the Horizon?" *Marketing Mistakes and Successes* (New York: Wiley, 1998), p. 273.

15. Farland Chang, "Western Ideas, Asian Empire," *CNNfn: Entrepreneurs Only*, June 7, 1999.

16. Al Labita, "Jollibee to Open More Fast Food Outlets in U.S.," *Business Times* (Singapore), March 22, 1999, p. 20.

17. Robert F. Hartley, *Marketing Mistakes and Successes* (New York: Wiley, 1998), p. 237.

18. Robert D. Buzzell, "Can You Standardize Multinational Marketing?" *Harvard Business Review*, November–December 1968, pp. 102–113.

19. Warren J. Keegan, *Global Marketing Management*, 7th ed. (Upper Saddle River, N.J.: Prentice Hall, 2001), pp. 421–426.

20. "Starbucks May Have Run out of Steam in Japan," *Financial Times*, July 9, 2002, p. 17

21. Craig and Douglas, *International Marketing Research*, pp. 16–19.

22. Erin White, "Market Research on the Internet Has Its Drawbacks," *The Wall Street Journal*, March 2, 2000.

23. "China: What's in a Number? Worries About Reliability Plague All Who Use Chinese Statistics," *East Asian Executive Reports*, September 15, 1997, pp. 8, 14.

24. "The Use of Secondary Information Published by the PRC Government," *Journal of Market Research Society*, July 1, 1999, p. 355.

25. "The Good Statistics Guide," *Economist*, September 11, 1993, p. 65.

26. "Russia's Unemployment Rate Rises Year-On-Year," *Interfax News Agency*, June 21, 1999, p. 1.

27. Jeffery D. Zbar, "Need Seen for Standard in TV Audience Data," *Advertising Age International Supplemen: i32*, March 11, 1996, p. 131.

28. *World Bank Atlas 2002*. (Washington, D.C.: World Bank, 2002), p. 46.

29. "Few Damned Lies," *Economist*, March 30, 1996, p. 54.

30. "The Unmeasurable Lightness of Being," *Economist*, November 23, 1996, pp. 85–86.

31. "Crunch Debates for Anti-Smoking Week," *Vietnam Investment Review*, May 28, 2001, p.2.

32. Craig and Douglas, *International Marketing Research*, p. 132.

33. "Wired but Wary," *Business Wire*, November 9, 1999.

34. Robin Cobb, "Marketing Shares," *Marketing*, February 22, 1990, p. 44.

35. David Ricks, *Blunders in International Business*, 3d ed. (United Kingdom: Blackwell, 1999), p. 39.

36. Ibid., p. 1.

37. Kevin Reagan, "In Asia, Think Globally, Communicate Locally," *Marketing News*, July 19, 1999, pp. 12–14.

38. Emanual H. Demby, "ESOMAR Urges Changes in Reporting Demographics, Issues Worldwide Report," *Marketing News*, January 8, 1990, p. 24.

39. James Heckman, "Marketers Waiting, Will See on EU Privacy," *Marketing News*, June 7, 1999, p. 4.

40. "EU Denies Breakdown in Data Privacy Talks with the U.S.," *Dow Jones International*, May 31, 1999, p. 1.

41. Stephen Connell, "Travel Broadens the Mind–The Case for International Research," *International Journal of Market Research*, January 1, 2002, vol. 44, no. 1, p. 97.

42. Gilbert A. Churchill, Jr., and Dawn Iacobucci, *Marketing Research Methodological*, 8th ed. (New York: Harcourt College, 2002), p. 459.

43. W. Boyd Harper, Jr., Ronald E. Frank, William F. Massy, and Mostafa Zoheir, "On the Use of Marketing Research in the Emerging Economies," *Journal of Marketing Research*, November 1964, vol. 1, pp. 20–23.

44. Richard D. Robinson, *Internationalization of Business*, 2d ed. (Chicago, Ill.: Dryden Press, 1984), p. 36.

45. Franklin R. Root, *Entry Strategies for International Markets* (New York: Jossey-Bass, 1999), p. 41.

46. Gilbert D. Harrell and Richard O. Kiefer, "Multinational Strategic Market Portfolios," *MSU Business Topics*, Winter 1981, pp. 5–15.

47. Iqbal Singh Ahmedabad, "Swatch May Launch Low-End Watches," *Business Standard*, April 6, 1999, p. 8.

48. Peter Marsh, "Japan's Komatsu to Enter U.S. Heavy-Equipment Market," *Financial Times*, December 7, 1998, p. 19.

49. C. K. Prahalad and Gary Hamel, "The Core Competence of the Corporation," *Harvard Business Review*, May–June 1990, pp. 79–91.

50. Ibid.

51. Benjamin Gilad, "The Role of Organized Competitive Intelligence in Corporate Strategy," *Columbia Journal of World Business*, Winter 1989, p. 32.

52. "High Price of Industrial Espionage," *Times of London,* June 5, 1999, p. 31.

53. Michael E. Porter, *Competitive Strategy: Techniques for Analyzing Industries and Competitors* (New York: Free Press, 1980), p. 4.

54. Xavier Gilbert and Paul Stebel, "Taking Advantage of Industry Shifts," *European Management Journal,* 1990, vol. 7, no. 4, p. 399.

55. V. Kumar and Anish Nagpal, "Segmenting Global Markets: Look Before You Leap," *Marketing Research,* Spring 2001, vol. 13, no. 1, pp. 8–13.

56. Shelly Branch, "ACNielsen Gives 43 Brands Global Status," *The Wall Street Jouranl,* October 31, 2001, p. B8.

57. "ESOMAR, Annual Report of the Market Research Industry 2000," *ESOMAR,* 2001, p. 3, *www.esomar.nl;* accessed on May 30, 2002.

58. "ESOMAR, Annual Report of the Market Research Industry 2000," *ESOMAR,* 2001, p. 21, *www.esomar.nl;* accessed on November 22, 2002.

59. "ESOMAR, Annual Report of the Market Research Industry 2000," *ESOMAR,* 2001, p. 8, *www.esomar.nl;* accessed on May 30, 2002.

60. Kenneth Wylie, "100 Leading Research Companies," *Advertising Age,* May 20, 1996, p. 39.

61. Jagdish N. Sheth, "A Conceptual Model of Long-Range Multinational Marketing Planning," *Management International Review,* 1971, vol. 4, no. 5, pp. 3–10.

62. Bob Violino, "Extended Enterprise—Coca-Cola Is Linking Its IT System with Those of Worldwide Bottling Partners as It Strives to Stay One Step Ahead of the Competition," *Information Week,* March 22, 1999, pp. 46–54.

63. David A. Ricks, *Blunders in International Business,* 3d ed., p. 159.

64. United Nations Conference on Trade and Development, *Investment Policy Review* (Geneva: United Nations, 2002), *http://www.unctad.org/en/pub/investpolicy.en.htm.*

Part III

Developing Global Marketing Opportunities

COMPETENCE LEVEL	GLOBAL ENVIRONMENT
ENVIRONMENTAL COMPETENCE	*Understanding the Global Marketing Environment*
	2 3 4
ANALYTIC COMPETENCE	*Analyzing Global Marketing Opportunities*
	5 6
STRATEGIC COMPETENCE	*Developing Global Marketing Strategies*
	7 8 9
FUNCTIONAL COMPETENCE	*Designing Global Marketing Programs* 10
	11 12 13 14 15
MANAGERIAL COMPETENCE	*Managing the Global Marketing Effort*
	16 17

Companies are being asked more and more often to design their marketing strategies from a global point of view. Globalized marketing strategies require an ability to look at business and competitive developments on a worldwide basis and to incorporate often conflicting information into a single, workable global marketing plan. Global marketing strategies require skills and conceptual understanding that are different from those required for developing domestic marketing strategies.

In Part III, we concentrate on the global marketing strategies that firms must be able to develop to be successful. No company can be all things to all people, and global marketing managers have to learn to focus and build on their company's strengths. Global marketing managers must have the strategic competence necessary to develop global marketing programs that will ensure the success of their firms.

Chapter 7 deals with the global mindset required of future global marketing managers. Chapter 8 concentrates on the major strategic decisions faced by firms active in global marketing. The chapter introduces the most recent concepts on globalization of marketing strategies. Alternative market entry strategies will be the subject of Chapter 9.

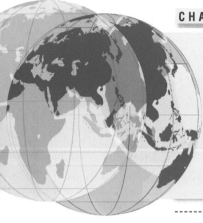

Developing a Global Mindset

The slogan "Think globally, act locally" is frequently used to describe the managerial challenge faced by global marketers.[1] It captures the need to think in global terms about a business or a market while at the same time tailoring a product or service to meet the particular requirements of the local customers. In this chapter, we give some background information on what is meant by thinking globally. If this thinking is truly different, and thus requires a new mindset (namely, a global one), one should be able to differentiate it from a more traditional mindset. Therefore, we have decided to offer detailed ideas about what this new global marketer with a global perspective ought to be able to do, how he or she should be able to think, and what kind of skills could be expected from such a person. This chapter is different from others because it does not focus primarily on existing business practice. Instead, we concentrate on developing new analytic tools that will make the adoption of a global perspective more likely.[2]

CATEGORIZING GLOBAL MARKETING MINDSETS

The mindset is the outlook or frame of mind that the marketer carries around the world. The global perspective, or mindset, is characterized by a different view of the opportunities and the facts of the world market. The global marketing perspective is more encompassing than the domestic, international, multinational, or even panregional perspective.[3] It is a new, truly different dimension in managerial thinking that transcends traditional labels and shapes the outlook of global marketers. See Figure 7.1 for a detailed illustration of the concepts discussed in this chapter.

Figure 7.1: Elements of the Global Mindset

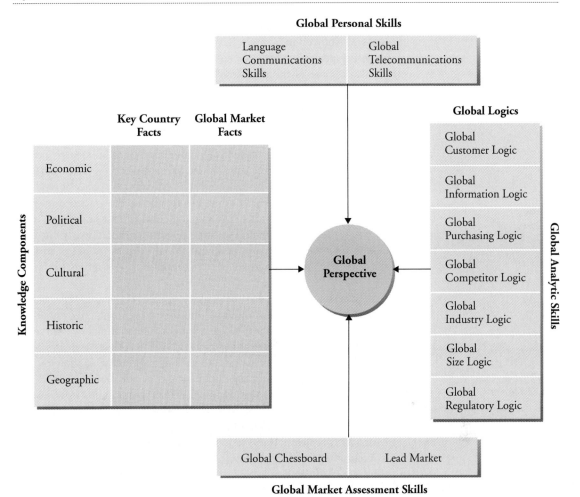

DOMESTIC MINDSET

The *domestic perspective,* or *domestic mindset,* is characterized by the fact that all basic anchor points for a marketer are based on a single-country experience: his or her domestic market. A marketing executive growing up in the United States and professionally active in the U.S. market has only a single-country, domestic mindset. The same is true for a Dutch manager growing up and living in Holland only. Thus, the domestic mindset is always single-country in nature. As we all know, marketers must constantly refer to their own experience as they make marketing decisions. Facts are not always spelled out completely, and executives typically fill in the blanks from their own cultural experience. The domestic mind tends to fill in those blanks from its own domestic market or cultural perspective.

Falling back on one's own cultural or domestic experience base comes naturally to executives. As we showed in Chapter 3, violating cultural norms in another country is commonplace because executives, or companies, go to a different country and automatically transfer some of their underlying assumptions to the new locale. The reverse, however, is also true. When data from a different country are available, executives with a domestic perspective often find that set of data meaningless, or discomfiting, preferring instead the business data from their own country.

The concept of the domestic perspective is not new to global marketing. For some time, executives have referred to such a perspective as ethnocentric, or culturebound.[4] This reaction of spurning data, facts, or readings from elsewhere is sometimes referred to as the not-invented-here (NIH) syndrome, a concept well known in engineering and scientific circles. It generally results in the rejection of new ideas that are not homegrown and stands in the way of adopting best practice in marketing, particularly when the idea originated in some distant market. Clearly, for marketing professionals to become effective in our new global economy, they must be able to step out of a domestic mindset and adapt a different, more open type of thinking.

INTERNATIONAL MINDSET

Marketing executives with an international mindset have broadened their reference points to other markets, typically through a longer international or overseas stay. A Japanese executive who has spent four years with a U.S. subsidiary can be expected to have broadened his or her perspective to an international one, allowing for incorporation of Japanese and U.S. reference points in his or her mind.

In many firms, executives are sent on international assignments for the single purpose of enhancing their perspective. Although working overseas provides a new perspective for the manager, substantial barriers limit opportunities. For one, sending a manager overseas is typically three to four times more costly than hiring locals.[5] The extra costs include cost-of-living allowances, different taxation schemes, and the expense of sending an entire family to a different country, including tuition for private schools.

An international experience for aspiring global marketers can take several different forms. Many students spend some time abroad in overseas university programs. International experience is gained if they have contact with the local environment. Likewise, the large numbers of international students in U.S. business schools gain international experience through their stay in the United States. At many business schools, an international experience is a requirement for graduation.

Sometimes, the impetus for international experience can be an unforeseen event. Mark Merson, a United Kingdom–based accountant with a major international accounting firm, was transferred by his firm from the United Kingdom to Tokyo, Japan, shortly after his promotion to partner. The firm wanted to make a major investment into training partners for its growing presence in Asian countries. For Mark Merson, this was his very first overseas posting, and his first experience with a very different cultural business environment. Speaking little Japanese, he had to learn how to work with local partners and adapt to their very different style of business. Because much of the work is done in international firms and in English, the absence of speaking

Japanese is not a major handicap. However, he still needs to adapt to Japanese behavioral patterns.[6]

All such experiences provide an international perspective as the student or executive gains in-depth knowledge of a foreign country. Although it is international experience in just one country, many experts believe that such a manager would be less subject to the NIH syndrome. By broadening the domestic, single-country perspective to an international (dual-country) view, the individual would in all likelihood respond more openly to an initiative in a new country than would the domestic-minded executive, for whom any international contact would be a first-time experience.

MULTINATIONAL MINDSET

Some executives, having gone through several overseas experiences or assignments, have reached a multinational perspective. These executives know more than one overseas country well. Often their assignments span a region, or even more than one region. In many large international firms, such as Citigroup, Nestlé, Unilever, and Shell, executives undertake a series of assignments, each of which may extend three to four years, in different locations. These executives not only become knowledgeable about one market or culture, but they have also learned how to master new cultures.

The cadres of executives with a multinational mindset are still largely bound, however, by their cultural and foreign experiences. Their skill derives from the detailed knowledge of those markets, knowledge gained from personal experience. While characterizing the multinational perspective as incorporating a greater quantity of in-depth international experience is fair, it still should not be confused with a global perspective, the unique mindset we describe in more detail in a following section.

Some executives believe that a multinational mindset is developed as a result of a series of single-country assignments. Even when executives move around the world assuming ever greater responsibility, however, they frequently receive these assignments in the context of a single-country market. It would not be unusual for an executive to be "promoted" from smaller to larger countries but still have assignments that limit responsibility to the assigned country. Therefore, the development of a truly global outlook, encompassing many different countries or markets at the same time, is stifled. A global mindset is not merely the accumulation of a series of single-country experiences; instead, it goes far beyond this approach and reflects a different type of thinking.

PANREGIONAL MINDSET

The panregional mindset is a variant of both the multinational and the global mindset. It incorporates the ability to encompass an entire region, such as Europe, and incorporate the realities of several countries at once. A marketing manager with extensive experience across many European markets would be called a pan-European manager. Panregional managers gain their experience from exercising marketing responsibility across numerous markets. In the case of Europe, this experience might include more than twenty different countries. Other panregional experiences might be gained in Asia and Latin America. Because of the nature of their responsibilities, panregional managers are much closer to the thinking of marketing managers with a global mindset because the need to think across many markets simultaneously is a precursor to the global mindset. Therefore, we shall move next to our fifth and final mindset.

GLOBAL MINDSET

With the global mindset, we are stepping into a type of perspective fundamentally different from the four previously described. The global perspective encompasses *all* cultures or nationalities; it might be described as a mind hovering like a satellite over the earth.[7] The global mindset calls for a manager with a capability to maintain equal "mental" distance from all regions of the world. However, such a manager should not be construed as a person without any cultural anchor. Rather, the executive with a global perspective maintains that point of view with respect to his or her business or profession. A personal cultural anchor point is still required for personal balance. Marketing managers with a global mindset can keep the entire global opportunity for a business in mind and can think across multiple markets rather than compartmentalize issues on one market at a time. They are able to see the "big picture" and are sensitive to the links between markets and trends across the world.

International, panregional, and multinational mindsets depend on experience gained from direct contact with one or several other countries and cultures. The marketing executive with a global mindset achieves that view for the entire world, even for areas where no direct prior experience exists. This ability is essential because managers who act with global responsibility for a product, segment, category, or some other project cannot possibly be personally exposed to all countries.

Although we have not yet said so explicitly, the global mindset is also an attitude. Executives with a global mindset display an innate curiosity about world developments. They recognize a need for continued, permanent, lifelong learning because much of what they know becomes obsolete over time. Executives who aspire to a global mindset need to recognize the integration of industries into a global economy. In this new global economy, they must see their industry as an interconnected whole and appreciate that events generated in this dynamic shape their industry and their customers' needs over time. This global mindset, then, is both an attitude as well as a cognitive capability to exercise a certain set of new analytic skills.

A marketing executive who wants to achieve a global mindset will have to think differently about the worldwide opportunity. The following sections of this chapter define those differences in thinking more clearly. We will concentrate on the particular knowledge required for a global mindset, the new global analytic skills to be applied, the strategic concepts to be understood, the personal skills to be mastered, and the managerial capabilities to be acquired.

KNOWLEDGE COMPONENTS FOR THE GLOBAL MINDSET

In the previous section, we described the kind of outlook, or mindset, a marketing manager with a global perspective brings to an assignment. Although such an outlook is important, it alone cannot suffice. The marketing manager with a global mindset will need knowledge about the world markets. The knowledge components described in this section represent core knowledge but are not necessarily complete. The components we discuss, however, will most likely account for a vast majority of the necessary factual knowledge. They might serve as a guide to aspiring global marketing managers who are in the process of acquainting themselves with the world.

Again, with the world constantly changing, such knowledge can never be viewed as final or static; it is in constant need of updating.

KEY MARKET KNOWLEDGE

With the world consisting of more than two hundred countries and territories, it would be impossible for anyone to have firsthand and factual knowledge of all these markets. Instead, knowledge of *key markets* will have to suffice. Key markets are the top twenty markets in a given industry. Keep in mind, however, that the top twenty markets might vary depending on the line of business. In most industries, 80 percent or more of the economic activity can be expected to come from the top twenty country markets, so we have structured the knowledge components around such a list. For the purpose of this book, we use the list of the top twenty countries determined by gross domestic product (GDP) and adjusted by purchasing power parity (see Table 7.1). Because these markets are of strategic value, marketing managers need to understand the parameters that shape the market dynamics.

Table 7.1 Top 20 Countries Ranked by Gross Domestic Product		
Ranking	Country	US$ Billions
1	United States	9,728
2	China	5,386
3	Japan	3,384
4	India	2,510
5	Germany	2,075
6	France	1,455
7	United Kingdom	1,437
8	Italy	1,388
9	Brazil	1,319
10	Russia	1,280
11	Mexico	881
12	Canada	865
13	Korea	846
14	Spain	790
15	Indonesia	662
16	Australia	503
17	Taiwan	496
18	Argentina	448
19	Turkey	419
20	Netherlands	413

Source: The World Competitiveness Yearbook 2002, Lausanne: IMD Institute, 2001, p. 350.

ECONOMIC KNOWLEDGE

Although statistical knowledge has some value, marketing managers need to have an understanding of the economic dynamics in a key market. It is important to know the present stage of the economic cycle. Another piece of required knowledge is the type of economic system and the structure of the economy. Understanding a country's monetary system and foreign exchange regime is important, as is up-to-date knowledge of foreign exchange trends. The marketer with a global perspective must know economic developments in the key markets so that a clear tapestry of the economic activity emerges. Key areas of market economic knowledge are listed in Table 7.2. Real understanding comes from combining these facts into a composite understanding of the present and future economic situation of any key market.

POLITICAL KNOWLEDGE

The global marketing manager needs to know the current and future political trends for each key market. This knowledge will certainly include knowledge about the important political institutions and how the country is governed. Among other things, managers need to know the importance of the various political parties, their political programs, something about the country's political leaders, and a sense of the leaders' electoral chances for success. As it has been practiced traditionally, country analysis will not be sufficient to understand the dynamics in key markets. Companies have to understand the key drivers in the industrial policies of countries. Increasingly, governments strive for added competitiveness, often in the form of generating more exports. The resulting economic policies affect players in that country and, given today's global economy, often extend their influence into other countries.

Executives used to be concerned about political risk as it related to expropriations, or loss of assets; today's global marketing manager worries more about opportunities lost or missed. The future development of the political system in China is of great interest to companies with major plants there, not because they are anxious about losing them but because political policy affects their future growth or profitability. The same can be said for Russia or any other part of the world where major changes might occur. The executive with a global mindset is always alert to relevant developments in the leading markets of the company's industry.

CULTURAL KNOWLEDGE

Each key market has its own cultural heritage.[8] A manager with a global mindset is expected to understand those major cultural traits and how they can shape customers

Table 7.2 Key Areas of Market Economic Knowledge

GNP	Export volume
GNP growth	Import volume
GNP per capita	Foreign trade position
Major industrial sectors	Monetary policies
Inflation rate	Foreign reserve position
Interest level	Employment level

or business executives in the market. Such cultural knowledge will certainly include an understanding of the language or languages spoken—for example, in the case of Brazil, Portuguese is the official language, whereas for Belgium it is French and Flemish (Dutch). In some companies, foreign language competency is critical. Matsushita, a leading Japanese firm, began to require that all of its managers pass an English competency test to be promoted. The company implemented this policy because it felt it would aid in globalizing its Japanese managers. Other Japanese firms, such as Toyota Motors, NEC, Hitachi, and Komatsu, have implemented similar policies.[9]

Additional knowledge of literature, the arts, or music might be important. In the case of Japan, for example, it would imply some understanding of traditional arts such as kabuki and No. Each country values its own leading artists, writers, and composers, and familiarity with the work of these people is integral to understanding the culture of any country. Included in cultural knowledge is an understanding of the religious background of the country. As we explained in detail in Chapter 3, the business environment is significantly affected if the country has a Christian, Muslim, or other religious tradition. For many countries, some understanding of the more popular local sports may be part of knowing the local culture.

HISTORIC KNOWLEDGE

Executives often underestimate the value of appreciating a country's history. Many developments that appear to be of a short-term political nature are driven by the long-term historical experiences of a country. How groups of executives relate to each other is also influenced by that heritage. Although global marketers typically know the historical background of their own country, few know the key historical developments or defining moments that shaped the present in their relevant key markets. Marketers need not know history for history's sake, but they should learn the relevant historical facts that still shape, or influence, the political and economic life of a country in the present. Looking over the list of the top twenty economies in Table 7.1 indicates where gaps exist. As the developments in a country such as the former Yugoslavia demonstrate, present actions are often rooted in history and can date back as many as six hundred years.[10] Commenting on the defining historic moments of Finland, some observers believe that knowledge of Finland's history—and especially its 1939 war with the Soviet Union—is important in understanding the determination that some Finnish companies apply to the conquering of world markets.[11]

GEOGRAPHIC KNOWLEDGE

Part of a thorough understanding of a key market is knowledge of its main geographic features. This knowledge may include the locations of key cities and the logistics of getting in and out of the country. Knowing the size of a country, its key dimensions, and its topography is also essential. Another critical component of the geographic knowledge of a key market is an understanding of its transportation infrastructure (which might include seaports and airports for freight shipments, and rail, water, and highway systems) and the telecommunications infrastructure.

UNDERSTANDING GLOBAL MARKET FACTS

Up to now, we have discussed knowledge about a company's key markets. Those facts are about individual countries only. A much larger body of knowledge about the global economy, politics, history, culture, and geography embraces all countries and plays an increasingly important role in today's business environment. A marketing manager with a global mindset appreciates this overarching global structure just as much as each individual key market.

Understanding *global economic forces,* rather than individual-country economic forces, requires knowledge about world trade, international economic structures, and the various international institutions that play a role in the creation of the global economy. Many international institutions—including the International Monetary Fund (IMF), the World Trade Organization (WTO), the Group of Seven (G7, consisting of the leaders of the seven largest economies of the world), and regional bodies such as the European Union (EU), the North American Free Trade Agreement (NAFTA), and the Association of South East Asian Nations (ASEAN)—have been described thoroughly in earlier chapters. In this category, we include understanding the current global economic trends that will shape the structure of the world economy over the next decades.[12]

The equivalent body of knowledge in the political realm consists of understanding how *global political forces* affect the global marketing environment. This knowledge goes beyond the political structures of any individual country but includes the role played by bodies such as the United Nations and an appreciation of the geopolitical realities of the day. The disappearance of communist regimes in eastern Europe cannot be treated as a single-country event but has to be understood in the context of world political forces.[13]

Country-specific history has its equivalent in a new body of knowledge that we could describe as world history. The understanding required is not the knowledge of just one country but the historical trends and developments over time, including a group of countries, a region, or even the entire world. Paul Kennedy's *Rise and Fall of the Great Powers* is but one example of the compilation of historical knowledge that aims at a global perspective in history.[14] In the same vein would be Denis de Rougemont's comprehensive work on the history and development of Europe, which incorporates the philosophical and historical development of an entire continent or region.[15] Equivalent works exist in the following areas: *world culture,* where the current media trends might be included; *world geography,* where a clear understanding of world trade patterns and trade routes could be included; and the history of *world trade.*

THE IMPORTANCE OF ACQUIRING GLOBAL KEY MARKET KNOWLEDGE

To some extent, the knowledge we are describing in this section may be viewed as strictly factual, the kind contained in a library. However, executives do not always consult their library when making decisions about the importance of key markets. Any decisions can be made based on erroneous, unverified knowledge and thus can result in less than optimal global marketing strategies. Significantly underestimating a country's population without checking current figures might lead to the elimination of a market that otherwise should be part of a global marketing strategy. Some studies have shown that knowledge about key markets or world affairs varies considerably between countries and that U.S. managers particularly may be approaching global marketing battles with less factual knowledge than managers from other countries.

A realistic strategy of acquiring knowledge of key markets and the global marketplace thus can be an important ingredient in the success of individual executives and companies. Sources such as the *World Competitive Yearbook* are readily available and contain valuable information.[16]

ANALYTICAL GLOBAL MARKETING SKILLS

Acquiring a global marketing perspective is much more than mastering global marketing facts. Marketing managers who want to plot strategy with a global mindset will be challenged to process the vast amount of data they acquire in different ways. In this section, we examine the thinking and analytic routines that executives have to go through as they chart global marketing strategies from a large set of data.

For space reasons, we do not give a complete summary of the analytic competence required by global marketers. Basic marketing analysis, used for both single-country and multicountry situations, is not covered here. We concentrate on some of the unique marketing analytic skills, concepts, and tools that are relevant primarily in global marketing. These topics are grouped around the concept of *global logic,* with special emphasis on how it applies to global marketing.[17]

THE GLOBAL LOGIC CONCEPT

We use *global logic* as an imperative *in the marketplace that requires a company to adopt a global strategy.* When the global logic is very strong, it creates a mandate to pursue marketing operations on a global scale, accommodating the global imperative. Alternatively, if the global logic were disregarded, the firm presumably would suffer negative competitive consequences. The company facing a global logic in its business must accommodate that logic or suffer competitively.

Whereas the global logic applies to the entire business strategy of a firm, the more specific *global marketing logic* describes the forces that demand the adoption of a global marketing strategy. The global marketer must understand the source of the global marketing logic because the strategic response might differ. The sources of a global marketing logic might rest with the customer base, thus creating a global *customer* logic or a global *information* logic. They may also come from the purchasing approaches, resulting in a global *purchasing* logic. The industry environment generates its own global logic sources. The strategies pursued by competitors are at the source of the global *competitor* logic. The industry and the relevant key success factors can combine to create a global *industry* logic. The presence of a strong critical mass requirement can lead to the global *size* logic. And finally, we can identify a global *regulatory* logic relating to the regulatory environment. We will now explore each of these sources of global marketing logic in more detail.

CUSTOMER-BASED GLOBAL LOGICS

Customer-based global logic was at the beginning of marketing globalization. In the early 1980s, many firms began to review their globalizing customers and determine the need for globalization from their customer base. As a result, it does make sense to begin our review of globalization drivers from the customer angle. Different from the approaches taken initially, we have divided the customer-based global logic into several different specific logics that may not all apply equally for each industry. In fact, it is important to recognize that the pressure for globalization not only stems from what customers want to buy, but also from how they buy it and where they get their information.

GLOBAL CUSTOMER LOGIC

A company faces a global customer logic when customers demand a similar product in most countries and, in particular, when the same customer purchases a given product or service in many different locations, or countries. In few cases, however, is the nature of demand so homogeneous that there are virtually no differences among countries. More likely, levels of similarities and dissimilarities exist. How does the marketer answer the question, "Do we have a global customer?" (See Figure 7.2.) Analyzing the nature of the demand across countries is a starting point. Traditionally, companies have segmented their business or markets along product/market and country/geographic territories. This traditional matrix, depicted in Figure 7.3, captures the view that, as a company moves from one country to the next, significant changes occur in its marketing environment. The traditional view, emphasizing the country or geographic differences, is characterized through the presence of thick vertical lines, each representing significant country differences. A company viewing its business this way would constantly emphasize the difference in its global marketing strategies. Due to the differences, once a company is in a given country, experience gained there can be applied to other product lines, a process we call leveraging on the vertical axis.

The opposite view may be taken. A company may find that, while country differences exist, still larger and more significant differences exist across segments,

Figure 7.2: Global Customer Logic

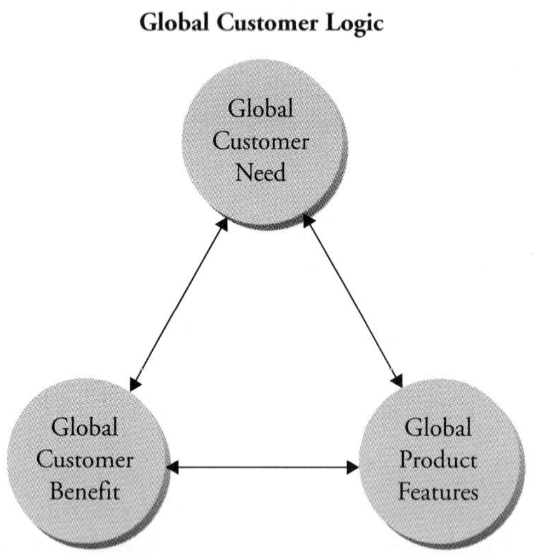

Global Customer Logic

Figure 7.3: Global Market Segmentation Matrix

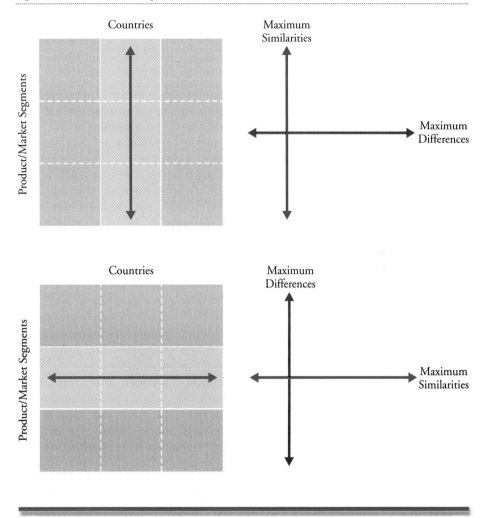

product lines, or industry sectors. In that situation, the horizontal lines between the segments are thick and solid, with the vertical lines separating countries fine and broken. In such a situation, the emphasis on the analysis is on the horizontal axis, where leverage occurs across a segment, product line, or sector. Similarities across countries are significant and can be exploited. We describe this as the horizontal view.

The marketer with a global mindset will discern between geographic differences and segment-specific similarities. For products more rooted in customs, such as food, differences along geographic lines may be greater than those across segment lines. As one moves toward new technological products and into industrial products and services, the geographic differences are often smaller than the segment or industry differences. The particular matrix faced by a company, with its specific grid of lines on either the geographic or segment level, depends on the type of industry. We therefore cannot speak of a generalized matrix; instead, the global marketer must be able to determine the relevant type of matrix that confronts his or her company.

Although such an analysis might show to what extent a market may differ across many countries, a company has other ways to test for global customer logic. More likely, a partial global customer logic may exist. Few products, particularly consumer products, are demanded by consumers in exactly the same form because the comparison across countries is lacking. The ultimate form of global product, which entails essential similarity in features and form, is rarely achieved, a function of the differences in requirements among countries.

If a given underlying need for a product or service exists across many countries, it is called a *global need.* A product or service subject to global need would show its presence worldwide, with consumers in most countries indicating such a need. Many generic needs, such as the need for communications, food, and so on, are global needs. Marketing products that fit a global need could be undertaken with multidomestic approaches, offering each country its own version of that product bundle. Whether or not a product or service would be subject to a still more powerful global logic would depend on other things.

The second phase of customer globalization occurs at the benefit level. Companies whose customers derive the same benefit from a product or service will face a much more far-reaching form of global logic. Benefits touch on the content of marketing communications. When a company needs to accommodate a *global benefit,* it will move sooner or later toward some form of global communication. When customers desire similar features in products, a company is said to face a *global product logic.* Similarity in features allows companies to standardize products and to market more homogeneous products across world markets.

Not all companies face identical customer logic. A company may face a global product logic, requiring homogeneous products, but encounter significant differences in benefits sought among customers. For other firms, the opposite may be true; a customer base seeks similar benefits around the world but requires different product features. Companies have to be ready to accommodate different levels and intensity of global logic, with corresponding differences in their strategic response.

GLOBAL INFORMATION LOGIC

Another type of logic that is different from the first but also relates to the customer base is defined as the *information acquisition strategy* of a company's customers.[18] By information acquisition, we mean the way customers scan the environment, the type of media they read or are exposed to, and to what extent they go to obtain information about products and services a long distance from home. Traditional coverage of information acquisition is well documented in standard marketing texts. Typically, consumers or business customers scan the local media before making a particular purchasing decision. There was very little, if any, global information logic in the customer base that influenced international firms.

More recent developments, however, have made such influences more pervasive and thus affect the presence of a global information logic. Many business-to-business customers in technology-driven sectors tend to read specific magazines or publications, mostly from the United States, thus making that information available to buyers in other countries. A Belgium buyer reviewing a U.S.-based industry publication thus acts to acquire information on a global scale, not just locally. This is particularly true for sectors such as information technology, communications, computers, electronic commerce, and medical instruments, where the U.S. market is viewed as the lead market and developments in the United States are quickly spotted elsewhere.

As a next step, buyers might go to specific trade shows with a global attendance. Such shows exist in both the United States and Europe, and for some industries they are the most important events. Telecom is a major trade show taking place every four years in Geneva, Switzerland. Visitors come from all over the world, thus creating a global information acquisition opportunity. Other important trade shows can be identified for many specific industries. Frequent travel by business executives exposes many buyers to information outside their home country. To the extent they follow up and actively pursue such information, a global information logic exists.

In consumer industries, this development has been even more pronounced. Information sources have spread through cable TV channels and satellite TV, making it possible for consumers to sit in their living room in the Netherlands and watch a program transmitted from the United Kingdom. To reach such consumers, companies in the Netherlands may have to advertise via a foreign channel, although the customer is in many ways viewed as a domestic customer. Sports events, such as the Olympics or world championships, create other strong global information logics. The commitment of advertisers to the Olympics in Sidney, Australia, was not primarily driven by the potential exposure to event visitors or even the Australian market. Instead, these companies were pursuing customers "joining in" via television from many countries. The actual event site is immaterial. Global companies are primarily interested in the audience generated by the event.

Possibly the most important change in our information acquisition is the development of the Internet and the World Wide Web (WWW). This new electronic network has rapidly become a new mode for researching product or service information. Consumers anywhere can enter the WWW and locate product information in a different country, thus creating strong global information logic.

Any company seeking to understand thoroughly the forces that shape the global marketplace must recognize the changing way by which customers acquire information. Neglecting global information logic in a business would put the company's entire communications strategy at risk, and any global strategy needs to be based on a thorough understanding of this logic.

GLOBAL PURCHASING LOGIC

Across the world, customers show different types of purchasing behavior and processes. A company is subject to a global purchasing logic to the extent that its customers search the world for best products as opposed to purchasing within a given local market only. In many industries, a customer no longer buys within the confines of one country only. Although this is less the case in consumer goods markets, industrial buyers are becoming accustomed to look for the best bargain on a regional or even a worldwide basis.

Automobile companies' purchasing behavior for parts used in assembling cars provides an example. Total parts costs traditionally account for 45 percent of total product costs for car makers.[19] Typically, parts purchases were sent out for bid each year, splitting supply contracts among several companies to bid down prices. In recent years, these companies have begun to pay more attention to parts costs as a way to increase efficiency. In some of the high-technology sectors of parts (for example, automotive electronics, which includes automatic breaking systems or engine management systems), research costs have amounted to about 10 percent of parts costs for parts suppliers. With each part supplier paying for its own research to fit components into specific car models, car companies have in fact paid for the same set of research costs several times. This situation has led some companies—GM was first among them—to concentrate parts purchases on fewer suppliers, at times even a single supplier, per car model and to give them a contract over the entire model life cycle.

Parallel to this development, car companies have begun to insist on best prices and now engage in worldwide sourcing. Rather than purchasing from nearby plants, a car company will source a greater distance away for lower costs. In some cases, parts are flown in by cargo aircraft from long distances on a regularly determined schedule, "just in time." This setup has changed the way companies purchase parts and locate plants, making the entire world the shopping plaza for firms that no longer source in the same country or nearby. Thus, the automotive parts and components industry has become subject to a strong global purchasing logic wherein buyers, car companies in this case, search the world for the best bargain. Many car components suppliers have had to adjust to this demand, often turning local firms into global suppliers, if they wanted to survive.[20] The presence of global sourcing or global purchasing practices in an industry is therefore one of the strongest indications of the presence of a significant global purchasing logic.

The presence of a gray market is another indicator. Gray markets exist where prices for a given product or service between two countries are widely different. Customers aware of that price difference begin to purchase in the low-price area and move the products into the high-price area. These gray-market activities are not illegal, and in Chapter 10 we explore this phenomenon in greater detail. We need to understand, however, that industries in which such activities persist are subject to a global purchasing logic. Many international firms experience this phenomenon constantly. When Sony launched its PlayStation 2, the game machine was first introduced in Japan and later in the U.S. market. Asian licensed dealers did not get the machine until much later. Still, PlayStation 2 had been available in Hong Kong and Taiwan for some time, with pirated versions of the software widely available.[21] Professional traders are likely to fill the void left by global companies for products that are subject to global demand, indicating the presence of a strong global purchasing logic.

This test of global purchasing logic is often present therefore in industry or business-to-business markets. It happens far less in consumer marketing because individual consumers usually buy a given product or service in one location only. Citicorp, the leading U.S.-based international bank, has encountered similar requirements among its wealthy customers looking for private banking services. The company began to offer a Citigold service to upwardly mobile Asian private customers with access to banking services wherever Citicorp has a branch—worldwide.[22] For some leisure or travel-related products, such as films, hotels, or even telephone services, a global purchasing logic exists because travelers can purchase these services from different locations if the price is right.

INDUSTRY-BASED GLOBAL LOGICS

When the debate on the merits of globalization began in the early 1980s, the predominant assumption among proponents of globalization was the belief that consumers, or customers, were becoming more similar, thus driving the trend toward globalization. In previous editions, this section was largely devoted to these trends and explained in detail sources of the various pressures that might compel firms to adopt some form of a global marketing strategy. However, there are still many firms for which pressure from the customer base itself is not sufficiently strong to warrant all-out global marketing strategies. Instead, as the experience of countless other firms has shown, different forces, often related to an industry's competitive behavior, or inherent industry economics may outshine customer-based forces as a source for globalization. These industry-based global logics in the form of global competitor logic, global industry logic, global size logic, and global regulatory logic will be our focus for this section.[23]

GLOBAL COMPETITOR LOGIC

When the need to develop a global marketing strategy stems from the behavior of a company's major competitors, we are speaking of a *global competitor logic.* Global pressures rooted in competitive actions can be observed from specific competitive patterns. First and foremost, a firm might face global competitor logic when the firm encounters the same competitors consistently wherever it markets. In some industries, particularly those of industrial equipment, a small set of internationally active companies pursue major orders, such as for aircraft, power plants, turbines, and similar large installations. Whenever a large public tender is opened, the same sales teams pursue the contract, no matter the country in question. This situation is a clear sign of global competitor logic. The presence of other globally active players who can reach into most markets requires all players to adopt a global marketing strategy to remain competitive themselves.

In extreme situations, leading companies engage in what we call a *global chess game*. Picturing the world market as a chessboard, the global chess game implies a consistent, direct, and competitor-oriented move that is highly cognizant of the various market positions of each player. The competitive situation of Kodak versus Fuji Film has continued over many years and has taken place both in the United States and in Japan. Kodak wants to protect its business in the United States and Fuji aims to maintain its lead in Japan. In China, where the market dominance is up for grabs, Kodak signed an agreement with the Chinese government in 1997 to invest more than $1 billion into production assets in the country, with the government in return banning other foreign firms from producing locally for several years.[24] The battle of Caterpillar versus Komatsu is another typical example of such competitive games, in which two players face off worldwide and pursue competitive advantages in many territories.[25] Over the years, Caterpillar had been able to navigate the turbulences in the international environment to its advantage while keeping its rival in check. One of the most intense global competitive battles being waged presently pits Coca-Cola

Co. against PepsiCo, armed with their leading brands of Coke and Pepsi, respectively. Pepsi found itself outmaneuvered when its bottler in Venezuela was acquired overnight by Coke, resulting in a complete loss of local distribution for Pepsi. In addition, the global fight has extended to mineral water. Pepsi is leading in the United States with its Aquafina brand versus Coca Cola's Dasani brand, extending the same type of intensive competitive battle to other beverage categories.[26] As in a chess game, the competitors' moves are very open and visible, and each company continually takes into account the next move of the opponent.

The presence of significant global competitor logic is derived from the number of relevant competitive theaters. Companies must understand when they are competing in a single, global competitive theater, or arena, in which the eventual outcome or ranking denotes their competitive position on a worldwide basis. In one global competitive arena, it will make sense to consider market share on a global, not on a national, basis. Indicating the presence of a single competitive arena is the fact that the outcome in the world market race is more important than the ranking in any single national market. For a company such as Boeing, the global market share for wide-bodied passenger jets is more important than the market share in any given country. The U.S. company will therefore view any threat by its European rival Airbus as serious, particularly also in the important sector for low-cost airlines in the United States and Europe, where Airbus managed to crack a previous airtight Boeing monopoly.[27]

A company might find many individual-country theaters rather than one global theater, thus calling for country-by-country competition. In such a case, looking at market share and competitive position on a country-by-country basis would be more relevant. Intermediate strategies are required by regional competitive theaters, where the relevant unit of analysis then becomes the region, such as Europe, North America, or Asia. Global competitor logic is strongest where the company faces one single relevant global theater and weakest when the relevant competitive theater is one country only (see Figure 7.4).

Recent developments in some industries have shown, however, that care must be exercised in the analysis of global competitive theaters. An analysis in the white goods industry in 1980 might not have found much presence of any global competitor logic because main players were confined to regions (e.g., U.S. firms to the United States and European firms to parts of Europe). The aggressive competitive behavior of one single player, in this case Electrolux of Sweden, led to the acquisition of Zanussi, a major Italian producer, and White Westinghouse, a major U.S. company, in the 1980s, purchases that transformed an entire industry. Major U.S. firms reacted. Maytag purchased Hoover of the United Kingdom, Whirlpool acquired the appliance business of Philips of the Netherlands, and GE entered into a close agreement with GEC of the United Kingdom.[28] These moves were triggered by a perceived threat to their position by Electrolux. As a result, an entire industry with little global competitor logic was transformed into an industry with an overwhelming global competitive logic. For Maytag and GE Appliances, the globalization strategies did not create permanent positive results and Maytag later disinvested itself of its European acquisitions. On the other hand, Bosch Siemens, originally active only in Europe, has now announced several acquisitions in the U.S. market and made it clear that any major player needed to be among the top firms both in Europe and the United States. Clearly, firms without any accommodation of that global competitive logic risk

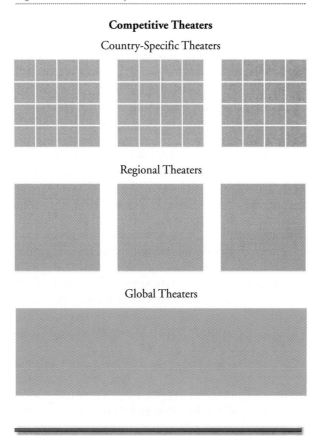

Competitive Theaters

Country-Specific Theaters

Regional Theaters

Global Theaters

competitive disadvantage over the long term. In many other industries as well, a sudden move by one major player has brought about a complete competitive reorganization and a sudden emergence of a global competitive logic.

GLOBAL INDUSTRY LOGIC

Conceptually, every industry requires some basic dos and don'ts for its participants. A company that violates these competitive rules invariably suffers competitive disadvantage and, in the long run, goes out of business. These basic rules of competition, required of any player that wants to be a member of a particular industry, have traditionally been called *key success factors* (KSFs).[29] When an industry is characterized by similar KSFs across the world, a global industry logic exists that would make transferring this experience from one country to another important.

Each company, successful in its home market, has learned how to deliver on the KSFs in its industry. An important indicator of global industry logic is the transferability of these KSFs across the world. If the lessons of competition and the basic competitive requirements for a company to sustain itself in an industry are essentially the same, the first and most important condition for a global industry logic exists. When a company competes in a global industry, applying any experience across many countries becomes of great importance. Firms that do so effectively gain a competitive advantage.

The presence of a significant global industry logic will often draw competitors into leveraging their experience into other countries, therefore also creating a secondary effect in the global competitor logic. The experience in the white-goods industry serves as an example. As mentioned above, Electrolux was the first player to pursue a global strategy, prompting many competitors to follow suit for fear of competitive disadvantage. Electrolux's original intent to change its strategy from essentially a country-by-country or even regional one (centering on Scandinavia) to a broader global strategy rested on some new assumptions. The Electrolux managers were not tempted by a sudden emergence of customers who all wanted the same appliances. Instead, they realized that, while appliances were different on the outside from country to country, the important components hidden from view were essentially the same. When costs for appliances became an important element, the costs for key components could be driven down only if the company gained economies of scale on compressors, pumps, and other elements present in millions of appliances.[30]

Electrolux believed that a competitive cost position for large component volume depended on gaining market share by acquiring other appliance makers in foreign countries. Electrolux was able to combine its component manufacturing with that of the acquired firms, reducing costs and investing in new models otherwise not affordable. This fundamental economic logic in the appliance business was not restricted to Electrolux's local market but applied to the world market as a whole. The company acted on this global industry logic, causing a competitive effect that changed the entire industry worldwide. Leveraging this type of component system may play a role in one industry, but in other industries, companies may be able to leverage other parts of the value chain. Whether a strong global industry logic exists in a given industry will depend on the presence of such leverage points.

GLOBAL SIZE LOGIC

A very particular logic is the one driven by *critical mass*. For many firms, a *minimal size* of a key activity needs to be sustained before they can safely compete in a given industry. The presence of some form of critical mass in the economics of an industry therefore easily relates to a global logic if that necessary critical mass can no longer be achieved in a single market. When companies need to pursue global markets to get over the critical mass hurdle, a global size logic exists.

Such critical mass issues exist in many industries. In the commercial airplane building business, the development of a new passenger jet requires huge sums of money. Boeing, together with Airbus (the leading builder of commercial airliners), estimates that a new model such as its planned high-speed Sonic Cruiser would cost about $10 billion.[31] No single domestic market is large enough to provide sufficient volume to justify such an investment, thus creating a global size logic that drives for maximum market coverage to recoup investment costs. In the pharmaceuticals industry, the development of a new drug, ranging from compound development through toxicology and clinical testing, tends to cost about $400 million in cash outlays. If the imputed interest for opportunity costs on the accumulated research outlay

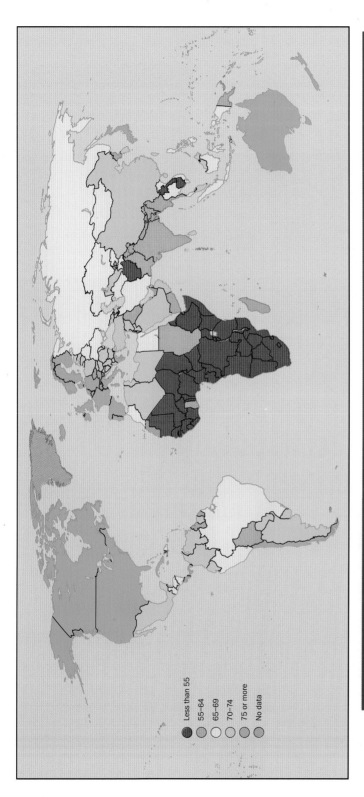

Life expectancy

Less than 55
55–64
65–69
70–74
75 or more
No data

Life expectancy at birth, 2000

The average number of years a newborn baby would live if patterns of mortality prevailing for all people at the time of its birth were to stay the same throughout its life.

Distribution of world population among economies grouped by life expectancy at birth

- Less than 55
- 55–64
- 65–69
- 70–74
- 75 or more
- No data

11%
25%
16%
31%
17%

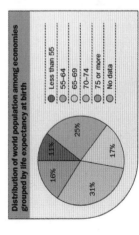

Life expectancy at birth, 2000, years

East Asia & Pacific — 69
Europe & Central Asia — 69
Latin America & Caribbean — 70
Middle East & North Africa — 68
South Asia — 62
Sub-Saharan Africa — 47
High income — 78

0   20   40   60   80   100

Life expectancy at birth, 2000, years

	Economies	GNI $ billions 2000	Population millions 2000	GNI per capita $ 2000
Less than 55	44	298	643	460
55–64	17	651	1,500	430
65–69	32	1,635	1,055	1,550
70–74	53	3,500	1,907	1,840
75 or more	50	25,219	952	26,500
No data	11	12	1	16,990

Source: Adapted from the 2002 World Bank Atlas. Copyright © 2002 the International Bank for Reconstruction and Development/The World Bank. Reprinted by permission.

Infant mortality

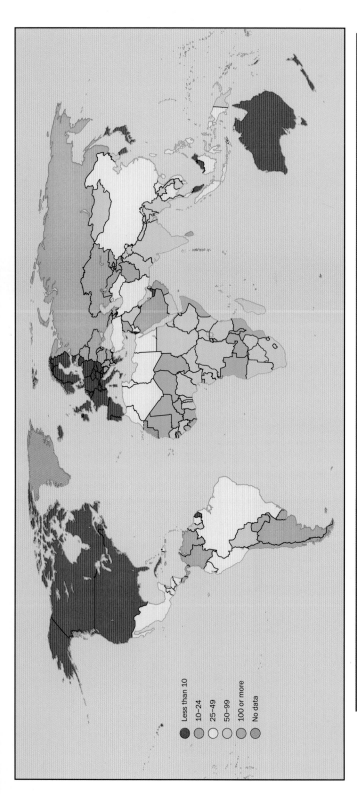

Infant mortality rate, 2000

The number of deaths of children under one year of age per thousand live births.

Legend:
- Less than 10
- 10–24
- 25–49
- 50–99
- 100 or more
- No data

Infant mortality rate, 2000, per 1,000 live births

Economies	GNI $ billions 2000	Population millions 2000	GNI per capita $ 2000
Less than 10	50	25,846	1,057	24,450
10–24	49	1,290	538	2,390
25–49	31	3,216	2,315	1,390
50–99	43	906	1,974	460
100 or more	19	44	172	260
No data	15	14	1	14,930

Infant mortality rate, 2000, per 1,000 live births

East Asia & Pacific	35
Europe & Central Asia	20
Latin America & Caribbean	29
Middle East & North Africa	43
South Asia	73
Sub-Saharan Africa	91
High income	6

Distribution of world population among economies grouped by infant mortality rate

- Less than 10 — 9%
- 10–24 — 33%
- 25–49 — 38%
- 50–99 — 17%
- 100 or more — 3%
- No data

Source: Adapted from the *2002 World Bank Atlas.* Copyright © 2002 the International Bank for Reconstruction and Development/The World Bank. Reprinted by permission.

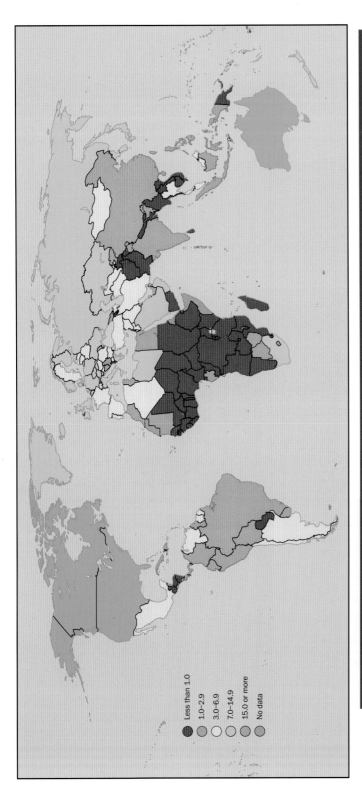

Greenhouse gas

Carbon dioxide emissions per capita, 1998

Emissions of CO_2 from the burning of fossil fuels and the man-ufacture of cement, divided by the population, expressed in metric tons.

Map legend:
- Less than 1.0
- 1.0–2.9
- 3.0–6.9
- 7.0–14.9
- 15.0 or more
- No data

Carbon dioxide emissions per capita, 1998, metric tons

Economies	GNI $ billions 2000	Population millions 2000	GNI per capita $ 2000
Less than 1.0	63	401	1,139	350
1.0–2.9	37	2,769	3,001	920
3.0–6.9	40	4,647	710	6,550
7.0–14.9	33	12,585	834	15,100
15.0 or more	15	10,883	344	31,600
No data	19	31	29	1,050

Carbon dioxide emissions per capita, 1998, metric tons

East Asia & Pacific	2.4
Europe & Central Asia	6.8
Latin America & Caribbean	2.6
Middle East & North Africa	3.9
South Asia	0.9
Sub-Saharan Africa	0.8
High income	12.6

Distribution of world population among economies grouped by carbon dioxide emissions per capita

- Less than 1.0 — 50%
- 1.0–2.9 — 12%
- 3.0–6.9 — 14%
- 7.0–14.9 — 6%
- 15.0 or more — 1%(?)
- No data

Source: Adapted from the 2002 World Bank Atlas. Copyright © 2002 the International Bank for Reconstruction and Development/The World Bank. Reprinted by permission.

Income per person

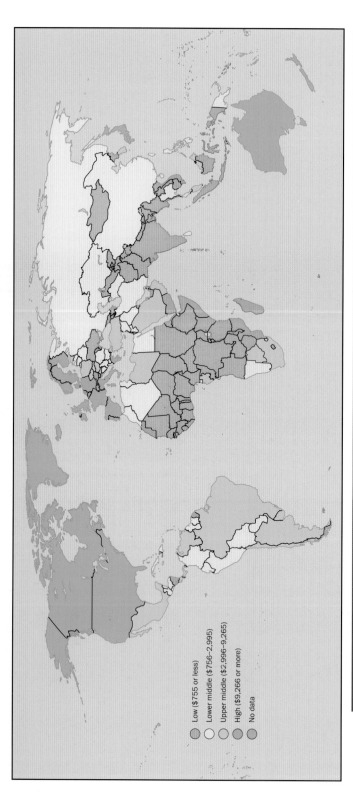

Low ($755 or less)
Lower middle ($756–2,995)
Upper middle ($2,996–9,265)
High ($9,266 or more)
No data

GNI per capita, 2000

Gross national income (formerly referred to as GNP)—the sum of gross value added by resident producers (plus taxes less subsidies) and net primary income from nonresident sources—divided by midyear population.

Distribution of world population among economies grouped by GNI per capita

- Low ($755 or less) — 41%
- Lower middle ($756–2,995) — 15%
- Upper middle ($2,996–9,265) — 11%
- High ($9,266 or more) — 34%

GNI per capita, 2000, $

East Asia & Pacific	1,060
Europe & Central Asia	2,010
Latin America & Caribbean	3,670
Middle East & North Africa	2,090
South Asia	440
Sub-Saharan Africa	470
High income	27,680

0   10,000   20,000   30,000

GNI per capita, 2000, $

	Economies	GNI $ billions 2000	Population millions 2000	GNI per capita $ 2000
Low ($755 or less)	63	997	2,460	410
Lower middle ($756–2,995)	54	2,324	2,048	1,130
Upper middle ($2,996–9,265)	38	3,001	647	4,640
High ($9,266 or more)	52	24,994	903	27,680
World	207	31,315	6,057	5,170

Source: Adapted from the *2002 World Bank Atlas.* Copyright © 2002 the International Bank for Reconstruction and Development/The World Bank. Reprinted by permission.

Income growth

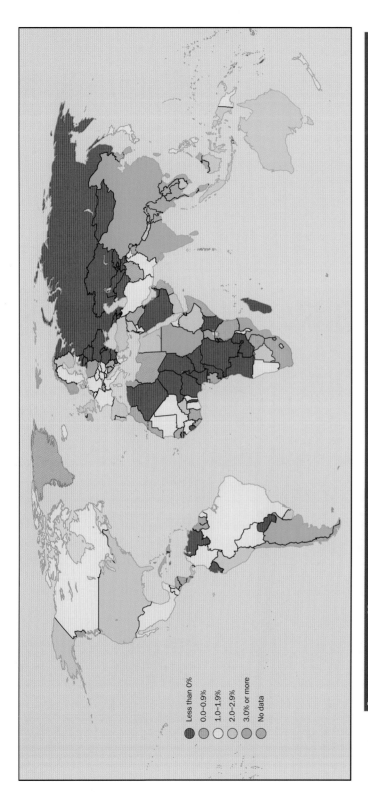

Less than 0%
0.0–0.9%
1.0–1.9%
2.0–2.9%
3.0% or more
No data

GDP per capita growth, 1990–2000

The average annual percentage change in a country's real GDP per capita. To exclude the effects of inflation, constant price GDP is used in calculating the growth rate.

GDP per capita annual growth rate, 1990–2000, percent	Economies	GNI $ billions 2000	Population millions 2000	GNI per capita $ 2000
Less than 0%	53	943	752	1,250
0.0–0.9%	17	496	166	2,980
1.0–1.9%	41	12,578	1,122	11,210
2.0–2.9%	31	13,550	975	13,890
3.0% or more	36	3,618	2,933	1,230
No data	29	129	108	1,190

Index of GDP per capita, 1980–2000, 1980 = 100

East Asia & Pacific
Latin America & Caribbean
Middle East & North Africa
South Asia
Sub-Saharan Africa

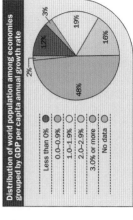

Distribution of world population among economies grouped by GDP per capita annual growth rate

- Less than 0%
- 0.0–0.9%
- 1.0–1.9%
- 2.0–2.9%
- 3.0% or more
- No data

2% 17% 3% 19% 16% 48%

Source: Adapted from the *2002 World Bank Atlas.* Copyright © 2002 the International Bank for Reconstruction and Development/The World Bank. Reprinted by permission.

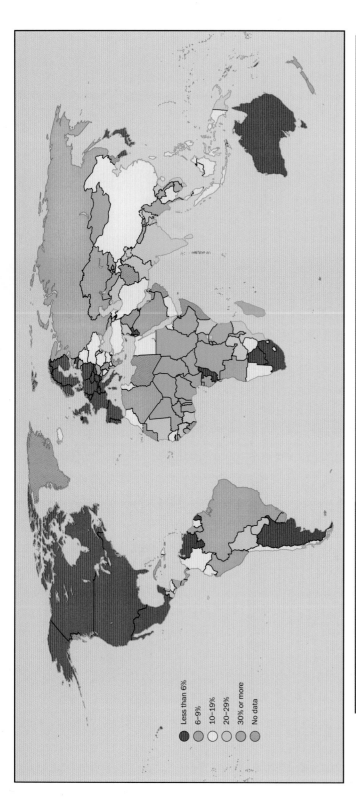

Less than 6%
6–9%
10–19%
20–29%
30% or more
No data

Agriculture

Agriculture share in GDP, 2000

The value added in a country's agricultural sector as a percentage of gross domestic product.

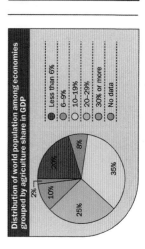

Distribution of world population among economies grouped by agriculture share in GDP

- Less than 6%
- 6–9%
- 10–19%
- 20–29%
- 30% or more
- No data

2%
10%
20%
8%
25%
35%

Agriculture share in GDP, 2000, percent

World	5
Low-income economies	24
Middle-income economies	9
Low- & middle-income economies	12
High-income economies	2

0 5 10 15 20 25 30

Agriculture share in GDP, 2000, percent

	Economies	GNI $ billions 2000	Population millions 2000	GNI per capita $ 2000
Less than 6%	48	26,350	1,194	22,060
6–9%	25	1,469	485	3,030
10–19%	41	2,308	2,121	1,090
20–29%	25	708	1,535	460
30% or more	35	154	603	250
No data	33	326	119	2,740

Source: Adapted from the *2002 World Bank Atlas.* Copyright © 2002 the International Bank for Reconstruction and Development/The World Bank. Reprinted by permission.

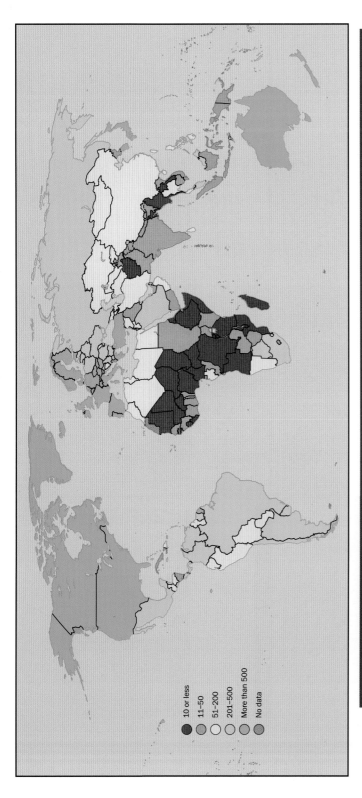

Telephones

Telephone lines and mobile phones per 1,000 people, 2000

Telephone lines connecting a customer's equipment to the public switched telephone network and mobile phones, per 1,000 people.

Distribution of world population among economies grouped by telephones per 1,000 people

- 10 or less
- 11–50
- 51–200
- 201–500
- More than 500
- No data

Fixed lines and mobile telephones per 1,000 people, 2000

East Asia & Pacific	171
Europe & Central Asia	314
Latin America & Caribbean	271
Middle East & North Africa	122
South Asia	31
Sub-Saharan Africa	32
High income	1,136

Fixed lines and mobile telephones per 1,000 people, 2000

Economies	GNI $ billions 2000	Population millions 2000	GNI per capita $ 2000
10 or less	27	162	250
11–50	36	1,758	460
51–200	42	1,806	1,020
201–500	42	2,727	3,390
More than 500	55	25,763	24,690
No data	5	9	2,640

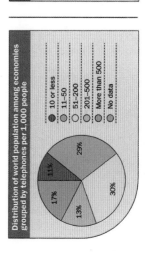

Source: Adapted from the *2002 World Bank Atlas.* Copyright © 2002 the International Bank for Reconstruction and Development/The World Bank. Reprinted by permission.

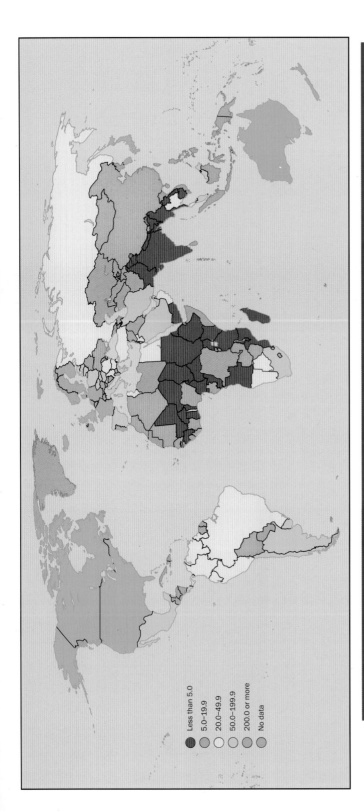

Personal computers

Personal computers per 1,000 people, 2000

The estimated number of self-contained computers designed to be used by a single individual, per 1,000 people.

Personal computers per 1,000 people, 2000

Economies	GNI $ billions 2000	Population millions 2000	GNI per capita $ 2000
Less than 5.0	30	684	1,729	400
5.0–19.9	32	1,583	2,021	780
20.0–49.9	24	1,660	684	2,430
50.0–199.9	38	3,704	507	7,300
200.0 or more	29	23,430	834	28,090
No data	54	254	282	900

Personal computers per 1,000 people, 2000

East Asia & Pacific	21.7
Europe & Central Asia	45.4
Latin America & Caribbean	43.6
Middle East & North Africa	31.2
South Asia	4.2
Sub-Saharan Africa	9.2
High income	392.7

0 100 200 300 400 500

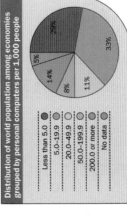

Distribution of world population among economies grouped by personal computers per 1,000 people

- Less than 5.0 — 29%
- 5.0–19.9 — 5%
- 20.0–49.9 — 14%
- 50.0–199.9 — 8%
- 200.0 or more — 11%
- No data — 33%

Source: Adapted from the *2002 World Bank Atlas.* Copyright © 2002 the International Bank for Reconstruction and Development/The World Bank. Reprinted by permission.

is included, total development doubles to $800 million.[32] In both instances, the amount of money a company may pay for research and development is limited. In few industries does this limit exceed 10 percent of sales revenue, and in the pharmaceuticals industry, it was estimated to have reached 20 percent of sales.[33] Whatever the acceptable percentage in a given industry, the relationship determines the volume the company needs to sell to pay off the entire development of a system or new product. In many industries, the minimal sales level to be achieved over the product life cycle exceeds the volume a company can expect to obtain in even as large a market as the United States.

The desire to achieve relevant size on a global basis has fueled several recent mergers in the pharmaceutical industry. Recent mergers and acquisitions include Bristol-Myers Squibb's acquisition of DuPont's pharmaceutical business, Johnson & Johnson's acquisition of Alza, and Abbott Laboratories' purchase of BASF's Knoll pharmaceutical unit. In each of these cases, the acquiring company attempted to increase its size to improve its competitive posture in a global competitive battle.[34]

The pursuit of new markets to pay off initial large investments for development is at the heart of the global size logic. What many of these companies have found is that the development or adjustment of an initial product to new markets is minor once the first step has been taken. Although we have cited mostly high-technology companies or industries so far, the same development can be seen in the motion picture industry, where true profitability often can be achieved only from foreign sales. Critical mass may be encountered in many ways. It may consist of a computer reservations system in one industry or a logistics system for another. Each industry must be analyzed separately and may show different patterns.

GLOBAL REGULATORY LOGIC

It has become apparent recently that governments, through their regulatory influence, can significantly affect the rationale for pursuing global strategies. Although in the past, government regulations have always had an impact on business, they tended to be country-specific in scope and, in general, did not push a company to pursue global marketing strategies. In several industries, recent trends toward deregulation, which implies a lowering of the regulatory threshold, have opened markets to foreign competitors and thus provided an impetus to globalization. Furthermore, some countries are treading the path of trade liberalization, allowing for more international entries into previously prohibited markets; this trend has also stimulated the growth of global logic. The recent entry of China into the WTO is a good example of such developments.

Such deregulation has had major repercussions in the international airlines industry. New types of accords, so-called open-sky agreements, have been signed between the United States and Italy, Korea, and the Czech Republic, giving more access to international airlines in both the U.S. and the foreign markets.[35] Such trends are causing some airlines to seek links with former competitors. The Star Alliance is an alliance among Lufthansa of Germany, United Airlines of the United States, Air Canada, Thai International, Scandinavian Airlines, and nine other airlines covering 729 airports in 124 countries. The Star Alliance resulted in a substantial increase of interline revenues for United, and about 8 percent of United passengers traveled Star Alliance partners.[36] Star Alliance members account for 24 percent of the world passenger market, and the alliance covers code share systems with other airlines, a frequent flyer program, ground services, and common lounge facilities at many airports. One airline member, Thai International, claims to have received benefits worth $90 million from the alliance in 2001.[37]

One of the industries most affected by recent regulatory activity is the telecommunications industry. With deregulation sweeping the world and resulting in most governments selling off their stakes in state monopolies, telecommunications companies suddenly have access to many more markets than before. The deregulatory fever, often taking the form of privatization of government-owned phone companies, is rapidly expanding the telecommunications market in many countries. It is being followed by a market opening that allows for multiple carriers in a given country. These trends are supported by new regulations or deregulation by the European Union (EU) and the World Trade Organization (WTO).

The market openings created many new opportunities for formerly government-owned phone monopolies. Both in Germany (Deutsche Telekom) and France (France Telecom), the phone companies were privatized, entered in the stock market, and encouraged to pursue opportunities abroad. Both Deutsche Telekom and France Telecom had acquired a combined stake of 22 percent in Sprint, only to sell their shares when the firms had to reduce debt loads in the wake of the telecommunications industry stock collapse in 2001.[38] Deregulations proceeded much more slowly in other countries. In Japan, where the government still owns a 45.9 percent stake in Nippon Telephone & Telegraph (NTT), foreign ownership was restricted to 20 percent.[39] NTT still controls 64 percent of DoCoMo, Japan's leading mobile phone company. Forced to allow competitors to enter the Japanese market, DoCoMo has made numerous investments in overseas mobile phone companies itself and tried to commercialize its new third-generation wireless service.[40] Foreign competitors would like to see the Japanese government reduce further its ownership of NTT and NTT reduce its ownership in DoCoMo to give them more access to those firms' purchasing of equipment and services. In Mexico, foreign telephone companies were also finding it difficult to enter. Although ostensibly privatized, Telmex, the formerly government-owned firm, still has a substantial hold on the Mexican market, allowing it to charge high access fees. Those favoring further deregulation point out that Mexico's phone density, with thirteen lines per 100 people, was below that of poorer countries such as Brazil, Columbia, and Costa Rica. A study by an international organization, OECD, found that of its thirty member nations, Mexico had the highest charge for a single phone line. However, Telmex is already preparing investments in the United States as a way to blunt further expected inroads into its domestic market, which were made possible by further deregulations.[41]

As these examples demonstrate, governments or other regulatory bodies can become major drivers forcing companies to take a global view of their markets. A company may thus have to review its situation carefully and monitor regulatory pressure for indications of impending changes in the world market.

INTEGRATING GLOBAL LOGICS INTO A COMPOSITE VIEW

So far in this section, we have focused on major global logics and how they might influence companies in designing global marketing strategies. We have described seven prototype, or generic, global logic forces, forces that we have found extremely useful for explaining the globalization pressures in a large number of industries. Conceivably, there could be others that might be more or less appropriate for a given industry. Although we have discussed these global logics one at a time, a company will of course be exposed simultaneously to several, and some will be more important than others. By plotting them on a single graph (see Figure 7.5), an analyst can get an impression of the nature of the pressures. Some firms might find the customer or purchasing logics stronger; other firms might find industry-based logics exerting greater pressure. Most likely, the graphs (spider webs) created would be different from industry to industry. Judging from the graphs, a firm facing a large footprint, exhibited by a larger area covered by the connected points, is said to face greater global logic than one facing a smaller footprint.[42]

Any firm must have a clear understanding of the particular set of forces it faces. Global logic patterns are rarely symmetrical, and it is important to isolate the dominating global logic in any given industry. In Chapter 8, we make a direct connection between the particular set of global logic forces faced by a firm and the suggested generic global marketing strategy best suited to that situation.

Global logic forces are not static. A company might well be able to describe the present constellation of global logic forces it faces. Equally important, however, are the trends and the expected forces that will enter the picture in the future. A company would thus be advised not only to analyze the present situation but also to understand the nature of the constellation as it will evolve in a particular industry. Effective global marketing strategies need to take into account the predicted constellation as the dominant factor.

The fundamental importance of the concept of global logic is its general validity. Once a global marketing logic exists in a given industry, all firms in the world market

Figure 7.5: Global Logic Patterns

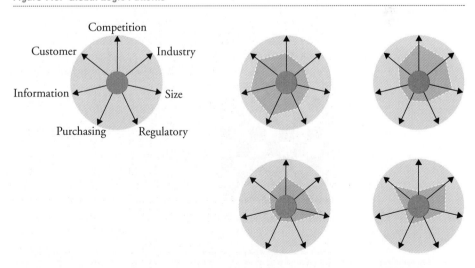

become subject to that imperative. A company facing considerable global logic pressures simply cannot avoid taking relevant action because global logic must be accommodated. Eventually, and inevitably, firms that disregard global logic forces face substantial competitive penalties over time.

GLOBAL MARKET AND OPPORTUNITY ASSESSMENT

To bring a global perspective to the analysis of marketing opportunities requires a new approach to the analysis of data. Traditionally, international marketers performed a considerable amount of analysis on a country-by-country basis. By contrast, marketing with a global mindset requires that additional analytic market assessment skills be acquired. This section introduces the global chessboard and lead markets as two new skills and concepts. They are to be viewed as additional skills beyond those already described in Chapter 6.

THE WORLD MARKET AS A GLOBAL CHESSBOARD

In the section on global competitor logic, we spoke of competition as a form of global chess. Rather than describing the rules of this game, we will concentrate on drawing analogies between the world market and the chessboard (see Figure 7.6). The global chessboard is not a square board consisting of sixty-four equal squares. Rather, it consists of many squares, one for each of the approximately two hundred countries that presently exist. Also, contrary to regular chess, in which each space is of equal size, the spaces on the global chessboard vary in size. In this game, square size represents market size, or typically, gross national product (GNP): countries with large GNPs are represented by large squares; countries with small GNPs are represented by correspondingly smaller squares. The United States, as the country with the largest GNP (representing about 20 percent of world GNP), would make up 20 percent of this global chessboard. Other countries would follow, each in proportion to its GNP.[43]

Figure 7.6: The Traditional Versus the Global Chessboard

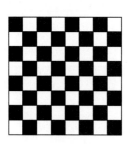

The Global Chessboard Differs

Has One Square for Each Country (200 plus)

The Squares Are Not All Equal in Size (Driven by GNP or Related Metric)

The Board Changes During Play (Political and Economic Developments)

Figure 7.6: The Traditional Versus the Global Chessboard (*continued*)

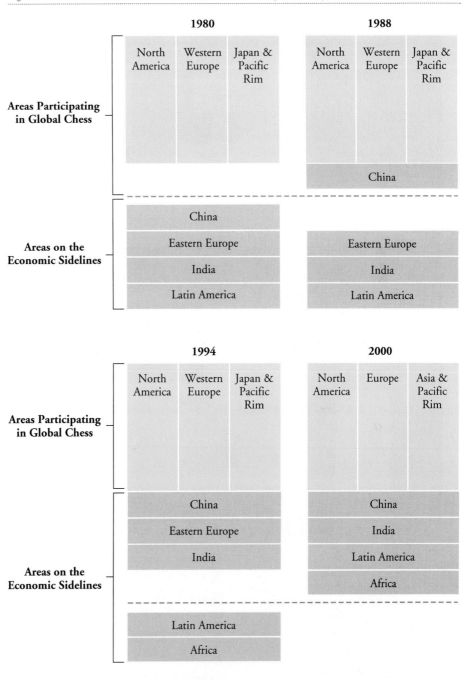

Figure 7.6: The Traditional Versus the Global Chessboard (*continued*)

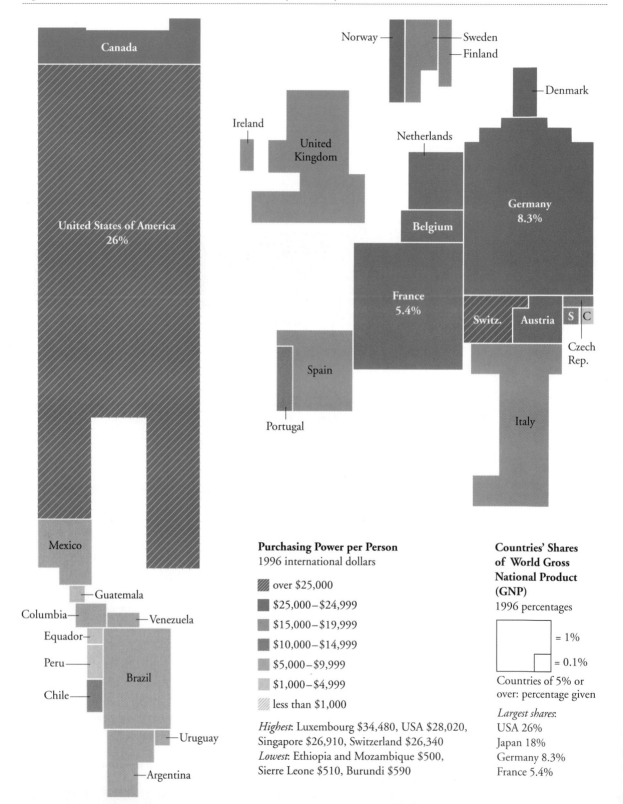

Canada

United States of America
26%

Mexico

Guatemala

Columbia—

Equador—

Peru—

Chile—

—Venezuela

Brazil

—Uruguay

—Argentina

Norway — Sweden
— Finland

Ireland

— Denmark

United Kingdom

Netherlands

Germany
8.3%

Belgium

France
5.4%

Switz.

Austria

S C

Czech Rep.

Spain

Italy

Portugal

Purchasing Power per Person
1996 international dollars

- over $25,000
- $25,000–$24,999
- $15,000–$19,999
- $10,000–$14,999
- $5,000–$9,999
- $1,000–$4,999
- less than $1,000

Highest: Luxembourg $34,480, USA $28,020,
Singapore $26,910, Switzerland $26,340
Lowest: Ethiopia and Mozambique $500,
Sierre Leone $510, Burundi $590

Countries' Shares of World Gross National Product (GNP)
1996 percentages

= 1%

= 0.1%

Countries of 5% or
over: percentage given

Largest shares:
USA 26%
Japan 18%
Germany 8.3%
France 5.4%

Figure 7.6: The Traditional Versus the Global Chessboard (*continued*)

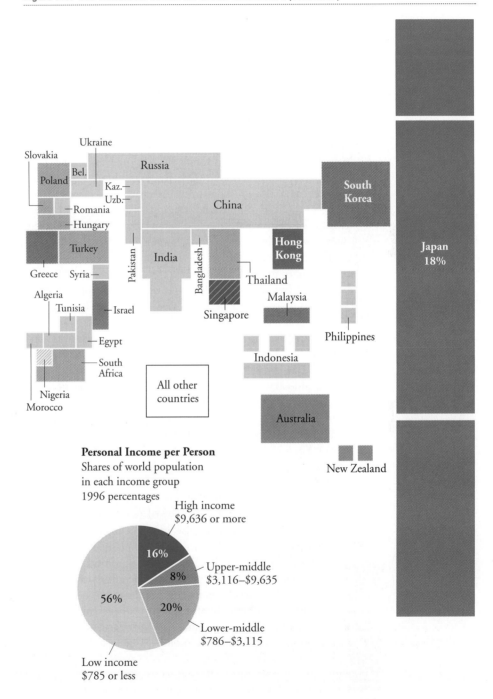

Personal Income per Person
Shares of world population
in each income group
1996 percentages

High income
$9,636 or more

Upper-middle
$3,116–$9,635

Lower-middle
$786–$3,115

Low income
$785 or less

Source: The State of the World Atlas, Sixth Edition by Dan Smith. Copyright © 1999 by Dan Smith; illustrations copyright by Myriad Editions Limited. Used by permission of Penguin, a Division of Penguin Putnam, Inc.

The rules of the game in global chess require the capture of the most important strategic spaces on the board. Contrary to regular chess, however, the global chessboard is a moving board, with the various squares subject to constant change, determined by the particular dynamics of the changing economic circumstances of the countries involved. Despite the large number of global chess squares, the ones that really count are those squares where companies can move products, services, people, capital, and profits freely across borders. Countries that are behind insurmountable trade barriers or that do not allow free transfer of imports or exports are excluded from the global chessboard because any market position in those countries cannot be leveraged to other countries.

Traditionally, the major members of the global chessboard were markets considered part of the triad, contributing some 75 percent of world GNP.[44] Consisting of Europe (western Europe then), the United States, and Japan, the triad market area was crucial for any global marketer. Having a strong position in at least two of the three areas and a credible presence in the third was viewed as essential for global success. L'Oréal, the world's largest cosmetics company, was market leader in Europe but enjoyed a much smaller share in the United States. Leadership in cosmetics was hotly contested by Procter & Gamble of the United States and Unilever, another European firm. In the important hair care segment, L'Oréal had boosted its market share in the United States from 34 percent to 41 percent. To enhance its own position, Procter & Gamble acquired Clairol from Bristol-Myers Squibb for about $5 billion, boosting its market share from 34 to 44 percent and edging L'Oréal from the number 1 spot. In global terms, the acquisition propelled Procter & Gamble to the leading worldwide position in hair colorants, and Clairol was a close second to L'Oréal.[45]

With the United States representing the largest single market in the global cosmetics industry, eventual global leadership will be decided on the outcome of the U.S. market battle. The U.S. market has become, therefore, a must-win market for L'Oréal and Procter & Gamble, causing them to invest disproportionately more in the United States than in other countries.

For Kenichi Ohmae, the triad concept was helpful to create a sense of priorities among the many existing countries. In some ways, it consisted of selecting a few key markets from the global chessboard. That global chessboard, however, has undergone substantial changes in the past few years. Not only has it gained many additional markets, pushing the total up toward two hundred, but the world marketplace has also seen different countries rise in importance and others decline. If we define the relevant part of the chessboard as those countries open to free trade, we thus see a boom in the emergence of new relevant markets.

The tremendous political changes leading to liberalization, privatization, and deregulation have led to many countries joining the global chessboard. In addition to the traditional industrialized members, consisting of western Europe, the United States, Canada, Japan, Australia, and New Zealand, other major countries are surging into prominence. These new members include the group of Asian countries (South Korea, Taiwan, Hong Kong, Singapore) typically dubbed the "Asian tigers" for their aggressive export drive. Recent newcomers to the global chessboard also include China (where relatively open trade is now possible), India, and several Latin American countries (notably Brazil, Mexico, Argentina, and Chile). As all of these countries begin to abandon their formerly restrictive trade practices, they become important pieces in the global chess game for market dominance. The same is the case for many eastern European countries. Over the last decade, the major expansion in the global chessboard has forced a rethinking of the triad concept. The relevant free market is now centered around three major trading regions: North America, consisting of the United States, Canada, and Mexico, bound together in NAFTA; Europe, consisting of the EU countries and the associate countries; and finally Asia, consisting of Japan, China, India, and the many Asia/Pacific Rim countries that are growing rapidly.

The dynamics of the global chessboard are not limited to new countries joining the game through trade liberalization. Some of these countries, particularly China and India, are experiencing remarkable growth, as we explained in earlier chapters. That growth is represented with an ever larger square on the global chessboard. In the case of China, this change has enhanced its importance in the competitive calculations of global firms. Both China and India would gain even more importance if the counties are listed at GNP adjusted for purchasing power parity (PPP), rather than expressed in nominal terms. A market such as China, if shut off from the rest of the world economy and not accessible to international firms via imports or exports, would be a far less important square on the global chessboard.

Although we can imagine the world as a global chessboard with each country represented by its size of GNP, individual firms competing in their own specific industry will see the chessboard as it is shaped by their industry's perspective: each country, or local market, represented with respect to market size, or relevant industry metric, for that industry. The chessboard for Volkswagen will be determined by the size of the automotive market in the various countries. The chessboard of HP-Compaq or Apple will be represented by the size of the computer markets. Global marketers, therefore, face chessboards that differ by industry, and the chessboard for each industry will have its own key markets as determined by size.

The telecommunications market provides an excellent example of the shifting importance of individual countries on the overall global chessboard. China has become the fastest growing market for telecommunications installations, and its annual spending was expected to reach $80 billion by 2005. This figure contrasts with only $2 billion per year in 1990. According to informed forecasts, China is expected to have 230 million fixed phone users and about 350 million mobile phone users by 2005.[46] Telecommunications firms that must invest large sums of money to develop the next generation of digital systems will find it critical to participate in the Chinese market for future competitiveness. Some experts have indicated that China has become the largest single market for telecommunications networking and infrastructure equipment. As a result, the Chinese market has become the cornerstone of any global marketing strategy for telecommunications firms, raising it to the status of a must-win market where future global leadership is determined.

Global marketers aspiring to a global mindset will need to evaluate the state of the global chessboard constantly. This evaluation, gauging the importance of key markets, not only will have to be made on present data but will need to consider growth rates and the state of the chessboard many years into the future. This survey must occur at both the macroeconomic level and the particular industry level relevant to the company. Marketers will have to develop a new sense of understanding and assess countries one at a time, and they must also be able to judge the importance of each piece of the global chessboard versus the rest of the pieces.

UNDERSTANDING LEAD MARKETS

Once the global chessboard relevant to a particular industry and a particular company has been determined, the marketer with a global mindset will need to understand the interrelationships of those markets. The first step in achieving this understanding is to identify the lead market, or markets, relevant to a particular part of the business. The *lead market* is the particular geographic market, or country, that is ahead in its development of the rest of the world and where initial new developments set a trend for other markets to follow. The lead market thus serves the function of a bellwether.[47]

The identification of a lead market has strategic importance for companies. Those who can identify their own lead markets relevant to their industry will be able to leverage learning from those markets for the rest of their international or global operations. Knowledge about lead markets gives the global marketer a window on future opportunities. It also helps identify those countries as strategic in importance.

One can distinguish several types of lead market categories. First, there are customer-driven lead markets based on the location of the country with the most advanced customers. A company would have to look at its industry and try to evaluate the location of its most advanced customers. If those customers are concentrated in one particular country or region, the company has determined the presence of a lead market with respect to customer demand. Charting the demand coming from that lead market might tell the future demand of the rest of the customers in other parts of the world.

One can distinguish among other types of lead markets as well. Operations-based lead markets are markets that contain the most efficient participants in an industry, particularly with respect to producing the products or services in question. A third category consists of the product lead market, which contains the country where the most advanced products in that industry emerge. Again, the emphasis is on industry participant, not on customer. And finally, one may distinguish the lead market based on management systems and the companies that consistently apply the most advanced management systems in that industry. More recently, we have applied the term *benchmarking* for measuring a company's performance against others that are best in its category. The lead market, by definition, contains the firms against which others benchmark their own operations. What is different in global terms is the requirement that these benchmark operations must in fact be leading the world, or of a world-class stature.

When the U.S. government undertook a major effort to reform the U.S. health care system in 1993, the impact of some of those discussions was felt around the world. Already, many companies involved in health care, such as insurance companies, hospitals, pharmaceutical firms, and medical equipment manufacturers, had long been under pressure to become more cost-effective. In the United States, the health maintenance organization (HMO) was founded as a way to replace fee-for-service care with managed care. By 1990, less than 10 percent of Americans were covered by managed care contracts. By 1996, this number had grown to 75 percent of Americans under managed care of some form. This trend, coming as a result of the cost pressures of ever-increasing medical expenses, was also present in European and other overseas markets. Now that governments elsewhere are trying to rein in health expenditures, they are looking to the United States for answers and its new types of care options. In this way, the U.S. health industry is becoming the lead market for other countries, and firms that successfully adapt to its demands are likely to find that they can do the same elsewhere.[48]

As with many of the concepts described earlier in this chapter, lead market identification is not a one-time exercise. Marketers who aspire to a global perspective have to monitor the performance of their lead markets continuously. Most lead markets were at one time concentrated in the United States, but they have become dispersed, with many countries sharing in some of them over time. A company must therefore understand the migration pattern of lead markets and adjust its understanding of the global chessboard accordingly. The search for lead markets is an attempt to identify the driving wheel of a complicated machine in which each country, or market, is characterized by a single cog wheel in a complex structure (see Figure 7.7). Marketers who understand the process and can clearly identify the driving market have an advantage. Chapters 8 and 9 include special sections dealing with strategic actions by which global firms can take advantage of their presence in lead markets.

Figure 7.7: Lead-Market Relationships

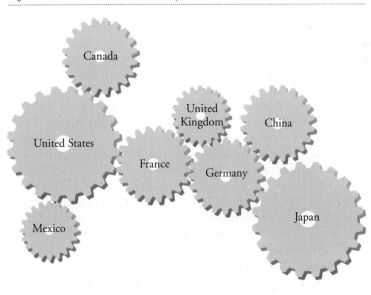

INDIVIDUAL SKILLS FOR A GLOBAL MINDSET

Most of the previous section described analytic and conceptual requirements for a marketer with a global mindset. We believe that certain individual requirements are also indispensable. These skills have been identified over the years through the authors' own interactions with many international executives. Some of them come from the authors' experience with sending many students on overseas assignments. These skills themselves do not alone form a global mindset. Without them, however, even the conceptual understanding of a global perspective on marketing can be diminished.

GLOBAL LANGUAGE COMMUNICATIONS SKILLS

The first category of skills can be grouped under global language communications skills. Here we want to emphasize the language aspects, treating them separately from the technological aspects of communications. Presumably, the global manager must be a multilingual manager. Although this is typically the case with managers from many countries, English is becoming the global business language. The use of English as the global business language has been further reinforced through the development of the Internet. In our new global world, what then is the value of learning and speaking a foreign language?

Typically, a major benefit of learning a foreign language comes from also learning about the foreign culture. However, in this global world, with many major markets speaking many different languages, which one should a manager learn? This choice has baffled many students of global management. Will the language acquired also be the language that is needed sometime in the future? Companies hiring young executives for future overseas assignments often emphasize that having learned one language is an indication of the young executive's promise to learn another for the next international appointment.

This pattern is illustrated by the career patterns of three former students, both of whom were hired by international firms. The first student, a U.S. national, joined a U.S. company in Latin America. The student won this assignment because of his proven Spanish language skills. After a few years, the student found himself transferred to Italy, for which he had no prior knowledge. His proven language skills in Spanish were used as an indication that he would acquire another language quickly. Our second student, also a U.S. national, had acquired some French during his undergraduate years. He was hired by the head office of a Swiss international firm in which the business language was English. The company hired him because his learning of French indicated to it that he had the capacity of being able to function in different environments. After an initial training period of two years, this student found himself in a newly formed subsidiary in Moscow, where again a very different language applied. Our third student was raised in Asia (English being the main language), then attended boarding school in Switzerland, and finally attended business school in the United States. Eventually, he founded a business in Poland, where he learned to speak Polish, a language entirely new to him. These three situations illustrate the advantage of learning one foreign language, while cautioning those who do so that their particular choice of language may have little bearing on their first real overseas assignment.

While learning a foreign language is still needed for longer stays in a country, most marketing executives who act in the global marketplace tend to spend little time in any one market. Moving about, making many brief trips, invariably causes them to use English as the key language in international business. Although executives in many parts of the world are increasingly familiar with English, this does not mean that their understanding is perfect. Those who work within the network of a U.S.-based international company can expect to find most written documents produced everywhere to be in English. Executives working for an international firm's operation in the United States, however, may find themselves limited if they cannot speak some of the language of the head-office country. This is especially true for French, Italian, and German firms; firms located in smaller countries, such as the Netherlands, Sweden, and Switzerland, tend to use English as their corporate language. When meeting local customers abroad, particularly those who are not engaged in international business per se, knowing the local language can still be important. Of course, that capability would be present in a company's local subsidiary or with a distributor or agent who can speak English.

Native English speakers use many idiomatic expressions that are not clear to those for whom English is a second language, however perfectly they may speak it. Misunderstandings thus can arise. A proven strategy is to eliminate such local, idiomatic expressions from the English spoken to arrive at something we call "global English." It is estimated that English is the primary language of 575 million people, and an even greater number speak English at near-native fluency. Over one-fifth of the world's population have achieved reasonable competency in English.[49] This capability will become more important, as we shall show in later chapters, when dealing with new forms of global organizations and global teams. Even more important is the use of non-idiomatic English when using email or similar forms of communication. It is important to recognize that foreign-language skills will help managers gain cultural empathy with another culture, but it is also necessary to realize that a marketing executive with a global mindset will still need to know the key markets for that industry. Knowledge described in the first part of our chapter will be required and can be acquired even without foreign-language skills for that particular market.

GLOBAL TELECOMMUNICATIONS SKILLS

A second set of important communications skills is more technical in nature. The communications revolution has brought about new forms of international telecommunications possibilities that have substantially changed the nature of international marketing transactions. For marketers who aspire to a global perspective, such knowledge is critical. We cannot describe these new forms of technology here in great detail, and it is not the purpose of this text to equip all readers with that knowledge. We can give some background, however, and will point out the application of these techniques to the way global marketing is conducted. To the detriment of their global marketing positions, many firms do not yet use the full technological capabilities.

Much international communication traffic travels over telephone lines. In global marketing, making international phone connections is now an everyday occurrence. With direct-access dialing to most countries, the phone has become an easy way to overcome communication gaps. Between 1980 and 1991, international calls into and out of the United States grew from 200 million to 6.6 billion per year.[50] The telephone, however, can bridge only the distance gap; both initiator and recipient of the call must be there at the same time. When calls have to be made from New York to Japan (Tokyo is fourteen hours ahead of New York), it becomes difficult to make calls at a time when both parties are in their offices. Even with Europe, where the time difference is only six hours for the East Coast of the United States, common office-time overlaps amount to only two to three hours each day.

With much of global marketing taking place in different time zones, companies have had to use other means of communicating. In the past, they used telex machines, or more recently fax machines. The use of international courier services such as FedEx, UPS, or DHL can speed documents across continents overnight, whereas transmittal used to take weeks through regular mail.

More recently, data communication over both fixed and mobile networks is placing telephones into the hands of business executives in even remote areas. Combining telephones with mobile data transmission capabilities has extended telephone networks to many parts of the world. What we have come to expect in terms of on-the-desk transmission (for example, credit card purchases) is now available through mobile networks. The effect of this new technology is to extend the reach of many firms beyond their own natural borders, bridging distance and time gaps so that round-the-clock processing of orders is becoming a possibility. Ecommerce, or ebusiness, is the latest form, bringing two business partners closer together and bridging both the distance and the time gap in dramatic ways.

Electronic mail, once used only to communicate within the premises of a single firm, is now available via regular phone lines and the Internet for communicating with clients and companies worldwide. By many accounts, email has exceeded phones as the preferred method of communications in business, greatly affecting how global firms reach other markets. For the U.S. market, it was estimated that about 3.4 trillion email messages were delivered in 1998, or 9.4 billion per day. However, only about 2.1 billion per day were actual communications messages; the rest were unsolicited commercial messages. For the average email users in the United States, outgoing messages averaged about twenty-six per day. Growth is still exponential for email.[51]

More and more companies avail themselves of an Internet gateway for their in-company electronic mail systems; executives thus have instant access to the Internet's thousands of computer networks. The popularity of the World Wide Web (WWW) has spawned a huge number of company web sites on the Internet. Although many of these sites only disseminate information, more and more firms have begun to transact business online. The Internet is better able to provide place and time independence than phone or fax and is more immediate in response. The Internet is also more cost-effective and offers worldwide access to smaller firms without any established distribution system. Even smaller companies can take advantage of ecommerce capabilities. In many business-to-business marketing areas, access to the World Wide Web is used to build stronger supply partnerships and to integrate supply chains across international borders. These developments are likely to revolutionize the ease of doing business globally, and to make global marketing and purchasing much more common than in the past. On a global basis, business-to-business (B2B) and business-to-consumer (B2C) electronic commerce is expected to multiply and to reach about 6.8 trillion in volume by 2004, with about half accounted for by North

America, and Western Europe and Asia accounting for 25 percent each.[52] This amount would represent almost 27 percent of global trade in goods and services.[53]

The development of new groupware software, such as Lotus Notes, allows many users within a single company to share information simultaneously. Immediate updates are provided as if everyone were connected to the same computer or workstation. Groupware has allowed firms to create virtual teams whose members may in fact be located in different offices in different countries. The number of corporate collaborative email users was estimated at 250 million worldwide.[54]

Another recent development in telecommunications is videoconferencing. Through connections over special telephone lines, companies have installed video systems that allow teams of managers to see each other as they talk although they are separated by thousands of miles. With participants sitting in front of cameras and with a separate projector for documents, such conferences are becoming the norm to avoid costly and time-consuming travel. Teleconferencing also allows firms to provide scarce technical specialists to the offices of their clients to support products or services and thus gain a competitive advantage. Although it does bridge the distance gap, videoconferencing still requires executives at both ends to be present at the same time. In the wake of the September 11, 2001, terrorist attacks, videoconferencing increased substantially because it was used in lieu of travel.[55]

CONCLUSIONS

As we pointed out in Chapter 1, a growing need for marketers with global mindsets exists in today's global business environment. In this chapter, we explained in more detail the components of such a global mindset, or global perspective. It is important nevertheless to indicate here that the need for marketers with a global mindset is not limited to companies operating in the major industrialized nations. The need for a global perspective extends to marketers from all parts of the world, from both developed and emerging countries.

The need for a global perspective results from the pervasiveness of the global logic. Any company that is part of the global economy and operating in an industry with some form of global logic will require marketing managers with a global mindset. Since the global logic is felt by companies large and small and is independent of the company's location, the need for the type of skills, knowledge, and concepts explained in this chapter is considered universal.

Acquiring a global mindset is aided by gaining knowledge about key markets and an understanding of the wider framework of the global economy and politics. Understanding the concepts of global logics and having the ability to determine their presence in a company's industry are part of the second prerequisite. Marketers with a global perspective will also have to adopt new ways for understanding and prioritizing the world market, such as through the analogy of the global chess game. And finally, the global mindset is gained through the acquisition of special communications skills that help overcome time and place differences and allow companies to use their skills beyond their own borders.

What separates the global mindset from other approaches to international and global marketing is the ability to think about the entire global opportunity at once, and to view each individual market in relationship to the whole world economy. This perspective, combined with a sense of strategic necessity, will allow global marketers to set the right priorities and to guide their firms through a mass of potential or theoretical possibilities, not all of which can realistically be pursued. This is a sharp departure from the long-standing tradition of analyzing individual markets one at a time. Although the single-market analysis competency will still be part of the necessary tool kit of the global marketer, that alone will no longer suffice as a guide through the multitude of possibilities.

As many more firms find themselves drawn into the global economy and forced to pursue global marketing strategies, the need for marketing managers with a capability to adopt the global perspective can be expected to rise dramatically over the next decade. A global mindset can be acquired; it is not an innate skill. Marketing managers from all countries face the same challenges, or the same hurdles, in acquiring it. Those who do better at it are likely to gain a competitive advantage over their peers who lack it. And finally, firms with a larger cadre of marketing executives who have cultivated a global mindset can be expected to outperform those who lack this key human resource.

Questions for Discussion

1. How does a global perspective differ from an international or multinational perspective?

2. Explain the concept of a global logic.

3. In the automobile manufacturing industry, where do you find a global logic? Which of the sources of the global logic predominates?

4. What is the managerial meaning of the concept of the global chessboard?

5. Select a country and complete a factual analysis that satisfies the section on global key markets.

6. What differentiates a single-market assessment from a global market assessment?

7. Select an industry and complete a global chessboard analysis for it. Determine relevant metrics and identify lead markets.

8. Select an industry and complete a global logic analysis on it (use Figure 7.5 as a framework). What implications can you draw from your spider web?

For Further Reading

Bartlett, Christopher A., and Sumantra Ghoshal. "What Is a Global Manager?" *Harvard Business Review,* September–October 1992, pp. 124–132.

Dyer, Jeffrey H., Dong Sung Cho, and Wujin Chu. "Strategic Supplier Segmentation," *California Management Review,* January 1, 1988, vol. 40, p. 57.

Jeannet, Jean-Pierre. *Managing with a Global Mindset.* London: Financial Times/Prentice Hall, 2000.

Ohmae, Kenichi. *Triad Power: The Coming Shape of Global Competition.* New York: Free Press, 1985.

Porter, Michael E., ed. *Competition in Global Industries.* Boston: Harvard Business School Press, 1986.

Pucik, Vladimir. "Creating Leaders That Are World-Class," *Australian Financial Review,* October 28, 1998, p. 10.

Short, John Rennie, et.al., "Cultural Globalization, Global English, and Geography Journals," *Professional Geographer,* vol. 53, no. 1, 2001, pp. 1–11.

Taylor, William. "The Logic of Global Business: An Interview of ABB's Percy Barnevik," *Harvard Business Review,* March–April 1991, pp. 91–105.

Tung, Rosalie L. "American Expatriates Abroad," *Journal of World Business,* June 22, 1998, vol. 33, no. 2, p. 125.

Endnotes

1. Gurcharan Das, "Local Memoirs of a Global Manager," *Harvard Business Review*, March–April 1993, pp. 38–47.

2. This chapter is based substantially on Jean-Pierre Jeannet, *Managing with a Global Mindset*, (London: Financial Times/Prentice Hall, 2000), Chapters 1–8.

3. Ibid., Chapter 3.

4. Howard V. Perlmutter, "The Tortuous Evolution of the Multinational Corporation," *Columbia Journal of World Business*, January–February 1969, p. 12.

5. "Global Leaders Wanted," *Workspan*, April 2001, pp. 37–41.

6. "Working in Japan—Mind Your Manners," *Accountancy* (London), February 2002, p. 38.

7. Kenichi Ohmae, *The Borderless World* (London: Collins, 1990), pp. 17–31.

8. Vern Terpstra and Kenneth David, *The Cultural Environment of International Business*, 3d ed. (Cincinnati, Ohio: Southwestern, 1991).

9. "Japanese Firms Want English Competency," *The Wall Street Journal*, June 11, 2001, p. B7A.

10. Ferdinand Schevill, *A History of the Balkans* (New York: Dorset, 1991).

11. Jutikkala Eino and Pirinen Kauko, *A History of Finland*, 4th ed. (Espoo: Eino & Kauko, 1984).

12. Robert B. Reich, *The Works of Nations* (New York: Knopf, 1991).

13. Henry Kissinger, *Diplomacy* (New York: Simon & Schuster, 1994).

14. Paul Kennedy, *The Rise and Fall of the Great Powers* (New York: Random House, 1987). See also Paul Kennedy, *Preparing for the Twenty-First Century* (New York: Random House, 1993).

15. Denis de Rougemont, *The 28 Centuries of Europe* (Paris, France: Payot, 1996).

16. *IMD World Competitive Yearbook 2002* (Lausannne, Switzerland: IMD, 2002).

17. Jean-Pierre Jeannet, *Managing with a Global Mindset* (London: Financial Times/Prentice Hall, 2000), pp. 45–80.

18. Ibid., pp. 52–54.

19. George Raedler, Jan Kubes, and Ulrich Steger, "*The Global Automotive Industry,*" (Lausanne, Switzerland: IMD Institute, 2001), Case GM 911.

20. Jean-Pierre Jeannet, *Siemens AT: Brazil Strategy* (Lausanne, Switzerland: IMD Institute, 1993).

21. "Companies Shy from Releasing Consoles in Asia," *The Asian Wall Street Journal*, November 19, 2001, p. 13.

22. "Capturing the Global Consumer," *Fortune*, December 13, 1993, p. 166.

23. Jeannet, *Managing with a Global Mindset*, pp. 55–66.

24. "No Lucky-Fuji Film Deal Yet," *Asiainfo Daily China News*, March 12, 2001, p. 1.

25. Stephen Allen, Case Series: "Note on the Construction Machinery Industry" (ECCH no. 393-068-5, 1993); "Caterpillar and Komatsu in 1988" (ECCH no. 393-069-1, 1993); "Caterpillar and Komatsu in 1993" (ECCH no. 393-070-1).

26. "Liquid Assets: In a Water Fight, Coke and Pepsi Try Opposite Tacks," *The Wall Street Journal*, April 18, 2002, p. A1.

27. "Airbus Gets Break in Europe Sector Boeing Dominates," *The Wall Street Journal*, May 3, 2002, p. A3.

28. Stephen Allen, Case Series: "Note on the European Major Home Appliance Industry—1990" (ECCH no. 393-091-5); "Whirlpool Corporation" (ECCH no. 393-095-1, 1993); "Electrolux" (ECCH no. 393-094-1, 1993); "General Electric: Major Appliances" (ECCH no. 393-093-1, 1993).

29. Kenichi Ohmae, *The Mind of the Strategist* (New York: McGraw-Hill, 1992), Chapter 3.

30. Christopher Lorenz, "The Birth of a Transnational," *McKinsey Quarterly*, Autumn 1989, p. 72.

31. "Boeing Rethinks Next Step," *Asian Wall Street Journal*, June 11, 2002, p. A8.

32. "Examining Drug Costs," *Drug Discovery & Development*, March 2002, vol. 5, p. 17.

33. "Pharma M&A Declines, but Financing Picks Up," *Chemical Week*, March 20, 2002, p. 30.

34. Ibid.

35. "SkyTeam Tops Oneworld, Alitalia Boosts Network," *Aviation Daily*, July 30, 2001, p. 3.

36. "United Posts Interline Revenue Growth Thanks to Star Membership," *Aviation Daily*, May 15, 2002, p. 1.

37. "Star Alliance Continues to Widen Market Lead with Three Additional Airlines," *Knight Ridder Tribune Business News*, June 7, 2002, p. 1.

38. "The 2001 Deals of the Year: Sprint's Dash for Cash," *Institutional Investor*, January 2002, p. 76.

39. "Deconstructing NTT," *Tele.Com*, May 28, 2002, p. 18.

40. "Japanese Phone Giant Fights to Keep Control of Fast-Growing Unit," *The Wall Street Journal*, December 18, 2001, p. A1.

41. "Mexican Connection: Telmex, Defying Telecom Slump, Defends Its Empire," *The Wall Street Journal*, May 16, 2002, p. A1.

42. Jeannet, *Managing with a Global Mindset*, pp. 67–80.

43. Jeannet, *Managing with a Global Mindset*, Figure 7.1, p. 84.

44. Kenichi Ohmae, *Triad Power: The Coming Shape of Global Competition* (New York: Free Press, 1985), pp. 122–124.

45. "Fast Growing Business," *Economist*, May 26, 2001, p. 68; and "P&G's Pantene Pitch Taps Performers' Cachet," *The Wall Street Journal*, June 11, 2002, p. A10.

46. "Olympic Games Spur Development of China's Communications Industry," *Fiber Optics Weekly Update*, September 28, 2001, pp. 1–2.

47. Jeannet, *Managing with a Global Mindset*, pp. 95–104.

48. "The Managed Care Remedy," *Financial Times*, September 9, 1996, p. 17.

49. John Rennie Short, Armando Boniche, Yeong Kim, and Patrick Li Li, "Cultural Globalization, Global English, and Geography Journals," *Professional Geographer*, vol. 53, no. 1, 2001, pp. 1–11.

50. *Global.factive.com/en/arch/*; accessed on June 12, 2002.

51. "An Unfounded Rumor That Should Be True," *Denver Post*, April 10, 2001, p. B07.

52. "E-Business Chips in," *Tele.Com*, September 3, 2001, pp. 35–41.

53. "Productivity Gains," *Internet World*, January, vol. 8, no. 1, 2002, p. 4.

54. "Pushing the Envelope," *Federal Computer Week*, December 10, 2001, pp. 30–32.

55. "Companies Turn to Teleconferencing," *The Asian Wall Street Journal*, November 5, 2001, p. 10.

Chapter 8

Global Marketing Strategies

I n this chapter, we introduce you to the complex choices faced by companies as they develop global marketing strategies. Companies need to make more than one decision about whether or not to adopt a global marketing strategy; more important, they also need to select from different generic global marketing strategies. First, companies have to review and consider their internationalization patterns, ranging from opportunistic or unplanned patterns, to fully planned patterns of globalization, which involve subjecting a pattern to global logics. Second, firms have to select an appropriate expansion strategy, which might result either in global market reach through market coverage or in globalizing their asset base through building companies in many markets. Third, companies must determine the desired geographic concentration strategy, which includes a selection of the markets the company intends to cover. The chapter ends with a review of the various generic global marketing strategies and their selection criteria. Figure 8.1 summarizes the topics discussed in this chapter.

PATTERNS OF GLOBALIZING MARKETING OPERATIONS

Whether to compete globally is a strategic decision that will fundamentally affect the firm, including its operations and its management. For many companies, the decision to globalize remains an important and difficult one. Typically, many issues form the basis for a company's decision to begin to compete in foreign markets. For some firms, going abroad is the result of a deliberate policy decision; for others, it is a reaction to a specific business opportunity or a competitive challenge.

Figure 8.1: Global Marketing Decision Elements

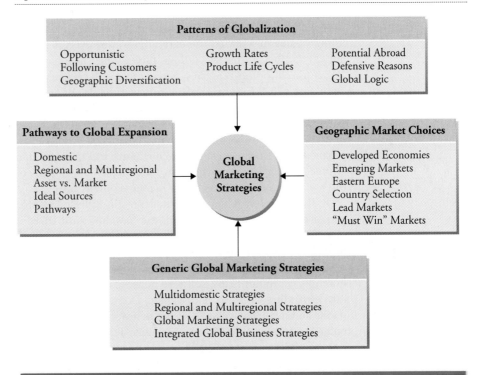

OPPORTUNISTIC GLOBAL MARKET DEVELOPMENT

Probably the most common reason for global expansion is the recognition that opportunities exist in foreign markets. Many companies, particularly those in the United States, promote their products in trade journals or through other media to their U.S. customers. These publications are also read by foreign business executives, who place orders that are initially unsolicited. Because these transactions are usually more complicated and more involved than a routine shipment to domestic customers, the firm has to make the decision whether to respond at that time. The company can also adopt a more aggressive policy and actively pursue foreign customers, moving beyond filling unsolicited orders. Thus, some firms have built sizable foreign businesses by first responding to orders and then taking a more proactive approach later. Most large, internationally active companies were built initially around an opportunistic strategy, although today these firms have moved to a more orchestrated and deliberate strategy in their approach to global marketing. Furthermore, smaller, growing firms and start-up companies are increasingly taking a planned approach to their internationalization because the strategic value of expanding globally is becoming more important for them.

FOLLOWING CUSTOMERS ABROAD

For a company whose business is concentrated on a few large customers, the decision to globalize is usually made when one of its key customers moves abroad to pursue international opportunities. Many of the major U.S. automobile component suppliers are operating plants abroad to supply their customers in foreign locations. PPG Industries is a major U.S.-based supplier of car body paints to the U.S. automobile industry and did little overseas business, other than licensing its technology to other foreign paint makers. In the early 1980s, however, it followed its major customers abroad and began to service them directly in Europe and elsewhere. The company began to sell to non-U.S. car companies as well and achieved the leading position in supplying paints to car manufacturers worldwide. By making a series of target acquisitions in the paint sectors for automotive OEMs and automotive refinish, the company was able to extend its market leadership from the United States, where it leads in both sectors, to become number 2 in Europe.[1] Similar trends can be observed as Japanese and European automobile manufacturers set up their own operations in the United States. These moves were followed by a series of component suppliers who did not want to lose out on a new business opportunity.

R. R. Donnelley & Sons Co., the largest U.S.-based printer of magazines, catalogs, and directories, was a largely domestic company until 1978, when it made its first foreign acquisitions. Years later, international revenue was still only 5.5 percent of its more than $5.3 billion in sales in 2001.[2] International business developed primarily on the strength of customer requests. Some of Donnelley's main client groups (for example, computer firms, software houses, and telecommunications firms) were rapidly expanding overseas and wanted Donnelley to go with them, supplying documents and manuals overseas. At the behest of one of its U.S. customers, the company entered into a venture with the Shanghai Telephone Directory Company, for the purpose of transforming the traditional yellow pages directory format into a comprehensive guidebook on communication, commerce, investment, and shopping.[3] Overall, investments in other countries, such as Argentina, were subject to sales declines due to the difficult economic circumstances over the past year.

The service sector has seen similar expansions triggered by client moves overseas. The establishment of international networks of major U.S. professional services firms, such as Deloitte Touche Tohmatsu, was motivated by a desire to service key domestic clients overseas. Deloitte has 29,000 employees and professionals in its U.S. operation, and another 66,000 spread over approximately 140 country operations. Many of the firm's service lines have adopted a globalized structure, such as the secure ebusiness practice. International revenue reached about 50 percent of the global total of $12.4 billion.[4]

PURSUING GEOGRAPHIC DIVERSIFICATION

A need to diversify beyond a single country can also be behind moves to internationalize a company. Although diversification is a lesser factor for U.S.-based companies, firms in other parts of the world often do not want their operations to be dominated or to become overly dependent on the economy of a single country. Saint-Gobain is a large French company founded by King Louis XIV about 330 years ago and has a long-standing tradition in glass and building materials. For years, it followed a strategy to break out of its France-only position. Acquiring large companies in the same field in Germany and the United Kingdom, the company was able to reduce French sales to 25 percent of corporate sales. The acquisition of Norton Company, a U.S.-based maker of abrasives and ceramics, and Carborundum of Canada significantly strengthened

Saint-Gobain's position in the United States. The company now ranks as the number 1 worldwide producer for several business lines, including flat glass, insulation, ductile iron pipes, major industrial ceramics, and abrasives, and it ranks as the number 2 worldwide producer in containers, reinforcements, and building materials for roofing and cladding products.[5] The company achieved global sales of $27 billion in 2001, and about three-quarters of its 173,000 employees are non-French nationals.[6]

EXPLOITING DIFFERENT ECONOMIC GROWTH RATES

Economic growth rates are subject to wide variations among countries. A company based in a low-growth country may suffer a competitive disadvantage and may want to expand into faster growing countries to take advantage of growth opportunities. The area of the Pacific Rim (which includes South Korea, Taiwan, China, Hong Kong, Thailand, Singapore, Malaysia, and Indonesia) experienced above-average growth rates in the 1990s, which in turn prompted many international firms to invest heavily in expanding in that region. Although the region suffered from a substantial economic recession in 1998, many of the region's economies have rebounded and are rapidly making up for lost ground.[7]

The chemicals industry in Asia has experienced above-average annual growth rates, ranging between 12 percent for China and 7 to 9 percent for several other Asia/Pacific Rim countries. This enormous growth allowed the Asian plastics additives market to become the largest in the world, with a share of 35 percent in value for 2000, compared to North America, with 28 percent, and Europe, with 25 percent.[8] Overall, the Asian chemicals market is expected to reach about 40 percent of global demand by 2010. This growth has attracted investments by many chemicals companies from the United States and Europe.[9] Bayer, a large German-based chemicals company, plans to invest about $6 billion in Asia by the year 2010. Bayer expects its Asian sales to reach about 25 percent of corporate sales, compared to 16 percent for 2001. Major investments are planned in Southeast Asia and China, where the company has already invested in a dozen specialized joint ventures.[10]

EXPLOITING PRODUCT LIFE CYCLE DIFFERENCES

When the market for a firm's product becomes saturated, a company can open new opportunities by entering foreign markets where the product may not be very well known. Thus, adding new markets extends the product's life cycle. Among firms following this strategy are many fast-moving consumer goods marketers, such as Coca-Cola and PepsiCo. They often target markets where the per capita consumption of their products is still relatively low. With economic expansion and the resulting improvement in personal incomes in the new market, these companies expect to reap substantial growth over time—although operations in the United States are showing little growth.

In 2001, Coca-Cola sold 419 eight-ounce servings per person annually in the United States. Only Mexico was able to surpass this figure, with 462 servings; most other developed countries consumed between 100 and 300 servings.[11] China trailed, with seven servings per capita, although the average is much higher in Beijing or Shanghai, where it has reached about seventy servings per capita.[12] The company is driven by the fact that in regions holding 44 percent of the world's population, the per capita consumption for Coke is only 1 percent of the current U.S. level.

Essentially, Coca-Cola would have tapped into only half of its global market opportunity and can fuel growth by pursuing low penetration markets.[13]

PURSUING POTENTIAL ABROAD

Some firms maximize their domestic market and then reach out for more potential abroad. With a 1998 market share of 45 percent in the United States, Anheuser-Busch dominates the U.S. beer market. However, with opportunities for growth outside the United States more attractive, Anheuser-Busch has also entered several major international markets and is trying to build a global brand for Budweiser, something no other brewery has been able to pull off. A latecomer to international expansion, the company did not even establish an international department until 1982. Since then, the company has built up major stakes in key international markets, although international volume is still only about 7 percent of total corporate volume.[14] Anheuser-Busch introduced several of its brands in Japan. In China, where Budweiser is priced two to three times higher than locally brewed premium brands, the company is building both brewing capacity and local distribution capabilities. China has become one of Anheuser's largest overseas markets. Anheuser-Busch has managed to make its Budweiser brand into the leading foreign premium brand in China, the second largest beer market worldwide and on the way to becoming the largest. The company has about seven hundred employees in China. It markets its brand through regional sales offices and a network of sixty-seven independent wholesalers covering more than forty key markets.[15] Long term, the potential in China far outstrips any growth opportunities the company has in the saturated U.S. market.

GLOBALIZING FOR DEFENSIVE REASONS

Sometimes companies are not particularly interested in pursuing new growth or potential abroad but decide to enter the international business arena for defensive reasons. When a domestic company sees its markets invaded by foreign firms, that company may react by entering the foreign competitor's home market in return. As a result, the company can learn valuable information about the competitor that will help in its operations at home. A company may want to slow down a competitor by denying it the cash flow from its profitable domestic operation, which could otherwise be invested in expansion abroad. For these reasons, companies who did not need to compete internationally find themselves suddenly forced to expand abroad.

With the Japanese market offering only limited opportunities, Hitachi, a large Japanese multinational, has made success in its home market contingent on success in the global market. With overseas operations accounting for 30 percent of sales in 2001, Hitachi considers itself lagging behind major competitors, that are at 40 percent and target themselves at 50 percent of corporate sales. With the Japanese market increasingly becoming a piece of the total global market, the ability to compete globally has become a necessity for domestic survival. As part of this globalization drive to defend its domestic market, Hitachi has eliminated the distinction between domestic and international sales operations for all of its 126 business groups.[16]

PURSUING A GLOBAL LOGIC OR IMPERATIVE

In Chapter 7, we covered the concept of the global logic. The strong presence of a global logic in a company's business or industry can be a major force propelling a firm to establish international and global operations. If a global logic is ignored, the firm is likely to suffer negative competitive implications, such as lower long-term profitability.

Many of the reasons for internationalization cited earlier in this section represent choices companies can make, but they do not represent compelling rationales that would lead to competitive disadvantages in case of inaction. The situation is different, however, for companies facing strong global logics. The stronger a global logic in a given area or along a given dimension, the stronger is the necessity to accommodate and comply.

A strong global logic thus creates an imperative for a firm to globalize its marketing operation. At this point, the steps to globalize are no longer voluntary, opportunistic, or based on what a company might like to do. Global marketing under the pressures of the global logic becomes a necessity. The global imperative or global logic demands accommodation, and steps to globalize the marketing operations have become necessary for competitive survival. This type of pressure is becoming more and more typical for many firms, thus driving globalization of marketing operations.

PATHWAYS TO GLOBAL EXPANSION

To succeed in global marketing, companies need to look carefully at their geographic expansion. To some extent, a firm makes a conscious decision about the extent of its globalization by choosing a posture that may range from entirely domestic (without any international involvement) to a global reach, where the company devotes its entire marketing strategy to global competition. Each level of globalization will profoundly change the way a company competes and will require different strategies with respect to marketing programs, planning, organization, and control of the international marketing effort.[17]

DOMESTIC MARKETING STRATEGIES

A company with a strictly domestic marketing strategy has decided not to involve itself actively in any global marketing. Clearly, such companies are not the main interest for our text, but nevertheless there are situations in which a company should not or cannot become an active participant in global marketing.

When a company has a very limited product range that appeals only to its own local market, global marketing is not advisable unless the company is prepared to expand its product line. In many service-oriented businesses, customer relations are such that business is done only within a narrow or limited geographic trading range. To expand to new business centers, other affiliates would have to be built, again requiring considerable capital assets. Also, some industries are substantially domestic, with individual companies not directly competing beyond their own local markets. And newly started companies may not be in a position to expand abroad before their domestic market is satisfied.

Over the past decades, an ever-increasing number of domestic industries have become subject to an increasing global logic (see Chapter 7). These developments may have been triggered by a foreign company's arrival on the scene, an event that changes the competitive situation. The major appliance industry serves as an excellent example of an industry that has turned from purely domestic to international in scope. According to many industry observers, the entry of Sweden-based Electrolux into the United States through the 1986 acquisition of a major U.S. domestic company is credited with its true transition from primarily domestic to an international and global industry.[18] Electrolux's transition triggered a reaction among the leading U.S.-based firms: GE Appliances, Whirlpool, and Maytag. Whirlpool joined the fight for global leadership and began to expand its business rapidly in Europe, acquiring major business from Philips of the Netherlands in 1989. Maytag also invaded Europe and acquired the operations of Hoover. These investments did not meet expectations, however, and Maytag later divested its Hoover assets in Europe and Australia. GE Appliances followed a more tentative strategy, engaging in a series of alliances and joint ventures in Europe but not entering the battle for control of that market.

Ten years later, the strategies of most major players in the appliance industry have changed. Whirlpool and Electrolux continue their battle for global leadership. Whirlpool is the leading global appliance company: it is a leader in the U.S. market, it is a strong number 3 in Europe, and it is well positioned in other areas of the world. The company has manufacturing operations in thirteen countries and markets its eleven major brands in more than 170 countries.[19] To benefit from its global strategy, Whirlpool moved from many regional products, or product platforms, to establish global product platforms built with the same key parts and systems. The company has increased its overall sales revenue from $8.5 billion to $10.3 billion in five years (ending in 2001) largely because of international expansion. Overseas sales account for one-third of total sales, and global expansion is continuing even in difficult trading situations, as evidenced by new acquisitions in Mexico and Poland.[20] Clearly, Whirlpool is no longer in a position to run a strictly domestic marketing strategy.

Many well-known firms with large domestic shares have had to align themselves with other firms to make up for lack of international coverage. Gerber Foods, a well-established U.S.-based producer of baby foods, was acquired by Sandoz of Switzerland (now a unit of Novartis Nutrition), which had an extensive overseas marketing network to sell Gerber products. Gillette acquired Duracell, a leading U.S.-based battery manufacturer, reasoning that it could introduce Duracell batteries in the many overseas markets where Gillette had experience, such as Brazil, India, China, and Indonesia. Duracell did not have the necessary resources to grow overseas on its own.[21] Kao of Japan, a leading maker of detergents, soaps, and toiletries, has also had a largely domestic history. Confronted with a shrinking domestic market, the company has expanded its international marketing operations to push international sales to 22 percent over several years.[22]

With more and more industries subject to the global logic, fewer companies can safely select purely domestic marketing strategies. Increasingly, firms will have to accommodate the global logic by pursuing various levels of globalization. The following sections describe different globalization pathways that companies may adopt.

REGIONAL AND MULTIREGIONAL MARKETING STRATEGIES

Mapping out a regional marketing strategy implies that a company will concentrate its resources and marketing efforts on one or possibly two of the world's regions. Emphasizing North America or Europe can be the result of a regional strategy. Other regions where a company may want to concentrate are Latin America, the Pacific Basin, and Asia. In such a situation, the company has expanded beyond a domestic environment but, as we will show later, has not yet reached a multinational or global state.

Companies pursue a pathway toward a regional marketing strategy for several reasons. Such firms are competing in the region where their home market is located; neighboring markets within the same region are invaded because of market or product similarity, and few adaptations are required. Regional strategies are also encouraged when customer requirements in one region are substantially different from customer requirements in others. Under those circumstances, different sets of competitors and market structures may exist, and industry participants may not invade each other's regions or market territories. When such a fragmentation exists, a firm can compete on the basis of knowing its own region best by being closer to its customers. As we have already observed in some of the industries moving from domestic to global, the global logic often does not stop at the regional level. Although an improved strategy for some firms, regional marketing strategies may only be a stopgap on the way toward a more completely global direction. Some firms (and the appliance industry serves again as our example) compete for market share globally but operate their businesses in distinct regional groupings. Electrolux, which operates a European appliance group and a North American one, is a case in point.[23]

ASSET GLOBALIZATION VERSUS MARKET GLOBALIZATION

International and global pathways can be classified along two dimensions. The *geographic dimension* describes a company's geographic reach for a marketing operation or market coverage into several countries. Along the geographic dimension, we can identify pathways ranging from domestic to international, regional, or global. Companies may adopt various patterns of geographic strategies. Along a second axis, the *asset distribution*, companies' pathways may be described in terms of their asset distribution strategies. The asset strategy describes a company's investment patterns in terms of plants, logistics operations, and other physical assets. Asset strategies may range from domestic, or single-country, to regional and eventually global, reflecting the way a company's assets are distributed around the world.

Companies' strategies may therefore fall into several categories.[24] (See Figure 8.2 for a matrix of the patterns.) Global market strategies are pursued by those firms that serve the entire world market with marketing operations that stretch across the world. Global asset strategies are pursued by firms that distribute their plants, support operations, and other fixed assets across the world. Clearly, combinations are also possible. The company with a local market and asset strategy is the typical domestic company, both producing and marketing in only one market. The company with a global market strategy but local asset strategy would be the typical exporter, marketing all over the world but producing in a single market. Boeing, the passenger aircraft manufacturer, exemplifies such a strategy. When a company markets globally and its assets are also distributed globally, we may speak of a truly global company. And finally, some firms whose markets are largely domestic pursue a global asset strategy by sourcing products overseas. Such firms may be classified as classic importers. Pacific Cycle, the largest importer of quality bicycles in the United States, would best fit that type of strategy. The company imports bicycles into the United States from mostly Asian sources and markets them under brands such as Schwinn, Pacific, Roadmaster, Mongoose, and Mongoose Pro.[25]

Figure 8.2: Market Coverage Versus Asset Distribution

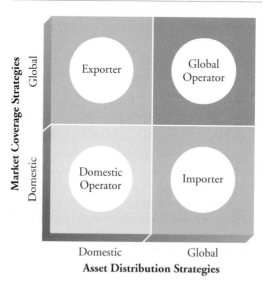

IDEA SOURCING: THE THIRD DIMENSION

In addition to market coverage and asset distribution, we can identify a third dimension, which we call *idea sourcing*. By idea sourcing, we refer to the sources of new business ideas for the creation of new enterprises. Traditionally, business ideas have come from nearby, typically the home or domestic market of the company founder. While concentrating on homegrown ideas is appropriate if an entrepreneur lives in the lead market for a given industry, executives and entrepreneurs elsewhere in the world benefit from importing ideas, or new business concepts, and realizing them locally. In retailing, entertainment, ecommerce, and many service businesses, local entrepreneurs all over the world pick up new ideas from lead market countries, frequently the United States, and implement them locally. A firm relatively new to idea sourcing is Submarino, a Brazil-based Internet bookseller. The company, originally started as Booknet in São Paulo, emulated Amazon.com's U.S. strategy by acting as an Internet-based distributor for Spanish and Portuguese books. With financing from some U.S.-based venture capital firms, the company embarked on an aggressive growth strategy and has opened offices in Spain, Argentina, and Mexico. Submarino's long-term strategy was to become the leading online shopping destination in the Spanish- and Portuguese-speaking world. Two years after launch, Submariono.com is said to be close to breaking even and has avoided the financial disaster that struck so many other Internet firms, domestic and international.[26]

A domestic idea sourcing strategy is limiting, whereas a global idea sourcing strategy entails scouring the entire world for the best new ideas. Again, the market exploitation and asset distribution of the resulting business might be either domestic or global. It is important to remember that pursuing a global marketing strategy does not require a physical presence in every country. We need to accept that different types of geographic strategies exist but that they all have a global context and they all require marketing managers with the global mindset described in Chapter 7. This situation comes about as close as we can to the often used expression "think globally, act locally."

STAGES OF GLOBAL MARKET DEVELOPMENT PATHWAYS

Tracking the development of large global corporations today reveals a recurring, sequential pattern of expansion. Typically, these companies began their business development phase by entrenching themselves first in their domestic markets. Often, international development did not occur until maturity was reached domestically. After that phase, these firms became companies with some international business, usually on an export basis. As the international side of their sales grew, the companies increasingly distributed their assets into many markets and achieved the status of what was once termed a multinational corporation (MNC). Pursuing multidomestic strategies on a market-by-market basis, companies began to enlarge and build considerable local presence. Only during their latest phase did these firms begin to transform themselves into global marketing behemoths whose marketing operations are closely coordinated across the world market rather than developed and executed locally.

This traditional sequencing of growth from domestic to international, to multi-domestic or multinational to global, seems typical for most firms, and also for many newly formed companies. However, some newer firms are jumping right into the latest category, the global category, and not going through the various stages of development (see Figure 8.3). This leap reflects two trends. First, the time that companies have to get their global market positions in key markets is getting much shorter, forcing many newly formed companies to attempt to conquer domestic and global markets at the same time. Second, newer firms realize that they do not have to learn in the same sequence that older ones did; they can take advantage of the most recent forms of market development—global forms. One example is Logitech, a Swiss-based computer-input device maker. Logitech's market coverage and its marketing strategy were global almost from its inception, skipping many of the earlier,

Figure 8.3: Sequencing Internationalization Strategies

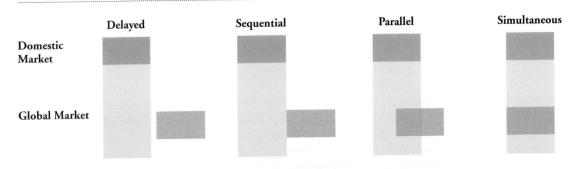

intermediate forms of international market development. The company not only opened sales offices rapidly throughout the world but also added factories in Taiwan, the United States, and Switzerland.[27] Logitech built its business into the world's leading PC mouse maker, with an annual output of 76 million mice made from plants in Taiwan and China, and global sales of $735 million for 2001.[28]

GEOGRAPHIC MARKET CHOICES

Once a company commits to extending its business internationally, management is confronted with the task of setting a geographic or regional emphasis. A company may decide to emphasize developed nations, such as Japan or those of Europe and North America. Some companies may prefer to pursue primarily developing countries in Latin America, Africa, or Asia. Management must make a strategic decision to direct business development so that the company's overall objectives are congruent with the particular geographic mix of its activities.

EMPHASIZING DEVELOPED ECONOMIES

Developed economies account for a disproportionately large share of world gross national product (GNP) and thus tend to attract many companies. In particular, firms with technology-intensive products have concentrated their activities in the developed world. Although competition from other international firms and local companies is usually more intense in those markets, doing business in developed countries is generally preferred over doing business in developing nations, primarily because the business environment is more predictable and the investment climate is more favorable. Developed countries are located in North America (the United States and Canada), western Europe, and Asia (Japan, Australia, and New Zealand). Although some global firms such as IBM operate in all of these countries, many others may be represented in only one or two areas. Very early in their development, U.S. international companies established strong business bases in Europe, then more recently in Japan. Japanese firms tend to start their overseas operations in the United States and Canada and then move into Europe.

The importance of developing a competitive position in the major developed markets was first articulated by Kenichi Ohmae. Ohmae maintained that, for most industries, it was important to compete effectively in the three parts of the "triad" of the United States, Europe, and Japan. Companies were said to need a strong presence in at least two areas and have a representation in the third; "real" global competitors were advised to have strong positions in all three areas. The three areas of the strategic triad account for about 80 percent of most industries, and are thus major determinants in the outcome of the competitive battle.[29] Even more so, ten of the most international-trade-minded developed countries (the United States, Canada, the United Kingdom, Germany, France, the Netherlands, Sweden, Switzerland, Japan, and Australia) account for 50 percent of the world's international trade, attract 70 percent of the world's investments, and account for 90 percent of its foreign direct investment. As a result, companies that see themselves as world-class marketers cannot afford to neglect these pivotal markets.[30]

Because of the importance of the triad countries in international trade, global companies expend great efforts to balance their presence so that their sales begin to mirror the relative size of the three regions. A company underrepresented in one area or another will undertake considerable investment, often in the form of acquisitions, to balance the geographic portfolio. Alcatel, a leading European manufacturer of telecommunications equipment, had staked out the enterprise market for communications equipment as an area of expansion. With 50 percent of the global opportunity for this market located in the United States, the company began a major investment drive into the LAN-switching business and acquired two California-based firms.[31] (LAN is an acronym for "local area network.")

Europe, the third member of the triad, has been the focus of investment from U.S. and Japanese companies. The attraction of Europe for Japanese firms was enhanced through the adoption of the common currency (euro), with final implementation as of January 2002. Eleven of the fifteen EU countries have chosen to adopt this common currency (see Chapter 4). The EU imported about euro (E) 84.7 billion from Japan, whereas Japan imported about E 44.6 billion from EU countries. Aside from the United States, this market is the second most important trading relationship for the EU, and for the United Kingdom in particular.[32]

Although the triad concept was first understood as referring to the United States, western Europe, and Japan, more recent use of the concept tends to emphasize three regions rather than countries. With the advent of the North American Free Trade Agreement (NAFTA) in 1992, North America has become a more relevant concept than just the United States. In Europe, the relevant concept is the European Union (EU), which has been expanded to fifteen western European countries. And finally, many firms refer to the third member of the triad as the Asia Pacific region rather than just Japan. Including other rapidly growing Asian countries in the triad has brought about a considerably increased focus. Most European and U.S. global firms, traditionally weak in that part of the world, have undertaken considerable efforts to balance their market positions. In a recent survey among managers of international firms, investment in the Asia Pacific region was rated as highest in importance, ranking equal to investment in their home countries and ahead of any other region.

EMPHASIZING EMERGING MARKETS

Emerging markets differ substantially from developed economies by geographic region and by the level of economic development. Markets in Latin America, Africa, the Middle East, and Asia are also characterized by a higher degree of risk than are markets in developed countries. Because of the less stable economic climates in these areas, a company's operation could possibly suffer greater uncertainty and fluctuation. Furthermore, the frequently changing political situations in developing countries often affect operating results negatively. As a result, some markets that may have experienced high growth for a few years may suddenly experience drastic reductions in growth. In many situations, however, the higher risks are offset by higher returns, largely because competition is often less intense in those markets. Consequently, companies need to balance the opportunity for future growth in the developing nations with the existence of higher risk.

Unilever, the large Dutch-British consumer goods company, met intensive competition in its traditional markets in Europe and the United States, where it generates about two-thirds of its volume. Faced with lower growth in those markets, the company moved aggressively into emerging markets, where annual growth has averaged 5 percent or more in most of its core business categories. The company declared five geographic areas as top targets: central Europe, eastern Europe, Latin America, India, and Southeast Asia.[33] By 2001, Unilever had been able to lift sales in the Asia Pacific region to $7.5 billion, or 17 percent of corporate total. The company has about twenty ventures in China alone, representing an investment of about $800 million.[34]

Banco Santander Central Hispano (SCH), the leading Spanish commercial and investment bank, decided to pursue emerging markets based on the belief that traditional markets in Europe and North America had too many banks. As a result, the company launched a major drive to develop its competitive position in Latin America. As a result of numerous acquisitions in several Latin American countries, SCH has become the region's leading commercial bank.[35]

Hyundai, the largest of Korea's three major car manufacturers, with sales of 1.6 million units in 2001, has also pursued emerging markets aggressively. The company operated joint ventures in India, Turkey, China, and Malaysia and maintained technical agreements with producers in Egypt, Venezuela, Pakistan, Indonesia, and Taiwan. All these countries have small car markets, and they have few competitors in place.[36]

The past experience of international firms doing business in developing countries has not been especially positive. With the present trend toward global trade liberalization and privatization, many formerly closed countries have opened their borders. Many firms were seriously affected by the economic crisis in Mexico in the early 1990s, or by the situation in Argentina in 2001–2002. Although the market potential is usually superior in emerging markets, global companies have to expect annual fluctuations that far exceed those experienced in the developed markets of North America or Europe. General Motors spent several hundred millions of dollars on investments in its Argentine operations during the 1990s and employed about one thousand people locally. The company indicated that it would wait out the current negative economic climate based on the expectation that the Argentine economy would bounce back from its recession.[37]

EXPANDING IN EASTERN EUROPE

During the past decade, the economic liberalization of eastern European countries opened a large new market for many international firms. The market typically represents about 15 percent of the worldwide demand in any given industry, about two-thirds of that figure accounted for by Russia and other countries of the former Soviet Union. Although many companies consider this market as having long-term potential with little profit opportunity in the near term, several firms have taken advantage of opportunities in areas where they were once prohibited from doing business.

The first wave of investments in eastern Europe was led by companies marketing industrial equipment, such as U.S.-based Otis. In Poland, where Otis has been operating since 1975, the company had reached a market share of 30 percent. Otis was attracted to the Polish market because its operating elevators were mostly old, and thus the replacement and service markets were promising.[38]

Companies marketing consumer goods tended to enter the region later. One of the first was Procter & Gamble, the U.S.-based consumer products company. P&G set up regional centers for each product line, for example, making the Czech Republic its center for detergents and Hungary its center for personal care products.

Procter & Gamble began its Russian operations in August 1991. P&G interviewed more than fifty thousand consumers in the region and conducted market tests with products carried around in suitcases. The company became the largest consumer goods company in the region, marketing more than thirty brands. Many of the brands rank among the top two or three in their respective categories. P&G envisioned continued growth, leading to a business of about $2 billion within the next three to five years.[39]

The behavior of international car manufacturers demonstrates an aggressive approach in eastern Europe. Low labor costs, at rates only a fraction of what they are in western Europe, attracted international firms to build cars in eastern Europe (see Table 8.1). Initial low sales levels promised substantial future growth as the income levels of the populations of eastern European countries improved. Few companies

Table 8.1 Operations of Automobile Firms in Eastern Europe

Company Name	Country	Type of Operation	Investment[a]
GM/Opel	Poland	Car assembly New car plant	DM 30 mio DM 500 mio
	Hungary	New engine and car plant	DM 1.0 bio
	East Germany	New car plant	DM 1.0 bio
Ford Motor	Poland	Car and van assembly	DM 54 mio
Volkswagen	Poland	Car and van assembly	DM 54 mio
	Hungary	New Audi engine and car plant	DM 1.0 bio
	Slovakia	Assembly and gearbox plant	DM 215 mio
	Czech	Skoda acquisition (70% stake), new car plant and models	DM 3.7 bio
	Eastern Germany	2 plants, new engine and cars	DM 3.2 bio
Fiat	Poland	FSM (78% stake) new plant and models	DM 1.8 bio
Suzuki	Hungary	New car plant (80% stake)	na
Daewoo	Poland	Acquisitions of FS Lublin and FSO, new plants and models	DM 1.34 bio

a. Some investments staged over several years into 2000–2002 period.
Source: Financial Times, February 13, 1997, p. 11. Reprinted by permission.

can match Volkswagen's success in its expansion into eastern Europe. Aside from setting up assembly plants, new car plants, and engine plants, the German company also invested in a new model range through its stake in Skoda, the leading Czech company with a long tradition in the automotive industry. In central and eastern Europe (not including Russia), Volkswagen (VW) has achieved a market share of 21 percent, with a volume of about 275,000 cars in 1999.[40] VW's success is based largely on the growth at Skoda, its Czech unit, where volume has tripled from 1991 to 2000 (to 435,000 units). Skoda had achieved almost a 50 percent market share in the Czech Republic, and its export performance accounted for nearly 10 percent of Czech exports. VW is increasingly using Skoda as an export product, marketing it in sixty-four countries. Added to the overall corporate volume of VW, sales in eastern Europe increase the overall global position of the entire Volkswagen group.[41]

COUNTRY SELECTION

At some point, the development of any global marketing strategy will come down to selecting individual countries in which a company intends to compete. There are more than two hundred countries and territories from which companies can select, but very few firms compete in all of these markets. The decision about where to compete, the country selection decision, is one of the components of developing a global marketing strategy.

Why is country selection a strategic concern for global marketing management? Adding another country to a company's portfolio always requires additional investment in management time and effort and in capital. Although opportunities for additional profits are usually the driving force, each additional country also represents a new business risk. It takes time to build business in a country where the firm has not previously been represented, and profits may not be realized until much later. Consequently, companies need to go through a careful analysis before they decide to move ahead.

ANALYZING THE INVESTMENT CLIMATE.   A complete understanding of the investment climate of a target country will help in the country selection decision. The investment climate of a country includes its political situation, legal structure, foreign trade position, and attitude toward foreign investment or the presence of foreign companies. In general, companies try to avoid countries with uncertain political situations. (The impact that political and legal forces can have on the operations of a foreign company was described in detail in Chapter 4.)

A country's foreign trade position can also determine the environment for foreign firms operating there. Countries with a strong balance of payments surplus or strong currencies that are fully convertible are considered good places to invest. Countries with chronic balance of payments difficulties and those with great uncertainty about the transferability of funds are viewed as risky and are thus less favored by foreign investors. (These topics were described in greater detail in Chapter 2.) Consequently, assessing a country's investment climate will require a thorough and skillful analysis. However, investment climate is not the only determinant for the selection of a country for entry.

DETERMINING MARKET ATTRACTIVENESS. Before a country can be selected for addition to a firm's portfolio of countries, management needs to assess the overall attractiveness of that country with respect to the firm's products or services. Initially, this assessment requires a clear indication of the country's market size. It may consist of analyzing existing patterns of demand. Also needed are data on growth—past and future—that will allow a firm to determine market size not only as it relates to the present situation but also with respect to potential.

Analyzing demand patterns allows a company to plot the location of a given product or service on the product life cycle. A firm may also want to analyze potential competitors in that country to achieve an understanding of how it can compete. Finally, companies should get to know a new country's market well enough to be able to determine if their methods of competing and marketing are allowed in that country. Some markets may be very attractive, but if the firm's key strength cannot be employed, success is questionable.

The analytic approach required for an in-depth assessment of a country's market attractiveness was covered in great detail in Chapters 5, 6, and 7. Analyzing international markets and the company's prospective international buyers—the ability to perform marketing research and analysis on an international scale—is a prerequisite to sound country selection decisions.

TARGETING LEAD MARKETS

In Chapter 7, we introduced the concept of a lead market and its importance to global marketing strategists. In the context of selecting markets for special emphasis, the lead market concept can help in identifying those countries where a company should place extra emphasis.

By 1994, the United States was no longer the only lead market in many key industries (see Figures 8.4 and 8.5). In electronics and in semiconductor manufacturing, Japan has captured the lead in several segments. This loss of leadership, first to Japan and later to other countries, such as Korea, Taiwan, and most recently China, has become pronounced in many areas of the electronics industry. Table 8.2 depicts the various eras covering the semiconductor industry from its inception, with the initial innovations by Bell Labs in the United States in 1947, to the most recent developments in China.[42] The history of semiconductor manufacturing clearly demonstrates that leadership in certain technologies is likely to change, and an ever-growing list of countries are functioning in the leadership positions. These changes in industry rankings affect many players. First, the competitors in other markets need to recognize such shifts of lead markets. Second, purchasers need to calibrate purchasing, or importing strategies, which is also a global marketing task. And finally, suppliers of chip-producing machinery need to find new clients when the lead moves to another country, and they must set up sales and service operations to cover new territories.

It is essential for globally competing firms to monitor lead markets in their industries or, better yet, to build up some relevant market presence in those markets. Toray Industries, a leading Japanese company in the plastic and textile industries, runs its artificial leather affiliate, Alcantara, from Italy. Although Japanese firms have traditionally stayed away from Italy as a market for investment, Alcantara is highly successful, primarily because it depends on design for its leather products, and Toray

Figure 8.4: U.S.-Based Firms Lead in Most World Markets . . . But Trail in a Few

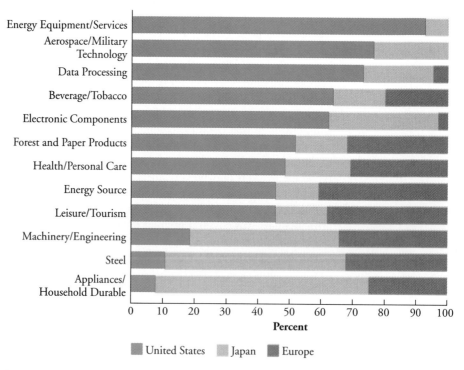

management considers Italy number 1 in the world in design. The result is excellent styling for new Toray products, which are strong enough to attract customers on looks alone. Thus, locating in lead markets gives companies lessons to learn for other markets and at the same time makes them more competitive on a worldwide basis.[43]

TARGETING "MUST WIN" MARKETS

As global marketers research the array of countries available for selection, they soon become aware that not all countries are of equal importance on the path to global leadership. Markets that are crucial to global market leadership, markets that can determine the global winners among all competitors, and markets that companies can ill afford to avoid or neglect—such markets are "must win" markets.

The starting point for analyzing which markets are "must win" markets is the relevant global chessboard that best depicts the industry in question. Not all industries show the same countries as "must win" markets, and absolute size is typically an important criterion for their selection. In the past, the United States has been the largest single market for many industries, thus becoming the decisive piece in global competitive struggles. With the rapid rise of China, its ongoing industrialization, and the sheer size of its 1.2 billion population, that giant is increasingly assuming a key role. When China opened its markets, it was pulled into the global chessboard, and sales in many consumer goods areas are growing rapidly. Procter & Gamble of the United States had just a few products and $50 million in sales in China; by 2001, sales had grown to more than $1 billion. Among its products in China, P&G's best-selling brand is Head & Shoulders shampoo.[44] The company has invested more than $300 million in China since 1988, created eleven joint ventures, and launched more than twenty brands.[45] In 1998, P&G opened a dedicated research facility in

Figure 8.5: Leading Research Nations

Field	Rank				
	1	2	3	4	5
Astrophysics	USA	SWI	NET	CHL	GBR
Biochemistry	USA	SWI	SWE	GBR	DEN
Chemistry	USA	SWI	ISR	NET	SWE
Earth Sciences	USA	AUS	GBR	SWI	FRA
Immunology	SWI	USA	BEL	GBR	SWE
Computer Science	ISR	USA	SWI	CAN	DEN
Engineering	DEN	SWE	USA	SWI	AUS
Multidisciplinary	USA	SWI	DEN	SWE	CAN
Agriculture	SWE	GBR	DEN	CAN	NET
Materials Science	USA	DEN	NET	ISR	SWI
Mathematics	DEN	NOR	GBR	USA	NET
Clinical Medicine	USA	CAN	GBR	SWE	DEN
Microbiology	USA	SWI	GBR	NET	ISR
Molecular Biology	SWI	USA	DEN	GBR	ISR
Neuroscience	SWE	USA	SWI	GBR	DEN
Ecology	SWE	NOR	USA	SWI	AUS
Plant and Animal Science	GBR	SWE	DEN	USA	AUS
Pharmacology	SWI	NZL	GBR	USA	SWE
Physics	SWI	DEN	USA	NET	ISR
Psychology	USA	SWE	DEN	GBR	CAN

AUS = Australia
BEL = Belgium
CAN = Canada
CHL = Chile
DEN = Denmark
FRA = France
GER = Germany
GBR = Great Britain
ISR = Israel
NET = Netherlands
NZL = New Zealand
NOR = Norway
SWE = Sweden
SWI = Switzerland
USA = United States

Source: Tages Anzeiger (Zurich, Switzerland), February 11, 1997, p. 6. Reprinted by permission.

Table 8.2 Lead Markets for the Semiconductor Industry

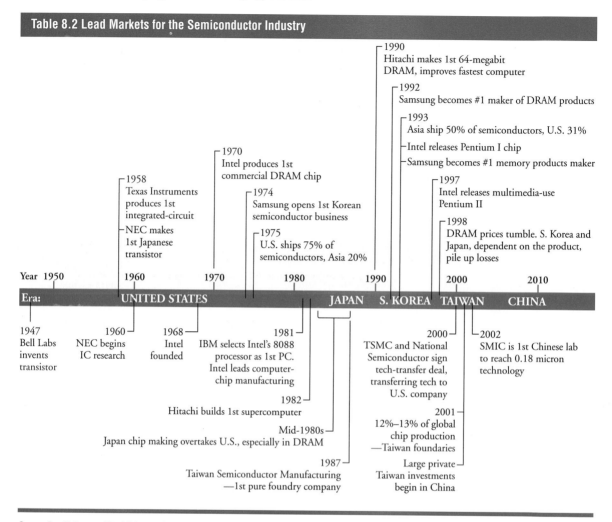

1990
Hitachi makes 1st 64-megabit
DRAM, improves fastest computer

1992
Samsung becomes #1 maker of DRAM products

1993
Asia ship 50% of semiconductors, U.S. 31%
Intel releases Pentium I chip
Samsung becomes #1 memory products maker

1970
Intel produces 1st
commercial DRAM chip

1997
Intel releases multimedia-use
Pentium II

1958
Texas Instruments
produces 1st
integrated-circuit
NEC makes
1st Japanese
transistor

1974
Samsung opens 1st Korean
semiconductor business

1998
DRAM prices tumble. S. Korea and
Japan, dependent on the product,
pile up losses

1975
U.S. ships 75% of
semiconductors, Asia 20%

Year 1950   1960   1970   1980   1990   2000   2010

Era: UNITED STATES   JAPAN   S. KOREA TAIWAN   CHINA

1947
Bell Labs
invents
transistor

1960
NEC begins
IC research

1968
Intel
founded

1981
IBM selects Intel's 8088
processor as 1st PC.
Intel leads computer-
chip manufacturing

2000
TSMC and National
Semiconductor sign
tech-transfer deal,
transferring tech to
U.S. company

2002
SMIC is 1st Chinese lab
to reach 0.18 micron
technology

1982
Hitachi builds 1st supercomputer

2001
12%–13% of global
chip production
—Taiwan foundaries

Mid-1980s
Japan chip making overtakes U.S., especially in DRAM

Large private
Taiwan investments
begin in China

1987
Taiwan Semiconductor Manufacturing
—1st pure foundry company

Source: Ben Dolven and David Kruger, "Silicon Rush," *Far Eastern Economic Review,* February 14, 2002, p. 32.

China to allow it both to adapt products to the local market and to tap into China's pool of scientists.[46] P&G's vision for greater China for the year 2020 is to become the largest consumer products company in China, surpassing $35 billion in sales and covering every household through its sales network.[47] Similarly, McDonald's views China as one of its biggest single opportunities. It built twenty-seven restaurants in China between 1990 and 1995, and the fast-food company expects to double its size every year until it reaches six hundred restaurants in early 2003. In Beijing alone, McDonald's ran about thirty-four outlets and expected to have as many as one hundred in a short period of time.[48]

China's automotive industry is also growing rapidly. In 1991, fifty thousand cars were sold in China. By 2000, the number had grown to 750,000 and was expected to double to 1.5 million by 2006.[49] Volkswagen was one of the first foreign automotive companies to set up in China, starting with a joint venture as early as 1984. In the first five months of 2000, it boasted a 38 percent market share in China. Success of both its Volkswagen and Audi lines prompted the company to announce plans to invest another $1.6 billion in China over the next few years.[50] The number of passenger cars in China will likely increase from 2 million in 1994 to 22 million by 2010. This increase would mean production of as many as 3.5 million units annually, a feat that would make China the fourth largest producer behind the United States, Japan, and Germany. Car manufacturers not investing in China are rightfully anxious that they may miss the chance of a lifetime. Any producer entrenched there would also be able to capitalize on the large volume advantage in the export business, beating competitors all over the world on the basis of cost. Volkswagen is likely to benefit enormously from a growing Chinese market, adding to its worldwide production total and expanding its market power elsewhere at the same time.

Competing for a "must win" market such as China is of great importance in new sectors, such as mobile telephones or information technology. By 2002, China had surpassed every country in terms of mobile phone users, with 167 million subscribers. In April 2002 alone, 6 million Chinese became new subscribers. And this number represented a penetration rate of only 13 percent of China's 1.1 billion people. By comparison, the United States, the world's second largest market, has 136 million subscribers.[51] When it comes to the Internet, China has the second largest number of home users, with 56 million households connected, second only to the United States, with 166 million Internet users.[52] Clearly, for many firms China will be a "must win" market, where future global market leadership will be determined. Considerable investment will be required in this huge market. With global leadership at stake, many companies believe they simply cannot afford to ignore this market.

IDENTIFYING GENERIC GLOBAL MARKETING STRATEGIES

Generic global marketing strategies are general classifications of prototype strategies that help us understand different approaches to globalization.[53] The concept of generic strategies has been widely used by writers on business and corporate strategies, including Michael E. Porter.[54] Generic strategies, such as differentiation, cost leadership, and the like, are archetypes that describe fundamentally different ways to compete. Believing that firms can select from among a great many different fundamental types of global strategies, we would like to offer a way to conceptualize the different types. See Figure 8.6 for a framework to help understand the choices today's companies face.

To many readers, the term *global marketing strategy* probably suggests a company represented everywhere and pursuing more or less the same marketing strategy. However, global marketing strategies are not to be equated with global standardization, although the two may be identical in some situations. *A global marketing strategy represents the application of a common set of strategic marketing principles across most world markets.* It may include, but does not require, similarity in products or in marketing processes. A company that pursues a global marketing strategy looks at the

Figure 8.6: Level of Geographic Marketing Strategy Integration

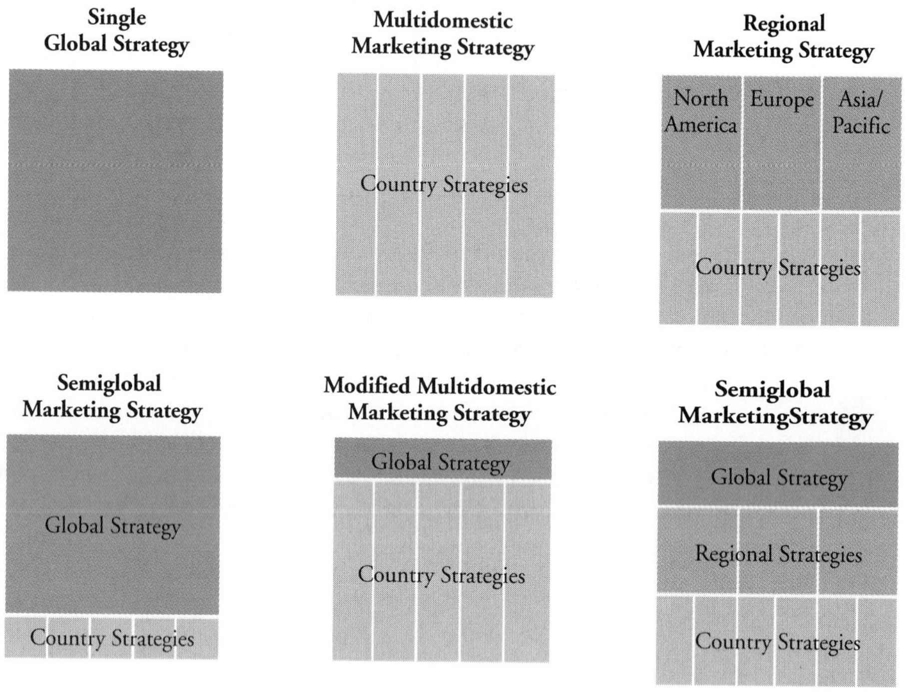

world market as a whole rather than at markets on a country-by-country basis. The latter approach is more typical for multinational firms.

Standardization deals with the amount of similarity companies want to achieve across many markets with respect to their marketing strategies and marketing mix. Standardization may also apply to general business policies or the modes of operation a company may want to pursue. *Globalization,* on the other hand, deals with the integration of the many country strategies and the subordination of these country strategies to one global framework. As a result, it is conceivable that one company may have a globalized approach to its marketing strategy but leave the details for many parts of the marketing plan to local subsidiaries.

Few companies want to globalize all of their marketing operations. The difficulty then is to determine which elements of the marketing operations will gain from globalization. Such a modular approach to globalization is likely to yield greater returns than a total globalization of a company's marketing strategy.[55] Globalization of a firm's marketing operations may take several forms. Major drivers are the differences in the environment and the different sources of global logic, as described in Chapter 7. The major sources of global logic can be grouped into two distinctive sets. Customer-based global logics, consisting of global customer, information, and purchasing logics, tend to affect the marketing variables such as product design, branding, and communications. Such globalization patterns frequently take place "in public" because globalization of products, communications, and brands is visible to all concerned. Industry-based global logics, such as competitive, industry, and size (critical mass) logics, mostly affect the integration aspects of global operations, ranging from manufacturing to research and development, logistics, and distribution. Because this type of globalization path takes place within the organization, these aspects are often hidden from view.

The two forces—customer-based logics and industry-based logics—combine into various paths of globalization, which explains the differences in global marketing practices among international firms. When the global logic is low for both customer- and industry-based factors, companies tend to opt for multidomestic marketing strategies. Faced with strong customer-based global logic but weak industry-based global logic as a result of differences in the competitive and industry structures across many markets, companies can pursue global marketing mix strategies. Confronted with different customer pressures across the world but high industry-based global logic, companies may adopt a global leverage strategy by concentrating on synergy in operations. Finally, when both sets of global logics, industry-based and customer-based, are strong, a firm may find an integrated global business strategy most appropriate. Figure 8.7 depicts the different globalization patterns.

Figure 8.7: Generic Global Marketing Strategies

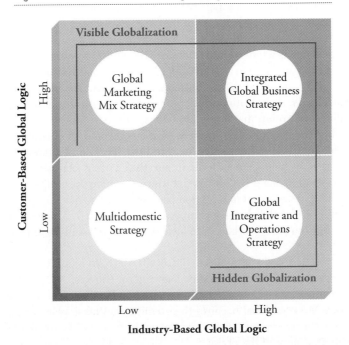

MULTIDOMESTIC MARKETING STRATEGIES

Although we explore organization issues in more detail in Chapter 16, some general principles for the organization of multidomestic firms should be introduced at this point. To a large extent, international firms operating as multidomestic firms have organized their businesses around countries or geographic regions. Some key strategic decisions with respect to products and technology are made at the central or head office, but the implementation of marketing strategies is left largely to local-country subsidiaries. As a result, profit and loss responsibility tends to reside in each individual country. At the extreme, this leads to an organization that runs many different businesses in several countries—hence the term *multidomestic*. Each subsidiary represents a separate business that must be run profitably.

As we discussed in Chapter 1, multinational corporations tend to be represented in a large number of countries and the world's principal trading regions. Many of today's large, internationally active firms may be classified as pursuing multidomestic strategies. Many of today's global firms have traditionally operated multidomestic marketing strategies, including well-known firms such as General Motors, Ford, IBM, Gillette, General Electric, and Kodak, as well as major service businesses, including CitiGroup and Morgan Chase, two of the largest U.S.-based financial services organizations. Overseas firms with long international experience, such as Unilever, Royal Dutch-Shell, and Nestlé, who have established subsidiary networks in many countries, have also tended to operate under the multidomestic marketing mode. Unilever's chairman explained his company's marketing strategy as "multi-local multinational" based on his observation that "there is no such thing as a global consumer, I have never met one. Every consumer is local."[56]

Nestlé, the world's largest food company, is represented in most markets of the world and is a typical practitioner of the multidomestic strategy. Including its operating companies, such as Carnation, Rowntree, and Buitoni, among others, it has traditionally practiced a decentralized approach to management. Local operating managers, thought to be much more in tune with local markets, are given the freedom to develop marketing strategies tailored to local needs. In the foods business, where considerable differences exist among countries' cultures and consumer habits, competitive environments, market structures, and practices, decentralization was judged by management to be imperative.[57] Many companies pursuing a multidomestic strategy have begun a move toward a more centralized management structure, which has resulted in a reorganization around major business lines. To reap the benefits of global leverage, companies realize that the multidomestic business model leaves too many initiatives to local levels, thus resulting in missed opportunities.

REGIONAL AND MULTIREGIONAL STRATEGIES

Regional marketing strategies focusing on Europe, Asia, or Latin America represent a halfway point between multidomestic and truly global strategy types. Conceptually, they are not global because the coordination takes place across a single region only. Pan-European strategies stand out as the first real regional marketing strategies, created because of the opportunities presented by the European Union and its increasing integration.

Regional strategies are essentially marketing strategies across several countries, although most are in close proximity. For Europe, the overall market might include about fifteen different main markets. The fact that several countries are involved with a closely coordinated strategy means that regional marketing strategies are no longer multidomestic either. The thought process that companies go through to determine their appropriate regional strategy across, say, ten Asian markets is identical to the analysis a company would apply to determine the best global marketing strategy across its top twenty global markets. The global mindset is thus closely related to a pan-European mindset, at least on a conceptual level. The major difference stems from the type of markets included in the analysis, but not from the type of conceptual approach. The many different regional marketing strategies (see Figure 8.8) typically center on any one of the three large trading blocs of North America (United States, Canada, and Mexico), Europe, and the Asia Pacific area (Japan and the Pacific Rim countries). A global strategy, by comparison, would include all the major triad regions. Regional strategies may be structured around penetrating just one regional market or several markets.

We speak of a North American strategy if a company has integrated its marketing strategy for the United States, Canada, and Mexico. The creation of NAFTA caused many firms to adopt an integrated North American strategy by merging operations of the three signature countries. A pan-European strategy occurs when a firm

Figure 8.8: Regional Marketing Strategies

Global Triad Strategy

Asia Pacific | North America | Europe

Integrated Regional Strategies

Pan-Asian Strategy | North American Strategy | Pan-European Strategy

Multiregional Strategies

Trans-Pacific Strategy | Trans-Atlantic Strategy

integrates its strategy across Europe. And finally, a firm adopting a pan-Asian strategy integrates its marketing strategy across the Asia Pacific region. Companies may also integrate two regions into a trans-Pacific strategy or a trans-Atlantic strategy.

GLOBAL MARKETING STRATEGIES

In the early phases of development, global marketing strategies were assumed to be of one type only. Typically, these first types of global strategies were associated with offering the same marketing strategy across the globe. The debate centered on whether a company could gain anything from this strategy and what its preconditions would be. As marketers gained more experience, many other types of global marketing strategies became apparent. Some strategies were much less complicated and exposed a smaller aspect of a marketing strategy to globalization. In this section, we explore the various generic types of global marketing strategies and indicate the conditions under which they may best succeed (see Figure 8.9).

INTEGRATED GLOBAL MARKETING STRATEGY. When a company pursues an integrated global marketing strategy, most elements of the marketing strategy have been globalized. Globalization includes not only the product but also the communi-

Figure 8.9: Level of Global Marketing Strategy Integration

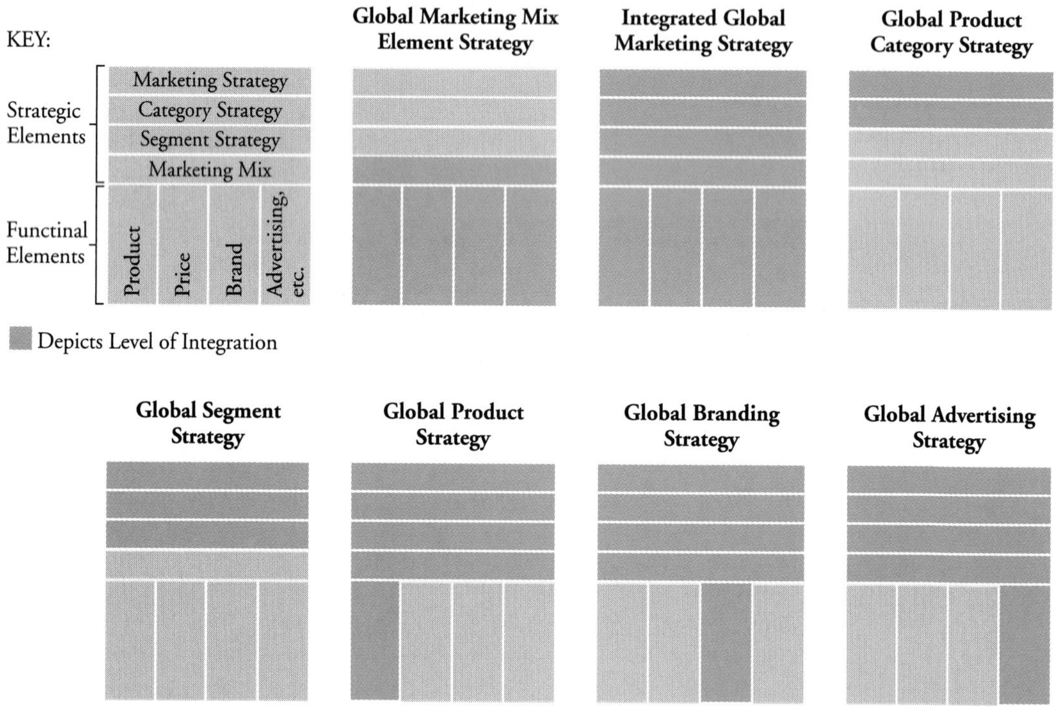

cations strategy, pricing, and distribution, as well as strategic elements such as segmentation and positioning. Such a strategy may be advisable for companies that face largely globalized customers along the lines defined earlier. It also assumes that the way a given industry works is highly similar everywhere, thus allowing a company to unfold its strategy along similar paths country by country.

One company that fits the description of an integrated global marketing strategy to a large degree is Coca-Cola. Coca-Cola has achieved a coherent, consistent, and integrated global marketing strategy that covers almost all elements of its marketing program, from segmentation to positioning, branding, distribution, bottling, and more. This globally integrated marketing strategy is also aided by a constant and intensive global logic faced by Coca-Cola from both its customers and the industry, as evidenced by the relentless competitive struggle with its archrival PepsiCo. We cover this classic global battle in more detail later in this chapter.

Reality tells us that completely integrated global marketing strategies will continue to be the exception. However, there are many other types of partially globalized marketing strategies. Each may be tailored to specific industry and competitive circumstances.

GLOBAL PRODUCT CATEGORY STRATEGY. Possibly the least integrated type of global marketing strategy is the global product category strategy. Leverage is gained from competing in the same category country after country and may come in the form of product technology or development costs. Selecting the form of global product category implies that the company, while staying within that category, will consider targeting different segments in each category, or varying the product, advertising, and branding according to local market requirements. Companies competing in the multidomestic mode are frequently applying the global category strategy and leveraging knowledge across markets without pursuing standardization. That strategy works best when there are significant differences across markets and when few segments are present in market after market. Several traditional multinational players who had for decades pursued a multidomestic marketing approach—tailoring marketing strategies to local market conditions and assigning management to local management teams—have been moving toward the global category strategy. Among them are Nestlé, Unilever, and Procter & Gamble, three large international consumer goods companies doing business in food and household goods.

For decades, Nestlé relied on regional executives who supervised many local companies. Now it has adopted a series of strategic business units (SBUs) along product categories, such as beverage, confectionery, or milk products. Senior executives at the head office took on responsibility for those categories. The confectionary business unit, centered around the Nestlé Crunch and Kitkat brands, has focused on key markets (Russia, India, China) for growth.[58] The water business, with a global market share of 16 percent, is devoted to making Nestlé the leading bottled water brand around the world.[59] Other product groups have similar goals and strategies. A similar move has been made by Procter & Gamble, the U.S.-based producer of consumer goods. For several of its categories, such as disposable baby diapers, senior head-office executives now carry out the function of coordinating and sharing information across one category on a global basis. Most recently, Procter & Gamble decided to structure its entire organization around seven product categories with global responsibility.[60]

Unilever, the Dutch-British company in similar businesses as Nestlé and Procter & Gamble, is focusing its business on about fourteen main categories.[61]

GLOBAL SEGMENT STRATEGY.   A company that decides to target the same segment in many countries is following a global segment strategy. The company may develop an understanding of its customer base and leverage that experience around the world. In both consumer and industrial industries, significant knowledge is accumulated when a company gains in-depth understanding of a niche or segment. A pure global segment strategy will even allow for different products, brands, or advertising, although some standardization is expected. The choices may consist of always competing in the upper or middle segment of a given consumer market or always competing for a particular technical application in an industrial segment.

Segment strategies are relatively new to global marketing. Industrial firms in particular have begun to adopt them. The former ICI Nobel Explosives, a world leader in explosives for use in various types of mining, adopted a global segmentation strategy according to key mining segments, such as deep mining, surface mining, and so on. Since the mining companies are increasingly pursuing global strategies themselves, it has begun to make sense for ICI Nobel to coordinate its strategies by segments and to leverage products, experience, and sales activities around the world. Serono, a Swiss-based biotech company, has structured its global marketing operation around several key segments. Serono markets around its reproductive health segment, where the company is the global leader, as well as around the multiple sclerosis (MS) segment, where the company has built the lead in Europe and is also expanding in the United States.[62] Among financial services firms, several companies have adopted global segment strategies. Citibank, a unit of recently formed CitiGroup, runs several segment strategies for different categories of private banking clients. Deloitte Touche Tohmatsu, a leading professional services firm, has adopted global strategies for several key client segments, such as for the financial services industry and telecommunications.

GLOBAL MARKETING MIX ELEMENT STRATEGIES.   These strategies incorporate globalization along individual marketing mix elements, such as pricing, distribution, communications, or product. They are partially globalized strategies that allow a company to customize other aspects of its marketing strategy. Although various types of strategies may apply, the most important are global product strategies, global advertising strategies, and global branding strategies. Typically, companies globalize those marketing mix elements that are subject to particularly strong global logic forces. A company facing strong global purchasing logic may globalize its account management practices or its pricing strategy. Another firm facing strong global information logic will find it important to globalize its communications strategy. DSM, a global Dutch chemical company, faced strong purchasing logic in its engineering plastics sector. The requirements of more and more customers who expected a coordinated global approach led to the formation of a new global account management structure, with responsibilities that cut across geographic lines.

GLOBAL PRODUCT STRATEGY.   Pursuing a global product strategy implies that a company has largely globalized its product offering. Although the product may not be completely standardized worldwide, key aspects or modules are in fact globalized.

The company may elect to add a global product strategy if the product or services offered fit the description of global products discussed earlier. Global product strategies require that product use conditions, expected features, and required product functions be largely identical so that few variations or changes are needed. Companies pursuing a global product strategy are interested in leveraging the fact that all investments for producing and developing a product have already been made. Global strategies will yield more volume, which will make the original investment easier to justify.

Volkswagen (VW) of Germany has adopted a global product strategy using a limited number of car platforms as the basis for many of its models. The platform is the basic chassis, or powertrain, of a car, with different models built onto it. Although VW markets different brands, such as the Volkswagen brand, Audi, Seat, and Skoda, the underlying powertrain is often the same for efficiency reasons. Similar platform concepts are used by Whirlpool Corporation, the U.S. major appliances firm, for its product lines in different parts of the world. Although global product strategies might lead to standardized products, many firms use the platform concept to pursue a partial global product strategy, allowing for differentiation at the local level but preserving key components globally for cost reasons. Other companies with relatively homogeneous products have already achieved global product status. For example, in the mobile phone handset industry, the products are largely standardized phones, with the exception that they be refitted to different local telecommunications standards. Although features may differ from country to country, substantial modules, or elements, of the products are identical.

GLOBAL BRANDING STRATEGIES. Global branding strategies consist of using the same brand name or logo worldwide. Companies want to leverage the creation of such brand names across many markets because the launching of new brands requires a considerable marketing investment. Global branding strategies are advisable if the target customers travel across country borders and are exposed to products elsewhere.

U.S.-based athletic shoe manufacturer Reebok spent about $140 million on its brand name and embarked on a global branding strategy, consolidating all of its advertising under the Leo Burnett advertising agency. The company wants to become a leading sports and fitness brand in the athletic shoe market, estimated at $12 billion, and in the process achieve a 30 percent world market share.[63]

Global branding strategies also become important if target customers are exposed to advertising worldwide. This situation is often the case for industrial marketing customers, who may read industry and trade journals from other countries. Increasingly, global branding has become important also for consumer products, where cross-border advertising through international television channels has become common. Even in some markets such as eastern Europe, many consumers had become aware of brands offered in western Europe before the liberalization of the economies in the early 1990s. Global branding allows a company to take advantage of already existing goodwill. Companies pursuing global branding strategies may include luxury product marketers, who typically face a large fixed investment for the worldwide promotion of a product. In Chapter 12, we look at the various choices of global branding in more detail.

GLOBAL ADVERTISING STRATEGY. Globalized advertising is generally associated with the use of the same brand name around the world. A company may want to use different brand names, however, partly for historic purposes. Many global firms have made acquisitions in other countries, resulting in several local brands. These local brands have their own distinctive market, and a company may find it counterproductive to change those brand names. Instead, the company may want to leverage a certain theme or advertising approach that may have been developed as a result of global customer research. Global advertising themes are most advantageous when a firm wants to market to customers around the world who are seeking similar benefits. Once the purchasing reason has been determined as similar, a common theme may be created to address it. The difficulties encountered with selecting common themes are discussed at length in Chapter 12. Procter & Gamble's advertising for its Pantene hair care line offers an example of how a global advertising strategy works. Originally started in 1999 in Latin America, the company began to feature endorsements by actresses and soap opera stars speaking in a woman-to-woman conversational tone. This approach represented a departure from traditional Pantene advertising elsewhere, in which advertisements emphasized specific product claims. The new approach more than doubled Pantene sales in Latin America. P&G decided to use the same approach elsewhere, but replaced the actresses and soap opera stars with locally known personalities.[64]

HYBRID GLOBAL MARKETING STRATEGY. The above descriptions of the various global marketing models can give the impression that companies might be using one or the other generic strategy exclusively. Reality shows, however, that few companies consistently adhere to only one strategy. More often, companies adopt several generic global strategies simultaneously. A company might follow a global brand strategy for one part of its business while at the same time using local brands in other parts of its business. The earlier descriptions were deliberately offered in pure form to give you a clearer understanding. This simplification was not intended to disguise the fact that many firms are a mixture of different approaches, thus the term *composite*. When companies use composite global marketing strategies, one generic strategy usually dominates, and other generic strategies tend to be a lower priority.

INTEGRATED GLOBAL BUSINESS STRATEGIES

A company that faces a high degree of both customer-based and industry-based global logics is in a position to consider an integrated global business strategy. In this case, not only the marketing strategy, as discussed in the previous section, is globalized but so are other aspects of the business strategy. Typically, globalization also involves research and development (R&D), production, logistics, information technology, finance, accounting, and many other key functions relevant to the business.

In the context of global marketing, as we perceive it here, the issues of globalizing nonmarketing functions are beyond the scope and purpose of this text.[65] However, global marketers need to understand the challenge of fitting into a global business strategy. This challenge stems from relating marketing to other core functions, particularly product development, research and development, and manufacturing. Integration means that those functions, like the marketing function, do not exist on a single-country basis only, but that several or all regions share in common manufacturing, research, or development.

In the early phases of a firm's international development, the marketing responsibility is frequently the first to globalize. Manufacturing, research, and other core functions tend to remain attached to the domestic, or original, home market. In a true international business strategy, this umbilical cord would be cut and the functions would serve all markets on an equal basis, without bias toward home markets. Such resource sharing, or integration, makes sense if the firm faces a strong industry, competitive, or size logic, as described in the previous chapter.

When it comes to global business strategies, companies have several choices to make. We explain two main forms in the next section: the global focus strategy and the global business unit.

FORMULATING GLOBAL FOCUS STRATEGIES. As outlined earlier in this chapter, geographic extension is one of two key dimensions in the strategy of an international company. The second dimension is concerned with the range of a firm's product and service offerings. To what extent should a company become a supplier of a wide range of products aimed at several or many market segments? Should a company become the global specialist in a certain area by satisfying one or a small number of target segments, and doing so in most major markets around the world?

Even some of the largest companies cannot pursue all available initiatives. Resources for most companies are limited, often requiring a tradeoff between product expansion and geographic expansion strategies. Resolving this tradeoff is necessary to achieve a concentration of resources and effort in areas where they will bring the most return. We can distinguish between two models: on the one hand, we have the broad-based firm marketing a wide range of products to many different customer groups, both domestic and overseas; on the other hand, we have the narrowly based firm marketing a limited range of products to a homogeneous customer group around the world. Both types of companies can be successful in their respective markets.

Companies such as Procter & Gamble, Unilever, and Nestlé are all examples of consumer goods firms practicing a broad-based product strategy. In most markets, these firms offer many brands and product lines. Among industrial marketers, General Electric follows a similar strategy. Some of these firms, however, are broken down into a large number of strategic business units, or divisions with a limited product range aimed at a limited market segment. Within each business unit, the chosen strategy may be much more focused.

Firms with a narrow product range include Hertz and Avis, the U.S. car rental companies, and Rolex, the Swiss watch manufacturer. These firms have a common strategy of a narrow and clearly focused product line, with the intent of dominating the chosen market segment across many countries. Many specialty equipment manufacturers in the fields of machine tools, electronic testing equipment, and other production process equipment tend to fit this pattern of niche, or focus, marketing.

The trend today is for companies to expect their businesses to develop a worldwide position and for some (such as GE) to become number 1 or 2 worldwide in any category where they compete. This expectation requires a business to develop its competitive position across all key markets, in particular across the major regions of North America, Asia Pacific, and Europe. The preference is for businesses (or strategic business units in large corporations) to focus on a particular line or segment by extending that offering around the globe. This has also led companies to pursue global marketing strategies for each business line rather than for the corporation as a whole. Rather than having a single global strategy for one corporation, companies will let each operating division set the appropriate type of global strategy best suited to the division's markets and industry environment.

A company such as GE may pursue many different global marketing strategies, not just one. Each business develops its own, and there may well be different generic global marketing strategies for different businesses. In this sense, each business is given a global mandate, which means that it is required to develop its business on a worldwide basis. As a result, each operating division, such as GE Appliances, GE Capital, GE Plastics, and GE Medical Systems, develops and implements its own form of global strategy. GE Capital, which concentrates on financial services, is one of the largest units of its kind and consists of twenty-eight operating units specializing in different segments of the financial services market. GE Capital has invested heavily in Europe, where it became involved with GPA, the large Irish aircraft leasing firm, and the card finance companies of several European retailers. The company also invested in financing companies in Asia and in Japan specifically, where it acquired loans from several banks, including Japan's Long-Term Credit Bank.[66] Needless to say, the global marketing strategy of GE Capital will have to be quite different from the global marketing strategy of other GE units, such as GE Plastics.

CREATING GLOBAL BUSINESS UNITS. Many firms have come to realize that a strong global presence in one given product was becoming a strategic requirement. Since traditional multinational firms, often competing through a multidomestic strategy, have realized the weakness of their unfocused patterns of global coverage, they have begun to assemble business units that have a better global focus. Many firms are striving to change their business to reflect a more coherent market position, whereby a business consists of strong units in major markets. To avoid globally unfocused strategies, international firms have either retrenched to become regional specialists or changed their business focus to adopt global niche strategies, selective globalization, or complete globalization (see Figure 8.10).

A strategy of *complete globalization* is selected by firms that essentially globalize all of their business units. This pattern is typical of companies such as General Electric of the United States (as discussed earlier) and Siemens of Germany. Such firms end up with a dozen or more globally positioned businesses, each charting its own global marketing strategy. *Selective globalization* is adopted by firms that globalize several businesses but also exit from others because financial resources may be limited. Examples of selective globalization include ICI of the United Kingdom, where some units, such as manmade fibers, polyurethane, and acrylics, were sold off to strengthen the market positions of other units. *Global niche strategies* are selected by firms that focus on one or very few businesses worldwide and exit from others because of a lack of resources. Nokia, the Finnish telecommunications company, employs such niche strategies. The company exited from computers, paper, and other sectors to concentrate on cellular phones and telecommunications infrastructure.[67] Nokia eventually became a global leader in both sectors, beating both Motorola and

Figure 8.10: Global Business Strategies

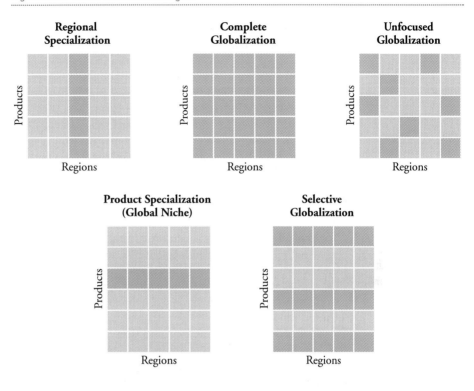

Ericsson, which had traditionally been strong in those businesses. Although largely focused on mobile handsets and mobile infrastructure, the handset business, Nokia Mobile Phones, has been further subdivided into nine different business units, each with a global mandate and a narrow segment focus.[68]

In general, companies with a narrow product or business focus that are globally marketed are considered to perform better than firms with a broad product line. Because the establishment of strong global marketing positions requires substantial resources, many firms have begun to adopt the narrow focus model by reorganizing business no longer viewed as part of the company's core operations or strategy. On the other hand, we have also seen firms conjure up irrelevant number 1 marketing positions by combining different businesses into newly created and at times artificial categories. The combination of pharmaceutical and agrochemical companies into life sciences businesses is a case in point. Pioneered by Monsanto, many other companies followed suit and combined several businesses under one corporate umbrella to pursue the leading position in life sciences. When these market positions failed to yield any positive results, a major trend toward focus emerged and many agrochemical businesses were reorganized into separate firms. Syngenta, formed from Novartis and AstraZeneca agrochemical businesses, is an example.[69]

COMPETITIVE GLOBAL MARKETING STRATEGIES

As firms compete globally for markets, the competitive game changes and different elements, rather than those characterizing traditional single-market competition, become the focus. The purpose of this section is to give some background on the shifting and varied competitive game by highlighting some well-known battles in the global marketplace. Two types of games are of particular interest to us. First, there are several heated global marketing duels in which two firms compete with each other across the entire global chessboard. The second game pits a global company versus a local company—a situation frequently faced in many markets. Both are discussed in depth here for illustrative purposes.

GLOBAL FIRM VERSUS GLOBAL FIRM

One of the longest-running battles in global competition is the fight for market dominance between Coca-Cola and PepsiCo, the world's largest soft-drink companies.[70] Traditionally, the two have been relatively close in the U.S. market, but Coca-Cola has long been the leader in international markets. With international markets growing much more rapidly than the domestic market, the advantage continues to shift in favor of Coca-Cola. Coca-Cola, with its Coke brand, outsells Pepsi in most of the world's ten largest markets. Pepsi is holding its own in the United States and the United Kingdom.[71]

The battle for global market share is an ongoing one that erupts simultaneously on several fronts. One of the most dramatic actions took place in Latin America. Venezuela was the only market in Latin America where Pepsi led Coke by a substantial margin (76 percent share versus 13 percent), thanks to its long-standing ties with the local bottler. In a dramatic play for share, Coca-Cola negotiated with PepsiCo's Venezuelan bottler to acquire a controlling interest in that company. The day after the deal was announced, on August 16, 1996, the Venezuelan bottler was switched to bottling Coke, and Pepsi lost its distribution literally overnight.[72] It took Pepsi thirty months and a combined investment of more than $500 million to reestablish itself in the country.[73] PepsiCo's other large Latin American bottler, Argentina-based Baesa, with operations in several Latin American markets, also suffered when it found itself unable to dislodge Coke in Brazil, one of the world's largest markets, where Coke leads Pepsi with a five-to-one advantage.

Coca-Cola and PepsiCo are fighting it out in other competitive arenas as well. In Europe, Coca-Cola consolidated its bottling with a few major bottlers with regional and international reach. Coca-Cola was able to concentrate its own activities on brand building and franchise creation while its bottling partners were running distribution and local operations. In eastern Europe, where Pepsi traditionally was ahead of Coke, Coca-Cola was able to change its strategy following the extensive liberalization that began around 1990.

A final major arena, and potentially the largest prize, is Asia. While its U.S. market was growing slowly, Coca-Cola believed that in the major markets of China, India, and Indonesia, which together are home to almost half the world's population, Coca-Cola would be able to double its business every three years for the indefinite future.[74] Although Coca-Cola and PepsiCo were relatively evenly matched at the outset, Coca-Cola was able to pull ahead of PepsiCo in China by a substantial margin in major cities.

Finally, Coca-Cola had left India many years ago when it was forced to give up control of its business. On its return in 1993, Coca-Cola found PepsiCo already established. In the race for local dominance, Coca-Cola acquired a leading local soft-drink firm, Parle, with fifty-four bottling plants. Coca-Cola is rapidly building up its Indian operation and has already overtaken PepsiCo in this large market. It is expected to invite another anchor bottler into India from among its established Asian bottlers.

Many other well-known matchups mirror the soft-drink global marketing wars. Unilever, a Europe-based firm, and Procter & Gamble of the United States clash in many markets, particularly in laundry products. The two firms compete with each other in most world markets, and action in one market easily spills over into others, causing observers to describe the competitive action as "The Great Soap Wars."[75]

An equally bruising battle is under way between Kodak of the United States and Fuji of Japan. Fuji has successfully entered the U.S. market and gained about 25 percent share, which puts pressure on Kodak at home. The U.S. firm has also had great difficulty expanding in Japan. Despite efforts by the U.S. government, the World Trade Organization has not found any evidence of unfair practices in the Japanese market on the import of foreign film.[76]

LOCAL COMPANY VERSUS GLOBAL FIRM

As we have shown, global firms can leverage their experience and market position in one market for the benefit of another. Consequently, the global firm is often a more potent competitor for a local company. As many examples show, however, there are smart local companies that can, sometimes with fewer resources, offer strong resistance to the encroachment of international firms into their local markets. The beer market in China, fast becoming the premier beer market by volume, knows many local and international competitors. Foreign brewers flock to China in search of the last frontier and encouraged by the huge potential volumes. Tsingtao, China's oldest brewery and one of its strongest brand names, has acquired the interests of international brewers piling up huge losses in the emerging Chinese market. Foreign brewers, arriving in China with their own international brand names, often retire the brands of the acquired local companies. Tsingtao, on the other hand, appreciates the Chinese adherence to long-time local names and instead revives those local brands, rather than replacing them with a national brand. Its strategy has allowed Tsingtao to purchase the interests of foreign-owned brewers. It then works on improving the local brand or the quality of the beer and does not change the name. The company aims at reaching a 10 percent share of the China market, a volume large enough to join the ranks of the top ten brewers worldwide.[77]

Although global firms have superior resources, they often become inflexible after several successful market entries and tend to stay with standard approaches when flexibility would be a better approach. In general, the global firms' strongest local competitors are those that watch global firms carefully and learn from their moves in other countries. Some global firms require several years before one of their products is introduced in all markets. Local competitors in some markets can take advantage of the advance notice produced by such time lags to build defenses or launch a preemptive attack on the same segment.

CONCLUSIONS

Any company engaging in global marketing operations is faced with several very important strategic decisions. At the outset, a decision needs to be made about committing the company to some level of internationalization. Increasingly, firms find that the presence of a strong global logic demands that global marketing must be pursued for competitive reasons and that it is often not an optional strategy. Once committed, the company needs to decide where to go, both in terms of geographic regions and specific countries.

During the 1990s, a changing competitive environment considerably affected these choices. In the past, companies have moved from largely domestic or regional firms to become global. As multidomestic companies, these firms competed in many local markets and attempted to meet the local market requirements as best they could. Although many firms still approach their international marketing effort this way, an increasing number are taking a global view of their marketplace.

The global firm operates differently from the multidomestic or regional company. Pursuing a global marketing strategy does not necessarily mean that the company is attempting to standardize all of its marketing programs on a global scale. A global marketing strategy also does not imply that the company is represented in all world markets. Rather, a global marketing strategy requires a new way of thinking about global marketing operations. Global companies are fully aware of their strengths across as many markets as possible. Consequently, the global company builds its marketing strategy on the basis of a thorough understanding of global logic pressures and enters any markets dictated by the overall global logic it faces in any given industry.

A global company is also keenly aware of the value of global size and market share. As a result, several strategic decisions, such as which markets to enter, becomes subject to the overall global strategy. Rather than making each market pay its way separately, a global firm may aim to break even in some markets if this strategy helps its overall position by holding back a key competitor. As strategy begins to resemble that of a global chess game, companies have to develop new skills and learn about new concepts to survive. Understanding and exploiting the lead market principle will become more important.

Globalization of many industries today is a fact. Some companies have no choice but to become globalized; once key competitors in their industries are globalized, other firms must follow. This situation leads to a rethinking of the strategic choices and inevitably leads to new priorities. Globalization is not simply a new term for something that has existed all along; it is a new, competitive game requiring companies to adjust to and learn new ways of doing business. For many companies, survival depends on how well they learn this new game.

As we have seen in this chapter, *globalization* has become a multifaceted term requiring companies to monitor their markets carefully. Globalization may occur in several parts of a firm's business and may require different responses, whether it occurs at the customer, market, industry, or competitor level. As a result, there are many types of generic global marketing strategies a firm may choose from, moving the fundamental choice away from *whether* a global marketing strategy should be pursued toward *which* global marketing strategy should be adopted.

In the future, we can expect to see global marketing strategies adopted by firms from all parts of the world. As markets become increasingly accessible to all firms, the trend toward globalization will continue. Firms in developing and emerging economies, which are as affected by the global logic as those based in the developed world, will begin to concentrate on their own strengths and develop global marketing strategies for a particular sector. This trend is a key reason why managers in emerging markets will need a global mindset as much as their peers in developed countries.

Global marketing strategies are also becoming an issue for firms not typically associated with globalization. Smaller firms, although *focused*, increasingly find benefits from a global marketing strategy. To make the best of their limited resources, these firms will likely select niche strategies but pursue global reach in many key markets. Furthermore, many of the new venture start-ups will join the global game from the outset as they compete for key markets globally. Such venture firms will implement global marketing strategies early and by design, in contrast with earlier international companies such as Nestlé, Unilever, and others, which often became global *accidentally* rather than as the result of an explicit and intentional strategy.

Questions for Discussion

1. Why should small firms pursue a global strategy? Should they pursue such a strategy at all?

2. Investigate the geographic portfolio of three large *Fortune* 500 companies. What differences do you see, and what do you think accounts for these differences?

3. Contrast global with other types of geographic expansion strategies. In particular, how does a global expansion strategy differ from a multinational strategy?

4. How can a local company best compete against global firms?

5. What are the major advantages of a global niche strategy?

6. Why should firms in emerging countries pursue global marketing strategies?

7. Contrast global integration strategies with global marketing strategies.

8. Contrast regional with global marketing strategies.

For Further Reading

Abegglen, James C. *Sea Change*. New York: Free Press, 1994.

Alahutta, Matti. "Growth Strategies for High Technology Challengers." *Acta Polytechnica Scandinavica*, Electrical Engineering Series No. 66, Helsinki University of Technology, Helsinki, Finland, 1990.

Bartlett, Christopher A., and Sumantra Ghoshal. *Managing Across Borders*. Boston: Harvard Business School Press, 1989.

Ghoshal, Sumantra. "Global Strategy: An Organizing Framework." *Strategic Management Journal*, 1987, vol. 8, pp. 425–440.

Guido, Gianluigi, "Implementing a Pan European Marketing Strategy." *Long Range Planning*, 1991, vol. 24, no. 5, pp. 23–33.

Haikio, Martti. *Nokia: The Inside Story*. Helsinki: Edita/Pearson, 2002.

Jeannet, Jean-Pierre. *Managing with a Global Mindset*. London: Financial Times/Pitman, 2000.

Ohmae, Kenichi. *Triad Power: The Coming Shape of Global Competition*. New York: Free Press, 1985.

Pavlinek, Petr, and Adrian Smith. "Internationalization and Embeddedness in East-Central European Transition," *Regional Studies*, October 1, 1998, p. 619.

Porter, Michael E., ed. *Competition in Global Industries.* Boston: Harvard Business School Press, 1986.

Porter, Michael E. *The Competitive Advantage of Nations.* New York: Free Press, 1990.

Reich, Robert B. "Who Is Them?" *Harvard Business Review,* March–April 1991, pp. 77–88.

Thomsen, Stephen, and Malko Miyake. "Recent Trends in Foreign Direct Investments." *Financial Market Trends,* June 1, 1998, p. 95.

Endnotes

1. "PPG Industries," Lehman Brothers, Global Equity Research, June 18, 2002, p. 15.

2. Donnelley (R.R.) & Sons Co., Merrill Lynch, March 27, 2002, stock market analyst report, p. 2.

3. "China Gets the Message," *Journal of Commerce* (Special), September 23, 1998, p. 1C.

4. Deloitte & Touche, "Facts and Figures," *www.deloitte.com.*

5. "Compagnie de St.-Gobain," *Industry Week,* June 7, 1999, p. 38.

6. Saint-Gobain 2001, *Annual Report,* 2001.

7. "Buoyant Tiger Returns to High Growth and Reform," *Financial Times,* November 4, 1999, Special Survey on Taiwan, p. I.

8. "Plastics Additives Makers Hope for a Better Mix in 2002," *Chemical Market Exporter,* April 8, 2002.

9. "Asia Still Offers the Most Growth," *Chemical Week,* March 20, 2002, p. 34.

10. "Bayer to Boost Growth in Asia," *Wall Street Journal Europe,* June 20, 2001, p. 4.

11. The Coca-Cola Company, *Annual Report,* 2001.

12. "Head of Coke China Says Company Focusing on Water Conversation," *Cox Newspapers,* October 9, 2000, *www.coxnews.com.*

13. Drip Portfolio Report, *The Motley Fool.com (www.fool.com),* August 6, 1997.

14. "This Bud's for Them: Anheuser-Busch Takes Closer Aim at Foreign Markets," *New York Times,* June 23, 1999, p. C1.

15. Anheuser-Busch International, Inc., "International Beer Operations," *www.anheuser-busch.com/overview/international.html;* accessed on June 18, 2002.

16. "Globalizing for Future Growth," *Hitachi Today,* March-April 2001, no. 58, p. 2.

17. For a background on the concept of global pathway, see "Pathways to Global Success: Globalization Strategies for Financial Services Companies," Jean-Pierre Jeannnet et. al., Deloitte Touche Tohmatsu International and IMD Institute, New York, 2000.

18. "Globalization: The Second Decade," *Appliance Manufacturer,* May 1, 1999, p. 34.

19. "Whirlpool Corporation Announces Key Steps in Extension of Global Business Strategy," *Business Wire,* January 6, 2000.

20. "Whirlpool Corporation," Equity Research, Morgan Keegan, New York, July 10, 2002, p. 2

21. "Gillette to Buy Duracell for $7 Billion," *New York Times,* September 13, 1996, p. D1.

22. "Jewel of Japan," *Barron's,* November 5, 2001, p. 32.

23. "Globalization: The Second Decade," *Appliance Manufacturer,* May 1, 1999, p. 34.

24. Vijay Jolly, "Global Competitive Strategies," in *Strategy, Organizational Design, and Human Resource Management,* ed. Charles C. Snow (Greenwich, Conn.: JAI Press, 1989), pp. 55–110.

25. "Pacific Cycle Acquires Schwinn/GT," company press release, September 10, 2001, *www.mongoose.com;* accessed on June 18, 2002.

26. "No, They Didn't Name It Mississippi," *New York Times,* June 24, 2002, p. C4.

27. Vijay Jolly, "Logitech International (A)," Case (Lausanne, Switzerland: IMD International, 1991).

28. "Logitech," Global Equity Research, Lehman Brothers, July 12, 2002.

29. Kenichi Ohmae, *Triad Power: The Coming Shape of Global Competition* (New York: Free Press, 1985).

30. "Subramanian Rangan: Seven Myths to Ponder Before Going Global," *Financial Times,* Mastering Strategy, Part 10, November 29, 1999, p. 2.

31. "Alcatel Open to More Acquisitions," *Business World,* March 25, 1999.

32. "EU/Japan: Ten Year Action Plan Ushers in New Era," *European Report,* July 4, 2001, p. 1

33. "China: Unilever Seeks Market in China," *China Daily,* June 21, 1999, p. 5.

34. "Unilever to Expand Business in China," *Asiainfo Daily China News,* October 22, 2001, p. 1.

35. "Derivatives Structuring Capabilities," *Euromoney,* March 2002, p. 5.

36. Hyundai Motors, *Annual Report,* 2001, p. 29.

37. "US Companies Assess Damage in Argentina," *Asian Wall Street Journal,* January 10, 2002, p. 2.

38. "Otis Signs $5 Million Contract with TPSA," *Polish Press Agency,* June 9, 1999.

39. "P&G Dived into Eastern European Market," *Enquirer Business Coverage,* November 7, 1999.

40. "VW Maintains Its Pole Position," FT Auto 2000, International Perspectives, *Financial Times Survey,* 2000.

41. "Czech Carmaker Skoda Moving Up," *USA Today,* April 23, 2001.

42. "Silicon Rush," *Far Eastern Economic Review,* February 14, 2002, p. 30.

43. "Manager's Hands-Off Tactics Right Touch for Italian Unit," *Nikkei Weekly,* February 3, 1997, p. 17.

44. "Local Brands in China Challenge Global Rivals," *European Wall Street Journal,* May 25, 2001, p. 26.

45. "P&G Fortifies Foothold in China," *Asiainfo Daily China News,* June 27, 2001, p. 1.

46. "P&G China Lag Has Global Role," *Research Technology Management,* September-October 2001, pp. 4–5.

47. "P&G Fortifies Foothold in China," *Asiainfo Daily China News,* June 27, 2001, p. 1.

48. "Fast Food, Western Colas Highlight China Growth," *National Catholic Reporter,* January 29, 1999, p. 15.

49. "Volkswagen Shifts Gears in China," *Wall Street Journal Europe,* April 8, 2002, p. A12.

50. "Volkswagen to Invest Another $1.63 Billion in China," *China Online,* June 21, 1999.

51. "China Leads World in Mobile Phone Subscribers," *Nua Internet Surveys,* June 18, 2002.

52. "China Number Two in Home Net Usage," *Nua Surveys* (Reuter), June 18, 2002.

53. This section has been adapted from Jean-Pierre Jeannet, *Managing with a Global Mindset* (London: Financial Times/Prentice Hall, 2000), pp. 121–167.

54. First published in Michael E. Porter, *Competitive Strategy: Techniques for Analyzing Industries and Competitors* (New York: Free Press, 1980); more recently in Michael E. Porter, *The Competitive Advantage of Nations* (New York: Free Press, 1990), pp. 39–40.

55. John Quelch, "Customizing Global Marketing," *Harvard Business Review,* May–June 1986, pp. 59–68.

56. "Everything from Soup to Soap," *Wall Street Journal Europe,* January 31, 2002, p. 10.

57. Helmut Maucher, "Global Strategies of Nestlé," *European Management Journal,* 1989, vol. 7, no. 1, pp. 92–96.

58. Presentation on Nestlé Confectionary Business Unit, Nestlé corporate web site (*www.ir.Nestle.com*), 2002.

59. Presentation of Nestlé Water, Nestlé corporate web site (*www.ir.Nestle.com*), 2002.

60. "P&G Moves Forward with Reorganization," *Chemical Market Reporter,* February 1, 1999, p. 12.

61. "Giant Breaks Free from the Shackles," *Financial Times,* February 12, 1997, p. 20.

62. "Serono Reported a 14 Percent Jump in Sales for the First Quarter—Focus Is on Future in Multiple Sclerosis," *Wall Street Journal Europe,* May 3, 2001, p. 25.

63. "Why Reebok Fired Chiat, Once and for All," *Advertising Age,* September 20, 1993, p. 3.

64. "P&G's Pantene Pitch Taps Performer's Cachet," *Wall Street Journal Europe,* June 11, 2002, p. A10.

65. For more details on nonmarketing functions, see *Managing with a Global Mindset,* by Jean-Pierre Jeannet, op. cit.

66. "GE Profit Jumped 15 Percent to $2.82 Billion," *Wall Street Journal,* July 9, 1999, p. A3

67. Dan Steinbock, *The Nokia Revolution* (Amacom, 2001).

68. "Nokia's Next Act," *Business Week,* July 1, 2002, pp. 56–58.

69. "Syngenta Tries to Grow Profits in 2002," *Chemical Market Reporter,* March 4, 2002.

70. "Pepsi Gets Back in the Game," *Time Magazine,* April 26, 1999, p. 44.

71. "Near As Damn It," Marketing Week, April 11, 2002, p. 25.

72. "How Coke Is Kicking Pepsi's Can," *Fortune,* October 28, 1996, pp. 70–84.

73. "PepsiCo's Venezuelan Joint Venture Inaugurates $32 Million Plant," *Financial Times,* May 27, 1999, p. 19.

74. "Coke Pours into Asia," *Business Week,* October 28, 1996, p. 72.

75. "Unilever: Bureaucracy Buster," *Forbes,* January 25, 1999, p. 40.

76. "U.S. Urges Japan to Further Open Up the Film Market," *Wall Street Journal,* August 8, 1998, p. A4.

77. "A Thirst for Success," *Far Eastern Economic Review,* December 28, 2000, p. 106.

Chapter 9

Global Market Entry Strategies

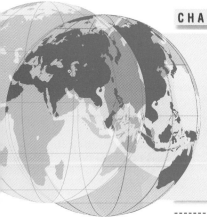

Companies pursuing a global marketing strategy must determine the type of presence they expect to build in every market where they intend to compete. One major choice concerns the method of entering any selected market. A company may want to export to the new market, or it may prefer to produce locally. A second major choice involves the amount of direct ownership desired. Should the company strive for full ownership of its local operation, or is a joint venture preferable? These initial decisions about market entry tend to be of medium- to long-term importance, leaving little room for change once a commitment has been made. Therefore, it is important to treat these decisions with the utmost care. The financial return to the company is not the only issue at stake. The extent to which the company's marketing strategy can be employed in the new market also depends on these decisions.

In this chapter, we concentrate on the major entry strategy alternatives by explaining each one in detail and citing relevant company experiences. We also treat the entry strategy from an integrative point of view and offer guidance about how a specific strategy may be selected to suit a company's needs. For an overview of all chapter topics, see Figure 9.1.

EXPORTING AS AN ENTRY STRATEGY

Exporting to a foreign market is a strategy many companies follow for at least some of their markets. Many countries do not offer a large enough opportunity to justify local production, so exporting allows a company to manufacture its products centrally for several markets and, therefore, to obtain economies of scale. Furthermore, exports add volume to an already existing production operation located elsewhere, so the marginal profitability of such exports tends to be high.

Figure 9.1: Market Entry Strategies

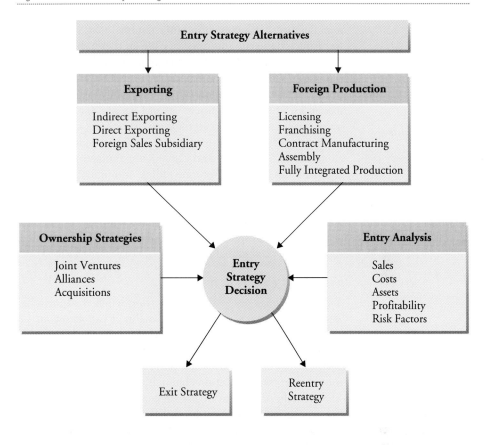

Invensys Energy Systems (NZ) Ltd. serves as an example of a company driven by exporting. Based in New Zealand and part of a larger global group (BTR), the company sells more than 90 percent of its volume (US $35 million) to more than thirty countries in Asia, the Pacific, Africa, the Americas, Europe, and the Middle East. Invensys is a leader in the design and manufacture of standby DC power equipment for the telecom industry. Invensys relies on local support to market and service its products. Sales are assisted by other group companies. Although the sales to export ratio is very high, this is a typical example of a small to medium-sized, specialized company based in a small home market (New Zealand) and marketing niche products worldwide.[1]

A firm has two basic options for carrying out its export operations. It can contact foreign markets through a domestically located (in the exporter's country of operation) intermediary—an approach called *indirect exporting,* or it can use an intermediary located in the foreign market—an approach termed *direct exporting.* The use of various types of export intermediaries is described in detail in Chapter 15.

INDIRECT EXPORTING

Several types of intermediaries located in the domestic market are ready to assist a manufacturer with contacting international markets or buyers. The major advantage for using a domestic intermediary lies in that individual's knowledge of foreign market conditions. Particularly for companies with little or no experience in exporting, the use of a domestic intermediary provides the exporter with readily available expertise. The most common types of intermediaries are brokers, combination export managers, and manufacturers' export agents. Group selling activities can also help individual manufacturers in their export operations.

Browne & Dreyfus International is a firm serving as indirect exporting channel for about fifteen U.S.-based and Canadian manufacturers. Located in New York City, the company has been marketing welding equipment and automatic tools in Europe for its client firms for about forty years. In many markets, it is using distributors.[2] For its clients, Browne & Dreyfus acts as the market link, thus sharing its exporting skill with several smaller firms that would find it difficult to maintain their own exporting organizations. Despite their efficiency for small firms, indirect exporters represent a small part of total global marketing.

DIRECT EXPORTING

A company engages in direct exporting when it exports through intermediaries located in the foreign markets. Under direct exporting, an exporter must deal with a large number of foreign contacts, possibly one or more for each country the company plans to enter. Although a direct exporting operation requires a larger degree of expertise, this method of market entry provides the company with a greater degree of control over its distribution channels than it could exercise in indirect exporting.

Successful direct exporting depends on the viability of the relationship between the exporting firm and the local distributor or importer. By building the relationship on a solid foundation, the exporter saves considerable investment costs. However, success is not always ensured. Pacific World Corp. is a small California-based manufacturer of artificial fingernails and nail care products. The company began exporting its products in 1992. Exporting became a profitable activity only after the company took care to develop a strategic export plan in 1995. Although the company is still small, with thirty-five employees, its Nailene brand is now one of the most widely distributed artificial nail brands in the world. With exports at 15 percent of sales, and growing rapidly, the export share is expected to reach 25 percent over the next few years. The company believed it was successful by building long-term relationships with distributors, agents, and other overseas partners. Additional market intelligence was made available by the U.S. Department of Commerce.[3]

INDEPENDENT DISTRIBUTOR VERSUS SALES SUBSIDIARY. The independent distributor earns a margin on the selling price of the products. Although the independent distributor does not represent a direct cost to the exporter, the margin the distributor earns represents an opportunity that is lost to the exporter. By switching to a sales subsidiary to carry out the distributor's tasks, the exporter can earn the same margin. For example, a manufacturer of video projection equipment exports products priced at $10,000 each (at the factory in Boston). With airfreight, tariffs, and taxes amounting to $2,000, the product's landed costs amount to $12,000 for each piece of video projection equipment at the country of destination. An independent distributor will have to price the products at $18,000 to earn a desired gross margin of $33\frac{1}{3}$ percent. Instead, the exporter can set up a wholly owned sales subsidiary, in this case, consisting of a manager, a sales manager, several sales agents, clerical staff, a warehousing operation, and the rental of an office and warehouse location. If the total estimated cost amounts to $480,000 annually, then the point at which the manufacturer can switch from an independent distributor to a company-owned sales subsidiary is calculated as follows:

$$\frac{\text{Annual fixed cost}}{\text{Unit sales contribution}} = \text{Breakeven unit volume}$$

$$\frac{\$480,000}{\$6,000} = 80 \text{ units}$$

As a result, the exporter of video projection equipment would be able to set up its own sales organization in a given country if the annual sales volume were at least eighty units, or more. With increasing volume, the incentive to start a sales subsidiary grows. On the other hand, if the anticipated sales volume is small, the use of independent distributors will be more efficient because sales are channeled through a distributor who maintains the necessary staff for several other product lines. Sega, the Japanese video game company, experienced cost pressures from exports in its European operation. Following rapid growth, European sales declined, and the slump immediately affected Sega's cost structure. As a result, Sega had to restructure its European operation, and its sales subsidiaries in Austria, Belgium, and the Netherlands were closed. In those countries, as in many other European markets, Sega continued to market through independent agents, serving only the United Kingdom, France, Germany, and Spain through sales subsidiaries. The total cost of this restructuring amounted to $245 million.[4]

The lack of control frequently causes exporters to shift from an independent distributor to wholly owned sales subsidiaries. Volkswagen (VW), at the time the leading importer into Japan, had used Yanase as its exclusive importer to Japan for almost forty years. In 1992, Volkswagen wanted to expand to a level of 100,000 units annually. In the belief that its existing distribution arrangements would not get it to that higher level, VW replaced Yanase by creating its own sales subsidiary, Volkswagen Audi Nippon. VW also entered into an arrangement with Toyota to open additional channels. Upset by this approach, Yanase signed as the importer of Opel, General Motors' German subsidiary, abandoning its long-standing relationship with VW. As a result, Opel had to switch its previous relationship with Isuzu, a General Motors (GM) affiliate located in Japan that had performed below expectations. Following the switch, Volkswagen sales took a 40 percent plunge. The company reasoned that its $300 million predelivery inspection center, opened in Japan in 1992, was scaled for 100,000 cars to be imported each year. Since the existing dealer arrangement did not promise to reach that volume, the company had to go it alone and create its own sales subsidiary and network. Although sales continue to improve, 1997 volume amounted to only 49,340 units.[5] In the meantime, GM had been able to expand its links with Yanase, adding Cadillac and Saab to its Opel brand in Japan, and planning for a volume of eighty thousand Opels in 2000.[6] Although the strategic rationale for the shift was clear, this example shows that such distribution changes are difficult to accomplish.

THE COMPANY-OWNED SALES OFFICE (FOREIGN SALES SUBSIDIARY). Many companies export directly to their own sales subsidiaries abroad, sidestepping independent intermediaries. The sales subsidiary assumes the role of the independent distributor by stocking the manufacturer's products, selling to buyers, and assuming the credit risk. The sales subsidiary offers the manufacturer full control of selling operations in a foreign market. Such control may be important if the company's products require the use of special marketing skills, such as advertising or selling. The exporter thus finds it possible to transfer or export not only the product but also the entire marketing program, which often makes the product a success.

The operation of a subsidiary adds a new dimension to a company's international marketing operation. It requires the commitment of capital in a foreign country, primarily for the financing of accounts receivables and inventory. Also, the operation of a sales subsidiary entails numerous general administrative expenses that are essentially fixed in nature. As a result, a commitment to a sales subsidiary should not be made without careful evaluation of all the costs involved.

When General Motors began to plan for the export of its Saturn car to Japan, the GM division opted to open its own sales subsidiary. With the eventual goal of selling about thirty thousand vehicles annually, the company sidestepped Yanase, its Japanese importer, and recruited its own dealerships for the launch. But Saturn could find only about ten dealers and ended up with a volume of only 1,400 units in its first sixteen months of operations in Japan.[7] Clearly, going on its own in a difficult market turned out to be much harder than Saturn had anticipated.

LOCAL PRODUCTION AS AN ENTRY STRATEGY

Many companies realize that, to open a new market and serve local customers better, exporting into that market is not a sufficiently strong commitment for creating a strong local presence. As a result, these companies look for ways to strengthen their base by entering into one of several manufacturing arrangements. The following section explores the various types of local manufacturing arrangements that can be made—ranging from licensing all the way to fully integrated production facilities. The purpose of this section is to relate manufacturing to market entry and not to treat international or offshore production in a disconnected way. Our interest lies only in establishing production for the purpose of securing a local market. Many companies engage today in offshore production, which is simply a way of maximizing product supply or minimizing costs. A company building a new factory in Taiwan with the purpose of creating access and thus lowering cost production and then exporting its products to the United States is not truly entering the Taiwan market for enhanced presence, and this arrangement would not be of interest to us as global marketing executives. However, a firm building a new factory in Brazil with the expressed strategy of improving its own Brazilian market position is of interest to us. The foreign production section is intended for these latter types of companies.

LICENSING AS A MARKET ENTRY STRATEGY

Under licensing, a company assigns the right to a *patent* (which protects a product, technology, or process) or a *trademark* (which protects a product name) to another company for a fee or royalty. Using licensing as a method of market entry, a company can gain market presence without a major investment. The foreign company, or licensee, gains the right to exploit the patent or trademark commercially, on either an exclusive (the exclusive right to a certain geographic region) or an unrestricted basis.

Licenses are signed for various time periods. Depending on the investment needed to enter the market, the foreign licensee may insist on a longer licensing period to pay off the initial investment. Typically, the licensee will make all necessary capital investments (machinery, inventory, and so forth) and market the products in the assigned sales territories, which may consist of one or several countries. Licensing agreements are subject to negotiation and tend to vary considerably from company to company and from industry to industry.

REASONS FOR LICENSING. Companies use licensing for several reasons. For one, a company may not have the knowledge or the time to engage more actively in international marketing. The market potential of the target country may also be too small to support a manufacturing operation. A licensee has the advantage of adding the licensed product's volume to an ongoing operation, thereby reducing the need for a large investment in new fixed assets. A company with limited resources can gain advantage by having a foreign partner market its products; both would sign a licensing contract. Licensing saves capital because no additional investment is necessary and allows scarce managerial resources to be concentrated on more lucrative markets. Also, some smaller companies with a product in high demand may not be able to satisfy demand unless licenses are granted to other companies with sufficient manufacturing capacity. In some countries where the political or economic situation appears uncertain, a licensing agreement will avoid the potential risk associated with investments in fixed facilities. Both commercial and political risks are absorbed by the licensee. In other countries, governments favor the granting of licenses to independent local manufacturers as a means of building up an independent local industry. In such cases, a foreign manufacturer may prefer to team up with a capable licensee, despite a large market size, because other forms of entry may not be possible.

The French pharmaceutical company Sanofi has become a major user of licensing. Volume under license, but attributable to its licensees, accounted for as much as 60 percent of Sanofi's sales of about $2 billion. A new entrant into the drug business, the company realized that it could do only a limited number of research projects if it had to bring them from the lab to trial and eventual market entry. Sanofi therefore decided to engage in active licensing, letting other pharmaceutical companies market its newly discovered drugs. As a result of licensing and sharing, Sanofi was able to advance many more research and development projects. With this strategy, Sanofi advanced to twenty-fifth place in the pharmaceutical industry and achieved sales of $3.5 billion.[8] With the acquisition of Sterling Winthrop in the United States and Synthelabo of France, Sanofi was able to expand its employment base in the United States and become less reliant on licensing to enter the U.S. market.[9]

DISADVANTAGES OF LICENSING. A major disadvantage of licensing is the company's substantial dependence on the local licensee to produce revenues, or royalties, usually paid as a percentage on sales volume only. Once a license is granted, royalties are paid only if the licensee can perform an effective marketing job. The local company's marketing skills may be less developed, so revenues from licensing may suffer accordingly. Another disadvantage is the resulting uncertainty about product quality. A foreign company's image may suffer if a local licensee markets a product of substandard quality. Ensuring uniform quality requires additional resources from the licenser that may reduce the profitability of the licensing activity. Miller Brewing, one of the leading U.S. brewers, marketed Genuine Draft as its main international brand. Because Miller did not own any distribution systems in foreign markets, the company used licensing to get around the roadblocks. Miller had licensing agreements in place for countries such as Russia, Poland, Canada, the United Kingdom, Ireland, Germany, Brazil, Turkey, and the Philippines. Miller Brewing was acquired by South African Breweries, and the new parent company is likely to make its wide local distribution networks available to Miller, thus improving sales overseas beyond what Miller could accomplish through licensing alone.[10]

The possibility of nurturing a potential competitor is viewed by many companies as a disadvantage of licensing. With licenses usually limited to a specific time period, a company has to guard against the prospect of a licensee using the same technology independently after the license has expired and, therefore, turning into a competitor. Although there is great variation from one industry to the next, licensing fees in general are substantially lower than the profits that can be made by exporting or local manufacturing. Depending on the product, licensing fees may range anywhere between 1 percent and 20 percent of sales, with 3 to 5 percent being more typical for industrial products.

Conceptually, licensing should be pursued as an entry strategy if the amount of the licensing fees exceeds the incremental revenues of any other entry strategy, such as exporting or local manufacturing. A thorough investigation of the market potential is necessary to estimate potential revenues from any one of the entry strategies under consideration.

USING FRANCHISING TO ENTER MARKETS

Franchising is a special form of licensing in which the franchiser makes available a total marketing program, including the brand name, logo, products, and method of operation. Usually, the franchise agreement is more comprehensive than a regular licensing agreement because the total operation of the franchisee is prescribed.

Numerous companies that successfully exploited franchising as a distribution form in their home market are exploiting opportunities abroad through foreign entrepreneurs. Among these companies are McDonald's, Kentucky Fried Chicken, Burger King, and other U.S. fast-food chains, with operations in Latin America, Asia, and Europe. About 70 percent of all McDonald's restaurants worldwide are franchised. Service companies such as Holiday Inn, Hertz, and Manpower have also successfully used franchising to enter foreign markets.

BUILDING A LOCAL MANUFACTURING BASE

A common form of market entry is the local manufacturing of a company's products. Many companies find it advantageous to manufacture locally instead of supplying the particular market with products made elsewhere. Numerous factors such as local costs, market size, tariffs, laws, and political considerations may affect the choice to manufacture locally. The actual type of local production depends on the arrangement made; it may be contract manufacturing, assembly, or fully integrated production.

Because local production represents a greater commitment to a market than other entry strategies, it deserves considerable attention before a final decision is made.

Some international firms with plants in Korea, Malaysia, Thailand, and other foreign countries have little intention of penetrating these markets with the help of their new factories. Instead, they locate abroad to take advantage of favorable conditions that reduce manufacturing costs, and the products are slated for markets elsewhere. This cost savings strategy has been employed by many U.S. companies in the electronics industry, and it has been adopted more recently by Japanese and European firms as well. The motivation behind the location of plants in foreign countries may be related to cost savings rather than to entering new markets. Such decisions, of a sourcing or production nature, are not necessarily tied to a company's global marketing entry strategy and therefore are not of concern to us here.

CONTRACT MANUFACTURING.   Under contract manufacturing, a company arranges to have its products manufactured by an independent local company on a contract basis. The manufacturer's responsibility is restricted to production. Afterward, products are turned over to the international company, which usually assumes the marketing responsibilities for sales, promotion, and distribution. In a way, the international company "rents" the production capacity of the local firm to avoid establishing its own plant or to circumvent barriers set up to prevent the import of its products. Contract manufacturing differs from licensing with respect to the legal relationship of the firms involved. The local producer manufactures based on orders from the international firm, but the international firm gives almost no commitment beyond the placement of orders.

Nokia, the world leader in mobile phones, is using outsourcing of its manufacturing in some markets. South Korea's Telson Electronics Co. is producing Nokia handsets for the Korean market, with some being exported to other countries as well.[11] Acer, a Taiwan-based company and leader in PCs and electronics, split itself into two parts. Wistron, one of the two units, is specializing in contract manufacturing for other computer brands.[12]

Contract manufacturing is typically chosen for countries with a low-volume market potential combined with high tariff protection. In such situations, local production appears advantageous to avoid the high tariffs, but the local market does not support the volume necessary to justify the building of a single plant. These conditions tend to exist in the smaller countries in Central America, Africa, and Asia. Of course, whether an international company avails itself of this method of entry also depends on its products. Usually, contract manufacturing is employed where the production technology involved is widely available and where controlling the marketing effort is of greater importance than are manufacturing skills in the success of the product. Furthermore, a considerable amount of off-shore manufacturing takes place in low-cost economies for export to global markets. Those strategies by global companies are part of their overall global supply chain maximization and have little to do with entry into a single, specific market.

ASSEMBLY.   By moving to an assembly operation, the international firm locates a portion of the manufacturing process in the foreign country. Typically, assembly consists only of the last stages of manufacturing and depends on the ready supply of components or manufactured parts to be shipped from another country. Assembly usually involves heavy use of labor rather than extensive investment in capital outlays or equipment. Motor vehicle manufacturers have made extensive use of assembly operations in numerous countries. General Motors has maintained major integrated production units only in the United States, Germany, the United Kingdom, Brazil, and Australia. In many other countries, disassembled vehicles arrive at assembly operations that produce the final product on the spot.

The opening of the Vietnam market in 1991 led to a series of car assembly operations. The Vietnamese government controlled very tightly the number of parts to be imported and prohibited the construction of large-scale plants. To protect their interests in this low-volume but high-potential market, car makers have signed numerous agreements about assembly operations, most of them on a joint venture basis. Several of these agreements involve many of the world's leading auto manufacturers. As of 1999, fourteen different car ventures were operating in Vietnam, with a combined total output of 140,000 units. With annual demand estimated at only thirty-five thousand new units per year, it will take some time until the market is large enough to support full-scale manufacturing operations for most car companies.[13] BMW, which operates assembly units in Indonesia, Malaysia, Thailand, the Philippines, and Vietnam, estimates that it required an annual volume of about fifteen hundred to eight thousand units to justify the establishment of a local assembly unit.[14] UAZ, a Russian manufacturer of four-wheel drive vehicles, is planning to establish assembly plants in Jordan with a volume target of ten thousand vehicles, and in Vietnam with a volume target of four thousand vehicles. Of its annual output of 110,000 vehicles, the Russian company exports about twenty-five thousand units.[15] Local assembly plants based on kits will allow the company to expand into markets where tariff and other local hurdles cannot be overcome with an export strategy based on assembled vehicles.

Often, companies want to take advantage of lower wage costs by shifting the labor-intensive operation to the foreign market; this tactic results in a lower final price of the products. In many cases, however, the local government forces the setting up of assembly operations either by banning the import of fully assembled products or by charging excessive tariffs on imports, sometimes as much as 300 percent.[16] As a defensive move, foreign companies begin assembly operations to protect their markets. However, successful assembly operations require dependable access to imported parts. When this access is not guaranteed, supply interruptions can occur.

FULL-SCALE INTEGRATED PRODUCTION. Establishing a fully integrated local production unit represents the greatest commitment a company can make for a foreign market. Since building a plant involves a substantial outlay in capital, companies do so only when demand appears assured. International companies may have any number of reasons for establishing factories in foreign countries. Often, the primary reason is to take advantage of lower costs, thus providing a better basis for competing with local firms or other foreign companies already present. Also, high transportation costs and tariffs may make imported goods uncompetitive.

Establishing Local Operations to Gain New Business. Some companies want to build a plant to gain new business and customers. Such an aggressive strategy is based on the fact that local production represents a strong commitment and is often the only way to convince clients to switch suppliers. Local production is of particular importance in industrial markets, where service and reliability of supply are main factors in the choice of product or supplier.

When the Indian government began to liberalize its car market by allowing importation of parts and participation of foreign firms, many international car companies began to review their position in the Indian market. With duties on imported parts still at 50 percent, the economic benefit from setting up local plants was great. Many companies announced major investments. Hyundai of Korea committed to a major investment and in 1999 was producing at a rate of 6,500 units monthly, a level close to breakeven, and had captured about 10 percent market share. Some products were also exported.[17] Toyota entered the market with plans to launch a purposely built car for India in early 2000 and a target volume of twenty thousand units annually.[18] Finally, Honda, another foreign car company to set up in India, was planning to begin exporting locally assembled units to Sri Lanka and steering wheel subassemblies to Thailand.[19]

Establishing Foreign Production to Defend Existing Business. Many times, companies establish production abroad not to enter new markets but to protect what they have already gained through exporting. Changing economic or political factors may make such a move necessary. The Japanese car manufacturers, which had been subject in the United States to an import limitation of assembled cars from Japan, began to build factories there in the 1980s to protect their market share. In 1982, Honda became the first Japanese car manufacturer to set up production in the United States. In 1993, Japanese car manufacturers produced, for the first time, more cars in the United States than they exported to that country from Japan. Toyota, Honda, Nissan, Mitsubishi, Mazda, and Suzuki have also built production capacities in Europe and in Asia.

The Japanese manufacturers' reasons for the local production were partly political: the United States imposed import targets for several years. Also, with the value of the yen increasing in relationship to the U.S. dollar, exports from Japan became uneconomical compared to local production. To defend their market positions, Japanese car companies instituted a longer-term strategy of making cars in the region where they are sold. Despite their efforts at establishing local production plants, Japanese firms still maintain an active export business from their Japanese plants, ranging from one-third of output for Honda to almost one-half for Toyota.[20]

Moving with an Established Customer. Moving with an established customer can also be a reason for setting up plants abroad. In many industries, important suppliers want to keep a relationship by establishing plants near customer locations; when customers build new plants elsewhere, suppliers also move to those locations. The automobile industry, with its intricate network of hundreds of component suppliers feeding into the assembly plants, is a good example of how companies follow customers. As Japanese car manufacturers have built plants in the United States and in Canada, Japanese parts suppliers have become concerned that U.S. production will partially replace car shipments from Japan and that a reduction in parts volume will result. To counter this possibility, Japanese suppliers have built about four hundred component plants in the United States and in Canada in the early 1990s.[21] In similar fashion, Detroit's major automotive parts and component suppliers, such as tire companies and battery manufacturers, long ago opened manufacturing facilities abroad to supply General Motors' and Ford's various foreign facilities.

Shifting Production Abroad to Save Costs. When Mercedes-Benz was looking at new opportunities in the automotive market, the company targeted the luxury sports vehicle segment. In the United States, its major market, the company was suffering a 30 percent cost disadvantage against major Japanese and U.S. competitors. Mercedes-Benz decided to locate a new factory for such sports vehicles outside Germany, despite the fact that the company had never before produced cars abroad. Mercedes-Benz chose the United States because it expected total labor, components, and shipping costs to be among the lowest in the world. By 1999, the plant had already reached a volume of eighty thousand units annually and was employing about fifteen hundred workers.[22] Similarly, Honda built a full-scale plant in Thailand, and from this location it is shipping some cars back to Japan for local sale. Honda's Thai plant is more than an assembler of knocked-down kits, however. Sourcing the majority of its components from Southeast Asia, the Thai plant offers a low-cost site not only for the Thai market, but for other markets as well.[23] However, we are primarily concerned with creating markets globally, so for the purposes of this text, the cost savings issue is less of a concern.

OWNERSHIP STRATEGIES

Companies entering foreign markets have to decide on more than the most suitable entry strategy. They also need to arrange ownership, either as a wholly owned subsidiary (discussed above), as a joint venture, or—more recently—in the form of a strategic alliance.

FORMING JOINT VENTURES

Under a joint venture (JV) arrangement, the foreign company invites an outside partner to share stock ownership in the new unit. The particular participation of the partners may vary, with some companies accepting either a minority or majority position. In most cases, international firms prefer wholly owned subsidiaries for reasons of control; once a joint venture partner secures part of the operation, the international firm can no longer function independently, which sometimes leads to inefficiencies and disputes over responsibility for the venture. If an international firm has strictly defined operating procedures, such as for budgeting, planning, and marketing, getting the JV company to accept the same methods of operation may be difficult. Problems may also arise when the JV partner wants to maximize dividend payout instead of reinvestment, or when the capital of the JV has to be increased and one side is unable to raise the required funds. Experience has shown that JVs can be successful if the partners share the same goals, with one partner accepting primary responsibility for operations matters.

REASONS FOR ENTERING INTO JOINT VENTURES. Despite the potential for problems, joint ventures are common because they offer important advantages to the foreign firm. By bringing in a partner, the company can share the risk for a new venture. The JV partner may also have important skills or contacts of value to the international firm. Sometimes, the partner may be an important customer who is willing to contract for a portion of the new unit's output in return for equity participation. In other cases, the partner may represent important local business interests with excellent government contacts. A firm with advanced product technology may also gain market access through the JV route by teaming up with companies that are prepared to distribute its products.

Many international firms have entered Japan with JVs. During the 1960s and 1970s, the Japanese market was viewed as a difficult environment, much different from other industrialized markets, and government regulations tightly controlled equity participation in ventures. When McDonald's entered Japan in 1971, it did so in a joint venture with Fujita & Company, a trading company owned by a private Japanese businessman, Den Fujita. He insisted on some practices that differed from the typical U.S. approach of McDonald's, such as opening the first store in the fashionable Ginza shopping district rather than going to a suburban location, and owning most of the stores rather than franchising. The chain grew enormously, with about 3,800 restaurants operating in Japan by 2002 and 2001 sales of more than $2.76 billion.[24] McDonald's Japan went through an initial public offering (IPO) in 2001, raising about $400 million for a 20 percent stake for private investors. The company is still on a growth track and planning for a ten thousand store system and $8 billion in revenue within a decade.[25]

At one time, JVs were the only way an international firm could hope to establish a base in Japan. Many of the existing ventures, therefore, were formed in the 1960s and 1970s. Today, international firms do find it possible to have full ownership. Despite this change, however, new joint ventures continue to be signed when companies enter markets unknown to them. America Online entered Japan in 1996 via a JV with Mitsui & Co., a large trading company, and Nihon Keizai Shimbun, a large publisher, with America Online holding 50 percent of the equity. Growth has been substantial, with 200,000 subscribers in early 1999.[26]

Joint Ventures for Entering China.   Given the country's large economic potential, many foreign firms have been attracted to China. Within two years of the adoption of China's law on joint ventures in 1979, more than four hundred joint venture contracts had been signed between Chinese and foreign firms. By 1991, about ten thousand joint ventures involving foreign investors had been formed in China. At least one hundred of them had been closed in the first 10 years after formation, not including a number of ventures fallen into a dormant state.[27]

Swiss-based Schindler, a leading elevator manufacturer, was the first foreign firm to take advantage of China's new law on joint ventures, in 1979. The company took a 25 percent equity position, with the goals of becoming a major supplier of elevators in China and using the venture as a production base for its growing business in the Far East. Selling a total of thirty thousand elevators over the first eighteen years of operation, the JV has become one of China's leading elevator suppliers. Other leading firms, such as Otis, Thyssen, Mitsubishi, and Hitachi, all maintain JVs in China.[28] Schindler did get to use its Chinese JV as an export base, exporting about four hundred elevators to other countries and, as a result, maintaining its number 1 position in China.[29]

Few companies can match the experience of Thailand's Charoen Pokphand Group (CP) with JVs in China (see Chapter 8). Most observers consider the Thai company, with its 110 joint ventures, the largest foreign investor in China. With Heineken, CP started to produce beer in Shanghai in 1989. With another Chinese partner, Shanghai Motor Corp., CP set up one of the world's largest motorcycle plants, with a planned capacity of 2 million units, accounting for up to 20 percent of China's market. Other ventures are in the areas of banking, retailing, and agrobusiness. The company's top management credits its success to its ethnic Chinese contacts as well as its ability to make decisions quickly and not to bog down business discussions in voluminous details, something western firms typically do before they sign. Although the company went through some restructuring in China in 1999, selling some non-agro-industry businesses, CP remains the largest foreign investor, employing about sixty thousand workers, with assets exceeding $4 billion and revenues of $3.6 billion.[30]

When China first opened its market to international firms, JVs were the only alternative. Today, with ownership laws more liberalized, international firms can own either all or a majority of a venture. As those firms become more experienced at operating in China, the value and the need of relying on a JV partner might decrease over time. However, JVs remain the primary ownership model for China.

Joint Ventures in Eastern Europe. With the liberalization of industry and trade in eastern Europe over the past decade, many international firms have pursued joint ventures in those countries. Originally, western firms were not allowed to own any stock, capital, or real estate, and joint ventures were thus the norm. Restrictions on foreign investments were lifted in many countries, although the political and economic situations were still in flux, and foreign firms were allowed to start new companies with full ownership. Because of the difficulties of operating in unknown environments, however, many foreign firms nevertheless continue to form JVs with local partners.

The difficulties of running a JV in Russia are considerable because Russia does not yet have a fully developed market economy, as is typical for western Europe. Because of often unreliable supplies, lack of modern machinery, and lack of technological know-how, ventures that intend to exploit cheap Russian labor or raw material often fail. Ventures aimed largely at satisfying domestic demand, with exports a secondary goal, have much greater chances for success.[31] Since 1987, when the first JVs with western firms were allowed, more than ten thousand ventures have been registered. However, only about 20 percent of those actually began business operations. Because many Russian JVs fail during the first year of operation, the average survival rate of Russian JVs is only about 2.5 years.[32]

The structure of the McDonald's venture in Russia is a classic way of operating as an island within the country and as independently of local suppliers as is possible. With its partner, the city of Moscow, McDonald's built a $45 million processing plant to make its own beef patties, pasteurize its own milk, and bake its own buns. Raw materials for this plant are obtained from Russian sources, however, and the company has several specialists working with suppliers on quality. Transportation is arranged with its own trucks. The initial restaurant is the world's busiest McDonald's; in 1999 it served twenty thousand customers a day.[33] In 2001, McDonald's served about 84 million Russian customers. With a total investment of $230 million, the company operated seventy-three restaurants in twenty-three Russian cities and employed nine thousand people.[34]

A very successful JV operates in St. Petersburg between Gillette of the United States and Leninets, a Russian consumer products company. Gillette built a $60 million plant and received a 65 percent stake in the operation. Designed for an output of 860 million blades a year, the operation employs five hundred people and has annual revenues of $200 million. With the older, double-edged blades still accounting for 80 percent of volume, there was still substantial growth for Gillette's twin-blade systems. A new expansion was announced in 1998 that would employ another 350 workers.[35]

Gillette began to develop the Russian market with small-scale imports in 1989 and grew its Russian business so that Russia became one of the company's top ten markets. Russia, with its 2 billion blade volume, was the third largest blade market in the world and thus of critical importance to Gillette. By 1999, it was Gillette's fastest growing market, with growth rates of 40 percent. The reason for entering a JV in 1993 with the local partner was based on the experience that Gillette had gained in other parts of the world, such as China. Gillette was first helping the local partner to market it own local brand, Sputnik. Through market observance and experience, the company began to launch its own brands and eventually built a modern production facility in 2000. That production facility allows Gillette to circumvent high tariffs, and the JV partners helped Gillette to avoid local red tape and to deal with authorities.[36]

Not all companies have been so successful. U.S. firms make up the largest share of foreign investment in Russia, with more than five hundred U.S. firms operating directly in the country. Following economic difficulties in 1997, about fifty firms left or closed operations. Among those were Dunkin' Donuts, Pizza Hut, and Ben and Jerry's Ice Cream.[37] Researchers have determined that success was enhanced if the local partner firm and the international company possessed a similar organizational culture and climate. In addition, it was important that the organizational climate of the local JV was more similar to the foreign partner's own climate, rather than the local partner.[38]

JOINT VENTURE DIVORCE: A CONSTANT DANGER. Not all joint ventures are successful and fulfill their partners' expectations. One study found that between 1972 and 1976, about ninety major ventures failed in Japan alone. Many of these ventures involved large U.S.-based firms such as General Mills, TRW, and Avis. Another study revealed the failure of 30 percent of investigated joint ventures formed before 1967 between U.S. companies and partners in other industrialized countries. In most cases, the ventures were either liquidated or taken over by one of the original partners.[39]

Not all joint ventures in Japan end as failures. One of the most successful is the collaboration between Caterpillar of the United States and Mitsubishi Heavy Industries. For years, Caterpillar had a JV with Mitsubishi for the production of bulldozers and other heavy construction equipment. However, the market in Japan, where building operations must take place under very tight space limitations, became increasingly attractive for excavators. These machines were never at the center for Caterpillar; so when the market took off in Japan, the company decided to form a second JV, Shin Caterpillar-Mitsubishi. But the new JV was not only for Japan. It was also made responsible for hydraulic excavator design worldwide for both Caterpillar and Mitsubishi and included the Mitsubishi manufacturing in Japan. Outside Japan, Caterpillar was to remain independent for manufacturing and distribution, while all excavator products were to carry the name Caterpillar. Excavator sales of the combined company grew 75 percent worldwide in four years; in Japan, Mitsubishi recovered its declining market share. Based on this success, Caterpillar assigned additional responsibility to the JV and now sources key components from Japan for its operations elsewhere.[40]

Despite the difficulties involved, it is apparent that the future will bring many more joint ventures. Successful international and global firms will have to develop the skills and experience to manage JVs successfully, often in different and difficult environmental circumstances. And in many markets, the only viable access is through JVs.

FORGING STRATEGIC ALLIANCES AND COLLABORATIVE STRATEGIES

A more recent phenomenon is the development of a range of strategic alliances. Alliances are different from traditional joint ventures, in which two partners contribute a fixed amount of resources and the venture develops on its own. In an alliance, two entire firms pool their resources directly in a collaboration that goes beyond the limits of a joint venture. Although a new entity may be formed, it is not a requirement. Sometimes, the alliance is supported by some equity acquisition of one or both of the partners. In an alliance, each partner brings a particular skill or resource—usually, they are complementary—and by joining forces, each expects to profit from the other's experience. Typically, alliances involve distribution access, technology transfers, or production technology, with each partner contributing a different element to the alliance.

TECHNOLOGY-BASED ALLIANCES. Most technology-based alliances are in the biotechnology and information technology industries. The most commonly cited reasons for entering such an alliance were access to markets, exploitation of complementary technology, and a need to reduce the time taken for an innovation.

One of the companies most experienced with technological alliances is Toshiba, a major Japanese electronics company. The company's first technological alliances go back to the beginning of this century, when it contracted to make light bulb filaments for U.S.-based General Electric. The company has since engaged in alliances with many leading international companies, among them General Electric, IBM, United Technologies/Carrier, Apple Computer, Sun Microsystems, Motorola, and National Semiconductor, all of the United States, and European firms such as Infineon, Electrolux, Kone, and SGS. Toshiba entered a wide-ranging alliance with the U.S.-based Carrier Company, a leader in air conditioning equipment. Both Toshiba and Carrier placed their respective Japanese units into the alliance and formed a new company, 60 percent of which is owned by Toshiba. The Japanese company's $1.1 billion air conditioning equipment unit was merged with Carrier's Japanese unit. As part of this wide-ranging alliance, the two firms also formed manufacturing JVs in the United Kingdom and Thailand. Toshiba sales organizations in several Asian and European countries were also merged with Carrier units. Carrier, traditionally strong in the larger systems, obtained access to Toshiba's leading technology in lighter and commercial air conditioning equipment.[41]

PRODUCTION-BASED ALLIANCES. Particularly in the automobile industry, numerous alliances have been formed over the past years. These alliances fall into two groups. First, there is the search for efficiency through component linkages, which may include engines or other key components of a car. Second, companies have begun to share entire car models, either by producing jointly or by developing them together. U.S. automobile manufacturers have been very active in creating global alliances with partners, primarily in Japan. Many of these alliances are production based.

To compete more effectively in the super-small car segment in Europe, Peugeot of France and Toyota of Japan are collaborating on the building of a new production plant located in Kolin, Czech Republic. Investing about $1.5 billion in this facility, the companies will create three thousand new jobs. Owned jointly at 50 percent each, the plant will be designed to build 1,000 to 1,400 cc sized subcompact cars and to have an annual capacity of 300,000 units. The two partners will share the same body design but will use exterior modifications to differentiate their models. The firms plan to go into production by 2005, and both will market the models separately, and thus are likely to compete against each other through their own sales and distribution networks. By joining forces, both manufacturers will gain economies in a very price sensitive market segment.[42] (For several examples of other U.S. firms engaged in production alliances, see Figure 9.2.)

DISTRIBUTION-BASED ALLIANCES. Alliances with a special emphasis on distribution are becoming increasingly common. General Mills, a U.S.-based breakfast cereals producer, had long been number 2 to Kellogg's in the important U.S. market. With no effective position outside the United States, the company entered into a global alliance with Nestlé of Switzerland, forming Cereal Partners Worldwide (CPW), which is owned equally by both companies. General Mills used the local distribution and marketing skills of Nestlé in Europe, the Far East, and Latin America. In return, General Mills provided the food technology and experience of competing against Kellogg's. CPW was formed as a full business unit with responsibility for the entire world except the United States. General Mills initially invested $103 million but has since invested more than $300 million annually to expand the business.[43] CPW reached $880 million in sales in 2001. Market share for cold cereals outside the United States reached 21 percent for CPW, and operations covered eighty countries. General Mills was also active in eight other alliances, including Snack Ventures Europe with PepsiCo, with 2001 sales of about US $990 million. Overall, General Mills' international alliances generated sales of $1.870 billion (consolidated at $945 million) out of the corporate total of $6.7 billion. The company's own international sales through wholly owned subsidiaries amounted to $333 million in 2001. At present growth rates, sales are expected to reach $4 billion by 2010.[44]

Nestlé formed a different alliance with Coca-Cola. Forming Beverage Partners Worldwide (BPW) in 2001 (formerly Coca-Cola Nestlé Refreshments, or CCNR), the two partner companies created their alliance initially in 1991 to market Nestlé's new ready-to-drink coffees and teas (Nestea and Nescafé ready-to-drink) through the

Figure 9.2: International Alliances of U.S. and Japanese Automobile Manufacturers (as of March 1993)

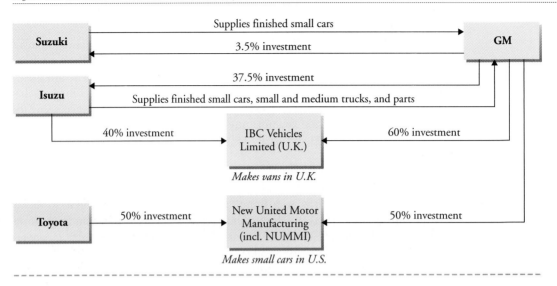

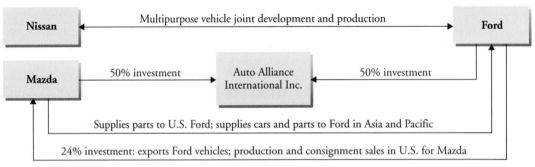

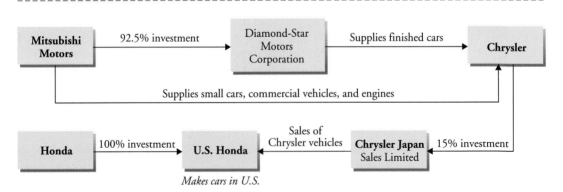

Source: "Japan Braces Itself for the U.S. Roadshow," Financial Times, August 19, 1993. Reprinted by permission.

Coca-Cola distribution system worldwide. Nestlé had developed the products and already held a leading position in instant coffee. But ready-to-drink products were sold mainly through vending machines. This latter distribution channel was well known to Coca-Cola, whose Georgia brand canned coffee is a leading product in Japan. BPW was set up as new company, with its own management based in Zurich and a head office staff of sixty. In addition to the Nestlé brands, BPW will also market Coca-Cola's Tian Yu Di and Yang Guang tea businesses, and Nestlé added its Belte tea already marketed in Italy. BPW had a volume of 250 million cases, operated in about twenty-four countries, and operated worldwide (with the exception of Japan, where both partner firms had their own operations in this sector).[45]

THE FUTURE OF ALLIANCES. Although many older alliances were spawned by technology exchange and were formed among manufacturing companies, some of the most innovative arrangements are signed by service firms. Many of these have proved to be short-lived, however, in a never-ending rearrangement among the world's leading players. In telecommunications, the global logic of both the operating business and client needs has driven companies to create a series of new organizations. Large telecommunications carriers compete in groups of constantly shifting alliances. Global One, a collective effort of France Telecom, Deutsche Telekom, and Sprint (of the United States), did not survive the self-interests and mergers of the industry. Concert, a grouping formed before AT&T and BT from the United Kingdom, was not a lasting effort.[46] Likewise, alliances among international airline companies have been subject to constant changes and shifts.

Although many global alliances have been forged in a large number of industries, the evidence is not yet in about whether these alliances will become successful business ventures. Experience suggests that alliances with two equal partners are more difficult to manage than those with a dominant partner. Many observers question the value of entering alliances with technological competitors, such as between western and Japanese firms. The challenge in making an alliance work lies in the creation of multiple layers of connections, or webs, that reach across the partner organizations. Eventually such connections will result in the creation of new organizations out of the cooperating segments of the partners. In that sense, alliances may very well be just an intermediate stage until a new company can be formed or until the dominant partner assumes control.

ENTERING MARKETS THROUGH MERGERS AND ACQUISITIONS

International firms have always made acquisitions, but the need to enter markets more quickly than through building a base from scratch or entering some type of collaboration has made the acquisition route extremely attractive. This trend has probably been aided by the opening of many financial markets, making the acquisition of publicly traded companies much easier. Most recently, even unfriendly takeovers in foreign markets are now possible.

Reckitt & Coleman of the United Kingdom had always had a business in household cleaners in the United States. Competing with Procter & Gamble, however, the company was always a distant player. The company therefore jumped at the chance to acquire L&F Household, which included the U.S. brand Lysol and accounted for $360 million in sales. Bringing in several other brands and adding about $775 million in new volume, Reckitt & Coleman considered the acquisition both faster and cheaper than building the same business on its own.[47] In 1999, Reckitt & Coleman merged with Benckiser, a Dutch firm, forming Reckitt Benckiser and creating the world's largest household cleaning products company, surpassing its old rivals Procter & Gamble and Unilever with dominant positions in fabric care, surface care, personal care, and home care. Using the merger route allowed Reckitt Benckiser to achieve its leading global position much more quickly than would have been possible if it had tried to achieve this position on its own through internal growth.[48]

Mergers are also transacted among leading international firms. Even more complex are mergers of two firms with a wide range of geographic interests. Coca-Cola acquired the worldwide beverage interests of Cadbury Schweppes and all related brands in about 155 countries. Because of specific regulatory difficulties, however, not all country operations could be acquired by Coca-Cola. Those in the United States, Norway, Switzerland, and some European Union member states were excluded.[49] DaimlerChrysler, itself the product of a merger between Daimler Benz of Germany and Chrysler of the United States, acquired a 34 percent stake in Mitsubishi Motors Corp. of Japan. DaimlerChrysler also acquired a 10 percent stake in Hyundai Motors of Korea, giving the German-U.S. firm a presence in Asia and access to the production of small, fuel-efficient cars at low cost. In addition, the Hyundai deal also gave DaimlerChrysler a chance to form a new venture with Hyundai on trucks for the Asian market. Pursuing the acquisition route, even in the form of minority stakes, was viewed as a faster way to build a market presence in Asia than building from scratch on its own.[50]

In general, global mergers with overlapping interests frequently force the acquiring company to divest other units to satisfy regulators, thereby reducing the overall value of the merger. When Nestlé of Switzerland acquired Ralston Purina Co. of the United States, Nestlé hoped to combine its global $3.7 billion pet food business with Ralston's $2.25 billion in sales, of which $450 million were international. Nestlé, which was strong in the canned pet food market, was interested in Ralston's position in the fast growing dry pet food segment and in expanding it around the world through its own sales network. Because this merger would have resulted in a combined market share of 45 percent in the dry cat food segment, the U.S. Federal Trade Commission (FTC) required Nestlé to dispose of two of Ralston's cat food brands.[51] It has become quite common for firms to negotiate, either with the U.S. FTC or its European equivalent, for permission to merge. Sometimes the requirements for approval are considered too restrictive, as was the case with the planned merger between Honeywell and General Electric. The requirements imposed by the European Commission were deemed too restrictive by General Electric, which declined the merger.[52]

Nevertheless, international mergers and acquisitions remain a commonly used avenue for building market presence globally. During the period 1989 to 1991, cross-border mergers and strategic investments grew fivefold, to $798 billion annually. The United Kingdom was the most acquisitive country globally, followed by the United States, Germany, and France. About fifty thousand cross-border transactions were covered in the survey.[53] Given the recent developments at various stock exchanges, merger activity is expected to decline in the near future, and this avenue of building global market presence may become less important compared to other options.

PORTAL OR EBUSINESS ENTRY STRATEGIES

The technological revolution of the Internet, with its wide range of connected and networked computers, has given rise to the virtual market entry strategy. Using electronic means, primarily web pages, email, file transfers, and related communications tools, firms have begun to enter markets without touching down. A company that establishes a server on the Internet and establishes a web page can be contacted from anywhere in the world. Consumers and industrial buyers who use modern Internet browsers, such as Netscape, can search for products, services, and companies and in many instances can even make purchases online.

Whatever the forecasts, most experts agree that the opportunity for Internet-based commerce will be huge. Although the cost of creating a web presence is small, global marketing alone is beyond a mere web page. Once a business has a web address, interested buyers from anywhere in the world can contact the address. Consequently, the Internet will eliminate some of the hurdles that plagued smaller firms from competing beyond their borders. Although it is difficult to guess the actual trading done by international customers at all Internet sites, the trend is clear if one follows some major Internet companies.

Amazon.com, the leading Internet retailer, established a presence overseas early. Following its web presence in the United States, it opened a second one in the United Kingdom (Amazon.co.uk) by acquiring Bookpages, an existing U.K. Internet book retailer. In Germany (Amazon.de), the company purchased Telebuch. The German site is entirely in German, and the merchandise inventory is specific to the different markets. Amazon.com also offers a French site (Amazon.fr), a Japanese site (Amazon.co.jp), and one for Canada (Amazon.ca) and for Austria (Amazon.at). All international web sites are patterned after the U.S. site, thus providing the same look and feel. Although established first in the United States, Amazon is typically encountering established foreign competitors in overseas markets. Each of its operations has its own fulfillment operation that packages and ships from local stocks. A customer can always order from the United States but will have to pay the extra charges for shipment and delivery. However, there are many customers who can now order from Amazon.com who would not otherwise have access to the company's wide range of books, CDs, and other products. Via the Internet, Amazon.com can compete globally without a presence in every market.

The power of the Internet not only helps competitors from large markets. It also shapes the access to many overseas markets for smaller companies from emerging markets. Streetmarket.Com Sdn Bhd is an electronic retailing company based in Malaysia and specializes in Malaysian-made consumer products, marketing them to the world. The company plans to set up online retailing outlets in several countries, such as the United Kingdom and Australia. The outlets will be equipped with terminals and sample merchandise, and customers can order goods and receive them within seven days.[54]

A new group of major Internet players with global ambitions are service providers, such as Schwab and Merrill Lynch. Although the first wave of Merrill's online trading was targeted for U.S. brokerage clients, the future points toward using this service abroad.[55] However, financial services firms battle with legal restrictions and the need to obtain regulatory approval for offering certain services to a given country. On the other hand, it is almost impossible for governments to police the access. Most likely, financial services firms will have to provide special access, or qualifying service, to local customers before they can enter the market. Given the low cost of the Internet, it is very likely that many more established firms will use it as the first point of contact for countries where they do not yet have a major base.

There are many challenges to would-be Internet-based global marketers. One of the biggest is language. One research company estimated that by 2002, 60 percent of the world's Internet users and 40 percent of the ecommerce revenue will be from outside the United States, mostly from non-English-speaking areas. Although many people can surf the Internet in English, they still prefer to complete transactions in their local language. The second big challenge is the fulfillment side of the ebusiness. Here we are dealing with completing a sale, shipping, collecting funds, and providing after-sales service to customers all over the world.[56]

The real issue in portal entry strategies deals with the ease of setting up and covering a market. If the costs of establishing a virtual presence remain so much lower than the traditional entry strategy modes, it will invariably change the options for global marketers. Firms with a smaller resource base should now have a chance to reach out to global markets. Also, location plays a lesser role because an entrepreneur anywhere can suddenly reach into any market, nearby or distant. The technical development of the Internet will therefore bring the practice of global marketing to many more consumers and marketers around the world.

PREPARING AN ENTRY STRATEGY ANALYSIS

Of course, assembling accurate data is the cornerstone of any entry strategy analysis. The necessary sales projections have to be supplemented with detailed cost data and financial need projections on assets. The data need to be assembled for all entry strategies under consideration (see Figure 9.3). Financial data are collected not only on the proposed venture but also on its anticipated impact on the existing operations of the international firm. The combination of the two sets of financial data results in incremental financial data incorporating the net overall benefit of the proposed move for the total company structure.

For best results, the analyst must take a long-term view of the situation. Asset requirements, costs, and sales have to be evaluated over the planning horizon of the proposed venture, typically three to five years for an average company. A thorough sensitivity analysis must also be incorporated. Such an analysis may consist of assuming several scenarios for international risk factors that may adversely affect the success of the proposed venture. The financial data can be adjusted to reflect each new set of circumstances. One scenario may include a 20 percent devaluation in the host country, combined with currency control and the difficulty of receiving new supplies from foreign plants. Another situation may assume a change in political leadership, to a group less friendly to foreign investments. With the help of a sensitivity analysis approach, a company can quickly spot the key variables in the environment that will determine the outcome of the proposed market entry. The international company then has the opportunity to add to its information on such key variables or at least to monitor their development closely.

In this section, we provide a general methodology for the analysis of entry decisions. It is assumed that any company approaching a new market is looking for profitability and growth. Consequently, the entry strategy must support these goals. Each

Figure 9.3: Considerations for Market Entry Decisions

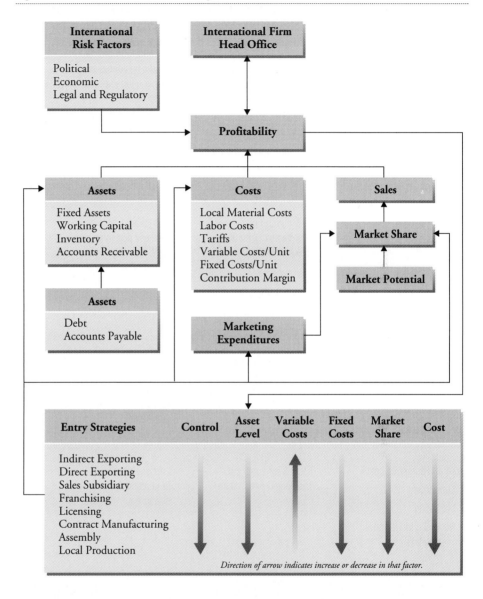

project has to be analyzed for the expected sales level, costs, and asset levels that will eventually determine profitability (see Table 9.1).

ESTIMATING SALES

An accurate estimate of the market share or sales volume is crucial to the entry strategy decision. Sales results will depend mostly on the company's market share and the total size or potential of the market. The market share to be gained is primarily

Table 9.1 Financial Analysis for Entry Strategies			
Financial Variables	**Local Values**	**Decreases Elsewhere (Due to New Operation)**	**Incremental Value**
ASSETS	New amount of assets needed to sustain chosen entry strategy in local market	Assets liquidated or no longer needed due to shift of operation	Net new assets required
Cash			
Accounts receivable			
Inventory			
Equipment			
Buildings			
Land			
TOTAL			
LIABILITIES	New amount of liabilities incurred due to entry strategy	Reduction or change in liabilities due to shift in operation	Net liabilities incurred
Accounts payable			
Debt			
TOTAL			
NET ASSETS			
			Net asset requirement
COSTS			
Unit variable costs (VC)	Amount of VC in newly selected operations	Diseconomies of scale due to volume loss by shifting production to new subsidiary	Net variable costs across all subsidiaries resulting from new entry mode
Material costs			
Labor costs			
Purchases			
TOTAL			
Fixed and semifixed costs	Local fixed costs due to selected entry mode	Lost contribution if production shifted elsewhere	Net fixed burden of new entry mode Incremental total costs
Supervision			
Marketing			
General administrative expenses			
TOTAL			
TOTAL UNIT COSTS			
SALES	Local sales of chosen entry mode	Lost sales in other units of the MNC subsidiary network	Net additional sales of entry strategy
TOTAL SALES			

determined on a competitive basis. The foreign company can influence the market share through a strong marketing mix, which in turn depends on the level of financial commitment for marketing expenditures. The various types of entry strategies also allow a foreign firm to aim for varying degrees of market share. Typically, direct or indirect exporting results in a lower market share than do local sales subsidiaries or local production because of a weaker market presence. This weaker presence causes a loss of control over local intermediaries; also, the exporter must depend to some extent on independent firms for carrying out its marketing functions.

Of course, market potential is not subject to the influence of the international firm seeking entry. The size of a local market combined with the expected market share often determines the outcome of an entry strategy analysis. Local assembly or production, with correspondingly high levels of assets and fixed costs, needs large volumes to offset these costs, whereas exporting operations can usually be rendered profitable at much lower sales volumes than can other entry strategies.

Particularly in markets with considerable growth potential, it becomes essential to forecast sales over a longer period of time. A low expected volume right now may indicate little success for a new subsidiary, but data on volume expected in, say, three to five years may suggest a change in the future entry strategy. It is often impossible to shift quickly into another entry mode once a firm is established, so special attention must focus on the need to ensure that the chosen entry strategy offers a long-term opportunity to maximize profits.

ESTIMATING COSTS

The international firm will have to determine the expected costs of its operation in a foreign country with respect to both manufacturing and general administrative costs. Unit variable costs may vary depending on the chosen strategy: local production, assembly, or exporting. To establish such costs, analysts must take local material costs, local wage levels, and tariffs on imports into consideration. Again, unit variable costs should be expected to vary according to the entry strategy alternatives considered.

Necessary fixed costs represent another important element in the analysis. Administrative costs tend to be much smaller for a sales subsidiary than for a local manufacturing unit. Through use of a contribution margin analysis, breakeven for several levels of entry strategies can be considered. Government regulations and laws may also affect local costs and substantially change costs over time.

Cost levels may differ substantially from country to country. The task of estimating and forecasting costs in the international environment requires the added awareness that environmental factors of a political, economic, or legal nature can render a careful analysis invalid. Such possibilities always need to be considered from the outset.

ESTIMATING ASSET LEVELS

The level of assets deployed greatly affects the profitability of any entry strategy. The assets may consist of any investments made in conjunction with the entrance into (or exit from, for that matter) the new market. Such investments may include working capital in the form of cash, accounts receivable, and/or inventory, or fixed assets such as land, buildings, machinery, and equipment. The amount of assets required depends to a great extent on the particular entry strategy chosen. Exporting and sales subsidiaries require an investment in working capital only, with little additional funds for fixed facilities. Local assembly and production, however, demand substantial investments. Often, local financing can reduce the net investment amount of the international firm. For an adequate comparison of the various entry strategies, an asset budget should be computed for each alternative considered.

FORECASTING PROFITABILITY

Conceptually, a company should maximize the future stream of earnings, discounted at its cost of capital. Other companies may prefer to concentrate on return on investment (ROI) as a more appropriate measurement of profitability. In either case, profitability depends on the level of assets, costs, and sales. Several exogenous international risk factors influence profitability and therefore must be included in the analysis. The outcome of such an analysis determines the selection of the entry strategy. In the following sections, each of these factors will be described, and their possible impact on profitability will be indicated.

ASSESSING INTERNATIONAL RISK FACTORS. Aside from the normal business risk factors that every company confronts in its home market, the existence of more than one economy or country involves additional risks. Each country hosting a foreign subsidiary may take political, economic, and/or regulatory actions that can completely obliterate any carefully drawn-up business plan. As discussed in Chapter 4, political turmoil in many parts of the world greatly affects business and investment conditions. For example, following the departure of the shah of Iran in 1979, the country's political stability deteriorated to such an extent that business could not be conducted as usual. Many foreign operations were taken over by the government or ceased to exist. Similar effects on businesses were seen in other countries, particularly Nicaragua (in 1979) and Turkey (1978 to 1980).

As we explained in Chapter 2, different economic systems add to uncertainties, which are reflected in currency changes or diverging economic trends. Manufacturing costs are particularly sensitive to various changes. Many times, a company has shifted production from one country to another on the basis of the latest cost data only to find out a few years later that costs have changed because of fluctuations in macroeconomic variables beyond company control. Local labor costs, for example, are very sensitive to local inflation and foreign currency changes; they have fluctuated considerably over the years.

MAINTAINING FLEXIBILITY. The ability to switch from one mode of entry to another may be an important requirement of the initial arrangement. As we can see from the earlier analysis, different sales volume levels dictate different entry strategies for maximum efficiency. A company might therefore prefer to start with a small investment through exporting, move toward employing a local distributor, gravitate to a sales subsidiary, and possibly add local production in a later phase. However, this step-by-step approach neglects the difficulty of switching from one entry mode to another for legal reasons, essentially locking a company into the original entry mode. To avoid such an occurrence, a global company may want to consider legal flexibility, or forego earlier phases to maintain the potential for full deployment at a later time.

ASSESSING TOTAL COMPANY IMPACT. Once profitability on a local level has been established and the relevant international risk factors included, analysis must turn to the company as a whole. The expected profits of the new market entry have to be analyzed along with the overall impact on the total organization. Replacing imports with local production may cause a loss of sales or output at the existing facility, which may counterbalance the new profits gained from the plant opening. Such an impact may also exist with respect to assets, costs, and sales, depending on the entry strategy. As a result, the global firm plans to maximize incremental profits achieved on incremental assets and sales. A promising opportunity abroad may suddenly appear less attractive when allowances are made for displacement in other parts of a global company.

ENTRY STRATEGY CONFIGURATION

This chapter has been dedicated to explaining the various entry strategies available to international and global firms. In reality, however, most entry strategies consist of a combination of different formats. We refer to the process of deciding on the best possible entry strategy mix as *entry strategy configuration*.

Rarely do companies employ a single entry mode per country. A company may open a subsidiary that produces some products locally and imports others to round out its product line. The same foreign subsidiary may even export to other foreign subsidiaries, combining exporting, importing, and local manufacturing into one unit. Furthermore, many international firms grant licenses for patents and trademarks to foreign operations, even when they are fully owned. This strategy is followed for additional protection or to make the transfer of profits easier. In many cases, companies have bundled such entry forms into a single legal unit, in effect *layering* several entry strategy options one on top of the other.

Bundling of entry strategies is the process of providing just one legal unit in a given country or market. In other words, the foreign company sets up a single company in one country and uses that company as a legal umbrella for all its entry activities. However, such strategies have become less typical—particularly in larger markets, many firms have begun to unbundle their operations. When a company *unbundles*, it essentially divides its operations in a country into different companies. The local manufacturing plant may be incorporated separately from the sales subsidiary. With this option, companies may select different ownership strategies, for instance, allowing a JV in one operation while keeping full ownership in another part. Such unbundling becomes possible in the larger markets, such as the United States, Germany, Japan, and China. It also allows the company to run several companies or product lines in parallel. Siemens, the large German electrical equipment company, operates dozens of subsidiaries in the United States that report to different product line companies in Germany and are independently operated. Global firms granting such global mandates to product divisions will find that each division needs to develop its own entry strategy for key markets.

EXIT STRATEGIES

Circumstances may make companies want to leave a country or market. Other than the failure to achieve marketing objectives, there may be political, economic, or legal reasons for a company to want to dissolve or sell an operation. International companies have to be aware of the high costs attached to the liquidation of foreign operations;

substantial amounts of severance pay may have to be paid to employees, and any loss of credibility in other markets can hurt future prospects. Sometimes, an international firm may need to withdraw from a market to consolidate its operations, such as a consolidation of factories from many to fewer such plants. Production consolidation, when not combined with an actual market withdrawal, is not really what we are concerned with here. Rather, our concern is a company's actual abandonment of its plan to serve a certain market or country.

In the past, some U.S.-based firms had to retrench from their international operations and shrink back to a U.S. base. This retrenchment is usually done when the company needs to conserve resources. Gateway, the U.S. PC company, faced such a situation when it had to reduce costs. The company decided to withdraw from most international markets and concentrate on the domestic market (in the United States) instead. Such retrenching may not occur as a result of unprofitable international businesses but instead is often driven by other factors.[57]

Yahoo, a leading U.S.-based portal, decided to withdraw from the European auction business and sell most of its interest to eBay, its major competitor. Although Yahoo had superior traffic to its European sites, most visitors came for information and searches, not for auctions. It withdrew from the United Kingdom, Ireland, France, Germany, Italy, and Spain, but the company decided to hold on to its suites in Denmark, Sweden, and Norway, where it enjoyed a stronger position.[58]

Changing political and economic situations may at times force companies to leave markets. With the economies of several Latin American countries subject to considerable fluctuations, it should not be surprising for us to see companies departing that region when profitable operations no longer appear to be assured. Fiat, the Italian car manufacturer, announced its withdrawal from the Argentine market. CellStar, a U.S.-based distributor of wireless products, decided to exit Peru and Argentina for economic reasons. The company remained in Mexico, where its business was on a more stable foundation.[59]

Exit strategies can also be the result of negative reactions in a firm's home market. When the political situation in South Africa was open to challenge on moral grounds, many global companies exited that country by abandoning or selling their local subsidiaries. In 1984, about 325 U.S. companies maintained operations in South Africa. Two years later, this number had decreased to 265. Among the U.S. firms that left was Coca-Cola; others included General Motors, IBM, Motorola, and General Electric. Some European firms also withdrew from South Africa.[60]

REENTRY STRATEGIES

Several of the markets left by international firms over the past decades have changed in attractiveness, making companies reverse their exit decisions and enter those markets a second time. In India, for example, the government relaxed its restrictive ownership legislation in view of its overall policy of economic liberalization. When the restrictive Foreign Exchange Regulation Act was introduced in India in 1973, about two hundred of five hundred companies with large investments exited, selling their stakes to local companies. Following liberalization in August 1991, approximately one hundred firms raised their equity stakes to the allowable 51 percent. Typical of this strategy is Gillette, which had entered India with a minority stake in the mid-1980s.[61] Coca-Cola, after having left the market completely in 1977, reentered in 1993 to counter the earlier first-time entry of rival PepsiCo. Coca-Cola accomplished its return to the Indian market by acquiring Parle, India's leading local cola company.[62]

The changing situation in South Africa is largely a function of the political evolution in that country. International sanctions, as well as sanctions imposed by the U.S. government and about 150 cities, states, and counties, resulted in 214 U.S. firms exiting between 1984 and 1991.[63] Since July 1991, when the ban on investing in South Africa was lifted, some of those firms have returned. Today, U.S. companies have again taken a substantial lead with investment in South Africa, accounting for almost 86,000 directly related jobs.[64]

Although the examples cited concerning India and South Africa are of major strategic impact, companies exit and reenter markets regularly. Renault of France decided to reenter Peru, a market it had left many years earlier, after it concluded its alliance with Nissan of Japan. Nissan maintains a sales channel in Peru and is therefore able to use its partner's distribution channel.[65] Acer, the Taiwan-based PC manufacturer, returned to the Chinese market, after a five-year absence, with a new line of PCs.[66] Matsushita pulled out of the U.S. cell phone business in 1998 but returned to the United States two years later with an adapted product line.[67] NEC of Japan returned to the U.S. cell phone market, after an absence of only one year, with a new cell phone generation.[68] And finally, Toshiba of Japan left the Chinese market for refrigerators and washing machines in 1994, when the Chinese government imposed high tariffs to curb imports; however, it returned six years later when it became clear that China would enter the WTO and would have to give foreign firms greater market access under the new trading rules.[69]

With the fortunes of markets shifting ever-more rapidly, global companies will frequently have to reconsider positions in major markets. However, companies need to review disruptions to their customers if they leave a market and consider the costs of reestablishing a presence years later.

CONCLUSIONS

The world contains more than two hundred individual countries or markets. Thus, entry decisions are the strategy decisions that international companies must make most frequently. Since the type of entry strategy can clearly affect later market success, these decisions need to be based on careful analysis. Companies often find it difficult to break out of initial arrangements, another reason why special attention must be given to this type of decision. In some of the more difficult markets, such as Japan, making the correct entry decision can become a key competitive advantage for a firm and can unlock markets otherwise inaccessible to a foreign company.

To survive in the coming global battles for market dominance, companies have to become increasingly bolder and more creative in their entry strategy choices. Long gone are the days when entry was restricted to exporting, licensing, foreign manufacturing, and joint ventures. New concepts such as global alliances have become common, and international firms will have to include acquisitions, venture capital financing, and complex government partnerships as integral elements in entry strategy configurations. The myriad of new entry alternatives has raised the level of complexity in international marketing, and decisions about these entry alternatives will remain an important challenge for managers.

This added complexity will make detailed analysis and comparisons of entry strategy alternatives more difficult. For adequate analysis, companies must consider not only present cost structures but also the ever-changing economic and political environment. Rapidly fluctuating foreign exchange rates have changed the cost of various entry alternatives and have forced companies to shift their approach. Economic changes are likely to continue, and companies will be forced to reevaluate their entry strategy decisions on an ongoing basis. Entry strategies will rarely be permanent but will have to be adapted to the most recent situation.

Most companies have preferences about which entry strategy they would pursue, given no objections or obstacles, but firms will more and more often have to adopt a flexible approach. Establishing a sales subsidiary may be the best alternative for entering some countries, whereas joint ventures may be necessary to enter other countries. Managers will be forced to learn to manage with various entry strategies, and they will be less able to repeat the same entry patterns all over the world. A high degree of managerial flexibility will thus be required of international companies and their executives. We can also expect that the future will bring other types of entry strategies that will challenge international managers anew.

Questions for Discussion

1. Contrast the entry strategies practiced by Boeing and IBM. What differences do you find, and what explains these differences?

2. Would entry strategies differ for companies considering Germany, Japan, and China? If so, how would these strategies differ and why?

3. How will the entry strategy of a new start-up firm differ from that of a mature multinational company?

4. What difficulties and special problems can be expected for a firm practicing only franchising as an entry strategy?

5. Complete a literature search on alliances and try to determine the reasons why particular alliances were formed.

6. It has been speculated that alliances between Japanese and western firms work primarily to the benefit of Japanese companies. Explain.

7. Explain the concept of entry strategy configuration and the strategies of layering, bundling, or unbundling entry strategies.

For Further Reading

Bleeke, Joel, and David Ernst. "The Way to Win in Cross-Border Alliances." *Harvard Business Review*, November–December 1991, pp. 127–135.

Erramilli, Krishna M., and C. P. Rao. "Service Firms' International Entry-Mode Choice: A Modified Transaction–Cost Analysis Approach." *Journal of Marketing*, July 1993, vol. 57, pp. 19–38.

Fey, Carl F., and Paul W. Beamish. "Organizational Climate and Performance: International Joint Ventures in Russia," *Organizational Studies* (Berlin), vol. 22, no. 5, 2001, pp. 853–882.

Harrigan, Kathryn R. *Strategies for Joint Ventures*. Boston: D.C. Heath, 1985.

Kanter, Rosabeth Moss. *When Giants Learn to Dance*. New York: Simon & Schuster, 1989.

Kogut, Bruce, and Harbir Singh. "The Effect of National Culture on the Choice of Entry Mode." *Journal of International Business Studies*, Fall 1988, pp. 411–432.

Lawrence, Paul, and Charalambos Vlachoutsicos. "Joint Ventures in Russia: Put the Locals in Charge." *Harvard Business Review*, January–February 1993, pp. 44–54.

Parkhe, Arvind. "Interfirm Diversity, Organizational Learning, and Longevity in Global Strategic Alliances." *Journal of International Business Studies*, 4th quarter 1991, pp. 579–601.

Root, Franklin R. *Entry Strategies for International Markets*, revised and expanded ed. Lexington, Mass.: D.C. Heath, 1994.

Shan, Weijan. "Environmental Risks and Joint Venture Sharing Arrangements." *Journal of International Business Studies*, 4th quarter 1991, pp. 555–578.

Yoshino, Michael Y., and U. Srinivasu Rangan. *Strategic Alliances*. Cambridge: Harvard Business School Press, 1995.

Endnotes

1. "DHL Major Exporter of the Year Award," *Nz Business*, December-January, 2001, p. N6.

2. "The European Minefield," *World Trade*, September 1999, pp. 36–40.

3. "Turning the Corner on Export Profits," *World Trade*, April 1999, p. 104.

4. "Sega to Scale Down European Sales Operations," *Financial Times*, February 28, 1996, p. 1.

5. "Sato to Retire from VW's Japan Unit," *Automotive News*, June 29, 1998, p. 43.

6. "GM to Strengthen Marketing Ties in Japan," *Nikkei/Dow Jones International News*, March 9, 1999; "GM Japan, Yanase Team Up to Promote GM's Opel Cars in Japan," *Dow Jones International News*, June 10, 1998.

7. "How Does GM's Saturn Sell Cars in Japan? Very Slowly," *Wall Street Journal*, August 25, 1998, p. B1.

8. "French Drug Maker Reaps Profits with Offbeat Strategy," *Wall Street Journal*, November 14, 1996, p. B4.

9. "The Expanding Partnership Role of Information Services at Sanofi," *Pharmaceutical Executive*, March 1999, pp. 70–78.

10. "SABMiller to Focus on Marketing Overseas," *Knight Ridder Tribune Business News*, June 11, 2002, p. 1.

11. "Slowing Mobile Phone Sales Spark and Outsorcing Trend," *Asian Wall Street Journal*, June 19, 2002, p. A7.

12. "Acer Anticipates 30 Percent Rise in Sales," *Asian Wall Street Journal*, June 20, 2002, p. M2.

13. "Ford Vietnam Targets Bigger Automobile Market Slide," *Saigon Time Daily*, July 2, 1999.

14. "BMW Testing Waters for Local Facility," *Businessline* (Islamabad), May 17, 2002.

15. "UAZ Car Plant to Open Assembly Lines in Jordan, Vietnam," *Itar-Tass News Wire* (New York), January 31, 2002.

16. "As China Surges, Asean Trade Zone Gains New Urgency: BMW's Thai Plant Hindered by the Region's High Tariffs," *Asian Wall Street Journal*, April 1, 2002, p. A1.

17. "Hyundai to Step Up Production of Euro-II Santro," *The Hindu*, July 3, 1999.

18. "India Launch of Toyota Model in January 2000," *Business Standard*, February 13, 1999, p. 16.

19. "Honda Increasing Transactions Between Asian Units," *Dow Jones News Service*, July 5, 1999.

20. "Japan Car Makers Find a Friend in Weaker Yen—Up to a Point," *Wall Street Journal*, January 28, 2002, p. A12.

21. "Successful Transplants," *Financial Times*, Survey, Automotive Components, March 27, 1991, p. 2.

22. "Picking Up an ML320 at Factory Adds to Fun," *Washington Times*, April 23, 1999, p. E13.

23. "Honda to Sell Thai-Made Car in Japan", *Automotive News*, February 4, 2002, p. 28.

24. "McD's Japan to Close 130 Units, Curb Growth by 23 Percent," *Nation's Restaurant News*, April 1, 2002.

25. "McD Co. of Japan's IOP Netws $400 Million," *Nation's Restaurant News*, August 6, 2001.

26. "AOL Japan Subscribers Top 2000,000," *Asia Pulse*, January 22, 1999.

27. "Foreigners Find China Ventures Difficult to Quit," *Wall Street Journal*, March 12, 1991, p. A15.

28. "China Elevator Maker Lifts Performance Expectations," *China Daily*, June 1, 1998.

29. "Toppest Export Recorded in Schinler Elevator of Suzhou," *AsiaPort Daily News/China Market News*, July 27, 1998, p. 5.

30. "CP Committed to Businesses in China," *Bangkok Post*, July 1, 1999, p. 2.

31. Jeffrey M. Hertzfeld, "Joint Ventures: Saving the Soviets from Perestroika," *Harvard Business Review*, January–February 1991, pp. 80–91.

32. "Successful Joint Ventures in Russia," *World Trade*, August 1, 1998, p. 42.

33. "Russian McWorkers Have Beef with McDonald's," *Wall Street Journal*, June 25, 1999.

34. "Russia: McDonald's Plans to Open New Restaurants in Russia," *Inzhenernaya Gazeta*, January 29, 2002.

35. "Gillette Expands in Russia with New Blade Plant," *Business Wire*, March 30, 1998.

36. "Hearts, Minds, and Beards Pursuing Its Overseas Growth Strategy, Gillette Opens Factory in St.Petersburg," *Boston Globe*, June 7, 2000, p. C.1.

37. "Many U.S. Firms Leaving Russia," *Times Union* (Albany, NY), April 6, 1999, p. E4.

38. Carl F. Fey and Paul W. Beamish, "Organizational Climate Similarity and Performance: International Joint Ventures in Russia," *Organization Studies* (Berlin), 2001, vol 22, no. 5, pp. 853–882.

39. J. Peter Killing, "How to Make a Global Joint Venture Work," *Harvard Business Review*, May–June 1982, p. 121.

40. "American Companies in Japan," *Japan-U.S. Business Report*, January 30, 1999, vol. 1999, no. 352.

41. "Carrier and Toshiba Make It Official, Form Global Strategic Alliance," *Business Wire*, April 1, 1999.

42. "Toyota, Peugeot Break Ground for Czech Plant," *Jiji Press News Service*, April 10, 2002.

43. "Is the Cereal Bowl Half Full or Half Empty," *Star-Tribune* (Minneapolis-St. Paul), August 16, 1998, p. 1D.

44. General Mills, *Annual Report*, 2001, p. 15.

45. "Coke, Nestle, Launch BPW," *Financial Times*, January 31, 2001.

46. "Japan and Europe—Worlds Apart?" *Telecommunications International*, March 2002, pp. 38–40.

47. "Cleaning Up Its Act to Fight the Giants," *Financial Times*, September 27, 1994, p. 17.

48. "Reckitts Deal Will Lead to Brand Cull," *Marketing* (London), July 29, 1999, p. 1.

49. "Coca-Cola Completes Acquisition of Schweppes Brands in 155 Countries," *Dow Jones Business News*, July 30, 1999.

50. "Why Daimler Is Driving Hard into Korea," *Business Week*, July 10, 2000, p. 158.

51. "Nestlé's Acquisition of Purina Secrues U.S. Endorsement—Regulators Require Companies to Sell Two Cat Food Brands," *Wall Street Journal*, December 12, 2001, p. 4.

52. "Doubts Over GE Appeal," *Financial Times*, September 14, 2001.

53. "Merging Across Borders," Survey by KPMG Corporate Finance, *Reuters*, February 29, 2000.

54. "Streetmarket.Com Adopts Niche e-Retail Strategy," *Business Times* (Kuala Lumpur), September 20, 2000.

55. "Joining Crowd, Merrill to Offer On-Line Trades," *Herald Tribune International*, June 3, 1999, p. 13.

56. "Idiom App Speaks Your Language," *Computer World*, May 31, 1999, p. 66.

57. "Gateway Slices Staff, Operations," *Internetweek.Com*, August 29, 2001.

58. "Yahoo Cedes Most of Europe to eBay," *Wall Street Journal*, May 23, 2002, p. A.3.

59. "CellStar Corp: Move Is Announced to Quit UK, Peru, Argentina Markets," *Wall Street Journal*, June 6, 2002, p. B.2.

60. "South Africa: Time to Stay—or Go?" *Fortune*, August 4, 1986, p. 45; "If Coke Has Its Way, Blacks Will Soon Own 'The Real Thing,'" *Business Week*, March 27, 1987, p. 56; "High Risks and Low Returns," *Financial Times*, November 25, 1986, p. 10.

61. "Back in Charge," *Far Eastern Economic Review*, July 8, 1993.

62. "Coca-Cola Invasion Starts to Worry Businessmen," *Financial Times*, November 9, 1993, p. 6.

63. "As US Firms Return to Land of Apartheid, Lotus Feels its Way," *Wall Street Journal*, May 26, 1993.

64. "US Still SA's Biggest Investor," *Business Day* (South Africa), February 15, 1999, p. 2.

65. "European Companies," *Wall Street Journal*, January 10, 2001, p. 5.

66. "Acer to Re-Enter into China Mainland PC Market," *AsiaInfo Daily China News*, June 25, 2002.

67. "Japan's Cellphone Leader to Re-Enter US Market," *Wall Street Journal*, November 16, 2000, p. A23.

68. "NEC to Reenter US Mobile Phone Market," *Jiji Press English News Service*, April 5, 2002.

69. "Toshiba to Reenter China Consumer Electronics Mart," *Jiji Press English News Service*, January 13, 2000.

Part IV

Designing Global Marketing Programs

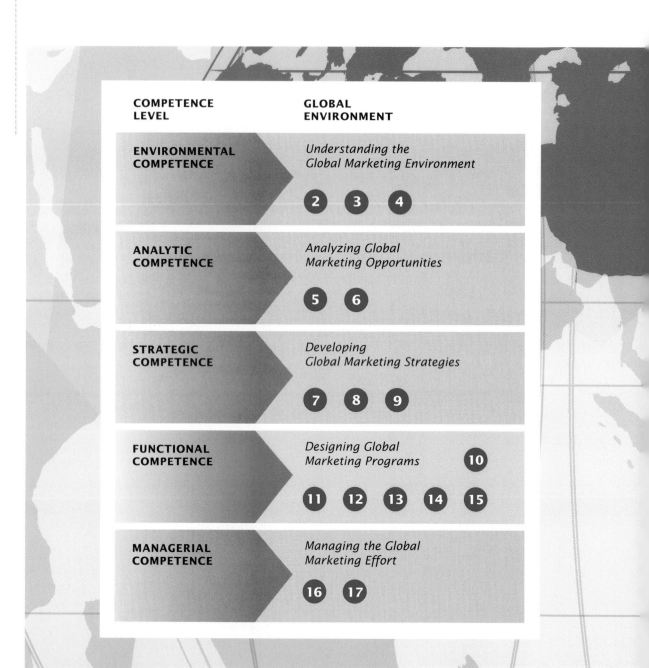

COMPETENCE LEVEL	GLOBAL ENVIRONMENT
ENVIRONMENTAL COMPETENCE	*Understanding the Global Marketing Environment* 2 3 4
ANALYTIC COMPETENCE	*Analyzing Global Marketing Opportunities* 5 6
STRATEGIC COMPETENCE	*Developing Global Marketing Strategies* 7 8 9
FUNCTIONAL COMPETENCE	*Designing Global Marketing Programs* 10 11 12 13 14 15
MANAGERIAL COMPETENCE	*Managing the Global Marketing Effort* 16 17

Assembling a global marketing program requires an analysis of how the environment affects the four marketing mix elements: product, distribution, pricing, and communications. In Part IV, we focus on how companies adapt to different marketing environments by adjusting certain elements of their marketing programs to ensure market acceptance. Learning about these issues will help you increase your functional competence. Marketing managers must not only be knowledgeable about the global environment; they must also possess the solid, functional skills necessary to compete successfully in the global marketplace. They must adapt to local conditions when necessary and provide a global solution when possible.

Chapter 10 outlines the differences between domestic and global pricing, and how companies can deal with problems arising from different prices in different markets. In Chapter 11, we provide an overview of communications strategies, sales force management, and promotional policies for global companies. Chapter 12 looks at global advertising and the challenges faced by companies running advertising programs simultaneously in many countries. Chapter 13 concentrates on product and service strategy issues for global markets. In Chapter 14, we discuss how to manage the new-product development process in a global environment. Important distribution and channel decisions are covered in Chapter 15.

Chapter 10

Pricing for Global Markets

This chapter provides an overview of the key factors that affect pricing policies in a global environment. We assume that you already understand the basic pricing decisions that companies must make in a single-country or domestic environment. In this chapter, we focus on the unique aspects of global pricing. See Figure 10.1 for a chapter overview.

The material is organized around six major issues. First, we look at internal factors and company policies as they affect global pricing strategies. Costs and how they affect price determination are major concerns. The second section is devoted to the market factors that companies must consider when setting prices. These factors include competition and the income levels of various countries. The third segment focuses on the environmental variables, such as foreign exchange rates, inflation, and legal constraints, that are not controlled by individual firms but that play an important role in shaping pricing strategies. The fourth section covers managerial pricing issues, such as transfer pricing—price arbitrage and countertrade—issues of great concern to companies active globally. The chapter ends with sections on two financing issues: risks and financial sources. These financing issues are critical areas that have received increased attention from global firms.

Global marketers are measured by their results, which ultimately means sales and profit. The pricing strategy of a firm significantly influences the level of sales and the resulting profit. Several factors push firms to consider standardized pricing worldwide, but opportunities still exist to maximize total profit based on obtaining the best price in each country. Global marketers must understand all the factors affecting pricing so they can make the best decisions, given all the internal and external factors.

Figure 10.1: Global Pricing Strategies

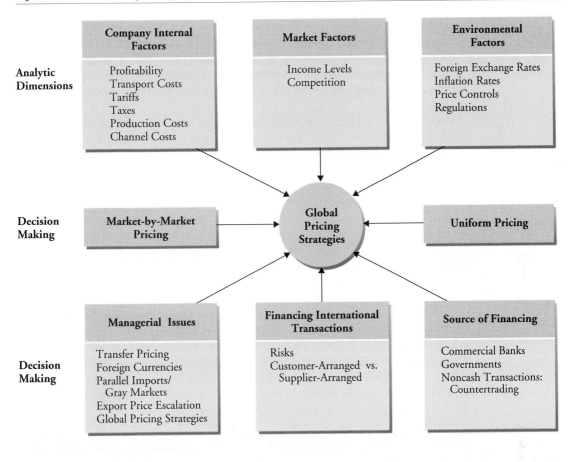

COMPANY INTERNAL FACTORS

Most companies begin pricing deliberations based on their own internal cost structure. Therefore, it makes sense to look at internal costs before considering other issues. Included under internal factors are profits and the requirement for profits as they affect internal pricing procedures.

Also of concern are country-to-country transfer costs, such as tariffs, transportation, insurance, taxes, and local channel costs. Such costs frequently make exported products more expensive than domestic ones, and this fact must be taken into consideration if a company wants to compete effectively. However, such costs do not have to be taken as permanent. Through various actions, companies can affect the level of these costs. The purpose of this section is to point out the options available to companies when they manage their global costs.

PROFIT AND COST FACTORS

The basis for any effective pricing policy is a clear understanding of the cost and profit variables involved. Experience shows that clear definitions of relevant costs and of profits are often difficult to achieve. On the other hand, the field of global marketing offers many examples of firms that have achieved substantial profits through flexible or unconventional costing approaches. Therefore, understanding the various cost elements can be considered a prerequisite for a successful global pricing strategy.

According to standard accounting practice, costs are divided into two categories: fixed costs and variable costs. Fixed costs do not vary over a given range of output, whereas variable costs change directly with output. The relationship of these variables is shown in Table 10.1. The table uses a fictitious example, Western Machine Tool, Inc., a manufacturer of machine tools selling at $60,000 per unit in the U.S. market.

The total cost of a machine tool is $54,000. The company will achieve a profit of $6,000 before taxes from the sale of each unit at $60,000 apiece. If one additional unit is sold (or not sold), however, the marginal impact amounts to more than an additional profit of $6,000 (or loss of the same amount) because the extra cost of an additional unit will be limited to its variable costs only, or $26,000, as shown in Table 10.2. For any additional units sold, the marginal profit is $34,000, or the amount in excess of the variable costs. This amount may also be referred to as the *contribution margin*.

Another example is used to illustrate the relationships among variable costs, fixed costs, and contribution margin. Western Machine Tool has a chance to export a unit to a foreign country, but the maximum price the foreign buyer is willing to pay is $50,000. Machine Tool, using the full cost pricing method, argues that the company will incur a loss of $4,000 if the deal is accepted. However, only $26,000 of additional variable cost will be incurred for a new machine because all fixed costs are incurred

Table 10.1 Profit and Cost Calculation for Western Machine Tool, Inc.

Selling price (per unit)			$60,000
Direct manufacturing costs			
Labor	$10,000		
Material	15,000		
Energy	1,000	$26,000	
Indirect manufacturing costs			
Supervision	5,000		
Research and development contribution	3,000		
Factory overhead	5,000	13,000	
General administrative cost			
Sales and administrative overhead	10,000		
Marketing	5,000	15,000	
Full costs			54,000
Net profit before tax			$ 6,000

Table 10.2 Marginal Profit Calculation for Western Machine Tool, Inc.		
Selling price (per unit)		$60,000
Variable costs		
Direct manufacturing costs		
Labor	$10,000	
Material	15,000	
Energy	1,000	26,000
Total variable costs		26,000
Contribution margin (selling price minus variable costs)		$34,000

anyway and are covered by all prior units sold. Thus, the company can go ahead with the sale and claim a marginal profit of $24,000 using a contribution margin approach. In such a situation, a profitable sale may easily be turned down unless a company is fully informed about its cost composition.

Cost components are subject to change. For example, if growing export volume adds new output to a plant, a company may achieve economies of scale that allow operations at lower costs, both domestically and abroad. Furthermore, as the experience curve indicates, companies with rapidly rising cumulative production may reap overall unit cost reductions at an increasing rate because of the higher output resulting from exporting.[1]

TRANSPORTATION COSTS

Global marketing often requires the shipment of products over long distances. Because all modes of transportation, including rail, truck, air, and sea, depend on a considerable amount of energy, the total cost of transportation has become an issue of growing concern to global companies. High-technology products are less sensitive to transportation costs than are standardized consumer products or commodities. In the latter case, the seller with the lowest transportation costs often has the advantage.

For commodities, low transportation costs can be the deciding factor for determining who gets an order. For expensive products, such as computers or sophisticated electronic instruments, transportation costs usually represent only a small fraction of total costs and rarely influence pricing decisions. For products between the two extremes, companies can substantially affect unit transportation costs by selecting appropriate transportation methods. The introduction of container ocean vessels has made large-scale shipment of many products possible. Roll-on, roll-off ships (ro-ro carriers) have reduced ocean freight costs for cars and trucks to very low levels, making exporters more competitive vis-à-vis local manufacturers. World seaborne trade increased 3.6 percent in 2000, to 5.88 billion tons, and is dominated by oil, grain, iron ore, coal, and other bulk commodities. Containerized cargo increased 1 percent in 2000, to 1.75 billion tons.[2] The international firm must continuously search for new transportation technologies to reduce unit transportation costs and thus enhance competitiveness.

TARIFFS

When products are transported across national borders, tariffs have to be paid unless a special arrangement exists between the countries involved. Tariffs are usually levied on the landed costs of a product, which include shipping to the importing country. Tariffs are normally assessed as a percentage of the value. Tariff costs can have a rippling effect and can increase prices considerably for the end user. Intermediaries, whether they are sales subsidiaries or independent distributors, tend to include any tariff costs in their cost of goods sold, and they add any operating margin to this amount. As a result, the impact on the final end-user price can be substantial whenever tariff rates are high.

Managing shipments through duty and regulations sometimes requires scientific, engineering, or similar technical data. For example, "if a retailer ships women's hosiery into the US, it must first determine whether the hosiery is full-length or knee-length. It then must determine whether the yarn used to make the hosiery measures less than 67 decitex per single yarn. If so, the importer must ascertain whether the hosiery contains 70% or more by weight of silk or silk waste."[3] Tariffs always penalize someone. In 1999, the United States imposed a 100 percent tariff on printed bed linens from Europe in retaliation for the European Union tariffs on Latin American bananas. The linen producers in Italy, France, and Portugal lost sales, as did the retailers in the United States who specialize in this product.[4] BMW faced a similar situation in Egypt, which imposes duties of 135 percent of the value of the car, plus a 45 percent sales tax. BMW set up an assembly plant in a duty-free zone near Cairo, and monthly sales increased from thirty-five to one hundred cars.[5] Although tariffs have declined over recent years, they still influence pricing decisions in some countries. As we explained in Chapter 9, companies have shipped components only and established local assembly operations, because tariffs on components are frequently lower than on finished products, to avoid paying high duties. The automobile industry is a good example of how companies can reduce overall tariff costs by shifting the place of production and shipping knocked-down cars to be assembled on the spot. Such a move may be necessary when tariffs are especially high.

TAXES

Local taxes imposed on imported products also affect the land cost of the products. Various taxes may be imposed. One of the most common is the value-added tax (VAT) used by member countries of the European Union (EU). Each EU country sets its own value-added tax structure (see Figure 10.2). Common to all, however, is a zero tax rate (or exemption) on exported goods. A company exporting from the Netherlands to Belgium does not have to pay any tax on the value added in the Netherlands. However, Belgian authorities do collect a tax on products shipped from the Netherlands at the Belgium rate. Merchandise shipped to any EU member country from a nonmember country, such as from the United States or Japan, is assessed the VAT rate on landed costs, in addition to any tariffs that may apply to those products.

LOCAL PRODUCTION COSTS

Up to this point, we have assumed that a company has only one producing location from which it exports to all other markets. However, most global firms manufacture

Figure 10.2: European VAT Rates, September 2002 (in Percentages)

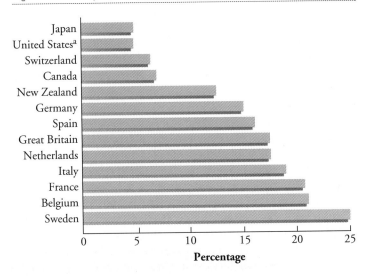

products in several countries. In such cases, operating costs for raw materials, wages, energy, or financing may vary widely from country to country, allowing a firm to ship from a particularly advantageous location to reduce prices or costs. Increasingly, companies produce in locations that give them advantages in freight, tariffs, or other transfer costs. Consequently, judicious management of sourcing points may reduce product costs and thus result in added pricing flexibility.

CHANNEL COSTS

Channel costs are a function of channel length, gross margin, and logistics. Many countries have long distribution channels, which means an increase in the number of intermediaries and thus results in higher total costs and end-user prices. In addition, gross margins at the retail level tend to vary from country to country because of the different logistics systems. All these factors can add extra costs to a product that is marketed globally.

Campbell Soup Company, a U.S.-based firm, found that its retailers in the United Kingdom purchased soup in small quantities of twenty-four cans per case of assorted soups. The assortment in each case required each can to be handpacked for shipment. In the United States, the company sold one variety to retailers in cases of forty-eight cans per case, which were purchased in large quantities. To handle small purchases in England, the company had to add another level of distribution and new facilities. As a result, distribution costs are 30 percent higher in England than in the United States.[6]

MARKET FACTORS AFFECTING PRICING

Companies cannot establish pricing policies in a vacuum. Although cost information is essential, prices must also reflect the realities of the marketplace. The challenge in pricing for global markets is the large number of local economic situations to be considered. Two factors stand out and must be analyzed in detail: income levels and competition.

INCOME LEVELS

The income level of a country's population determines the amount and type of goods and services bought. When detailed income data are not available, income is expressed by gross national product (GNP) or gross domestic product (GDP) divided by the total population. This measure, *GNP per capita* or *GDP per capita,* is a surrogate measure for personal income and is used to compare income levels among countries. With this method, all GNPs/GDPs must be converted to the same currency. If you look at the table on the inside back cover of this book, you will see that GNP per capita figures for key countries are expressed in U.S. dollars.

We explained in Chapter 6 that this method—GNP/GDP per capita converted to dollars based on market exchange rates—tends to understate the true purchasing power of a country's consumers. It is more accurate to look at developing countries' GNP or GDP per capita converted to dollars based on purchasing power parity. The World Bank's latest estimate of China's GNP/GDP based on purchasing power parity is $4.8 trillion, which is higher than that of Japan and approximately one-half that of the United States.[7] To respond to the purchasing power of different countries, Coca-Cola prices its product as a proportion of disposable income.[8]

Because of widely differing income and price levels, elasticity of demand for any given product can be expected to vary greatly. Countries with high income levels often display lower price elasticities for necessities such as food, shelter, and medical care. In part, these lower elasticities reflect a lack of alternatives. One example is the fact that buyers in these countries often can't "do for themselves" (they don't grow their own food or build their own houses), which forces them to purchase such goods at even higher prices. In many countries with low income levels, a considerable part of the population has the additional alternatives of providing their own food or building their own shelters should they have insufficient money to purchase products or services on a cash basis. Availability of such options increases price elasticity because these consumers can opt out of the cash economy more easily than can consumers in developed economies. Global companies theoretically set product price by considering the price elasticity in each country. However, there are forces at work that do not always allow this practice because prices may vary widely across several countries. The danger of disparate price levels is examined later in this chapter, under the heading "Managerial Issues in Global Pricing."

COMPETITION

The nature and size of competition can significantly affect price levels in any given market. A firm acting as the sole supplier of a product in a particular market enjoys greater pricing flexibility. The opposite is true if that same company has to compete against several other local or global firms. Therefore, the number and type of competitors greatly influence pricing strategy in any market. The public postal, telephone, and telegraph (PTT) services of some countries are a public monopoly, allowing them to charge high rates with no threat of competition. As the Japanese telecommunications market has opened up, U.S. suppliers and others have been quick to respond. AT&T World Access offered international calling opportunities at approximately half the standard rate offered by Japanese providers.[9] The opening of telecom markets is destroying the fortresses previously held by the PTTs. For example, after the German telecom market was opened in 1998, fifty-one new companies entered the field, taking one-third of the market from Deutsche Telekom and dropping long-distance rates by 90 percent.[10]

Also important is the nature of the competition. Local competitors may have different cost structures from those of foreign companies, resulting in different prices. Market prices for the same product may vary from country to country, based on the competitive situation. In China, local tax structures favor local competitors. For example, in Wuhan, an industrial city, officials have given tax breaks to anybody who buys cars made in the local car plant.[11]

However, foreign companies do not always have to compete at a disadvantage with local companies. In the wake of the substantial strengthening of the Japanese yen in 1998, Japanese car manufacturers did not cut prices in the United States. They enjoyed strong sales in the U.S. market. The profits were repatriated to Japan and will help the weak markets in Asia.[12]

Occasionally, price levels are manipulated by cartels or other agreements among local competitors. Cartels are forbidden by law in the United States, but some governments allow cartels, provided they do not injure the consumer. Following a five-year investigation, the European Union fined twenty-three western European chemical companies $80 million for the price fixing of two plastic products. The companies were found guilty of forming secret pricing cartels to keep up the price of polyvinyl chloride (PVC) and low-density polyethylene.[13] The U.S. Justice Department found four graphite electrode manufacturers guilty of conspiring to suppress and eliminate competition between 1992 and 1997. The two Japanese companies, one German company, and one U.S. company paid fines totaling $284 million.[14] Cartels may be officially recognized by a local government or they may consist of competitors following similar pricing practices. In general, new market entrants must decide whether to accept current price levels or to set price levels different from those of the established competition. The U.S. government has a very strict approach to cartels, and any cartel such as those described above clearly would be against existing U.S. laws. U.S. companies may find themselves in violation of U.S. laws if they actively participate in any foreign cartel.

ENVIRONMENTAL FACTORS AFFECTING PRICE

We have thus far treated pricing as a matter of cost and market factors. Several environmental factors also influence pricing on the global level. These external variables, uncontrolled by any individual company, include the general economic environment, foreign exchange, inflation, government price controls, and government regulations. These factors restrict company decision-making authority and can become dominant concerns for country managers.

EXCHANGE RATE FLUCTUATIONS

One of the most unpredictable factors affecting prices is the foreign exchange rate. As the exchange rate moves up and down, it affects all producers. A company's costs are often in its domestic currency. As this currency weakens, the company's goods are cheaper in another currency. For example, when the euro was launched in January 1999, each euro was valued at $1.20. By July 1999, the euro had dropped to $1.00. Therefore, Cotherm, a French producer of thermostats and sensors that exports to China and Brazil, was able to reduce prices and maintain profits and market share.[15] (In Chapter 2, we explained the reasons behind these foreign currency fluctuations.)

Though foreign exchange fluctuations can present new opportunities, they may also make operations more difficult, particularly for companies operating in countries with appreciating currencies. As the dollar and the pound became stronger against the euro, items manufactured in the United States or the United Kingdom were more expensive in the eleven euro countries and therefore export demand was expected to drop. The Confederation of British Industry estimated that fifteen thousand to twenty thousand jobs were lost in the United Kingdom by August 1999 because of the strong pound sterling.[16] In 1999, Korean shipbuilders were able to offer prices well below that of Japanese shipbuilders because of the fast appreciation of the yen versus the Korean won. Korean shipbuilding volume increased 37 percent in 1999 over 1998, even though world orders declined 15 percent.[17]

INFLATION RATES

The rate of inflation can affect product cost and may force a company to take specific action. Inflation rates have traditionally fluctuated over time and, more important, have differed from country to country. In some cases, inflation rates have risen to several hundred percent. When inflation is this high, payment for products may be delayed for months, harming the economy because of the local currency's rapid loss of purchasing power. A company would have to use a last-in, first-out (LIFO) method of costing or, in the extreme, a first-in, first-out (FIFO) approach to protect itself from eroding purchasing power. A company can usually protect itself from rapid inflation if it maintains constant operating margins (gross margin, gross profit, net margin) and makes constant price adjustments, sometimes on a monthly basis.

Historically, inflation has been a problem in countries like Brazil. The United States and Europe have successfully managed inflation by raising interest rates whenever the economy starts to heat up, keeping inflation at 0 to 2 percent. One exception is Greece, where consumer prices rose 5 percent in 1998 and were estimated to rise only 3 percent in 1999, the country's lowest inflation rate since 1972.[18]

In countries with extremely high inflation, companies may price in a stable currency, such as the U.S. dollar, euro, or yen, and translate prices into local currencies on a daily basis. Vision Express, which has been very successful in Russia, charges customers in dollars to avoid the inflation that lifts prices rapidly. Most of the customers, entrepreneurs and businesspeople, seem to be able to get dollars. In fact, a 1998 study by the Russian central bank found that 20 percent of transactions in its economy were in dollars.[19] The U.S. dollar was reasonably strong in 1999, appreciating against most currencies except for some Asian currencies, such as the Indonesian rupiah, the Japanese yen, the Australian dollar, and the South Korean won (see Figure 10.3). One of the big losers against the dollar in the beginning of 1999 was the Brazilian real, which dropped 34 percent versus the dollar since the end of 1998.

PRICE CONTROLS

In some countries, government regulatory agencies influence the prices of products and services. Controls may be applied to an entire economy to combat inflation; regulations may be applied only to specific industries, such as the pharmaceutical industry. In the European Union, where many aspects of the countries' economies are coordinated, methods of controlling prices for drugs may vary considerably. In

Figure 10.3: Currencies Against the Dollar, Percentage Change, December 31, 2001, to August 14, 2002

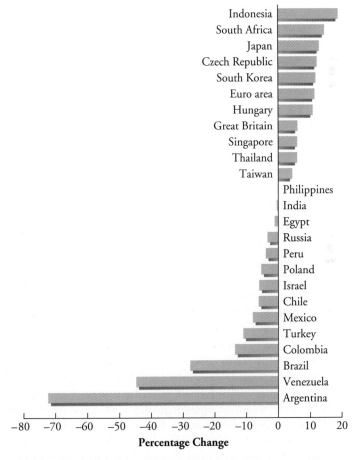

Romania, a chronic shortage of medicines in 1989 led to an advantageous pricing structure for importers but threatened the long-term sustainability of domestic producers. The average price of a locally manufactured drug in Romania is 50 cents and the average price of an imported drug is $3.10.[20] Italy uses a similar restrictive list combined with price controls and varying levels of reimbursements. France uses a method of strict price controls to contain overall health costs, and Germany also maintains a restrictive list for some drugs but otherwise lets the companies set their own prices. In contrast, U.S. prices for some drugs are established through negotiations between the drug company, the federal Medicare program, and several private insurance companies that reimburse their customers for drug costs. Because of the strong government policy limiting prices of drugs in many countries, consumers pay less than they do in the United States. The same $100 worth of drugs in the United States would cost $76 in Canada, $67 in the United Kingdom, $47 in Sweden, and $32 in Australia.[21]

The European Union is attempting to stabilize EU car prices without resorting to price controls. Twice a year, car manufacturers must publish comparative EU price lists for selected new cars. In each EU country, car prices are expected to be within 12 percent over the long term and within 18 percent over periods of a year. Nevertheless, there is still great disparity among European car prices, with the United Kingdom having the highest, 50 percent higher than car prices in Denmark.[22] If car manufacturers do not stay within these differentials, they may lose the right to use selective dealer distribution. BMW, the owner of the U.K.-based Rover, announced in 1999 that it would cut price differentials on all its new cars to less than 10 percent.[23] A report by the EU found cars sold in the United Kingdom were priced 35 percent higher than those in the Euro-zone countries in 2000. EU competition commissioner, Mario Monti, said that he will prosecute violations of EU competition rules when the car-sales exception from the EU law expires in 2002.[24]

REGULATORY FACTORS: DUMPING REGULATIONS

The practice of selling a product at a price below actual costs is referred to as *dumping*. Because of potential injuries to domestic manufacturers, most governments have adopted regulations against dumping. Antidumping actions are allowed under provisions of the World Trade Organization (WTO), as long as two criteria are met: "sales [are] less than fair value" and "material injury" to a domestic industry exists.[25] The first criterion is usually interpreted to mean selling abroad at prices below those in the country of origin. However, the WTO rules (originally adopted by the General Agreement on Tariffs and Trades [GATT] in 1968) prohibit assessment of retroactive punitive duties and require all procedures to be open. The United States differs from the WTO in its antidumping regulations, determining "fair market value" and "material injury" sequentially rather than simultaneously. Also, the U.S. government will assess any duty retroactively and has, on numerous occasions, acted to prevent antidumping practices from injuring domestic manufacturers.

The U.S. government and other governments have taken dumping actions on numerous occasions over the past decade. Antidumping cases have tripled since the 1980s. Fifty-three safeguard investigations were initiated in 2001, up from five in 1996, and twenty-four countries initiated 348 antidumping investigations involving 139 different products.[26] The United States is not alone in taking antidumping actions. Twenty-six countries opened 225 WTO antidumping cases in 1998. In the 1980s and early 1990s, 80 percent of antidumping charges were brought by the United States, Canada, the European Union, and Australia, often against Asian countries. Many of the new antidumping cases have been brought to the WTO by developing countries such as South Africa, India, Brazil, Indonesia, and Mexico, with the United States, the European Union, Canada, and Australia bringing less than one-third of the cases. Forty-three of the cases were brought against the European Union and its members.[27] Global marketers have to be aware of antidumping legislation that sets a floor under export prices, limiting pricing flexibility even in the event of overcapacity or industry slowdown. On the other hand, antidumping legislation can work to a company's advantage, protecting it from unfair competition.

MANAGERIAL ISSUES IN GLOBAL PRICING

Now that we have given you a general overview of the context of global pricing, we direct your attention toward managerial issues. The following recurring issues require constant management attention because they are never really considered solved: transfer pricing, quoting in foreign currencies, gray-market pricing, and export price escalation.

DETERMINING TRANSFER PRICES

A substantial amount of global business takes place between subsidiaries of the same company. It is estimated that in-house trading between subsidiaries accounts for one-third of the volume among the world's eight hundred largest multinationals. The cost to the importing or buying subsidiary depends on the negotiated transfer price agreed on by the two participating units of the international firm. How these prices are set is a major issue for global companies and governments. Because negotiations on transfer prices do not represent arm's-length negotiations between independent participants, the resulting prices frequently differ from free-market prices.[28]

Companies may deviate from arm's-length prices for two reasons. They may want to (1) maximize profits by shifting their tax burden to low-tax countries and/or (2) minimize risk and uncertainty by shifting profits to stable, predictable countries.[29] To pursue a strategy of profit maximization, a company may lower transfer prices for products shipped from some subsidiaries while increasing prices for products shipped to others. The company will then try to accumulate profits in subsidiaries where it is advantageous and keep profits low in other subsidiaries. All governments want to receive the appropriate tax revenue from any company operating within their borders; therefore, it is not surprising that transfer prices receive much attention from tax officials. In a survey of 638 global companies in twenty-two countries, 85 percent of the finance/tax directors reported that transfer pricing was their most important international tax issue. Twenty-nine percent of the same directors reported that transfer pricing was considered part of strategic corporate planning.[30]

IMPACT OF TAX STRUCTURE. Different tax, tariff, or subsidy structures from country to country frequently cause companies to modify transfer prices. By accumulating more profits in a low-tax country, a company lowers its overall tax bill and thus increases profit. Likewise, tariff duties can be reduced by quoting low transfer prices to countries with high tariffs. When countries use different exchange rates for the transfer of goods as opposed to the transfer of capital or profits, advantages can be gained by increasing transfer prices rather than transferring profits at less advantageous rates. The same is true for countries with restrictions on profit repatriation. A company may also want to accumulate profits in a wholly owned subsidiary rather than in one that is minority owned; by using the transfer price mechanism, it can avoid sharing profits with local partners.

Companies may also use the transfer price mechanism to minimize risk or uncertainty by moving profits or assets out of a country with chronic balance-of-payment problems and frequent devaluations. Because regular profit remittances are strictly controlled in such countries, many firms see high transfer prices as the only way to repatriate funds and thereby to reduce the amount of assets at risk. The same practice may be employed if a company anticipates political or social disturbances or a direct threat to profits through government intervention.

INTERNAL CONSIDERATIONS. Rigorous use of the transfer pricing mechanism to reduce a company's income taxes and duties and to maximize profits in strong currency areas can create difficulties for subsidiary managers whose profits are artificially reduced. In such cases, managers may be subject to motivational problems when the direct-profit incentive is removed. Company resource allocation may become inefficient because funds are distributed to units whose profits are artificially increased; conversely, resources may be denied to subsidiaries whose income statements are subject to transfer price–induced reductions. It is generally agreed that a transfer price mechanism should not seriously impair either employee morale or resource allocations because gains incurred through tax savings may be lost easily through other inefficiencies.

EXTERNAL PROBLEMS. Governments do not look favorably on transfer pricing mechanisms aimed at reducing their tax revenues. Tax law, particularly Section 482 of the Revenue Act of 1962, governs U.S. government policy on transfer pricing. The act is designed to provide an accurate allocation of costs, income, and capital among related enterprises to protect U.S. tax revenue.

U.S. transfer pricing regulations have continued to evolve. If a comparable arm's-length transaction cannot be located, the IRS can use the comparable profits method to gauge the appropriate tax burden. In addition, the IRS requires all companies to maintain detailed explanations of the rationale and analysis supporting the transfer pricing policy. Because of the U.S. IRS tax regulations, the countries of the Organization for Economic Cooperation and Development (OECD) have agreed to a new set of transfer pricing guidelines that are close to the U.S. rules.[31] According to a study by the General Accounting Office, 67 percent of all the foreign-controlled companies doing business in the United States, or 40,195 companies, do not pay any U.S. taxes. In the same report, the largest 15,363 U.S. companies pay an average of $8.1 million per year in taxes, whereas the large 2,767 foreign companies pay only $4.2 million per year. Senator Byron L. Dorgan (Democrat, North Dakota) estimates that foreign-controlled companies doing business in the United States are failing to pay $45 billion owed in U.S. taxes. Transfer pricing is the primary method used to avoid taxes.[32]

Given the strengthening of government regulations all around the world, it is necessary for global businesses to document the arm's-length principle. According to a global survey of 814 companies and their subsidiaries, 65 percent had a transfer pricing audit within the previous two years.[33] In 1992, the U.S. IRS developed the Advanced Pricing Agreement (APA) program, which became effective on December 31, 1993. Under this program, a company can obtain approval from the IRS for its transfer pricing procedures. This new process, completed in an open, nonadversarial atmosphere, reduces the expense and uncertainty around transfer pricing.[34] Asia, Australia, Japan, and Korea all have formal advanced pricing arrangements, and China, India, and New Zealand have informal programs.[35] The introduction of the euro resulted in greater price transparency from country to country. This transparency, combined with the heightened scrutiny of Canada, the United States, the United Kingdom, Germany, France, and Japan, means that global companies face increased risk of transfer price audits and income adjustments.[36]

QUOTING PRICE IN A FOREIGN CURRENCY

For many global marketing transactions, it is not always feasible to quote in a company's domestic currency when selling or purchasing merchandise. Although the majority of U.S. exporters quote prices in dollars, customers may sometimes prefer quotes in their own national currency. For most import transactions, sellers usually quote the currency of their own country. When two currencies are involved, a change in exchange rates may occur between the invoicing date and the settlement date for the transaction. This risk, the foreign exchange risk, is an inherent factor in global marketing and clearly separates domestic from international business. In 2001, the Japanese electronics company Sharp gained 300 million yen ($2.3 million) every time the yen fell by one against the dollar.[37] A research study of 671 companies in the United States, Finland, and Sweden found that companies that respond to customer's currency requests benefit from a larger volume of export business.[38] Even though the United Kingdom retained its national currency, retailers Harrods and Marks & Spencer said they would accept euros along with the pound.[39] In such circumstances, special techniques are available to protect the seller from the foreign exchange risk.

The tools used to cover a company's foreign exchange risk are either (a) hedging in the forward market or (b) covering through money markets. As we discussed in Chapter 2, for most major currencies, international foreign exchange dealers at major banks quote a spot price and a forward price. The *spot price* determines the number of dollars to be paid for a particular foreign currency purchased or sold today. The *forward price* quotes the number of dollars to be paid for a foreign currency bought or sold 30, 90, or 180 days from today. The forward price, however, is not necessarily the market's speculation about what the spot price will be in the future. Instead, the forward price reflects interest rate differentials between two currencies for maturities of 30, 90, or 180 days. Consequently, there are no firm indications about what the spot price will be for any given currency in the future. (For a review of foreign exchange markets, see Chapter 2.)

A company quoting in foreign currency for purchase or sale can simply leave settlement until the due date and pay whatever spot price prevails at the time. Such an uncovered position may be chosen when exchange rates are not expected to shift or when any shift in the near future will result in a gain for the company. With exchange rates fluctuating widely on a daily basis, even among major trading markets such as the United States, Japan, Brazil, and the United Kingdom, a company will expose itself to substantial foreign exchange risks. Because global firms are in business to make a profit from the sale of goods rather than from speculation in the foreign exchange markets, management generally protects itself from unexpected currency fluctuations.

One such protection lies in the forward market. Instead of accepting whatever spot market rate exists on the settlement in thirty or ninety days, the corporation can opt to contract for future delivery of foreign currency at a firm price, regardless of the spot price actually paid at that time. This strategy allows the seller to incorporate a firm exchange rate into the price determination. Of course, if a company wishes to predict the spot price in ninety days and is reasonably certain about the accuracy of its prediction, a choice may be made between the more advantageous of the two: the expected spot or the present forward rate. However, such predictions should be made only under the guidance of experts familiar with foreign exchange rates.

An alternative strategy, covering through the money market, involves borrowing funds to be converted into the currency at risk for the time until settlement. In this case, a company owes and holds the same amount of foreign currency, resulting in a corresponding loss or gain when settling at the time of payment. As an example, an exporter holding accounts receivable in Japanese yen and unwilling to absorb the related currency risk until payment is received may borrow yen for working capital purposes. When the customer pays in the foreign currency, the loan, also denominated in that same currency, is paid off. Any fluctuations will be canceled, resulting in neither loss nor gain.

HOW TO INCORPORATE A FOREIGN EXCHANGE RATE INTO A SELLING PRICE QUOTE. To illustrate the incorporation of a foreign exchange rate into a price quote for export, assume that a U.S. company needs to determine a price quote for its plastic extrusion machinery to be sold to a Canadian customer. The customer requested billing in Canadian dollars. The exporter, with a list price of U.S. $250,000, does not want to absorb any exchange risk. The daily foreign exchange rates on July 15, 2002, are U.S. $.6524 spot price for one Canadian dollar and $.6486 in the sixty days forward market.[40] The exporter can calculate the Canadian dollar price by using the forward rate, resulting in an export price of $383,200.49 in Canadian currency. On shipping, the exporter would sell at $385,445.57 (in Canadian money) forward with sixty days delivery and, with the rate of $.6486 per Canadian dollar, receive U.S. $250,000. Wherever possible, quotes in foreign currencies should be made based on forward rates, with respective foreign currency amounts sold in the forward market.

SELECTION OF A HEDGING PROCEDURE. To illustrate the selection of a hedging procedure, assume that a U.S. exporter of computer workstations sells ten machines valued at $200,000 to a client in the United Kingdom. The client will pay in British pounds quoted at the current (spot) rate (as of July 15, 2002) of $1.5517, or £128,890.89. This amount will be paid in six months. As a result, the U.S. exporter will have to determine how to protect the incoming amount against foreign exchange risk. Although uncertain about the outcome, the exporter's bank indicates that there is an equal chance for the British pound spot rate to remain at $1.5517 (Scenario A), to devalue to $1.45 (Scenario B), or to appreciate to $1.65 (Scenario C). As a result, the exporter has the option of selling the amount forward in the six months forward market, at $1.5343.

	A	**B**	**C**
Spot rate as of July 16, 1999	$1.5650	$1.5650	$1.5650
Spot rate as of September 16, 1999 (estimate)	1.45	1.65	$1.5650
U.S. dollar equivalent of £15,335.46 at spot rates on July 16, 1999	24,000.00	22,236.42	25,303.51
Exchange gain (loss) with hedging	0	(1,763.58)	1,303.51

Source: "Foreign Exchange," *Wall Street Journal,* July 16, 1999, p. C15. Copyright © 1999 Dow Jones & Co. Used with permission.

The alternative available to the exporter is to sell forward the invoice amount of £128,890.89 at $1.5343 to obtain a sure $197,757.29, a cost of $2,242.71, on the transaction. In anticipation of a devaluation of the pound, such a hedging strategy would be advisable. Consequently, the $2,242.71 represents a premium to ensure against any larger loss. However, the company would also forgo any gain if Scenario C prevailed. Acceptance for hedging through the forward market depends on the expected spot rate at the time the foreign payment is due. Again, keep in mind that the forward rate is not an estimate of the spot rate in the future.

DEALING WITH PARALLEL IMPORTS OR GRAY MARKETS

One of the most perplexing problems that global companies face is the phenomenon of different prices between countries. When such price differentials become large, individual buyers or independent entrepreneurs step in and buy products in low-price countries to re-export to high-price countries, profiting from the price differential. This arbitrage behavior creates what experts call the "gray market," or "parallel imports," because these imports take place outside the regular trade channels controlled by distributors or company-owned sales subsidiaries. Such price differences can occur because of company price strategy, margin differences, or currency fluctuations. Levi Strauss sells its 501 jeans in Paris at twice the price paid in the United States; therefore, it is not surprising that EU retailers are buying much of their Levi's inventory from unofficial sources outside the EU. The current EU legislation allows for parallel trading between countries within the EU but does not allow parallel imports of unofficial branded products from outside the EU. Levi is suing twenty-four European retailers, including Tesco, the U.K. supermarket giant, for parallel importing from outside the EU. The brand owners argue that parallel imports hurt the consumer because the goods are old, damaged, made from different specifications, or even fakes. Consumer groups and retailers argue that parallel imports increase competition, give the consumer more choices, and lead to lower prices.

EU commissioners are considering elimination of the law banning parallel trading from outside the E.U.[41]

Parallel importing has become a big problem in the European pharmaceutical industry. Wholesalers buy truckloads of branded ulcer and cancer drugs at bargain-basement prices in Spain and Portugal and resell them in Britain and Germany, where prices are higher. The northern European countries have paid the higher prices to support the higher costs of research and development. The practice costs the pharmaceutical industry about $3 billion in sales a year, according to industry estimates. Pfizer, the pharmaceutical company, estimates that half of its U.K. sales of Lipitor, a cholesterol blockbuster, come from intermediaries who originally purchased the drug in other European countries.[42]

As the European Union transitions to a common currency, two events occurred. First, pricing has become more transparent, and customers expect lower prices. For example, a pack of twenty aspirin cost 11 cents in Spain and 19 cents in Germany in 1997. Retailers in Germany expect a price close to the Spanish price, or they will buy from a Spanish distributor.[43] Second, there will be no foreign exchange cost. Heinz-Walter Kohl, head of corporate finance at Bayer, estimated the common European currency will save Bayer up to DM 50 million ($28.5 million) in exchange costs each year.[44]

Fluctuating currency values can also create opportunities for parallel imports, as observed earlier in this chapter. The fluctuating currency value in Indonesia has led to a flourishing parallel import trade. With the value of the dollar fluctuating between Rp 14,000 and Rp 17,000, customers can buy Epson inkjet printers and Toshiba notebooks on the gray market for $5 to $50 less than from an authorized dealer.[45] For the United States alone, parallel, or gray-market, annual volume was estimated at $130 billion. A typical example of a gray market is Lanza Research Company, which sold shampoo at a 40 percent discount to Libya and Malta. When Quality King International purchased the shampoo in Malta and reimported it into the United States, Lanza sued Quality King in federal court based on copyright law but lost the suit in the U.S. Supreme Court.[46] In a similar case, the European Court of Justice in Luxembourg decided that Tesco Stores Ltd. did not have a right to sell "gray market" Levi Strauss products in the European Economic Area (EEA). Tesco purchased the Levi goods from sources outside the EEA, but it could not prove that it had Levi's permission to purchase these goods from outside the EEA.[47]

Corporate users of international telecommunications services have begun to enjoy the benefits of parallel trading of long-distance telephone services. Although long-distance service from Japan to the United States is available through Kokusai Denshin Denwa (KDD) at a cost of $4.36 per minute, companies can use callback service for a rate of $1.77 per minute or less. The caller simply dials a number in the United States, which recognizes the call without answering it, then calls back and allows the user to take advantage of inexpensive phone rates.[48]

Global companies can deal with parallel, or gray, markets reactively or proactively. Once such practices occur, a firm may use several strategies in a reactive way. These strategies range from confronting the culprit to price-cutting, supply interference, and emphasis of product limitations all the way to acquisition of the culprit involved. Proactive strategies may be implemented to prevent the practice from occurring at all. A company may provide product differentiation solely to prevent gray markets from developing. Strategic pricing may be used to keep prices within limits. Cooperation may be achieved with dealers willing to cooperate. And, finally, companies may use strict legal enforcement of contracts and can even resort to lobbying governments with the aim of adding regulations that may prevent the practice. For example, international drug companies argued in hearings before the Israeli Knesset (parliament) that parallel imports endanger public health because of fake and fraudulent medicines.[49]

The pricing situation in the EU is especially interesting because of the introduction of the euro, which allows easy price comparisons from country to country. A study by the French *L'Express* found prices within Europe could vary by up to 500 percent. For example, a 1.5 liter of Coca-Cola cost .7 euro in Portugal and 1.9 euro in Finland; a Sony premium 180-minute videocassette cost 1.98 euro in Portugal and 10.52 euro in France. A proactive strategy to develop a European pricing corridor is recommended by some experts. The price corridor would take into account the price elasticities of different markets and maximize the potential European profit margin rather than gravitating to the lowest price in Europe.[50]

Product arbitrage will always occur when price differentials get too large and when transport costs are low in relation to product value. Global companies will have to monitor price differentials more closely for standardized products in particular. Products that are highly differentiated from country to country are less likely to be traded in the parallel market.

MANAGING EXPORT PRICE ESCALATION

The additional costs described earlier may raise the end-user price of an exported product substantially above its domestic price. This phenomenon, called export price escalation, may force a company to adopt either of two strategic patterns. First, a company may realize its price disadvantage and adjust the marketing mix to account for its "luxury" status. By adopting such a strategy, a company sacrifices volume to keep a unit price high. For example, in Guangzhou, China, Pizza Hut found that the typical price per person per meal was 40 to 50 renminbi (RMB), whereas a value meal at McDonald's was 16 to 25 RMB. Pizza Hut determined it was necessary to position itself as a casual dining restaurant with table service, rather than counter service, to differentiate its offerings from the fast-food restaurants.[51] Or a company may grant a "discount" on the standard domestic price to bring the end-user price more in line with prices paid by domestic customers. Such discounts may be justified under marginal-contribution pricing methods. Because of reduced marketing costs at the manufacturer's level, particularly when a foreign distributor is used, an export price equal to a domestic price is often not justified. Legal limits such as antidumping regulations prevent price reductions below a certain point. Customary margins, both wholesale and retail, may differ considerably among countries, with independent importers frequently requiring higher margins than domestic intermediaries do.

GLOBAL PRICING STRATEGIES

As global companies deal with market and environmental factors, they face two major strategic pricing alternatives. Essentially, the choice is between the global single-price strategy and the individualized country strategy.

To maximize a company's revenues, it seems logical to set prices on a market-by-market basis, looking in each market for the best combination of revenue versus volume to maximize profit. This strategy was common for many firms in the early part of their international development. For many products, however, noticeable price differences between markets are taken advantage of by independent companies or channel members, who see a profit from buying in lower-price markets and exporting products to high-price markets. For products that are relatively similar in many markets and for which transportation costs are not significant, substantial price differences will quickly result in the emergence of the gray market. As a result, fewer companies have the option of pricing on a market-by-market basis. As the markets become more transparent, the information flows more efficiently, and products become more similar, the trend away from market-by-market pricing is likely to continue.

McDonald's, the leading U.S. fast-food chain, has taken the route of pricing its products according to local market conditions. Its key product, the Big Mac, priced at $2.49 in the United States, ranged from $.89 in Malaysia to $3.06 in Switzerland. The third column in Table 10.3 shows the cost of a Big Mac in each country divided by its cost in the home market, giving the implied purchasing power of the local currency. Comparing these figures to the actual exchange rate, you can see which currencies are overvalued or undervalued based on the Big Mac; for example, the Swiss franc is overvalued by 53 percent, whereas the Argentine peso is undervalued by 68 percent and the South African rand is undervalued by 64 percent. Even though hamburgers are not a completely accurate measure of purchasing-power parity, and local prices may be distorted by trade barriers on beef, sales taxes, or discrepancies in property costs, academic studies of the Big Mac index have concluded that the strategy of investing in the most undervalued of the main currencies each year is profitable.[52] (See Table 10.3 for more comparisons.) Certainly, McDonald's can maximize its pricing according to the competitive forces of each individual country without much fear of parallel imports.

For many consumer products, there are still substantial price differences across many countries. For a price comparison of the cost of a movie ticket in major European cities, see Figure 10.4. Many theorize that large differences in prices will cause consumers to cross the border for a lower price. Thus, if a Swatch costs 39.2 euros in Belgium and 25.7 euros in Italy, or a bottle of Chanel No. 5 perfume is 42.2 euros in the Netherlands and 34.8 euros in Belgium, consumers will cross the border to spend less. However, the price differences often reflect the value-added tax (VAT), labor rates, regulatory burdens, transportation, or real estate cost differences. Mr. Jan Haars, group treasurer of Unilever, predicts about a 10 percent price difference will remain across Europe.[53]

The factors influencing pricing strategy standardization were studied in the manufacturing subsidiaries of global companies. The extent of international pricing strategy standardization is correlated to the degree of similarity between the home country and the host countries in terms of economic conditions, legal environment, customer characteristics, and stage of the product life cycle.[54] Employing a uniform pricing strategy on a global scale requires that a company, which can determine its prices in local currency, will always charge the same price everywhere when the price is translated into a base currency. In reality, this standardization becomes very difficult to achieve whenever different taxes, trade margins, and customs duties are involved. As a result, there are likely to be price differences due to factors not under the company's control. Keeping prices identical, even without uncontrollable factors,

Table 10.3 The Hamburger Standard

	Big Mac Prices		Implied PPP[a] of the Dollar	Actual $ Exchange Rate as of 30/03/99	Under (−)/ Over (+) Valuation Against the Dollar, %
	In Local Currency	In Dollars			
United States[b]	$2.49	2.49	—	—	—
Argentina	Peso12.60	.78	1.00	3.13	−68
Australia	A$3.00	1.62	1.20	1.86	−35
Brazil	Real3.60	1.55	1.45	2.34	−38
Britain	£1.99	2.88	1.25[c]	1.45[c]	+16
Canada	C$3.33	2.12	1.34	1.57	−15
Chile	Peso1400	2.16	562	655	−14
China	Yuan10.50	1.27	4.22	8.28	−49
Denmark	DKr24.75	2.96	9.94	8.38	+19
Euro area	Euro2.67	2.37	0.93[d]	.89[d]	+5
Hong Kong	HK$11.20	1.40	4.50	7.80	−42
Hungary	Forint459	1.32	184	272	−32
Indonesia	Rupiah16,000	1.71	6,426	9,430	−32
Japan	¥29.2	2.01	105	130	−19
Malaysia	M$5.04	1.33	2.02	3.80	−47
Mexico	Peso21.9	2.37	8.80	9.28	−5
New Zealand	NZ$3.95	1.77	1.59	2.24	−29
Poland	Zloty5.90	1.46	2.37	4.04	−41
Russia	Rouble39.00	1.25	15.70	31.20	−50
Singapore	S$3.30	1.81	1.33	1.82	−27
South Africa	Rand9.70	.87	3.90	10.90	−64
South Korea	Won3,100	2.36	1,245	1,304	−5
Sweden	SKr26.0	2.52	10.40	10.30	+1
Switzerland	SFr6.30	3.81	2.53	1.66	+53
Taiwan	NT$70.0	2.01	28.1	34.8	−19
Thailand	Baht55.0	1.27	22.1	43.3	−49

a. Purchasing-power partiy: local price divided by price in United States.
b. Average of New York, Chicago, San Francisco, and Atlanta.
c. Dollars per pound.
d. Dollars per euro.
Source: "The Hamburger Standard," *Economist,* April 3, 2002, p. 27. Copyright © 2002 The Economist Newspaper Ltd. All rights reserved. Reprinted with permission. Further reproduction prohibited. www.economist.com

Figure 10.4: Price of a Movie Ticket in Major European Cities and New York City

Euro-zone cities

Source: From "Prices at the Europlex," *The Economist*, March 27, 1999, p. 110. Copyright © 1999 The Economist Newspaper Ltd. Reprinted with permission. Further reproduction prohibited. www.economist.com

is a challenge. Firms may start with identical prices in various countries but soon find that prices must change to accommodate often substantial currency fluctuations.

Although it is becoming increasingly clear for many companies that market-by-market pricing strategies will cause difficulties, many firms have found that changing to a uniform pricing policy is rather like pursuing a moving target. Even when a global pricing policy is adopted, a company must carefully monitor price levels in each country and avoid large gaps that can cause problems when independent or gray-market forces move in and take advantage of large price differentials.

FINANCING GLOBAL TRANSACTIONS

As many global marketers have observed, the ability to make financing available at low cost can become the deciding factor when it comes to beating competitors. In the context of global marketing, financing should be understood in its broadest sense (see Figure 10.5). Not only does it consist of direct credits to the buyer, it also includes a range of activities that enable the customer to afford the purchase. In this section, we examine financing provided by the selling company, as well as financing through the financial community and government-sponsored agencies.

RISKS

Financing global marketing transactions involves a host of risks over and above those encountered by strictly domestic operations. Global companies have to be aware of these risks and understand the methods available for reducing risk to an acceptable

Figure 10.5: Financing Global Marketing Transactions

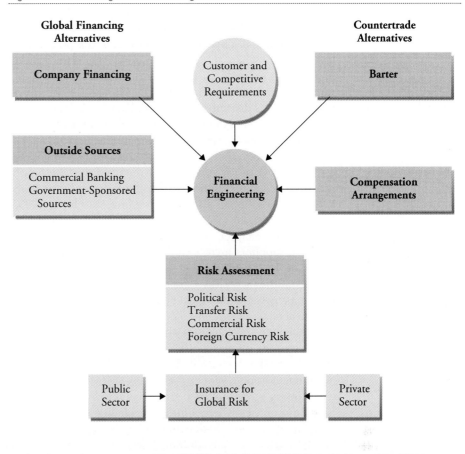

level. The four major risks are commercial risk, foreign currency risk, transfer risk, and political risk.

Commercial risk refers to the buyer's ability to pay for the products or services ordered. This risk is also typical for a domestic operation. As a result, companies are accustomed to checking the financial stability of their customers and may even have internally approved credit limits. Although checking credit references in a domestic environment poses no great difficulty, credit information is not always available in every market. Companies can rely on their banks or on credit reporting agencies where such organizations exist. Past experience with a commercial customer abroad may often be the only indicator of a firm's financial stability.

Foreign currency risk exists whenever a company bills in a currency other than its own.[55] For U.S. companies billing in Japanese yen, a currency risk exists because the value of the yen versus the dollar is subject to market fluctuations and therefore cannot be determined at the outset. Foreign currency risk grows with the length of credit terms and with the instability of a foreign currency. For example, in June 1998, the dollar was worth 142 yen, a drop of 40 percent from the 1995 high of 102 yen to the dollar. This weakening of the yen meant that all countries exporting to Japan found their product more expensive when prices were converted to yen. Also, South Korea and Taiwan, whose products compete with Japanese exports, found lower prices when the weak yen was converted to dollars, sterling, or Swiss francs.[56] For example, in 1997, Andrew Carol Jr., president and CEO of the American Automobile Association, stated, "The free fall of the yen is becoming a serious problem that is disrupting business planning and threatening many U.S. exports opportunities. Having depreciated more than 50 percent from its peak in 1995, it has become a run-away train that is threatening serious market disruptions."[57] On the other hand, when the yen started to recover in 1999, its appreciation made Japanese exports more expensive. Sony reported that the 5 percent appreciation in the yen cost the firm 54 billion yen in the last quarter of 1998. Nissan predicted a 60-billion-yen loss for its fiscal year ending March 31, 1999.[58] Suppliers can protect themselves against foreign currency fluctuations, as we described in more detail earlier in this chapter.

When suppliers invoice in their own currency, they shift the currency risk to the customer. The customer may not be in a position to cover that risk, as is the case in many countries with less sophisticated financial markets. In such a case, the exporting company frequently must choose between selling in a foreign currency or having no deal at all.

Although the customer may be able to pay, payments are often delayed by bureaucracies, creating a *transfer risk*. Transfer delays prevail in countries where the foreign exchange market is controlled and where the customer has to apply for the purchase of foreign currency before payment takes place. Delays of up to 180 days beyond the credit terms agreed to are not unusual and add to the costs of the exporter or supplier. In countries where a foreign exchange shortage prevents immediate payment of all foreign currency—denominated debts, complex debt restructuring negotiations may take place, causing additional delays. Many countries, including Brazil, Mexico, Argentina, Turkey, Poland, and Zaire, have had to negotiate such extensions at one time or another.

Financing for global marketing operations is also subject to *political risk*, which includes war, revolution, insurgency, or civil unrest, any of which may result in nonpayment of accounts receivable. For example, Argentina underwent significant turmoil in 2001 and 2002, when five presidents came and went in a two-week period, and all savings accounts were frozen, crippling the banking system, and forcing the withdrawal of foreign banking subsidiaries like Credit Agricole of France and Scotiabank of Canada. The banking crisis resulted in consumer demonstrations and rioting, a rise in unemployment to 23 percent, and a decline in the economy by 10 to 15 percent. As the Argentine congress considered converting all savings to bonds and reducing the size of the government, President Duhalde attempted to reach an agreement with the International Monetary Fund (IMF). The political and economic situation in Argentina resulted in major losses for most companies.[59]

The global marketer needs to understand the risks of providing financing to customers. In cases when the supplier assumes all global risks, companies may want to build extra costs into their prices. Smaller price adjustments may be required when only a portion of the global credit risk is carried.

CUSTOMER-ARRANGED VERSUS
SUPPLIER-ARRANGED FINANCING

As discussed in this section, financing arranged by suppliers goes beyond the open-account practices. In this context, supplier financing is viewed as any term beyond the usual thirty to ninety days, which is customary for open-account shipment.

Because credit risks are higher for clients abroad, companies prefer shorter payment terms with foreign clients. However, many customers may not be able to purchase under shortened credit terms. Consequently, companies may charge an interest rate on the outstanding amount. When companies cannot obtain at least market interest rates, they may try to capture the additional cash through higher prices. Most clients today are adept at comparing total costs themselves, however, and opportunities for hiding interest costs behind higher list prices are limited.

Most companies do not consider themselves to be in the business of financing their customers, and they prefer to assist clients in finding suitable financing opportunities. One such exception is financing without recourse (explained below), a relatively new method for financing shipments abroad.

SOURCES OF FINANCING

Companies can choose from a wide selection of alternatives to finance global marketing transactions: traditional financing through commercial banks, government-sponsored loans, or countertrade. The global marketer is increasingly expected to be knowledgeable about complicated financial arrangements. Buyers compare acquisition costs, including any necessary financing, and providing such financing thus becomes a matter for marketing management to handle. The following sections offer a general background on the most common financing alternatives practiced by many global companies today.

COMMERCIAL BANKS

Commercial banks, whether domestic or foreign, are usually willing to finance transactions only to first-rate credit risk companies. This fact makes financing unavailable to all but the largest companies. Furthermore, commercial banks avoid long-term financing and prefer short maturities. When selecting a commercial bank, inquire about the following: the size of the global department, the number and locations of foreign branches or correspondent banks, charges for letters of credit, and experience with government financing programs.

Commercial banks that have loaned heavily to developing countries have recently experienced difficulties with repayment and interest payments on outstanding loan portfolios. Therefore, banks located in developed countries have hesitated to lend additional sums to developing countries, forcing exporters to look elsewhere to help their clients find financing.

Clients outside the developed countries of Europe and Asia have also found local financing difficult. Foreign buyers in developing countries are increasingly dependent on financing from abroad, especially for puchases in currencies other than their own. With commercial banks only partially able to close the gap, both buyers and suppliers are availing themselves of other financing sources.

FORFAITING: FINANCING WITHOUT RECOURSE.[60] *Forfaiting*, or financing without recourse, means that the seller of merchandise can transfer a claim, resulting from a transaction in the form of a bill of exchange, to a forfaiting house by including the term *without recourse* as part of the endorsement. The collection risk is thus transferred to the forfaiting house, and the seller, on presentation of documents, receives the full amount minus a discount for the entire credit period. Generally, the forfaiting houses prefer working with invoices guaranteed by foreign banks or governments.[61] The discount varies with the country risk and the currency chosen for financing. Typical maturities range from six months to several years. Forfaiting specialists include Holbrook Forfaiting Limited (www.holbrookforfaiting.co.uk), London Forfaiting Company PLC (www.londonforfaiting.com), or Credit Suisse (www.credit-suisse.ch). The Association of Forfaiters in the Americas (www.afia-forfaiting.org) is also an excellent source of information.

Nonrecourse financing offers the advantage of selling products over the medium term at market rates. Such transactions are not possible through commercial banks. An exporter may obtain a firm quote on a business deal ahead of time, allowing inclusion of the discount rate into the price calculation. This practice ensures that the net payout meets normal profitability standards. Forfaiting has become very popular for companies in developed countries selling to developing markets in eastern Europe and Latin America. The export forfaiting market is estimated to be $30 to $50 billion, or 5 percent of world trade.[62] For example, when Sortex, a California manufacturer of agricultural processing equipment, sold $100,000 worth of equipment to a company in Argentina, it turned to London Forfaiting. The forfaiting loan was guaranteed by the buyer's bank, and the equipment was shipped. After Sortex received the paperwork from the customer and its local bank that the equipment had arrived in Argentina, London Forfaiting paid Sortex.[63]

GOVERNMENT-SPONSORED FINANCING: THE EXPORT-IMPORT BANK

With the ability to assemble the best financing package often determining the sale of capital equipment or other large-volume transactions, governments all over the world have realized that government-sponsored banks can foster exports and therefore employment. Government-subsidized financing now exceeds financing formerly provided by commercial banks and exporters. For this purpose, the United States created its Export-Import Bank (Eximbank) in 1934. Other countries, particularly members of the Organization for Economic Cooperation and Development (OECD), have established their own export banks, also aimed at assisting their respective exporters with the financing of large transactions. Japan committed funds to provide 15 trillion yen of insurance coverage per year for developing countries and political risk insurance for Japanese companies investing overseas. The export insurance plan was to cover up to 97.5 percent of the value for prepaid contracts.[64]

The Export-Import Bank (www.exim.gov) and affiliated institutions, the Foreign Credit Insurance Association (www.fcia.com), and the Private Export Funding Corporation (www.pefco.com) offer several services to U.S. exporters. Eximbank has special services for short-, medium-, and long-term financing requirements. In 2002, the Eximbank authorized $12.6 billion in loan guarantees and insurance, which supported $15.5 billion of U.S. exports.[65]

SHORT-TERM FINANCING. Financing requirements of 180 days or less are considered short-term. For such commitments, Eximbank does not make direct financing available. Instead, it offers export credit insurance to the U.S. exporter. This insurance covers the exporter for commercial risk, such as nonpayment by the foreign buyer; political risk, such as war, revolution, insurrection, and expropriation; and currency inconvertibility. The cost of such insurance averages less than half of 1 percent per $100 of gross invoice value. With such insurance, the exporter has the choice of carrying accounts receivable on the company records or refinancing with a commercial bank at domestic interest rates. In general, commercial risks are insured up to 90 percent of the invoiced value. Political risks are covered for up to 100 percent of the merchandise value, depending on the type of policy selected.

MEDIUM-TERM FINANCING. Eximbank classifies terms ranging from 181 days to five years as medium-term. It has four special programs to serve exporters: the medium-term export credit insurance programs (FCIA), the U.S. Commercial Bank Guarantee Program, the Discount Loan Program, and the Cooperative Financing Facility.

Several insurance alternatives are available through FCIA. Eximbank will insure each specific transaction, provided the foreign buyer makes a cash payment of 15 percent on or before delivery, subject to a deductible of 10 percent. Through the cooperation of nearly three hundred U.S. commercial banks, Eximbank organized the U.S. Commercial Bank Guarantee Program. Under this program, Eximbank offers protection against commercial and political risks on debts acquired by U.S. banks from U.S. exporters. This coverage is now extended to more than 140 countries. The interest rate is set by the commercial bank according to prevailing domestic market conditions. For example, in 2002, Eximbank approved a $3 million medium-term loan guarantee for the sale of Caterpillar equipment to OAO Stroytransgaz, a pipeline developer in Moscow.[66]

LONG-TERM FINANCING. Long-term financing by Eximbank extends from five to ten years. Under special circumstances, as in the case of conventional or nuclear power plants, financing may be arranged for longer periods. Financing is arranged either by direct credit to the foreign buyer or by a guarantee of repayment of private financing arranged by the buyer. Eximbank requires a 15 percent down payment by the foreign buyer and assurance that private financing is not possible on similar terms. In the past, foreign airlines and utilities have made frequent use of such terms to finance purchases of aircraft and power-generating equipment.

In general, Eximbank programs do not extend direct financing to the U.S. exporter. Rather, the bank closes the gap between commercial bank financing and foreign buyer needs by offering guarantees or financing for the foreign buyer.

THE VALUE OF EXIMBANK LOANS TO U.S. EXPORTERS. Eximbank has supported more than $400 billion worth of exports over sixty years. In June 2002, President Bush signed the reauthorization legislation to fund Eximbank until September 2006. Supporting approximately $15 billion in export sales per year, 90 percent of the bank's transactions and 18 percent of the dollar value is for small businesses.[67] A U.S. company that relied heavily on Eximbank financing was J. I. Case.

Ellen Robinson, Case Corporation's vice president for communications and government affairs, identified over 235 companies in thirty states that had benefited as sub-suppliers to Case on Eximbank-financed exports.[68]

Eximbank support of U.S. exporters depends on funding from the U.S. government. In the past, U.S. exporters have lobbied heavily to expand Eximbank funding, hoping to receive more loans at more favorable rates. However, many critics argue that Eximbank serves large firms that are already profitable. The political debate surrounding Eximbank is expected to continue, and its lending authority will vary as Congress appropriates differing fund levels from year to year. The Office of Management and Budget (OMB) has recommended that the federal government overhaul U.S. export functions by merging Eximbank of the United States with two other agencies: the Overseas Private Investment Corp., which provides political risk insurance, and the Trade and Development Agency, which develops feasibility studies for overseas export and investment in emerging markets.[69]

Eximbank has created a program that is used by over 1,100 U.S. small business exporters per year. Small businesses can use the short-term interest rates of Eximbank (6.5 to 7.5 percent in mid-1999) to offer attractive credit terms to their overseas customers. Also, the Eximbank Insurance Program, which costs about $940 on a $100,000 order, protects the business against payment default. Eximbank will pay 95 percent of the invoice if the buyer goes bankrupt, or 100 percent if the buyer cannot pay for political reasons, such as war.[70]

FINANCIAL ENGINEERING: A NEW MARKETING TOOL. With financing costs becoming ever-more important for capital goods, many companies have moved toward exploiting the best financial deal from bases around the world. A company with manufacturing bases in several countries may bid on a contract from several subsidiaries and thus let the client select the most advantageous package, or it may preselect the subsidiary that will bid based on available financing. Devising such financial packages is known as *financial engineering,* and it is practiced by independent specialists located in leading financial centers and by international banks that have developed expertise in this field.

Massey-Ferguson, Ltd., a Canadian farm machinery manufacturer, is an example of a firm that uses financial engineering.[71] Massey-Ferguson had traditionally supplied tractors to Turkey from its U.K. plants. Turkey experienced balance-of-payments difficulty, and the company had problems obtaining credit for the country. Massey-Ferguson looked to its other manufacturing bases for new sources of financing. The best deal was offered by the government of Brazil, a country eager to expand its exports. Brazilians helped convince the Turkish customer Mafer to buy Brazilian-made equipment in U.S. dollars. Massey-Ferguson sold 7,200 tractors worth $53 million to a Brazilian agency, which in turn sold to the Turkish buyer. Massey-Ferguson was to be paid cash, and a Brazilian state agency guaranteed payment. Thus, Brazil was able to take business of about twenty thousand tractors annually from the United Kingdom because it assumed all risk for Massey-Ferguson.

Other companies are now institutionalizing financial engineering in their global operations. Some maintain full-time specialists at their global divisions, specialists who are prepared to advise operating divisions on financial engineering opportunities in bidding. Allowing customers to select the best financing options from any

tanker ships ranging from 28,000 to 65,000 tons. The proceeds of these transactions were to be used to expand the ongoing PepsiCo business in Russia by expanding Pepsi-Cola into national distribution and to fund the expansion of the Pizza Hut restaurant chain.[79]

COMPENSATION ARRANGEMENTS. Compensation arrangements are transactions that include payment in merchandise or foreign exchange. Depending on the type of arrangement, the method or structure of the compensation transaction may change. One usually speaks of a compensation transaction when the value of an export delivery is offset by an import transaction, or vice versa. Compensation transactions are typical for large governmental purchases, such as for defense, when a government wants to obtain some extra exports for the import of defense systems.[80] Compensation transactions may be classified into several categories, as described below.

Full Versus Partial Compensation.   Full compensation is similar to barter because a 100 percent mutual transfer of goods takes place. However, deliveries are made and paid for separately. By signing the sales agreement, the exporter commits to purchasing products or services at an amount equal to that specified in the export contract. An option exists to sell such a commitment to a third party who may take over the commitment from the exporter for a fee. For example, Indonesia agreed to barter crude palm oil in exchange for Indian rice and railroad tracks.[81]

Under *partial* compensation, the exporter receives a portion of the purchase price in hard currency and the remainder in merchandise. The exporter will not be able to convert such merchandise into cash until a buyer can be found, and even then only at a discount. A partial compensation transaction was concluded in 1998 by an Italian company building electric services in Thailand. The Italian company agreed to take 30 percent of the value of the contract, or 218 million baht, in agricultural products, including rubber, rice, and tapioca.[82]

Parallel Deals.   In a parallel deal, the exporter agrees to accept the merchandise equivalent of a given percentage of the export amount. Payment is received on delivery. This arrangement is intended to offset the outflow of wealth from the country when a very large purchase has been made. Within a given amount of time, the exporter searches for a specific amount of merchandise that can be bought from the country or company that purchased the products originally. Eastern European countries often include a penalty fee in case the western exporter defaults on the countertrade portion of the arrangement. Boeing agreed to increase its purchases of titanium from Russia's Verhnyaya Salda metallurgical plant from 2,000 to 2,200 tons in a deal that secured Boeing's sale of ten 737-400s to Aeroflot Russian International Airlines. Offset deals are a type of parallel agreement gaining popularity today, because all parties are benefiting.[83]

Linked Deals.   Linked deals, sometimes called junctions, are a form of countertrade not frequently used. A western importer finds a western exporter willing to deliver merchandise to a country in eastern Europe or to a developing nation. At the same time, the importer is released from a counterpurchase agreement by paying a premium to the exporter, which in turn organizes the counterpurchase.

Triangular Compensation. Triangular compensation arrangements, also called *switch trades*, involve three countries. The western exporter delivers hard goods (salable merchandise) to an importing country, typically in eastern Europe. As payment, the importing country may transfer hard goods (easily salable merchandise) or soft goods (heavily discounted merchandise) to a third country in the West or in eastern Europe, which then reimburses the western exporter for the goods received. Such negotiations may become complex and time consuming. The assistance of skilled switch traders is often required to ensure profitable participation by the western exporter.

Marc Rich & Co., a Swiss commodities firm, has been very successful in the republics of the former Soviet Union with complicated triangular arrangements. For example, in one deal, the company bought seventy thousand tons of raw sugar in Brazil and shipped it to Ukraine to be processed. It paid for the processing with some of the sugar, then shipped thirty thousand tons of the refined sugar six thousand miles to several huge Siberian oil refineries, which needed the sugar for their work force. Strapped for hard currency, the oil refineries paid with 130,000 tons of low-grade A-76 gasoline, which was shipped to Mongolia. The Mongolians paid for the gasoline with thirty-five thousand tons of copper concentrate, which was shipped across the border to Kazakhstan, where it was refined to copper metal and shipped to a Baltic port. Marc Rich & Co. then sold the copper on the world market for hard currency and a profit.[84]

Offset Deals. One of the fastest-growing types of countertrade is the offset deal. In an offset transaction, the selling company guarantees to use some products or services from the buying country in the final product. These transactions are particularly common when large purchases, such as public utilities or defense-related equipment, from government-type agencies are involved. The South African government has used offset deals very effectively to stimulate local industrial development in exchange for purchasing military equipment. In 1998, Saab and British Aerospace completed the sale of twenty-eight Gripen fighter planes by agreeing to industrial purchasing and investment in South Africa, valued at 480 percent of the contract value.[85]

Cooperation Agreements. Cooperation agreements are special types of compensation deals extending over longer periods of time. They may be called product purchase transactions, buyback deals, or pay-as-you-earn deals. Compensation usually refers to an exchange of unrelated merchandise, such as coal for machine tools. Cooperation usually involves related goods, such as payment for new textile machinery with the output produced by these machines.

Although sale of large equipment or of a whole factory can sometimes be clinched only by a cooperation agreement involving buyback of plant output, long-term negative effects must be considered before any deal is concluded. In industries such as steel or chemicals, the effect of high-volume buyback arrangements between western exporters of manufacturing technology and eastern European importers has been devastating. Western countries, especially in Europe, have been flooded with surplus products. European Union members established a general policy on cooperation arrangements to avoid further disruption of their domestic industries.

International Harvester is one U.S. company with experience in buyback arrangements.[86] In 1973, the company sold the basic design and technology for a tractor crawler to Poland. At the same time, International Harvester agreed to buy back tractor components manufactured by the Polish plant. These components were shipped to a subassembly plant in the United Kingdom that served the European market. In 1976, the company sold Hungary the design for an axle. To offset this sale, the company agreed to purchase complete axles for highway trucks.

DANGERS IN COMPENSATION DEALS. The greatest danger in compensation arrangements stems from the difficulty of finding a buyer for the merchandise accepted as part of the transaction. Such transactions are often concluded with organizations of countries in which industry is under government control. Because prices for goods in these countries are not determined by the supply-and-demand forces of a free-market economy, merchandise transferred under compensation arrangements is often overvalued compared to open-market products. In addition, such merchandise, obviously not salable on its own, may be of low quality. As a result, the exporter may be able to sell the merchandise only at a discount. The size of these discounts may vary considerably, from 10 percent to 33 percent of product value.[87] The astute exporter will raise the price of the export contract to cover such potential discounts on the compensating transaction.

The experience of a multinational chemical company serves as a good example of the difficulties encountered in barter deals. The company had sold $8 million worth of chemicals to Zimbabwe and agreed to take payment in tobacco, which was sold to Egypt along with another $12 million worth of chemicals. To pay for this transaction, Egypt offered a whole range of basic commodities and materials in lieu of the $20 million cash price. A specialty company was engaged to select appropriate products, find buyers elsewhere in the world, and collect the cash. All told, the $20 million deal with Egypt involved ten different countries and six different product categories (see Figure 10.7).[88]

PRECAUTIONS FOR COUNTERTRADE. A study of fifty-seven British companies involved in countertrade reported that the most difficult problems with it were that there was no in-house use for the goods offered and the negotiations were complex and time consuming.[89] At the conclusion of the sales agreement, the exporter should obtain a clear notion of the merchandise offered for countertrade. The description, origin, quality, quantity, delivery schedules, price, and purchasing currency in local or hard currency should be determined. With a detailed description given to a specialized trader, an estimate on the applicable discount may be rendered. The sale price of merchandise offered may be structured to include the difference between purchase amount and actual cash value. It is paramount that the western exporter not agree to any price before these other items are determined. Maintaining flexibility in negotiations requires skill and patience.

ORGANIZING FOR COUNTERTRADE. International companies are moving toward organizing countertrade for higher leverage. Many larger firms have established specialized units whose single purpose is to engage in countertrade. A study of organizations conducting countertrade found that the purchasing function of many companies

Figure 10.7: Countertrade with International Chemical Company

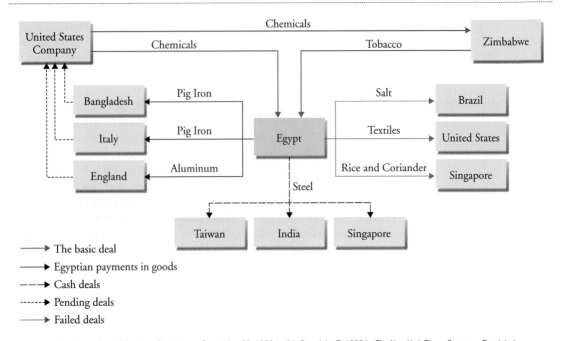

Source: *New York Times*, Special Business Supplement, September 25, 1988, p. 34. Copyright © 1988 by The New York Times Company. Reprinted by permission.

was often unaware of the opportunity for countertade transactions, and the legal departments and treasury departments were not farmiliar with the countertrade processes.[90] The countertrade associations can provide information on the industry itself and on industry specialists. Countertrade associations include International Reciprocal Trade Association (www.irta.com), American Countertrade Organization (www.countertrade.org), Australian Countertrade Association, and Asia Pacific Countertrade Association (http://www.apca.net). Many independent trading companies offer countertrading services.

Daihatsu, a Japanese automobile manufacturer, offers a good example of how a willingness to engage in countertrade can lead to a competitive advantage. Although the company was the smallest Japanese automobile manufacturer, Daihatsu managed to become the market leader for imported cars in eastern European countries such as Poland and Hungary. In Hungary, the company went as far as to schedule its parties for retiring Japanese workers through Hungary, allowing that country to earn additional foreign exchange, which resulted in the sale of another forty cars. The extravagant parties were planned in Japan, but all expenses were paid by Daihatsu Hungary, which was given hard currency by Daihatsu Japan.[91]

FINANCING EXPORT OPERATIONS

Although cash transactions can be desirable, this form of payment is rarely used. The shipment may be in transit for weeks or even months at a time, thus tying up the importer's capital. Also, the importer does not really know what was shipped until the products are in possession. Consequently, most forms of payment are designed to protect both parties. When an exporter knows the foreign clients and fully trusts their financial integrity, shipments on *open account* may be arranged. Usually, the terms are arranged so that the foreign client can wait to make payment until the goods have arrived at their final destination. In this case, however, the exporter will have risked capital in the transaction.

Consignment sales is the method whereby credit is extended by the exporter. The exporter is not compensated until the products are physically sold by the importer. The consignment goods are often held in free trade zones or in a bonded warehouse until they are sold by an agent or needed by the buyer. With appropriate payment, the consigned goods will be released to the buyer. This approach increases the exporter's capital costs because no funds are received until the goods are collected by the buyer.

To control both ownership and payment terms for international shipments, traders have developed the *draft* or *bill of exchange*. The draft is a formal order that the exporter issues to the importer, specifying when the sum is to be paid to the third party, usually the exporter's bank. A triangular relationship is established with the issuer of the draft, the exporter as drawer, the importer as drawee, and the payee as the recipient of the payment. Because the draft is a negotiable instrument, it can be sold, transferred, and discounted, and the exporter can use it to finance the shipment.

Exporters may use either a *sight draft* or a *time draft*. Sight drafts are used when the exporter desires to control the shipment beyond the point of original shipment, usually to ensure payment. In practice, the exporter endorses the bill of lading (B/L) and adds a sight draft on the correspondent bank of the exporter's bank. Along with the bill of lading and sight draft, other documents, such as the packing list, invoice, consular invoices, and certificate of insurance, will be provided. Once the documents have arrived, a transfer, by way of endorsement to the importer, will be made on payment in full at that bank. Consequently, the importer cannot take possession of the goods until payment has been made (on sight of documents). But the importer is assured that the goods have actually been shipped, as indicated by the accompanying documents.

Transactions can also be made in time drafts. This method specifies the period in which the payment is to be made. The payment period, beginning on receipt of the documents, may be thirty, sixty, or ninety days, or longer. Not only will drafts allow the exporter to control the shipment until proper payment occurs, but they also allow further financing by having the properly signed draft discounted with a bank before the agreed-upon payment term expires. In such a case, the banking system assumes the role of the creditor, thus reducing the capital risks of the exporter.

Also used quite frequently is a financial instrument called a *letter of credit*. With a letter of credit, the importer, or foreign buyer, finances the transaction, thus alleviating the credit burden for the exporter. With a letter of credit, the responsibility is in the hands of the importer. Once informed that the exporter will ship with a letter of credit (L/C), the importer will ask the bank to write an irrevocable L/C with a bank specified by the exporter on the latter's behalf. The importer will usually instruct the bank on the conditions of payment, typically submission of all necessary documents, including a bill of lading. When the exporter has placed the shipment on the appropriate vessel, the exporter will go to the bank and turn over all documents associated with the transaction. When satisfied, the exporter's bank will pay out the funds and debit the importer's bank, which will in turn debit the importing company.

Overall, the irrevocable L/C has distinct advantages for the exporter because it represents a firm order that, once issued by the bank, cannot be canceled or revoked. For example, a company that sells machinery built to order can use the irrevocable L/C to guarantee that payment will be made. Time limits are placed on the L/C to protect the importer against an open-ended transaction. Should the exporter fail to ship and submit documents before the expiration date, the L/C would expire without any further responsibility on the part of the importer to finance the transaction. Any bank charges associated with the transaction are usually paid by the buyer. Letters of credit are normally prepared at commercial banks by a staff of back-office clerks. The paperwork required for each letter of credit, as well as the possibility of typing errors, can make the issuing of these instruments slow. Pressure from exporters has motivated many banks to automate this process with computer technology, thus speeding up the process so payments can proceed quickly.[92]

Letters of credit are widely used instruments, and they have developed into several specialized forms over and above the standard, irrevocable L/C described above. The following additional forms exist:

Revolving or *periodic letters of credit* allow for a repetition of the same transaction as soon as the previous amount has been paid by the bank that originated the L/C.

Cumulative letters of credit cover payments of partial shipments and/or the use of the unused portion of the L/C for another transaction between the same parties.

Red clause letters of credit permit partial cash payments to the beneficiary, or exporter, as an advance on the shipment without any documentation. Final payments are made only against full documentation, however.

Back-to-back letters of credit are based on an earlier L/C. This procedure may be done if an exporter, in whose name an L/C was opened by a foreign client, will use the original L/C as a basis or security to issue a second L/C for a supplier of materials connected with that particular transaction.

Circular letters of credit are issued without designating any particular bank. The exporter may send documents to the issuing bank or present them to any bank, which will send them on for collection.

Performance letters of credit guarantee the completion of a contract undertaken abroad. They can be drawn upon if the exporter fails to meet performance requirements; thus, they are also known under the term *performance bonds*.[93]

Letters of credit can be a costly and time-consuming way to do business. The World Trade Centers Association is a not-for-profit group that provides trade-related services to 500,000 companies through a network of 327 centers in ninety-seven countries, and it has developed an electronic letter of credit alternative. The new approach, called TradeCard, reduces paperwork by 80 percent and shortens processing time by 60 percent. The product is available through www.tradecard.bm.[94] In addition to TradeCard, several banks now allow customers to initiate, amend, and track letters of credit through the bank web site on the Internet.[95] It is expected that export documentation, financing, and insurance will all eventually be done via the Internet.

When a company exports to a politically volatile area or to a new customer, guaranteeing payment of invoices is always a concern. A letter of credit is a relatively safe instrument for guaranteeing payment. In some cases, letters of credit may not be acceptable to the buyer, or they may not be practical. In the United States, exporters can turn to the Foreign Credit Insurance Association (FCIA) for assistance. The FCIA is an association of fifty marine and insurance casualty companies created in 1961 to insure U.S. exporters of goods and services against commercial and political risks. There are numerous risks associated with any foreign buyer. The firm can go out of business, the local government can change standards, or natural disasters such as floods or earthquakes can eliminate the buyer's ability to pay. FCIA offers insurance to protect against a buyer's failure to pay. Most developed countries have some type of export insurance program similar to FCIA.

Some companies that market major infrastructure projects, such as roads, airports, telecommunication systems, and ports, find that few companies or customers can go directly to capital markets for financing. In 2000, for example, Chile was the only Latin American country still considered an investment-grade risk by U.S. rating agencies. In February 2000, Moody's Investor Service announced it might grant Mexico investment-grade status.[96] For most other projects, customers or suppliers will have to find loans from international commercial banks. Helping customers gain access to international financing can often be the key to clinching a major project or deal.

As we have seen, numerous options are available for arranging for payment in export transactions. The exporting company can, of course, select the particular type of transaction, always keeping in mind the needs and requirements of the buyer—who may, if offered better credit terms elsewhere, decide to place an order with a different company. The payment process is an important part of the transaction between the buyer and the seller in an export situation; it can minimize the risks of exchange rate fluctuations and the process of dealing with a distant buyer or seller. Experienced exporters study government assistance and financing programs, looking for creative ways to use these programs for the benefit of the buyer. Australian companies can rely on the government-owned Export Finance and Insurance Corporation (EFIC) to assist in both the financing of exporters' capital needs and the financing of customers' purchases. EFIC underwrites about $6 billion worth of exports annually. Australian exporters of ferries were able to use EFIC finance and thus compete effectively with exporters elsewhere to secure several contracts in Asia. Without the creative use of EFIC, these contracts would not have been concluded.[97]

CONCLUSIONS

Managing pricing policies for a global firm is an especially challenging task. The global marketer is confronted with several uncontrollable factors deriving from the economic, legal, and regulatory environments, all of which have an impact on how prices are established in various countries. Though these influences are usually quite manageable in any given country, pricing across many markets means coping with price differentials that evolve out of environmental factors at work in various combinations in different countries. Managing these price differentials and keeping them within tolerable limits are major tasks in global pricing.

One of the most critical factors affecting price levels is foreign exchange rates. Today, managers find currencies moving both up and down, and the swings have assumed magnitudes that may substantially affect the competitiveness of a company. Understanding the factors that shape the directions of the foreign exchange market and mastering the technical tools that protect firms against large swings have become required skills for the global marketer. If a company can make itself less vulnerable to exchange rate movements, compared to its competitors, it may gain additional competitive advantage.

Because the relevant factors that affect price levels on an international scale are always fluctuating, the global pricing task is a never-ending process in which each day may bring new problems to be resolved. If a company is slow to adapt or makes a wrong judgment, the market is very quick at adapting and at exploiting these weaknesses. As long as uncontrollable factors such as currency rates and inflation are subject to considerable fluctuations, the pricing strategies of international companies will have to remain under constant review. The ultimate goal is to minimize the gap between the price levels of various markets.

In this chapter, we have also examined the rather technical aspects of trade financing and countertrade. Many executives have realized that they cannot leave these trade forms to the occasional specialist but must use them proficiently as a competitive weapon in the aggressive global arena. If knowledge of financial engineering and countertrade is to become a competitive advantage, marketing executives negotiating such transactions must master the relevant techniques. Global companies will be forced to train their executives in these aspects of trade. We can expect an increasing amount of world trade to involve one or the other of these techniques.

As competition in many industries increases, companies that have maintained a policy of "cash or no deal" now face the situation of "countertrade or no deal." Companies established in industrialized countries have seen that expansion into developing countries and countries poor in hard currency requires a willingness to engage in countertrade. Understanding countertrade has become a prerequisite for a global marketing executive.

Questions for Discussion

1. Discuss the difficulty or desirability of having a standardized worldwide price for a company's products.

2. Why should a company avoid pricing its products in each market according to local factors?

3. How will the establishment of the euro affect consumer pricing in Europe?

4. You are an exporter of industrial installations and you have received a $100,000 order from a Japanese customer. The job will take six months to complete and will be paid in full at that time. Now your Japanese customer has called you to request a price quote in yen. What will you quote him or her?

5. What factors may influence McDonald's to price its Big Mac differently throughout the countries of Latin America?

6. What strategies, other than through pricing, do companies have for combating parallel imports?

7. What should be the U.S. government's position on the issue of parallel imports? Should the government take any particular actions?

8. What is meant by the term *financial engineering*?

9. How should a firm approach the decision on whether to insure its exports?

10. Explain the major forms of countertrade. Under what circumstances should a company enter into such transactions?

11. What are the major risks to a firm engaging in countertrade?

For Further Reading

Assmus, Gert, and Carsten Wiese. "How to Address the Gray Market Threat Using Price Coordination." *Sloan Management Review,* 1995, vol. 36, no. 3, pp. 31–42.

Cavusgil, S. Tamer. "Pricing for Global Markets." *Columbia Journal of World Business,* Winter 1996, pp. 66–78.

Davis, H. Thomas, Jr. "Transfer Prices in the Real World—10 Steps Companies Should Take Before It Is Too Late." *CPA Journal,* October 1994, vol. 64, no. 10, pp. 82–83.

Dolan, Robert J., and Hermann Simon. *Power Pricing.* New York: Free Press, 1996.

Forman, Howard, and Richard Lancioni. "The Determinants of Pricing Strategies for Industrial Products in International Markets." *Journal of Business to Business Marketing,* 2002, vol. 9, no. 2, pp. 29–64.

Frazer, Jill Andresky. "Controlling Global Taxes." *Inc.,* August 1993, p. 35.

Glowacki, Roman, and Leon Zurawicki. "Marketing for Hard Currency in Polish Domestic Markets." *Journal of Global Marketing,* vol. 4, no. 4, 1991, p. 85.

Horlick, Gary N., and Eleanor C. Shea. "The World Trade Organization Antidumping Agreement." *Journal of World Trade,* February 1995, vol. 29, no. 1, pp. 5–31.

Huddleson, Patricia, and Linda K. Good. "The Price-Quality Relationship: Does It Hold True for Russian and Polish Consumers?" *International Review of Retail, Distribution and Consumer Research,* 1998, vol. 8, no. 1, pp. 35–51.

Marin, Dalia, Monika Schnitzer, and Masahiko Aoki, *Contracts in Trade and Transition: The Resurgence of Barter.* Cambridge, Mass.: MIT Press, 2002.

McGowan, Karen M., and Brenda J. Sternquist. "Dimensions of Price as a Marketing Universal: A Comparison of Japanese and U.S. Consumers." *Journal of Inter-*

national Marketing, November 1998, vol. 6, no. 4, pp. 77–83.

McKee, Michael J., Robert C. Miall, and W. Scott McShan. "Transfer Pricing at a Time of Economic Downturn." *International Tax Review,* March 2002, vol. 13, no. 3, pp.19–21.

Nagle, Thomas, and Reed Holden. *Strategy and Tactics of Pricing,* 3rd edition. Englewood Cliffs, N.J.: Prentice Hall, 2002.

Platt, Gordon. "Currency Hedging Helps Companies Control Risks in a Volatile Global Economy." *Global Finance,* November 2001, vol. 15, no. 12, p. 43.

Royal, Weld, and Allison Lucas. "Global Pricing and Other Hazards." *Sales & Marketing Management,* August 1995, vol. 147, no. 8, pp. 80–83.

Samiee, Saeed, Patrick Anckar, and Abo Akademi. "Currency Choice in Industrial Pricing: A Cross-National Evaluation." *Journal of Marketing,* July 1998, vol. 62, no. 3, pp. 112–128.

Simon, Hermann, and Eckhard Kucher. "The European Pricing Time Bomb: And How to Cope with It." *European Management Journal,* June 1992, pp. 136–144.

Sinclair, Stuart. "A Guide to Global Pricing." *Journal of Business Strategy,* May–June 1993, pp. 16–19.

Theodosiou, Marios, and Constantine S. Katsikeas. "Factors Influencing the Degree of International Pricing Strategy Standardization of Multinational Firms." *Journal of International Marketing,* vol. 9, no. 3, pp. 1–18.

Weekly, James K. "Pricing in Foreign Markets." *Industrial Marketing Management,* May 1992, pp. 173–179.

Wrappe, Steven C., and George H. Soba. "A Practical Guide to the U.S. Advance Pricing Agreement Process." *Tax Executive,* November-December 1998, vol. 50, no. 6, pp. 442–446.

Endnotes

1. Chris Malburg, "Competing OnCost," *Industry Week*, October 16, 2000, p. 31.

2. "The Review of Maritime Transport, 2001: United Nations Conference on Trade and Development," *United Nations Publication*, 2001, pp. 4, 9.

3. Damon Pike and Giovanni DiCenso, "US Customs Finally Meets Its Match," *International Tax Review*, December 2001-January 2002, vol. 13, no. 1, p. 38.

4. Brent Felgner, "Bed Imports Look to Peel Away Tariff," *Home Textiles Today*, April 26, 1999, pp. 1, 46.

5. "BMW Invests to Avoid Tariffs," *Corporate Location*, September-October 1997, p. 57.

6. Philip R. Cateora and John L. Graham, *International Marketing*, 10th ed. (New York: Irwin McGraw Hill, 1999), p. 562.

7. *World Bank Atlas 2002*, (Washington, D.C.: World Bank, 2002), pp. 46–47, 28–29.

8. "The Ascent of Everest: Coca-Cola's Plans for a New Global Sales Assault," *Financial Times*, January 16, 1992, p. 10.

9. Joshua Ogawa, "AT&T Adds Corporate Call Back Service," *Nikkei Weekly*, November 4, 1996, p. 9.

10. Gautam Naik and William Boston, "Deregulation Dismays Deutsche Telekom," *Wall Street Journal*, January 14, 1999, p. 1.

11. "Business: Leave It to the locals; Cars in China," *Economist*, April 13, 2002, pp. 61–62.

12. William Dawkins, "A Yen for Appreciation," *Financial Times*, November 12, 1996, p. 15; Lisa Shuchman and Gregory L. White, "Japan Car Makers to Hold U.S. Prices," *Wall Street Journal*, June 18, 1999, p. A15.

13. "Don't Save the Yen," *Economist*, February 8, 1997, p. 18.

14. "Bruce Ingersoll, "Germany's SGL to Pay $135 Fine," *Wall Street Journal*, May 5, 1999, p. B12.

15. David Woodruff, "Weakened Euro May Enliven Economies," *Wall Street Journal*, April 15, 1999, p. A17.

16. Helene Cooper, "British Exports Suffer as Euro Goes Forward," *Wall Street Journal*, September 14, 1998, p. A1.

17. Lee Jong-Seung, "Competitive Prize Edge Sinks Rivals," *Business Korea*, January 2000, pp. 24–25.

18. "Greece," *Economist*, February 13, 1999, p. 106.

19. George Melloan, "Another Russian Crisis," *Wall Street Journal*, June 2, 1998, p. A23.

20. McAleer, "Romania Drug Sector Swallows Bitter Pill," *Financial Times*, June 14, 2002, p. 20

21. Carol Gentry, "Bay State May Negotiate Price of Pharmaceuticals," *Wall Street Journal*, December 9, 1998, p. NE1.

22. "Car Prices in UK Still Outpacing Rest of EU," *Financial Times*, February 3, 2001, p.5

23. Tim Burt, "BMW to Smooth Price Variations," *Financial Times*, July 1, 1999, p. 7.

24. Brandon Mitchener, "European Commission Raids Offices of Renault in Antitrust Probe," *Dow Jones Business News*, April 19, 1999, p.1.

25. Franklin R. Root, *International Trade and Investment*, 3rd ed. (Cincinnati, Ohio: Southwestern, 1973), p. 296.

26. "When One Man's Dumping Is Another Man's Good Price," *Financial Times*, May 9, 1990, p. 10.

27. "World Trade: Poorer Nations Starting More Dumping Cases," *Financial Times*, May 6, 1999, p. 21.

28. For a conceptual treatment, see *Transfer Pricing* (Washington, D.C.: Tax Management, Inc., 1995).

29. Virginia Anne Taylor, "Analytic Framework for Global Transfer Pricing," *Journal of American Academy of Business*, March 2002, vol. 1, no. 2, pp. 308–313.

30. "Overlooking Transfer Pricing," *Practical Accountant*, January 2002, vol 35, no. 1, pp. 6–8.

31. Michael C. Durst, "United States: Transfer Pricing," *International Tax Review* (London), February 1999, pp. 56–60.

32. William Glanz, "Foreign Firms Skirt U.S. Tax Laws," *Washington Times*, April 15, 1999, p. 14.

33. Daniel M. Hrisak, "Companies Miss Tax Opportunities When They Ignore Transfer Pricing," *Managing the General Ledger*, January 2002, Issue 1523–5270.

34. Steven Harris, "U.S. Programme Sets the Standard," *International Tax Review* (London), April 1999, vol. 10, no. 4, pp. 35–38.

35. Michael Happell, "Asia: An Overview," *International Tax Review*, February 1999, pp. 7–9.

36. Steven Felgran and Mito Yamada, "Transfer Pricing: A Truly Global Concern," *Financial Executive*, November 2001, vol. 17, no. 8, p. 21.

37. Peter Landers, "Japan Likely to Hold Currency Steady for Now," *The Wall Street Journal*, January 16, 2002, p.22

38. Saeed Samiee, Patrick Anckar, and Abo Akademi, "Currency Choice in Industrial Pricing: A Cross-National Evaluation," *Journal of Marketing*, July 1998, vol. 62, no. 3, pp. 25–27.

39. Elliot Blair Smith, "Single Currency Could Boost Sluggish Economies," *USA Today*, December 26, 2001, p.14.

40. "Currency Trading," *Wall Street Journal*, July 15, 2002, p. C11.

41. "Parallel Imports: Hardly the Full," *Economist*, February 27, 1999, p. 72.

42. Vanessa Fuhrmnas and Scott Henseley, "Drug Makers Try to Curtail Cheap Imports," *Wall Street Journal*, April 11, 2002, p.1.

43. "When the Walls Come Down," *Economist*, July 5, 1997, p. 61.

44. "EMU Boost for Bosch," *Financial Times*, July 8, 1997, p. 2.

45. "Parallel Imports Take a Chunk Out of Distributor Profits," *Asia Computer Weekly*, December 21, 1998, p. 3.

46. "Gray Goods Cleared by Court," *Chain Store Age* (New York), April 1998, p. 34.

47. Charles Goulding, "International Taxation," *Corporate Business Taxation Monthly*, February 2002, pp. 46–48

48. Joshua Ogawa, "Call Back Market Ringing Up a Storm," *Nikkei Weekly*, October 21, 1996, pp. 1, 19.

49. "Israel Adopts Dutch Drug Import Pricing System," *Marketletter* (London), February 23, 1998, p. 1.

50. Stephan A. Butscher, "Maximizing Profits in Euro-Land," *Journal of Commerce*, May 5, 1999, p. A5.

51. Author's interview on June 16, 1999, Guangzhou, China, with Henry Yip, General Manager of Pizza Hut Southern China.

52. "Big Mac Currencies," *Economist*, April 27, 2002, p. 27

53. G. Pascal Zachary, "Euro Is Unlikely to End Differences in Prices Soon," *Wall Street Journal*, January 1, 1999, p. A16.

54. Marios Theodosiou and Constantine Katsikeas, "Factors Influencing the Degree of International Pricing Strategy Standardization of Multinational Corporations," *Journal of International Marketing*, 2001, vol. 9, iss. 3, pp. 1–18.

55. Keith Redhead, "Exchange Rate Risk Management—Part 3," *Credit Control*, 2001, vol. 22, no. 5, pp. 27–32.

56. "The Yen: Asian Nightmares," *Economist*, June 13, 1998, p. 68.

57. "Worth Repeating," *Fortune*, March 3, 1997, p. 27.

58. Robert L. Simison, "Japan's Nissan Reports Wider Loss," *Wall Street Journal*, May 21, 1999, p. 1; Bill Spindle, "Weak Sales Prove Drag on Results for Sony," *Wall Street Journal*, January 1, 1999, p. A13.

59. "Scraping Through the Great Depression; Argentina's Collapse," *Economist*, June 1, 2002, p. 35; and "Return to the Dark Ages; Argentina's Collapse," *Economist*, April 27, 2002, p. 36.

60. This section is based on Carol Lustig, "Forfaiting: A European Customer Finance Technique Comes to the U.S.," *Business Credit*, November-December 1998, pp. 26–29.

61. Riccardo Striano, "Forfaiting as a Risk Mitigation and Sales Tool," *Business Credit*, November-December 2000, p. 52.

62. Rupert Wright, "Forfaiting for Fun and Profit," *Euromoney*, December 1997, pp. 140–141.

63. Daniel S. Levine, "Forfaiting," World Trade, December 1998, pp. 55–56.

64. "Japan to Make Trade Insurance Operations into Independent Agency," *Dow Jones International News*, January 6, 1999, p.16.

65. "President George W. Bush Signs Ex-Im Bank Reauthorization," press release, Export-Import Bank of the United States, June 14, 2002, *www.exim.gov.*

66. "New Russian Bank Deal Approved," *Ex-Im Bank News*, July 2002, vol. 2, no. 8, p.2.

67. "President George W. Bush Signs Ex-Im Bank Reauthorization," press release, Export-Import Bank of the United States, June 14, 2002, *www.exim.gov.*

68. "Ex-Im Bank, Trade Groups Work Together to Meet U.S. Export Financing Needs," press release, Export-Import Bank of the United States, March 12, 1999, *www.exim.gov.*

69. David Sanger, "U.S. Backs Export Groups," *International Herald Tribune*, January 25–26, 1997, p. 10.

70. "Ex-Im Bank Support for Small Business Exporters," press release, Export-Import Bank of the United States, May 13,1999, *www.exim.gov.*

71. "How Massey-Ferguson Uses Brazil for Export Financing," *Business Week*, March 17, 1978, p. 86.

72. "Countertrade," *Business Credit*, April 2002, vol. 103, no. 4. p. 65.

73. "Countertrade Comes Out of the Closet," *Economist*, December 20, 1986, p. 89.

74. "Turkmenistan to Reconstruct Export Gas Pipeline," BBC Monitoring Former Soviet Union, December 27, 2001, from ITAR_TASS news agency.

75. Pompiliu Verzariu, "Risk Mitigating Roles for Countertrade Techniques in Project Finance," *Journal of Project Finance* (New York), Fall 1998, pp. 57–62.

76. Darren McDermott and S. Karene Witcher, "Bartering Gains Currency in Hard-Hit Southeast," *Wall Street Journal*, April 6, 1998, p. A10.

77. The terminology used in this section is based on *Barter, Compensation and Cooperation*, vol. 47, no. IV (Zurich: Credit Suisse, 1978).

78. Jan Norman, "Bartering Can Be Valuable for Business," *Knight Ridder Tribune Business News*, March 25, 2002, p.1.

79. "Pepsi Will Be Bartered for Ships and Vodka in Deal with Soviets," *New York Times*, April 9, 1990, p. 1.

80. "Excitement of Bartering Is Fading Away," *Financial Times*, June 1, 1989, sec. 3, p. 111.

81. "Countertrade to Fight Drop in Indonesian CPO Exports to India," *Asia Pulse*, March 6, 2002.

82. "Countertrade: Farm Goods Swapped for Italian Electricity," *Bangkok Post*, July 23, 1998, p. 1.

83. Jonathon Bell, "Plane Trading," *Airfinance Journal*, June 1998, pp. 34–6.

84. "Commodity Grant: Marc Rich & Co. Does Big Deals at Big Risk in the Former USSR," *Wall Street Journal*, May 13, 1993, pp. 1, A6.

85. Robert Koch, "Saab-British Aerospace Take Big Step Ahead of Competitors," *Agence France-Presse*, November 18, 1998, p. 1.

86. "Countertrade," *Commerce America*, June 19, 1978, p. 1.

87. "Algeria: When Barter Is Battery," *Economist*, October 3, 1981, p. 80.

88. "Barter Is His Stock in Trade," *New York Times*, September 25, 1988, Special Business Supplement, pp. 32–36.

89. David Shipley and Bill Neale, "Industrial Barter and Countertrade," *Industrial Marketing Management*, February 1987, p. 6.

90. Dan West, "Countertrade," *Business Credit*, April 2002, vol. 104, no. 4, p. 50.

91. "Daihatsu Sets Sights on Europe," *Financial Times*, March 5, 1986, p. 4.

92. Jon Marks, "Letters of Credit Are Beginning to Change, a Rich Link with the Past," *Financial Times*, June 1, 1989, Export Finance Section, p. 7.

93. Endel J. Kolde, *International Business Enterprise*, 2nd ed. (Englewood Cliffs, N.J.: Prentice Hall, 1973), p. 294.

94. David Bieederman, "Here Comes TradeCard," *Traffic World*, March 8, 1999, p. 25.

95. Robb Evans, "Best Practices in Global Payments and Collections," *TMA Journal*, January 1, 1999, pp. 51–52.

96. Geri Smith, "Mexico Isn't Investment Grade Yet," *Business Week*, March 13, 2000, p. 140.

97. "EFIC Eases Risk Burden," *International Business Asia*, April 19, 1996, p. 7.

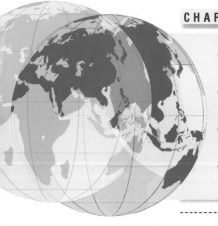

Chapter 11

Global Communications Strategies

M anaging the communications process for a single market is no easy task. The task is even more difficult for global marketers, who must communicate to prospective customers in many markets. In the process, they struggle with different cultures, habits, and languages. In this chapter, we describe the communications process when more than one country is involved and explore how a company structures its global communications mix. Advertising, a key element of the communications mix, will be covered in detail in Chapter 12. After a closer look at the differences between single-country and multicountry communications processes, we will turn to the challenge of developing a personal selling effort on a global level. Various methods of sales promotion are analyzed, and special problems involving the selling of industrial goods, including the effects of the Internet and the World Wide Web on global marketing operations, are highlighted.

THE SINGLE-COUNTRY COMMUNICATIONS PROCESS

Before discussing the various tools available to firms in the global promotion area, we first need to discuss the country-to-country dimension of the communications process. From studying basic marketing, you are already familiar with the generalized single-country communications process. Communications flow from a source, in this case, the company, through several types of channels to the receiver, in this case, the customer. Channels are the mass media, both print and electronic, and the company's sales force. Communication takes place when intended content is received as the perceived content by the receiver or customer. Through a feedback mechanism, the communication sender verifies that the intended and perceived content are in fact identical.

This communications process is typically hindered by three potentially critical variables. A *source effect* exists when the receiver evaluates the received messages based on the status or image of the sender. Second, the *level of noise* caused by other messages being transmitted simultaneously tends to reduce the chances of effective communication. Finally, the messages have to pass through the receiver's, or target's, *perceptional filter*, which keeps out any messages that are not relevant to or consistent with the receiver's experience. Consequently, effective communications require that the source, or sender, overcome the source effect, noise level, and perceptional filter. This communications process is familiar to most marketers in a domestic, or single-country, situation.

THE MULTICOUNTRY COMMUNICATIONS PROCESS

Research evidence and experience have demonstrated that the single-country/domestic communications model can also be applied to consumers in other countries. We find some additional barriers to overcome, however, in the multicountry communications process: the cultural barrier, different source effects, and various noise levels. Figure 11.1 presents a multicountry communications model, with cultural barriers arising at different times in the process.

What is a cultural barrier? In any multicountry communications flow, the source and the receiver are often located in different countries and thus have different cultural environments. The kind of influence that culture can have on the marketing environment has already been discussed at length in Chapter 3. The difficulty of communicating across cultural barriers, however, lies in the danger of substituting, or falling back on, one's own self-reference criteria in situations in which no particular information exists. This danger is particularly acute for executives who are physically removed from the target country. By moving additional decision-making responsibility into the local market, the cultural barrier may be overcome at a point closer to the source.

Figure 11.1: Barriers in the Multicountry Communications Process

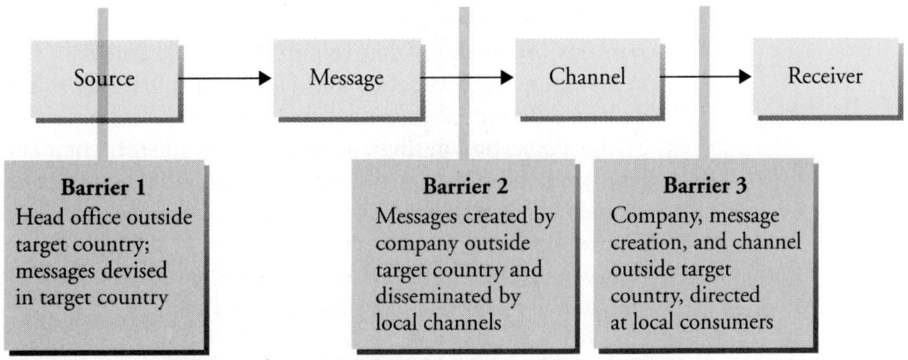

Even when a local subsidiary has substantial decision-making authority, some input comes from a regional or corporate head office operation. For most firms, a deliberate effort to overcome this cultural barrier will have to be made. In almost all cases, certain executives are charged, often informally, with bridging two cultures. Global companies need to avoid the trap of "corporate imperialism," which entails the ill-advised enforcement of head office culture or communications methods in weaker market subsidiaries. The consequences of not successfully bridging this communications gap can be failure and underperformance in a global or local market opportunity.

Multicountry communications may also have an impact on the source effect. A foreign company's communications may trigger different reactions than do the communications of a local firm. In cases where a positive reference group effect exists, an international company may want to take advantage of that situation. Frequently, however, the reaction to international firms is negative, forcing companies to de-emphasize their foreign origins.

The noise level may differ because of different economic and competitive circumstances. In highly developed countries, noise from companies competing for the attention of target customers is extremely high. In some developing countries, fewer companies may vie for the attention of prospective clients. With media availability differing widely from country to country, the nature of channels used to reach target customers tends to vary. And finally, the feedback mechanisms may be subject to additional delays because of the distances involved.

Consequently, we can characterize the multicountry communications process as similar to the single-country process, although it is subject to considerable additional difficulties that make the task highly challenging. The purpose of this chapter is to suggest strategies that global companies can employ to overcome these additional difficulties and barriers. Therefore, we begin our analysis by concentrating first on the different elements of the communications mix.

GLOBAL COMMUNICATIONS STRATEGIES

How to manage the communications mix globally is a critical question for many companies. Most firms conduct business in a certain way and do not rethink their promotion mix regularly. However, global marketers cannot take the full availability of all promotion elements for granted. As a result, many companies find themselves in countries or situations that require an adjustment or a substantial change in their promotion mix. This section and the sections that follow are devoted to understanding how different international environments affect promotion mix decisions.

In a domestic, or single-country, environment, companies achieve a balance in their promotion mix on the basis of experience, costs, and effectiveness. For most companies, communications mix decisions require the selection of an appropriate balance between advertising and personal selling. This choice translates into a push-versus-pull strategy decision (see Figure 11.2). How different is the company's approach to marketing its products globally?

PUSH-ORIENTED STRATEGY

In a domestic setting, *push-oriented marketing strategies* emphasize personal selling rather that advertising in their communications mix. Although very effective as a pro-

Figure 11.2: Global Communications Strategies

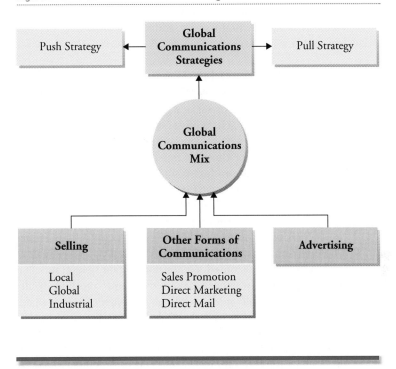

motion tool, personal selling requires intensive use of a sales force and is costly. Companies marketing industrial or other complex products to other firms or governmental agencies have relied on personal selling. Personal selling is usually more effective when a company is faced with a short channel. Global marketers basically look at the personal selling requirements in the same way that marketers do in a domestic situation. However, some of the key inputs into the decision-making process need to be reviewed.

The complexity of a product usually influences how extensively personal selling is used. The level of complexity has to be compared with the product knowledge of the clients. A company selling the same products domestically and abroad may therefore find that more personal selling may be necessary abroad because some foreign clients are less sophisticated than are domestic clients. A U.S. company may use the same amount of personal selling in Europe as it does in the United States, but it may need to expend a greater personal selling effort in developing countries, where the product may not be well understood.

Though they may prefer personal selling as a promotion mix, many companies are increasingly using advertising to avoid the high cost of maintaining a personal sales force. These costs, which are estimated to have passed $300 for a typical sales call, have motivated some companies to shift part of the selling job to advertising.

Channel length can also be an important factor in determining the amount of personal selling or push strategy to be used. If a company faces the same channel length abroad as it does in the domestic market, no change is needed in the push strategy. However, when a company faces a longer channel because other intermediaries, such as local distributors, are added, the firm may be better off shifting to a pull campaign.

PULL-ORIENTED STRATEGY

Pull strategy is characterized by greater dependence on advertising directed at the end user of a product or service. Pull campaigns are typical for consumer goods firms that need to approach a large segment of the market. For such companies, the economies of using mass communications such as advertising dictate a reliance on pulling the product through the distribution channel. Pull campaigns are usually advisable when the product is widely used by consumers, when the channel is long, when the product is not very complex, and when self-service is the predominant shopping behavior. Increased or decreased reliance on pull campaigns for global markets depends on several factors. Most important are access to advertising media, channel length, and the leverage the company has with the distribution channel.

Marketers accustomed to choosing among several media options may find choices limited in some overseas markets. For many products, pull campaigns work only if access to electronic media, particularly television, is available. In Japan and in some developing countries, radio and television stations tend to be commercially operated. In other areas, such as some European countries, liberalization of the media and full commercial access are relatively new. This trend was sparked by the advent of satellite radio and television in Europe and Asia, which allowed commercial operators to beam signals into countries where commercial media were previously nonexistent. As a result, most areas of the world are now accessible to both electronic and print media advertising.

In other countries, access to those media is restricted through time limits imposed by governments. Consequently, companies will find it difficult to duplicate their promotional strategies when moving from an unregulated environment to more restricted environments. Although in many countries a company may be able to shift advertising from one medium into another, it is nevertheless true that the unfolding of a fully developed pull campaign can be more difficult to do in some countries.

Channel length is another major determinant of the feasibility of a pull campaign. Companies in complex consumer markets often face long channels and thus try to overcome channel inertia by directing their advertising directly to end users. When a company enters other markets, it may face an even longer channel because local distribution arrangements are different. In Japan, for example, channels tend to be much longer than those in the United States. As a result, greater reliance on a pull strategy may be advisable or even necessary.

Distribution leverage is also different for each company from market to market. Getting cooperation from local selling points, particularly in the retail sector, is often more difficult than in the domestic market. The fight for shelf space may be intense; shelf space in most markets is limited because carrying several competing brands of a product category is not customary. Under these more competitive situations, the reliance on a pull campaign becomes more important. If consumers are demanding the company's product, retailers will make every effort to carry it.

PUSH VERSUS PULL STRATEGIES

In selecting the best balance between advertising and personal selling for the pull versus push decision, companies have to analyze the markets to determine the relative need for these two major communications mix elements. However, as we have seen, the availability of, or access to, any one of several media may be limited. This scenario is particularly true for firms depending a great deal on pull policies. Many such companies find themselves limited in the use of the most powerful communications tools. How must a company adjust its communications policy under such circumstances?

When lack of access to advertising media makes the pull strategy less effective, a company may have to resort to more of a push strategy (and make greater use of personal selling). In some instances, limited access to television advertising may force a company to use less effective media forms such as print advertising. In such circumstances, a company can employ a larger sales force to compensate for the reduced efficiency of consumer-directed promotions.

Limited ability to unfold a pull strategy from a company's home market has other effects on the company's marketing strategy. Reduced advertising tends to slow the product adoption process in new markets, thus forcing the firm to accept slower growth. In markets crowded with existing competitors, newcomers will find it difficult to establish themselves when avenues for pull campaigns are blocked.

Consequently, a company entering a new market may want to consider such situations for its planning and adjust expected results accordingly. A company accustomed to a certain type of communications mix usually develops an expertise or a distinctive competence in the media commonly used. When a company is suddenly faced with a situation in which that competence cannot be fully applied, the risk of failure or underachievement increases. Such constraints can even affect entry strategies or the market selection process.

PERSONAL SELLING

Personal selling takes place whenever a customer meets a representative of the marketing company in person. When doing business globally, companies must meet customers from different countries. These customers may be accustomed to different business customs and may speak a different language. Thus, personal selling in an individual context is extremely complex and requires special skills on the part of the salesperson.

In this section, we differentiate between global selling and local selling. When a company's sales force travels to other countries and meets directly with clients abroad, it is practicing *global selling*. This type of selling requires an ability to manage across several cultures. Much more often, however, companies engage in *local selling:* they organize and staff a local sales force of local nationals to do the selling in only one country. Managing and operating a local sales force involves different problems than those encountered when managing multicountry salespersons.

GLOBAL SELLING THROUGH A MULTICOUNTRY SALES FORCE

The job of the global salesperson seems glamorous. One imagines a professional who frequently travels abroad, visiting a large number of countries and meeting a large number of different businesspeople with various backgrounds. However, this type of work is quite demanding and requires a special set of skills. Global salespeople are needed only when companies deal directly with their clients abroad, which is usually the case for industrial equipment or business services, and rarely for consumer products or services. Consequently, for our purposes, global sales will be described in the context of industrial selling.

PURCHASING BEHAVIOR. In industrial (business-to-business) selling, one of the most important parts of the job is finding the right decision maker in the client company. The seller must locate the key decision makers, who may hold different positions from company to company or from country to country. In some countries, the purchasing manager may have different responsibilities, or the engineers may play a greater role. The global salesperson must be able to identify and deal effectively with buying units that differ by country. For example, when selling in Japan, the salesperson must recognize that the decision process will be slower than in other countries because the members of the buying unit will want to explore and debate alternatives, while at the same time striving for unity and collegiality among the buyers. Japanese buying behavior will require a different set of sales skills tailored to the culture.[1]

BUYING CRITERIA. In addition to different purchasing patterns, the global salesperson may have to deal with different decision criteria or objectives on the part of the purchaser. Buyers or users of industrial products in different countries may need to meet different goals. However, for standardized uses for specific industries, relatively little difference between countries applies. Particularly for high-technology products, such as production equipment for semiconductor components used in the electronics industry, the applications are almost identical, regardless of whether the factory is located in Taiwan or Germany.

LANGUAGE. Overcoming the language barrier is an especially difficult task for the global salesperson. The personal selling effort is markedly enhanced if the salesperson speaks the language of the customer. For some of the products marketed by a global sales force today, two trends have emerged. First, the dependency on the local language for many industries is not as strong today as it was just one or two decades ago. For many new and highly sophisticated products (for example, biotechnology, IT), English is the business language spoken by most customers. Consequently, with more and more executives speaking English in many countries, more firms have been in a position to market their products directly, without local intermediaries. English is widely spoken in Europe, particularly in the Nordic area, and it is the leading second language in Asia and Latin America. Consequently, we now see that the ability to speak one or more foreign languages is less of a necessity. Learning a foreign language can be an excellent way, however, to understand a foreign culture. Also, language proficiency continues to have a very favorable impact on the sales process.

In industries in which knowledge of the local language is important, companies tend to assign sales territories to salespersons on the basis of language skills. A European multinational manufacturer of textile equipment assigns countries to its sales staff according to the languages the salespeople speak. Speaking another language is more important in the traditional industries such as textile manufacturing, in which businesses are more local in orientation and in which English is not spoken that well by management.

Even executives who speak fairly proficient English may not understand all the details of product descriptions or specifications. As a result, a company can make an excellent impression by having its sales brochures translated into key languages. European companies routinely produce company publications in several languages. Such translations may not be needed for Scandinavia but may go a long way in other parts of the world where the level of English language skills is not that high.

BUSINESS ETIQUETTE.   Global marketers selling to many markets are likely to encounter a diverse set of business practices as they move from one country to another. Since interpersonal behavior is intensely culture-bound, this part of the salesperson's job will vary by country. Many differences exist in local customs for making appointments, deciding if and how an introduction is made, and arranging lead time when making appointments. The salesperson must also know whether or not gifts are expected or desired. When a salesperson travels to the same area repeatedly, familiarity with local customs can be expected. But for newcomers or experienced executives traveling to a new area, finding out the correct cultural information is still necessary.

For example, visiting businesspeople must attend long banquets when negotiating with the Chinese. These banquets may start in the late morning or early in the evening. Sitting at a round table, the visitors will normally be seated next to the host, who is expected to fill the visitor's plate at regular intervals. Foreigners are cautioned that frequent toasts are the norm and that many Chinese business hosts expect the guest to become drunk; otherwise, the guest is believed not to have had a good time. Also, business etiquette can differ from one country to another. Although it is acceptable for visitors to arrive late in China, India, or Indonesia, it is not acceptable in Hong Kong. Lateness causes the visitor to "lose face," which is an extremely serious matter among Hong Kong businesspeople.

There are countless rules on business etiquette, and they vary from country to country. The following list was accumulated only for illustrative purposes. It should not be considered complete, nor can such lists be completely free of misconceptions. This list is based on the experience of a globally active sales manager for a consulting company[2]:

Kuwait

- Kuwaiti officials are prohibited by tradition from working more than six hours per day. Mornings are thus best for appointments.
- Of several persons present at a meeting, the person asking the most questions is likely to be the least important. The real decision maker is probably a silent, elderly Kuwaiti who watches everything but never speaks to you directly.

China

- Use black and white for your collateral materials because colors have great significance for the Chinese. Gold is the most prestigious color.
- Never place a person's business card in your wallet that you then place in your back pocket.

Israel

- Note that when a schedule is agreed upon in terms of months, the Israelis may think in terms of twenty-eight-day months (versus thirty-day months for Europeans or North Americans).

France

- Most French citizens get four to five weeks vacation time each year, and the vacations are frequently scheduled for August. Avoid making appointments during that time.
- Eye contact among the French may be much more intense than is customary for Americans.

Norway

- When you are invited to a Norwegian home, wait to be asked in, then wait again until you are asked to sit down.

United States

- The United States is much more informal than other countries. Use of first names in other countries is much less common, or automatic. When in doubt, it is safer in other countries to use a formal address.[3]

Since no manager can be expected to know the business customs of every country, important information can be obtained from special sources. The company's own foreign market representatives or sales subsidiary can provide important information or suggestions. When such access is not available, governments often collect data on business practices through their commercial officers posted abroad. For example, the U.S. Department of Commerce publishes a regular series entitled *Doing Business in . . .* , which offers a wealth of helpful suggestions. Some business service companies, such as global accounting firms or global banks, also provide customers with profiles of business practices in foreign countries.

Foreign business people receiving visitors from other foreign countries rarely expect the foreign visitor to be familiar with all local customs. However, it is always appreciated when the visitor can indicate familiarity with the most common practices and some willingness to try to conform. Learning some foreign customs helps to generate goodwill toward the company and can therefore increase the chance of doing business.

NEGOTIATIONS STRATEGIES. Negotiations in the global arena are complicated because the negotiating partners frequently come from different cultural backgrounds. As a result, misunderstandings or misjudgments can occur and can lead to failure. To increase the chances of a successful outcome in the often difficult and protracted negotiations, global sales personnel must be in tune with the cultural differences.

The conceptualization developed by E.T. Hall along low-context and high-context cultures has often been identified as a driving force in determining buyers' and sellers' negotiation styles.[4] The United States, and many Western countries, are viewed as low-context cultures, whereas a country such as the Philippines is viewed as a high-context culture. In low-context cultures, which support the "western logic" of negotiation, negotiators start with the identification of a systematic starting point to the activity, and the negotiation terminates when an agreement is reached, preferably in writing. Negotiators from high-context cultures show a greater reliance on verbal communication.[5]

Although several negotiation strategies exist, concentrating on mutual needs rather than on the issues is an often used approach. In global marketing, the salesperson, or negotiator, must first determine the true objectives and needs of the other party. When negotiating within an unknown cultural setting, this determination is often a challenging task. However, careful assessment of the negotiating party's needs can enhance the chance for success.

Understanding the *mindscape* of the counterpart can be very important for successful negotiation. Wenlee Ting, a noted anthropologist, defined mindscape as "a structure of reasoning, cognition, perception, design, planning, and decision making that may vary from individual to individual and from culture to culture."[6] Research indicates that Hong Kong businesspeople negotiated well in eastern and western cultures. Skilled Hong Kong negotiators were able to engage in reasoning with western counterparts while simultaneously employing other reasoning and negotiation techniques when dealing with local groups, family members, and other business associates.[7] This observation suggests that successful negotiation may depend on the foreign businessperson's ability to discover the foreign counterpart's mindscape.

Careful background preparation on the cultural norms prevalent in the foreign country is the starting point to successful negotiation and selling. A fifteen-year study of the negotiation styles of seventeen cultures found significant differences from culture to culture. For example, the Japanese were the least aggressive, with few threats or warnings, whereas the French and Brazilians were aggressive, using warnings, threats, and interruptions frequently. The research found that cultural differences caused misunderstandings, which could be reduced with cross-cultural awareness.[8]

Timing is also an important component of negotiating abroad. In some countries, such as China, negotiations tend to take much more time than in the United States or some other western countries. One European company that operated a joint venture in China observed that during one annual meeting, two weeks were spent in a discussion that elsewhere might have taken only a few hours. In this situation, however, much of the time was used for interdepartmental negotiations among various Chinese agencies rather than for face-to-face negotiations with the European company. In another instance, a European firm negotiated with a Middle Eastern company over several months for the delivery of several hundred machines. When the European representatives went into the Middle Eastern country for the final round of negotiations, they found that a competing firm had already been there several weeks before their arrival. The European firm's representatives decided to prepare themselves for long negotiations and refused to make concessions, figuring that the competitor had most likely been worn down in the prior weeks. That assessment turned out to be correct, and the European company won the order by outstaying its competitor in a rather difficult negotiating environment. Unprepared sales executives may lose to competitors if they do not understand the negotiation customs of a foreign country as they relate to the amount of time necessary to conclude a deal.

LOCAL SELLING USING A SINGLE-COUNTRY SALES FORCE

When a company can maintain a local sales force in each country where it does business, many of the difficulties of bridging the cultural gap with clients are minimized. Local sales forces are usually staffed with local nationals. The local sales force can be expected to understand the local customs, which helps the global company gain additional acceptance in the market. Many challenges remain, however, and the management of a local sales force often requires different strategies from those used in running a sales force in the company's domestic market.

ROLE OF THE LOCAL SALES FORCE AND CONTROL. When a company has decided to build a local sales force, the decision has already been made for forward integration in its distribution effort. As we learned in Chapter 9, establishing a sales force means that the company has assumed the full role of a local sales subsidiary, thus sidestepping the independent distributor. Depending on the distribution strategy adopted, the company may sell directly, as is often the case for many industrial products or business services, or indirectly through local wholesalers, as is the case for many consumer products and services. Although global companies will not make such a move unless current business volume justifies it, substantial benefits are associated with having one's own sales force.

Control over a firm's sales activities is a frequently cited advantage for operating a company-owned local sales force. With its own sales force, the company can emphasize the products it wants to market at any time, and the company has better control over the way it is represented. In many cases, price negotiations, in the form of discounts or rebates, are handled uniformly, and these decisions are not left to an independent distributor with different interests. Having a company sales force also ensures that the personnel are of the necessary level and qualification. Control over all of these parameters usually means higher sales compared with using a distributor's sales force.

Also, a local sales force can represent an important bridge with the local business community. For industries in which the buying process is local rather than global, the sales force speaks the language of the local customer, can be expected to understand the local business customs, and thus can bring the global firm closer to its end users. In many instances, local customers, though they may not object to buying from a foreign firm, may prefer to deal with local representatives of that firm. As a result, the ability of the global company to make its case heard with prospective customers is substantially enhanced.

However, local sales forces are single-country, or single-culture, by nature. Although the members of the local sales force speak the language of the local customers, they may not speak any other language. The local sales force may have a very limited understanding of the language used in the head office. That limited understanding is, in general, not sufficient to conduct business in the language of the head office. Furthermore, a local sales force cannot be expected to speak the languages of neighboring countries sufficiently to deal directly with customers from those countries. In Europe, where this problem is particularly acute, language competency usually precludes a German firm from sending its sales force into France or a French firm from sending its sales force into Italy or Spain. In some countries, such as the Netherlands, Switzerland, and Belgium, several different languages are spoken, further enhancing the mobility of the sales force located in those countries.

LOCAL SALES JOB. The type and extent of local sales effort that a company will need depend on its own distribution effort and the relationship of distribution to the other communications mix elements. For firms that still use distributor sales forces to a large extent, a missionary sales force with limited responsibilities may suffice. This missionary sales force concentrates on visiting clients together with the local distributor's sales force. If the global company's sales force needs to do the entire job, a much larger sales force will be necessary. As for the global firm's domestic market, the size of the local sales force depends mostly on the number of clients and the desired frequency of visits. This frequency may differ from country to country, which means that the size of the sales force will differ from country to country.

The role of the local sales force needs to be coordinated with the promotion mix selected for each market. As many companies have learned, advertising and other forms of promotion can be used to make the function of the sales force more efficient. In many consumer goods industries, companies prefer a pull strategy, thus concentrating their promotion budget on the final consumer. In such cases, the role of the sales force is restricted to gaining distribution access. As we have mentioned previously, however, access to communications media in some countries is severely restricted. As a result, companies may place greater emphasis on a push strategy utilizing the local sales force, which affects both role definition and size.

FOREIGN SALES PRACTICES. Although sales forces are employed almost everywhere, the nature of their interaction with the local customer is unique to each market and may affect local sales operations. For most westerners, Japanese practices seem substantially different. The following example was reported by Masaaki Imai, president of Cambridge Corporation, a Tokyo management consulting and recruiting firm.

When Bausch & Lomb Japan introduced its then new soft-lens line in Japan, the company targeted influential eye doctors in each sales territory for its introductory launch. Bausch & Lomb assumed that, once these leading practitioners signed up for the new product, marketing to the majority of eye doctors would be easier. One particular salesperson was quickly dismissed by a key customer. The doctor said that he thought very highly of Bausch & Lomb equipment but preferred regular lenses for his patients. The salesperson did not even have a chance to respond; he decided to extend his visit, however, since it was his first to this clinic. He talked to several assistants at the clinic and to the doctor's wife, who was handling the administration of the practice, as is typical for Japanese businesses.

The next morning, the salesperson returned to the clinic and observed that the doctor was very busy. He talked again with the assistants and joined the doctor's wife when she was cooking and talked with her about food. When the couple's young son returned from kindergarten, the salesperson played with him and even went out to buy him a toy. The wife was very pleased with this attention to her son. She later explained to the salesperson that her husband had very little time to listen to any sales presentations during the day, so she invited him to come to their home in the evening. The doctor, obviously primed by his wife, received the salesperson very warmly, and they enjoyed *sake* together. The doctor listened patiently to the sales presentation and responded that he did not want to use the soft lenses on his patients right away. However, he suggested that the salesperson try them on his assistants the next day. So, on the third day, the salesperson returned to the clinic and fitted soft lenses on several of the clinic's assistants. The reaction was very favorable, and the doctor placed an order on the third day of the sales call.[9]

It is probably fair to say that salespeople in many countries would have taken the initial negative response as the final answer from the doctor and would have tried elsewhere for success. In Japan, however, the customer expects a different reaction. Japanese customers often judge from the frequency of the sales calls they receive whether the company really wants to do business. Salespeople who make more frequent calls to a potential customer than the competition does may be regarded as more sincere. This perception also means that companies doing business in Japan have to make frequent sales calls to their top customers, often only for courtesy reasons. Customers are visited twice a year, usually in June and December, without necessarily discussing any business. Although this contact may occasionally be only a telephone call, the high frequency of visits significantly affects the staffing levels of the company-owned sales force in Japan.

RECRUITING. Companies have often found recruiting sales professionals quite challenging in many global markets. Although the availability of qualified sales personnel is a problem even in developed countries, the scarcity of skilled personnel is even more acute in developing countries. Global companies, accustomed to having sales staff with certain standard qualifications, may not find it easy to locate the necessary salespeople in a short period of time. One factor limiting their availability in many countries is the local economic situation. Depending on the economic cycle, the level of unemployment may be an excellent indicator for the difficulty of finding prospects. This will limit the number of people a company can expect to hire away from existing firms unless a substantial increase over present compensation is offered.

More important, sales positions don't enjoy uniformly high prestige from country to country. Typically, sales as an occupation or career has a relatively favorable image in the United States. This favorable image allows companies to recruit excellent talent, usually fresh from universities, for sales careers. These university recruits can usually consider sales as a career path toward middle-management positions. Such an image of selling is rare elsewhere in the world. In Europe, many companies continue to find it difficult to recruit university graduates for their sales forces, except in highly technical fields such as computers, where the recruits are typically engineers. When sales is a less desirable occupation, the quality of the sales force may suffer. If the company wants to insist on top quality, the time it will take to fill sales positions can be expected to increase dramatically.

COMPENSATION. In their home markets, where they usually employ large sales forces, global companies become accustomed to handling and motivating their sales forces in a certain way. In the United States, typical motivation programs include some form of commission or bonus for meeting volume or budget projections, as well as vacation prizes for top performers. When a global company manages local sales forces in various countries, the company must determine the best way to motivate them. Not all cultures may respond the same way, and motivational practices may differ from country to country.

One of the frequently discussed topics in motivating salespeople is the value of the commission or bonus structure. U.S. companies, in particular, tend to use some form of commission structure for their sales force. Although this practice may fluctuate from industry to industry, U.S. firms tend to use more of a flexible and volume-dependent compensation structure than European firms. Japanese firms use a straight salary type of compensation more often. To motivate the sales force to achieve superior performance, the global company may be faced with using different compensation practices, depending on the local customs.

ALTERNATIVES TO A LOCAL SALES FORCE. Because building a local sales force is both costly and time consuming, some companies have looked for alternatives without necessarily falling back on independent distributors. When competitive pressures require a rapid access to a sales force, piggybacking on some other company's already existing sales force (as described in Chapter 15) has been practiced by some companies.

Recently, companies have entered into a wide variety of international distribution alliances (see Chapter 9). The sales alliance format differs from other ventures because the two firms that join forces do so as independent firms and not necessarily in the form of a limited joint venture. In an alliance, two companies may swap products, with one company carrying the other firm's products in one market, and vice versa. Such swaps have been used extensively in the pharmaceutical industry. The short period of time left for marketing once the products have been approved and before the patents expire calls for a rapid product rollout in as many countries as possible.

BUSINESS-TO-BUSINESS SELLING

Many of the promotion strategies discussed so far are geared toward the marketing of typical consumer goods and industrial goods. However, some specific promotion methods oriented toward the business-to-business market play an important role in the global marketing of such products. The use of global trade fairs, bidding procedures for global projects, and consortium selling all have to be understood if an investment or industrial products company wants to succeed in international markets.

GLOBAL TRADE FAIRS

Participation in global trade fairs has become an important aspect of marketing industrial products abroad. Trade fairs are ideal for exposing new customers and potential distributors to a company's product range and have been used extensively by both newcomers and established firms. In the United States, business-to-business customers can be reached through a wide range of media. One example is a specialized magazine with a particular industry focus. In many overseas countries, markets are too small to allow for the publication of such trade magazines. As a result, prospective customers usually attend trade fairs regularly. Trade fairs also offer companies a chance to meet with prospective customers in a less formal atmosphere. For a company that is new to a certain market and does not yet have any established contacts, participation in a trade fair may be the only way to reach potential customers. There are an estimated six hundred major international trade shows in seventy countries every year. The Hanover Fair is considered the largest industrial fair in the world. With over 7,100 exhibitors in engineering and technology from over seventy countries, the fair attracts 330,000 visitors.[10] Other large general fairs include the Canton Fair in China and the Milan Fair in Italy.

Specialized trade fairs concentrate on a certain segment of an industry or on a user group. Such fairs usually attract limited participation in terms of both exhibitors and visitors. Typically, they are more technical in nature. Some of the specialized trade fairs may not take place every year. One of the leading specialized fairs is the Achema for the chemical industry in Germany; it is held every three years. The Domotechnica Trade Fair in Cologne, Germany, is a leading trade fair for the household appliance industry. About 1,800 exhibitors from fifty-seven countries attracted seventy-two thousand professional visitors from 121 countries. Manufacturers used the four-day trade show to display their latest innovations.[11] The Light+Building trade show held in Frankfurt, Germany, is a newcomer to the schedule of international fairs. In its second running, this international trade fair for architecture and technology attracted 118,500 visitors and 2,200 exhibitors from ninety-seven countries.[12]

Participation in trade fairs can save both time and effort for a company that wants to break into a new market and does not yet have any contacts. For new-product announcements and/or demonstrations, the trade fair offers an ideal forum for display. Trade fairs are also used by competitors to check on one another's most recent developments. They can give a newcomer an idea of the potential competition in some foreign markets before actual market entry. Consequently, trade fairs can provide information about selling products and can offer a company important and useful market intelligence. Therefore, marketers with global aspirations should research the relevant trade fairs directed at their industry or customer segment and attend relevant fairs regularly.

Global exhibits may require additional planning compared to domestic trade shows. First, planning should begin twelve to eighteen months in advance because international shipping may involve delays. Second, show attendance should be checked because it is common for many shows to allow the public to visit; marketers may therefore want to plan a separate and private area for qualified prospects. Third, in the United States, a show may be staffed by salespeople and middle managers. At many global shows, customers expect to see the CEO and senior management. Finally, local distributors, consultants, or sales representatives are typically engaged to help with the logistics of bridging to the local culture.

SELLING THROUGH A BIDDING PROCESS

The bidding process for industrial products is more complicated than that for consumer products, particularly when major industrial equipment is involved. Companies competing for such major projects have to pass through several stages before negotiations for a specific purchase can even take place. Typically, companies conduct a search process for new projects, then move on to prequalify for the particular project before a formal project bid or tender is submitted. Each phase requires careful management and the appropriate allocation of resources.

During the search phase, companies want to make sure that they are informed of any project that is related to their product lines and that is worth their interest. For particularly large, government-sponsored projects, full-page advertisements may appear in leading international newspapers. More likely, companies will have a network of agents, contacts, or former customers who will inform them of any project being considered.

In the prequalifying phase, the purchaser will frequently ask for documentation from interested companies that would like to make a formal tender. At this phase, no formal bidding or tender documents are submitted. Instead, a more general company background, which may describe other or similar projects the company has finished in the past, will be required. At this stage, the company will have to sell itself and its capabilities. A large number of companies can be expected to pursue prequalification.

In the next phase, the customer will select the companies—usually only three or four—to be invited to submit a formal bid. Formal bids consist of a proposal showing how to solve the specific client problem. For industrial equipment, this phase of the process usually requires personal visits on location, special design of some components, and the preparation of full documentation, including engineering drawings for the client.[13] The bid preparation costs can be enormous, even up to several million dollars for some very large projects. The customer will select the winner from among those submitting formal proposals. Normally, it is not simply the lowest bidder who will obtain the order. Technology, the type of solution proposed, and the financing arrangements all play a role (see Chapter 10).

Once an order is obtained, the supplying company may be expected to insure its own performance. For that purpose, the company may be asked to post a performance bond, which is a guarantee that the company will pay certain specified damages to the customer if the job is not completed within the agreed-on specifications. Performance bonds are usually issued by banks on behalf of the supplier. The entire process, from finding out about a new prospect until the order is actually received, may take from several months to several years, depending on the project size or industry.

A special situation exists when the customer is a governmental institution. Marketing to governmental bodies had been characterized in the past by protectionism and favoritism, and has been driven more by connections or the strength of contacts than by the strength of the offer. Over the past decade, primarily because of liberalization processes within the European Union and the World Trade Organization (WTO), many restrictive purchasing practices have been struck down and the government procurement process in many sectors is now much more open to outside bidders. This restructuring, still going in on many countries, can be expected to continue and is likely to open more competition for companies that want to pursue their opportunities globally.

CONSORTIUM SELLING

Because of the high stakes involved in marketing equipment or *turnkey* projects (a plant, system, or project in which the buyer acquires a complete solution so that the entire operation can commence at the "turn of a key"), companies frequently combine forces to form a consortium. A *consortium* is a group of firms that share in a certain contract or project on an already agreed-on basis but act almost as one company toward the customers. Joining a consortium can help companies share the risk in some very large projects. A consortium can enhance the competitiveness of the members by offering a turnkey solution to the customer.

Most consortiums are formed on an ad hoc basis. For the supply of a major steel mill, for example, companies supplying individual components may form a group and offer a single tender to the customer. The consortium members have agreed to share all marketing costs and can help one another with design and engineering questions. The customer gets a chance to deal with one supplier only, which simplifies the process substantially. Ad hoc consortiums can be found for some very large projects that require unique skills from their members. The consortium members frequently come from the same country and thus expect a greater chance at obtaining the contract than if they operated on their own. In situations in which the same set of skills or products is in frequent demand, companies may form a permanent consortium. Whenever a chance for a project arises, the consortium members will immediately prepare to qualify for the bidding.

Consortium selling is frequently practiced by companies joining together to obtain telecommunications licenses in foreign countries. The consortium members might include a local firm with its local connections, combined with one or two international telephone operating companies with expertise in running a network. On occasion, such a consortium may include equipment suppliers who want to ensure that their equipment will be included in any eventual contract. When the consortium members represent companies from different countries, a considerable management challenge exists in keeping the consortium together and on track.

GLOBAL ACCOUNT MANAGEMENT

Account management was traditionally performed on a country-by-country basis. This practice invariably led to a country-specific sales force, which was typical even for large global firms. Over the last few years, an emerging trend has developed in which companies organize their sales force into global account teams. The global team services an entire global customer base (realistically, in all countries where a customer relationship exists). Global account teams may comprise members in different parts of the world, all serving segments of a global account and coordinated through a global account management structure.

The trend toward global account management is rooted in ever-increasing global purchasing logic among customers, primarily industrial customers (see Chapter 7). Companies that purchase similar components, raw materials, or services in many parts of the world realize that they can obtain substantial savings by combining the purchasing function and managing it more centrally. Companies are scanning the global market for the best buy, and they want to deal with the source that can offer the most advantages.

The system of global account management is practiced widely in the professional service sectors. Globally active banks like Citibank have maintained global account structures for years. Advertising agencies also offer global clients global account management with seamless coordination across many countries.[14] And finally, the world's largest accounting firms, such as Deloitte Touche Tohmatsu, have long-standing traditions of leading their engagements for international clients from one place. At Deloitte, the system of lead client service partners (LCSPs) is well developed. The LCSP is empowered, for example, to direct a global audit engagement for a large multinational account across all countries where the work must be performed.[15]

Global account management is greatly enhanced by sophisticated information technology. With members of the team dispersed around the globe, it becomes essential to coordinate all actions meticulously. The development and rapid spread of videoconferencing, electronic mail, and groupware applications have greatly extended the reach of a management team beyond the typical one-location office. Many customers who want to conduct business around the world but who prefer to deal with fewer suppliers will demand this new sales approach. Many of the national selling organizations now maintained by international firms will inevitably be transferred, or transformed, into smaller, globally active account teams.

OTHER FORMS OF MARKETING COMMUNICATIONS

So far, our discussion has concentrated on personal and industrial selling as key elements of the communications mix. Aside from advertising, however, various other forms of marketing communications play a key role in marketing. Usually combined under the generic title of global sales promotions, they may include elements such as in-store retail promotions and coupons. Many of these tools are oriented toward consumer goods and are used less often in industrial goods marketing. In this section, we look at sales promotion activities, as well as sports promotions and sponsorships.

SALES PROMOTION

The area of sales promotion has mostly a local focus. Although some forms of promotions, such as coupons, gifts, and various types of reduced-priced labels, are in use in most countries, strict government regulations and different retailing practices serve to limit the options for global firms (see Table 11.1).

In the United States, coupons are the leading form of sales promotion. Consumers bring product coupons to the retail store and obtain a reduced price for the product. Second in importance are refund offers. Consumers who send a proof of purchase to the manufacturer receive a refund in the form of a check. Also used, but less frequently, are cents-off labels or factory-bonus packs, which encourage customers to buy large quantities because of the corresponding price reduction. U.S. marketers of consumer goods, the primary users of these types of sales promotion, find a full array of services available to run their promotions. Companies such as AC Nielsen specialize in managing central locations for coupon redemption, so that all handling of promotions can be turned over to an outside contractor.

Couponing varies significantly from country to country. Coupon distribution is popular and growing in Italy. In the United Kingdom and Spain, couponing is declining. Couponing is in its infancy in Japan, with restrictions on newspaper coupons lifted in 1991. Couponing is limited in Germany, Holland, Switzerland, and Greece. The European Commission is working toward a policy of allowing pan-European sales promotion as long as the practices are legal in the country of origin, therefore requiring each country to recognize the laws of the other countries. This new policy, if approved, will significantly increase sales promotion across Europe.[16]

In most overseas markets, price reductions in the store are usually the most important promotional tool, followed by reductions to the trade, such as wholesalers

Table 11.1 Concise Guide to Promotion Techniques and Restrictions

Country	Top Three Sales Promotion Techniques	Restrictions on Sales Promotion Techniques
Argentina	Reduced price in store Trade discounts In-store displays, promotions	Rules on lotteries, special prizes Products such as pharmaceuticals cannot be promoted through prices
Australia	Reduced price in store Trade discounts Promotional pack sizes with extra free product	Individual state coupon restrictions Promotions and trade support must be available for all stores Lotteries and games of chance subject to government authorization Some restrictions on proof of purchase
Austria	Reduced price in store Open competitions Trade discounts	No coupons Restrictions for on-pack deals
Belgium	Reduced price in store Trade discounts Extra product free	No free draws No sweepstakes
Brazil	Gift-banded packs Reduced price in store	Distribution of prizes via vouchers, contests, etc., is subject to government authorization
Canada	Reduced price in store Trade discounts Coupons	Ethical products, alcoholic beverages, cigarettes, cigars not permitted any type of sale promotion
France	Reduced price in store Trade discounts Coupons	Games of chance are usually forbidden Premiums and gifts are limited to 5% of product value and no more than 1% off
Germany	Reduced price in store Displays Trade discounts	No coupons Free goods restricted to value of about DM 0.10 No in-pack premium or cross-product offers No free-draws or money-off vouchers
Great Britain	Reduced price in store Trade discounts Coupons	Legislation on bargain offers, lotteries, sweepstakes Competitions must include a degree of skill No price promotion on categories such as pharmaceuticals

(continued)

Table 11.1 Concise Guide to Promotion Techniques and Restrictions (cont.)

Country	Top Three Sales Promotion Techniques	Restrictions on Sales Promotion Techniques
Sweden	Co-op advertising and money off Local activities Coupons	No premium redemption plans Competitions must include a degree of skill Mixed offers are restricted In-pack or on-pack cross-coupons not allowed
Switzerland	Reduced price in store Trade discounts Merchandising contribution to manufacturers to trade	Laws against unfair competition No competition, free draws, sweepstakes, money-off vouchers, or money off next purchase
United States	Coupons Refund offers Cents-off label, factory packs, and bonus packs	All promotion and trade support must include a degree of skill Mixed offers are restricted In-pack or on-pack cross-coupons not allowed

Source: From William J. Hawkes's presentation of A.C. Nielsen Company material to the International Marketing Workshop. AMA/MSI, March 1983. Reprinted by permission of A.C. Nielsen Company. Updated December 1990.

and retailers. Also of importance in some countries are free goods, double-pack promotions, and in-store displays.

Most countries have restrictions on some forms of promotions. Frequently regulated are any games of chance, but games in which some type of skill is required are usually allowed. When reductions are made available, they often are not allowed to exceed a certain percentage of the product's purchase price. Because global firms will encounter a series of regulations and restrictions on promotions that differ among countries, there is little opportunity to standardize sales promotion techniques across many markets. This lack of standardization has caused most companies to make sales promotions the responsibility of local managers, who are expected to understand the local preferences and restrictions. Sales promotion can also be influenced by local culture. A study of consumer attitudes regarding sales promotion found significant differences among Taiwan, Thailand, and Malaysia. The Taiwanese consumer preferred coupons over sweepstakes and had a low level of embarrassment when using coupons. The Malaysians and Thais both preferred sweepstakes over coupons, and although they were generally price conscious, this sensibility did not influence their sales promotion attitudes.[17]

SPORTS PROMOTIONS AND SPONSORING

With major sports events increasingly being covered by the mass media (by television, in particular), the commercial value of these events has increased tremendously over the last decade. Today, large sports events, such as the Olympics or world championships in specific sports, cannot exist in their present form without funding by companies. Companies provide this funding either through advertising or through different types of sponsorships.

In the United States, companies have for some time purchased television advertising space for regularly broadcast sports events such as baseball, basketball, and American football. Gillette is one company that regularly uses sponsorship of the World Series to introduce new products. This tactic is just another extension of the company's media strategy to air television and radio commercials at times when its prime target group can be found in large numbers watching television or listening to the radio. More recently, companies have purchased similar time slots for the Olympics when they are broadcast in the United States.

About two-thirds of the television rights revenue for the Olympic Games comes from the U.S. market. The cost of purchasing the rights to broadcast the Olympics on television in the United States continues to escalate. NBC acquired the television rights for the United States in a long-term contract with the International Olympic Committee (IOC), through the 2008 Olympic Games, for a total of $2.3 billion. The summer 2000 (Sydney, Australia) and winter 2002 (Salt Lake City, Utah) games went for $1.25 billion. For the 2008 games, NBC agreed to pay $894 million and 50 percent of the advertising revenue. As a result, the typical thirty-second television spot for U.S. broadcasting was expected to increase from $380,000 for the 1996 Atlanta games to $445,000 for the 2000 games, and to $608,000 for the 2008 games.[18] Similarly, the rights to broadcast the Olympics elsewhere were sold to the European Broadcasting Union, which covers Europe, North Africa, and the Middle East, through the 2008 games for a reported $1.44 billion.[19] About half of the broadcast revenues flow to the host city for the games; the other half goes to the International Olympic Committee for its activities. For the Olympic Winter Games 2002 in Salt Lake City, about sixty-five sponsoring companies contributed a total of $859 million, or about two-thirds of the total event budget.[20]

To circumvent restrictions on commercial television during sports programs, companies have purchased space for signs along the stadiums or the arenas where sports events take place. When the event is covered on television, the cameras will automatically take in the signs as part of the regular coverage. No mention of the company's product is made in any way, either by the sports announcer or in the form of commercials. The visual identification is what the firms are looking for.

Aside from purchasing advertising spots or signage space in broadcast programs, individual companies can also engage in sponsorship. Main sponsors for the Olympic Games pay a fee of $40 million to the IOC. Coca-Cola, one of the companies that became a sponsor for the 1996 summer games in Atlanta, spent another estimated $100 million on purchasing commercial time slots from NBC, the owner of the U.S. broadcast rights. The company spent another $100 million on promotional actives surrounding the winter games in Salt Lake City in 2002.[21] Already, the company is gearing up for the summer Olympic Games to be held in China in 2008. China has moved from purchasing just 4 million cases of Coca-Cola to absorbing 450 million cases in 2001, so the company is interested in using sponsorships to increase its volume in what now represents already its sixth most important market.[22] Coca-Cola also sponsors many other sports events, such as the European and world football (soccer) championships, and the Tour de France, the famous multistage bicycle race.

To take advantage of global sports events, a company should have a logo or brand name that can become recognizable to a global audience. It is not surprising to find that the most common sponsors are companies producing consumer goods with a global appeal, such as soft-drink manufacturers, consumer electronics producers, and film companies. To purchase sign space, a firm must take into consideration the popularity of certain sports. Few sports have global appeal. Football (soccer) is the number 1 spectator sport in much of the world. MasterCard International has renewed its official sponsorship of the World Cup football games, held in 2002 in Japan and South Korea. Between 1999 and 2002, MasterCard was the sponsor of four hundred championship matches, with a projected cumulative television audience of 50 billion people.[23] In contrast, baseball and American football have little appeal in Europe or parts of Asia and Africa. Many other sports also have only local or regional character, which requires a company to know its market and its interests—even the athletic interests—of its target audience.

In 1996 in China, Philip Morris sponsored the newly formed football (soccer) league, which it named the Marlboro League, for $2 million annually. Within a short period of time, the league teams increased their per-game revenue to $150,000. In 1999, Pepsi beat Coca-Cola for the sponsorship of the fourteen-team China football league. Pepsi paid a reported $11 million for advertising exposure to the 400 million football fans in China.[24]

Korean global firms have used sports sponsorship abroad extensively. Typically, Korean firms have underwritten individual teams overseas. Samsung is sponsoring ten sports teams or events in eastern Europe, eight in Latin America, and two each in Asia and the Middle East. The company increased its $2.8 million budget in 1996 to $4 million in 1997. Among the Samsung-sponsored teams are twelve foreign football (soccer) teams; the company plans to invite them to Korea for a Samsung tournament. Other Korean firms are active too. Hyundai supports eastern European and African football (soccer) teams, and the LG Group has been very active in sponsoring local sports teams. These Korean firms consider sports sponsorship a cost-effective way to boost their brand or company recognition in emerging or untapped markets.[25] In 2002, Korea and Japan jointly hosted the world football championship.

Aside from sponsoring sporting events, companies have also moved more aggressively into sponsoring direct competitors or teams. Manufacturers of sports equipment have for some time concentrated on getting leading athletes to use their equipment. For sports that have achieved global reach, such as tennis, skiing, or football, an endorsement of sports products by leading athletes can be a key to success. This success is why manufacturers of sports equipment have always attempted to get world-class athletes to use their equipment. Nike, which has rolled out about seventeen models under the Jordan name, has even created a separate Jordan Division, with annual sales of $300 million.[26] Tiger Woods, one of the most recognizable sports figures in the world today, was recently signed by Nike to a five-year contract extension for $100 million.[27]

As part of its aggressive plan to raise its profits in sports sponsorship, the U.S. firm Nike has moved beyond the sponsorship of individual superstars to sponsor entire teams. For a sum of $200 million, Nike obtained sole sponsorship of the Brazilian national teams at all levels for ten years, including the football (soccer) world championships and the Olympic Games.[28] Finally, Nike captured the largest known sponsoring deal in sports history. Under a contract that started in 2002, Nike will pay Manchester United, one of the world's leading football clubs, $450 million over a thirteen-year period. The company will, in addition, take over the club's retail stores and pass on half of all profits from merchandise sales. Nike's logic is to attach its brand to the most famous and best supported teams in the world and watch as everybody benefits.[29] With football (soccer) the most popular sport worldwide, Nike aims to increase its competitiveness against major rivals like Reebok and Adidas.

To exploit the media coverage of spectator sports, many manufacturers besides those who produce sporting goods have also sponsored specific athletes or teams. These firms intend to exploit the visual identification created by the media coverage. Parmalat, a leading Italian dairy company with global operations, serves as a case in point. The company began with the sponsorship of the world Ski Cup in 1975, and and then sponsored Formula One motor car racing through Niki Lauda, world champion, in 1976 and 1977. The company owned and sponsored the local professional football club, AC Parma, and became the main sponsor for a Brazilian club, Palmeiras, which became Brazilian champion in 1999.[30] Parmalat brought the combination of sports sponsorship and brand building to the United States by sponsoring the New York/New Jersey MetroStars, a major soccer club. Parmalat used the following slogan on its milk cartons: "official milk of the MetroStars."[31] Parmalat has used a particular marketing mix that makes heavy use of sports sponsorship in many of its markets and has successfully become the largest UHT milk processor in the world, operating in thirty-one countries.[32]

Many will remember the pictures of winning race car drivers with all the various corporation names or logos on their uniforms. Although these promotions were once mostly related to sports products, sponsors increasingly have no relationship to the sports. Sponsoring a team for competition in the sixteen Grand Prix races all over the world is estimated to cost about $45 to $60 million for one year. The main sponsor is expected to pay about one-half to two-thirds of the cost and gets to paint the cars in its colors and with its logo. The expenses are substantial because the winners do not get very high purses; yet leading race car drivers are reported to get salaries as high as $9 million for one year. In 1988, the races were broadcast in eighty-one countries over 100,000 minutes and attracted 3.3 billion viewers, resulting in about 17 billion "viewings." Major sponsors were tobacco companies (Marlboro, Camel, John Player, Gitanes/Loto) and other consumer goods firms (Benetton).

Through the intensive coverage of sports in the news media all over the world, many companies continue to use the sponsorship of sporting events as an important element in their global communications programs. Successful companies have to track the interest of various countries in the many types of sports and to exhibit both flexibility and ingenuity in the selection of available events or participants. In many parts of the world, sports sponsorship may continue to be the only available way to reach large numbers of prospective customers.

DIRECT MARKETING

Direct marketing includes several marketing approaches that involve direct access to the customer. Direct mail, door-to-door selling, telemarketing, and the Internet are the primary direct marketing tools used around the world. Some companies have achieved considerable success in their fields through aggressive direct marketing. Many of these firms realize that not all markets respond equally well to direct marketing.

The leading agencies practicing direct marketing now generate more than half their revenue from overseas. This figure is a good indicator of how fast this type of selling has grown globally. In 2001, U.S. spending on direct mail, a key component of direct marketing, amounted to $40.8 billion. By comparison, spending in Europe was $35.5 billion, and in Japan, it was $3.3 billion.[33]

Regionally, Europe claims the largest portion of direct marketing volume outside the United States. However, Asia and Latin America are growing rapidly. Asia is benefiting from a new and advanced telecommunications infrastructure with modern postal, telecommunications, cellular, and interactive capabilities. In Latin America, many global firms have begun to use direct marketing. Both Nestlé and IBM did so in Brazil, where seventy-two direct marketing agencies operate, as did American Express in Argentina, where about ten agencies are active. Direct marketing volume is expected to grow 30 percent annually. It is especially useful in overcoming large distances and compensating for less developed traditional physical distribution capabilities.

DIRECT MAIL

Largely pioneered in the United States, direct mail is used extensively in many countries. Successful mail-order sales require an efficient postal system and an effective delivery system for the shipped products. Retail organizations and other service organizations, such as *Reader's Digest* and credit card suppliers, use direct mail in countries where these preconditions exist.

The U.S.-based catalog house Lands' End has maintained local-language catalogs for France and the Netherlands since 1994. The company entered the German market in 1996 with a German-language version of its catalog, including prices in local currency. The company was attracted to Germany as one of the top three mail-order countries, next to Japan and the United States. German consumers were known to purchase more apparel per person through mail order than any other buyers. To support its operation, Lands' End established a fifty-person telephone/customer service facility near the borders of France, Luxembourg, and Germany, where customers may order toll-free on a twenty-four-hour basis. All merchandise was shipped from a Lands' End European distribution center in the United Kingdom, and the merchandise reached German customers in four to five days.

Global mail-order companies have also begun to target Japan. Japanese consumers were estimated to have ordered $26.1 billion worth of merchandise in 1997 alone. With Japanese per capita mail-order sales about half that of the United States, Japan is an attractive market for U.S. and other non-Japanese mail-order companies.[34] Foreign catalogs accounted for about 10 percent of the Japanese direct mail market. David Rio, a San Francisco–based food gifts mailer, launched a Japanese-language catalog in 1997 and mailed a second edition in 1998. Despite a deterioration of the yen versus the U.S. dollar, average orders held up, at $175 per order. For a foreign mail-order company to succeed in Japan, decisions have to be made about the issue of a Japanese-language catalog, whether or not to price in local currency (yen), and whether or not to open a local call center. All of these decisions

Company	Japanese-Language Catalog	Yen Pricing	Japan-Based Call Center
Bass Pro Shop (U.S.)	No	No	Yes
California Gold (U.S.)	Yes	No	No
Coldwater Creek (U.S.)	Yes	No	No
Cyrillus (France)	Yes	No	Yes
David Rio (U.S.)	Yes	No	No
Delia's (U.S.)	Yes	No	No
Eddie Bauer (U.S.)	Yes	Yes	Yes
Freemans (U.K.)	No	No	Yes
GB Data (U.S.)	Yes	No	No
Griot's Garage (U.S.)	No	No	Yes
Hanna Andersson (U.S.)	Yes	No	Yes
Lands' End (U.S.)	Yes	Yes	Yes
Littlewoods (U.K.)	No	No	Yes
L. L. Bean (U.S.)	Yes	No	Yes
Neiman Marcus (U.S.)	No	No	Yes
Patagonia (U.S.)	Yes	Yes	Yes
Paul Fredrick (U.S.)	Yes	No	Yes
REI (U.S.)	Yes	No	No
Victoria's Secret (U.S.)	No	No	Yes

Table 11.2 A Selection of Foreign Catalogs Working to Build a Presence in Japan

Source: Catalog Age, March 1, 1999, vol. 16, no. 3, p. 77.

could substantially increase the cost of entry for direct mail companies.[35] See Table 11.2 for a selection of foreign catalogs working to build a presence in Japan.

There is a great variety of mailing lists in both the United States and Europe. There are also list brokers and lists available in most markets. Direct mail offers an opportunity for companies that want to extend their business beyond a limited location and even into foreign countries. In general, however, shipping packages abroad always involves the receiver country's customs system, which tends to delay parcels. And companies that want to engage in direct mail will have to ensure that their mail pieces or catalogs are translated into the respective foreign language.

DOOR-TO-DOOR SALES

Avon, a leader in the field of door-to-door retailing, has long emphasized international markets. In 2001, the company's revenue in international markets was 62 percent of total worldwide revenue of $5.95 billion. Avon has been able to employ its selling concept successfully in forty-five markets outside North America. Avon has encountered some difficulties because its brand name is less well known than local brands. In April 1998, Avon, together with direct sales companies, was forced to cease direct selling in China. Avon now employs a store-based sales operation, with independently owned Avon stores, in China. Sales have surpassed $100 million and continue to grow rapidly.[36] In Korea, where Avon and Mary Kay only recently established direct sales forces, the leading Korean firm, LG Household & Health Care, was forced to change its strategy by entering the direct sales channels that became dominant for expensive cosmetics imported through Avon and Mary Kay.[37]

The concept of door-to-door selling is not equally accepted in all countries. It is also not equally accepted everywhere to make a profit from selling to friends, work colleagues, or neighbors. The ability to find suitable part-time salespeople may also be limited because in some countries, women or even students are not necessarily expected to work. As a result, door-to-door selling may work best only in the United States.

TELEMARKETING

To make telephone sales effective, an efficient telephone system is a requirement. Telephone sales for individual households may become practical when a larger number of subscribers exist and when their telephone numbers can be easily obtained. However, not all countries accept the practice of soliciting business directly at a person's home. In western Europe, where the economic pressures on selling are the same as they are in the United States, companies can expect gains from the effective use of telemarketing. Because of the language problems involved, companies must make sure their telemarketing sales forces not only speak the language of the local customer but do so fluently and with the correct local or regional accent.

Telemarketing is already a big business in Europe and other areas of the world. Lands' End, the U.S.-based catalog house, opened its European call center at the junction of the French, German, and Luxembourg borders. Employing fifty people, the call center operates twenty-four hours a day and was established to offer support to shoppers and to answer questions. Telemarketing has also been intensifying elsewhere. In Latin America, growth has been substantial, with thirty-six telemarketing firms reported in Brazil, twenty-five in Argentina, and fifteen in Chile. Call centers have grown very fast in Brazil, where the market for telemarketing center software and hardware exceeds $500 million per year.[38]

Major issues in telemarketing are privacy concerns and the different regulations between the United States and Europe. According to EU rules, telemarketers must get permission from the consumer in advance for everything they want to do, including using a customer's personal financial information. That situation is quite different in the United States, where the customer can opt out of telemarketers' lists but otherwise does not have to ask permission. Informing the customer in the United States of the company's adopted privacy policy is sufficient. U.S. and other non-European firms will have to adapt their privacy policies to conform to EU rules, even to the point where they may have to maintain two different databases.[39]

On a global level, telephone sales may be helpful for business-to-business marketing when decision makers can be contacted quickly and when they can be identified from available directories. Because costs for overseas travel are considerable and direct dialing is now possible for international calls in many countries, telemarketing on a cross-country or global basis may be possible.

GLOBAL MARKETING VIA THE INTERNET AND THE WORLD WIDE WEB

The emergence of the commercial use of the Internet, along with the rapid expansion of World Wide Web applications, has been one of the most important developments affecting global marketing in this decade. In 2001, ACNielsen estimated that 429 million people worldwide had Internet access; 59 percent of these Internet users were outside the United States and Canada.[40] The Internet offers companies an entirely new vehicle for communicating and interacting with current and potential customers.

The availability of Internet technology is of particular importance to global marketers. With it, firms can eliminate the time and distance gaps that hinder many international dealings. A company anywhere in the world can establish a web site on the Internet and be instantly available to potential customers from anywhere in the world. This immediate availability, of great importance to all firms, gives a particularly valuable opportunity to smaller firms that lack established international sales channels.

The potential power of the Internet is demonstrated by both large and small companies. DSM, the Dutch chemicals group, announced in early 2000 that, within three years, 100 percent of its purchases and 50 percent of its sales would be conducted via the Internet. Peter Elverding, DSM chairman, said the Internet would increase sales and reduce costs. DSM would also increase its Internet-based dealings with customers and suppliers. Also, it plans to trade through ChemConnect, an Internet exchange for chemicals in which DSM has equity ownership. According to Elverding, "If you don't go down this road, you will be out of business."[41]

The use of the Internet is also increasing in areas such as Latin America. Business to business (B2B) was expected to increase to $6.7 by 2004, compared to revenue in 2000 of only $ 3.6 billion for all forms of ecommerce. The leading country was Brazil, with about 3.9 million Internet users. Brazil thus accounts for about 40 percent of the Latin American potential. Brazil, together with Mexico and Argentina, represents 65 percent of the 9.9 million Latin American users. Use of the Internet is expected to increase even more with the increase in PC ownership in Latin America, which is still low by international standards. PC ownership in Lain America ranges between a low of 3 percent for Peru and 10 percent for Argentina.[42]

A major collateral impact of the Internet will be market harmonization. By creating a common trading channel with broad reach, real-time information, and new revenue opportunities, Forrester Research predicts that Europe will become a single market more quickly with the Internet; a European eZone that will support cross-border commerce will likely be created.[43]

The impact of the Internet on global marketing will be pervasive. Small and large companies alike will be able to reach customers across the world almost instantly, and vice versa. Answers to questions, transmitted via email, will arrive in seconds. Small firms that previously had little chance to reach global markets will be able to do so. Electronic commerce will bring global competition to small or domestic firms, which will suddenly see their markets invaded. The result will be pressures on prices in markets where margins are high. The ultimate winner may be the world's large number of consumers, who will suddenly have an astonishing array of purchasing options.

CONCLUSIONS

Communications in a global context are particularly challenging because managers must communicate with customers from different cultural backgrounds. This situation adds to the complexity of the communications task, which demands a particular sensitivity to culture, habits, and at times even different types of rational reasoning.

Aside from the cultural differences that largely affect the content and form of communications, global firms also encounter a different set of cost constraints for the principal communications mix elements, such as selling or advertising. Given such diversity from country to country with respect to sales force costs or media costs, global firms have to design their communications mix carefully to fit each individual market. Furthermore, the availability of any one individual communications mix element cannot be taken for granted. The absence of one mix element, due to either legal or economic development considerations, will force the global firm to compensate with a greater reliance on other mix elements.

When designing effective sales forces for local markets, global marketers need to consider the challenge of global sales and the requirements for success. Such global sales efforts can usually be maintained for companies selling highly differentiated and complex products to a clearly defined target market. In most other situations, in which the products are targeted at a broader type of industrial or consumer customer group, global firms typically have to engage a local sales force for each market. Local sales forces are usually very effective in reaching their own market or country, but they are not always able to transfer their skills to another country because of language limitations. Building and managing a local sales force are challenging tasks in most foreign markets and require managers with a special sensitivity to local laws, regulations, and trade practices.

All forms of direct and interactive marketing apply to the global market as well. As we have seen, many firms have succeeded by adopting U.S.-based or U.S.-originated direct marketing ideas and using them skillfully abroad. With the global telecommunications infrastructure developing rapidly, the applications for the World Wide Web and Internet-based interactive marketing will continue to expand and will undoubtedly become ever-more important communications mix elements for globally active firms, large or small.

Questions for Discussion

1. What factors affect the extension of push or pull policies in global markets?

2. Under what circumstances should a company pursue a global versus a local selling effort?

3. What factors most often differentiate local selling from country to country?

4. What patterns can you detect in the use of sales promotion tools from country to country?

5. To what types of companies would you suggest sponsorship in the next Olympic Games? Which sports would you recommend to them? How would such firms profit from their association with the Olympic Games?

6. What role will the Internet play in global promotion?

For Further Reading

Chang, Lieh-Ching. "Cross Cultural Differences in Styles of Negotiation Between North Americans (U.S.) and Chinese." *Journal of American Academy of Business,* March 2002, vol. 1, no. 2, pp. 179–187.

Cook, Roy A., and Joel Herche. "Assessment Centers: An Untapped Resource for Global Sales Management." *Journal of Personal Selling and Sales Management,* Summer 1992, pp. 31–38.

Corcoran, Kevin J., et al. *High Performance Sales Organizations: Achieving Competitive Performance in the Global Marketplace.* New York: McGraw-Hill, 1995.

Deighton, John. "Interactive Marketing." *Harvard Business Review,* November–December 1996, p. 151.

Federation of European Direct Marketing Associations. *The Handbook of International Direct Marketing,* 4th ed. London: Kogan Page, 1999.

Kamins, Michael A., Wesley J. Johnston, and John L. Graham. "A Multi-Method Examination of Buyer-Seller Interactions Among Japanese and American Businesspeople." *Journal of International Marketing,* Spring 1998, pp. 27–38.

Kashani, Kamran, and John A. Quelch. "Can Sales Promotion Go Global?" *Business Horizons,* May-June 1990, vol. 33, no. 3, pp. 37–43.

McDonald, William J. "International Direct Marketing." *Direct Marketing,* March 3, 1999, pp. 44–45.

Miller, Russell R. *Selling to Newly Emerging Markets.* Westport, Conn.: Quorum Books, 1998.

Mintu-Wimsatt, Alma, and Julie B. Gassenheimer. "The Moderating Effects of Cultural Context in Buyer-Seller Negotiation." *The Journal of Personal Selling & Sales Management,* vol. 20, no. 1, Winter 2000, pp. 1–9.

Paik, Youngsun, and Rosalie L. Tung. "Negotiating with East Asians: How to Attain "Win-Win" Outcomes." *Management International Review* (Wiesbaden), 2d quarter 1999, vol. 39, no. 2, pp. 103–122.

Simintiras, Antonis C., and Andrew H. Thomas. "Cross-Cultural Sales Negotiations: A Literature Review and Research Propositions." *International Marketing Review,* 1998, vol. 16, no. 1, pp. 10–28.

Volkema, Roger J., and Maria Tereza Leme Fleury. "Alternating Negotiation Conditions and the Choice of Negotiation Tactics: A Cross-Cultural Comparison." *Journal of Business Ethics (Dordrecht),* April 2002, vol. 36, no. 4, pp. 381–398.

Wilson, Kevin, Nick Speare, and Sam Reese. *Successful Global Account Management,* London: Kogan Page, 2001.

Zhao, Jensen J. "The Chinese Approach to International Business Negotiation." *The Journal of Business Communication* (Urbana), July 2000, vol. 37, no. 3, pp. 209–237.

Endnotes

1. Paul Romani, "Selling in the Global Community: The Japanese Model," *American Salesman,* October 1998, pp. 21–25.

2. "Culture of Commerce: US Executives, Foreigners Learn to Negotiate a Two-Way Street," *The Atlanta Journal-Constitution,* April 3, 2002, p. E1.

3. "Etiquette Tips for Today's Global Economy," *Direct Marketing,* March 1999, pp. 22–23.

4. Edward Hall, *Beyond Culture* (Garden City, N.Y.: Anchor Press/ Double Day, 1976).

5. Mintu-Wimsatt, and Julie B. Gassenheimer, "The Moderating Effects of Cultural Context in Buyer-Seller Negotiation," *The Journal of Personal Selling & Sales Management* (New York), Winter 2000, vol. 20, no. 1, pp. 1–9.

6. Wenlee Ting, *Business and Technological Dynamics in Newly Industrialized Asia* (Westport, Conn.: Greenwood, 1985); Magorah Maruyama, "Mindscapes and Social Theories," *Current Anthropology,* 1980, pp. 589–608.

7. Alf H. Walle, "Conceptualizing Personal Selling for International Business: A Continuum of Exchange Perspective," *Journal of Personal Selling and Sales Management,* November 1986, pp. 9–17.

8. William Briggs, "Next for Communicators: Global Negotiation," *Communication World,* December 1, 1998, pp. 1–3.

9. "Salesmen Need to Make More Calls Than Competitors to Be Accepted," *Japan Economic Journal,* June 26, 1979, p. 30.

10. "Welcome to Europe's Biggest Industrial Fair: Hannover Messe 1998," *Modern Materials Handling,* March 1998, p. E3.

11. "Domo Delights," *Appliance Manufacturer* (Chicago), May 1999, vol. 47, no. 5, pp. 27–32.

12. "Thirteen Percent Increase in Trade Fair Visitors," *Businessworld,* May 9, 2002, p. 1.

13. Iris Kapustein, "Selling and Exhibiting Across the Globe," *Doors and Hardware,* September 1, 1998, p. 34.

14. Jean-Pierre Jeannet and Martha Lanning, *Euro RSCG: Global Brand Management in Advertising,* Case (Lausanne, Switzerland: IMD, 2001).

15. Jean-Pierre Jeannet and Robert Collins, *Deloitte Touche Tohmatsu International Europe*, Case (Lausanne, Switzerland: IMD, 1993).

16. David Murphy, "Sales Promotion: Cross-Border Conflicts," *Marketing*, February 11, 1999, p. 30.

17. Lenard C. Huff and Dana L. Alden, "An Investigation of Consumer Response to Sales Promotion in Developing Markets," *Journal of Advertising Research*, May-June 1998, pp. 47–57.

18. "NBC, IOC Chase Long-Term Deals," *Advertising Age*, December 18, 1995, p. 3.

19. "Murdoch Loses Bidding for Olympic Television Rights," *Financial Times*, January 31, 1996, p. 1.

20. "Union Pacific Gets Higher Profile from Olympics Sponsorship," *Knight Ridder Tribune Business News*, February 7, 2002.

21. "Lord of the Rings," *Dollars & Sense*, March-April 2002, pp. 4–5; and "Coca-Cola on Ice Chill from Corporate Clutter Is Challenge for Leading Olympic Sponsor," *The Atlanta Journal-Constitution*, January 23, 2002, p. D1.

22. "Cashing in on the World Cup," *Far Eastern Economic Review*, June 6, 2002, p. 43.

23. "MasterCard Renews Commitments with FICA World Cup Through 2002," *Comline Pacific Research Consulting*, March 19, 1999, pp. 1–2.

24. "Pepsi Scores over Coke in China Battle," *Stadium and Arena Financing News*, February 22, 1999, p. 1.

25. "Chaebol Takes a Sporting Chance, Raises Spending on Advertising," *Nikkei Weekly*, January 27, 1997, p. 26.

26. "Advertisers Prepare Full-Court Press if Jordan Plays," *USA Today*, August 29, 2001, p. B10.

27. "Woods, His Agent and Nike Top Leaderboard of Golf's Power Brokers," *Denver Post*, August 5, 2001, p. C12

28. "Nike Puts Its Hands on Ultimate Trophy," *Financial Times*, December 14-15, 1996, p. 5.

29. "Nike Learns the Flipside of Associating with Success," *Marketing Week* (London), November 30, 2000, p. 37.

30. "Brazil's Cash-Strapped Soccer Teams Look to Manchester United for Inspiration," *Financial Times*, June 19, 1999, p. 4.

31. "Parmalat Teams with MetroStars for U.S. Soccer Debut," *Brandweek*, January 8, 2001, p. 37.

32. "Making More of Milk," *Dairy Field*, February 2002, p. 7.

33. "In Industry's Gloom, Direct Marketing Is One Bright Spot," *Wall Street Journal*, April 10, 2002, p. A8.

34. "How US Mail Order Companies Do Business in Japan," *Fareast Direct*, *www.fareastdirect.com;* accessed on July 8, 2002.

35. "Surviving and Thriving in Japan today," *Catalog Age*, March 1, 1999, p. 77.

36. Avon, *Annual Report*, 2001.

37. "Cosmetics Hit the Road in Korea with Surge in Door-to Door Sales," *Asian Wall Street Journal*, May 23, 2002, p. A8.

38. "Brazil: Boom in the Call Centers Market," *Gazeta Mercantil*, May 31, 1999, p. 1.

39. "US, EU Still Don't Agree on Data Handling," *Marketing News* (Chicago), August 13, 2001, pp. 5–6.

40. "429 Million People Are on the Net Worldwide," *Direct Marketing*, September 2001, p. 18.

41. "DSM Set to Expand Web-based Dealings," *Financial Times*, February 24, 2000, p. 17.

42. "Study Examines E-Commerce/Internet Use in Latin America," *Direct Marketing*, April 2001, p. 9.

43. "Internet Will Speed European Market Harmonization," *Strategic Finance*, May 1999, p. 20.

Chapter 12

Managing Global Advertising

At the beginning of this book, we defined global marketing as consisting of those marketing activities that applied simultaneously to more than one country. In the case of global advertising, the volume of activity directed simultaneously toward targets in many countries is actually small. The majority of global advertising activity still tends to be directed toward one country at a time. Despite the "local" nature of global advertising, it is important to recognize that the initial input, in terms of either the product idea or the basic communications strategy, originates in another country. Although there is a largely local aspect to most global advertising, there is also a global country-to-country aspect to consider.

Two important questions must be answered in global advertising: (1) how much of a local versus a global emphasis should there be? and (2) what should be the nature and content of the advertising itself? The first part of the chapter is organized around the explanation of key external factors and their influence on global advertising. The rest of the chapter focuses on the major advertising decisions and helps to explain how external factors affect specific advertising areas. The chapter organization is depicted in Figure 12.1.

The diversity of views and approaches to global advertising are best described with two recent examples: Coca-Cola and Kleenex. Coca-Cola and Kimberly-Clark (maker of Kleenex) have chosen diametrically different approaches and strategies for their global advertising. Kimberly-Clark (K-C) once spent a considerable amount of time developing commercials that fit many countries for its Kleenex brand campaign "Thank Goodness for Kleenex." K-C spent months and became involved with many parties from different countries while creating numerous spots to serve many markets. In its recent approach, the company used a small team of executives teamed with its agency and created a single spot (the visuals) in a short time to be used in all

Figure 12.1: Global Advertising

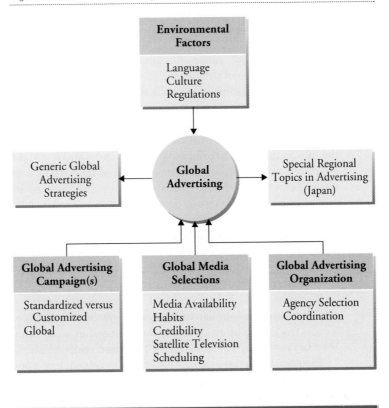

markets. The resulting commercials outperformed existing ads in tests in both the United States and Europe. The initial flight of centrally planned spots could grow to many more, leading later to tailoring in individual markets.[1] Coca-Cola, which has considerable experience making commercials for its leading Coke brand, produced just one global ad to go with the 1998 World Cup (soccer). For the 2002 version of the World Cup, the company reused a re-edited version of the earlier ad but decided to augment it with about twenty-five commercials tailored to individual markets. Although the company still pursues a strategy of leveraging its marketing skills globally, the company believes that producing a single, perfect global ad for many markets may take an inordinate amount of time and resources to produce.[2]

CHALLENGES IN GLOBAL ADVERTISING

Probably no other aspect of global marketing has received as much attention as advertising. Many mistakes have been made in translating advertising copy from one language to another. Most of these mistakes occurred, however, in the 1960s, when global advertising was in its infancy. Today, most companies and advertising agencies have reached a level of sophistication that reduces the chances of translation error.

This level of sophistication does not mean that language is not a factor to consider in today's global communications strategy. However, the industry has moved from a primary concern about translation to concerns about ways to be more efficient and effective.

A second major cause of global advertising mistakes has traditionally been the neglect of the cultural attitudes of consumers in foreign countries. Benetton, the Italian clothing manufacturer, sells through stores all over the world. It ran into cultural problems with its advertising when it launched a campaign under the theme "United Colors of Benetton," which had won awards in Europe. The ads had started conventionally in 1983 featuring models of different races in Benetton clothes, with the images intended to promote racial harmony and world peace. The ads became increasingly controversial when one appeared in 1992 showing an AIDS patient moments before death; subsequent advertisements showed a newborn baby with its umbilical cord still attached, or prison inmates sentenced to death. Relatives of victims depicted or other groups offended by the ads began to sue the company. The controversial ads were partly to blame for Benetton's declining sales in the United States, so the company changed course. In its most recent campaign, Benetton went out of its way to be less controversial by featuring models in colorful knitwear in its advertisements.[3]

In another case, Nike found that its flame logo on shoes offended Islamic followers. The flame was similar to the Arabic symbol for Allah, and in Islam the feet are seen as unclean. The two images shown together were interpreted as disrespectful. Nike has now withdrawn the use of the flame symbol.[4]

Such examples show that, even when the language or translation hurdle is cleared, firms still need to consider the cultural and social background of the target market. Mistakes based on a misinterpretation of cultural habits are more difficult to avoid, although substantial progress has been made by global marketers in steering clear of the most obvious violations. Merely avoiding translation or cultural errors, however, does not guarantee an effective advertising campaign. In this chapter, we concentrate initially on ways to overcome cultural difficulties; later in the chapter, we cover the critical issues related to organizing effective global advertising campaigns.

OVERCOMING THE LANGUAGE BARRIER

Most of the translation blunders that plagued global advertising in the past were the result of literal translations completed outside the target country. The translators, not always in contact with the culture of the target country, were unable to judge the actual meaning of the translated copy for the target audience. Furthermore, the faulty translation could not be checked by the executives involved because they too were from a different culture and did not possess the necessary language skills.

Today, the trap of faulty translations can be avoided through the involvement of local nationals or language experts. Typically, global marketers have translations checked by either a local advertising agency, their own local subsidiary, or an independent distributor located in the target country. Because firms are active in a large number of countries and thus advertise in many languages, today's global marketers can find an organizational solution to avoid many of the translation errors of the past.

In the European Union (EU), many official languages are spoken. As a result, much advertising puts a special emphasis on communicating visually rather than through the various languages. Graphics are used more effectively in print media, too.[5] Satellite TV channels have discovered that not everyone in Europe speaks English well enough to understand English commercials and that, if given a chance, most people like to watch programs in their own language. Super Channel moved to trilingual program services. Rather than offer pan-European programs, operators of satellite channels in Europe have moved toward multiregional programming. There are economies-of-scale benefits if a campaign can be run in several countries with a multilanguage approach. For example, Pepsi ran a multilanguage campaign that centered on an on-pack promotion for exclusive Spice Girl prizes in nine countries, with a menu of redemption options tailored to the market needs and legal requirements of each country.[6]

Adjusting to a local language often requires changes in the product name or its positioning. For example, Coca-Cola was first rendered as *Ke-kou-ke-la* in Chinese, which meant "bite the wax tadpole" or "female horse stuffed with wax," depending on the dialect. After the problem was discovered, Coca-Cola researched forty thousand Chinese characters and found *Ko-kou-ko-le* a close phonetic representation for Coca-Cola. The Chinese phrase means "happiness in the mouth."[7]

OVERCOMING THE CULTURAL BARRIER

When global marketers fail because of misinterpretation of the local culture, they usually do so because they advocated an action inconsistent with the local culture or because they chose an appeal inconsistent with the motivational pattern of the target culture. Advocating the purchase of a product whose use is inconsistent with the local culture will result in failure, even if the appeal itself does not violate that culture. Companies can also fail if the appeal, or message employed, is inconsistent with the local culture, even if the action promoted is not. Consequently, a foreign company entering a new market has to be aware of both cultural aspects: the product's use and the message employed.

Sara Lee, the U.S.-based global firm that owns lingerie brands such as Playtex, Cacharel, and Wonderbra, faced intensive opposition to a series of billboards in Mexico. The company launched a global Wonderbra campaign that featured a Czech model posing in the bra on all of its outdoor advertising. In Mexican cities, citizens protested the ads because they considered them offensive. Pressured by the public, the company redesigned its billboards; for Mexico, the model wore a suit. Sara Lee learned that in some countries it had to change the visual of the global campaign on a case-by-case basis.[8]

Renault, the French car manufacturer, used a government-created French cartoon character, a mascot of the French government's national traffic center in the form of a "smart buffalo," for an ad. A Native American depicted in the ad was intended as a reference to the French national cartoon character. The character, "Bison," gives traffic directions on French television during the evenings of long weekends when extensive traffic problems typically occur. French television viewers immediately made a positive connection with the character. Other audiences, such as those in the United States, did not have prior exposure to the cartoon character, and had a different view of it. The ad was found offensive to members of the Native American community, which prompted Renault and its advertising agency to withdraw the advertisement and issue an apology.[9]

To ensure that a message is in line with the existing cultural beliefs of the target market, companies can use resources similar to those used to overcome translation barriers. Local subsidiary personnel or local distributors can judge the cultural content of the message. Also helpful are advertising agencies with local offices. Global marketers cannot possibly know enough about all the cultures with which they will come into contact to assess the appropriateness of advertising appeals. It is the responsibility of the international executive, however, to make sure that knowledgeable local nationals have been given enough input so that the use of an inappropriate advertising appeal in any given culture will be avoided.

Sometimes, global companies have to use advertising to overcome expressed cultural biases, or attitudes, that can be harmful to their business. McDonald's, the largest French restaurant chain with about eight hundred outlets and sales of 1.5 billion euros, found itself in the midst of a debate unleashed by anti-globalizing forces. The company resorted to a full-fledged advertising campaign in France emphasizing its "local" roots and the use of French supplies and foods, such as beef, to prepare its hamburgers.[10]

Judging the appropriateness of a product or service for a culture is substantially more difficult than making a judgment only on the type of advertising to be employed. In Chapter 3, we discussed the nature of cultural and social forces; we covered the evaluation of market potential for products in Chapter 6. Here, we restrict ourselves to a discussion of the advertising aspects of cultural analysis.

THE IMPACT OF REGULATIONS ON GLOBAL ADVERTISING

There are numerous situations in which differing customer needs require tailor-made advertising campaigns. In many instances, the particular regulations of a country prevent firms from using standardized approaches, even when they would appear desirable. In countries such as Malaysia, regulations are a direct outgrowth of changing political circumstances. Malaysia is a country with a large Muslim population, and it outlawed ads showing women in sleeveless dresses and pictures showing underarms. Given the strict rules in Malaysia governing the production and screening of commercials, Unilever found it most advantageous to film its Lipton Yellow Label Tea commercial in Malaysia. Using local talent and internationally acceptable scenery, Unilever was able to shoot three versions of the commercial on the same storyline for fifteen European and Asian countries, at a substantial savings over doing local commercials in each market.[11]

Advertising for cigarettes and tobacco products is strictly regulated in many countries. Members of the World Health Organization are negotiating a treaty that will establish global regulations on cigarette advertising; limits will be set on where smoking will be allowed, and cigarette taxation will be raised in all countries. The treaty will be the first binding global treaty on social behavior and is scheduled to be implemented in 2003.[12] Brazil, home to about 30 million smokers, has even surpassed Europe with its regulations against advertising for smoking or cigarettes. The country instituted one of the most comprehensive bans on advertising, gradually forbidding advertising everywhere except at the counters where cigarettes are sold. Furthermore, Brazil adopted a ban on terms such as *light* or *mild* from appearing on cigarette packs, a ban it adopted ahead of Europe.[13]

The European Union is debating a series of rulings that could have great impact on advertising in Europe. The discussions involve efforts toward both greater harmonization and the extent of regulation. Greater harmonization is generally viewed as desirable throughout Europe and could potentially result in uniform regulations for advertising. This harmonization would greatly enhance the potential for pan-European marketing campaigns and bring greater advertising efficiency. With Sweden taking over the presidency of the EU in 2001, the push to harmonize advertising regulations in the EU on the basis of the most restrictive national regulations on pharmaceuticals, food, and advertising to children (as they already are in force in Sweden) was expected to be renewed.[14]

Self-regulation plays a big role in advertising, with watchdogs established in many countries that will call on any advertiser that supposedly violates established norms. In France, the issue was advertising portraying women and the depiction of the human body. Europe's leading fashion houses were singled out for portraying women in a degrading way. But the self-regulation is directed at firms that use advertising agencies. Those companies that produce their own ads are often exempt from the pressure of voluntary regulations. Benetton of Italy refused to withdraw an ad showing a young woman in a suggestive pose.[15]

Other regulations that companies may encounter cover the production of advertising material. Some countries require all advertising, particularly television and radio, to be produced locally. As a result, it has become a challenge for global advertisers to find campaigns that can be used in as many countries as possible and thus save on production costs. Such campaigns are possible, however, only if a marketer has sufficient input from the very beginning on the applicable legislation and can thus take all regulations into account.

SELECTING A GLOBAL ADVERTISING THEME

STANDARDIZATION VERSUS CUSTOMIZATION

For marketers with products sold in many countries, the basic decision often centers around the appropriate level of standardization for the advertising theme and its creative execution. Because inexperienced companies that employed a completely standardized approach experienced so many failures, companies shifted to the other extreme by allowing each market to design its own campaign. In the mid-1960s, European-based advertising executives started to discuss the possibility of greater standardization. Erik Elinder was among the first to advocate the benefits of a more standardized approach. Elinder argued that European consumers were increasingly living under similar conditions, although they read and spoke different languages thus making it possible to pursue greater standardization.[16]

ADVANTAGES OF STANDARDIZING GLOBAL ADVERTISING. Because creative talent is scarce, a single effort to develop a campaign will likely produce better results than forty or fifty separate efforts. This situation applies particularly to countries for which the marketing or advertising experience is limited. A second advantage centers around the economics of a global campaign. To develop an individual campaign in many countries creates costs for photographs, layouts, and the production of television commercials. In a standardized approach, these production

costs can be reduced, and more funds can be spent on purchasing space in the media. In addition, the fewer messages to be produced can be created with higher production budgets, thus increasing communication effectiveness. A third reason for a standardized approach is found in global brand names. Many companies market products under a single brand name in several countries within the same region. With the substantial amount of international travel occurring today and the considerable overlap in media across national borders, companies are interested in creating a single image to avoid any confusion caused through local campaigns that may conflict with each other.

Patek Philippe, the prestigious watchmaker, has supported its brand with a global print and television campaign using the following theme: "You never actually own a Patek Philippe. You merely look after it for the next generation." The campaign has been successful in many markets, including the United States, Europe, China, Japan, Singapore, and Taiwan.[17]

Procter & Gamble (P&G) launched Pringles potato chips in the 1970s. For fifteen years, the company experienced little significant penetration in the salty-snack market, which was dominated by Frito-Lay. Between 1995 and 1999, however, P&G doubled the sales of Pringles to $1.0 billion. Now one of P&G's top three global brands, Pringles potato chips are sold in over forty countries. P&G attributes the global success of Pringles to a uniform package, product, and advertising message aimed at young children (six to eleven years old) and teens (twelve to seventeen years old). The message used around the world is "Once you pop, you can't stop." P&G allows some local tactical differences, including some flavor variations, from one market to another, but the bulk of the advertising and merchandising is global.[18]

Warner Lambert Co. decided to revitalize the image of Chiclets gum. Past advertisements were created on a country-by-country basis with no central theme. Research had shown that Chiclets faced low visibility in many countries. The new positioning ad campaign was targeted to the eighteen- to twenty-four-year-old consumer. The commercial, shot in the sand dunes of northern Brazil, included a desert shack occupied by a young man and a monkey. By rattling a Chiclets box, he summoned an international audience ranging from Japanese geishas to English schoolboys. The tag line in English was "Chiclets make cool things happen." By using the ad worldwide, Warner Lambert maximized the impact of its advertising expenditures.[19]

Taco Bell, a U.S.-based chain with seven thousand restaurants, featured Gidget, the talking Chihuahua dog, in advertisements in the United States. The company found that Gidget could not be used in Asia, where many consider dogs a delicacy, or in Muslim countries, where it is taboo to touch a dog.[20] As all the preceding examples show, specific factors will either allow or prevent standardization of some parts of an advertising campaign. The nature of these factors is the topic of the following section.

REQUIREMENTS FOR STANDARDIZED CAMPAIGNS. For a company to launch a worldwide standardized campaign, some requirements with regard to the product name, packaging, awareness, competitive situation, and consumer or customer attitudes must first be met. The need for a standardized brand name or trademark is viewed by many companies as a prerequisite to a standardized campaign. Not only should the name always be written in the same format, it should be pronounced identically.

Table 12.1 The World's Top Ten Most Valuable Brands

Brand	Brand Value 2001 ($m)	Brand Value 2000 ($m)	Percentage Change	Market Cap	Brand Value as Percentage Market Cap
Coca-Cola	68,945	72,537	−5	113,400	61
Microsoft	65,068	70,197	−7	380,000	17
IBM	52,752	53,184	−1	198,700	27
GE	42,396	38,128	11	498,600	9
Nokia	35,035	38,528	−9	104,200	34
Intel	34,665	39,049	−11	202,200	17
Disney	32,591	33,553	−3	60,000	54
Ford	30,092	36,368	−17	45,900	66
McDonald's	25,289	27,859	−9	35,400	—
AT&T	22,828	25,548	−11	148,950	15

Source: From Interbrand/BusinessWeek, August 2002. Copyright © 2002 Interbrand/BusinessWeek. Used with permission.

Trademarks or corporate logos can also help in achieving greater standardization of corporate campaigns. Well-known logos such as Kodak's, Sony's, and General Electric's are used the world over. The power of a company's brand name has a considerable influence on whether the company can use a standardized campaign. Few brand names are known universally. A research firm reviewed some of the best-known brands and examined them according to its brand valuation model which includes four key elements: financial forecasting, role of branding, brand strength, and brand value calculation. The results are shown in Table 12.1.

Whirlpool acquired the Philips business in 1991 following an earlier joint venture, and the firm thus became the world's largest appliance maker, overtaking Electrolux of Sweden. Because Whirlpool was largely unknown to European consumers, the company undertook a pan-European advertising campaign conducted over several years. The advertising was the result of some exhaustive testing of housewives in the United Kingdom, France, Spain, and Austria. Whirlpool maintained its share of the European market. The company focused most of its advertising efforts on promoting the Whirlpool brand name at the expense of some locally acquired brands, such as Bauknecht in Germany.[21] Following eight years of success in Europe, Whirlpool took the campaign, consisting of four thirty-second spots and one sixty-second brand treatment, and adapted it to the United States. The campaign's feature of the "spirit of the all-powerful female, made even more powerful with Whirlpool products by her side," tested well in focus groups held with U.S. women. The campaign was extended to Latin America and ran in more than forty countries.[22] This campaign was successful in many markets because the purchasing criteria, and the purchase motivation, of women customers were sufficiently similar.

To aid the prospective customer in identifying the advertised product with the actual product placed in retail stores, consumer products manufacturers in particular use standardized packages. Despite differences in sizes, these packages carry the same design in terms of color, layout, and name. Nonstandardized packages cannot be featured in a standardized campaign. Naturally, this concern is of interest to consumer products companies because the package has to double as a protective device and as a promotional device.

Because products may be at different stages of their product life cycles in different countries, different types of advertising may be required to appeal to the various levels of customer awareness. Typically, a campaign during the earlier stages of the product life cycle concentrates on the product category because many prospective customers may not have heard about the product. In later stages of the product life cycle, with the accompanying intensive competition, the campaign tends to shift toward emphasizing the product's advantages over competitive products.

As companies enter new markets, they can expect to find different competitive situations that require an adjustment in the advertising campaign. Competing against different groups of competitors and placed in the situation of an outsider often demand a change from the advertising policy used in the domestic market, where these firms might well have a strong position. Perrier entered the U.S. market using a premium appeal. Emphasizing the product's noncaloric attributes, Perrier was positioned as an alternative to soft drinks and alcoholic beverages. With its premium price, Perrier was geared toward more affluent adults. In European markets, where Perrier was already well entrenched and the drinking of mineral water is already accepted by a large number of consumers, such an approach would not have yielded the same results.

These examples involve companies with solid leadership positions at home entering foreign markets as outsiders. They were forced by this circumstance to develop advertising programs substantially different from those used in their home markets.

SPECIAL REGIONAL TOPICS IN GLOBAL ADVERTISING

ADVERTISING IN THE JAPANESE MARKET.   Japan is the world's second largest advertising market after the United States, with spending in 2000 of $52 billion.[23] The dominant style of advertising in Japan uses an image-oriented approach, or "soft sell," compared with the more factual or "hard sell" approach that is typical in the United States, or the "wit" that is prevalent in the United Kingdom.[24]

Because different cultural backgrounds produce varying consumer attitudes, it is quite normal to expect differences in advertising appeals. Japan offers several examples that contrast with experiences in the United States or Europe. In Japan, consumers tend to be moved more by emotion than by logic, in contrast to North Americans or Europeans.[25] According to Western observers, the Japanese are culturally oriented to consider the mood, style, and sincerity demonstrated by a deed as more important than its content. Consequently, consumers are searching for ways to be emotionally convinced about a product. This cultural feature leads to advertising that rarely mentions price, occasionally even omits the distinctive features or qualities of a product, and shies away from advertising aimed at diminishing the products of competing firms. This type of advertising is further supported by the Japanese language, which even has a verb *(kawasarern)* to describe the process of being convinced to buy a product contrary to one's rational judgment.

Traditionally, Japanese advertising has a strong nonverbal component; uses contemporary Japanese language; frequently shows man-woman, mother-child, or even father-daughter relationships; demonstrates Japanese humor; and above all stresses long-term relationships. There is also some evidence of the individual's place in Japanese society in the use of evocative pictures or events. With respect to the emotional component, the use of nonverbal communication and inference seems to prevail. Also important is the product origin and the need to present the product as being right for the Japanese. These characteristics require a strong corporate identity program to establish a firm's credibility in the Japanese market.

Although one may conclude that U.S. products do not sell in Japan, reality shows that this is not necessarily so. Japanese television commercials are full of U.S. themes, use many U.S. stars or heroes, and frequently have U.S. landscapes or backgrounds. By using U.S. stars in their commercials, Japanese companies give the impression that these products are very popular in the United States. Given the Japanese interest in and positive attitudes toward many U.S. cultural themes, such strategies have worked out well for Japanese advertisers. U.S. movie and pop stars are sought after for appearances in Japanese television commercials, resulting in payments of $2 to $3 million for each commercial produced. Movie stars such as Meg Ryan, Brad Pitt, and Demi Moore may be seen in Japan endorsing face cream, blue jeans, and protein drinks.[26] In contrast to U.S. testimonials, however, Japanese advertisers tend to use foreign stars as actors using the product rather than openly endorsing it.

A trend in Japanese advertising is to strive for product awareness only; Japanese advertisements are thus often devoid of any mention of the product itself. As a result, comparative advertising rarely exists in Japan; before-and-after claims are also seldom used. According to some experts, western advertising is designed to make the product look superior, whereas Japanese advertising is aimed at making it desirable.

Using an approach new to Japan, Sega was able to recover market share lost to Sony's PlayStation and Nintendo 64. A series of commercials played on the poor performance of Sega. The first commercial began with one junior high school boy saying to another, "Sega sucks. Let's go play with PlayStation," while a senior Sega executive, Hidekazu Yukawa, overhears the conversation. Commercials that followed showed Yukawa losing battles with disheartened workers, a bottle of booze, and tough guys on the street before stumbling home to his wife. The last commercials showed that Sega was able to challenge PlayStation with the launch of Dreamcast. According to Yasumichi Oka, the creative director at the ad agency Dentsu, if the commercials had started by saying everything was fine at Sega, no one would have believed it. The series of seven commercials successfully launched Dreamcast with sales of 3 million units in the first month, compared with only 5 million units of Sega's previous product, Saturn, over forty months.[27]

Advertising in Japan also differs from western practice in its management and structure. In Japan, the conflict-of-interest rules do not apply, and competing brands can be handled by the same agency. The market is dominated by Dentsu, by far Japan's largest advertising agency and one of the world's largest as well. Dentsu is the Japanese media's biggest single customer, accounting for about 20 percent of all billings in Japan and 50 percent of prime-time television. Dentsu usually commands the best price and the best space in the press.[28] None of the other major advertising markets in the world is so dominated by a single local agency.

ADVERTISING IN CHINA. China is a country that makes standardized approaches difficult. Research has shown that the Chinese display sharply different attitudes in three areas. First, Chinese consumers emphasize respect and harmony more than U.S. consumers do. Second, the Chinese view health in broader terms than do Americans: the Chinese concept of health includes sleeping well and peace. Third, the Chinese place a higher priority on family life within the home.

Driven by the relentless growth in its economy, the Chinese advertising market has grown to the second largest in Asia, after Japan, with total spending surpassing $11 billion in 2001. This amount makes the Chinese advertising market tied with the corresponding markets in Germany and the United Kingdom. At present growth rates, China would surpass Japan by the end of the decade and assume the role of the second largest market in the world, behind the United States.[29] Growth was fueled in part by local companies that invested heavily in television advertising. Among the top product categories were several personal care groups, also dominated by local brands.[30] The growth in advertisement spending became a concern of the government, and the tax code was changed to make sure that only advertisement spending up to 2 percent of sales could be deducted as a business expense. This change was instituted due to concerns that some firms might spend themselves out of business.[31]

The experience of international firms in China demonstrates that careful research pays off. De Beers, the South Africa–based diamond marketing company, spent three years carefully studying Chinese attitudes toward love and marriage. The results indicated that De Beers could not use its tried and proven approach of selling diamonds for wedding rings as a symbol of romance in China. Instead, the company depicts diamonds as a symbol of a couple's bright, prosperous future, something the company has not tried anywhere else. The results of the strategy are encouraging. After running these ads, one in three couples in Shanghai bought a diamond ring, compared to only one in ten in Beijing and Guangzhou, and even less in rural Chinese provinces.[32]

Procter & Gamble, one of the most successful international marketers in China, found it had to pull an ad for its Rejoice shampoo. The original ad featured an airline hostess, who had to be replaced in subsequent ads with a woman working as an airline mechanical engineer. The change was influenced by the result of surveys that showed women had become more career-focused. The company has changed its approach again, however. Its most recent ads for Rejoice feature a girl playing beach volleyball. This second change came after it was discovered that many Chinese women want to fulfill other aspirations besides career success. The traditional archetypes for Chinese women were the ingénue and the caregiver, but these images are rapidly yielding to new archetypes, such as woman as hero, woman as lover, or woman as creator and explorer.[33] Clearly, such changes will have to be reflected in advertising messages.

The experience of TCBY frozen yogurt in China indicates that a more regionalized approach may at times be necessary. The company maintains that each Chinese city is different, and that even within China, a single commercial was not feasible. Thus, TCBY advertisements try to address the interests of Chinese consumers in each separate city or province.[34]

THE ADVERTISING ENVIRONMENT IN EASTERN EUROPE. With the political and economic liberalization in eastern Europe over the past ten years, advertising suddenly became available to foreign companies and developed into an acceptable economic activity. Its growth has been hampered by the fact that commercial advertising, as it is known in a market economy, had been used previously for political purposes and to advertise surplus merchandise only. When the markets in eastern

Table 12.2 Twenty-Five Advertising Firms in Europe[a]			
Agency (Multinational Network)	1998 Gross Income	Percentage Change from 1997	1998 Billings
Euro RSCG Worldwide	$647.4	8.7	$4,109.1
BBDO Worldwide	634.8	53.1	4,742.7
McCann-Erickson Worldwide	627.5	16.2	5,473.9
Publicis Worldwide	586.8	36.6	3,726.2
Young & Rubicam	516.3	11.0	4,686.6
Ogilvy & Mather Worldwide	498.1	9.7	4,753.5
DDB Needham Worldwide	480.4	8.0	3,421.4
Grey Advertising	433.1	6.6	3,055.9
J. Walter Thompson Co.	431.7	9.0	3,102.3
TBWA International	357.9	17.7	2,441.0
Ammirati Puris Lintas	334.0	6.8	2,445.5
D'Arcy Masius Benton & Bowles	301.3	−4.5	2,784.4
Bates Worldwide	272.7	7.4	3,208.5
Leo Burnett Co.	257.5	15.2	2,119.1
Lowe & Partners Worldwide	212.3	9.0	1,475.5
Saatchi & Saatchi	154.4	2.2	1,979.7
Brann Worldwide	148.1	37.9	987.8
Rapp Collins Worldwide	116.0	NA	773.4
Foote, Cone & Belding	104.8	NA	758.3
TMP Worldwide	89.1	33.0	593.8
Bozell Worldwide	78.9	4.4	521.3
Campus	72.5	59.9	594.4
FCA/BMZ	69.5	3.2	457.6
Carlson Marketing	44.5	25.9	519.2
Draft Worldwide	44.4	61.6	554.6

a. All figures are in millions of dollars.
Source: Reprinted with permission from Advertising Age International. Copyright, Crain Communications, Inc. 1999.

Europe opened up, changes came both in the media policy of these countries and in the acceptability of commercial advertising. In the words of one expert, "The last hundred years of western advertising [experience] have been compressed into just four years for us."[35] Differences between Czech and western consumers are said to be the smallest among eastern European countries, but significant differences persisted elsewhere. In most eastern European nations, advertising is in the early phases of development. The present infrastructure is still not what global firms are used to. Many western agencies established local offices, some as joint ventures with local account managers. Table 12.2 shows the top European advertising firms, most of which operate also in eastern Europe.

A study of twelve thousand consumers in central and eastern Europe revealed three general mindsets for consumers there: (1) optimists—not afraid of change, enjoy life, usually opinion leaders; (2) engaged—hopeful, early adopters of new ideas; and (3) defeatist—lacking financial security, believe lives are changing for the worse, prefer communism.[36] Each eastern European country had 40 to 50 percent optimists and engaged, who together are the most willing to buy new products. The greatest percentage of optimists were in Russia and the Ukraine.[37]

As eastern European markets make the transition to market economies, western firms have significant opportunities to build brand awareness quickly. As Russia's population of 218 million grows more prosperous, opportunities for marketing consumer products will grow. Procter & Gamble is exporting several brands to Russia, among them Crest toothpaste and Camay soap. With strong interest among global firms to build a presence in the large Russian consumer market, several global advertising agencies have set up shop in Moscow.

GLOBAL ADVERTISING

Global advertising received a considerable amount of attention in the 1980s and is now considered the most controversial topic in global marketing. The debate was triggered by Professor Theodore Levitt, who argues in an article and in his book, *The Marketing Imagination*, that markets are becoming increasingly alike worldwide and that the trend is toward a global approach to marketing.[38]

Levitt's ideas were applied to the field of global advertising by Saatchi & Saatchi, a British advertising agency that rose to prominence on the basis of its global campaigns. Saatchi & Saatchi claimed that worldwide brands would soon become the norm and that such an advertising challenge could be handled only by worldwide agencies. Saatchi & Saatchi purchased several privately held agencies, including Ted Bates of the United States, in 1986. In response, the industry began a period of consolidations that resulted in large global agencies, including WPP Group, Omnicom, Interpublic, and Saatchi & Saatchi. Saatchi & Saatchi has had financial difficulty because of its large debt, but its initial philosophy led to the development of several global advertising firms. In 2000, Saatach & Saatchi was acquired by Publicis, a competing French agency network. The Saatchi & Saatchi head offices were transferred to New York, where the company still runs a network of about 150 offices in about ninety countries. The original founders of the British agency, Maurice and Charles Saatchi, left in 1995 and created a new rival network, under the M&C Saatchi name, with a smaller number of offices. Some key accounts, such as British Airways, moved to the new agency.[39]

The fervent advocates of global advertising argue that consumer tastes, needs, and purchasing patterns are converging. This viewpoint can be supported by the converging trends in demographics across many countries. At the forefront of these trends has been the decline of the nuclear family, both in North America and in many countries around the globe. In most countries, more women are working. Divorce trends are helping to fuel the decline of the nuclear family in North America, Europe, and other developed countries. This trend has changed the role of women in society almost everywhere. Standards of living have risen in many countries, and earlier differences among nations have been reduced. In addition to these demographic trends, common media such as films, television, and music are creating cultural convergence as well. These developments are said to reduce cultural barriers among countries; such barriers are expected to diminish even further through satellite television networks beaming identical programs to many countries.

One of the strong initial believers in global advertising, British Airways, broke new ground in its industry by airing the well-known "Manhattan" television commercial in 1983. Designed by Saatchi & Saatchi, the spot showed a plane's flight across the Atlantic and its landing on the island of Manhattan. The ad was an expression of British Airways flying as many passengers annually across the Atlantic as there were people living in Manhattan. In 1989, the same advertising agency designed a new global campaign for British Airways. It featured a cast of about four thousand people greeting each other and interspersed with the creation of a smiling face when viewed from the air. The commercial was produced in the U.S. Midwest and was directed by a well-known movie director. The company believed that the strong visual image allowed the advertisement to be used everywhere, resulting in a global campaign production cost of about half the traditional cost of creating advertising for each market.[40] A recent campaign continued British Airways' global advertising approach. The company split the emphasis, however, between business and leisure travel, launching the new advertising simultaneously in 133 countries. The company moved from a single global campaign with one overall image to two global campaigns directed at two separate types of air traveler.[41] When British Airways resumed its emphasis on global corporate advertising in 1997, it did so with a visual campaign named "Global Images." It featured Dutch pottery, African tribal art, and Chinese calligraphy on its planes' tail fins. Although widely popular outside the United Kingdom, the campaign failed to impress British Airways' domestic customer base. This situation resulted in a new design for about half its fleet: a new wavy Union jack flag design inspired by Admiral Neslon's flag used in the 1805 Battle of Trafalgar.[42]

Practioners of global advertising found that visual ads were more universally understood. Visuals have the obvious advantage of not being culturally specific. Most global ads are linked to the brand, with the visual image helping to register the brand in the consumer's mind. Cartier, the French luxury products firm, launched its global campaign in 123 countries with global positioning. The 1996 magazine advertising campaign featured minimal copy language and emphasized dramatic photography so that the same message could be conveyed in Brazil, Japan, Russia, and dozens of other countries. Although designed and executed centrally, the campaign budgets were dispersed to Cartier's twenty-five subsidiaries.[43]

For a global strategy to be successful, experience indicates that four requirements must be fulfilled. First, the product must be able to deliver the same benefit in each market. Second, the market or the product category development in each market must be at the same level in terms of product life cycle, penetration, and use. Third, the competitive environment—that is, the type of competition and the nature of the competitive products encountered—must be similar in each market. And fourth, the heritage of the brand must not be restricted to particular countries, and the brand history must be similar in the various markets.

Global campaigns do appear to work if the target market is relatively narrowly defined. Sprite is a brand owned by Coca-Cola Company. Central to the brand's global advertising strategy is the fact that the meaning of Sprite as a brand—what it stands for in the eyes of consumers—is exactly the same globally. Many Sprite ads are run unchanged worldwide, while others are tailored locally. All share the same basic theme of self-reliance and trusting one's instincts. The company found that despite cultural differences, there was strong global similarity among teenagers, no matter what country they were from. The entire global campaign was thus built on the apparently universal teenage attitude toward soft drinks and similar products, and toward what Sprite "symbolizes."[44] Sprite was a U.S. campaign exported around the world, but Fanta, another Coca-Cola brand and the number 5 global soft drink brand, has its strength in overseas markets. Coca-Cola launched a campaign building on overseas market positions and emphasizing Fanta as a fashion statement.[45]

For its main brand, Coke, Coca-Cola moved from a global campaign with few ads to a more regional or locally driven campaign that was built around the understanding that the product was basically consumed in many different local communities. As a result, Coca-Cola moved toward more local control and approaches at a time when many other companies, and some of its other brands, moved toward global campaigns. To compensate, Coca-Cola created an advisory council with its lead agency, Interpublic Group, whose subsidiary McCann-Erickson has worked on the Coke account since 1942 and creates ads in about eighty-nine countries. Interpublic's role is to develop, refine, and focus strategies to ensure that relevant and consistent messages are being used around the world by the ten agencies that work on the Coke account in more than 200 countries.[46]

A number of companies have begun the process of developing regional or global brands:

- L'Oréal, the French cosmetics company, runs global advertising campaigns for Maybelline, Ralph Lauren perfumes, Helena Rubinstein cosmetics, and Redken hair care.[47]
- H.J. Heinz has launched a global campaign for Heinz ketchup that will develop consistency in its brand image and advertising worldwide. The global approach is seen as a way to shore up the brand in Heinz's biggest markets—the United States, the United Kingdom, and Germany—and to build sales in eastern Europe and South America.[48]
- "More power. More life." That was Duracell's tag line in its campaign to support the company's leading share of the battery business over its rival, Energizer.[49]
- Jaguar found that its S-type model would appeal to similar customers around the world. Thus, the company has launched the same campaign, "Chicago to Riyadh, Tokyo, and Berlin," in the United States, Saudi Arabia, Japan, and Europe with the intention of creating a consistent image worldwide and saving money by not developing different themes for each market.[50]

Reebok International has had a lot of experience with global advertising campaigns. Its most recent, the "Defy Convention" campaign, was created in the United States and exported to many European markets, as well as to Japan.[51] Boots' of the United Kingdom acquired the Clearasil brand from Procter & Gamble and is launching a global advertising campaign to reduce costs. The company believes the global ads will work because the skin needs of teenagers are similar around the world, which should allow the company to have global positioning and core brand equity.[52]

A modularized approach to global advertising may be more realistic. A company may select some features as standard for all its advertising, while other features will change based on local tastes. Coca-Cola's approach with Coke is clearly meant to preserve the overall advertising theme, or story, as a global one, but also to create an opportunity for local execution. The main issue for advertisers is to look at the entire advertising campaign and decide if all, or parts only, can be globalized. Different approaches may be taken for the theme, the execution, the creativity, or the tone of an ad, adding to the complexity of global advertising. Reebok International's "Defy Convention" campaign is an example of a global campaign with many local adaptations. The footage of the commercials shows athletes from all over the world, filmed in different environments, doing an activity that is different from their main sport. The design of the campaign was flexible enough to allow for the inclusion of local athletes while keeping the overall theme and template intact.[53]

GLOBAL MEDIA STRATEGY

When executing a global advertising strategy, the global marketer faces various media around the world. Difficulties arise because not all media are available in all countries, and the technical capability to deliver to the required audience may be limited, even if the desired medium is available. Therefore, global media decisions are influenced by the availability or accessibility of various media for advertisers and the media habits of the target country.

MEDIA AVAILABILITY

Advertisers in the United States and many European countries have become accustomed to the availability of a full range of media for advertising purposes. Aside from the traditional print media, consisting of newspapers and magazines, the U.S. advertiser has access to radio, television, billboards, cinemas, and the Internet. In addition, direct mail is available to most prospective client groups. This complete choice of media is not available in every country, so a company marketing its products in several countries may find itself unable to apply the same media mix in all markets. Even when some media are available, access may be partially restricted. For example, the use of commercials interspersed throughout programs on radio or television is common in North America, Japan, and Latin America, among others, but is less common in Europe.

The prevalence of media varies from country to country, partly reflecting regulatory and historical patterns. In the United States, television dominates, with 38 percent share, but newspapers are close behind, with 33 percent. By contrast, television leads with a much greater margin in Japan (46 percent) over newspapers (27 percent), whereas in Germany, newspapers dominate, with a 44 percent share. Among emerging markets, China is also a large television market (67 percent), as is Brazil (48 percent).[54] In countries with a long print history, expressed by a strong and prevalent daily press, print media play a much greater role. Global advertisers should have a flexible campaign with an ability to use both print and electronic media, depending on whichever is more easily accessible. See Table 12.3 for a comparison of the top ten advertising markets.

Table 12.3 Top Ten Advertising Markets				
Country	2001 Ad Spending[a]	2002 Ad Spending[a]	2001 Population	2001 GNP per Capita
United States	$135.7 billion	$133.6 billion	286.9 million	$36,055
Japan	$45.5 billion	$41.6 billion	127 million	$36,040
Germany	$17.2 billion	$17.5 billion	82 million	$25,900
United Kingdom	$15.2 billion	$15.3 billion	59.8 million	$24,650
France	$9 billion	$9 billion	60 million	$22,270
Italy	$7.2 billion	$7.4 billion	58 million	$19,298
Brazil	$6.4 billion	$6.4 billion	169.6 million	$6,772
South Korea	$5.9 billion	$6.1 billion	47.3 million	$10,600
Canada	$5.3 billion	$5.5 billion	31.2 million	$23,370
China	$5.0 billion	$5.5 billion	1.3 billion	$850

a. Estimated numbers.

Source: Reprinted with permission from *Ad Age Global.* Copyright, Crain Communications, Inc. 2002.

In some countries, the available time for commercials is regulated for various product groups, often regardless of the number of competitors or products in the market. For some competitive product categories, new products may be launched only by reallocating a company's television time among its existing products. This lack of flexibility inhibits new-product introduction in some consumer product categories for which television would be the most efficient advertising medium.

Global advertisers distinguish between international or local media channels. International media are those with the ability to reach target customers in multiple countries, whereas local media channels do so only within a limited geographic range. Global print media is dominated by well-known weekly magazines, such as *Business Week, The Economist, Forbes,* and *Fortune,* as well as by some special dailies *(Financial Times, International Herald Tribune).* A few selective magazines are also among that group *(Elle).*[55] However, the scene is dominated by large-circulation, local media magazines and newspapers. Among electronic media, the global or panregional television programs are far stronger. Because of satellite television and cable channels, many television channels have become quite accessible in most countries. MTV Networks, CNBC, CNN, TNT, and the Discovery channels are the global leaders.[56] See Table 12.4 for more information.

GLOBAL MEDIA HABITS

As the experienced media buyer for any domestic market knows, the media habits of the target market are major factors in deciding which media to use. The same applies on the international level. However, substantial differences in international media habits exist because of several factors that are of little importance to the domestic or single-country operation. First, the penetration of various media differs substantially from one country to another. Second, advertisers encounter radically different

Table 12.4 Global Television Programs and Stations

Network[a]	Ownership	Number of Households	Average Rate (:30 Spot)	Top Advertisers
Animal Planet Web: Yes	Discovery Communications; BBC	54.9 million[b]	N/A	N/A
BBC World Web: Yes	BBC Worldwide	60 million	$1,600	Iridium; Samsung Electronics, Union Bank of Switzerland
Cartoon Network Web: Yes	Time Warner	125.5 million	$5,000	Nintendo; Mattel; Hasbro
CNBC Web: Yes	NBC; Dow Jones & Co. (only 100% NBC-owned in U.S.)	136 million[c]	$5,500[d]	Iridium; Hewlett-Packard; Allianz
CNN International Web: Yes	Time Warner	221 million	$6,000	Volvo Car Corp.; American Express; Toyota
Discovery Networks International Web: Yes	Discovery Communications	144 million	N/A	Iridium
ESPN Web: Yes	Walt Disney Co.; Hearst Corp.	242 million	N/A	Anheuser-Busch; Chevron; Diners Club International
MTV Networks Web: Yes	Viacom	285 million	N/A	PepsiCo International; Levi Strauss & Co.; United International Pictures
TNT Web: Yes	Time Warner	140.2 million	$5,000	Anheuser-Busch; American Express

a. Web = ad supported web site.
b. Includes 45 million homes in the United States.
c. Excludes Latin Ameria.
d. Industry estimate.
Source: *Advertising Age International*, February 8, 1999.

(continued)

Table 12.4 Europe and Middle East Television Lineup (cont.)

Network	Ownership	Number of Households	Average Rate (:30 Spot)	Top Advertisers
Animal Planet Europe Web: Yes	Discovery Communications; BBC	6 million	N/A	N/A
BBC World Web: Yes	BBC Worldwide	42 million	$800	Oracle Corp.; Emirates: KPMG
Cartoon Network Web: Yes	Time Warner	42.8 million	$2,000	N/A
CNBC Europe Web: Yes	NBC; Dow Jones & Co.	52.2 million	$1,500	Hewlett-Packard; Airbus Industries; Siemens
CNN International Web: Yes	Time Warner	103.2 million	$3,000	BMW; Oracle Corp.; Vivendi
Discovery Channel Europe Web: Yes	Discovery Communications	17.6 million	N/A	Mitsubishi; Philips Electronics; Sony Corp.
Euronews Web: Yes	SECEMIE (European public broadcasters); ITN	94.3 million	$2,559[a]	Sony Corp.; Thomson Multimedia; Audi
Eurosport Web: Yes	ESPN; Canal Plus; TF1; European Broadcasting Union	80.5 million	$2,896[a]	Audi; Saudi Arabian Airlines; Sony Music
Middle East Broadcasting Centre Web: No	ARA Group International	50 million	$2,000	Haj Hussein Ali Reza; Saudi America Bank; Mahmoud Saed
MTV Networks Europe Web: Yes	Viacom	77 million	$150–$2,700	United International Pictures; Nokia; Suzuki
National Geographic Channel Europe Web: No	BSkyB/News Corp.; National Geographic Channels Worldwide	16 million	N/A	N/A
Orbit Satellite TV & Radio Network Web: Yes	Mawarid Group	280,000	$500	PepsiCo International; Ford Al Jazirah; Al Bustani
TNT Web: Yes	Time Warner	38.9 million	$2,000	N/A

a. Airtime sales begin second quarter 1999.
b. Web = ad supported web site.
c. Converted from euro currency at rate of E1 = $1,159.
d. A joint venture of National Geographic Society and NBC.
Source: Advertising Age International, media companies.

(continued)

Table 12.4 Asia-Pacific Television Lineup (cont.)

Network[a]	Ownership	Number of Households	Average Rate (:30 Spot)	Top Advertisers
Animal Planet Asia Web: Yes	Discovery Communications; BBC	350,000	N/A	N/A
BBC World Web: Yes	BBC Worldwide	15 million	Varies	DHL; Asia Brown Boveri; Singapore Airlines
Channel V Web: Yes	STAR TV/News Corp.; EMI; Sony Corp.; Time Warner; Bertelsmann	72 million	$1.200	Carlsberg; Coca-Cola Co.; Adidas; Procter & Gamble Co.; Unilever
CNBC Asia Web: Yes	NBC; Dow Jones & Co.	13 million	$900	Jaguar; Nokia; Singapore Airlines
CNN International Web: Yes	Time Warner	25.1 million	$2,000	N/A
Discovery Channel Asia Web: Yes	Discovery Communications	33.6 million	$1,000	Audi; Citibank; Ericsson; Nokia
ESPN STAR Sports Web: Yes	ESPN; STAR TV	76.2 million	N/A	N/A
MTV Mandarin Web: No	Viacom; PolyGram	44 million	$850	Ericsson; Siemens; Reebok International
MTV Southeast Asia Web: No	Viacom; PolyGram	23 million	$350	Za; Carlsberg; Reebok International
National Geographic Channel Asia Web: No	National Geographic Channels Worldwide[b]	10 million[c]	$400–$780[d]	Hong Kong Bank; Acer; General Electric
Phoenix Chinese Channel Web: Yes	Phoenix Satellite Television	45 million[e]	$2,400[f]	Nokia; Lucent Technologies; Philips Electronics; BMW
STAR Movies Web: Yes	STAR TV/News Corp.	72 million	$1,000	Lever Bros.; Seagram & Co.; Cadbury; Colgate-Palmolive
STAR Plus Web: Yes	STAR TV/News Corp.	72 million	$1,700	Ponds; Johnson & Johnson
STAR World Web: Yes	STAR TV/News Corp.	72 million	$500	Hindustan Lever; Philips Electronics; Seagram & Co.
TNT/Cartoon Network Web: Yes	Time Warner	17 million	$1,000	N/A

a. Web = ad supported web site.
b. A joint venture of National Geographic Society and NBC.
c. Includes 655,000 homes in Australia.
d. Excludes Australia.
e. China only distribution.
f. Prime time.

Source: Advertising Age, February 8, 1999. Reprinted with permission from *Advertising Age International.* Copyright, Crain Communicaitons, Inc. 1999.

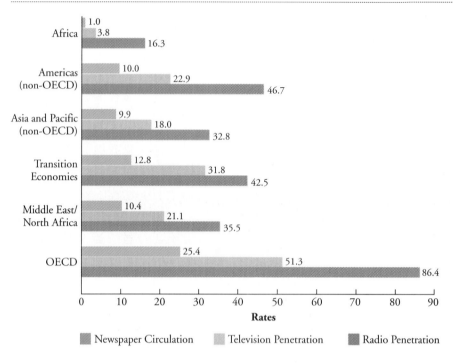

Figure 12.2: Media Penetration Rates by Region and by OECD Compared with Non-OECD Countries

Note: Newspaper circulation = daily newspapers circulated per 100 people; television penetration = sets per 100 people; radio penetration = radios per 100 people.
Source: World Development Report 2002: Building Institutions for Markets by World Bank. Copyright © 2002 by International Bank for Reconstruction and Development, The World Bank. Used by permission of Oxford University Press, Inc.

literacy rates in many parts of the world. And finally, they may find different cultural habits or traits that favor one medium over another, regardless of the penetration ratios or literacy rates. See Figure 12.2 for regional media penetration rates.

Ownership or use of television, radio, and newspapers and magazines varies considerably from one country to another. Whereas the developed industrial nations show high penetration ratios for all three major media carriers, developing countries have few radio and television receivers and low newspaper and magazine circulation. In general, the use or penetration of all these media increases with the average income of a country. In most countries, the higher-income groups avail themselves first of the electronic and print media. International marketers have to be aware that some media, though generally accessible for the advertiser, may be of limited use because they reach only a small part of the country's target population.

The literacy of a country's population is an important factor influencing media decisions. Although literacy is less of a concern for companies in the industrial products market, it is a crucial factor in consumer goods advertising. In countries where large portions of the population are illiterate, the use of print media is of limited value. (See Table 3.2 for the literacy rates of selected countries.) Both radio and television have been used by companies to circumvent the literacy problem. Other media that are occasionally used for this purpose are billboards and cinemas. The absence of a high level of literacy has forced consumer goods companies to translate their advertising campaigns into media and messages that communicate strictly by sound or demonstration. Television and radio have been used most successfully to overcome problems with illiteracy, but they cannot be used in areas where the penetration of such receivers is limited.

TECHNOLOGY AND THE EMERGENCE OF NEW COMMUNICATIONS CHANNELS

Satellite television channels are not subject to government regulations and have revolutionized television in many parts of the world. The impact of satellite television channels is felt most directly in Europe.

The leader in this field of privately owned channels is Sky Channel. Sky Channel is owned by Rupert Murdoch, who controls vast media interests in many countries. In 1993, Murdoch purchased the Star Satellite System, which serves millions of people, from Egypt to Mongolia. The Star Satellite System relies heavily on advertising revenue.

The Murdoch group is eyeing expansion in Asia. Through its News Corp, the company produces three Chinese-language news and entertainment channels from studios in Hong Kong. These channels can reach most of Asia. Similar to the twenty-one other foreign broadcasters sending signals into China, the programs are supposed to be seen only in hotels rated three stars and above, in housing complexes attracting international residents, and in offices. But Phoenix TV, which is the station sending the signals, can be picked up by many privately installed satellite dishes across China and in upscale local housing complexes.[57]

One of the most successful global satellite television ventures is the MTV Network. This music channel, launched in 1981 in the United States, reached 285 million households in more than sixty countries by 1999. Its MTV Mandarin reached about 44 million households, and MTV Southeast Asia accounts for another 23 million.[58] MTV Networks International, the music channel, and its sister operations, VH1 and Nickelodeon, reach 1 billion people in eighteen different languages in 164 countries. Eighty percent of all MTV viewers live outside the United States. Although the design and structure of every broadcast is similar, the music is adapted to the local requirements. The network, owned by the U.S. company Viacom, is highly profitable. With a reach that is twice that of CNN, it has become a truly global media channel of value to global companies.[59]

For satellite-shown commercials to be effective, companies must use a global brand name and a uniform logo. Also, language remains a problem. English is the common language of the majority of satellite channels; however, there is a trend toward local-language satellite programming. Satellite channels are now available in several European languages, such as German, French, and Swedish.

ONLINE ADVERTISING CHANNELS. Finally, the global reach of Internet properties must not be underestimated. The Internet can provide opportunities for electronic forms of advertising, such as banner ads used in connection with web sites. Measured in terms of the reach of the Internet population, the leading web sites are Microsoft Sites, AOL Network, and Yahoo Sites, with all three covering between 50 and 60 percent of the global Internet user population.[60] (See Table 12.5 for a list of the top ten digital properties.) Because these sites are used by a global population, they act as global media and allow advertisers to reach a global audience. Online advertising already accounts for about 5 percent of total U.S. advertising expenditures, but it accounts for only 1 percent in the next largest eight global markets. The U.S. market is larger because the Internet reaches a global audience through global web site properties. With about 50 percent of Internet users living outside the United States, web sites with global content are of great value to advertisers.[61] See Table 12.5 for more information on top digital properties.

CABLE TV. Cable TV networks have been installed in the more densely populated countries of Europe, a fact that carries considerable implications for global marketers. In Europe, close to 84 million of 148 million homes (or 57 percent) can be connected to cable. About 49 million of those homes subscribe to cable today. Some countries, such as Germany, the Netherlands, Belgium, and Switzerland, are fully connected to cable, whereas Italy and Greece have very little cable installed.[62] Access to cable networks eventually leads to access to broadband and the Internet, which will also affect a global company's ability to reach large audiences at lower cost.

MOBILE DEVICES. The growth of mobile, hand-held devices with Internet capabilities is opening a new market for entertainment, information, and advertising. Nokia, the largest manufacturer of mobile devices, has had discussions with both AOL and News Corporation about providing content for these devices.[63] The new use of mobile devices provides potential global advertising opportunities.

The emergence of multiple media and advertising channels on a global scale is both a commercial and technical challenge for global companies. Companies are beginning to create entire global campaigns across multiple platforms, or so-called cross-platform packages. When Toyota relaunched its leading model Camry with the intent of repositioning it as a car for a younger man (rather than its original position as a car for an older woman), the company teamed up with AOL Time Warner to buy a bundle of advertisements in magazines, cable TV channels, and web sites. Time proposed the idea of letting Toyota sponsor an entire issue of *Time* magazine written around a theme of "Music Goes Global." Time Warner convinced its sister publications *People, Entertainment Weekly, Fortune,* and *Style* to publish concurrent articles about global music and to accept advertising from Toyota. In addition, Toyota sponsored music shows on the CNN and TNT cable channels (although those shows were scheduled prior to the Camry launch deal).[64]

SCHEDULING GLOBAL ADVERTISING

The general rule in scheduling advertising suggests that the company more or less duplicates the sales curve or seasonality of its product. Depending on the complexity of the buying decision or the deliberation time, media expenditures tend to peak before the actual sales peak. This practice, though somewhat generalized here, applies to both domestic and global markets. Deviations from this general rule may exist, however, due to different sales peaks in the year, vacations or religious holidays, and differences in the deliberation time with regard to purchases.

Sales peaks are influenced both by climatic seasons and by customs and traditions. The winter months in North America and Europe are summer months in some countries of the Southern Hemisphere (Australia, New Zealand, South Africa, and

Table 12.5 Top Digital Properties

Top Ten Global Digital Properties

August 2000

Rank	Property	Unique Audience	Reach %
1	Microsoft Sites	82,931	61.3
2	AOL Network	81,252	60.0
3	Yahoo Sites	78,806	58.2
4	Lycos	46,836	34.6
5	Excite Network	34,323	25.4
6	Go Network	23,628	17.5
7	About the Human Internet	19,814	14.6
8	AltaVista Network	19,522	14.4
9	Real.com Network	18,309	13.5
10	Amazon	16,015	11.8

Total digital media: 135,360,000

Audience numbers are in thousands

Top Ten European Digital Domains

August 2000

Rank	Domain	Unique Audience	Reach %
1	Yahoo	8,021	33.0
2	MSN.com	7,111	29.2
3	Microsoft.com	6,959	28.6
4	T-Online.de	4,339	17.8
5	AOL Proprietary	3,942	16.2
6	Freeserve.com	3,777	15.5
7	Passport.com	3,702	15.2
8	T-Online Application	3,486	14.3
9	Lycos.com	3,267	13.4
10	AltaVista.com	3,207	13.2

Total digital media: 24,314,000

Audience numbers are in thousands

Top Ten U.S. Digital Domains

September 2000

Rank	Domain	Unique Audience	Reach %
1	Yahoo.com	49,987	62.6
2	MSN.com	41,065	51.4
3	AOL.com	33,414	41.8
4	Microsoft.com	29,954	37.5
5	Lycos.com	26,263	32.9
6	Passport.com	22,681	28.4
7	Hotmail.com	21,354	26.7
8	Go.com	20,589	25.8
9	Netscape.com	18,529	23.2
10	Excite	15,486	19.4

Total digital media: 79,859,000

Audience numbers at home and at work are in thousands

Top Ten Japanese Digital Domains

September 2000

Rank	Domain	Unique Audience	Reach %
1	Yahoo.co.jp	12,479	70.2
2	Nifty.com	10,568	59.5
3	Biglobe.ne.jp	8,343	46.9
4	Microsoft.com	8,174	46.0
5	Geocities.co.jp	7,967	44.8
6	So-net.ne.jp	6,594	37.1
7	DTI.ne.jp	6,535	36.8
8	MSN.co.jp	5,682	32.0
9	Hi-ho.ne.jp	5,371	30.2
10	MBN.or.jp	4,847	27.3

Total digital media: 17,776,000

Audience numbers at home and at work are in thousands

Methodology. **REACH:** The number of visitors to a site expressed as a % of total Internet populataion. **UNIQUE VISITOR:** We count a visitor to a given site only once, regardless of the number of visits they make. **DOMAIN:** Individual site (amazon.co.uk or amazon.de). **GLOBAL DOMAIN:** Measures brand strength and combines all site addresses for one brand name, i.e. Amazon.com, .de, .fr, etc. Duplications are removed. **DIGITAL MEDIA:** Software, hardware, proprietary e-mail services (like AOL online). **PROPERTIES:** Combines all the sites that are majority owned (i.e. more than 50.1%) by the same company. **CATEGORIES:** In this section we group sites together by their market sector classification.

Source: Ad Age Global, November 2000. Reprinted with permission from Ad Age Global. Copyright, Crain Communications, Inc. 2000.

Argentina, to name a few). This seasonal difference substantially influences the purchase of many consumer goods, such as clothing, vacation services, and travel. Vacations are particularly important for some European countries. In Europe, school summer vacations tend to be shorter than those in the United States. But European employees are typically granted four to five weeks of vacation, which is more than the vacation time granted to the average U.S. employee. Religious holidays may also affect the placement or timing of advertising. During the Islamic Ramadan, usually celebrated for over a month, many Muslim countries do not allow the placement of any advertising.

For industrial products, the timing of advertising in support of sales efforts may be affected by the budgetary cycles prevailing in a given country. For countries with large state-controlled sectors, industrial producers may need to pay particular attention to the period before a new national or sector plan is developed. Private-sector companies tend to be more influenced by their own budgetary cycles, usually coinciding with their fiscal years. In Japan, many companies begin their fiscal year in June rather than in January. If capital budgets are completed before the new fiscal year commences, products that require budgetary approval will need advertising support before budget completion.

The time needed to think about a purchase has been cited as a primary factor in deciding on the appropriate time by which the advertising peak is to precede the sales peak. A company may have become accustomed to a given purchase deliberation time by its domestic customers. The deliberation time may be determined by income levels or other environmental factors, so other (that is, international) markets may show different patterns. The purchase or replacement of a small electrical household appliance may be a routine decision for a North American household, and the purchase may occur whenever the need arises. In a country with a low income level, such a purchase may be planned several weeks or even months ahead. Consequently, a company engaged in international advertising needs to evaluate the underlying assumptions of its domestic advertising policies carefully and not automatically assume that they apply elsewhere.

ORGANIZING THE GLOBAL ADVERTISING EFFORT

A major concern for global marketing executives centers on the organization of their company's global advertising effort. Key concerns are the role of centralization at the head office versus the roles that subsidiaries and the advertising agency should play. Marketers are aware that a more harmonious approach to the global advertising effort may enhance both the quality and efficiency of the total advertising effort. Thus, organizing the global advertising effort deserves as much time as individual advertising decisions about individual products or campaigns. In this section, we examine in greater detail advertising agency selection and the managerial issues of running a global advertising effort in a multinational corporation.

ADVERTISING AGENCY SELECTION
Global companies face several options with respect to selecting an advertising agency. Many companies first develop an agency relationship domestically and eventually must decide if they expect their domestic agency to handle their global adver-

tising business as well. In some foreign markets, companies need to select foreign agencies to work with them—a decision that may be left to the local subsidiaries or made by the head office alone. Recently, some agencies have banded together to form international networks to attract more global business.

WORKING WITH DOMESTIC AGENCIES. When a company starts to grow internationally, it is not unusual for the domestic advertising agency to handle the international business as well. However, this additional advertising business is possible only when the domestic agency has global experience and capability. Many smaller domestic agencies do not have global experience. Thus, companies are forced to make other arrangements. Frequently, the global company starts to appoint individual agencies in each of the various foreign markets in which it operates. This selection may be done with the help of the local subsidiaries or through the company's head-office staff. Before long, the company may have a series of advertising agency relationships that may make global coordination difficult.

Sometimes, a domestic agency can do better than the international counterpart. Skoda UK, the U.K. distributor of Czech Skoda cars and part of VW Group, was dissatisfied with the pan-European advertising campaign created by the VW European agency. Skoda UK management believed it had to tackle old, outdated beliefs about Skoda cars head-on, and that the pan-European campaign was too bland. Local management decided to pursue a local campaign that was witty and that confronted prejudice head on through the use of self-deprecating humor to convince consumers to reevaluate their view of Skoda cars. The campaign was highly successful, won many awards, and resulted in the U.K. company achieving 60 percent of the year's sales targets in just three months.[65]

WORKING WITH LOCAL AGENCIES. The local-agency relationship offers some specific advantages. First of all, the local advertising agency is expected to understand the local environment and thus have the ability to create advertising targeted to the local market. However, many firms question the expertise and professionalism of local agencies, particularly in countries where advertising is not as developed as in the major markets of North America and Europe. Despite their in-depth knowledge, local agencies often lose to international networks as part of agency realignments. In the case of Jaguar and Land Rover, not even exceptional work could save the local agency. Land Rover America discontinued its relationship with GSD&M, a small Austin-based firm handling the $50 million account in the United States only. Even though GSD&M was doing an exceptional job, the company wanted to consolidate its advertising under one global agency to gain a global perspective. It also wanted to create efficiencies across both the Jaguar and the Land Rover accounts because both are owned by Ford Motor.[66]

Motorola, a leading U.S.-based company in various technology and communications sectors, recently consolidated its global advertising under a single agency. Prior to the consolidation, Motorola had sixty-seven agency relationships, covering both business and consumer products.[67] Ogilvy & Mather, the appointed global agency, will have to direct the $400 million account around the "One Motorola" concept. Although the company had done well over the years, it had slipped compared to others in brand ranking; for example, it was listed as number 49 compared to Nokia's number 5 in brand equity by Interbrand's 1999 survey.[68] Consolidation of all marketing and advertising efforts under a single agency was considered a necessity by management.

WORKING WITH GLOBAL AFFILIATES IN LOCAL MARKETS. Increasingly, global companies have the option of working with local affiliates of global agencies. Often these agencies were locally founded and at some time sold a minority stake to larger foreign agencies. More recently, global agencies have acquired majority stakes or started new branches from scratch. The capabilities of these agencies depend on the extent to which they can be supported by the owner's network. This trend has brought new sophistication and expertise to countries where little existed.

Global agencies are favored in eastern Europe, where in some markets up to 90 percent of the advertising is handled by affiliates of global firms. In many eastern European countries, which suffer from very little local expertise in advertising, global agencies have become a repository of advertising knowledge. These affiliates can rely on the skills of their global networks and can therefore leverage on their vast knowledge and transfer much-needed skills. McCann-Erickson has become the primary global agency network operating in eastern Europe and has attracted business from leading firms such as Coca-Cola, Nestlé, and Unilever.[69]

WORKING WITH GLOBAL ADVERTISING NETWORKS. Many companies with extensive global operations find it too difficult and cumbersome to deal simultaneously with a large number of agencies, both domestic and global. For that reason, global firms have tended to concentrate their accounts with some large advertising agencies that operate complete global networks. In the past, each network was identical to a separate company. Over the past two decades, the advertising industry has changed with the creation of agency holding firms or groups comprising several networks.[70] Leading firms among those agency holding companies include Interpublic (McCann-Erickson and Lowe Lintas networks), Omnicom (TBWA, BBDO, and DDB), WPP (Ogilvy & Mather, J. Walter Thompson, Young & Rubicam), Havas (Euro RSCG and Campus), and Publicis Groupe (Publicis, Saatchi & Saatchi, Burnett, D'Arcy).[71] Each of these agency holding companies also operates a series of additional services, ranging from public relations (PR) agencies to direct marketing. Table 12.6 lists several leading global firms and their main agency relationships.

The first generation of global networks was created by U.S.-based advertising agencies in the 1950s and 1960s. The major driving forces were their clients, who encouraged their U.S. agencies to move into local markets where the advertising agencies were weak. Leaders in this process were J. Walter Thompson, Ogilvy & Mather, BBDO, and Young & Rubicam. The second wave of global networks was dominated by British entrepreneurs Saatchi & Saatchi and WPP, which assembled a series of global agency networks under one corporate name. The most recent networks are being built by two of the French media groups, Publicis and Havas. Japanese agencies are also building their own networks through acquisition.[72]

As companies develop global business, they are likely to change agencies. In 1995 Colgate-Palmolive became the first packaged goods company to consolidate its entire worldwide $500 million advertising accounts in the hands of a single agency. For the monumental task, it appointed Young & Rubicam (Y&R), an agency it had worked

Table 12.6 Major International Firm/Agency Relationships[a]

Agency \ Client	American Home Products	Bayer Corp.	Bristol-Meyers Squibb Co.	British American Tobacco Co.	Coca-Cola Co.	Danone	Diageo	Ford Motor Co.	General Motors Corp.	Gillette Co.	Henkel	Hewlett-Packard Co.	Johnson & Johnson Co.	Kellogg Co.	Kraft Foods	L'Oreal	Mars Inc.	Nestlé	Novartis	Philip Morris Cos.	Procter & Gamble Co.	Siemens	SmithKline Beecham Corp.	Sony Corp.	Unilever	Warner-Lambert Co.
Ammirati Puris Lintas					X				X				X					X							X	
Bartle Bogle Hegarty																									X	
Bates Worldwide				X	X								X					X			X					X
Batey Ads																										
BBDO Worldwide		X								X	X				X									X		
Bozell Worldwide			X																							
D'Arcy Masius Benton & Bowles		X			X		X		X									X			X					
DDB Worldwide		X			X				X				X					X							X	
Dentsu																		X								
Dentsu Young & Rubicam															X										X	
EURO RSCG Worldwide	X	X	X			X	X										X	X	X							X
FCA! BMZ International											X															
FCB Worldwide			X																							
Grey Advertising				X	X												X		X		X		X			
Hakuhodo																										
Leagas Delaney																										
Leo Burnett Co.					X									X	X					X	X					
Lowe & Partners Worldwide					X				X	X	X															
McCann-Erickson Worldwide	X				X				X	X		X	X			X		X							X	X
Ogilvy & Mather Worldwide			X	X				X	X									X	X	X		X	X	X	X	
Publicis Communication					X								X			X		X						X		
Saatchi & Saatchi							X					X	X					X			X				X	
Scholz & Friends																										
TBWA Worldwide											X								X						X	
J. Walter Thompson Co.							X	X						X	X			X	X				X		X	X
Wieden & Kennedy																										
Y&R Advertising						X		X							X					X				X		

a. Top multinational advertisers are ranked by number of ad markets handled by agency networks.

Source: Ad Age International, September 1999. Reprinted with permission from Advertising Age International. Copyright, Crain Communications, Inc. 1999.

with for about twelve years. The move was further aided by the fact that Colgate spent all but $82 million of its advertising outside the United States, where it also generates two-thirds of its sales. In return for a single, huge account, the company expected more creative effectiveness for its fifteen global campaigns. Y&R set up several centers of excellence, spread throughout the world, which assembled global teams to handle the many Colgate campaigns.[73]

Shell International Petroleum also concentrated its advertising account. Using about thirty-five main agencies around the world, Shell reduced its roster to one agency, J. Walter Thompson (JWT), which handles Shell's advertising in forty-five countries. Shell measured its progress by doing consistent research of its advertising, comparing it both against others in the same category and across different categories. In both areas, Shell believes it has clear evidence that the superior production and quality of a major, pooled account has produced superior advertising.[74]

Some companies, such as Unilever, assign global work by brand and might therefore maintain several global advertising agency relationships. Following the acquisition of Bestfoods, Unilever reorganized its sauces and dressing brands around two major global brands, Knorr and Hellman's, and assigned responsibility for each brand globally to different agencies. The selected agencies were all members of international networks.[75]

International advertising networks are sought after because of their ability to spread advertising quickly around the globe with one single campaign. Usually, only one set of advertisements will be made and then circulated among the local agencies. Working within the same agency guarantees consistency and a certain willingness to accept direction from a central location. If a company tries to coordinate a global effort alone, without the help of an international network, the burden of coordination largely rests with the company itself. Not all firms are equipped for such an effort. Therefore, the international network is a convenience to multinational firms. Table 12.7 provides a list of the world's top fifty advertising agencies. Table 12.8 provides a list of the world's top twenty-five advertising agency brands.

Not all companies find that a network is a necessity. Some advertisers argue that a company may profit from a single strategy but that the execution of this strategy in the various markets should be left to local agencies that are willing to work in an ad hoc network responsive only to the company's needs. At a time when many global companies are moving in the direction of global campaigns through global agency networks, Coca-Cola has moved in the opposite direction. The company decided to appoint a global agency (Interpublic) for the development of a global brand message while keeping its local agencies in place for the local adaptations. To help in the translation of the global message into tailored ones, Interpublic will help run eleven global hubs for Coca-Cola. Coca-Cola expects more efficiency from these arrangements while maintaining relevance for the local consumer.[76]

COORDINATING GLOBAL ADVERTISING

The role played by the global marketing executive in a company's global advertising effort may differ from firm to firm and may depend on several factors. Outside factors, such as the nature of the market or competition, and company internal factors, such as company culture or philosophy, may lead some firms to adopt a more centralized approach to global advertising. Other firms, for different reasons, may prefer to

Table 12.7 The World's Top Fifty Advertising Organizations (in Millions of Dollars)

Rank 1998	Rank 1997	Ad Organization	Headquarters	Worldwide Gross Income 1998	Worldwide Gross Income 1997	Percentage Change
1	1	Omnicom Group	New York	$4,812.0	$4,295.7	12.0
2	2	Interpublic Group of Cos.	New York	4,304.5	3,806.1	13.1
3	3	WPP Group	London	4,156.8	3,616.9	14.9
4	4	Dentsu	Tokyo	1,786.0	1,987.8	−10.2
5	5	Young & Rubicam	New York	1,659.9	1,497.9	10.8
6	7	Havas Advertising	Paris	1,297.9	1,183.6	9.7
7	6	True North Communications	Chicago	1,242.3	1,204.9	3.1
8	8	Grey Advertising	New York	1,240.4	1,143.0	8.5
9	9	Leo Burnett Co.	Chicago	949.8	878.0	8.2
10	12	Publicis	New York	930.0	721.8	28.8
11	13	Snyder Communications	Bethesda, Md.	904.2	700.6	29.1
12	11	MacManus Group	New York	859.2	842.6	2.0
13	10	Hakuhodo	Tokyo	734.8	848.0	−13.4
14	14	Saatchi & Saatchi	New York	682.1	634.6	7.5
15	15	Cordiant Communications Group	London	603.2	597.3	1.0
16	17	TMP Worldwide	New York	347.4	305.4	13.7
17	16	Asatsu-DK	Tokyo	343.4	392.5	−12.5
18	18	Carlson Marketing Group	Plymouth, Minn.	326.8	283.8	15.2
19	26	USWeb/CKS	Santa Clara	228.6	114.3	100.0
20	21	HA-LO	Niles, Ill.	224.0	163.0	37.4
21	20	Daiko Advertising	Tokyo	168.7	204.4	−17.5
22	19	Tokyu Agency	Tokyo	167.1	204.5	−18.3
23	22	Dentsu, Young & Rubicam Partnerships	Singapore	145.5	162.8	−10.6
24	28	Cyrk-Simon	Gloucester, Mass.	137.9	103.1	33.7
25	27	Nelson Communications	New York	130.8	107.1	22.1
26	29	Bronner Slosberg Humphrey	Boston	124.2	101.2	22.7
27	23	Cheil Communications	Seoul	106.0	154.1	−31.2
28	24	Yomiko Advertising	Tokyo	102.8	119.4	−13.9
29	31	Clemenger BBDO	Melbourne	101.8	94.1	8.2
30	44	Healthworld Corp.	New York	99.6	62.9	58.3
31	33	EPB Partners	New York	93.7	81.2	15.4
32	35	Harte-Hanks/DiMark	Langhorne, Pa.	90.5	75.6	19.8
33	25	I&S/BBDO	Tokyo	89.5	117.5	−23.9

(continued)

Table 12.7 The World's Top Fifty Advertising Organizations (in Millions of Dollars) (cont.)

Rank 1998	Rank 1997	Ad Organization	Headquarters	Worldwide Gross Income 1998	Worldwide Gross Income 1997	Percentage Change
34	34	Frankel	Chicago	$87.9	$77.7	13.1
35	48	IXL Enterprises	Atlanta	87.2	55.3	57.6
36	51	Deutsch	New York	86.9	53.3	63.2
37	30	Wieden & Kennedy	Porland, Ore.	86.9	96.3	−9.7
38	40	Doner	Southfield, Mich.	85.7	68.5	25.0
39	38	Incepta Group	London	78.2	70.3	11.2
40	43	Spar Group	Tarrytown, N.Y.	74.8	63.6	17.6
41	32	Asahi Advertising	Tokyo	74.6	85.6	−12.8
42	41	MDC Communications Corp.	Toronto	74.2	67.9	9.3
43	NR	Agency.com	New York	72.0	NA	NA
44	39	Duailibi Petit Zaragoza Propaganda	Sao Paulo	71.2	69.4	2.6
45	55	HMG Worldwide Corp.	New York	70.0	46.3	51.2
46	42	Fallon McElligott	Minneapolis	68.5	64.0	7.0
47	46	Fischer America Comunicacao Total	Sao Paulo	66.9	59.3	12.8
48	36	Oricom Co.	Tokyo	64.1	75.3	−14.8
49	52	Gage Marketing Group	Minneapolis	63.8	51.4	24.1
50	47	Springer & Jacoby Werbung	Hamburg, Germany	61.4	56.8	8.0

Source: Reprinted with permission from Advertising Age International. Copyright, Crain Communications, Inc. 1999.

delegate more authority to local subsidiaries and local agencies. Key factors that may cause a firm to centralize or decentralize decision making for global advertising will be reviewed in the sections that follow.

EXTERNAL FACTORS AFFECTING ADVERTISING COORDINATION. One of the most important factors influencing how companies allocate decision making for global advertising is market diversity. For products or services for which customer needs and interests are homogeneous across many countries, greater opportunities for standardization exist. For companies with relatively standardized products, pressures also point in the direction of centralized decision making. Consequently, companies that face markets with very different customer needs or market systems and structures will work more toward decentralizing their global advertising decision making, and local knowledge would be more important to the success of these firms.

The nature of the competition can also affect the way a global firm plans for advertising decision making. Firms that essentially face local competition or different sets

Table 12.8 World's Top Twenty-Five Advertising Agency Brands

Rank 1998	Rank 1997	Agency	Worldwide Gross Income 1998	Worldwide Gross Income 1997	1998–1997 Percentage Change	Worldwide Volume 1998	Worldwide Volume 1997	Percentage Change
1	1	Dentsu	$1,786.0	$1,987.8	–10.2	$13,032.9	$14,473.3	–10.0
2	3	McCann-Erickson Worldwide	1,640.1	1,414.8	15.9	13,610.5	10,880.0	25.1
3	3	BBDO Worldwide	1,304.2	1,193.0	9.3	10,910.1	9,640.2	13.2
4	4	J. Walter Thompson Co.	1,176.6	1,115.9	5.4	8,077.4	7,638.3	5.7
5	5	Euro RSCG Worldwide	1,018.7	938.1	8.6	7,340.9	7,069.1	3.8
6	6	DDB Needham Worldwide	1,007.1	928.0	8.5	7,800.5	6,999.0	11.5
7	7	Grey Advertising	942.8	918.3	2.7	6,289.0	6,431.6	–2.2
8	8	Leo Burnett Co.	933.7	867.8	7.6	6,708.0	5,908.8	13.5
9	11	Young & Rubicam	878.7	780.8	12.5	9,308.6	8,004.0	16.3
10	10	Ogilvy & Mather Worldwide	860.5	816.8	5.3	7,984.9	7,256.3	10.0
11	12	TBWA Worldwide	781.8	714.4	9.4	5,530.2	5,029.6	10.0
12	15	Publicis	764.7	570.3	34.1	5,105.9	3,742.9	36.4
13	9	Hakuhodo	734.8	848.0	–13.4	5,663.7	6,475.6	–12.5
14	13	Ammirati Puris Lintas	655.6	616.7	6.3	4,826.3	4,420.4	9.2
15	14	D'Arcy Masius Benton & Bowles	616.7	606.8	1.6	5,791.8	5,806.6	–0.3
16	16	Foote, Cone & Belding	510.0	481.0	6.0	5,645.4	5,509.6	2.5
17	18	Saatchi & Saatchi	444.8	416.1	6.9	5,727.9	5,358.5	6.9
18	22	Brann Worldwide	435.7	322.6	35.1	2,906.0	2,151.6	35.1
19	17	Bates Worldwide	431.0	439.2	–1.9	5,044.3	4,749.6	6.2
20	20	Bozell Worldwide	371.9	365.4	1.8	3,055.0	2,971.0	2.8
21	21	Lowe & Partners Worldwide	368.5	339.0	8.7	2,772.6	2,478.5	11.9
22	23	TMP Worldwide	349.3	298.4	17.1	3,328.7	2,664.9	24.9
23	19	Asatsu-DK	343.4	392.5	–12.5	2,726.6	3,097.2	–12.0
24	24	Carlson Marketing Group	326.8	283.8	15.2	2,591.8	2,244.8	15.5
25	25	Wunderman Cato Johnson	323.0	280.5	15.2	2,414.7	2,032.3	18.8

Source: Reprinted with permission from Advertising Age International. Copyright, Crain Communications, Inc. 1999.

of competitors from country to country will find it more logical to delegate global advertising to local subsidiaries. On the other hand, if a company is competing everywhere with a few firms, which are essentially global firms using a similar type of advertising, the need to centralize will be apparent.

INTERNAL FACTORS AFFECTING ADVERTISING COORDINATION. A company's internal structure and organization can also greatly influence its options for either centralizing or decentralizing global advertising decision making. The opportunities for centralizing are few when a company follows an approach of customizing advertising for each local market. When a company follows a standardized advertising format, however, a more centralized approach will be possible and probably even desirable.

Skill levels and efficiency concerns can also determine the level of centralization. Decentralization requires that the advertising skills of local subsidiaries and local agencies be sufficient to perform successfully. On the other hand, global advertising may not be centralized successfully for companies in which the head-office staff does not possess a full appreciation of the global dimension of the firm's business. Decentralization is often believed to result in inefficiencies or decreased quality because a firm's budget may be spread over too many individual agencies. Instead of one large budget in one agency, the firm has created mini-budgets that may not be sufficient to obtain the best creative talent to work on its products. Centralization will often give access to better talent, but knowledge of the local markets may be sacrificed.

The managerial style of the global company may also affect the centralization decision in advertising. Some companies pride themselves on giving a considerable amount of freedom to local subsidiary managers. Under such circumstances, centralizing advertising decisions will be counterproductive. It has been observed with many multinational firms that the general approach taken by the company's top management toward global markets relates closely to its desire to centralize or decentralize global advertising. Because the company's internal and external factors are subject to change over time, however, it can be expected that the decision to centralize or decentralize will never be a permanent one.

GENERIC GLOBAL ADVERTISING STRATEGIES

You are now familiar with the concept of generic global marketing strategies, which were introduced in Chapter 8. For our purposes, it is important to recognize that global firms can also select from a series of generic global advertising strategies. Table 12.9 shows the top 100 global marketers based on their media advertising expenditures outside the United States.

A company can adopt a single *global advertising campaign*, which consists of essentially equal execution across the globe. This type of single global campaign is not likely to be the rule, and other options exist. A company may also select a *global brand approach*, using essentially the same brand name, logo, and so on, but otherwise engaging different advertising apparatuses by country. This approach is used by Mercedes-Benz, as described earlier. Companies using a *global theme* employ a more coordinated approach, using the same advertising theme around the world but

Table 12.9 Top 100 Global Marketers by Media Ad Spending Outside the United States

Rank 1999	Rank 1998	Advertiser	Headquarters	Spending Outside U.S. 1999	Percent Change	Country Count
1	2	Unilever	Rotterdam/London	$3,110	8.1	66
2	1	Procter & Gamble Co.	Cincinnati	2,988	−4.7	68
3	3	Nestlé	Vevey, Switzerland	1,580	0.6	67
4	4	Coca-Cola Co.	Atlanta	1,178	5.3	69
5	7	Ford Motor Co.	Dearborn, Mich.	1,150	6.9	51
6	8	General Motors Corp.	Detroit	1,148	8.6	43
7	5	L'Oréal	Paris	1,120	0.2	47
8	6	Volkswagen	Wolfsburg, Germany	1,009	−8.2	33
9	9	Toyota Motor Corp.	Toyota City, Japan	1,007	−3.9	44
10	10	PSA Peugeot Citroen	Paris	906	−0.3	37
11	12	Sony Corp.	Tokyo	886	8.3	53
12	11	Mars Inc.	McLean, Va.	841	−3.4	37
13	14	Renault	Paris	809	5.7	31
14	13	Philip Morris Cos.	New York	767	−1.5	49
15	15	Henkel	Duesseldorf	728	−0.9	35
16	16	Nissan Motor Co.	Tokyo	657	−5.0	39
17	18	McDonald's Corp.	Oak Brook, Ill.	649	−0.3	54
18	17	Fiat	Turin, Italy	649	−2.2	26
19	23	Danone Group	Paris	642	18.9	24
20	21	Ferrero	Perugia, Italy	603	2.8	34
21	19	Colgate-Palmolive Co.	New York	591	−5.0	57
22	36	Deutsche Telekom	Bonn, Germany	578	82.7	5
23	24	DaimlerChrysler	Stuttgart, Germany	556	7.2	39
24	27	Reckitt Benckiser	Windsor, Berkshire, U.K.	543	24.1	39
25	26	Johnson & Johnson	New Brunswick, N.J.	486	6.4	52
26	42	Vodafone Group	Newbury, Berkshire, U.K.	467	63.2	8
27	50	Telefonica	Madrid	466	79.2	5
28	40	France Telecom	Paris	453	57.0	5
29	32	Seagram Co.	Montreal	435	24.0	28
30	22	Kao Corp.	Tokyo	426	−21.1	9
31	33	Beiersdorf	Hamburg, Germany	411	19.8	45
32	20	Honda Motor Co.	Tokyo	409	−32.2	35
33	38	Bertelsmann	Guetersloh, Germany	370	19.3	20
34	31	PepsiCo	Purchase, N.Y.	343	−3.6	47
35	28	Kellogg Co.	Battle Creek, Mich.	330	−13.4	27

(continued)

Table 12.9 Top 100 Global Marketers by Media Ad Spending Outside the United States (cont.)

Rank 1999	Rank 1998	Advertiser	Headquarters	Spending Outside U.S. 1999	Percent Change	Country Count
36	39	Time Warner	New York	$322	4.8	26
37	25	Mitsubishi Motors Corp.	Tokyo	321	−29.9	28
38	37	IBM Corp.	Armonk, N.Y.	318	2.0	27
39	48	Carrefour Group	Paris	303	13.9	11
40	34	SmithKline Beecham	London	302	−6.2	41
41	29	BMW	Munich	301	−19.1	30
42	35	Diageo	London	299	−6.7	27
43	67	Hyundai Motor Co.	Seoul	271	39.3	37
44	53	Daewoo Corp.	Seoul	262	6.2	36
45	43	British American Tobacco	London	258	−8.3	33
46	44	Matsushita Electric Industrial Co.	Osaka	253	−9.4	35
47	54	Mazda Motor Corp.	Hiroshima	247	4.2	27
48	41	News Corp.	Sydney	244	−14.9	17
49	46	Gillette Co.	Boston	243	−10.0	45
50	51	Walt Disney Co.	Burbank, Calif.	242	−6.7	21
51	55	British Telecommunications	London	234	1.6	4
52	49	Metro	Duesseldorf	232	−12.2	8
53	78	LG Group	Seoul	219	50.7	29
54	30	Philips Electronics	Eindhoven, Netherlands	212	−42.4	37
55	59	Wm. Wrigley Jr. Co.	Chicago	210	−0.6	33
56	97	Samsung Group	Seoul	208	81.8	28
57	56	Pfizer	New York	203	−11.5	33
58	52	Shiseido Co.	Tokyo	200	−19.7	6
59	58	Japan Tobacco Co.	Tokyo	199	−7.3	19
60	76	Interbrew	Leuven, Belgium	195	25.5	8
61	61	Hasbro	Pawtucket, R.I.	190	−9.7	18
62	72	Trucon Global Restaurants	Louisville, Ky.	189	7.8	28
63	98	Hewlett-Packard Co.	Palo Alto, Calif.	187	66.5	33
64	60	MG Rover	Bickenhill, U.K.	182	−13.8	15
65	66	EMI Group	London	181	−7.3	17
66	74	Compaq Computer Corp.	Houston	181	9.5	32
67	45	Lion Nathan	Sydney	168	−38.3	4
68	71	Ajinomoto Co.	Tokyo	167	−6.4	8
69	63	Bacardi Corp.	Hamilton, Bermuda	167	−17.3	14
70	203	Axel Springer	Hamburg	166	803.1	5

(continued)

Table 12.9 Top 100 Global Marketers by Media Ad Spending Outside the United States (cont.)

| Rank | | | | Spending Outside U.S. | | Country |
1999	1998	Advertiser	Headquarters	1999	Percent Change	Count
71	65	S.C. Johnson & Son	Racine, Wis.	$161	−19.6	37
72	64	Bayer	Leverkusen, Germany	159	−21.2	25
73	47	Mattel	El Segundo, Calif.	155	−42.0	20
74	96	Motorola	Schaumburg, Ill.	154	33.9	27
75	73	Nokia	Helsinki	152	−7.9	40
76	69	Suzuki Motor Co.	Hamamatsu, Japan	150	−20.5	25
77	68	C&A Brenninkmeyer	Amsterdam	148	−21.6	6
78	88	Cadbury Schweppes	London	140	9.6	23
79	70	Ericsson	Stockholm	137	−23.8	43
80	102	Seiko Group	Nagano, Japan	137	26.7	17
81	75	Kimberly-Clark Corp.	Irving, Texas	134	−15.1	16
82	79	Toshiba Corp.	Tokyo	134	−7.9	16
83	95	Lidl & Schwarz Stiftung & Co.	Bad Wimpfen, Germany	131	12.6	5
84	90	Tchibo Holding	Hamburg	128	2.9	16
85	87	Wal-Mart Stores	Bentonville, Ark.	127	−2.7	6
86	83	Sears, Roebuck & Co.	Hoffman Estates, Ill.	127	−8.1	5
87	84	Sara Lee Corp.	Chicago	126	−7.4	23
88	101	Heineken	Amsterdam	123	12.9	14
89	106	Aldi Group	Essen, Germany	119	19.2	6
90	82	Bristol-Myers Squibb Co.	New York	118	−14.5	18
91	115	Hitachi	Tokyo	117	37.9	9
92	105	Ingka Holdings	Humlebaek, Denmark	117	12.6	18
93	107	LVMH Moet Hennessy Louis Vuitton	Paris	115	15.7	20
94	92	Novartis	Basel, Switzerland	115	−5.2	23
95	89	American Home Products Corp.	New York	113	−9.6	19
96	80	Canon	Tokyo	111	21.8	26
97	93	Boots Co.	Nottingham, U.K.	108	−10.7	10
98	94	Siemens	Munich	106	−11.1	26
99	179	HSBC Holdings	London	104	246.5	14
100	127	Sharp Corp.	Osaka, Japan	104	45.2	13

Notes: Figures are in millions of U.S. dollars; 1998 rankings reflect data collected in 2000.
Country count is the number of countries where spending was reported for 1999.
Source: Reprinted with permission from Ad Age Global. Copyright, Crain Communications, Inc. 2000.

Table 12.10 Global Companies Agency Selection Strategies

Client	Agency	North America	U.S.	Canada	Latin America	Argentina	Bolivia	Brazil	Chile	Colombia	Ecuador	Mexico	Paraguay	Peru	Uruguay	Venezuela	Central America	Caribbean	Europe	Austria	Baltics*	Belgium	Czech Republic	Denmark	Finland	France	Germany	Greece	Hungary	Ireland	Italy	Netherlands	Norway	Poland
Procter & Gamble Co.	Bates																			X		X	X					X						
Procter & Gamble Co.	D'Arcy		X	X		X	X	X	X	X	X	X	X	X	X	X	X	X		X	X	X	X	X	X	X	X	X	X	X	X	X	X	X
Procter & Gamble Co.	Grey		X	X		X		X				X	X	X	X			X		X	X	X	X	X	X	X	X	X	X	X	X			X
Procter & Gamble Co.	Burnett		X	X		X		X	X	X		X				X	X	X		X		X	X			X	X	X	X	X	X			X
Procter & Gamble Co.	Saatchi		X	X								X	X					X		X	X	X	X	X		X	X	X	X	X	X			X
British Airways (cargo)	Grey		X																	X					X	X	X				X	X		
British Airways	M&C		X			X		X	X	X		X				X				X	X	X	X	X	X	X	X			X	X	X	X	X
British Airways	Publicis					X		X	X	X		X				X				X	X	X	X	X	X	X	X			X	X	X	X	X
Coca-Cola Co.	APL											X				X				X		X					X		X					
Coca-Cola Co.	Bates																											X						
Coca-Cola Co.	D'Arcy		X			X		X												X	X		X			X		X		X		X		
Coca-Cola Co.	Burnett		X	X		X		X	X			X	X		X								X					X	X	X	X		X	X
Coca-Cola Co.	Lowe		X	X		X			X			X													X				X	X				
Coca-Cola Co.	McCann		X			X	X	X	X	X	X	X	X	X	X	X	X	X		X			X			X		X	X	X				
Coca-Cola Co.	Publicis											X								X	X	X	X	X		X		X	X	X	X	X	X	X
Dell Computer Corp.	BBDO		X	X																X			X					X	X	X				
Dell Computer Corp.	Euro RSCG			X																														X
Ford Motor Co.	JWT		X			X		X	X	X	X	X	X	X					X		X	X			X	X	X	X	X			X			
Ford Motor Co.	O&M		X	X				X				X								X		X	X	X	X	X	X	X	X	X	X	X	X	X
Ford Motor Co.	Y&R		X	X																X		X	X	X	X	X	X				X			X
Gillette Co.	BBDO		X	X															X	X	X		X	X	X	X				X	X	X	
Gillette Co.	McCann		X			X	X	X	X	X	X	X	X	X	X	X	X	X		X		X			X	X			X	X	X		
Gillette Co.	O&M		X	X		X	X	X	X	X	X				X	X	X	X		X							X			X		X	X
Gillette Co. (Braun)	Lowe		X	X												X				X						X	X	X		X	X	X	X	X
Gillette Co. (Braun)	BBDO			X																X	X	X	X				X				X		X	X
Gillette Co. (Braun)	McCann					X		X	X			X															X		X					X
Gillette Co. (Oral-B)	Lowe		X	X				X	X	X		X																	X	X	X	X		
Microsoft Corp.	Euro RSCG																												X	X	X			
Microsoft Corp.	Grey			X																		X	X	X	X						X	X	X	
Microsoft Corp.	McCann		X					X				X	X					X														X		
Nestlé	APL		X					X				X		X			X		X			X				X	X	X	X		X	X		X
Nestlé	Dentsu		X																												X			
Nestlé	Euro RSCG		X																			X			X						X	X		
Nestlé	JWT		X	X		X	X	X	X	X	X		X	X	X			X	X		X	X	X	X	X	X	X	X			X	X	X	X
Nestlé	McCann		X	X		X	X	X	X	X	X	X	X	X	X	X	X	X		X	X	X	X	X	X	X	X	X	X		X	X	X	X
Nestlé	O&M		X					X																		X		X	X	X	X	X		
Nestlé	Publicis		X	X		X		X				X			X			X		X		X				X	X	X			X	X		
Nestlé	Saatchi																														X			
Nestlé (Pet food)	DDB							X												X			X	X	X	X					X	X	X	

(continued)

varying it with local execution. The localization typically involves the visuals, which are chosen specifically to suit each country or region.

Finally, companies need to adopt a strategy on *global coordination*. Global advertising coordination, usually done through a global advertising agency network, gives companies acceptable control and yet allows them to rely on the agency for the detailed coordination work. Table 12.10 shows how companies used international

Table 12.10 Global Companies Agency Selection Strategies (cont.)

Client	Agency	Europe (cont.)										Middle East			Africa		Asia-Pacific															
		Portugal	Romania	Slovakia	Soviet*	Spain	Sweden	Switzerland	Turkey	U.K.	Former Yugoslavia	Israel	Middle East	Saudi Arabia	South Africa	Other	Australia	China	Hong Kong	India	Indochina	Indonesia	Japan	Malaysia	New Zealand	Pakistan	Philippines	Singapore	South Korea	Sri Lanka	Taiwan	Thailand
Procter & Gamble Co.	Bates			X							X						X	X	X	X									X			
Procter & Gamble Co.	D'Arcy	X	X	X	X	X	X	X	X	X	X	X	X	X	X	X	X	X	X	X	X	X	X	X	X	X	X	X	X	X	X	X
Procter & Gamble Co.	Grey		X		X	X	X	X	X	X	X	X	X		X		X	X	X	X	X	X	X	X	X	X	X	X	X	X	X	X
Procter & Gamble Co.	Burnett	X	X	X	X	X	X			X	X		X	X	X		X	X	X	X		X	X	X	X	X	X	X	X		X	X
Procter & Gamble Co.	Saatchi	X	X		X	X	X			X	X	X	X	X	X	X	X	X	X	X		X	X	X	X	X	X	X	X		X	X
British Airways (cargo)	Grey				X	X	X			X																						
British Airways	M&C	X	X	X	X	X			X	X	X	X			X	X	X	X	X			X		X			X	X	X		X	X
British Airways	Publicis	X	X	X	X	X			X	X		X			X	X	X					X		X			X	X			X	X
Coca-Cola Co.	APL						X	X			X		X			X																X
Coca-Cola Co.	Bates		X												X		X		X		X							X				
Coca-Cola Co.	D'Arcy		X	X					X	X	X	X						X	X	X		X						X				
Coca-Cola Co.	Burnett	X				X	X		X	X					X			X	X	X		X						X				
Coca-Cola Co.	Lowe																	X														
Coca-Cola Co.	McCann	X	X			X	X		X	X	X	X		X	X	X	X		X	X	X	X	X	X	X	X	X	X				X
Coca-Cola Co.	Publicis		X	X	X		X	X	X	X	X				X																	
Dell Computer Corp.	BBDO								X																							
Dell Computer Corp.	Euro RSCG								X								X	X	X	X	X	X	X	X	X	X	X	X	X		X	X
Ford Motor Co.	JWT	X			X	X		X	X		X	X	X	X	X	X	X	X	X	X	X		X	X	X		X	X	X		X	X
Ford Motor Co.	O&M	X	X	X		X	X	X		X							X	X		X			X								X	X
Ford Motor Co.	Y&R	X				X	X			X							X			X												
Gillette Co.	BBDO	X			X	X	X	X		X					X			X					X									
Gillette Co.	McCann		X	X	X				X	X	X		X	X	X	X	X	X	X	X		X	X	X	X	X	X	X	X	X	X	X
Gillette Co.	O&M		X	X					X	X		X	X	X	X	X	X	X	X	X		X	X		X			X	X		X	X
Gillette Co. (Braun)	Lowe	X			X	X	X	X	X																							
Gillette Co. (Braun)	BBDO	X		X	X	X		X									X			X				X								
Gillette Co. (Braun)	McCann		X						X		X				X	X				X				X					X		X	X
Gillette Co. (Oral-B)	Lowe				X				X								X															
Microsoft Corp.	Euro RSCG								X									X		X								X			X	
Microsoft Corp.	Grey				X	X	X	X		X																						
Microsoft Corp.	McCann			X							X								X			X	X			X						X
Nestlé	APL	X			X	X			X			X		X		X	X	X	X	X		X	X	X	X	X		X				X
Nestlé	Dentsu								X	X							X	X			X					X			X		X	
Nestlé	Euro RSCG							X																								
Nestlé	JWT	X	X			X	X	X	X	X		X	X		X		X	X	X	X			X	X			X		X	X		
Nestlé	McCann	X	X		X	X	X	X	X	X	X	X	X			X	X	X	X	X	X	X	X	X	X	X	X	X	X	X	X	X
Nestlé	O&M		X			X			X	X					X	X	X			X		X		X	X	X			X	X	X	X
Nestlé	Publicis	X			X		X		X			X			X	X	X	X	X		X		X	X	X	X	X					X
Nestlé	Saatchi							X									X						X			X					X	
Nestlé (Pet food)	DDB				X	X	X		X																							

Source: Reprinted with permission from Advertising Age International. Copyright, Crain Communications, Inc. 1999.

agency networks to coordinate their advertising. Some companies prefer to do their own coordination. Should a company adopt a largely local advertising approach, the coordination requirement would be minimal or even redundant.

Companies involved in global advertising will have to determine which type of generic global advertising strategy to employ. It is important to recognize that the choice is not simply between global or local advertising, but rather that different aspects of a communications campaign may be globalized. This modular approach requires companies to select carefully which aspects of their communications to globalize and which to localize.

CONCLUSIONS

Few areas of global marketing are subject to more intense debate than is global advertising. The complexity of dealing simultaneously with a large number of different customers in many countries, all speaking their own languages and subject to their own cultural heritage, offers a real challenge to the global marketer. Global executives must find the common ground within these diverse influences so that coherent advertising campaigns can still be possible.

The debate in the field has recently shifted from one of standardization versus customization to one of global versus nonglobal advertising. Proponents of global advertising point to the convergence of customer needs and the emergence of the "world consumer," a person who is becoming more and more like his or her counterparts living in Paris, London, New York, and Tokyo. However, many aspects of the advertising environment remain considerably diverse. Although English is rapidly becoming a global language, most messages still have to be translated into local languages. Diverse regulations in many countries on the execution, content, and format of advertisements still make it difficult to offer standardized solutions to advertising problems. Also, media availability is substantially different in many parts of the world; so many companies still have to adapt their media mix to the local situation. Thus, many executives believe that local content is necessary and they will give the local country organizations substantial responsibility for input and decision making. Effective global advertising maintains a balance between the consistency of the global campaign and the creativity of the local campaign.

Most marketers realize that total customization is not desirable because it would require that each market create and implement its own advertising strategies. Top creative talent is scarce everywhere, and better creative solutions tend to be costly. As a result, companies appear to be moving toward modularization, in which some elements of the advertising message are common to all advertisements while other elements are tailored to local requirements. To make customization work, however, companies cannot simply design one set of advertisements and later expect to adapt the content. Successful modularization requires that companies, from the outset, plan for such a process by including and considering the full range of possibilities and requirements to be satisfied. The customization process offers a considerable challenge to global marketing executives and their advertising partners.

Questions for Discussion

1. What factors affect the extension of a domestic advertising campaign into several other countries?

2. Explain why some companies appear to be successful with very similar campaigns worldwide whereas others fail with the same strategy.

3. What advice would you give to a U.S. firm interested in advertising in Japan, and what would you suggest to a Japanese firm interested in advertising in the United States?

4. What future do you see for global advertising?

5. What will be the impact of increased commercial satellite television on global advertising, both in the United States and abroad?

6. How will the advertising industry need to react to the new trends in global marketing?

For Further Reading

Alden, Dana L., Jan-Benedict E. M. Steenkamp, and Rajeev Batra. "Brand Positioning Through Advertising in Asia, North America, and Europe: The Role of Global Consumer Culture." *Journal of Marketing,* January 1999, pp. 75–87.

De Pelsmacker, Patrick, and M. Geuens. "Reactions to Different Types of Ads in Belgium and Poland." *International Marketing Review,* 1998, vol. 15, no. 4, pp. 277–290.

Harker, Debra. "Achieving Acceptable Advertising: An Analysis of Advertising Regulation in Five Countries." *International Marketing Review,* 1998, vol. 15, no. 2, pp. 101–118.

Jo, Myung-Soo. "Contingency and Contextual Issues of Ethnocentrism-Pitched Advertisements: A Cross-National Comparison." *International Marketing Review,* 1998, vol. 15, no. 6, pp. 447–457.

Keillor, Bruce D., Stephen Parker, and T. Bettina Cornwell. "Using Advertising to Manage Consumer Satisfaction in an International Market." *Journal of Global Marketing,* 1998, vol. 12, no. 1, pp. 27–46.

McNeal, James U., and Mindy F. Ji. "Chinese Children as Consumers: An Analysis of Their New Product Information Sources." *The Journal of Consumer Marketing,* 1999, vol. 16, no. 4, pp. 345–365.

Melewar, T. C., and John Saunders. "Global Corporate Visual Identity Systems: Standardization, Control and Benefits." *International Marketing Review,* 1998, vol. 15, no. 4, pp. 291–308.

Moon, Young Sook, and George R. Franke. "Cultural Influences on Agency Practitioners' Ethical Perceptions: A Comparison of Korea and the U.S." *Journal of Advertising,* Spring 2000, vol. 29, no. 1, pp. 51–65.

Moss, Gloria A., and Vinten Garald. "Choices and Preferences: Testing the Effect of Nationality." *Journal of Consumer Behavior,* November 2001, vol. 1, no. 2, pp. 198–207.

Sandler, Dennis M., and David Shani. "Brand Globally but Advertise Locally: An Empirical Investigation." *International Marketing Review,* 1992, vol. 9, no. 4, pp. 18–31.

Sherry, John, Bradley Greenberg, and Hiroshi Tokinoya. "Orientations to TV Advertising Among Adolescents & Children in the US and Japan." *International Journal of Advertising,* 1999, vol. 18, no. 2, pp. 233–250.

Sirisagul, Kenya. "Global Advertising Practices: A Comparative Study." *Journal of Global Marketing,* 2000, vol. 14, no. 3, pp. 77–97.

Tian, Robert G., and Charles Emery. "Cross Cultural Issues in Internet Marketing." *Journal of the American Academy of Business,* March 2002, vol. 1, no. 2, pp. 217–224.

Whitelock, Jeryl, and Jean-Christophe Rey. "Cross-Cultural Advertising in Europe: An Empirical Survey of Television Advertising in France and the UK." *International Marketing Review,* 1998, vol. 15, no. 4, pp. 257–276.

Witkowski, T. H., and J. Kellner. "Convergent, Contrasting and Country-Specific Attitudes Towards Television Advertising in Germany and the United States." *Journal of Business Research* (USA), June 1998, vol. 42, no. 2.

Endnotes

1. "Global Kleenex Effort Breaks K-C Boundaries," *Advertising Age,* April 10, 2000, p. 3.

2. "Coke's Local World Cup Tactics," *Marketing,* May 30, 2002, p. 15.

3. "About Face," *Forbes,* March 19, 2001, p. 178.

4. Allyson L. Stewart-Allen, "Cultural Quandaries Can Lead to Misnomers," *Marketing News,* November 23, 1998, p. 9.

5. "The Picture Puzzle: Advertising's New Visual Language," *Communications Arts,* December 2001, p. 240.

6. Allyson L. Stewart-Allen, "Cross-Border Conflicts of European Sales Promotions," *Marketing News,* April 26, 1999, p. 10.

7. "Getting Lost in the Translation," *Computer Dealers News,* April 6, 1998, p. 56.

8. "Mexico Forces a Wonderbra Cover-Up," *Financial Times*, August 19, 1996, p. 4.

9. "Renault Apologizes to Tribes for Offensive Ads," *Knight Ridder Tribune Business News*, April 19, 2002, p. 1

10. "Hey, Why Do You Think We Call Them 'French Fries'?" *Wall Street Journal Europe*, December 9, 1999, p. 1.

11. Eirmalasare Bani, "Lipton Shoots Its Latest Commercial in Malaysia," *Business Times* (Malaysia), June 9, 1999, p. 15.

12. Frances Williams, "Curbs on Tobacco: WHO to Launch Talks on Treaty," *Financial Times*, October 26, 1999, p. 6.

13. "Smoking Offensive: Brazil's Strict Measures Open Unlikely Front in War on Cigarettes," *Wall Street Journal*, January 15, 2002, p. A1.

14. "Should These Ads Be Banned?" *Marketing*, March 23, 2000, p. 28.

15. "Clampdown on 'Porno-Chic' Ads Is Pushed by French Authorities," *The Wall Street Journal*, October 25, 2001, p. B4.

16. Erik Elinder, "How International Can Advertising Be?" *International Adviser*, December 1961, pp. 12–16.

17. "Patek Philippe: Tradition Anyone?" *Ad Age International*, January 11, 1999, p. 9.

18. Judann Pollack, "Pringles Wins Worldwide with One Message," *Ad Age International*, January 11, 1999, p. 14.

19. "Chiclets Tries New Language," *Advertising Age International*, April 19, 1993, p. I-1.

20. Normandy Madden and Andrew Hornery, "As Taco Bell Enters Singapore, Gidget Avoids the Ad Limelight," *Ad Age International*, January 11, 1999, p. 13.

21. "The New Europe: Whirlpool's European Sales Short-Circuit," *Asian Wall Street Journal*, April 15, 1998, p. 1.

22. "Whirlpool Asks Commerce to 'Just Immagine'," *Twice*, May 15, 2000, p. 38.

23. "Dentsu Ventures Abroad," *Asian Wall Street Journal*, March 29, 2001, p. N1.

24. Gregory M. Rose, Victoria D. Bush, and Lynn Kahle, "The Influence of Family Communication Patterns on Parental Reactions Toward Advertising: A Cross-National Examination," *Journal of Advertising*, January 1, 1998, p. 71.

25. "Emotion, Not Logic, Sways the Japanese Consumer," *Japan Economic Journal*, April 22, 1980, p. 24.

26. "Movie Stars Moonlight in Japan," *Forbes*, March 14, 2001.

27. "Sega's Sales Rise as Ads Play on Woes," *Ad Age International*, February 8, 1999, p. 1.

28. "The Dentsu Story," *Campaign*, April 9, 1999, p. 38.

29. "Nielsen Media Research—International Predicts Second-Half Rebound in Global Ad Sales," Press Release, Nielsen Media Research (International), *Business Wire*, May 31, 2002.

30. Ibid.

31. "Advertising Continues to Slump in Asia," *Asian Wall Street Journal*, August 9, 2001, p. 7.

32. "How Do I Love Thee?" *Far Eastern Economic Review*, March 18, 1999, p. 48.

33. "Chinese Women Find Evolving Roles Beget New Economic Clout," *Asian Wall Street Journal*, May 30, 2002, p. A6.

34. "Frozen Assets: TCBY Takes a Scoop Out of the China Market," *Far Eastern Economic Review*, November 14, 1996, p. 68.

35. "Full of Eastern Promise," *Financial Times*, June 8, 1995, p. 13.

36. "European Consumers Studied by Burnett," *Direct Marketing*, August 1998, pp. 14–15.

37. "Polish Advertising Most Effective Outside Media," *Polish Press Agency*, May 14, 1998, p. 1.

38. Theodore Levitt, "The Globalization of Markets," *Harvard Business Review*, May–June 1983, p. 92; *The Marketing Imagination* (New York: Free Press, 1983); interview with Theodore Levitt, *International Herald Tribune*, October 1, 1984, p. 7.

39. "M&C Saatchi Wins BA/Comair Account," *Marketing Web*, September 28, 2001.

40. "BA's Warm Approach," *Financial Times*, December 28, 1989, p. 8.

41. "BA's $150 Million Campaign Makes Worldwide Debut," *Advertising Age*, January 8, 1996, p. 33.

42. "British Air Launches Union Jack Livery After UK Complaints About Tail-Fin Art," *Wall Street Journal*, June 7, 1999, p. 6.

43. "Cartier Softens French Accent in International Campaign," *Advertising Age*, October 7, 1996, p. 12.

44. "Sprite Is Riding Global Ad Effort to No. 4 Status," *Advertising Age*, November 18, 1996, p. 30.

45. "Coca-Cola Touts Overseas Strength for Fanta Brand," *AdAge.com*, November 4, 1996.

46. "Coke Brands IPG as Global Ad Strategist," *AdAge.Com*, December 4, 2000.

47. "The Beauty of Global Branding," *Business Week*, June 28, 1999, p. 70.

48. "Heinz Re-enlists Leo Burnett for Global Campaign," *Pittsburgh Post-Gazette*, March 27, 1999, p. C1.

49. "Duracell Given More Life Is Launching $50 Million Global Campaign," *Adweek*, June 15, 1998, p. 84.

50. "Jaguar Goes Global," *Automotive News Europe*, April 12, 1999, p. V.

51. "Unconventional," *Adweek*, January 29, 2001, p. 28.

52. "Acne Products to Get New Face," *Wall Street Journal*, February 11, 2002, p. 12.

53. "Unconventional, *Adweek*, January 29, 2001, p. 28.

54. "Top 10 Global Ad Markets," *AdageGlobal*, April 2002, p. 18.

55. "Global Media," *Ad Age International*, February 8, 1999, p. 23.

56. "Global Media," *Ad Age International*, February 8, 1999, p. 23.

57. "Phoenix Rising," *Newsweek*, November 12, 2001, p. 46.

58. "Global Media," *Ad Age International*, February 8, 1999, p. 23.

59. "MTV's World," *Business Week*, February 18, 2002, p. 81.

60. "Top 10 Digital Properties," *Adageglobal*, November 2000.

61. "Going Global with Banner Ads," *www.sun.com;* accessed on July 16, 2002.

62. "Cable in Europe: Prospects for Development and Profitability," *IDATE Newsletter*, 3rd Quarter, 2000, no. 26.

63. "Nokia in 'Exploratory Talks' with News Corp. About Internet Tie-Up," *Financial Times*, February 2, 2000, p. 13.

64. "AOL Lands Toyota for Multimedia Pact," *Wall Street Journal*, August 28, 2001, p. B7.

65. "Think Global, Act Local?" *Marketing*, March 29, 2001, p. 24

66. "Chicago Tribune Marketing Column," *Knight Ridder Tribune Business News*, July 10, 2002, p. 1.

67. "Motorola Consolidates," *MC Technology Marketing Intelligence*, December 2000, p. 15.

68. "Motorola Strives for Brand Unity," *B to B*, September 25, 2000, p. 4.

69. "Agencies Expanding Eastern European Penetration," *Advertising Age International*, October 1996, p. I-8.

70. "Think Global, Act Local?" *Marketing*, March 29, 2001, p. 24.

71. "3 Ad Competitors Unite to Conquer," *New York Times*, March 8, 2002, p. C1.

72. Andreas Grein and Robert Ducoffe, "Strategic Responses to Market Globalisation Among Advertising Agencies," *International Journal of Advertising*, August 1, 1998, p. 301.

73. "$500 Million in Colgate Eggs in One Y&R Basket," *Advertising Age*, December 4, 1995, p. 1.

74. "Think Global, Act Local?" *Marketing*, March 29, 2001, p. 24.

75. "Unilever Realigns L200 Million Food Task," *Marketing*, February 15, 2001, p. 1.

76. "How a Coke Ad Campaign Fell Flat with Viewers," *Wall Street Journal*, March 19, 2001, p. B1.

Chapter 13

Global Product and Service Strategies

This chapter looks at the strategies that companies can pursue to adapt their products and services to global markets. The chapter discussion first centers on the many environmental factors that can prevent the marketing of uniform and standardized products across a multitude of markets. Attention then shifts to the various implications of selecting brand names for global markets. Global firms are concerned not only with determining appropriate brand names but also with protecting those names against abuse and piracy. Subsequent sections focus on packaging and managing product lines and support services. The chapter concludes with a section on the marketing of services on a global scale. We also highlight the enormous opportunities in the service industry and explain how various companies are pursuing these opportunities globally.

The global marketing manager is constantly balancing the need to tailor products and services to the local customer with the opportunity to identify similar needs across countries because these similar needs could support a global product or service. Of course, the local culture, regulations, and physical environment could all suggest the need for a local product or service. However, there can be significant economies of scale in manufacturing and marketing standardized products and services across multiple countries. Global marketers must always be aware of these competing issues. Figure 13.1 highlights the factors involved in global product strategy decisions.

PRODUCT DESIGN IN A GLOBAL ENVIRONMENT

One of the principal questions in global marketing concerns the types of products that can be sold in different markets. The international firm wants to know whether existing products have to be adapted to certain global requirements or whether they

Figure 13.1: Global Product Strategies

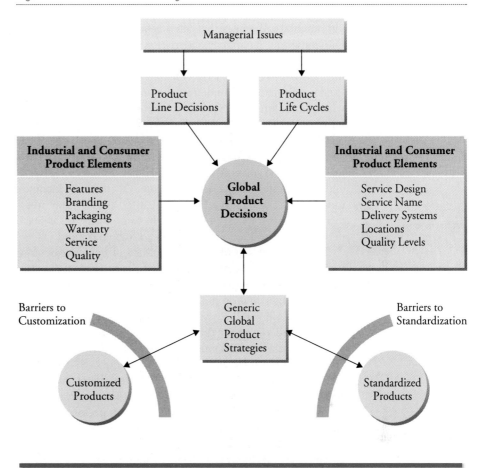

can be shipped in their present form. For new products, the firm must select the particular features that its products should incorporate and then determine the desired function and performance of these features. The major elements of product design are explained in the following sections, which emphasize the effect of global complexities of this topic.

Selecting the most desirable product features is an involved decision for global marketers. The approach taken should include a thorough review of all the environmental factors that may affect product use, such as the level of literacy, income, and technical skills of potential customers. Also to be considered are the climatic conditions, power level, and availability and quality of maintenance support because all will affect product performance. A thorough analysis should also include a review of the physical environment, a topic described in detail in Chapter 6. In all cases, however, a firm must picture its products in the targeted market and ask the question, "How would our product be used in that country?" In some situations, it may be necessary to test units in the various markets.

PRODUCT DIMENSIONS

Dimensions (as expressed by size, capacity, or volume) are subject to market and environmental influences that often require different approaches to any given market. One important factor, particularly for U.S. firms, is the selection of a metric versus a non-metric scale. The firm must go beyond a simple translation of non-metric into metric sizes to help users or consumers understand the design of products and meet legal requirements. Simple translations do not lead to round, standardized numbers, which often forces companies to change the physical sizes of their products to conform to new standards. With Europe (the only exception being the United Kingdom) and Japan operating on the metric standard, the United States is one of the few remaining major non-metric markets. Translation of product dimensions is therefore less of an issue for non-U.S. firms than it is for U.S.-based companies that normally operate on a non-metric basis at home. Of course as Japanese and European companies market their products in the United States, they need to provide non-metric measurements for U.S. consumers. In some cases this is just a matter of labeling, and in others the product dimensions need to be modified.

The different physical characteristics of consumers often influence product design. Swiss watch manufacturers have learned over the years to adapt their watchbands to different wrist sizes. The Japanese have smaller wrists than Americans; thus, design changes that do not necessarily change the function or look of the watch are required. Unilever, the consumer product company, found that the characteristics of hair in Brazil were very different from Thailand, a finding that required a much different formula for the same shampoo.[1] Ansell Edmont asked Japanese factory workers to test their new work gloves. They found that Japanese workers have smaller hands and shorter fingers than their counterparts in Europe and the United States and therefore require different gloves.[2] Domino's Pizza found that one size pizza did not fit all appetites. In Germany, consumers preferred a smaller individual pizza. By tailoring to local sizes and tastes, Domino's overseas sales increased from $16 million in 1986 to $503 million in 1996.[3]

Although product characteristics may have to be varied from market to market, companies also look for similarities across geographic boundaries. If market segments with similar product needs that cut across geographic products can be identified, the company can reduce the number of product variations needed to serve the global marketplace. For example, in one study of four different cultural and geographic markets, researchers identified three distinct segments of fruit-flavored-soda drinkers. The segments were based on sensory preferences: (1) weak aroma, light color, low sweetness, and low flavor; (2) stronger aroma, medium color, medium sweetness, and stronger flavor; (3) strongest aroma, darkest color, high sweetness, and strongest flavor.[4] Although products often must be tailored to the needs of different markets, more and more companies are looking for similarities across markets.

Product size is often affected by the physical surroundings of the location or space where the product will be used. In some countries, limited living space necessitates home appliances that are substantially smaller than those found in a country such as the United States, where people live in larger dwellings. Recently, U.S.-made major appliances have been imported in Japan by a few discount chains. Some wealthier Japanese consumers favor these large appliances, although the sales volume is still small by international standards. Some of the customers have had to return the appliances after purchase, however, because they could not fit the refrigerators through their apartment doors. In many countries, customers have come to expect certain products in certain sizes; thus, international firms are forced to adapt to meet these expectations.

DESIGN FEATURES

International firms find almost invariably that they must alter some components or parts of a product because of local circumstances. One worldwide manufacturer of industrial abrasives has had to adjust to different raw material supply situations by varying the raw material input according to country while still maintaining the performance standards of its abrasives. Food packaging may also need to be adapted to the climate and physical conditions of marketing to another country. For example, an American snack manufacturer designed a composite can that was environmentally friendly and lighter, and that could be vacuum packed to take into account the longer shelf life and shipping costs of marketing its products in Japan.[5]

Packaging color and numbers per unit have cultural significance to the global marketer. A slick black package with imprinted gold or silver is considered elegant and sophisticated in the United States, but that same package suggests death in parts of Africa.[6] Some countries may require a number of product features, but adding the desired features can strengthen a company's marketing effort and offset the added engineering and production costs. In some local markets, customers may even expect a product to perform a function that is different from the one originally intended. One U.S. exporter of gardening tools found that its battery-operated trimmers were used by the Japanese as lawn mowers on their small lawns. The batteries and motors did not last as long as they would have under the original intended use, which was trimming shrubbery. Because of the different function desired by Japanese customers (trimming small lawns), a design change was eventually required.

ADAPTING PRODUCTS TO CULTURAL PREFERENCES. Fashion and tastes differ by country, so companies often change the styling of their products. Color, for example, should reflect the values of each country. For Japan, red and white have happy associations, whereas black and white indicate mourning. Green is an unpopular color in Malaysia, where it is associated with the jungle and illness. Textile manufacturers in the United States that have started to expand their export businesses have consciously used color to suit local needs.[7] For example, the Lowenstein Corporation has successfully used brighter colors for fabrics exported to Africa.

Scent is also subject to change from one country to another. S. C. Johnson & Son, a manufacturer of furniture polishes, encountered resistance to its Lemon Pledge furniture polish among older consumers in Japan. Careful market research revealed that the polish smelled similar to a latrine disinfectant used widely in Japan in the 1940s. Sales rose sharply after the scent was adjusted.[8]

Food is one of the most culturally distinct product areas. Campbell Soup Company realized it had to change its traditional western-style cream recipes to broth-based recipes with fish as the primary ingredient to be successful in Japan. They relied on grassroots market research in formulating new products for the Japanese markets. Campbell employed staff to eat soup in local Japanese restaurants and report on the taste, the spices used, appearance, texture, color, and consistency.[9]

Of course, adaptation is not always necessary. Kentucky Fried Chicken (KFC) is doing very well in Pakistan, where chicken is a preferred meat. The menu is not substantially different than elsewhere, and in the two years following its initial market entry in 1997, KFC quickly grew to ten restaurants in two major cities.[10]

ADAPTING PERFORMANCE STANDARDS. Manufacturers typically design products to meet domestic performance standards. As we have already seen, such standards do not always apply in other countries, and product changes are required in some circumstances. Products designed in highly developed countries often exceed the performance needed in developing nations. Customers in developing nations often prefer products of greater simplicity, not only to save costs but to ensure better service over a product's lifetime. Companies have been criticized for selling excess performance when simpler products will do. Stepping into this market gap are companies from some of the less developed countries whose present technology levels are more in line with the consumers' needs.

The need for different product standards was behind a foreign acquisition by General Electric (GE). The U.S.-based company acquired the low-voltage business of GEC-Alsthom in the United Kingdom, with the strategic intent of positioning itself for competition under the International Electric Committee (IEC) electrical standard. Standards for electrical equipment in the United States differ from those adopted by many foreign countries, and relevant standards abroad were often set by the IEC. Rather than rebuild the U.S.-made controls, GE decided to acquire a European firm specializing in IEC standard controls for use in its equipment.[11] Of course, manufacturers from developing countries face the opposite challenge: companies must increase the performance of their products to meet the standards of industrialized countries. In general, the necessity of increasing performance tends to be more apparent, whereas opportunities for product simplification are frequently less obvious to the observer. Sometimes manufacturers have to build design changes into products for overseas sales, changes that are not apparent to the buyer. These internal design changes can increase product use or performance or adapt the product to a new environment. In the mobile phone market, different standards prevail in various regions or countries. The first generation of mobile phones had to be built to country-specific standards, resulting in low sales volumes. In Europe, there were two analog standards (TACS and NMT), whereas in the United States there was a single analog standard (AMPS). The second (and digital) generation was dominated by the GSM standard in Europe and different standards in the United States (TDNA, DCNA, and some GSM). Eventually, some companies began to offer dual-standard phones. The challenge of multiple standards continues, however, and it forces companies such as Motorola, Ericsson, and Nokia to decide how many different standards they want or can serve effectively.[12]

ADAPTING HIGH-TECHNOLOGY PRODUCTS. Technology-intensive and industrial products frequently face standards for product performance that differ from one country to the next. In telecommunications, the signaling standards used for U.S. switching systems differ from those used in Europe. As a result, significant barriers exist when a company wants to become an exporter. In effect, the exporter often faces the decision of becoming a multistandard firm. Designing and manufacturing such systems to several standards, or languages, adds to the total cost. Without minimum sales volume, a company may have to forgo export opportunities if the adaptation costs outweigh the business opportunity. 3Com, the U.S.-based maker of Palm Computing products and related devices, distributes its products to thirty-five different countries and supports many languages, including English, French, German, and Spanish. To continue building its global leadership, the company also entered an alliance to offer Japanese language support for its Palm Computing products. In Japan, the company will offer Japanese language software, as well as dictionaries covering the Japanese and English languages.[13] Accrue Software, Inc., a leading provider of enterprise ebusiness analysis software and services, entered the Japanese market with Sumitomo Electronics. It customized its software and thus offered it in the Japanese language.[14] Both 3Com and Accrue believed that they needed to enter the large Japanese market and yet also understood that such entry would not be successful unless their complicated software products were customized for Japanese customers.

Computer manufacturers also need to consider adapting products to different technologies. Apple Computer adapted its operating system and software for Office 98 to include Japan-specific features, including the direct entry of hiragana text and support for vertical text in documents. Help characters were also customized for Japanese users. Although Apple's overall market share in personal computers is small, the entire Asia Pacific region accounted for 20 percent of the company's corporate sales. In some specific applications, such as graphics, architecture, or medicine, Apple had a leading share, with up to a 70 percent market share in selected segments.[15] To protect that share, the company was eager to adjust and adapt its products.

CHANGING PROVEN PRODUCTS TO MEET FOREIGN REQUIREMENTS. One of the most difficult decisions for international companies to make is whether or not to change a proven product that has sold well in the past. Sometimes, a company may be in a position to change a proven design to gain a competitive advantage because other, more tradition-bound firms declined to do so.

The European Union's policies of deregulation and market opening are affecting how locomotives are designed and built. Because of the EU standardization policies, the technology of choice is the three-phase, asynchronous system and induction motor, without slip rings. The EU has a uniform European Train Control System, which reduces the cost of adapting locomotives for service on the various national systems.[16] Sometimes different standards are mandated by governments, leaving international marketers scrambling for compliance. Efforts to coordinate these kinds of standards within Europe are well under way and are even spreading to non-EU country markets. European companies have gained strategic advantages in the exporting of EU standards internationally.[17]

QUALITY

The quality of a product reflects the intended function and the circumstances of product use. As these circumstances change, it is sometimes necessary to adjust quality accordingly. Products that receive less service in a given country have to be redesigned and adapted to compensate for the lower service levels. At times, there may be an opportunity to lower product cost by reducing the built-in quality and, in turn, reducing the price to the customary purchase levels of the local market. However, such reductions in quality may be dangerous if the company reputation suffers in the process. Not marketing a product at all may be preferable.

Some companies go to great lengths to live up to different quality standards in foreign markets. The experience of BMW, the German automaker exporting to Japan, serves as an excellent example of the extra efforts frequently involved. BMW found that its customers in Japan expected the very finest quality. Typically, cars shipped to Japan had to be completely repainted. Even very small paint scratches were not tolerated by customers. And when the car needed service, it was picked up at the customer's home and returned when services and/or repairs were completed.

GLOBAL STANDARDS[18]

Most countries have some type of national organization that sets standards for business processes and practices. Groups such as the Canadian Standards Association, the British Standards Institute (BSI), and the American National Standards Institute (ANSI) all formulate standards for product design and testing. If products adhere to the standards, buyers are assured of a stated level of product quality.

Given the growth in global commerce, there are benefits to having global standards for items such as credit cards, speed codes for 35 mm film, paper sizes, screw threads, and car tires. Although the national standards institutes ensure consistency within countries, an international agency is required to coordinate the differences from one country to the next. The country-to-country differences become obvious, for example, when you try to plug your hair dryer into outlets in different countries.

The International Standards Organization (ISO), located in Geneva, Switzerland, coordinates the setting of global standards. To set a global standard, representatives from various countries meet and attempt to agree on a common standard. Sometimes they adopt a standard already set by a country. For example, the British standard for quality assurance (BS5750) was adopted internationally as ISO 9000. Initially a European standard, ISO 9000 is becoming recognized globally.

The unification of Europe has forced its citizens to recognize the need for multi-country standards. In areas where a European standard has been developed, manufacturers who meet the standard are allowed to include the EU certification symbol, "CE." Firms in and outside the EU are eligible to use the CE symbol, but they must be able to verify compliance with the EU standards. The financial services industry is the latest to implement a quality performance standard worldwide and is also working on subordinate standards for specific sectors, such as transfer agent operations and claims and check processing.[19] If Europe continues to dominate the creation of global standards through ISO, the United States and Japan will be under pressure to conform. The U.S. standards-setting process is much more fragmented than it is in Europe. In the United States, there are over 450 different standards-setting groups, all loosely coordinated by ANSI. After a standard is set by one of the 450 groups, ANSI certifies that it is an "American National Standard."

As we already stated, ISO 9000 is one of the most widely recognized standards. As the global quality standard, ISO 9000 ensures that an organization can consistently deliver a product or service that satisfies the customer's requirements. The number of ISO global standards has grown from 4,917 in 1982 to 8,651 in 1992, to 13,000 in 2002 in 140 countries around the world.[20]

The "standards wars" will have a great impact on global marketing for all firms, regardless of their home base. Regional standards, such as those put forth by the European Commission (EC), can become effective standards for firms in Asia or Latin America hoping to export to Europe. Particularly for international firms based in emerging markets, meeting these newly emerging, de facto global standards will become the basic requirement for securing export orders.

BRANDING DECISIONS

Selecting appropriate brand names for use globally is substantially more complex than deciding on a brand name for just one country. Typically, a brand name is rooted in a given language and may have either a different meaning or none at all if used elsewhere. Ideally, marketers look for brand names that evoke similar emotions or images around the world. From their past experiences, people worldwide have come to expect the same thing from brand names such as Coca-Cola, IBM, Minolta, and Mercedes-Benz. It has become increasingly difficult, however, for new entrants to become recognized unless the name has some meaning for the prospective customer. Language problems are particularly difficult to overcome.

Colgate-Palmolive, the large U.S.-based toiletries manufacturer, purchased the leading toothpaste brand in Southeast Asia, "Darkie." With a minstrel in blackface as its logo, the product had been marketed by a local company since 1920. After the acquisition, Colgate-Palmolive came under pressure from many groups in the United States to use a less offensive brand name. The company undertook a large amount of research to find both a brand name and logo that were racially inoffensive and yet close enough to be recognized quickly by consumers. The company changed the name to Darlie after an exhaustive search. In some markets where the Darkie brand had as much as 50 percent market share, the marketing challenge was success at getting customers to transfer brand loyalty from the old to the new name.[21]

SELECTION PROCEDURES

Brand name selection is critical. Global marketers must carefully evaluate the meanings and word references in the languages of their target audiences. Can the name be pronounced easily, or will it be distorted in the local language? Branding in Asia, and especially in China, is based on visual appeal, whereas speakers of English tend to judge a brand name on its sound. Asian firms spend extraordinary time and resources on the selection of brand names. Western firms can benefit from such extensive research. Good examples are Coca-Cola, which means "tasty and happy" in Chinese.[22] The Chinese equivalent for Mercedes-Benz means "speed on."[23] A study of the brand names used by a sample of Fortune 500 consumer products companies found that only 10 percent used their English brand name in the Chinese market.[24]

Given almost unlimited possibilities for names and the restricted opportunities for finding and registering a desirable one, international companies spend considerable effort on the selection procedure. One consulting company specializes in finding brand names with worldwide application. The company brings citizens of many countries together in Paris, where, under the guidance of a specialist, they are asked to state names in their particular language that would combine well with the product to be named.[25] Speakers of other languages can immediately react if a suggested name sounds unpleasant or has distasteful connotations in their language. After a few such sessions, the company may accumulate as many as one thousand names, which will later be reduced to five hundred by a company linguist. The client company then is asked to select fifty to one hundred names for further consideration. At this point, the names are subjected to a search procedure to determine which ones have not been registered in any of the countries under consideration. Only about ten names may survive this entire process; from these, the company will have to make the final selection. Although this process may be expensive, the cost is generally considered negligible compared with the advertising expenditures invested in the brand name over many years.

When confronted with the need to search for a brand name with global applications, a company may consider the following options:

1. An arbitrary or invented word not to be found in any standard English (or other language) dictionary, such as Toyota's Lexus.
2. A recognizable English (or foreign-language) word, but one totally unrelated to the product in question, such as the detergent Cheer.
3. An English (or other language) word that merely suggests some characteristic or purpose of the product, such as Mr. Clean.
4. A word that is evidently descriptive of the product, although the word may have no meaning to persons unacquainted with English (or other specific languages), such as the diaper brand Pampers.
5. A geographical place or a common surname, such as Kentucky Fried Chicken.
6. A device, design, number, or some other element that is not a word or a combination of words, such as 3M Company.[26]

After selecting a brand name based on these six options, another key question to be answered in global branding is, "Should the company use a single brand name worldwide or should it use different names in different countries adapted to the local language?"

SELECTION OF INTERNET DOMAIN NAMES

Selection of an Internet domain name poses even more problems. The registration of Internet domain names has been opened to all users worldwide, and because the cost of a registration is less than $100 for the first two years, many individuals and firms have begun registering names, regardless of prior or intended use. A company starting with a new product or company name thus faces the challenge of registering its Internet domain name at the same time that it registers the legal papers required for establishment of the company. Trade name registration and protection alone do not guarantee access to an Internet domain name. As a result, initial Internet domain name registration is fast becoming the first step before either a product or a company goes public. As of the beginning of 2002, there were already 36.3 million web sites worldwide.[27]

SINGLE-COUNTRY VERSUS GLOBAL BRAND NAMES

Global marketers must decide whether the brand name needs to be universal. Brands such as Coca-Cola and Kodak have universal currency and lend themselves to an integrated global marketing strategy. With worldwide travel a common occurrence, many companies do not think that they should accept a brand name unless it can be used universally. Brands provide a badge, emblem, or symbol that gives the product credibility and helps the consumer identify products and make choices. A brand that consumers know and trust helps them make choices faster and more easily.[28] Companies invest in their brands, both in brand identity and in product quality. One of the biggest success stories is Intel. After losing a trademark case to protect the "386" name in 1991, Intel launched the "Intel Inside" campaign through cooperative advertising. Awareness of the company's chip went from 22 percent to 80 percent in two years.[29] Since then, Intel has been able to transfer the brand equity into its Pentium processor brands and a whole list of licensing requirements that the company imposes on its chip clients for use in PCs.[30] A global brand name can be a huge asset as a firm enters new markets. For example, when McDonald's opened its doors in Johannesburg, South Africa, thousands of people stood in line. When Coke entered Poland, its red-and-white delivery trucks drew applause at traffic lights.[31]

Of course, using the same name elsewhere is not always possible, and a change in the home market may jeopardize the positive feelings for the original name, positive feelings that were hard-won after years of marketing efforts. In such instances, different names must be found. Procter & Gamble had successfully marketed its household cleaner, Mr. Clean, in the United States for some time. This name, however, had no meaning except in countries using the English language. The situation prompted the company to arrive at several adaptations abroad, such as Monsieur Propre in France and Meister Proper in Germany. In all cases, however, the symbol of the genie with his gleaming eyes was retained because it evoked responses abroad that were similar to those in the United States.

PRIVATE BRANDING STRATEGIES

The practice of private branding, or supplying products to a third party for sale under the original brand name, has become quite common in many domestic markets. In food retailing, private branding is very popular in Europe, with 40 to 50 percent of total store sales being store brands, versus only 10 to 15 percent in the United States.[32] Similar opportunities exist on a global scale and may be used to the manufacturer's advantage. Arranging for distribution of the firm's product through local distributors or companies with already existing distribution networks reduces the risk of failure and provides for rapid volume growth via instant market access. Some Japanese companies have used the private branding approach to gain market access in Europe and the United States. Ricoh of Japan, originally known as a manufacturer of cameras, entered the market for small plain-paper copiers (PPCs) in the early 1970s. Private branding supply contracts were signed with several U.S. and European firms. Ricoh used this strategy to enter the market when it was not yet well known, but later it switched its brands to its own name and acquired many of its initial partners.[33] The company is now a global leader for both small personal copiers and fax machines.

These private branding arrangements are also called original equipment manufacturer (OEM) contracts, in which the foreign manufacturer assumes the role of the OEM. As the market grows, these arrangements become difficult to manage from the manufacturer's point of view. Nevertheless, they open markets more quickly and at much lower investment cost than would be required if the company developed these markets on its own. LG, an international Korea-based firm that used to operate under the brand name Goldstar, has used various OEM relationships to help it expand into established markets. In the United States, the company acquired Zenith and is now supplying televisions under that brand name.[34] To build up the European market for its home appliances, televisions, and microwave ovens, the company relied on private branding. For its more recent products, such as digital televisions and DVDs, the company will use the LG brand name.[35] In Romania, where there was no strong local producer, LG entered the market directly under its own brand name.[36]

Private branding or OEM contracts come with drawbacks for the manufacturer. With control over marketing in the hands of the distributor, the manufacturer must depend on the distributor and can influence marketing only indirectly. For long-term profitability, companies often find that they need to sell products under their own names, even when the OEM has achieved substantial marketing success. Such partnerships often end because of conflicting interests.

GLOBAL BRANDS

Experts disagree on what constitutes a global brand. However, few brands are marketed in the same way, with the same strategy, and for identical products worldwide. Many products that are marketed as global brands with a largely identical strategy still have not yet received major recognition beyond their home regions. For example, Federal Express launched its courier business in the United States in the 1970s. The Federal Express name became synonymous with U.S. overnight delivery service. As Federal Express opened its international operations, however, its name became a problem. In Latin America, *federal* connoted corrupt police, and in Europe, the name was linked to the former Federal Republic of Germany. In 1994, Federal Express changed its name to FedEx, which now, in some cases, has become a verb meaning "to ship overnight."[37] When Pillsbury wanted to market Progresso, its U.S. brand of Italian-style food products, in foreign markets, it discovered that in South American markets, the name "Progresso" was easily associated with products other than food. So Pillsbury used the name "Frescarini" to market the Progresso products globally.[38]

Although several Japanese companies like Toyota, Panasonic, and Sony have built strong global brands, few other Asian companies have achieved such status. Acer Corp., the Taiwanese PC maker, has begun to build a global brand, and it is followed closely by LG, formerly known under Lucky–Goldstar, the Korean electronics company. LG Group, the $40 billion Korean conglomerate, hired Landor Associates to build its global image.[39] Samsung, the South Korean electronics manufacturing company, retained Vogt-Wein of Westport, Connecticut, to build its global brand image for VCRs, satellite dishes, personal computers, cameras, and automobiles.[40] The three largest soap manufacturers in Europe, Procter & Gamble (P&G), Unilever, and Henkel, have three distinct global branding strategies there. P&G's strategy is to increase the Europeanization of its brands. P&G has developed a European segmentation, along a quality/price dimension, with the policy of keeping only one brand per segment for all European countries, with a standardized marketing mix. As a consequence, P&G de-emphasizes or eliminates all local brands not fitting that desired portfolio. Unilever uses a multinational strategy by exploiting local equities to capitalize on consumer goodwill, while standardizing the product platforms as much as possible. The goal is to reduce all sources of unnecessary costs. Henkel maintains a balanced portfolio of global and local brands to exploit economies of scale while securing market penetration, calling its approach "glocally adaptive." In Europe it aims at creating global brands as much as possible: it sells Dixan and Persil in most European countries, but not in Spain, for instance, where Henkel operates two strong local brands (Wipp and Blanol). In such cases, instead of risking the loss of goodwill attached to these names, Henkel prefers simply to harmonize the product features with those of Dixan and Persil.[41]

Global brands have been very successful in China. In the cities of Beijing, Shanghai, Guangzhou, and Chengdu, foreign brands control 85 percent of the shampoo market, 72 percent of the chocolate market, and 81 percent of the carbonated soft-drink market. Although global brands control 40 percent of the laundry detergent sales in the top four Chinese cities, the local state-owned enterprise— Shanghai's White Cat—is putting up a fight. White Cat copied Unilever's Omo brand detergent right down to the red, blue, and yellow cardboard packaging.[42] White Cat is the Chinese market leader for detergents, with about 19 percent market share, well ahead of leading global brands such as Ariel, Tide, and Omo.[43]

The opportunity for global branding is partially driven by the presence of strong global information logic, a topic we explained in detail in Chapter 7. Customers who do not scan the world for brands are much less aware of globally launched brands. Increasingly, however, customers look elsewhere for products and are becoming more aware of brands offered internationally, even globally. As this awareness continues to expand, the payoff for global brands, with their strong appeal for perceived quality, will outweigh the difficulties of launching them.

PANREGIONAL BRANDS

Brands actively marketed in a geographic region, such as Europe, are considered panregional. (In the case of Europe, they are also called pan-European brands or Eurobrands.) In the strictest sense, packaged goods marketed across Europe with the same formula; the same brand name; and the same positioning strategy, package, and advertising are still said to account for a small portion of total sales volume in Europe. Examples of such products include P&G's Pampers and Head & Shoulders, Michelin tires, and Rolex watches. However, experts expect the Eurobrands' share of all brands to rise. Another group of products, marketed with semistandardized strategies but with changes in one or more of the marketing variables, is estimated to account for as much as 40 percent of the European consumer goods business. Consequently, purely national brands will decline in share, from more than 50 percent today to about 33 percent in the next decade. In Latin America, Brazil's Varig Airlines has undertaken a design and logo change to broaden its regional appeal. The revamped Varig logo is a modern design with warm colors, which supports the company's advertising program of well-rested passengers getting off their flights.[44] In Asia, the Shangri-La hotel chain, with thirty-four hotels, has built a strong regional brand. Shangri-La offers all the amenities of a luxury hotel, along with Asian hospitality. The staff uniforms reflect the local costumes. Shangri-La also uses its advertising to appeal to Asian executives, who are judged by the hotels they choose. The tag line on Shangri-La ads is "It must be Shangri-La."[45]

Electrolux, the Swedish white goods (household appliances) company, made more than one hundred acquisitions between 1975 and 1985, which left the company with more than twenty brands sold in forty countries. Large markets such as the

United Kingdom and Germany had as many as six major Electrolux brands. A study by Electrolux found a convergence of market segments across Europe, with the consumers' need for "localness" being defined primarily in terms of distribution channels, promotion in local media, and use of local names instead of the need for different product features. From this analysis, Electrolux developed a strategy with two pan-European brands and one or two local brands in each market. The Electrolux brand was targeted to the high-prestige, conservative consumers, and the Zanussi brand was targeted to the innovative, trendsetting consumers. The local brands were targeted to the young, aggressive urban professionals and the warm and friendly, value-oriented consumers.[46]

The introduction of the euro has elevated the importance of panregional branding in Europe, primarily because of price transparency. Panregional brand positioning has also become increasingly important in Europe. The increase of panregional branding in Europe requires local tailoring. Individual legislation varies depending on the country. In 2000, Kimberly Clarke ran a promotion in four European countries for its sanpro (sanitary napkins) product "Brevia," which featured different marketing promotions because of country-specific legal restriction. The promotional look was identical in the United Kingdom, the Netherlands, France, and Germany but the promotions varied. In France, Kimberly Clarke used money-off coupons, while in Germany, representatives gave away free samples. The company then ran two campaigns featuring vouchers in the Netherlands. And in the United Kingdom, promotions featured free samples and a free pack coupon. One of Universal's most successful panregional marketing campaigns was a cereal promotion featuring *Jurassic Park: The Lost World*. A fossil giveaway resulted in an increase in sales across Europe, and sales continued to rise after the promotion was over. Universal worked with several cereal brands because different countries eat different cereals. The company did not extend the promotion into Scandinavia because Scandinavians generally do not eat cereal.[47]

TRADEMARKS

Because brand names or trademarks are usually backed by substantial advertising funds, it makes sense to register such brands for the exclusive use of the sponsoring firm. However, registration abroad is often hampered by several factors. Trademarks still have to be registered one country at a time. Different interpretations exist in different countries and may affect filing. In some countries, registration authorities may object because the name lacks the inherent distinctiveness needed for registration or because the chosen word is too common to be essential to the promotion of the product, thus allowing other firms to continue to use the name in a descriptive manner. Other countries allow registration of trademarks and renewals for actual or intended use, thus increasing the possibility that other firms may have already registered the name. In countries where the first applicant always obtains exclusive rights, companies risk the possibility of having their brand names pirated by outsiders who apply for a new name first. The foreign company is then forced to buy back its own trademark. When a country does not allow registrations until all objections are settled, the registration process may continue for years.

Maintaining the Budweiser trademark has been an interesting saga for Anheuser Busch. In 1911, Anheuser Busch gave Budvar—a Czech brewery in Ceske Budejovice, a Czech town also known as Budweis—the rights to the Budweiser name in continental Europe. When Anheuser Busch decided to enter Europe, it tried to renegotiate with Budvar. When this failed, Anheuser Busch took Budvar to court and won in many European courts.[48] Although it seems Budvar may lose access to the Budweiser name in Europe, it still owns the name in Vietnam, causing Anheuser Busch to pull out of a $145 million joint venture there, and in the Czech Republic.[49] Anheuser Busch's attempt at acquiring the Czech brewery outright was thwarted. Anheuser Busch's legal strategy in the continuing fight was to block any export shipments of its Czech rival whenever they appeared in any area where Anheuser Busch can market its beer legally.[50]

TRADEMARK AND BRAND PROTECTION

Violations of trademarks have been an inescapable problem for global marketers. Many companies have found themselves subject to violations by people who use either the protected name or a very similar one. Deliberate violations can usually be fought in court, although often at great expense. Violations of trademarks, or counterfeit products, are estimated to account for 3 percent of world trade, according to the International Chamber of Commerce. The U.S. Department of Commerce estimates that about 750,000 U.S. jobs were lost because of foreign forgeries of U.S. products.[51] Some sources estimate the annual global trade in counterfeit products at $250 billion.[52] International trade in counterfeit products is worth $350 billion per year, or about 6 percent of overall world merchandise trade. The Internet has made it much easier for counterfeiters to reach a huge number of customers. Growth in the Internet counterfeit trade occurs in pharmaceuticals such as Viagra, Zyban, and Prozac.[53]

Recorded music has long suffered from pirating. Global sales of pirated music is estimated at $4.5 billion worldwide, and the products consist of about 400 million CDs and 1.6 billion cassettes. In 1998, pirated music was believed to outsell legitimate music in twenty countries, including Hong Kong, Malaysia, the Ukraine, Israel, Estonia, and Latvia. This number is up from fourteen countries a year earlier. The Ukraine has assumed the position of the music counterfeit capital of Europe; legislation is inadequate there, and the Ukrainian authorities lack the commitment to clamp down on the problem.[54] Other sectors affected by counterfeiting are toys and sporting goods, with an estimated loss of 13 percent of sales; perfumes and toiletries, with a 10 percent loss; and clothing and footwear, with 4 percent of total sales lost to pirated products.[55]

Gillette Philippines became concerned about counterfeit blades flooding the market, so it worked with the National Bureau of Investigation to launch a campaign to help consumers spot counterfeit products.[56] Computer software companies also battle piracy. Surveys conducted in 1999 indicated that about 40 percent of all new business software applications are pirated, resulting in a revenue loss of $11 billion. The biggest country offenders were Vietnam, with 97 percent; China, with 95 percent; and Indonesia, with 92 percent of all installed new software being pirated. Even in the United States, the piracy rate was estimated at 25 percent, resulting in about $2.9 billion of revenue loss. The problem was estimated to be far greater for consumer applications produced by Microsoft or Norton Utilities, for which illegal copies outsold legal copies.[57]

Counterfeiting injures both businesses and consumers. In some cases, trademark violations can result in potential harm to the customer. In India, some counterfeit pharmaceutical drugs were made of different chemical compounds, thereby posing serious threats to patients.[58] Glaxo Wellcome, a leading U.K. pharmaceutical company, worked on making its products and packaging unique so that they could not be copied by counterfeiters. Zantac, its leading ulcer drug, was made as a five-sided, peach-colored pill for the U.S. market. Prescribing doctors could look up the drug in the *Physicians' Desk Reference* to verify its features.[59]

Piracy of trademark-protected products flourishes in countries where legal protection of such trademarks is weak. In Vietnam, the nature of copyright infringement is open to interpretation. Enforcement there is weak because the government does not have the resources to enforce existing laws or to control its borders. Some international consumer goods companies doing business in Vietnam claim that their sales are reduced by as much as 50 percent because of illegal, and cheaper, products. Procter & Gamble is believed to have lost sales of up to 25 percent because illegal operators collected its containers and refilled them with counterfeit products. The same happened to brand name cognacs and whiskies. Reused bottles are known to be filled with sugar rum.[60]

Finally, the emergence of ebusiness has contributed to the growth of global counterfeit trade. Online counterfeit business volume was estimated at $25 billion, one-tenth of the total counterfeit volume. Internet counterfeiters use an estimated five thousand web sites and include shady overseas operators to local schoolchildren. Rolex, the Swiss-based luxury watch producer, regularly checks eBay auctions, where on any given day several hundred Rolex watches may be up for bid, and many are counterfeit. The manufacturers of many other luxury items also check the Internet regularly. Louis Vuitton regularly checks eBay for counterfeit products.[61]

International companies have gone on the offensive to thwart counterfeiting attempts. The United States passed the Trademark Counterfeiting Act of 1984, which makes counterfeiting punishable by fines of up to $250,000 and prison terms of up to five years. International companies are increasingly focusing on methods to stop counterfeiting. Many firms find that subcontractors, who know manufacturing processes, are becoming part of the problem. These companies may fulfill their regular contracts to an international company while selling extra volume on the black market. To stop such practices, new marketing systems are being developed to allow companies to monitor abuses and to allow customers to spot counterfeit products. Polaproof (by Polaroid) is one tamper-proof label; holograms are another. Many invisible marketing devices or inks exist on products to facilitate the detection of counterfeits. Given the difficulty of tracking counterfeiters and the obvious opportunities for making quick profits, however, counterfeiting will likely continue to be a problem for international companies.

PACKAGING FOR GLOBAL MARKETS

Differences in the marketing environment may require special adaptation in product packaging. Different climatic conditions often demand a change in the package to ensure sufficient protection or shelf life. The role that a package assumes in promotion also depends on the market retailing structure. In countries with a substantial degree of self-service merchandising, a package with strong promotional appeal is desirable for consumer products; however, these requirements may be substantially scaled down in areas where over-the-counter service still dominates. In addition, distribution handling requirements are not identical around the world. In high-wage countries of the developed world, products tend to be packaged so that further handling by retailing employees is reduced. For consumer products, mass merchandisers only need to place products on shelves. In countries with lower wages and less-developed retailing structures, individual orders may be filled from larger packaged units, entailing extra labor by the retailer.

The use of the word *diet* in the Diet Coke brand name necessitated the use of Coca-Cola Light as an alternate name because the word *diet* has either no relevance or an undesirable connotation in several countries. The challenge was to create a compelling branding system that would be consistently recognizable in 146 world markets, whether the product was named Diet Coke or Coca-Cola Light. Coca-Cola positioned its product as a soft drink that would help people look and feel their best, rather than as one solely centered on the notion of losing weight. Coca-Cola's plan was for consumers to be able to perceive these characteristics just by looking at the product's graphics, regardless of the name. The resulting combination of brand visuals and expression of product attributes not only transcends the name difference but can also be identified easily whether that name is rendered in English, Korean, Chinese, or Cyrillic characters.[62]

Specific packaging decisions affected by the particular foreign market for which the product is designated are size, shape, materials, color, and text. Size may differ by custom or by existing standards such as metric and non-metric requirements. Higher-income countries tend to require larger unit sizes because their populations shop less frequently and can afford to buy larger quantities each time they shop. In countries with lower income levels, consumers buy in smaller quantities and buy them more often. Gillette, the world's largest producer of razor blades, sells products in packages of five or ten in the United States and Europe, whereas single blades are sold in some emerging markets.

Packages can assume almost any shape, largely depending on the customs and traditions of each market. Materials used for packaging can also differ widely. Whereas Americans buy mayonnaise and mustard in glass or plastic containers, consumers in Germany and Switzerland buy these same products in tubes. Cans are the customary material for packaging beer in the United States, whereas most European countries prefer glass bottles. The package color and text have to be integrated into a company's promotional strategy and therefore may be subject to specific tailoring by country or region. The promotional effect is of great importance for consumer goods and has led some companies to attempt to standardize their packaging in color and layout. In areas such as Europe or Latin America, where the consumers frequently travel to other countries, standardized colors help identify a product quickly. This strategy depends on devising a set of colors or a layout with an appeal beyond one culture or market. An example of a company pursuing a standardized package color is Procter & Gamble, the U.S. manufacturer of the leading detergent, Tide. The orange-and-white box familiar to millions of U.S. consumers can be found in many foreign markets, even though the package text may appear in the language or print of the given country.

Consumers and governments have become more concerned about the environmental consequences of the disposal of excess or inappropriate packaging. One result is that companies are expected to develop packaging that is environmentally friendly. The European Union has put tight controls on manufacturers concerning the volume of packaging, including pallets and containers. European governments are pushing the expense of waste disposal for packaging materials back to the manufacturers. As of 2002, thirty countries have laws that regulate the producer's responsibility for packaging disposal, and twenty-four countries require manufacturers to pay a fee to waste-collection companies.[63]

MANAGING A GLOBAL PRODUCT LINE

In early sections of this chapter, we covered decisions about individual products in detail. Most companies, however, manufacture or sell many products. Some, such as General Electric, produce as many as 200,000 items. To facilitate marketing operations, companies group these items into product groups consisting of several product lines. Each product line consists of several individual items that share similarities. Johnson & Johnson (J&J) divides its business into three worldwide segments: consumer, pharmaceutical, and medical and diagnostics. The company practices decentralized management, and the executive committee is responsible for group operations. Certain committee members also serve as worldwide chairs of group operating committees, which are formed by managers representing key operations within the group. These committees in turn oversee and direct J&J's domestic and international companies related to the consumer, pharmaceutical, and medical and diagnostic businesses. Each of these businesses are headed by a chairperson, president, general manager, or managing director, who reports to the group operating committee. The company follows its decentralization policy by ensuring as much as possible that international subsidiaries are managed by the subsidiaries' national citizens.[64]

A company with several product lines is faced with the decision to select those product lines most appropriate for global marketing. As with each individual product or decision, the firm can either offer an identical line in its home market and abroad or, if circumstances demand it, make appropriate changes. In most cases, a firm looks at the individual items within a product line and assesses marketability on a product-by-product basis. As a result, the product lines abroad are frequently characterized by a narrower width than those found in a company's domestic market.

The circumstances for the deletion of products from product lines vary, but some factors predominate. Lack of sufficient market size is a frequently mentioned factor. Companies with their home base in large markets such as the United States, Japan, or Germany often find sufficient demand in their home markets for even the smallest market segments, justifying additional product variations and greater depth in their lines. Abroad, opportunities for such segmentation strategies may not exist because the individual segments may be too small to warrant commercial exploitation. Lack of market sophistication is another factor in product line variation. Except for the top twenty developed markets, many markets are less developed and sophisticated and may not demand some of the most advanced items in a product line. And finally, new-product introduction strategies can affect product lines abroad. For most companies, new products are introduced first in their home markets and then introduced abroad only after the product has been successful at home. As a result, the lag in introduction of new products in foreign markets also contributes toward a product line configuration that differs from that of the firm's domestic market.

Firms confronted with deletions in their product lines sometimes add specialized offerings to fill the gap in the line. They can either produce a more suitable product or develop an entirely new product that may only have application within a specific market. Such a strategy can be pursued only by a firm with adequate research and development strength in its foreign subsidiaries.

EXPLOITING PRODUCT LIFE CYCLES

The existence of product life cycles immediately opens opportunities for the international firm but, on the other hand, poses additional hurdles that may complicate product strategy. Experience has shown that products do not always occupy the same position on the product life cycle curve in different countries. New products receiving initial introduction in the world's developed markets tend to move into later life cycle stages before those in countries that receive the product at a later date. As you can see in Figure 13.2, it is possible for a product to be in different stages of the product life cycle in different countries. Other countries follow the home country, usually each according to its own stage of economic development. Although a product may be offered and produced worldwide, it is common for it to range over several stages in the product life cycle at any point in time. The principal opportunity offered to the firm is the chance to extend product growth by expanding into new markets and thus compensate for declining growth rates in mature markets. A risk arises when a company enters new markets or countries too quickly, before the local market is ready to absorb the new product. To avoid such pitfalls and to take advantage of long-term opportunities, international companies may follow several strategies.

Figure 13.2: Possible Product Life Cycle for a Product in Different Countries

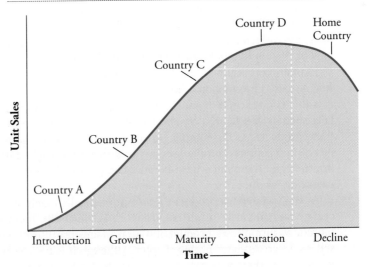

During the introductory phase, a product may have to be debugged and refined. This job can best be handled in the originating market or in a country close to company research and development centers. Also, the marketing approach will have to be refined. At this stage, the market in even the most advanced countries is relatively small, and demand in countries with lower levels of economic development can hardly be exploited commercially. Therefore, the introductory stage will be limited to the advanced markets, often the company's domestic, or home, market.

Once the product has been fully developed and a larger group of buyers has become interested, volume will increase substantially. Domestic marketing policies foresee price decreases due to volume gains and to the entry of new competitors, with a corresponding expansion of the entire market. At this stage, many firms start to investigate opportunities elsewhere by introducing the product in selective markets, where the product would be in the introductory phase. This step requires some adaptation of communication strategy to parallel earlier efforts in the home market because the approach designed for the second phase, the growth stage, cannot be used. In the late 1980s and early 1990s, U.S. white goods manufacturers faced a mature market in the United States, with a decline in total volume. This situation led Whirlpool, GE, Hoover, and Maytag to enter the European market, which is expected to grow with the European Union and the economic liberalization of eastern Europe.[65]

A product facing life cycle decline may be withdrawn from the market in stages, similar to its introduction. The most advanced countries will see such a withdrawal earlier than some of the less developed markets. Volkswagen, the German automaker, offers an example of how an old design may still sell in some countries while not in others. Its famous Beetle car, originally introduced in the 1930s, was withdrawn from production everywhere but Mexico. There, the Beetle remains the best-selling car and helps make VW a leading car producer. The model has been adapted for modern environmental requirements but comes only in a simple version without extras or options. More recently, VW has begun to export a totally redesigned Beetle from Mexico into the U.S. market. This new model was largely for export to the U.S. markets, not for local Mexican consumers. The new Beetle's success in the U.S. market increased Volkswagen's share of the U.S. market from 1 percent in 1992 to 5 percent in 2002.[66]

Exploiting product life cycles was a profitable strategy for Samsung Electronics, a Korean-based international firm. In the 1970s, Samsung deliberately produced products that had reached the declining stage of the product life cycle in developed markets such as the United States. Samsung was easily able to obtain technology for those products. As the company successfully assimilated new technologies, Samsung increasingly entered product segments with earlier product life cycle stages until the firm reached the point where it could compete with world-class companies on new, emerging products.[67]

As we have seen, a product cannot automatically reach the various stages in its life cycle simultaneously in all countries; thus, flexibility in marketing strategy is required. To introduce a product abroad in stages represents a strategic decision in itself, as described later in this chapter. Although it is typical, the phased introduction to foreign markets may not always be in the best interest of the firm because it may offer competitors a chance to expand locally.

GLOBAL WARRANTY AND SERVICE POLICIES

Buyers around the world, like domestic consumers, expect more than the physical benefits of a product. Consumers purchase products with certain performance expectations. In their purchase choice, consumers also consider company policies for backing promises. As a result, warranties and service policies have to be considered as integral components of a company's global product strategy. Companies interested in doing business abroad frequently find themselves at a disadvantage with local competitors in the area of warranties and service. With the supplier's plant often thousands of miles away, foreign buyers sometimes want extra assurance that the supplier will back the product. Thus, a comprehensive warranty and service policy can become a very important marketing tool for global companies.

PRODUCT WARRANTIES

A company must address its warranty policy for global markets either by declaring its domestic warranty valid worldwide or by tailoring it to specific countries or markets. Although declaring worldwide warranty with uniform performance standards would be simple from an administrative point of view, local market conditions often dictate a differentiated approach. In the United States, most computer manufacturers sell their equipment with a thirty- or sixty-day warranty, whereas twelve-month warranties are more typical in Europe or Japan.

Aside from the technical decisions about what standards should be covered under a warranty and for how long, a company should also consider the type of actual product use. If buyers in a foreign market subject the product to more stress or even wear, some shortening of the warranty period may become necessary. A company may be able to change the product design to allow for different standard performance requirements. In developing countries, where technical sophistication is below that found in North America or Europe, maintenance terms may not be adequate and may result in more frequent equipment breakdowns. Another important factor is local competition. An attractive warranty policy can be helpful in obtaining sales, so a firm's warranty policy should be in line with that of other firms competing in the local market.

The importance of global product warranty expectations can be demonstrated by the experience of Perrier, the French bottled-water company. In February 1990, the company had to withdraw its Perrier water from U.S. retail stores after the product was found to contain benzene in concentrations above the legal limit. This U.S. test result triggered similar tests by health authorities in other countries. Soon Perrier had to withdraw its products from other countries, eventually resulting in a worldwide brand recall. This situation illustrates the interdependence of many products in today's open and accessible markets. Failure to maintain quality, service, or performance in one country can rapidly have a negative impact in other countries.[68] Coca-Cola experienced a similar problem with bottling plants in Belgium, which led to a recall of many products, not only in Belgium but also in France. About two hundred consumers had complained of illness after drinking Coca-Cola products, leading to the largest product recall in Coca-Cola's history. Inadequate sanitation procedures resulted in recalls in Poland as well.[69]

GLOBAL PRODUCT SERVICE

No warranty will be credible unless it is backed with an effective service organization. Although important to the average consumer, service is even more crucial to the industrial buyer because any breakdown of equipment or of a product is apt to cause substantial economic loss. This risk has led industrial buyers to be conservative in their choice of products, always analyzing carefully the supplier's ability to provide service in case of need.

To provide the required level of service outside the company's home base poses special problems for global marketers. The selection of an organization to perform the service is an important decision. Company personnel are preferable because they tend to be better trained. However, use of company personnel is economically feasible only if the installed base of the market is large enough to justify such an investment. In cases in which a company does not maintain its own sales subsidiary, it is generally more efficient to turn to an independent service company or to a local distributor. Providing adequate services via independent distributors requires extra training for the service technician, usually at the manufacturer's expense. In any case, the selection of an appropriate service organization should ensure that fully trained service personnel are readily available within the customary time frame for the particular market.

Closely related to any satisfactory service policy is an adequate inventory of spare parts. Because service often means replacing some parts, the company must place sufficient inventory of spare parts within reach of its markets. Whether this inventory is maintained in regional warehouses or through sales subsidiaries and distributors depends on the volume and the required reaction time for service calls. Buyers will generally want to know how the manufacturer plans to organize its service operations before making substantial commitments.

Firms that demonstrate serious interest in a market by providing their own sales subsidiaries are often at an advantage over firms using distributors. One German truck manufacturer that entered the U.S. market advertised that 97 percent of all spare parts are kept in local inventory, thus assuring prospective buyers that they can get spare parts readily. In some instances, the difficulty with service outlets may even influence a company's market entry strategy. This was the case with Fujitsu, a Japanese manufacturer of electronic office equipment. By combining forces with TRW Inc., a U.S.-based company, Fujitsu was able to sell its office equipment in the U.S. market in conjunction with the extensive service organization of TRW. Because the guarantee of reliable and efficient service is such an important aspect of a firm's entire product strategy, investment in service centers at times must be made before any sales can take place. In this case, service costs must be viewed as an investment in future volume rather than as a recurring expense.

MARKETING SERVICES GLOBALLY

In 1998, global trade in services reached $1,290 billion worldwide. Services include business services, travel, transportation, and government services. One of the largest categories of service exports was business services. Export services in this category include communications, financial services, software development, database management, construction, accounting, advertising, consulting, and legal services. The export of business services took place primarily from developed economies such as the United States, the Netherlands, France, Japan, the United Kingdom, Germany, and Italy. The U.S. share of global service import trade amounted to about 12 percent, with 18 percent for service exports.[70]

Decisions about marketing services are related to the structure of the service itself. A firm has to decide which service to sell or offer and how the service should be designed. It also needs to decide on the content of the service that it wants to offer and the manner in which the service is to be performed or consumed. Again, the issue of standardization needs to be addressed, although there are fewer opportunities for economies of scale by standardizing services worldwide. Business services tend to be more standardized, and more in demand worldwide, because the needs of companies are more uniform than those of individual consumers. Personal services are subject to cultural and social influences to a much greater degree and exhibit a greater need for tailoring to local circumstances.

BUSINESS SERVICES

The services aimed at business buyers that are most likely to be exported are those that have already met with success. The experience of U.S.-based service companies can be used as an example. Some of the services marketed abroad most successfully include financial services. Commercial banks such as Citibank built extensive branch networks around the world, to the extent that foreign deposits and profits constitute nearly half of business volume. Advertising agencies have also expanded overseas, either by building branch networks or by merging with local agencies. Similar strategies were followed by accounting and management consulting firms. More recently, U.S.-based marketing research firms have expanded into foreign countries.

OPPORTUNITIES FOR NEW SERVICE FIRMS

The U.S. economy is slowly moving toward a service economy, and similar trends can be found in the economies of other developed countries in western Europe and Japan. Many types of services are in great demand abroad. For example, global courier services is an area in which several companies are vying for global positions. U.S.-based Federal Express built its overseas business by buying Flying Tiger, the largest international cargo airline, and merging it with FedEx's international small-documents and parcel service.[71] However, building its courier service worldwide initially resulted in tremendous losses. The company scaled back its European operations in 1991, but in 1996, it promised to become operational in 1999 via a major European hub.[72] In 2001, FedEx serviced areas accounting for 90 percent of global gross national product with its twenty-four- to forty-eight-hour door-to-door service. Shipping more than 3 million items to 211 countries each working day, the company employs more than 215,000 employees or contractors and flies 640 aircraft, with annual revenue of $19.6 billion.[73]

Another major company with global ambitions in the small-parcels business is United Parcel Service (UPS), which is using its considerable cash flow from U.S. operations to build its global network. It took UPS about twelve years to build its German operation, which now employees six thousand. To help its overseas strategy, UPS acquired several local courier companies in various countries. UPS grew its business in Europe more slowly than did FedEx, however, and was able to learn in the process. UPS is now pushing beyond Europe into Latin America and Asia and is scheduling its own overseas flights.[74]

International accounting and consulting services saw tremendous growth in the 1980s. Major firms started to think in global terms and to expand their operations into many markets. For the leading accounting firms, international revenue typically was larger than domestic (or U.S.) revenue. Several firms merged, so the former "Big Eight Accounting Firms" are now down to five. With the possible failures at Enron, Worldcom, and Tyco, the future of the accounting firm Arthur Andersen may be in jeopardy. Its demise would leave only four global accounting firms. Ernst & Whitney merged with Arthur Young because of the latter firm's strong international network. Peat Marwick merged with KMG, a company that was traditionally strong in Europe. Price Waterhouse merged with Coopers and Lybrand to form PricewaterhouseCoopers.[75] Overseas expansion is important to these U.S.-based firms because revenue is growing faster abroad and margins are also better for international business. Many of the firms' accounting clients have recently undergone globalization themselves and thus demand different services. Finally, the liberalization of trade in Europe has also boosted cross-national business and mergers.

British and U.S. law firms are also finding numerous opportunities overseas. The unification of Europe has accelerated cross-border mergers and acquisitions. The growth of the European Union in Brussels has created a demand for lawyers who are willing to lobby the EU, and privatization of many businesses in eastern Europe has created a legal gold mine. France and Japan have established local requirements to slow the growth of British and U.S. firms in their respective countries, but despite these regulations, the legal profession has become another global service industry. Many U.S. law firms are opening overseas branch locations, primarily in London, to capture business from investment banks and other financial services firms that require a presence in both New York and London, which are major capital market centers.[76]

SERVICES FOR CONSUMERS AND INDIVIDUAL HOUSEHOLDS

Marketing services to consumers turns out to be more difficult than selling to industrial users. Consumer purchasing and usage patterns differ from one country to another and to a greater degree than do industry usage patterns, so many services have to be adapted to local conditions to ensure their success. The U.S.-based fast-food chains were some of the first consumer service companies to pursue foreign opportunities. McDonald's, Kentucky Fried Chicken, Dairy Queen, and many others opened numerous restaurants in Europe and Asia. Although success came eventually, initial results were disappointing for McDonald's in Europe. The company had anticipated differences in consumer tastes across Europe by serving wine in France, beer in Munich and Stockholm, and tea in England, where the company also lowered the sugar content of its buns by 4 percent. However, McDonald's based its first store locations on U.S. criteria and moved into the suburbs and along highways. When volume did not develop according to expectations, McDonald's quickly moved into the inner cities. Once this initial problem concerning location was overcome, McDonald's grew very quickly abroad. In 1985, international revenue accounted for 24 percent of total revenue, but by 1992 it had grown to almost 50 percent.[77] Although some local food variations have been incorporated, the company uses the same standardized manual worldwide, indoctrinating all of its franchise operations abroad with the same operating culture.

Insurance companies have found significant opportunities in emerging markets. For example, in Shanghai, China, the American International Group (AIG) sold more than twelve thousand policies in eight months. Although it took AIG over ten years to receive licensing in China, the company believes that opportunities there are tremendous. AIG was granted the right to own 100 percent of its life insurance branches, a privilege denied other insurance companies. AIG has eight life and property insurance licenses in China, compared to only single licenses offered to other foreign insurance companies. Now that China is a member of the WTO, the EU is contesting the enviable position of AIG in China.[78]

CONCLUSIONS

To be successful in global markets, companies need to be flexible in product and service offerings. Although a product may have been very successful in a firm's home market, environmental differences can often force the company to make unexpected or costly changes. A small group of products may be marketed worldwide without significant changes, but most companies find that global success depends on a willingness to adapt to local market requirements. Additional efforts are frequently required in product support services to assure foreign customers that the company will stand behind its products. For companies that successfully master the additional international difficulties while showing a commitment to foreign customers, global success can lead to increased profits and more secure market positions domestically.

Questions for Discussion

1. Generalize about the overall need for product adaptations for consumer products versus high-technology industrial products. What differences exist? Why?

2. American fast food, music, and movies have become popular around the world, with little adaptation, whereas U.S. retailers, banks, and beer companies have had slower progress in global markets. Why?

3. What are the major reasons why a company would choose a worldwide brand name for its product?

4. Under what circumstances would using different brand names in different countries be advisable?

5. Are there any differences between the international marketing of services and the international marketing of products?

For Further Reading

Davidson, William H., and Richard Harrigan. "Key Decisions in International Marketing: Introducing New Products Abroad." *Columbia Journal of World Business,* Winter 1977, pp. 15–23.

Douglas, Susan P., Sam Craig, Edwin J. Nijssen. "Integrating Branding Strategy Across Markets: Building International Brand Architecture." *Journal of International Marketing,* 2001, vol. 9, no. 2, pp. 97–114.

Fan, Ying. "The National Image of Global Brands." *Journal of Brand Management,* 2002, vol. 9, no. 3, pp 180–192.

Gillespie, Kate, Kishore Krishna, and Susan Jarvis. "Protecting Global Brands: Towards a Global Norm." *Journal of International Marketing,* 2002, vol. 10, no. 2, pp 99–112.

Keillor, Bruce D., Douglas R. Hausknecht, and R. Stephen Parker. "Thinking Global, Acting Local: An Attribute Approach to Product Strategy." *Journal of the Euro-Marketing,* 2001, vol. 10, no. 2, pp. 27–48.

Kelz, Andreas, and Brian Block. "Global Branding: Why and How?" *Industrial Management & Data Systems,* 1993, vol. 93, no. 4, pp. 11–17.

Levitt, Theodore. "Globalization of Markets." *Harvard Business Review,* May–June 1983, pp. 92–102.

Roellig, Larry. "Designing Global Brands." *Design Management Journal,* Fall 2001, vol. 12, no. 4, pp. 40–45.

Samiee, Saeed, and Kendall Roth. "The Influence of Global Marketing Standardization on Performance," *Journal of Marketing,* April 1992, pp. 1–17.

Sorenson, Ralph Z., and Ulrich E. Wiechmann. "How Multinationals View Marketing Standardization." *Harvard Business Review,* May–June 1975, vol. 53, no. 3, p. 38.

Wilson, Steven R. "The Impact of Standards on Industrial Development and Trade." *Quality Progress,* July 1, 1999, vol. 32, no. 7, p. 71.

Endnotes

1. Robert Gray, "Local on a Global Scale," *Marketing,* September 27, 2001, pp. 22–24.

2. Robert Thomas, Vice President, Ansell Edmont, in a discussion with authors on July 13, 1987.

3. "Think Globally, Bake Locally," *Fortune,* October 14, 1996, p. 205.

4. Howard R. Moskowitz and Samuel Rubino, "Sensory Segmentation: An Organizing Principle for International Product Concept Generation," unpublished article.

5. Laurel Delaney, "A Checklist for Preparing Your Package to Go Global," *Brand Packaging,* July 2001, pp. 40–52.

6. Laurel Delaney, "A Checklist for Preparing Your Package to Go Global," *Brand Packaging,* July 2001, pp. 40–52.

7. Herbert E. Meyer, "How U.S. Textiles Got to Be Winners in the Export Game," *Fortune,* May 5, 1980, p. 260.

8. Vernon R. Alden, "Who Says You Can't Crack Japanese Markets?" *Harvard Business Review,* January–February 1987, pp. 52–56.

9. Charles Orton, "A Fine Kettle of Fish," *World Trade,* October 2001, p. 74.

10. "Foreign Fast Food Firms Flourish in Pakistan," *AFP,* March 22, 1999, p. 2.

11. "GEC Deal Boosts Power Control LV Market Share," *Electrical Review,* March 17, 1999, p. 1.

12. Jean-Pierre Jeannet, *Managing with a Global Mindset* (London: Financial-Times Prentice-Hall, 2000), p. 99.

13. "3Com Delivers Japanese Language Support for World-Leading Palm Computing Platform Products," *Business Wire,* February 3, 1999, p. 1.

14. "Accrue Software Expands into Japan Market," *Business Wire,* June 8, 1999, p. 1.

15. "Microsoft, Apple Court Macworld Tokyo Crowds," *MacWeek,* February 23, 1998, p. 1.

16. Heinz Kurz, "Rolling Across Europe's Vanishing Frontiers," *IEEE Spectrum,* February 1999, pp. 44–49.

17. Michelle Egan, "Setting Standards: Strategic Advantages in International Trade," *Business Strategy Review,* Spring 2002, pp. 51–64.

18. Charles Batchelor, "International Standards," *Financial Times,* October 14, 1993, pp. 23–25.

19. "Exporters Look to 12 Certifying Bodies to Boost Competitiveness," *Managing Exports,* April 6, 2002, pp.1–4.

20. *www.iso.org;* accessed on July 27, 2002.

21. "Darkie No, Darlie Yes," *South China Morning Post,* May 16, 1999, p. 2.

22. June N. P. Francis, Janet P. Y. Lam, Jan Walls, "Executive Insights: The Impact of Linguistic Differences on International Brand Name Standardization," *Journal of International Marketing,* June 2002, pp. 98–116.

23. "The Art of Brand Renaming," *Brand Strategy,* April 2002, p. 32.

24. June Francis, Janet P. Y. Lam., and Jan Walls, "The Impact of Linguistic Differences on International Brand Name Standarization: A Comparison of English and Chinese Brand Names of Fortune 500 Companies," *Journal of International Marketing,* 2002, vol. 10, no. 1, pp. 98–116.

25. "Trademarks Are a Global Business These Days, but Finding Registrable Ones Is a Big Problem," *Wall Street Journal,* September 4, 1975, p. 28.

26. George W. Cooper, "On Your 'Mark,'" *Columbia Journal of World Business,* March–April 1970, pp. 67–76.

27. "Number of Dot.Com Domains on Internet Declined by 130,000 in Last 3 Months of 2001," *Online Reporter,* January 7, 2002, p. 1.

28. "The Brand's the Thing," *Fortune,* March 4, 1996, p. 75.

29. Ibid.

30. "Inside Intel: Chip Maker's Restrictive Marketing Program and Millions in Subsidies Shackle PC Makers," *PC Week,* April 5, 1999, p. 12.

31. "The Brand's the Thing," *Fortune,* March 4, 1996, p. 75.

32. Bruce Winningham, "Private Label Grows Up," *Discount Merchandiser,* November 1999, vol. 39, no. 11, p. 109.

33. "Ricoh Distributes Whistle Communications' Award Winning Internet Solutions in Japan," *PR Newswire,* March 23, 1998, p. 1.

34. "LG Starts Digital TV Exports to US," *Comline Business News,* July 15, 1999, p. 1.

35. "LGE Reacts to Integration in Europe, Strengthens Own Brand Name Sales," *Korea Herald,* June 15, 1999, p. 3.

36. "LG Becomes Household Name Among Romanian Consumers," *Korea Herald,* June 25, 1999, p. 19.

37. "Landor: Experts on Identity Crisis," *Ad Age International,* March 1997, p. I-44.

38. Jonathan Asher, "Global Branding: Same, but Different," *Brandweek,* April 9, 2001, p. 25.

39. "Landor: Experts on Identity Crisis," *Ad Age International,* March 1997, p. I-44.

40. "Gaining Recognition for Asian Brands," *Ad Age International,* June 1996, p. I-36.

41. Jean-Noel Kapferer, "Is There Really No Hope for Local Brands?" *Journal of Brand Management,* January 2002, pp. 163–170.

42. "China's Brand-Name Cat," *Far Eastern Economic Review*, April 18, 1996, p. 70.

43. "China's Detergent Market Expands in 1998," *Asia Pulse*, January 25, 1999, p. 3.

44. "Regional Brands: Varig Eyes the Skies Outside of Brazil," *Advertising Age International*, March 1997, p. I-19.

45. "Shangri-La on Earth," *Advertising Age International*, March 1997, p. I-24.

46. Christopher A. Bartlett and Sumantra Ghosal, "What Is a Global Manager?" *Harvard Business Review*, September–October 1992, p. 125.

47. Rachel Miller, "Promotions Aim to Cross Borders," *Marketing*, May 21, 2001, pp. 31–32.

48. "U.S. Brewer Loses Budvar Fighting for Identity," *Financial Times*, November 1, 1996, p. 20.

49. "Anheuser Ends Czech Talks over the Budweiser Name," *New York Times*, September 24, 1996, p. D6.

50. "Budweiser Takes on the World," *New York Times*, June 24, 1999, p. C16.

51. "Stop, Thief," *International Management*, September 1990, p. 48.

52. "Sleaze E-Commerce," *Wall Street Journal*, May 14, 1999, p. W1.

53. "Fighting the Fakers," *Engineer*, April 26, 2002, p. 16.

54. "Music Piracy Remains Headache for Big Labels," *Wall Street Journal Europe*, June 11, 1999, p. UK16.

55. Ibid.

56. "Gillette Philippines Starts Campaign vs. Fake Products," *Businessworld*, June 25, 2002, p. 1.

57. "Software Piracy Costs Billions in Revenue," *Baltimore Sun*, June 13, 1999, p. 2D.

58. "Fake Drugs Numb Profits of Indian Pharmaceutical Industry," *Agence France-Presse*, July 16, 1999, p. 2.

59. "Businesses Battle Bogus Products," *AP Online*, January 26, 1999, p. 1.

60. "Vietnam's Prolific Counterfeiters Take a Walk on 'LaVile' Side," *Asian Wall Street Journal*, June 4, 1998, p. 1.

61. "Sleaze E-Commerce," p. w1.

62. Larry Roellig, "Designing Global Brands: Critical Lessons," *Design Management Journal*, Fall 2001, pp. 40–45.

63. Clyde Witt, "Producer Responsibility: A Global Concept," *Materials Handling Management*, April 2002, vol. 57, no. 4, p. 11.

64. "Striking a Balance," *European Cosmetic Markets*, May 2002, p. 19.

65. "The Deal Steps Up the U.S. Group's Drive into Europe, the Final Link in Whirlpool's Global Circle," *Financial Times*, June 7, 1991, p. 12.

66. "Beetlemania to the Rescue," *Business Week*, January 12, 1998, p. 46.

67. Seongjae Yu, "The Growth Pattern of Samsung Electronics: A Strategy Perspective," *International Studies of Management Organization*, January 1, 1998, vol. 28, no. 4, pp. 57–72.

68. "Brit Helps Perrier Move Beyond the Recall Crisis," *Advertising Age*, November 12, 1990, p. 12.

69. "Coca-Cola Poland Details Scope of Product Recalls," *Wall Street Journal*, July 14, 1999, p. A17.

70. "World Trade in Commercial Services by Selected Region and Economy," *World Trade Organization*, Trade in Services Section of the Statistics Division, March 1999, p. 1.

71. "A Fragile Air Freight Strategy," *New York Times*, September 6, 1989, p. D1.

72. "FedEx Rebuilds Operations," *Journal of Commerce*, March 23, 1999, p. 6A.

73. FEDEX, *Annual Report*, 2001, 2002.

74. "UPS Adjusts International Plans," *American Shipper*, December 1, 1998, p. 13.

75. "Big Five Accounting Firms Unlikely to Shrink, but the Possibility Exists," *Pittsburgh Business Times & Journal*, May 28, 1999, p. 33.

76. "US Law Firms Are on the Prowl in London," *Wall Street Journal Europe*, June 1, 1999, p. 4.

77. "Overseas Sizzle for McDonald's," *New York Times*, April 17, 1992, p. D1.

78. Geoff Winestock and Karby Leggett, "China to Enter WTO; Dispute on Insurance to Be First Test," *Wall Street Journal*, September 17, 2001, p. A14.

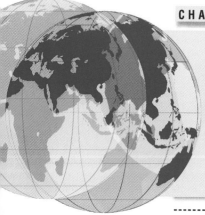

Developing New Products for Global Markets

In Chapter 13, we focused on individual product decisions. In Chapter 14, we concentrate on the strategic issues of product design and development for global markets. Following an analysis of the standardization versus adaptation issue, we cover a series of alternatives involving product extension, adaptation, and innovation strategies. This part of the chapter discussion includes a segment on global products that deals with the complexities of designing products for many markets simultaneously. The second part of the chapter is devoted to product development strategies for global companies. Here, we emphasize organizational issues, sources, and approaches that enhance a firm's ability to innovate in a changing marketplace. We conclude the chapter with a discussion of new-product launch issues. Figure 14.1 presents an illustration of the topics covered in this chapter.

Global marketers must understand how to implement both global and adapted product strategies. Before developing new products, the global marketer must understand the needs of local customers in multiple markets to be able to develop the appropriate product strategy. Then the global marketer works with research and development (R&D) to develop and deliver the desired new products and services. The process of developing new products for multiple markets requires an understanding of the many options for sourcing new products as well as the costs to develop these products for customers.

GLOBAL PRODUCT STRATEGIES

The purposes of this section are to outline the basic product strategies that a firm may select and to demonstrate their close relationship with a company's communications policy, particularly with respect to advertising.[1]

Figure 14.1: Global Product Development Strategies

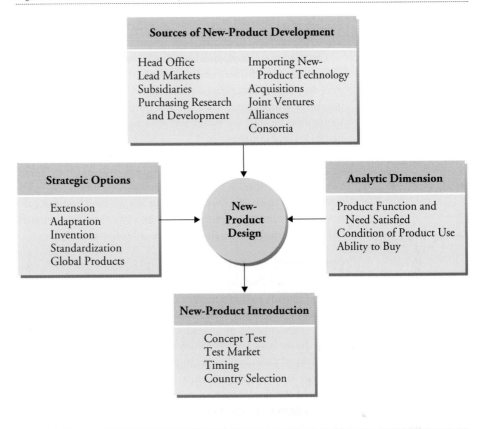

Sources of New-Product Development

Head Office
Lead Markets
Subsidiaries
Purchasing Research
   and Development

Importing New-
   Product Technology
Acquisitions
Joint Ventures
Alliances
Consortia

Strategic Options

Extension
Adaptation
Invention
Standardization
Global Products

New-
Product
Design

Analytic Dimension

Product Function and
   Need Satisfied
Condition of Product Use
Ability to Buy

New-Product Introduction

Concept Test
Test Market
Timing
Country Selection

ANALYTIC ISSUES: STANDARDIZATION VERSUS ADAPTATION

A company's decision to pursue a specific product strategy depends primarily on three factors: (1) whether the product function or the need satisfied is the same or different in a new market, (2) whether particular conditions surrounding product use can affect company strategy, and (3) whether target market customers can afford to buy the product. Because these three factors greatly influence the product strategy chosen, we examine each one before turning our attention to a company's strategic options.

PRODUCT FUNCTION, OR THE NEED SATISFIED. The key to the product function factor is the role that the product plays in a given market. Although certain types of products may be consumed by individuals in many countries, a company cannot automatically assume that the underlying motivation to purchase is identical in each country or individual. Take, for example, the difference between how Americans and Dutch purchase and use bicycles. Generally Americans purchase bikes for sport, to be used for cycling often on weekends. In Holland many consumers use bikes everyday to go to school or to work. As the country is flat, there is no need for many gears; but as it may be dark when going or returning from work, Dutch bikers need a light and bell to alert other bikers. Thus, the rationale for buying bikes and the functional needs can vary from country to country.

On the other hand, products for industrial use, such as plant machinery, are purchased the world over for similar intentions or reasons. Therefore, very little difference in product function or satisfied need is expected. There are also many consumer goods for which the need to be satisfied is similar from one country to the next. The motivation behind the purchase of razor blades, for example, is homogeneous across countries and cultures.

Differences in product function or satisfied need, even when present, do not necessarily call for a change in product design or features. The primary focus here is on the buyer and the motivation that triggers a purchase. As a psychological concept, motivation requires a corresponding response. Therefore, dissimilar purchasing motives require unique communications responses, or a change in a firm's advertising, to relate the product to these different motives.

CONDITIONS OF PRODUCT USE. Physical environmental variables combine into a physical event that determines the salient factors surrounding a product's actual use. If these events are identical within any two countries, a product may be marketed without any changes or alterations. The conditions of product use reflect the actual use or consumption of a product regardless of the motivation that triggered its purchase. In seeking opportunities for product standardization, marketers must consider the physical events surrounding product use that substantially determine the viability of the strategy. For example, paint coating on automobiles that are driven in areas with cold temperatures and snow would be different than the coatings used on automobiles driven in warm or hot climates.

ABILITY TO BUY. Purchasing power is generally not an issue in developed economies, but hundreds of millions of potential customers live in countries that simply do not have the economic resources found in more affluent markets. In such countries, the motivation to purchase a product and actual use conditions may be identical to those in affluent societies, but the products used to satisfy these demands are beyond the price that buyers can afford. Such situations may require an entirely different strategy. For example, the product can be changed so that it is sold at a much lower price. Thus, substantial differences in the nature of the economic event can have a significant influence on global product strategy.

Unilever, for example, expects revenues from developing and emerging markets to approach 50 percent of company sales in the next decade, so it has developed smaller packages to appeal to lower-income consumers. The small packages reduced the unit price to low-income consumers in Asia. The company has also introduced alternative packaging to bring the overall costs down. Unilever is recognized in Asia for its "multilocal, multinational" approach, and in 1999, it was among the top ten international firms operating throughout the Asia Pacific area.[2] During the 1998 economic crisis in Indonesia, Unilever offered tea, butter, and hand cream in smaller sachet sizes to maintain sales. Unilever found the smaller sizes actually increased sales, and after the economy recovered, sales in Indonesia more than doubled.[3]

ADVANTAGES OF PRODUCT STANDARDIZATION. Complete standardization of product design results in a substantial saving of production and research and development costs and allows a company to take advantage of economies of scale. Often, several markets can be supplied from a regional or central manufacturing plant with efficient and long production runs. Aside from these obvious advantages, production sharing and simultaneously supplying markets from several plants are important factors that support standardized output. While product standardization may benefit from economies of scale in manufacturing and R&D, it can also push companies to offer uniform prices. For example, Mandarina Duck, an Italian maker of fashionable handbags and accessories, could charge up to 15 percent more in Germany than in Italy or Spain. With the introduction of the euro and a standardized product strategy, Mandarina Duck found that it had to reduce the price differences from country to country. One event that helped the company during the price migration was the introduction of improved products, which customers would pay more for.[4] Obviously, the advantages gained from adaptation have to be compared with the overall loss in manufacturing flexibility.

Despite the advantages of economies of scale, few companies can standardize their products completely for the many markets they serve. To bridge the gap between various local adaptations and the need to standardize some components, some international firms have moved to a new type of product, the global product, which we discuss later in the chapter.

THREE STRATEGIC CHOICES: EXTENSION, ADAPTATION, INVENTION

A company can follow one of three basic strategies when moving into a foreign market. With respect to both its product and its communications policy, the firm can opt for an *extension* strategy, basically adopting the same approach as in its home market. The strategy of *adaptation* requires some changes to fit the new market requirements. When an entirely new approach is required, the company can adopt the strategy of *invention*. These three basic strategies can be further refined into the five strategies shown in Table 14.1. These five strategies are explained in the following sections.

STRATEGY ONE: PRODUCT EXTENSION—COMMUNICATIONS EXTENSION. One extension strategy calls for marketing a standardized product with the same communications strategy around the globe. Although this strategy has considerable attraction because of its cost effectiveness, it is rarely feasible for consumer products. The few exceptions include soft drinks and some luxury goods. Industrial products, with their greater homogeneity of buyers internationally, offer a somewhat greater opportunity for this strategy, but again the extension strategy is atypical.

The cost effectiveness of this strategy should not be underestimated. Product adaptations entail additional research and development expenses and tooling costs, and they do not allow economies of scale to the extent possible under a product extension strategy. Although less substantial, savings from the creation of only one communications strategy should also be considered. In any case, decision makers should consider the anticipated impact on demand in the foreign market if the product is *not* suited to local tastes or preferences, as well as the potential savings. Past experience

	Table 14.1 Global Product Strategies						
Strategy	**Product Function or Need Satisfied**	**Conditions of Product Use**	**Ability to Buy Product**	**Recommended Product Strategy**	**Recommended Communications Strategy**	**Rank Order from Least to Most Expensive**	**Product Examples**
1	Same	Same	Yes	Extension	Extension	1	Soft drinks
2	Different	Same	Yes	Extension	Adaptation	2	Bicycles, motor scooters
3	Same	Different	Yes	Adaptation	Extension	3	Gasoline, detergents
4	Different	Different	Yes	Adaptation	Adaptation	4	Clothing, greeting cards
5	Same	—	No	Invention	Develop new communications	5	Hand-powered washing machines

Source: From Warren J. Keegan, "Multinational Product Planning: Strategic Alternatives." Reprinted from *Journal of Marketing,* vol. 33, January 1969, pp. 58–62, published by the American Marketing Association. Reprinted by permission.

shows that rigidly enforcing a product and communications extension policy can lead to disaster and therefore should be adopted only if all requirements with respect to product function, satisfied need, use conditions, and ability to buy are met.

STRATEGY TWO: PRODUCT EXTENSION—COMMUNICATIONS ADAPTATIONS.

When the sociocultural event surrounding product consumption differs from country to country but the use conditions as part of the physical event are identical, the same product can be marketed with a change in the communications strategy. Examples can be found among bicycle and motorcycle manufacturers. In developing countries, a bicycle or a motorcycle is primarily a means of transportation, whereas the same products are used in sports or for recreation purposes in a developed market. This strategy is still quite cost-effective because communications adaptation represents a lower cost than does tailoring a product to a local market. In eastern Europe, tobacco companies have had great success developing local brands that appeal to national pride. The product is basically the same, but the brand and communications are adapted to each local market. BAT captured a significant share of the Polish market with its brand Jan Sobieski, named for the popular Polish figure.[5] R.J. Reynolds was also successful with its new Peter I brand in Russia, which captured 18 percent of the local market.[6]

STRATEGY THREE: PRODUCT ADAPTATION—COMMUNICATIONS EXTENSION.

Strategy three is appropriate when the physical event surrounding product use varies but the sociocultural event is the same as the one in the company's home market. Although changes in a product are substantially more costly than changes in the communications approach, a company will follow this course when the product may not sell in a foreign market otherwise. In some cases, product formulations may be changed without the consumer knowing it, as with detergents and gasoline, so that the product can function under different environmental circumstances.

STRATEGY FOUR: PRODUCT ADAPTATION—COMMUNICATIONS ADAPTATION. When both the physical and sociocultural events vary, a strategy of dual adaptation is generally favored. To make this strategy profitable, however, the foreign market or markets need to be of sufficient volume to justify the costs of dual adaptation. When Campbell Soup entered overseas markets, it found that tastes differed from market to market. U.S. products such as cream of mushroom and cream of chicken soup were successful in some markets, but in other markets these cream-based soups sat on the shelves. In 1995, Campbell teamed up with Nakano Vinegar Company in Japan. Nakano Vinegar Company helped them understand the market and develop many successful fish-based soups.[7]

STRATEGY FIVE: PRODUCT INVENTION. When the ability to purchase a product is generally missing, some companies invent an entirely new product, usually by re-designing the original product for a lower level of complexity. The resulting, substantially cheaper product leads to more purchases. An example is the strategy followed by Philips, the Dutch multinational corporation. In response to the desire of producers in many developing countries to own television manufacturing plants, the Dutch company redesigned its equipment and tools to suit the volume requirements of some of the world's poorest countries. Companies can also develop or invent entirely new products. For example, DaimlerChrysler found that traditional minivans were too big for Japanese streets, so they developed the Smart Car minivan to meet Japan's regulations and qualify for tax breaks for small cars, which propelled sales from 336 units in 2000 to 4,051 in 2001.[8]

GLOBAL PRODUCTS

In response to the pressure for cost reduction, and considering the relatively few opportunities for producing completely standardized products, many firms have moved to the creation of a *global product*. The global product is based on the fact that only a portion of the final design can be standardized and builds on flexibility in tailoring the end product to the needs of individual markets. This strategy represents a move to standardize as much as possible those areas involving common components or parts. This modularized approach has become of particular importance in the automobile industry. Both U.S. and European car manufacturers are moving toward the creation of world components to combat growing Japanese competition.

One of the first world cars was introduced by Ford during the 1981 model year. Ford's Escort model was assembled simultaneously in the United States, Great Britain, and Germany from parts produced in Japan, Spain, Brazil, Britain, Italy, France, Mexico, Taiwan, the United States, and West Germany. Ford saved engineering and development costs amounting to hundreds of millions of dollars because the design standardized engines, transmissions, and ancillary systems for heating, air conditioning, wheels, and seats. Still, the U.S. and European Escorts were two distinctly different cars.

Ford's second generation of the Escort was launched in 1991. With a budget of about $2 billion, Ford designed this second-generation Escort with Mazda, the Japanese car manufacturer that is partly owned by Ford. Ford engineers in the United States formulated the design, with the engineering and manufacturing planning performed by the Japanese engineers at Mazda. This new model was planned for assembly in twelve different locations where Ford sold the car under its Escort name, although Mazda used various different brand names (the 323, Protégé, or Familia). Ford's strategy was driven by the fact that product development duplication was a very costly process. By pooling development resources, Ford saved as much as $1 billion in development costs.[9]

Ford's global car, the Mondeo (called the Contour in the United States), was launched in 1993 in Europe and in 1994 in the United States. Ford invested $6 billion in the development of the new model, which included research and development as well as two new assembly plants and four new engine plants. Although sales in Europe were strong, the Mondeo-derived U.S. models did not sell very well. Although well designed for Europe, these models turned out to be too expensive for their segments in the U.S. market.[10]

For its latest version of world cars, Ford has changed its strategy. Instead of trying to build similar models in multiple markets, the company has moved toward building and launching different versions of cars on the same identical chassis (underpinning), creating a greater variety of car models while saving on the critical components and development of the drive train, transmission, and so forth. With this new strategy, Ford launched a new Escort, with European and U.S. versions, as part of its 1999 model range.[11]

Ford found that the global product strategy often resulted in the cars becoming too similar across brands, therefore reducing potential sales. Martin Leach, Europe's product development chief for Ford, said, "Ford has moved from one of platform definition to one of sharing technologies. In other words, Ford will no longer dictate that everyone shares this platform."[12]

One of the most significant changes in product development strategy in the 1990s has been modularity. This process involves the development of standard modules that can be connected easily with other standard modules to increase the variety of products. For example, General Motors has established a modular product architecture for all its global automobile projects. Future GM cars will be designed using combinations of components from seventy different body modules and about one hundred major mechanical components such as engines, power trains, and suspension systems. In the future, General Motors will share only parts such as engines, transmissions, and air conditioners.[13]

The challenge faced by Ford and other automobile manufacturers is similar to that faced by manufacturers and marketers of both industrial and consumer products all over the world. Cost pressures force them to standardize, whereas market pressures require more customization. Conceptually, these companies will gain from increasing the standardized components in their products while maintaining the ability to customize the final product for each market segment. Global firms will have to respond by achieving economies of scale on the core of their products—the key portion offered as a standard across all markets—by building on a series of standardized components. Different firms will have different levels of standardization, but rarely will one be able to standardize the product 100 percent. For one company, moving from a global core representing 15 percent of the total product to 20 percent of the total product may result in a considerable cost improvement, and this percentage may be the maximum level of standardization desirable. For another firm, the core may have to represent about 80 percent of the total product to achieve the same effect. These

Figure 14.2: Selecting Opportunities for Global Products

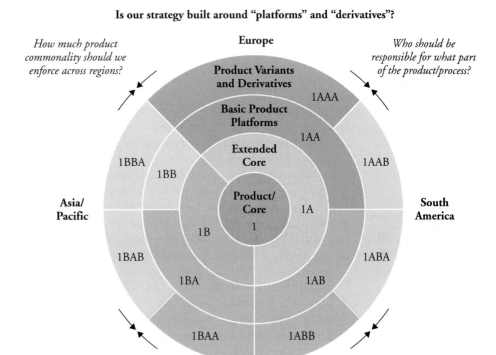

Is our strategy built around "platforms" and "derivatives"?

How much product commonality should we enforce across regions?

Who should be responsible for what part of the product/process?

Europe

Product Variants and Derivatives

Basic Product Platforms

Extended Core

Product/Core

1AAA

1AA

1AAB

1BBA

1BB

1A

1

South America

Asia/Pacific

1B

1BAB

1BA

1ABA

1BAA

1AB

1ABB

North America

levels will depend on the market characteristics faced by the company or industry. The limits to possible standardization were explained in the previous chapter.

The experience of many firms has led to the concept of building new products for global markets on the basis of "platforms" and "derivatives." The product core might be the same for all products in all regions. An extended core might apply for each region but differ across regions. Each region might support one or more basic platforms based on the extended-core concept. And finally, each region might launch product derivatives specific to the regional conditions. This "platform" strategy allows for different configurations while maintaining a stable product base, thus reducing basic development costs. However, such a global product strategy is possible only if a company has a coherent, well-planned global product development concept.[14] Figure 14.2 illustrates the concept of a core platform with product variants or derivatives for different markets. It is a strategy that continues to provide some manufacturing and R&D economies of scale while tailoring the product to local markets. A key element of this approach is the need to have a common interface between components. For example, National Bicycle of Japan uses modular architecture to provide bicycles that are tailored to the size and body proportions of individual customers. All the connection points are identical to allow easy assembly.[15]

NEW-PRODUCT DEVELOPMENT PROCESSES FOR GLOBAL MARKETS

Developing new products or services for global markets offers unique challenges to a firm. In contrast to the strictly domestic company, international firms must assign development responsibilities to any one of their often numerous international subsidiaries. Aside from the issue of who should perform development work, organizational problems resulting from participation by experts in many subsidiaries must be overcome. No doubt, the future success of international firms will depend to a substantial degree on how well these firms marshal their resources on a global scale to develop new products for multiple markets. A research study of 209 global companies with R&D expenditures of over $100 million found that 85 percent of the companies relied on external sources of technology, which was up from 40 percent in 1995. The same study also found that companies are spending more of their R&D budget outside the home region. In 2001, U.S. and European companies spent 35 percent of their R&D budget outside their home market, up from 25 percent in 1995. The most important sources of research were first the central corporate research and development department, then R&D in divisions or subsidiaries, then sponsored university research.[16]

THE ORGANIZATION OF HEAD OFFICE–SPONSORED RESEARCH AND DEVELOPMENT

Most companies currently engaging in research and development on a global scale originally conducted their development efforts strictly in centralized facilities in the firm's domestic market. Even today, the largest portion of research and development monies spent by global firms is in departments located in their home countries. As a result, new-product ideas are first developed in the context of the domestic market, with initial introduction at home followed by a phased-in introduction in the company's foreign markets.

There are several reasons for this traditional centralized approach. First, research and development must be integrated into a firm's overall marketing strategy. Such integration requires frequent contact and interfacing between research and development facilities and the company's main offices. Such contact is maintained more easily in close proximity. The argument for centralization of research and development is based on the concern that duplication of efforts will result if this responsibility is spread over several subsidiaries; centralized research and development is thought to maximize results from scarce research funds. A final important reason for centralization is the company's experience in its home, or domestic, market. Typically, the domestic market is very important to the company and is often the largest market. This is often the case for international companies based in the United States, Germany, and Japan. As a result, new products are developed with special emphasis on the domestic market, and research and development facilities, therefore, should be close by. For example, Gillette's global success is unquestionably the result of a hefty R&D investment. According to its CEO, "Good products come out of market research. Great products come out of R&D."[17] Traditionally, the level of R&D spent in a company or country was considered one of the best indicators of long-term growth. An Organization for Economic Cooperation and Development (OECD) study found that, although the investments in science and engineering were important, equally important was the diffusion of the new technology.[18]

Although there are many good reasons for centralizing product development at the company's head office, it will remain a challenge for the engineering and development staff of the firm to keep in mind all relevant product modifications before the design is finalized. Experience shows that later changes or modifications can be expensive. To keep a product acceptable in many or all relevant markets from the outset requires that the thinking of the product development staff become globalized early in the creation process. Only a globally thinking product development staff can ensure the global acceptability of a product by incorporating the maximum possible number of variations in the original product.

GLOBAL LEAD MARKETS AND RESEARCH AND DEVELOPMENT[19]

The first market for which a product is developed is referred to as a lead market. In general, a *lead market* is a market whose level of development exceeds that of the markets in other countries worldwide and whose developments tend to set a pattern for other countries. Lead markets are not restricted to technological developments as embodied in product hardware. The concept covers developments in design, production processes, patterns in consumer demand, and methods of marketing. Therefore, almost every phase of a company's operation is subject to lead market influences, although those focusing on technological developments are of special importance.

In the post–World War II period, many new developments in industry, marketing, and management emerged primarily in the United States. These developments, once accepted in the United States, were apt to be adopted later in other countries. This U.S. advantage was partially based on superior production methods, with the pioneering of mass production in the form of the assembly line. The U.S. advantage extended to management methods in general, and to access to new consumers in particular. The rapid development of U.S.-based international firms was based to a considerable degree on the exploitation of these advantages in applying new U.S. developments abroad and in creating extensive networks of subsidiaries across a large number of countries.

The U.S. lead over other countries did not last. Foreign competitors from Europe and Japan eroded the U.S. firms' advantages; as a result, no single country or market now unilaterally dominates the world economy. The United States has lost its lead in steel, television, radios, shoes, textiles, and automobiles, but it still leads the world in biotechnology, high-performance computing, and medical devices (see Figure 14.3). One area in which the United States has maintained supremacy is the Internet router market. Cisco Systems dominates the market, with an 85 percent share worldwide. Given the universal standards of the Internet, Cisco does not have a monopoly position. Cisco has maintained its position and doubled in size every year through constant innovation. By listening to customers and constantly developing new and faster products, Cisco has outdistanced all its smaller competitors.[20]

Figure 14.3: How the United States Stacks Up in a Dozen Emerging Technologies

Technology	Compared to Japan				Compared to Europe			
	R & D		New Products		R & D		New Products	
	Status	Trend	Status	Trend	Status	Trend	Status	Trend
Advanced Material	↔	↓	↓	↓	↑	↔	↔	↔
Advanced Semiconductor Devices	↔	↔	↓	↓	↑	↔	↔	↔
Artificial Intelligence	↑	↔	↑	↔	↑	↑	↑	↔
Biotechnology	↑	↓	↓	↓	↑	↑	↑	↔
Digital Imaging Technology	↔	↓	↓	↓	↔	↓	↓	↓
Flexible Computer-Integrated Manufacturing	↑	↔	↔	↔	↑	↓	↓	↓
High-Density Data Storage	↔	↔	↓	↓	↑	↔	↔	↔
High-Performance Computing	↑	↔	↑	↓	↑	↑	↑	↑
Medical Devices and Diagnostics	↑	↔	↑	↓	↑	↔	↑	↓
Optoelectronics	↔	↔	↓	↓	↔	↔	↑	↔
Sensor Technology	↑	↓	↔	↔	↑	↔	↔	↔
Superconductors	↔	↓	↔	↓	↔	↔	↔	↔

United States Status:

↑ Ahead   ↔ Even   ↓ Behind

United States Trend:

↑ Gaining   ↔ Holding   ↓ Losing

Source: U.S. Commerce Department. Reprinted from the June 15, 1990, issue of *Business Week* by special permission, copyright © 1990 by The McGraw-Hill Companies, Inc.

The fragmentation of lead markets led to a proliferation of centers, substantially complicating the task of keeping abreast of the latest developments in market demands, product design, and production techniques. Even formerly developing countries, such as South Korea, have reached lead market status in some categories. The South Korean company Samsung created the world's first 1-gigabyte computer chip, a major development that is bound to change the nature of the computer industry.[21]

To prosper in today's increasingly internationalized business climate, corporations must keep track of evolving lead markets as major sources for new product ideas and production techniques. New product ideas can stem from influences in demand, manufacturing processes, and scientific discoveries; no single country should expect to play a lead role in all facets of a firm's business. Any corporate research and development effort must look for new developments abroad, not just in the domestic market. Several global companies have invested heavily in R&D in China over the past five years. Procter & Gamble invested $10 million as part of its global strategy to adapt products to local markets. Its R&D facility is located adjacent to Tsinghua University, considered China's best in the field of science and technology. P&G hopes to identify new technologies in China that it can use around the world.[22]

THE ROLE OF FOREIGN SUBSIDIARIES IN RESEARCH AND DEVELOPMENT

Foreign subsidiaries of international firms rarely play an active role in research and development unless they have manufacturing responsibilities. Sales subsidiaries may provide the head office and/or the central research and development office with feedback on product adjustments or adaptations, but generally this participation does not go beyond the generation of ideas. Research has shown that subsidiaries may assume some research and development functions if the products require adaptation to the local market. The ensuing research and development capability is often extended to other applications unique to the local market. In many instances, however, the new product may have potential in other markets, and as a result these developments are transferred to other subsidiaries and to the central research and development staff.

International subsidiaries assume special positions when lead markets change from one country to another. Countries that can assume lead market status tend to be among the most advanced industrial nations of North America, Europe, and Asia. Larger international firms quite often have subsidiaries in all these markets. A subsidiary located in a lead market is usually in a better position to observe developments and to accommodate new demands. Consequently, international firms with subsidiaries in lead markets are in a unique position to turn such units into effective "listening posts." Unilever found that some countries of the world were very good at innovation in research and marketing, so it set up a global network of innovation centers. These centers were directed to expand their in-depth experience in research and marketing for Unilever's four categories of personal care products: dental, hair, deodorant, and skin. This expertise was then shared around the world.[23]

In the future, international companies will have to make better use of the talents of local subsidiaries in the development of new products. The role of the subsidiary as a selling or production arm of the company will have to be abandoned, and companies will have to find innovative ways to involve their foreign affiliates in the product development process. This involvement can be patterned around several role models. The *strategic leader* role for developing a new range of products to be used by the entire company may be assigned to a highly competent subsidiary in a market of strategic importance. Another subsidiary with competence in a distinct area may be assigned the role of *contributor*, adapting some products in smaller but nevertheless important markets. Most subsidiaries, because they are smaller in size and located in less strategic markets, will be expected to fulfill the roles of *implementers* of the overall strategy and will contribute less either technologically or strategically.

Nokia has established two R&D centers in China to support its position as a leading supplier of mobile and broadband network systems and mobile phones. The investments in advanced R&D help assure the Chinese government that Nokia is committed to China and will share its technology with local suppliers. Nokia has invested over 2.3 billion euros in China, has over twenty offices, operates eight joint ventures, and employs over five thousand people.[24]

PURCHASING RESEARCH AND DEVELOPMENT FROM FOREIGN COUNTRIES

Instead of developing new products through its own research and development personnel, a company may acquire such material or information from independent outside sources. These sources are usually located in foreign countries that have acquired lead market status. Managers commonly read literature published by lead markets. Also, through regular visits to foreign countries and trade fairs, managers maintain close contact with lead markets. These ad hoc measures are becoming increasingly insufficient, however, for maintaining the necessary flow of information in rapidly changing markets.

For companies without immediate access to new technology embodied in new products, the licensing avenue has been the traditional approach to gain new developments from lead markets. U.S. technology has been tapped through many independent licensing arrangements. Japanese companies have made extensive use of the licensing alternative to acquire technologies developed in countries that were lead markets from Japan's point of view. For example, Sony of Japan paid $28.5 million in 2002 to license all of the technology of InterTrust for use in Sony digital consumer products. The InterTrust technology is used to prevent the unauthorized copying of digital music and other content.[25] Although the advantage of licensing lies in its potential to develop new product technologies, typically some restrictions are attached, such as limiting the sale of such products to specific geographic regions or countries.

Technology licensing can also be used to speed up the adoption of new technologies and thus speed up market growth. Both Nokia and Ericsson are licensing their technology for 3G mobile phone networks to speed up the adoption of 3G technology. Traditionally, telecommunications companies develop their own network systems; however, this approach increases the cost and slows down the adoption of new technology. Nokia's licensing strategy should give it a bigger share of the base station marketplace, while all the mobile phone companies will continue to compete for the 3G phone business.[26]

ACQUISITIONS AS A ROUTE TO NEW PRODUCTS

Acquiring a company for its new technology or products is a strategy many firms have followed in domestic markets. International acquisition for the purpose of gaining a window on emerging technologies or products is becoming an acceptable strategy for many firms. Robert Bosch, a German firm, acquired an interest in American Microsystems, and Philips of the Netherlands purchased Signetics. In both cases, the foreign firms had to pay substantial premiums over the market value of the stock as the price for an inside look at new-product development.

Japanese companies illustrate how the acquisitions strategy can be used to gain access to new products and technologies. Japanese firms are reported to have invested approximately $350 million in about sixty deals for a wide range of minority positions in U.S.-based high-technology firms through joint ventures, licensing, or direct investment as minority shareholders. In 1989, Chugai Pharmaceutical acquired Gen-Probe of San Diego to gain access to the firm's products, including test kits for the detection of cancer and viral infections. Gen-Probe has since become a recognized world leader in the development, manufacturing, and commercialization of diagnostic products based on its patented genetic probe technologies.[27]

THE JOINT VENTURE ROUTE TO NEW-PRODUCT DEVELOPMENT

Forming a joint venture (JV) with a technologically advanced foreign company can also lead to new-product development, often at lower costs. Joint ventures are concluded today by firms from many different countries. GM operates a JV in Japan with Suzuki, a company in which it has a 10 percent share participation, and with Isuzu, a truck producer in which GM owns 49 percent. GM jointly develops cars with those firms for local markets.[28] GM is not a newcomer to JVs with Japanese car makers. It has operated a JV production unit in California with Toyota since 1984.[29] GM also signed an agreement to purchase low-emission engines from Honda Motors. In return, the Japanese firm will purchase diesel engines from Isuzu, a GM affiliate.[30] In 2002, DaimlerChrysler, Mitsubishi, and Korea's Hyundai signed a joint-venture agreement to form the Global Engine Alliance, which will develop 1.8-, 2.0-, and 2.4-liter aluminum engines. Together, the three companies will produce 1.5 million engines a year.[31]

Lilly established a clinical pharmacology center in Singapore with the Singapore National Science and Technology board and the National University of Singapore. The joint venture allows Lilly to tap the intellectual resources of leading Singaporean scientists.[32] Joint ventures often leverage the different strengths of the firms. Lilly combined their pharmacology resources with the academic research capabilities of the National University of Singapore.

ALLIANCES FOR NEW-PRODUCT DEVELOPMENT

Many companies are finding that alliances are a way to share technology and research and development for competitive advantage. Alliances are not as structured as joint ventures but include some type of mutually beneficial arrangement. For example, Electrolux, the Swedish appliance manufacturer, has concluded a broad-based alliance with Toshiba of Japan. The two firms plan to cooperate in household appliances (white goods) through the exchange of technology, product sourcing, and purchasing. The firms will also cooperate on developing technology that allows consumers to operate appliances remotely via the Internet. Toshiba will benefit from Electrolux's cost competitive position as the world's leading producer of white goods, and Electrolux will benefit from Toshiba's strengths in semiconductors and wireless communications. This alliance helps both companies gain access to information and technology that they would not have been able to obtain individually.[33] Alliances can sometimes be formed by firms for some segment of their business, although they remain competitors in other segments.

THE CONSORTIUM APPROACH

To share the huge cost of developing new products, some companies have established or joined consortia to share in new-product development. Under the consortium approach, member firms join in a working relationship without forming a new entity. On completion of the assigned task, member firms are free to seek other relationships with different firms.

Since the development of new aircraft is particularly costly, the aircraft industry offers several examples of the consortium approach to product development. The high development costs require that large passenger aircraft must be built in series of two hundred or three hundred units just to break even. Under these circumstances, several companies form a consortium to share the risk. One of the first highly successful efforts was the European Airbus, developed and produced by French, British, and German manufacturers.

For its latest generation of long-range aircraft, the 777, Boeing faced development and launch costs of about $4 billion. Such programs could not be justified unless several airlines, including foreign ones, could be involved from the outset with large capital commitments. To reduce the risk, Boeing sold a 21 percent share in the project to three Japanese companies: Mitsubishi Heavy Industries, Fuji Heavy Industries, and Kawasaki Heavy Industries. These companies are major suppliers of parts and components for every Boeing jetliner. It is believed that such Japanese participation was invited not only to share development costs but to help in the marketing of the planes. The fact that All Nippon Airlines is the largest operator of Boeing 767 planes outside the United States was linked to the strong participation of Japanese firms in the production of the plane. Both Japan Airlines and All Nippon Airlines are among the key accounts sought for the launch of the Boeing 777 model range.[34] Japan Airlines was already the world's largest operator of Boeing 747s. The fact that Japanese airlines are the largest buyers of long-range planes underscores the need to bring in Japanese partners in the early stages of any long-range passenger plane project.

Another advantage of a consortium approach lies in sales. The widespread participation of companies from the United States, Europe, and Japan gives partial assurance for future sales, thus further reducing the risk to each participating company. Airbus, a consortium competing with Boeing, was trying to enter the Japanese market for wide-bodied planes. The absence of strong consortium partners in the Japanese aircraft industry was viewed as a handicap for Airbus in signing major contracts. Airbus invested $12 billion to develop the A380, with orders for almost 100 aircraft going to Virgin Atlantic Airlines, Singapore Airlines, and Lufthansa. Airbus is especially interested in selling to JAL (Japan Airlines System Corporation), the world's largest purchaser of jumbo jets, which may explain why Airbus is buying components valued at over $1.5 billion from Mitsubishi Heavy Industries, Fuji Heavy Industries, Japan Aircraft Manufacturing Company, Toray Corp., and Sumitomo Metal Industries.[35]

The consortium approach is becoming increasingly popular in several technology-intensive industries. Companies in the automobile, computer, and biotechnology industries have formed cooperative agreements to share in the development and exploitation of technology. What is different about this trend today is that sometimes competitors will become partners, whereas previously such cooperation was unthinkable.

GLOBALIZATION OF THE PRODUCT DEVELOPMENT PROCESS

The previous section dealt primarily with the sources of product development. Total integration of the product development process for a multinational enterprise often requires the adoption of new organizational forms and the restructuring of the development process as a whole. The challenge in multinational product development is finding a way to combine domestic and foreign expertise so that truly global products can result.

The global approach to new-product development has changed significantly over the last twenty years. Twenty years ago, a German car manufacturer made cars for the German market. Then, fifteen years ago, the same manufacturer developed European cars. Ten years ago, the German manufacturer developed a world car. Now the German manufacturer owns an American car company and has financial relationships with U.K., Chinese, and Japanese car manufacturers. This shift from local to global development requires that the unique or special concerns of major markets be considered from the outset of the process, and a company no longer attempts to make various adaptations on the initial model or prototype. This early introduction of global considerations not only ensures that the product will achieve wide acceptance but also aims at maximizing the commonality of models to achieve economies in component manufacturing. A global product, then, is not identical in all countries. Instead, a world product is engineered from the outset, with the goal of maximizing the percentage of identical components, design, and parts to the point where local needs can be met with a minimum of additional costs in tooling, engineering, and development.

To globalize their research, Japanese companies have made heavy investments in U.S.-based research facilities. Hundreds of Japanese scientists already work side by side with Americans in research laboratories through exchange programs. The objective is to gain access to scientific talent in other countries. Companies chasing such talent around the world are opening development centers where the talent can be found. One example is China, where many western firms have opened development facilities to obtain access to Chinese scientific talent. Among those western firms are Intel and Microsoft, which have opened research centers near Beijing; many of China's leading universities are clustered in and around Beijing.[36] In 1998, Microsoft indicated it would spend about $80 million over a six-year period to expand its new research center, which will house one hundred employees. One of the main tasks of the research center is to find ways to make software more useful to Chinese computer users.[37]

The research and development process is stimulated by ideas for new products. Global companies must identify sources of new ideas from potential markets. Microsoft sponsored a nationwide contest in Russia to develop a Russian version of Microsoft Windows. Microsoft hopes to generate an attractive product for the Russian market as well as to stimulate product development.[38] In some markets, local competitors may be the best sources of product ideas. For example, in India, McDonald's needed to adapt to the Hindu custom of not eating beef and replicated other competitors' menus with the McDonald's touch. McDonald's developed the Maharajah Mac *two all-mutton patties,* made of lamb, and also offers its only vegetarian menu, for which a separate kitchen is used.[39]

To develop a global product also requires a different organizational structure. Changes instituted by General Motors (GM) reflect moves made by other international firms. With the advent of world cars, GM realized that the company needed more efficient coordination between its domestic units and its overseas subsidiaries. Therefore, it moved its overseas staff from New York to Detroit to speed up communication between domestic and international staffs and adopted the "project center" concept to manage its engineering effort. Each division or subsidiary involved in a new car design leads engineers to a centrally organized project center, which designs, develops, and introduces the new model. When the model is introduced into the market, the project center is disbanded. Of course, not every firm will find a project center approach feasible. Other alternatives include assigning primary responsibility to a subsidiary with special capability in the new-product field.

INTRODUCING NEW PRODUCTS TO GLOBAL MARKETS

Once a product has been developed for commercial introduction, several complex decisions still need to be made. Aside from the question of whether to introduce the product abroad, the firm has to decide on a desirable test-marketing procedure, select target countries for introduction, and determine the timing or sequence of the introduction. Given the large number of alternatives inherent in numerous possible markets, decisions surrounding new-product introduction often attain strategic significance. Determining which product to introduce abroad depends, of course, on sales potential. Following a careful analysis, a marketer develops a list of target countries. A company can then choose from among several paths leading to actual introduction in the target countries.

CONCEPT TESTS

Once a prototype or sample product has been developed, a company may decide to subject its new creation to a series of tests to determine commercial feasibility. It is particularly important to subject a new product to actual use conditions. When the development process takes place outside the country of actual use, a practical field test can be crucial. The test must include all necessary usage steps to provide complete information. For example, when testing dehydrated soups made by its newly acquired Knorr subsidiary, CPC International concentrated primarily on taste tests in the U.S. market to ensure that the final product suited U.S. consumers. Extensive testing led to soups that were different in formulation from those sold in Europe. CPC had neglected, however, to have consumers try the product at home as part of their regular cooking activities. Such a test would have revealed consumers' discontent with the relatively long cooking time—up to twenty minutes—compared to three minutes for comparable canned soups. The company realized these difficulties only after a national introduction had been completed and sales fell short of original expectations.

The concept-testing stage would be incomplete if the products were tested only in the company's domestic market. A full test in several major markets is essential so that any shortcomings can be alleviated early, before costly adaptations for individual countries are made. Such an approach is particularly important in cases when product development occurs on a multinational basis, with input from several foreign subsidiaries. When Volkswagen tested its original Rabbit models, test vehicles were made available to all principal subsidiaries to ensure that each market's requirements were met by the otherwise standardized car.

There may be some differences between concept testing for consumer products and concept testing for industrial products. Industrial products tend to be used worldwide for the same purposes under very similar circumstances. Factories using textile machinery are relatively standardized around the world, so a machinery test in one country may be quite adequate for most others. As a result, single-country market testing may be more appropriate for industrial products.

TEST MARKETING

Just as there are good reasons to test-market a product in a domestic market, an international test can give the firm valuable insights into potential future success. A key question is, Where should the market test be held? Companies in the United States have largely pioneered test-marketing procedures because it has been possible to isolate a given test-market city like the Columbus, Ohio market in terms of media and distribution. Such market isolation may not always be possible in smaller countries and even less so in countries. For example in Spain, T.V. media is national, not local. If a market test were considered in Barcelona with print media substituted for television, the test would not be a true replication of the actual full-scale introduction. As a result, test markets tend to include an entire country.In a larger country like India, test-marketing by cities is possible. Reebok India Company decided to test-market the Weebok range of shoes for toddlers and juniors only in Delhi and Mumbai. Based on the test-market results, the company adjusted the product range, finalized pricing, and determined if it should continue to import or manufacture locally.[40]

To overcome the shortage of test-market possibilities, international firms often substitute the experience in one country for a market test in another. Although market tests are typical for many U.S.-based firms in limited geographies in the U.S. market, companies use these early U.S. results as a basis for analysis. Such a strategy requires that at least one subsidiary of an international firm have actual commercial experience with a product or any given aspect of the marketing strategy before introducing the product elsewhere. Use of the U.S. market as a test market for other countries depends on the market situation and the degree to which results can be extrapolated to other countries. Circumstances are rarely exactly the same, so early U.S. results must be regarded with caution. Also, extrapolation may be appropriate only for other advanced countries in Europe and Asia. (See also our explanation of the comparative analytic approach in Chapter 6.)

Another approach to test marketing is to use a foreign country as a first introduction and proving ground before entering other markets. In Europe, smaller markets, such as the Netherlands, Belgium, Austria, and Switzerland, may be used to launch a new product. Because of their size, a test would include full national introduction, and results could then be applied to other countries.

Special attention should be given to the lead market as a potential test market. Any new product that succeeds in its lead market can be judged to have high potential elsewhere, as other markets for the product mature.

TIMING OF NEW-PRODUCT INTRODUCTIONS

A company will be faced very early in the introduction process with establishing the timing and sequence of its introduction. Timing determines when a product should be introduced in a foreign market. Sequencing becomes an issue when a firm deals with several countries and must decide on a phased or simultaneous entry approach. Traditionally, firms have introduced new products first in their domestic markets to gain experience in production, marketing, and service. Foreign market introductions are attempted only after a product has proven itself in the domestic market. Research has revealed a steadily decreasing time lag, however, between domestic and initial foreign market introduction.[41] From 1945 to 1950, only 5.6 percent of investigated firms introduced new products abroad within one year of introduction of a new product in the domestic market. By 1975, the percentage had increased to 38.7 percent, and about two-thirds were introduced abroad within five years. This reduction in time lag reflects the increased capability of U.S. firms to introduce products abroad rapidly. It also reflects the rapid economic development of many advanced countries, to the point where the United States no longer leads in several fields. The average time lag can safely be assumed to continue to decrease. Procter & Gamble (P&G) is one firm that does not believe it can compete successfully with long product introduction times. Having been confronted with an average of five years for global product rollouts, the company is reducing test marketing in multiple areas to eighteen months, followed by rollout of the product globally in key markets in another eighteen months. P&G's first use of this new timetable was to coincide with its new Dryel home dry-cleaning kit and Swiffer, a sweeper system.[42]

Some companies are now in a position to introduce products simultaneously in several countries. Simultaneous introduction depends on the company's foreign market development stage and its ability to satisfy demand. When the primary function of foreign subsidiaries is the sale of products shipped from one or a small number of centrally located manufacturing centers, simultaneous introduction is possible, as long as marketing efforts can be coordinated. This structure is typical for electronics firms. Other companies produce in many markets; thus, the manufacturing function would be strained if simultaneous introduction were attempted.

Companies have to invest ever-larger amounts for developing new technologies or products. As these investments rise, companies are finding they must launch globally to get a return on the investment before patent protections run out or until new competitors come out with similar products. As a result, companies have been forced into a rapid introduction of new products, so that we can now talk of a *global product rollout*. Global product rollout was practiced by Gillette with the introduction of its new Sensor and Mach 3 razors, with simultaneous introduction in both Europe and North America.

COUNTRY SELECTION

Although international firms have subsidiaries in numerous countries, product introductions have always been limited to the industrialized nations. Many U.S.-based international firms have used their European subsidiaries as stepping stones to Latin America or eastern Europe. One electronics manufacturer transferred an innovation first to its Italian subsidiary; the Italian subsidiary then introduced it in Spain through another subsidiary located in Spain. The same company has also used its Dutch subsidiary to transfer innovations to Poland.

The selection of countries for new-product launches is increasingly based on a single test market in possibly one or two countries, with a rapid move toward a global rollout. Most important, the test market may not even be the place of initial launch. IBM tested a new branding campaign for its Global Services line in Canada but launched it in the United States. Heinz also tested its new teenager-oriented ketchup campaign in Canada but rolled it out worldwide with minor creative modifications. Testing overseas prior to U.S. launch may be cheaper but requires an understanding of how to translate foreign results for use in U.S. markets. Global marketing is moving rapidly in a direction where testing in each individual country will not be possible; instead rollout in countries will be based on the test data from a few countries.[43]

CONCLUSIONS

When companies search for new markets for their products, they face the difficult task of adapting those products to new environments. Such adaptations are frequently expensive when they are incorporated after the product is introduced into a market for consumption. In the future, companies will increasingly consider global opportunities early in the development cycle of a new product. Incorporating global requirements and standards early will allow new products to be usable almost immediately in many markets. Such a move toward globalization of the product development cycle will result in the development of more global products. These products will be produced in modularized forms to include as many global components as possible, and they will also incorporate a set of unique components to fit the product needs of individual markets. The challenge for global marketers is to find the best tradeoff between the standardized global components of a product and the tailor-made components designed for specific markets.

Another increasingly influential factor in new-product development processes is speed. Companies want to be among the first, if not the first, to enter a market with a new product or service because early entrants tend to earn the biggest market share. To increase the speed of new-product introduction, companies work on collaborative development processes. The Internet has made it possible for companies to collaborate with other companies, suppliers, and customers within a virtual product development process. In this virtual space, different participants can contribute to the process from anywhere in the world, thus decreasing both the time to development and the time to global launch. They will also decrease the time it will take from first domestic introduction until worldwide launch. In the end, many firms will undertake multicountry launches or simultaneous global product rollouts. The risk increases with such global launches because less time is available to test the product, ensure that it meets the market performance needs, and tailor the product to a given country or market.

Questions for Discussion

1. Analyze three different products—freezers, compact discs, and contact lenses—according to the global product strategies listed in Table 14.1. What general marketing strategy recommendations would you suggest for each product?

2. In your opinion, what is the future for global products?

3. How should international firms organize their new-product development efforts today and in the future?

4. What is the impact of a loss of lead market position in several industries for U.S.-based corporations?

5. If you were to test-market a new consumer product today for worldwide introduction, how would you select test countries for Europe, Asia, and Latin America?

For Further Reading

Afriyie, Koti. "International Technology Transfers." In *Cooperative Strategies in International Business*, ed. Farok Contractor and Peter Lorange. Lexington, Mass.: D. C. Heath, 1987.

Arora, Ashish, and Andrea Fosfuri. "Wholly Owned Subsidiary Versus Licensing in the Chemical Industry." *Journal of International Business Studies*, 2000, vol. 31, no. 4, pp. 555–572.

Calantone, Roger J., and Yushan Sam Zhao. "Joint Ventures in China: A Comparative Study of Japanese, Korean and U.S. Partners." *Journal of International Marketing*, 2001, vol. 9, no. 1, pp. 1–23

Cheng, Joseph L. C., and Douglas J. Bolon. "The Management of Multinational R&D: A Neglected Topic in International Business Research." *Journal of International Business Studies*, 1st Quarter 1993, pp. 1–18.

Chryssochoidis, George M. "Why Do High-Tech Firms Suffer Delays in International New Product Rollouts?" *International Journal of Manufacturing Technology and Management*, (Geneva), 2000, vol. 2, no. 1–7, pp. 901–918.

Cooper, Robert Gravlin. *Winning at New Products: Accelerating the Process from Idea to Launch*, 3rd ed. New York: Perseus Books, 2001.

Crawford, Merle C. *New Products Management*, 6th ed. New York: McGraw-Hill, 1999.

Harrison, Norma J. "Managing Innovation for Competitive Advantage: A Global Survey." *International Journal of Entrepreneurship and Innovation Management*, 2002, vol. 2, no 1, pp. 1–16.

Kaikati, Jack G. "Domestically Banned Products: For Export Only." *Journal of Public Policy and Marketing*, 1984, vol. 3, pp. 125–133.

Kaplan, Nancy J., and Jonathan Hurd. "Realizing the Promise of Partnerships." *Journal of Business Strategy*, May 2002, vol. 23, no. 3, pp. 38–43.

Mabert, Vincent A., John F. Muth, and Robert W. Schmennor. "Collapsing New Product Development Time." *Journal of Product Innovation Management*, September 1992, pp. 200–212.

Manu, Franklyn A. "Innovation, Orientation, Environment and Performance: A Comparison of U.S. and European Markets." *Journal of International Business Studies*, 2nd Quarter 1992, p. 333.

Ogbuehi, Alphonso O., and Ralph A. Bellis, Jr. "Decent Sized R&D for Global Development: Strategic Implications for the Multinational Corporation." *International Marketing Review*, 1992, vol. 19, no. 5, pp. 60–70.

Roberts, Edward B. "Benchmarking Global Strategic Management of Technology." *Research Technology Management*, March-April, vol. 44, no. 2, pp. 25–36.

Wind, Yoram, and Vigay Mahajan. "New Product Development Process: A Perspective for Reexamination." *Journal of Product Innovation Management*, 1998, vol. 5, no. 4, pp. 304–310

Endnotes

1. This section is based on Warren J. Keegan and Mark C. Green, *Global Marketing*, 3d ed. (Englewood Cliffs, N.J.: Prentice-Hall, 2003), pp. 418–424.
2. "Unilever Among Asia's 10 Most Admired," *Manila Standard*, June 13, 1999, p. 12.
3. Cris Prystay, "To Unilever, Size Matters," *Wall Street Journal*, March 14, 2002, p. A12.
4. "The Common Good," *Economist*, December 1, 2001, pp. S8–S10.
5. "BAT–Rothmans Merger to Affect Polish Operations," *Polish News Bulletin*, June 16, 1999, p. 1.
6. "Japan Tobacco Wins RJR's Russia Unit," *Moscow Times*, March 11, 1999, p. 11.
7. Charles Wesley Orton, "A Fine Kettle of Fish," *World Trade*, October 2001, vol. 14, no. 10, p. 74.
8. "DaimlerChrysler Scores Hit in Japan with Smart Car," *Automotive News*, January 28, 2002, p. 74.
9. "How Ford and Mazda Shared the Driver's Seat," *Business Week*, March 26, 1990, p. 94.
10. "The Revolution at Ford," *Economist*, August 7, 1999, p. 51.
11. "Ford Motor Unveils Replacement of Ford Escort," *Knight-Ridder Tribune Business News*, March 3, 1998, p. 2.
12. "Ford Group Brands Won't Share Platforms," *Automotive News Europe*, October 8, 2001, p. 18.

13. "GM Says Its U.S., European Models Won't Share Common Structure," *Detroit Free Press,* March 6, 2002, p. 1.

14. Based upon conceptual work by Jean-Philippe Deschamps, (Lausanne, Switzerland, IMD).

15. Ron Ronchez, "Modular Architecture in the Marketing Process," *Journal of Marketing,* 1999, vol. 63, pp. 92–111.

16. Edward B. Roberts, "Benchmarking Global Strategic Management of Technology," *Research Technology Management,* March-April 2001, vol. 44, no. 2, pp. 25–36.

17. "Gillette Knows Shaving—How to Turn Out Hot New Products," *Fortune,* October 14, 1996, pp. 207–210.

18. "Playing Godmother to Invention," *Economist,* May 24, 1997, p. 76.

19. This section is based on Jean-Pierre Jeannet, "Lead Markets: A Concept for Designing Global Business Strategies," working paper, International Institute for Management Development (IMD), May 1986.

20. Richard Martin, "The Gospel According to John," *Industry Standard,* April 30, 2001, vol. 4, no. 17, p. 56.

21. "South Korea's Samsung Announces Next-Generation Computer Chip," *Agence France-Presse,* June 28, 1999, p. 1.

22. Daniel Walfish, "P&G China Lab Has Global Role," *Research Technology Management,* September-October 2001, vol. 44, no. 5, p. 4.

23. "Fanning Unilever's Flame of Innovation," *Advertising Age International,* November 23, 1992, p. I-3.

24. "Nokia to Supply GSM Network Expansion/MMS Trial to Zhejiang," *World Telecom,* June 1, 2002, vol. 14, no. 6, p. 1.

25. Don Clark, "InterTrust Technologies Signs a Licensing Deal with Sony," *Wall Street Journal,* May 24, 2002, p. N4.

26. David Pringle, "Nokia to License Technology to Rivals," *Asian Wall Street Journal,* February 12, 2002, p. 6.

27. "Gen-Probe Expands with a New State of the Art Manufacturing Facility," *Chemical Business NewsBase,* press release, May 17, 1999.

28. "GM Says Auto Plant in Japan Is Part of Long-Term Strategy," *Agence France-Presse,* August 6, 1999, p. 1.

29. "General Motors–Toyota Plant in Fremont, Calif. Thrives," *Knight-Ridder Tribune Business News* (*Contra Costa Times,* Walnut Creek, Calif.), July 20, 1999, p.1.

30. "Stand-Alone Honda Strikes a Deal," *Nikkei Weekly,* December 6, 1999, p. 8.

31. "Ford Joint Venture in Taiwan to Invest in New Product Development," *AFX News,* May 5, 1999, p. 2.

32. "Decision Made by Lilly to Establish R&D Center in Singapore," *Pharmaceutical Executive,* August 2001, vol. 21, no. 8, p. 24.

33. "Toshiba, Electrolux May Codevelop Appliances," *Jiji Press English News Service,* Tokyo, June 12, 2001, p. 1.

34. "Japanese Firms Sign on to Develop Materials for Boeing's Sonic Cruiser Project," *Knight Ridder Tribune Business News,* January 30, 2002, p. 1.

35. Todd Zaun, "Airbus Picks Japanese Parts Makers," *Wall Street Journal,* June 26, 2002, p. D3.

36. "China: Back to the Future," *Far Eastern Economic Review,* March 11, 1999, p. 10.

37. "Microsoft Lab in China, *Wall Street Journal,* November 6, 1998, p. 4.

38. Alexander Levinsky, "Forthcoming: Windows 2000 in Russian," *Moscow News,* February 23, 2000, Issue 7, pp. 7, B4.

39. "Gulliver's French Fries," *Wall Street Journal Europe,* May 10, 2001, p. 8.

40. Ratna Bhushan, "Reebok to Launch Kid's Range," *Business Line,* January 9, 2002.p.1.

41. William H. Davidson and Richard Harrigan, "Key Decisions in International Marketing: Introducing New Products Abroad," *Columbia Journal of World Business,* Winter 1977, p. 15.

42. "P&G Puts Two Cleaning Products on Its New Marketing Fast Track," *Wall Street Journal,* May 18, 1999, p. B6.

43. "Test It in Paris, France, Launch It in Paris, Texas," *Advertising Age,* May 31, 1999, p. 28.

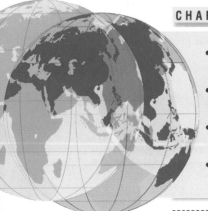

Chapter 15

Managing Global Distribution Channels

Global marketing distribution decisions are similar to the marketing distribution decisions made in a domestic setting. What differs, of course, are the environmental influences that, in the end, may lead to substantially different policies and channel options. Global marketers need to understand how environmental influences may affect these distribution policies and options. Using this knowledge, they must structure efficient channels for products on a country-by-country basis. In this chapter, we discuss the structure of global distribution systems; the process of developing a distribution strategy; and methods for selecting, locating, and managing channel members. We also explain the issues of gaining access to channels, global supply chain management, and global trends in distribution. Figure 15.1 presents an illustration of the topics covered in this chapter.

The global marketing manager's distribution decisions in multiple countries are very important. The channels of distribution are often the best sources of customer and competitor information in a country. The channels are often the voice of the firm to the customer, so selecting and managing distribution partners is critical to successful implementation of a marketing program. Finally, distribution agreements are often long term because they cannot be changed quickly, like advertising or pricing. For all these reasons, global marketers must understand the distribution options that are available and how to manage them.

THE STRUCTURE OF THE GLOBAL DISTRIBUTION SYSTEM

The structure of the distribution systems available in a country is affected by the level of economic development, the personal disposable income of consumers, and the quality of the physical infrastructure, as well as environmental factors such as cul-

Figure 15.1: Global Distribution

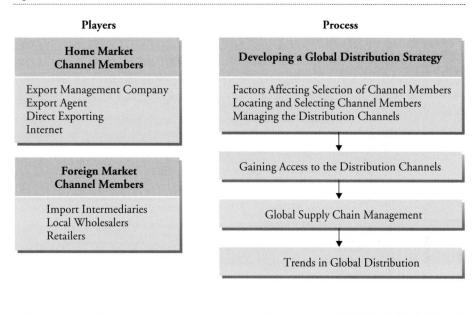

ture, physical environment, and the legal/political system. Marketers who develop a distribution strategy must decide how to transport the products from the manufacturing locations to the consumer. Although distribution can be handled completely by the manufacturer, products are often moved through intermediaries, such as agents, wholesalers, distributors, and retailers. An understanding of the structure of available distribution systems is extremely important in the development of a strategy. The various global distribution channels available to a manufacturer are shown in Figure 15.2.

There are two major categories of potential channel members: (1) those located in the home country and (2) those located outside the home country. In the home country, a manufacturer can utilize the services of an export management company or an export agent, or it can use company personnel to export products directly. In Chapter 9, we discussed which of these channel members should be used. In this chapter, our focus is on how to locate, select, use, and manage both home market and foreign market channel members.

HOME MARKET CHANNEL MEMBERS

Within a manufacturer's home market, several different types of export-related channel members can help with the export process. The most common are export management companies and export agents. A firm can choose to bypass the help of these specialists and use internal company expertise to export, or it can engage in ecommerce.

Figure 15.2: Global Marketing Channel Alternatives

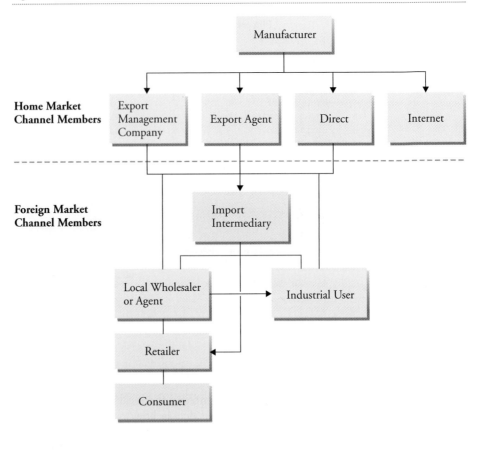

EXPORT MANAGEMENT COMPANY. An export management company (EMC) is a firm that handles all aspects of export operations under a contractual agreement. The EMC will normally take responsibility for the promotion of products, marketing research, credit, physical handling or logistics, patents, and licensing. The number of EMCs is estimated at 1,200 firms, representing about 10,000 manufacturers and accounting for 10 percent of U.S.-manufactured exports.[1] The Federation of International Trade Associations has a directory of 234 EMCs; the directory can be accessed at fita.org/emc/.html. Arrangements between an EMC and a manufacturer will vary, depending on the services offered and the volume expected. The advantages of an EMC are that (1) little or no investment is required to enter the global marketplace, (2) no company personnel are required, and (3) the EMC will have an established network of sales offices and international marketing and distribution knowledge. The main disadvantage is that the manufacturer gives up direct control of the international sales and marketing effort. Also, if the product has a long purchase cycle and requires a large amount of market development and education, the EMC may not expend the necessary effort to penetrate a new market.

EXPORT AGENTS. Export agents are individuals or firms that assist manufacturers in exporting goods. They are similar to EMCs, but they tend to provide more limited services and to focus on one country or one part of the world. Export agents understand all the requirements for moving goods through the customs process, but they do not provide the marketing skills that an EMC provides; these agents focus more on the sale and handling of goods. The advantage of using an export agent is that the manufacturer does not need to have an export manager to handle all the documentation and shipping tasks. The main disadvantage is the export agent's limited market coverage; to cover different parts of the world, a firm needs the services of numerous export agents.

DIRECT EXPORTING. Instead of using an EMC or export agent, a firm can export its goods directly, through in-house company personnel or an in-house exporting department. Because of the complexity of trade regulations, customs documentation, insurance requirements, and worldwide transportation alternatives, people with special training and experience must be hired to handle these tasks. Also, the current or expected volume must be sufficient to support the in-house staff.

THE INTERNET. Many smaller manufacturers have been establishing their own web presence. This presence allows foreign clients easier access to smaller firms and tends to mitigate the necessity of using some form of agent. To make the web presence worthwhile, the site needs to be constructed so that a foreign buyer can access information easily, obtain order forms, and send email questions. Experts also recommend that a web site be linked appropriately to search engines so that it shows up under certain relevant search words. Although a web presence goes a long way toward reaching and communicating with foreign markets, the manufacturer who wants to export still needs to deal with the entire logistics area and credit information. For logistics, companies such as FedEx, UPS, and Emery provide considerable online help, which is of great use to smaller companies without that particular expertise. For example, Samsung Electronics, a Korean firm, used the Internet to increase sales per salesperson by almost 300 percent. Use of the Internet allowed them to reduce order time and the number of documents to be handled.[2]

FOREIGN MARKET CHANNEL MEMBERS

As you saw in Figure 15.2, various channel alternatives are available in the marketplace once products have left the home market: import intermediaries, local wholesalers or agents, and retailers. Even with local manufacturing, the company still needs to get its products from the factory to the consumers.

IMPORT INTERMEDIARIES. Import intermediaries identify needs in their local market and find products from the world market to satisfy these needs. They will normally purchase goods in their own name and act independently of the manufacturers. As independents, these channel members use their own marketing strategies and keep in close contact with the markets they serve. A manufacturer desiring distribution in an independent intermediary's market area should investigate this channel partner as one of the ways to get its product to wholesalers and retailers in that area.

LOCAL WHOLESALERS OR AGENTS. A series of possible channel members in each country move manufacturers' products to retailers, industrial firms, or (in some cases) other wholesalers. Local wholesalers take title to the products, whereas local agents do not. Local wholesalers are also called distributors or dealers. In many cases, the local wholesaler has exclusive distribution rights for a specific geographic area or country.

The structure of wholesale distribution varies greatly from country to country. The number of wholesalers and the number of retailers per wholesaler vary according to the distribution structure and wholesale pattern of the country. For example, although Denmark and Portugal have approximately the same number of wholesalers, the Denmark wholesaler serves 1.3 retailers indirectly, whereas in Portugal a wholesaler serves 5.5 retailers.[3] Wholesale channels in Japan are very complex, with most products moving through as many as six intermediaries. This lengthy distribution channel increases prices in Japan—$20 for a bottle of aspirin, or $72 for a package of golf balls costing $26.80 in U.S. stores.[4]

The functions of wholesalers can also vary by country. In some countries, wholesalers provide a warehouse function, taking orders from retailers and shipping appropriate quantities to them. Wholesalers in Japan provide the basic wholesale functions but also share risk with retailers by providing financing, product development, and even occasional managerial and marketing skills.

RETAILERS. Retailers, the final members of the consumer distribution channel, purchase products for resale to consumers. The size and accessibility of retail channels vary greatly by country. In 1997, the population per retailer in Europe varied from a low of only forty-eight people per retailer in Poland to 564 people in Russia.[5] Japan has a large number of retailers, with thirteen per one thousand inhabitants, versus six in Europe or the United States. For example, in Japan, Shiseido, a maker of cosmetics, has twenty-five thousand outlets selling only its products, and Matsushita has nineteen thousand electrical appliance stores.[6] Until recently, all retailing in China was conducted through state-owned stores. As China prepared to enter the World Trade Organization (WTO), there has been a 27 percent decline in state-owned retail and wholesale enterprises and a 340 percent increase in privately owned retail and wholesale enterprises.[7] The global marketer must evaluate the available retailers in a country and develop a strategy around the existing structure.

DEVELOPING A GLOBAL DISTRIBUTION STRATEGY

The environmental forces of culture, physical environment, and the legal/political system, combined with the unique structure of wholesale and retail distribution systems, complicate the development of a global distribution strategy. A distribution strategy is one part of the marketing mix, and it needs to be consistent with other aspects of the marketing strategy: product policies, pricing strategy, and communications strategy (see Figure 15.3).

Figure 15.3: Distribution Strategy

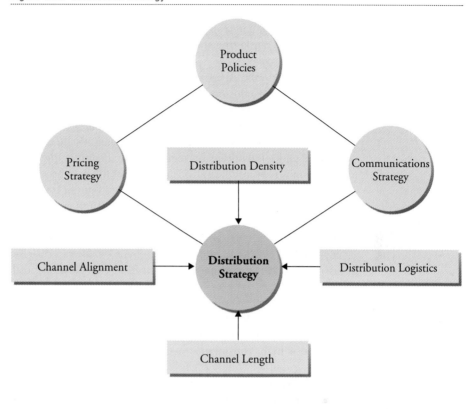

Within the structure of the marketing mix, the global marketer makes distribution decisions about each of the following variables:

1. *Distribution density.* Density refers to the amount of exposure or coverage desired for a product, particularly the number of sales outlets required to provide adequate coverage of the entire market.
2. *Channel length.* The concept of channel length involves the number of intermediaries involved in bringing a product to the market.
3. *Channel alignment.* The area of alignment deals with the structure of the chosen channel members to achieve a unified strategy.
4. *Distribution logistics.* Logistics involves the physical flow of products as they move through the channel.

These four decision areas cannot be approached independently. The decisions are interrelated, and they need to be consistent with other aspects of the marketing strategy. Although it is important to evaluate the distribution strategy logically, marketing managers must often work with an international distribution structure that previous managers have organized and put in place. That existing system may limit the flexibility of a company to change and grow; nevertheless, a creative marketer can usually find opportunities for circumventing or reorganizing the current arrangement. The following sections deal primarily with a company's distribution policies, dependence on distribution-specific variables, and the company's relationship to the other elements of the marketing strategy.

DISTRIBUTION DENSITY

The number of sales outlets or distribution points required for the efficient marketing of a firm's products is referred to as the *density of distribution.* The distribution density depends on the shopping or buying habits of the average customer. An optimum distribution network requires the marketer to examine how customers select dealers and retail outlets by segment. For consumer goods, an *extensive,* or wide, distribution is required if the consumer is not likely to exert much shopping effort. Such products, also called convenience goods, are bought frequently and in nearby outlets. Consumers shop for other products, such as appliances or clothing, by visiting two or more stores; these products require a more limited, or *selective,* distribution, with fewer outlets per market area. For specialty goods, products that inspire consumer loyalty to specific brands, a limited, or *exclusive,* distribution is required. It is assumed that the customer will search for the desired product and will not accept substitutes.

The key to distribution density, then, is the consumer's shopping behavior, or the effort expended to locate a desired item. This behavior may vary greatly, however, from country to country. In many developed countries, for example, where per capita income is high, consumers shop for many regular-use items in supermarkets, drugstores, and other widely accessible outlets. In other countries, particularly some with a much lower per capita income, the purchase of such items is likely to be a less routine affair, causing consumers to exert more effort to locate the items. This situation allows a less extensive distribution of products. Therefore, the international marketer must assess the shopping behavior of consumers in various countries. Yaohan, a large Japanese retailer, planned to open one thousand stores in China by 2005, but it has put growth plans on hold because it seems most shoppers in China are only window shopping. Although China has 1.2 billion potential customers, only 120 million urban Chinese have sufficient income (over $1,000 per year) to afford the packaged soap or prepared foods on Yaohan's shelves.[8]

Where consumers buy certain products also varies a great deal from country to country. In Germany, for example, contact lens solution is found only in stores that sell eyeglasses; in France, it is also found in most drugstores. Although magazines are sold in many grocery stores in the United States, in the United Kingdom, they are sold almost exclusively through news agents. It is important for marketers to find out early in the distribution analysis where consumers buy the types of products the firm plans to market.

Retailing is exploding in many parts of Asia, where a large portion of the population is crossing the income threshold at which they start to buy entirely new categories of goods, such as packaged foods, televisions, or mopeds. This phenomenon, called "magic moments," has hit Taiwan, Indonesia, Thailand, Malaysia, and China. When a country crosses the magic-moments threshold, distribution systems start to improve with modern stores. Ito-Yokado, which owns 7-Eleven, has been very successful. With twenty-three thousand 7-Eleven stores in 120 countries, the company continues to innovate. In Japan, where Ito-Yokado operates nine thousand stores, each store is restocked with fresh produce, meat, and fish every afternoon. This innovation has resulted in the inventory being turned over fifty times per year.[9] In China, with a population of 1.3 billion people, the market for cosmetics and toiletries is growing rapidly. From 1996 to 2000, the cosmetics and toiletries market grew by 46 percent. The fastest growing sectors included hair care, skin care, and color cosmetics.[10]

In the industrial sector, differences in buyer behavior or in the use of a particular product may require changes in distribution density. Industrial products applications are more uniform around the world as a result of similar customer needs and use conditions; thus, what constitutes capital equipment in one country typically is also classified as capital equipment in another. Differences may exist, however, among the decision makers. In the United States, for instance, radiology supply products are sold to hospitals and radiology departments through hospital supply distributors. In France, however, patients must pick up radiology supplies by prescription from a pharmacy before visiting the radiology department at the hospital. In this latter case, radiology supplies have to be presold to physicians and stocked at pharmacies to be successful, which is the same strategy pursued by pharmaceutical firms. Of course, the necessary distribution in France (selling to both physicians and pharmacies) is much more extensive than it is in the United States, where only hospitals are channel members.

CHANNEL LENGTH

The number of intermediaries directly involved in the physical or ownership path of a product, from the manufacturer to the customer, is indicative of the channel length. Long channels have several intermediaries, whereas short, or direct, channels have few or no intermediaries. Channel length is usually influenced by three factors: (1) a product's distribution density, (2) the average order quantities, and (3) the availability of channel members. Products with extensive distribution, or large numbers of final sales points, tend to have longer channels of distribution. Similarly, as the average order quantity decreases, products move through longer channels, with each stage of the distribution combining multiple items to make up for small shipments of single items.

Distribution density affects channel length, so it is clear that the same factors that influence distribution density—namely, the shopping behaviors of consumers—influence channel length. The average order quantity often depends on the purchasing power or income level of a particular customer group. In countries with lower income levels, people often buy food on a daily basis at nearby small stores. This contrasts sharply with more affluent consumers, who can afford to buy food or staples for one week or even a month and who don't mind traveling some distance to do this more infrequent type of grocery shopping. In the first case, a longer channel is required, whereas a shorter channel is adequate in the latter case. The type of distributors available in a country affects the channel length.

Also, the culture may demand a specific type of channel member. Japan is known for its lengthy, complex channels, which increase the cost of goods to consumers. Seiko Epson bypassed Japanese channel members and began a direct sales effort for its NEC and IBM-compatible PCs. Following the lead of Dell Computer, Seiko

Epson hoped to attract consumers by offering significant savings through its direct marketing effort.[11] Delta Computer, a Japanese company, also did very well with a direct sales approach in Japan, moving into second place overall behind Compaq and beating larger rivals such as IBM and NEC.[12]

Korean automaker Daewoo decided to sell directly to consumers rather than go through traditional dealers. It equipped its sales outlets with a multimedia touch-screen kiosk that allows consumers to "build" the car they want on the screen. This approach has positioned Daewoo as a manufacturer/dealer offering a hassle-free car-buying experience. In the United Kingdom, Daewoo representatives took cars directly to consumers' homes and completed the entire transaction in the customer's living room on a laptop computer.[13] When Ford began building the Ikon car in India, it encouraged European parts suppliers to establish joint ventures in India to reduce the distance and complexity of shipping to India and to meet the local content required in India.[14]

CHANNEL ALIGNMENT

One of the most difficult tasks of marketing is to get various channel members to coordinate their actions so that a unified approach can be achieved. The longer the channel, the more difficult it becomes to maintain a coordinated and integrated approach. On a global level, the coordinating task is made all the more difficult because the company organizing the channel may be a long distance from the distribution system, with little influence over the local scene. In each country, the strongest channel member will be able to dictate policies to the other channel members, although situations will vary by country. The international company will find it much easier to control the distribution channel if a local subsidiary with a strong sales force exists. In countries where the company has no local presence and depends on independent distributors, control is likely to fall to the independent distributor. This loss of control may be further aggravated if the international company's sales volume represents only a small fraction of the local distributor's business. Of course, the opposite will be true when a high percentage of the volume consists of the international corporation's products.

To achieve maximum efficiency in a channel of distribution, one participant must emerge as the channel captain, or dominating member. Differences exist among countries as to who typically emerges as the dominating member. In the United States, for example, the once-strong wholesalers have become less influential, with manufacturers now playing the dominant role in some channels. Large retailers like Home Depot or Wal-Mart have more and more often become channel captains in the United States. In Japan, on the other hand, wholesalers continue to dominate the channel structure. In many developing countries, independent distributors are dominant because they are the only authorized importers.

Some companies find it necessary to acquire the channel captain to increase the size of a market. For example, in 1994, Nike acquired Nissho Iwai Corp., the Japanese trading house that had been distributing Nike products in Japan. Nike felt that acquiring its Japanese distributor and converting Nissho Iwai to a wholly owned subsidiary would give Nike the increased control and expertise to penetrate the Japanese market more deeply.[15]

A different approach was chosen by Caterpillar, the large U.S. manufacturer of earthmoving equipment, for its entry into Japan. At first, the company's joint venture partner, Mitsubishi, suggested marketing equipment through existing channels. In Japan, manufacturers sell through large trading houses that resell and provide financing to dealers. The dealers are relatively small and leave parts inventory and service to independent repair shops. Caterpillar preferred to market its equipment through large, independent dealers that not only sold but also serviced the equipment and maintained a sufficient parts inventory. Caterpillar recognized that its distribution strategy was a critical global strength that was difficult for competitors to match, so it invested heavily in building and training its dealers. Shin Caterpillar Mitsubishi, the 50-50 joint venture between Caterpillar and Mitsubishi Heavy Industries, produces earthmoving and construction equipment in its factory at Sagamihara, Japan. Shin Caterpillar Mitsubishi is the leading supplier of earthmoving and construction equipment in Japan and will celebrate its fortieth anniversary in 2003.[16]

DISTRIBUTION LOGISTICS

Distribution logistics focuses on the physical movement of goods through the channels. Distribution logistics, an extremely important part of the distribution system, is discussed in detail later in this chapter.

FACTORS INFLUENCING THE SELECTION OF CHANNEL MEMBERS

After developing a distribution strategy, a marketer then needs to identify and select appropriate distribution partners to support the overall distribution strategy. The selection of distribution partners is an extremely important decision because the partner will often assume a portion of or the entire marketing responsibility for a set of markets. A poor decision can lead to lackluster performance. Because of local laws, it is often expensive or sometimes impossible to change a distribution partner. For example, in 1992, PepsiCo went through a year-long court battle to terminate its twenty-two-year contract with Perrier to bottle and distribute Pepsi in France. PepsiCo contended that Perrier had underperformed and had let Pepsi-Cola's share decline from 17 percent to 7 percent over the previous ten years. In December 1992 the two companies agreed that Pepsi would regain the right to market and distribute Pepsi in France, while Perrier would continue to produce and bottle Pepsi-Cola in France.[17] Also, the distribution partner is usually involved in the physical movement (logistics) of products to the customers. Therefore, the success of a firm's international efforts depends on the partners it selects. Several factors influence the selection of distribution partners. Those that have significant effect are:

1. Cost
2. Capital requirement
3. Product and product line
4. Control
5. Coverage
6. Synergy

COST

Channel costs fall into three categories: initial costs, maintenance costs, and logistics costs. The *initial costs* include all the costs of locating and setting up the channel, such as executive time and travel to locate and select channel members, cost of negotiating an agreement with channel members, and the capital cost of setting up the channel. (The *capital cost or requirement* is discussed separately in the next segment of this chapter.) The *maintenance costs* of the channel include the salaries of the company's salespeople and sales managers, travel expenses, and the cost of auditing and controlling channel operations, local advertising expenses, and the profit margin of the intermediaries. The *logistics costs* comprise the transportation expenses, storage costs, the cost of breaking bulk shipments into smaller lot sizes, and the cost for customs paperwork.

Although predicting all of these various costs when selecting different channel members is difficult, it is necessary to estimate the cost of various alternatives. High distribution costs usually result in higher prices at the consumer level, which may hamper entry into a new market. Companies often establish direct channels, hoping to reduce distribution cost. Unfortunately, most of the functions of the channel cannot be eliminated, so these costs eventually show up anyway. A study of five different international channels of distribution found that the least profitable is exporting directly to the retailers in the host country. The most profitable channel is selling to a distributor in a country that has its own marketing channels.[18]

CAPITAL REQUIREMENT

The capital cost of different channel alternatives can be very high. The capital cost includes the cost for inventories, the cost of goods in transit, accounts receivable, and inventories on consignment. The capital cost is offset by the cash-flow patterns from a channel alternative. For example, an import distributor will often pay for the goods when they are received, before they are sold to the retailer or industrial firm. On the other hand, an agent may not receive payment until the goods reach the industrial customer or retailer. This situation is also true of direct sales efforts. The establishment of a direct sales channel often requires the maximum investment, whereas use of distributors often reduces the investment required. The capital cost of various distribution channels affects the company's return on investment. In the early stages of the life cycle of organizations (see Chapter 16), companies often export through a distributor or agent because they cannot afford the capital cost of setting up a direct sales effort. Establishing its own channels can be a very expensive exercise for a company in many countries. For example, Wal-Mart evaluated the Japanese retail market and determined that the cost of locating new stores, along with developing the supplier relationships, would be very expensive. So Wal-Mart purchased 6.1 percent of Seiyu, with an option to acquire up to 66.7 percent over the next five years. This arrangement can give Wal-Mart a majority share of Seiyu's four hundred stores in Japan.[19]

PRODUCT AND PRODUCT LINE

The nature of a product can affect channel selection. If the product is perishable or has a short shelf life, then the manufacturer is forced to use shorter channels to get the product to the consumer faster. Delta Dairy, a Greek producer of dairy products and chilled fruit juices, was faced with increased transportation costs of shipping from Greece to France when the United Nations banned transit across the former Yugoslavia. In addition to a 25 percent increase in production costs, Delta lost five days of product shelf life, so it set up production in Switzerland to shorten the distance to the French market.[20]

A technical product often requires direct sales or highly technical channel partners. For example, Index Technology of Cambridge, Massachusetts, sells a sophisticated software product, called computer-aided systems engineering, that automates the development of software systems. The company entered the United Kingdom and Australia with a direct sales effort, but it used distributors to avoid start-up costs in France, Germany, and Scandinavia. Insufficient revenues from distributors led the company to set up its own sales efforts in France and Germany and to purchase the distributor in Scandinavia. The highly sophisticated nature of the product required a direct sales effort. Nonperishable or generic, unsophisticated products, such as batteries, that are available in many types of retail stores may be distributed through a long channel that reaches many different types of retailers.

The size of the product line also affects the selection of channel members. A broader product line is more desirable for channel members. A distributor or dealer is more likely to stock a broad product line than a single item. Limited product lines must often be sold through agents. If a manufacturer has a very broad, complete line, it is easier to justify the cost of a more direct channel. With more products to sell, it is easier to generate a high average order on each sales call. With a limited product line, an agent or distributor will group one firm's products together with products from other companies to increase the average order size.

CONTROL

Each type of channel arrangement offers a different level of control for the manufacturer. With a direct sales force, a manufacturer can control price, promotion, amount of effort, and type of retail outlet used. If these factors are important, the increased level of control may offset the increased cost of a direct sales force. Longer channels, particularly with distributors who take title to goods, often result in little or no control. In many cases, a company may not know who is ultimately buying the product.

Limited control is not necessarily a disadvantage, however. If the volume of sales is adequate, the manufacturer may not necessarily care where the product is used. Also, a manufacturer can increase its level of market knowledge, its influence on channel members, and its channel control by increasing its presence in the market. For example, the manager of international sales and marketing may be located in Europe and spend all of his or her time traveling with distributor salespeople.

COVERAGE

Coverage refers to the geographic coverage that a manufacturer desires. Although coverage is usually easy to obtain in major metropolitan areas, gaining adequate coverage in smaller cities or sparsely populated areas can be difficult. Selection of one channel member over another may be influenced by the respective market coverage. To determine an agent's, broker's, or distributor's coverage, the following must be determined: (1) the location of the sales offices, (2) the salesperson's home base, and (3) the previous year's sales by geographic location. The location of sales offices indicates where efforts are focused. Salespeople generally have the best penetration near their home base. Past sales clearly indicate the channel member's success in each geographic area.

SYNERGY

The choice of channel members or partners can sometimes be influenced by the existence of complementary skills that can increase the total output of the distribution system. This situation normally occurs where the potential distributor partner has some skill or expertise that allows quicker access to the market. For example, when Compaq entered the international personal computer market, it decided to sell only through a network of strong authorized dealers. While Compaq focused on developing market applications such as sales force automation, computer-aided design, and office productivity, it used the dealers to penetrate the marketplace. Compaq's international sales grew from $20 million in 1984 to $5 billion in 1996 through the combination of marketing and technical expertise from Compaq and sales and implementation expertise from the authorized dealers.

LOCATING AND SELECTING GLOBAL CHANNEL PARTNERS

Building a global distribution system normally takes one to three years. The process involves a series of steps, which are listed in Table 15.1. The critical steps in developing a successful system are locating and selecting distribution channel partners. The development of a global distribution strategy in terms of distribution density, channel length, channel alignment, and distribution logistics establishes a framework for the "ideal" distribution partners. The company's preference regarding key factors that influence the selection of channel partners (cost, capital requirements, product, control, coverage, and synergy) is used with the distribution strategy to establish criteria for the selection of partners. The strategy normally focuses on the selection of one or two types of channel partners—for example, an export manager's company and import distributors.

Selection criteria include geographic coverage, managerial ability, financial stability, annual volume, reputation, and so on. The following sources are useful in locating possible distribution partners:

1. *U.S. Department of Commerce.* The Agent Distributor Service is a customized service of the U.S. Department of Commerce that locates distributors and agents interested in a certain product line. The web sites are: http://www.doc.gov/ International_Trade/Export_Assistance/; http://www.export.gov/; http://www. trade. gov/td/tic/resources/index.html; http://www.usatrade.gov/.

Table 15.1 Process of Establishing a Global Distribution System

1. Develop a distribution strategy
2. Establish criteria for selecting distribution channel partners
3. Locate potential distribution channel partners
4. Solicit the interest of distributors
5. Screen and select distribution channel partners
6. Negotiate agreements

2. *Banks.* If the firm's bank has foreign branches, they may be able to locate distributors in other countries.
3. *Directories.* Country directories of distributors or specialized directories, such as those listing computer distributors, can be helpful.
4. *Trade shows.* Exhibiting at an international trade show or just attending a trade show exposes managers to a large number of distributors and their salespeople. Many government agencies help with international trade fairs.
5. *Competitor's distribution partners.* Sometimes a competitor's distributor may be interested in switching product lines.
6. *Consultants.* Some international marketing consultants specialize in locating distributors.
7. *Associations.* Associations of international intermediaries or country associations of intermediaries can offer assistance; for example, Japan has numerous industry associations. A list of international associations can be found at: http://fita.org/aboutfita.html.
8. *Foreign consulates.* Most countries post commercial attachés at their embassies or at separate consulates; these individuals are helpful in locating agents and/or distributors in their home countries.

After compiling a list of possible distribution partners, the firm may send each a letter with product literature and distribution requirements. The prospective distributors who are interested in the firm's product line can be asked to supply relevant information, such as lines currently carried, annual volume, number of salespeople, geographic territory covered, credit and bank references, physical facilities, relationship with the local government, and knowledge of English or other relevant languages. Firms that respond should be checked against the original selection criteria. Before making a final decision, a manufacturer's representative should visit the country and talk to the industrial end users or retailers to narrow the field to the strongest two or three contenders. While in the country, the manufacturer's representative should meet and evaluate the distribution partner candidates before making a final decision.

MANAGING GLOBAL DISTRIBUTION

Selecting the most suitable channel participants and gaining access to the market are extremely important steps in achieving an integrated and responsive distribution channel. Without proper motivation of and control over channel participants, however, sales may remain unsatisfactory for the foreign marketer. This section discusses the steps for gaining the full cooperation of all channel members and thus ensuring the flow of the firm's products through the distribution channel.

MOTIVATING CHANNEL PARTICIPANTS

Keeping channel participants motivated is an important aspect of global distribution policies. Financial incentives in the form of higher than average gross margins can be very powerful inducements, particularly for the management of independent distributors, wholesalers, and retailers. The expected gross margins are influenced by the cultural history of that channel. For example, if a certain type of retailer usually gets a

50 percent margin and the firm offers 40 percent, the effort may be less than expected. Inviting channel members to annual conferences and introductions of new products is also effective. By extending help to the management of distributorships in areas such as inventory control, collections, advertising, and so on, a firm can build goodwill that later can be advantageous. Special programs can also be instituted to train or motivate the channel members' sales forces.

Programs for motivating foreign independent intermediaries are likely to succeed if monetary incentives are considered along with efforts that help make the channel members more efficient and competitive. Of course, prosperous intermediaries is also in the interest of the international firm. These programs or policies are particularly important in the case of independents who distribute products on a nonexclusive basis. They are often beleaguered by the principals of the other products that they carry; each attempts to get the greatest possible attention from the distributor for its own purposes. Therefore, the international firm must have policies that make sure the channel members devote sufficient effort to its products.

The motivation of channel partners and the amount of effort devoted to the firm's product line are enhanced by a continuous flow of two-way information between the manufacturer and the distributor. The amount of effort an international firm needs to expend depends on the marketing strategy for that market. For example, if the firm uses extensive advertising to pull products through a channel, the intermediary may be expected only to take orders and deliver the product, without expending any real sales effort. If the marketing strategy depends on the channel member to develop the market or to push the product through the channel, then a significant sales effort is required. The manufacturer should send letters, public relations releases, product news, and so on, to encourage attention to its product line and reduce conflict as much as possible. More intense contact between the export manufacturer and the distributor is expected to result in better performance by the distributor.

In addition to telephone and mail communication, periodic visits to distribution partners can have a positive effect on their motivation and control. Visits can also provide other benefits. By visiting the distribution partner, the firm can resolve any difficulties in person. Also, sales volumes can be reviewed, and the most important products or types of customers can be emphasized. It is helpful to travel with a channel member salesperson to gain knowledge of the marketplace and to evaluate the skills of the salesperson. The most important benefit of a visit to the channel member is that it gives a clear message that the channel member's performance is important to the firm. Visits strengthen the personal relationship between the manufacturer and the channel member.

During these personal visits, the manufacturer can identify other ways to help and support the channel member. Strong advertising support through either national advertising or cooperative advertising can help strengthen the manufacturer's consumer franchise. Effective advertising makes it easier for the channel member to sell the manufacturer's products, which leads to increased sales and often more attention devoted to the product line.

Beware of strategies that cause conflict between manufacturers and channel members. The most common causes of channel conflict are (1) bypassing channels to sell directly to large customers, (2) oversaturating a market with too many dealers and/or distributors, (3) establishing too many levels in the distribution system (that is, requiring smaller distributors to buy from larger ones), and (4) opening new discount channels that offer the same goods at lower prices.[21] Research has shown that efforts by manufacturers to train and educate dealers in developing countries lead to increased revenue.[22] Caterpillar has faced the strong Japanese competitor Komatsu in the earthmoving equipment world market. Caterpillar found that dealer training developed a strong competitive advantage that was difficult for Komatsu to copy. In fact, during the pilot of the dealer sales training program, participating dealers increased revenue by 102 percent.[23]

CONTROLLING CHANNEL PARTICIPANTS

Although motivated intermediaries will expend the necessary effort on an international company's products, there is generally no assurance that these efforts will be channeled in the right direction. Therefore, the company should exert enough control over channel members to help guarantee that they interpret and execute the company's marketing strategies. The firm wants to be sure that the local intermediaries price the products according to the company's policies. The same can be said for sales, advertising, and service policies. The company's reputation in a local market can be tarnished when independent intermediaries handle local distribution ineffectively or inefficiently, so international companies must monitor the performance of local channel members closely. After the takeover of United Distillers by Guinness, the company reorganized to become a worldwide marketer of high-quality branded alcoholic drinks. In 1986, 75 percent of United Distillers' volume was sold through 1,304 distributors, and the company had very little control over the distribution of its products. By 1990, the number of distributors was reduced to 470, and through acquisition or joint ventures, United Distillers had gained direct control over 80 percent of its distribution.[24] In Japan, in 1998, the company reduced the number of its distributors to one, closed that one unit, and moved the business into a joint venture that had been set up in 1987 with the equity participation of Moet of France and Jardine of Hong Kong.[25]

One way to exert influence over international channel members is to spell out the specific responsibilities, including minimum annual sales, of each one in the distribution agreement. Attainment of the sales goal can be required for renewal of the contract. Also, the awarding of exclusive distribution rights can be used to increase control. Typically, business is channeled through one intermediary in one geographic area only, raising the firm's importance to the intermediary.

Frequently, exclusive rights are coupled with a prohibition against carrying directly competing products. The exclusive distributor's leverage is knowledge and expertise in the market. The leverage of the manufacturer is the patent on the product, the brand name, and possible economies of scale. Of course, the exclusive distributor can become too powerful and even evolve from a collaborator into a competitor. Many international companies limit the distribution rights to short time periods with periodic renewal. Caution is advised, however, because cancellation of distribution rights is frequently subject to local laws that prohibit a sudden termination.

Although termination of a distributor or agent for nonperformance or poor performance is a relatively simple action in the United States, termination of international channel members can be very costly in many parts of the world. In some countries, the termination of an agent may cost a multiple of the annual gross profits plus the value of the agent's investment, plus all kinds of additional payments. In other countries, termination compensation for agents and distributors can include the value of any goodwill plus expenses in developing the business, plus the amount of compensation claimed by discharged employees who worked on the product line. The minimum termination notices are frequently enforced. As a result, termination of a channel member can be a costly, painful process governed in almost all cases by local laws that tend to protect and compensate the channel member. Nissan of Japan became involved in a legal battle with its exclusive U.K. distributor, owned by British entrepreneur Octav Botnar, of twenty-one years when the company sent a fax to terminate the agreement at the end of 1990. Nissan Japan said there was a complete breakdown in the companies' business relationship which left no trust between them. The court case was dropped when Mr. Botnar was exposed for massive tax fraud in 1991 and departed the U.K. to live in exile in Switzerland. Nissan Japan formed Nissan GB in 1992 to service the 400,000 existing warrantee holders and to establish a new network of dealers.[26]

GAINING ACCESS TO DISTRIBUTION CHANNELS

Gaining access to distribution channels may well be the most formidable challenge in global marketing. Decisions on product designs, communications strategies, and pricing can be very complex and can pose difficult choices, but once a company has made the choices, their implementation requires significant management expertise and resources. The distribution system is critical to implementing the marketing strategy.

Entry into a market can be accomplished through various channel members (described earlier in the chapter; see Figure 15.1). Often, however, the most logical channel member already has a relationship with one of a firm's competitors, thereby limiting the firm's access and posing special challenges to the global marketer. This section illustrates alternatives available to companies that encounter difficulties in convincing channel members to carry their products.

THE LOCKED-UP CHANNEL

A channel is considered locked up when a newcomer cannot easily convince any channel member to participate, despite the fact that both market and economic reasons suggest otherwise. Channel members customarily decide on a case-by-case basis what products they should add to or drop from their line. Retailers typically select products that they expect to sell easily and in volume, and they can be expected to switch sources when better opportunities arise. Similarly, wholesalers and distributors compete for retail accounts or industrial users on economic terms. They can expect to entice a prospective client to switch by buying from a new source that can offer a better deal. Likewise, manufacturers compete for wholesale accounts with the expectation that channel members can be convinced to purchase from any given manufacturer if the offer exceeds those made by competitors.

Barriers often limit a wholesaler's flexibility in adding or dropping a particular line. The distributor may have an agreement not to sell competitive products, or its business may include a significant volume from one manufacturer, a relationship that it does not want to risk upsetting. In Japan, relationships among manufacturers, wholesalers, and retailers are long-standing and do not allow channel participants to change allegiance quickly to another source because of a superior product or price. Japanese channel members develop strong personal ties, and a sense of economic dependence develops. These close ties make it very difficult for any would-be participant to break channel-member relationships. In some cases, most existing wholesale or retail outlets may be committed already to business relationships, therefore a newcomer to the market may not find qualified channel participants.

Cultural forces may not be the only influences in blocking a channel of distribution. Competitors, domestic or foreign, may try to obstruct the entry of a new company, or the members of a channel may not be willing to take any risks by pioneering unknown products. In all of these instances, the result is a locked-up channel that stifles access to markets. Trade friction between the United States and Japan led to a bilateral accord on opening Japan's market for foreign cars and parts. Nissan started selling Ford cars through Tokyo Nissan, its largest dealer. The bottom line so far has not been pretty: Nissan has sold only four hundred Ford models and has accumulated debts of $2.8 million. Sales of foreign cars in Japan doubled from 5 percent to 10 percent between 1990 and 1995. Japanese dealers worried, however, that their brand-conscious consumers would not purchase Ford or GM cars, which are not as well known in Japan as other foreign cars like Mercedes and BMW.[27] When American Standard, the world's largest supplier of plumbing fixtures, tried to enter the Korean market, it found itself locked out of the normal channel distributors, who were controlled by local manufacturers. American Standard looked for an alternative distribution channel that served the building trade. It found Home Center, one of the largest suppliers of home building materials and appliances. With a local factory, American Standard circumvented the locked channels successfully.[28]

Manufacturers in the United States are not novices at dealing with the locked-up channel. Marketers of consumer goods developed the pull-type communications strategy to sidestep unresponsive channel members by concentrating advertising directly on consumers. Manufacturers of industrial products can usually contact independent manufacturers' representatives or agents to gain quick access to users. To use the same strategies abroad requires equally free access to communications channels in other countries. However, this access is restricted in some countries (see Chapter 12) by government regulations that forbid television or radio advertising or allow only limited availability of these media. In the case of industrial markets, the frequent entry of new entrepreneurs as independent agents is also considerably less prevalent.

ALTERNATIVE ENTRY APPROACHES

With fewer chances to entice unresponsive channels abroad, global marketers have developed new approaches to the difficult situation of gaining access to distribution channels.

PIGGYBACKING. When a company does not find any channel partners with sufficient interest in pioneering new products, the practice of piggybacking may offer an alternative option. *Piggybacking* is an arrangement with another company that sells to the same customer segment. The second company takes on the new products as if it were the manufacturer. The products retain the name of the manufacturer, and both partners normally sign a multiyear contract to provide for continuity. The new company is, in essence, piggybacking its products on the shoulders of the established company's sales force.

Under a piggyback arrangement, the manufacturer retains control over marketing strategy, particularly pricing, positioning, and advertising. The partner (the second company) acts as a "rented" sales force only. Of course, this arrangement is quite different from the private-label strategy, whereby the manufacturer supplies products to a marketer that places its own brand name on each product. This approach has become quite common in the pharmaceutical industry, in which rival companies sometimes get other firms involved for the launch of a particular new drug. Warner-Lambert, one of the leading pharmaceutical companies, launched its leading cholesterol-lowering drug Lipitor in the United States with the help of Pfizer. The drug has become one of the most successful drugs ever with sales of $7.4 billion in 2002, expected to reach $10 billion in 2005. Warner-Lambert and Pfizer merged in 2000.[29] Coca-Cola and Procter and Gamble (P&G) decided to work together and combine their expertise in snacks and juice drinks. The partnership will allow P&G to piggyback on Coca-Cola's global distribution system, while giving Coca-Cola access to P&G's snacks like Pringles and juices like Sunny Delight.[30]

JOINT VENTURES. When two companies agree jointly to form a new legal entity, it is called a *joint venture* (see Chapter 9). Such operations have been quite common in the area of joint production. Our interest here is restricted to joint ventures in which distribution is the primary objective. Normally, such companies are formed between a local firm with existing market access and a foreign firm that would like to market its products in the local firm's country, where it has no existing market access. One of the best ways to enter the Japanese market is through a joint venture with a Japanese partner that is in a similar but not competitive field. Many such joint ventures have been signed between Japanese firms and foreign companies eager to enter the Japanese market. Through access to the distribution channel, the Japanese partner either acts as a sales agent or provides contacts for the joint venture's sales force.

Many such joint ventures expand into production, although the original intention of the foreign partner clearly was to gain access to the distribution system. Kodak had competed with Fuji and Konica in the Japanese market for years, reaching only a 10 percent market share. To increase its market share in 2001, Kodak Japan began an alliance with Shashinya-san, a photo shop chain.[31] To enter the Brazilian appliance (white goods) market, Whirlpool formed a partnership with Brasmotor, a local manufacturer in São Paulo, purchasing 31 percent of the company. The partnership paid off, with Whirlpool reaching 39 percent of the white goods market in Brazil in 1996.[32]

The Mexican beer market is controlled by two companies—Femsa, with a 49 percent share, and Modelo, with 51 percent. These two domestic producers had tied up the retail outlets with exclusivity constraints, which explains why Anheuser-Busch decided to enter Mexico through a joint venture with Modelo rather than trying to build a distribution system from scratch. Positioned as the market leader, Anheuser-Busch continues to rely on this joint venture for distribution in Mexico.[33] Carlsburg of Denmark has used joint ventures as a way to enter markets. For example, Carlsberg owns 50 percent of Baltic Beverage Holding AB, which had twelve breweries in the Baltic countries, Ukraine, and Russia, and was also one of Europe's leading brands (Baltic) by volume.[34] Carlsberg also owns 50 percent of a brewery in Laos and has a joint venture in Korea. In 2002, Carlsberg formed a joint venture with Chang Beverages Pte Ltd of Thailand, which has 70 percent of the Thai beer market. The joint venture combines the strength of both companies in Asia.[35] Danone, the French water, biscuit, and yogurt company, had difficulty distributing its Evian water in the United States, until it reached an agreement with Coca-Cola to distribute Evian there.[36]

To build one's own distribution system is not only costly but also requires patience and time. Until recently, the Japanese retail market was highly regulated, with new stores over five hundred square meters needing permission from local store owners to open. Although now weakened, the Large-Scale Retail Stores Law remains an important element for foreign marketers in Japan. To overcome local hurdles, the U.S. retailer Toys "R" Us started a completely new joint venture with Den Fujita, the founder of the McDonald's chain in Japan. The joint venture prospered, and by 1998 Toys "R" Us had sixty-four stores in Japan.[37] Through the joint venture, Toys "R" Us ceded some equity to its local partner. On the other hand, it obtained invaluable help in navigating the complex Japanese retail legislation.

ORIGINAL EQUIPMENT MANUFACTURERS (OEMS). When an international manufacturer signs a supply agreement with a domestic or local firm to sell the international manufacturer's products but under the established brand name of the local firm, the arrangement is termed an *OEM agreement* (or *private labeling,* for consumer products). The foreign company uses the already existing distribution network of the local company, whereas the local company gains a chance to broaden its product lines. Japanese companies have been particularly adept at using the OEM strategy to build whole alliances of captive markets. In the computer field, Japanese companies have adopted strategies that differ from those customarily chosen by U.S. computer manufacturers. Hewlett-Packard (HP), a leader in the server market used for Internet applications, has had a long-standing OEM relationship with NEC, a major Japanese computer company. Under this arrangement, NEC purchases HP servers and related technology and resells them under the NEC name in Japan.[38] This relationship allows HP to sell in the vast Japanese market at a higher volume than it could on its own, while NEC gains access to more superior products than it might be able to develop alone.

Distributing in foreign markets under OEM agreements has its disadvantages. The local OEM puts its own label on the imported product, so the international company does not gain any access to local customers and therefore finds it difficult to achieve a strong identity in the market. This reliance on the local OEM can also pose problems when the local company's performance declines. An excellent example is the situation faced by Mitsubishi International Corporation, a large Japanese automobile manufacturer that supplied Chrysler Corporation with small cars under an OEM agreement. With Chrysler's weak financial situation from 1983 to 1985, Mitsubishi would have preferred to sell its cars directly to the U.S. market under Mitsubishi's brand name. As long as the agreement was in effect, however, Mitsubishi was prohibited from selling its cars directly, and its fortune in the U.S. market continued to depend on Chrysler's efforts. The OEM arrangement allows a company to reach a high volume more quickly by sacrificing independence and control over its own distribution system. Of course, a company selecting this route is partially motivated by the cost savings from not having to build its own distribution system.

ACQUISITIONS. Acquiring an existing company can give a foreign entrant immediate access to a distribution system. Although it requires a substantial amount of capital, operating results tend to be better than those with a new joint venture, which often brings initial losses. It is often less important to find an acquisition candidate with a healthy financial outlook or top products than one with a good relationship with wholesale and retail outlets. A good example of the acquisition strategy used for gaining access to distribution channels was Merck's purchase of 51 percent of Japan's Banyu pharmaceutical company.[39] Merck has since been able to expand its Japanese staff to four hundred.[40]

The Japanese car market is a difficult one to enter for foreign manufacturers. Ford Motor Company overcame the problem through a joint venture with Mazda; purchase of Autorama, a nationwide distributor; and an alliance with Nissan to sell Ford cars through their dealers. General Motors acquired 67 percent of Daewoo, the Korean car manufacturer, to gain access to the Korean car market, as well as access in India and Poland, where Daewoo has major operations.[41]

GLOBAL SUPPLY CHAIN MANAGEMENT

The logistics system, including the physical distribution of manufactured products, involves planning, implementing, and controlling the physical flow of materials and finished products from points of origin to points of use. On a global scale, the task becomes more complex because so many external variables have an impact on that flow of materials or products. As geographical distances to foreign markets grow, competitive advantages are often derived from a more effective structuring of the logistics system, by either saving time or costs or increasing a firm's reliability. The emergence of logistics as a means of gaining competitive advantage means that companies are focusing increased attention on this vital area. Many manufacturers and retailers are restructuring their logistics efforts and disbanding their in-house distribution divisions in favor of outside logistics specialists.

Logistics is a capital- and labor-intensive function outside the core business of most companies. Logistics has become increasingly complex and, for many companies, it represents 16 to 35 percent of total revenues. A survey by CapGemini Ernst & Young found that information sharing between suppliers and customers improved inventory strategies and innovation, and resulted in significant reductions of total logistics and inventory costs.[42]

LOGISTICS DECISION AREAS

In this section, we describe the objectives of a global logistics system and the individual organizational operations that have to be managed and integrated into an efficient system. The total task of logistics management consists of five separate though interrelated jobs:

1. Traffic or transportation management
2. Inventory control

3. Order processing
4. Materials handling and warehousing
5. Fixed facilities location management

Each of these five jobs, or decision areas, offers unique challenges to the international marketer and is described below in more detail.

TRAFFIC OR TRANSPORTATION MANAGEMENT. Traffic management deals primarily with the mode of transportation. Principal choices are air, sea, rail, and truck, or some combination thereof. Transportation expenses contribute substantially to the costs of marketing products globally, so special attention has to be given to the selection of the transportation mode. Such choices are made by considering three principal factors: lead-time, transit time, and cost. Companies operating with long lead-times tend to use slower and therefore lower-cost transportation modes, such as sea and freight. For short lead-time situations, faster modes of transportation, such as air and truck, are used. Also important are transit times. Long transit times require higher financial costs because payments arrive later, and normally higher average inventories are stocked at either the point of origin or the destination. Modes of transportation with long transit times are sea or rail, whereas air or truck transportation results in much shorter transit times. Costs are the third factor considered when selecting a mode of transport. Typically, air or truck transportation is more expensive than either sea or rail for any distance.

Local laws and restrictions can have a significant impact on transportation costs. For example, France restricted foreign truck drivers from traveling on Sundays. The Dutch Transport Association reports these bans cost $60 million in Holland and billions across Europe. The Dutch have asked the European Union (EU) to investigate the forty-seven different bans in Europe regarding transportation on holidays, Sundays, and summer vacation.[43] Rank Xerox found that, by centralizing inbound deliveries from fifteen different trucking companies to one, it reduced transport costs by 40 percent in its Holland plant. Through this and other moves to centralize logistics, it expected to save $200,000 a year, reducing transport cost, inventories, and warehouse costs while at the same time improving the management and control of the logistics system.[44]

Logistics in China continues to be difficult because of the poor planning; provincial protectionism, which often allows only local companies to deliver within many cities; and corruption, The American Chamber of Commerce in Shanghai estimates that logistics costs 16 percent of product cost versus 4 percent in many developed economies.[45]

INVENTORY CONTROL. The level of inventory on hand significantly affects the service level of a firm's logistics system. To avoid the substantial costs of tied-up capital, inventory is reduced (ideally) to the minimum level needed. In global operations, adequate inventories are needed as insurance against unexpected breakdowns in the logistics system. To reduce inventory levels, several companies have adopted the Japanese system of just-in-time (JIT) deliveries of parts and components. Companies are also developing regional manufacturing strategies to minimize cost. For example, Rank Xerox produces its models for the world market (except the U.S. market) in four European plants. Prior to adopting a just-in-time system, the company kept buffer stocks of ten to forty days and an inventory of finished goods of ninety days. Now there is no stock for just-in-time parts and components, and the inventory for finished goods is only fifteen days. The improvements are the result of a just-in-time strategy: a reduced number of suppliers, improved quality control, and a more efficient logistics system.[46]

ORDER PROCESSING. Because rapid processing of orders shortens the order cycle and allows lower safety stocks for the client, this area is a central concern for logistics management. The available communications technology greatly influences the time it takes to process an order. Managers cannot expect to find perfectly working mail, telephone, or fax systems everywhere around the world. To offer an efficient order-processing system worldwide represents a considerable challenge to any company today. The ability to offer efficient order processing is a competitive advantage, however, because customers reap added benefits from such a system, and satisfied customers mean repeat business.

Toshiba Semiconductors, a major chip supplier based in Japan and with global operations, is revamping its global supply chain network to obtain faster deliveries and to ship its products on the shortest possible notice from any supply point in the world. Its OEM customers require this level of service for just-in-time delivery. To obtain these benefits, the company is also using a third-party logistics provider in Europe.[47]

MATERIALS HANDLING AND WAREHOUSING. Throughout the logistics cycle, materials and products will have to be stored and prepared for moving or transportation. How products are stored or moved is the principal concern of materials-handling management. For international shipments, the shipping technology or quantities may be different, causing firms to adjust domestic policies to the circumstances abroad. Warehousing in foreign countries involves dealing with different climatic situations, and longer average storage periods may require changing warehousing practices. In general, international shipments often move through different transportation modes compared to those of domestic shipments. Substantial logistics costs can be saved if the firm adjusts shipping arrangements according to the prevalent handling procedures abroad.

Automated warehousing is a relatively new concept for the handling, storage, and shipping of goods. Warehouses are often adjacent to the factory, and all goods are stored automatically in bins up to twelve stories high. The delivery and retrieval of all goods are controlled by a computer system. Although automated warehouses require significant up-front capital and technology, they ultimately reduce warehousing costs significantly.

FIXED FACILITIES LOCATION MANAGEMENT. The facilities crucial to the logistics flow are, of course, production facilities and warehouses. To serve customers worldwide and to maximize the efficiency of the total logistics system, production facilities may have to be placed in several countries, which involves a tradeoff between economies of scale and savings in logistics costs. At times, advantages can be gained from shipping raw materials or semiprocessed products to a market for further processing and manufacture, instead of shipping the finished product. These advantages arise from varying transportation costs for given freight modes or from different rates for each product category. Some companies compare the costs for several operational alternatives before making a final decision. The location of warehousing facilities greatly affects the company's ability to respond to orders once they are received or processed. A company with warehouses in every country where it does business would have a natural advantage in delivery, but such a system greatly increases the costs of warehousing and, most likely, the required level of inventory systemwide. Thus, a company seeks a balance that satisfies the customer's requirements on delivery and at the same time reduces overall logistics costs. Microsoft opened a single warehouse and distribution center in Dublin, Ireland, to serve all of Europe. The distribution center removes the need for Microsoft to keep a warehouse and inventory in each country.[48]

MANAGING THE GLOBAL LOGISTICS SYSTEM

The objective of a firm's global logistics system is to meet the company's service levels at the lowest cost. Costs are understood as total costs covering all five decision areas (discussed above). Consequently, a company has to combine cost information into one overall budget, which typically involves many departments from several countries. The key to effective management is coordination. A situation in which all managers try to reduce costs in their individual areas will either reduce the service levels provided or force other areas to make up for the initial reduction by possibly spending more than the original savings. Consequently, companies have to look carefully at opportunities to save in one area by comparing the additional costs that accrue in another. This process of comparison has caused some managers to refer to the logistics system as tradeoff management.

High-quality logistics does pay off. Fifty percent of all customer complaints to manufacturers concern poor logistics, so well-managed logistics that result in better service can reap substantial rewards. Research by the Strategic Planning Institute revealed that companies with superior service received 7 percent higher prices and grew 8 percent faster than low-service companies. Also, they were twelve times more profitable, on average.[49]

With markets becoming more scattered over numerous countries, the opportunities for competitive advantages in global logistics increase. The firms that can combine the various logistics areas under the responsibility of one manager have a chance at achieving either substantial cost savings or enhanced market positions by increasing service levels at minimum costs.

TRENDS IN GLOBAL DISTRIBUTION

Distribution systems throughout the world are continually evolving in response to economic and social changes. A manager developing a worldwide distribution strategy must consider not only the state of distribution systems today but also the expected state of distribution systems in the future. Five major trends currently prevail throughout the world: (1) the growth of larger-scale retailers, (2) an increased number of globally active retailers, (3) the proliferation of direct marketing, (4) the growth of online retailing, and (5) the dominant role of information technology in the support of a distribution strategy.

THE GROWTH OF LARGER-SCALE RETAILERS

The trend today is toward fewer but larger-scale retailers. As countries become more economically developed, they seem to follow a pattern of fewer, larger stores. Three factors contribute toward this trend: an increase in car ownership, an increase in the number of households with refrigerators and freezers, and an increase in the number of working wives. Twenty years ago, the European housewife may have shopped two or three times a day in local stores. Today, however, the increase in transportation options, refrigerator capacity, and cash flow, and the reduction of available shopping time have increased the practice of one-stop shopping in supermarkets.

The entry of Wal-Mart in the United Kingdom, via its acquisition of Asda's 260 stores, offered consumers decreased prices and a growth in superstores. Wal-Mart has grown faster than any other retailer in the United Kingdom, and it is adding photo centers, jewelry centers, vision centers, and pharmacies. In Germany, Wal-Mart acquired twenty-one Wertkauf stores and seventy-four stores from Spar Handels in 1997 and 1998, respectively. After three years, Wal-Mart was at a break-even profit, only because it lost several good managers in the acquisition process. The growth of Wal-Mart in Europe, as well as its entry into Latin America, China, Korea, and Japan, all contributed to international sales of $35 billion.[50]

The second largest global retailer, Carrefour, acquired Promodes in 1999 for 15.6 billion euros. Carrefour was primarily known for its hypermarkets in France. The acquisition of Promodes gave Carrefour expertise with supermarkets and small-store formats, as well as with discount stores. Carrefour is growing in Latin America and parts of Asia, but it doesn't have a presence in Germany, the United Kingdom, or the United States.[51] Carrefour has twenty-seven stores in China and will open ten new stores in China in 2002.[52]

IKEA, the Scandinavian retailer, has been very successful in Europe, Asia, and the United States in luring customers into its 200,000-square-foot stores. The IKEA strategy of offering a narrow range of low-cost furniture that the customers select, carry away, and assemble themselves results in a lower price to the consumer. Once in the store, customers are given tape measures, catalogs, paper, and pencils. Strollers are available for young children, as are free diapers. Each store has a restaurant that serves Scandinavian delicacies such as smoked salmon and Swedish meatballs. Customers can also borrow roof racks to place on their cars for bringing furniture home. IKEA has created a fun shopping experience that encourages people to enjoy themselves and make purchases. Sales per square foot are three times higher than in traditional furniture stores. IKEA opened stores in Shanghai and Beijing in 1998, stores that had a 70 percent increase in turnover in 2000 over the previous year.[53] The company plans to expand in Russia and other Asian countries as well. With its strong influence on furniture retailing, the company is likely to influence the general retailing scene in the markets where it opens new stores.

AN INCREASED NUMBER OF GLOBALLY ACTIVE RETAILERS

The number of globally active retailers is increasing.[54] Most originate in advanced industrial countries and spread to the developed countries of the world. For example, Sears is now in Mexico, South America, Spain, and Japan; Walgreen's is in Mexico; Tandy is in Belgium, the Netherlands, Germany, the United Kingdom, and France. The globalization of retailing includes firms originating in the United States, Canada,

France, Germany, and Japan. The wave was started by several large retailers in mature domestic markets that saw limited growth opportunities at home compared with the potential opportunities overseas. This principal reason for the trend toward global retailing has led Wal-Mart, IKEA, McDonald's, Pizza Hut, KFC, Carrefour, and many others to seek opportunities in Europe, the United States, and Japan. Several factors have facilitated the path toward an international presence. These factors include enhanced data communications, new forms of international financing, and lower barriers to entry. The single European market and the increasing number of new global retailers entering their domestic markets have also motivated retailers to expand overseas.[55] The trend toward global retailing allows manufacturers to build relationships with retailers who are active in several markets. Retailers are also expanding their global operations through acquisition.

Asian markets have also been particularly attractive to global retailers. Unfortunately, some have found the Asian market problematic. Lane Crawford, a Hong Kong retailer; U.S.-based Kmart; and the French group Galeries Lafayette have withdrawn from Singapore due to a lack of sales and no profit. Wal-Mart also experienced difficulty in Asia. The two discount stores Wal-Mart opened in Hong Kong with the Thai conglomerate Charoen Pokphand failed, and the partnership was dissolved. Apparently Wal-Mart assumed that its winning formula in the United States could be transferred easily to Asia. However, the small homes of the people living in apartment blocks did not have room for the bulk purchases that Americans find so alluring. Wal-Mart learned from its early mistakes and had fifteen supercenters and three Sam's Clubs by 2001 and planned to open thirteen new stores in 2002. Wal-Mart was also experimenting with a Neighborhood Market, which is only 28,000 square feet. If successful, this new format will be tailored to crowded Chinese cities and will accommodate a higher customer traffic and smaller transaction sizes.[56]

Despite some difficulties, U.S.-based retailers are continuing to expand in Asia. Starbucks, the specialty coffee firm, has opened stores in China, Hong Kong, Japan, Malaysia, the Philippines, and South Korea and intends to be present in every major urban Asian market by 2003. European retailers have found it essential to establish a unique selling position. C&A, the privately owned Dutch chain of clothing stores; the Body Shop, the U.K. natural cosmetics group; Benetton, the Italian fashion chain; IKEA, the Swedish furniture store; and Aldi, the low-priced German food retailer, are all successful international retailers that have developed a distinctive style. Each has a clearly defined trading format and product range that enable it to distinguish itself in each European market. Retailing formats can be translated into other countries as long as the format, its positioning, and messages are clear.

PROLIFERATION OF DIRECT MARKETING

There has been a continuous growth of direct marketing around the world. The complex, multilayered Japanese distribution system has encouraged some foreign companies to skip the stores and sell directly to consumers. The growth in direct marketing in Japan is supported by several demographic and technical factors. The dramatic increase in working women, from 50 percent to 75 percent, resulted in fewer available shopping hours. The introduction of toll-free telephone numbers, cable TV, videotext, and smart cards has also made it easier to shop at home. But U.S.-type mail-order companies have had their share of difficulties in penetrating the Japanese market. Paul Fredrick Menswear, a small U.S.-based catalog of men's shirts and ties, was able to sell $8 million of merchandise in Japan in 1997, a considerable volume by comparison with other, much larger U.S. mail-order houses. The company adapted its products to the Japanese market, for example, offering sleeve lengths of 30 and 31 inches instead of the U.S. standard of 32 inches. The company also found out that Japanese men have different color preferences and thus require a different catalog. The catalog was also translated into Japanese, resulting in an immediate sales increase. Larger U.S. firms, such as Brooks Brothers, were unwilling to make similar changes in their merchandise or approach.[57] One of the most successful direct marketing companies in Japan is Amway. With sales of $1.5 billion in 1999, the company employs approximately 1.1 million independent distributors and uses a direct sales model.[58]

Although the United States is the global leader in direct marketing, with $230 billion in sales in 1996, the market is also growing elsewhere. France is comparably smaller, with sales of $8.15 billion in 1996. In the United States, the direct marketing segment is dominated by specialty catalogs, but in France, as in other European countries, the market is dominated by general merchandise catalogs. U.S. direct marketing companies can do well, however, in foreign markets such as France. Reader's Digest ($136 million in 1997) and Inmac ($52 million in 1995) are two typical examples. In 1998, U.S. mail-order firms accounted for 25 percent of French foreign direct marketing sales, second behind German companies, which took the largest share with 50 percent.[59]

Direct marketing is also beginning to play a role in emerging markets. In Russia, direct marketing is a new concept and tends to be viewed negatively, as one of those new western business ideas. The Russian infrastructure in terms of delivery and telecommunications is also lagging behind other markets and tends to hold back progress. In Brazil, direct marketing has begun to take off, with consumers in cities receiving an average of ten pieces of direct mail offers a month. Telemarketing is hampered by a lack of phones (only one in ten Brazilians has a phone). Brazil is nevertheless a large market and tends to be ahead of the rest of Latin America in direct marketing. India is also only at the beginning of developing a direct marketing community. Bertelsmann, the German-based media company, put its planned Book Club India project on hold after realizing that a segmentation exercise on India's twenty-three largest urban markets had yielded a total of only 297,000 potential club members, too few to pursue the opportunity.[60]

In China, direct marketing is also a new phenomenon, and the lack of a sophisticated infrastructure poses big problems for direct marketing firms. Amway, a U.S.-based company, had begun to build a major operation there, investing as much as $100 million in a direct selling organization. The Chinese authorities denied the right to sell door-to-door, however, and the only way for Amway to salvage its investment was to agree to market its products through regular retail stores.[61]

For direct marketing to be effective, a company must be able to rely on a specific infrastructure that supports it. Basic requirements are a reliable telecommunications system, access to several good mailing lists, a target market with wide ownership of credit cards, an efficient postal or package delivery system, and telemarketing facilities such as call centers. In developed countries such as the United States, these requirements can be met easily. In many other markets, particularly emerging ones, the infrastructure is still lacking. As developing countries expand and improve their general communications infrastructure, direct marketing can be expected to expand.

GROWTH OF ONLINE RETAILING

The Internet has opened an entirely new channel through which retailers and manufacturers can sell their products. The United States is the undisputed leader in online retailing, or ecommerce, with estimates of $72.1 billion in sales in 2002. This amount represents 3.2 percent of total retail sales, up from 1 percent in 1999.[62] Nevertheless, ecommerce is a fast-growing segment. U.S.-based online retailers such as Amazon.com have expanded abroad, with specific "stores" for the United Kingdom and Germany. Most online retailing crosses borders, however, because through the Internet, consumers can reach any store with a legitimate Internet address.

Online retailing continues to expand in other countries too. The second largest ecommerce market after the United States is Japan, with an estimated revenue for 2001 of $8 billion.[63] Germany is also showing rapid growth, with Europe's highest number of households online, estimated at 6.4 million as of 1999. Other large online groups are in the United Kingdom (3.6 million) and France (1.7 million). These numbers were expected to increase quickly, fueling online retail growth. In Germany, surveys found that about 27 percent of all Internet users had ordered or purchased a product online.[64] Online retailing will expand even more rapidly as the perceived security problems are resolved and more consumers feel secure using credit cards over the Internet. But other infrastructure issues remain. Online retailing requires a solid Internet network available at low prices. The United States still leads the world in low-cost Internet connections and phone service. This situation is not true in many other countries, and a lengthy Internet connection can turn into an expensive shopping foray, particularly if nothing is purchased.

Finally, online retailing requires a large Internet-connected population. As many ecommerce executives know, online retailing also depends on a solid fulfillment cycle that gets the ordered merchandise into the hands of the consumer quickly. When shipping must take place across borders, issues of taxation and duty crop up and slow down delivery systems. Many foreign markets do not yet offer reliable fulfillment centers for use by small online retailers. However, the trend is clearly in the direction of resolving this issue. Once the delivery problem is solved, many more consumers will shop in online stores in faraway places, potentially turning every online marketer into a global retailer.

THE DOMINANT ROLE OF INFORMATION TECHNOLOGY

The worldwide retail industry is moving quickly toward the use of electronic checkouts that scan the bar codes on products, thus speeding up checkout, reducing errors, and eliminating the need to put a price label on each item. Electronic checkouts also improve the stores' ability to keep track of inventory and purchase behavior. As retailers and manufacturers begin to share consumer scanner data, they will be able to improve profitability.[65] Procter & Gamble, which had 53 percent of the U.K. detergent market in 1997, plans to reduce its product range by 40 percent and to increase profits by 40 percent.[66] More and more companies are developing global networks to assist with their global business. The networks improve communication, coordination, and sharing of best business practices. An additional benefit for many users of global networks is the recovery of value-added taxes (VATs) paid in multiple countries.[67]

Computerized retail systems have led to improved monitoring of consumer purchases, lower inventories, faster turnover of stock, better assessment of product profitability, and the possibility of just-in-time retailing. Retailers are beginning to link the electronic point-of-sale terminals with input on promotion and marketing plans to generate more accurate orders. Marks and Spencer, a U.K. retailer, uses an electronic checkout system that links directly to suppliers, who replenish stock 3 to 4 times per day per store. Technology is one of the keys to the success in Japan of 7-Eleven, owned by Ito-Yokado Company, Japan's most profitable retailer. Store clerks keep track of customer preferences and inventory through a sophisticated tracking system. The store clerks enter the consumer's sex and approximate age, as well as the items purchased. 7-Eleven-Japan posted a pretax profit of $680 million on $1.44 billion in 1992.[68]

Some stores are experimenting with self-scanning as a way to speed up checkout and reduce costs. Royal Ahold of Holland, the parent company of Stop & Shop in the United States, introduced self-scanning in Europe and is now using it in the United States. The same applies to Shaw's, another U.S.-based supermarket chain with a European parent, J. Sainsbury of the United Kingdom.[69] Modern retailing systems are clearly developed in many parts of the world and their diffusion takes place much more rapidly. This trend changes the retailing environment in many countries toward a "best in class world standard."

CONCLUSIONS

To be successful in the global marketplace, a company needs market acceptance among buyers and market access via distribution channels. Companies entering foreign markets often do so initially without noteworthy acceptance. Consequently, the company must guarantee some degree of market access through either effective marketing programs or sheer financial strength. To achieve access, the firm must select the most suitable members, or actors, of a channel, keeping in mind that substantial differences exist among countries on both the wholesale and the retail levels. Major differences in distribution exist from country to country. Local habits and cultures, planning restrictions, and infrastructure can all affect success in a new country.

Proper distribution policies have to allow for the local market's buying or shopping habits. A company should not expect to be able to use the same distribution density, channel alignment, or channel length in all its markets. The logistics system must reflect both local market situations and the additional difficulties inherent in longer distances. Finding willing and suitable channel members may be extremely difficult; access may be achieved only by forging special alliances with present channel members or local companies with access to them. Once the distribution system has been designed, participants still have to be motivated and controlled to ensure that the firm's marketing strategy is executed properly.

A major technological revolution is taking place with the emergence of the Internet, online retailing, and the widespread use of the Internet by consumers. These trends are likely to reshape the global distribution system and the way companies tap into markets all over the world. Easy access to the Internet makes it simpler for business or household customers to contact faraway markets, thus raising the global purchasing logic for all players. This trend has far-reaching consequences for all global marketers and needs to be taken into consideration as the new world economy adapts to the challenges of the Internet over the next few years.

Questions for Discussion

1. Your firm is just beginning to export printing equipment. How would you assess the decision about using an export management company or an export agent versus direct exporting?

2. What are the key elements of a distribution strategy?

3. If you enter a new marketplace and decide to distribute the product directly to the consumer, what types of costs will you incur?

4. You have been assigned the task of selecting distributors to handle your firm's line of car batteries. What criteria will you use to select among the twenty possible distributors?

5. The performance of your agents and distributors in South America has been poor over the past three years. How can you improve the management of these agents and distributors and thus improve sales?

6. What are the elements of an international logistics system, and how will they differ from a domestic logistics system?

7. Your firm has just entered the South Korean market for automobile parts; the major distributor is owned by a competitor, another manufacturer of automobile parts. What strategies can you use to gain access to this market?

8. Given the trends in distribution, what distribution strategies should a worldwide manufacturer of women's clothing consider using?

9. What impact on global marketing do you predict from the development of ebusiness?

For Further Reading

Arnold, David. "Seven Rules of International Distribution." *Harvard Business Review*, November-December 2000, vol. 78, no. 6, pp. 131–137.

Bello, Daniel C., David J. Urban, and Bronislaw J. Verhage. "Evaluating Export Middlemen in Alternative Channel Structures." *International Marketing Review*, 1991, vol. 8, no. 5, pp. 49–64.

Cooper, James C. "Logistics Strategies for Global Business." *International Journal of Physical Distribution and Logistics Management*, 1993, vol. 23, no. 4, pp. 12–23.

Czinkota, Michael R., and Masaaki Kotabe. *The Japanese Distribution System*. Chicago, Ill.: American Marketing Association, 1993.

Frazier, Gary L. "Organizing and Managing Channels of Distribution." *Academy of Marketing Science*, Spring 1999, vol. 27, no 2, pp. 226–240.

Govindarajan, Vijay, and Anil K. Gupta. "Taking Wal-Mart Global: Lessons from Retailing's Giant." *Strategy & Business*, 4th Quarter 1999, no. 17, p. 14.

Johnson, Gregory S. "Survey: Companies Consider Logistics a Key to Profits." *Journal of Commerce*, May 31, 1995, p. 2B.

Kaynak, E., and A. Kara. "Channels of Distribution in Developing Countries: Some Research Propositions." *Journal of International Marketing and Marketing Research*, June 2001, vol. 26, no. 2, pp. 59–76.

Kim, Keysuk, and Changho Oh. "On Distributor Commitment in Marketing Channels for Industrial Products: Contrast Between the United States and Japan." *Journal of International Marketing*, 2002, vol. 10, no. 1, pp. 72–97.

McDonald, William J. "International Direct Marketing in a Rapidly Changing World." *Direct Marketing*, March 1, 1999, p. 44.

Murray, Janet Y. "Strategic Alliance-Based Global Sourcing Strategy for Competitive Advantage." *Journal of International Marketing*, 2001, vol. 9, no. 4, pp. 30–58.

Rapoport, Carla, with Justin Martin. "Retailers Go Global." *Fortune*, February 20, 1995, pp. 102–108.

Richardson, Helen L. "Going Global? Master Distribution First." *Transportation and Distribution*, October 2000, vol. 41, no. 10, pp. 43–48

Williams, David E. "Differential Firm Advantages and Retailer." *International Journal of Internationalization of Retail and Distribution Management*, 1991, vol. 19, no. 4, pp. 3–12.

Endnotes

1. Franklin R. Root, *Entry Strategies for International Markets* (New York: Jossey-Bass/Wiley, 1998), p. 93.

2. "Removing the E-trade Barriers," *Business Korea*, vol. 18, no. 11, p. 49.

3. *Retailing in the European Single Market 1993*, (Euromonitor Publications, London, 1993) Table EUR1a

4. "Revolution in Japanese Retailing," *Fortune*, February 7, 1994, pp. 143, 146.

5. *European Marketing Data and Statistics*, 32nd ed. (London: Euromonitor Publications, 1997), Table 1203.

6. "Marketing in Japan—Taking Aim," *Economist*, April 24, 1993, p. 74.

7. Aimin Chen, "The Structure of Chinese Industry and the Impact from China's WTO Entry," *Comparative Economic Studies*, Spring 2002, vol. 44, no. 1, p. 74.

8. "Window Shopping in Shanghai," *Economist*, January 25, 1997, p. 62.

9. "Reinventing Convenience: Seventy-Five Years After Developing the First Convenience, 7-Eleven Shapes a New Future," *Convenience Store News*, May 6, 2002, p. 20.

10. "Overview of the Current State and Potential of China's Cosmetics and Toiletries Market," *Household and Personal Products Industry*, February 2002, vol. 39, no. 2, p. 1.

11. "Seiko Epson Clones Strategy of U.S. Rival," *Nikkei Weekly*, January 17, 1994, p. 8.

12. "Global PC Shipments Rise 9.5 Percent in 1998," *The Yomuri Shimbun/Daily Yomuri*, January 14, 1999.

13. "Ding-Dong, It's Seat Calling," *The Age*, July 30, 1998, p. 9.

14. Jon Hilsenrath, "Ford Builds Car to Suit India's Tastes," *Wall Street Journal*, August 20, 2000, p. A17.

15. "Nike 'Just Does It' Alone with Buyout of Japan Partner," *Nikkei Weekly*, January 17, 1994, p. 10.

16. "Caterpillar in Agreement with Mitsubishi Heavy Industries," *Asian Pulse*, November 6, 2001, p. 1.

17. "PepsiCo Regains Right over Brand Marketing, Distribution in France," *Wall Street Journal*, December 21, 1992, p. B7.

18. Warren J. Bilkey, "Variables Associated with Export Profitability," paper presented at the 1980 Academy of International Business Conference, New Orleans, October 23, 1980.

19. Mike Troy, "Wal-Mart Invests in Japan, Buys 6% Share of Seiyu," *DSN Retailing*, March 25, 2002, vol. 41, no. 2, pp. 1, 23.

20. "Delta Dairy Streamlined Food Producer," *Financial Times*, July 8, 1993, p. 11.

21. Allan J. Magrath and Kenneth G. Hardy, "Avoiding the Pitfalls in Managing Distribution Channels," *Business Horizons*, September–October 1987, p. 31.

22. Gary L. Frazier, James D. Gill, and Sudhir H. Hale, "Dealer Dependence Levels and Reciprocal Actions in a Channel of Distribution in a Developing Country," *Journal of Marketing*, January 1989, pp. 50–69.

23. S. Tamer Cavusgil, "Importance of Distributor Training," *Industrial Marketing Management* 1990, vol. 19, pp. 1–5.

24. "Re-shaping United Distillers," *Financial Times*, June 13, 1990, p. 12.

25. "UK Distillers to Unify Japan Whiskey Sales," *Dow Jones International News*, January 19, 1998, p. 2.

26. "Nissan's Direct Route," *Marketing Week* (London), March 10, 1995, p. 28.

27. "Selling U.S. Cars in Japan: More Than a Matter of Trade Policy," *Financial Times*, September 19, 1996, p. 6.

28. "American Standard Succeeds in Korea by Outflanking Local Firms' Lockout," *Financial Times*, August 26, 1993, p. A6.

29. "On Its Way to $10 Billion Lipitor," *Pharma Business* (London), May 2002, no. 50, p. 38.

30. Nikhil Deogun and Betsy McKay, "Coca-Cola and P&G Establish Venture for Juice and Snacks," February 22, 2001, p. 24.

31. "Kodak Japan Focuses on Photo Shops," *Nikkei Weekly*, July 23, 2001, p. 11.

32. "Brasmotor's Success Draws Competitors," *Wall Street Journal*, July 11, 1997, p. A10.

33. "The Lure of Mass Markets," *Prepared Foods*, July 1, 1998, p. 33.

34. David Pringle, "Scottish & Newcastle to Buy Hartwall," *Wall Street Journal (Europe)*, February 15, 2002, p. A9.

35. Adeline Paul Raj, "Carsberg Sees Asia Among Priorities," *Business Times*, March 12, 2002, p. 13.

36. Betsy McKay, "Danone and Coca-Cola Near Pact to Distribute Evian Water," *Asian Wall Street Journal*, April 24, 2002, p. A8.

37. "U.S. Retailers Surmount Japanese Protectionism," *Arizona Republic*, February 1, 1998, p. D1.

38. "HP, NEC to Team on Next-Gen Internet Protocol Servers in Japan," *Electronic Engineering Times*, July 5, 1999, p. 14.

39. "You Can Make Money in Japan," *Fortune*, February 12, 1990, p. 45.

40. "Banyu to Build Up Research and Development Activities as Merck's Foothold in Japan," Chemical Business NewsBase: *Japan Chemical Week*, July 22, 1999, p. 8.

41. "EU Approves Daewoo Sale to General Motors," *The Daily Deal*, July 25, 2002, p. 1.

42. "Collaborative Strategies and Tools to Reduce Overall Supply Chain Inventory," *Managing Logistics*, February 2001, pp. 1, 4–7.

43. "Haulers Urge Brussels to Curb Lorry Bans," *Financial Times*, July 16, 1997, p. 4.

44. Ibid.

45. Ben Dolven, "The Perils of Delivering the Goods," *Far Eastern Economic Review*, July 25, 2002, p. 29.

46. "Rivals Draw Distribution Truce to Cover Costs," *Nikkei Weekly*, January 31, 1994, p.10.

47. "Toshiba Sets Fast-Forward System," *Electronic Buyer's News*, August 2, 1999, p. 10.

48. "Microsoft Alters Distribution Chain for Europe," *Financial Times*, November 12, 1993, p. 20.

49. Neil S. Novich, "Leading-Edge Distribution Strategies," *Journal of Business Strategy*, November–December 1990, p. 49.

50. "Continental Divide: U.K. OK, but Germany Still Ailing," *DSN Retailing Today*, June 10, 2002, p. 118.

51. "Carrefour Flexible Thanks to Promodes," *Grocer*, March 30, 2002, p. 12.

52. "Carrefour Gets OK to Expand in China," *DSN Retail Fax*, April 29, 2002, p. 1.

53. "Case Study: Slow and Steady," *Country Monitor*, July 2, 2001, p. 5.

54. "Shopping All Over the World," *Economist*, June 19, 1999, p. 59.

55. Alan D. Treadgold, "The Developing Internationalization of Retailing," *International Journal of Retail and Distribution Management*, 1990, vol. 18, no. 2, p. 5.

56. "Wal-Mart Tests New Food Format in China," *Drug Store News*, April 29, 2002, p. 6.

57. "Competing in Japan's Catalog Market," *Target Marketing*, April 1, 1998, p. 30.

58. "Amway Japan Announces Fiscal 1999 First Quarter," *PR Newswire*, July 14, 1999, p. 1.

59. "France: Catalog Sales Market," U.S. Department of State, U.S. and Foreign Commercial Service, April 1998.

60. "International Direct Marketing in a Rapidly Changing World," *Direct Marketing*, March 1, 1999, p. 44.

61. "Amway Gets Okay to Operate in China," *Grand Rapids Press*, July 21, 1998, p. A1.

62. Online Retailing Still Growing Despite Some Loses Last Year," *Wall Street Journal*, June 12, 2002, p.B4; "Boom in E-Commerce," *Il Sole*, August 11, 1999, vol. 24, p. 12.

63. "Japan's Retail E-Commerce," *U.S. Newswire*, June 22, 1999, p. 2.

64. "Germany: Europe's On-Line Front Runner," *Communications Week International*, March 15, 1999, p. 6.

65. "Industry Analysts Predict Technology Driven Changes for Grocery Shopping," *Knight-Ridder Tribune Business News* (*Miami Herald*), February 18, 1999, p. 1.

66. Marcia MacLeod, "A Complex Route to Customised Solutions," *Financial Times IT: Networking*, July 3, 1996, p. 5.

67. Ibid.

68. "Listening to Shoppers' Voices," *Business Week/Reinventing America*, 1992, p. 69.

69. "New Concepts Check Out: Self-Scanning Reduces Lines, Personal Scanning Checks Out," *Boston Herald*, January 25, 1999, p. 27.

Part V

Managing the Global Marketing Effort

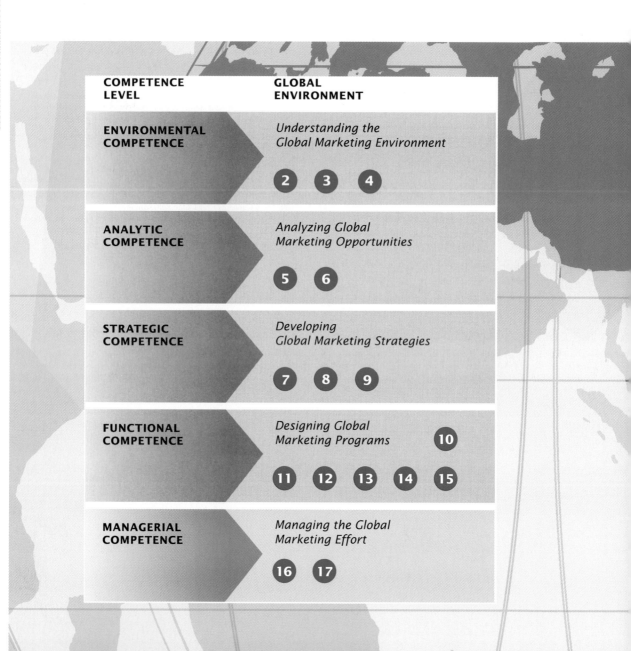

COMPETENCE LEVEL	GLOBAL ENVIRONMENT
ENVIRONMENTAL COMPETENCE	*Understanding the Global Marketing Environment* **2** **3** **4**
ANALYTIC COMPETENCE	*Analyzing Global Marketing Opportunities* **5** **6**
STRATEGIC COMPETENCE	*Developing Global Marketing Strategies* **7** **8** **9**
FUNCTIONAL COMPETENCE	*Designing Global Marketing Programs* **10** **11** **12** **13** **14** **15**
MANAGERIAL COMPETENCE	*Managing the Global Marketing Effort* **16** **17**

To be successful at global marketing, a company must do more than analyze markets and devise marketing programs. International companies run increasingly complex organizations with operating units in many different countries. The managerial challenges of running such diverse organizations are substantial, and these challenges require skills that are different from those required by single-country organizations.

The final part of our text, Part V, is devoted to issues involving the managerial competence of international and global marketing managers. Our goal is to show how managers can guide their operations more effectively in the very competitive global marketplace. In Chapter 16, we concentrate on organizational design issues for global firms; we also discuss where the decision-making process should be concentrated. Chapter 17 focuses on how global firms should control their operations and marketing programs.

CHAPTER 16
Organizing for Global Marketing

CHAPTER 17
Planning and Controlling Global Marketing

Chapter 16

Organizing for Global Marketing

An important aspect of global marketing is the establishment of an appropriate organizational structure. Any organization must be able to formulate and implement marketing strategies for each local market and also for the global market. The objective is to develop a structure that will allow the firm to respond to distinct variations in each market while utilizing the company's relevant experience from other markets and products. The key issue in establishing a global organization is deciding where to locate the global responsibility in the firm. The major dilemma facing global marketers involves the tradeoff between the need for an individual response to the local environment and the value of centralized knowledge and control. To be successful, companies need to find an appropriate balance between these two points of tension.

Several organizational structures are suitable for different internal and external environmental factors. No single structure is suitable under all circumstances. In this chapter, we examine the elements that affect the creation of global marketing organizations, the types of typical global organizational structures, emerging trends in global organization design, common phases through which organizations evolve, and the allocation of global mandates to different parts of the global marketing organization.

ORGANIZING: KEY TO GLOBAL MARKETING STRATEGY IMPLEMENTATION

To take advantage of global market opportunities, companies have to develop strategies to fit the needs of diverse markets while capitalizing on economies of scale in centralized operations, centralized control, and experience across many markets.

Such strategies require adaptation to the internal and external environment so that the company can prevail over competition.[1] Success of the strategy is influenced by the selection of an appropriate organizational structure for implementation of the global marketing strategy.

The structure of a global organization should be congruent with the tasks to be performed, the need for product knowledge, and the need for market knowledge. It is difficult to select an organizational structure that can implement a marketing strategy effectively and efficiently while responding to the diverse needs of customers and the corporate staff. Chapter 17, "Planning and Controlling Global Marketing," examines the simultaneous pressures for greater integration and greater diversity, whose interaction creates significant tension in the development and control of an ideal organizational structure.

ELEMENTS AFFECTING A GLOBAL MARKETING ORGANIZATION

The ideal structure of an organization should be a function of the products or services to be sold in the marketplace and the external and internal environments. Theoretically, the approach to developing such an organization is to analyze the specific tasks to be accomplished within an environment and then to design a structure that will complete these tasks most effectively. Several other factors complicate the selection of an appropriate organization. In most cases, a company already has an existing organizational structure. As the internal and external environments change, companies often change their existing structure. The search for an appropriate organizational structure must balance the forces for local responsiveness against the forces for global integration.[2]

It is important to understand the strengths and weaknesses of different organizational structures as well as the factors that usually lead to change in the structure. The diagram in Figure 16.1 depicts the elements that affect organizational design. In the following sections, we discuss each of these elements individually.

GLOBAL ENVIRONMENTAL FORCES

The most important global factors are geographic distance, time zone differences, types of customers, and government regulations. In the international environment, each issue should be examined to determine its effect on the organization.

GEOGRAPHIC DISTANCE. Technological innovations have eased the problems associated with physical distance. Companies primarily in the United States and other developed countries enjoy conveniences such as next-day mail and email, facsimile machines, videoconferencing, mobile phones, mobile data transmissions, and rapid transportation. However, these benefits cannot be taken for granted. Distance becomes a distinct barrier when operations are established in developing countries, where the telecommunications infrastructure is less developed. Companies invariably find it necessary to have key personnel make trips to engage in face-to-face conversations. Technology has thus shortened, but not eliminated, the distance gap.

Figure 16.1: Factors Affecting Organizational Design

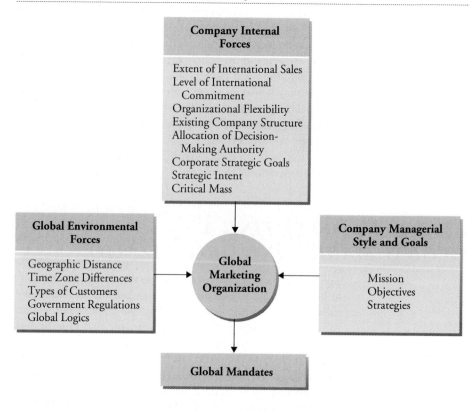

TIME ZONE DIFFERENCES. A problem even technology cannot completely resolve is time zone differences (see Figure 16.2). Managers in New York who reach an agreement over lunch will have a hard time finalizing the deal with their headquarters in London that same day because most executives in the United Kingdom will be on their way home for the evening. The five-hour time difference results in lost communication time, which impedes the rapid resolution of issues. Different time zones affect the relationship between a subsidiary and its headquarters if regular face-to-face meetings are required. Electronic mail has contributed substantially to overcoming time zone differences and facilitating interactions among far-flung business units, and its use is now standard for international companies.

GLOBAL LOGIC FORCES. In Chapter 7, we examined in great detail the various global logic forces that affect global marketing operations. Depending on the source of the global logic, companies may need to structure their global marketing organization differently. Companies facing very few global customers who are concentrated in one or a few locations and who thus create strong global purchasing logic will organize their global marketing efforts differently from firms that face a large number of customers in several different countries. In the former instance, when faced with extensive global customer or purchasing logic, firms tend to adjust their organizations and select their office locations according to where their customers are located. Many companies selling capital equipment or parts to automotive firms maintain marketing units near major concentrations of automotive production activity, such as in Detroit or in Stuttgart, Germany. On the other hand, companies that face large numbers of customers with little global logic tend to maintain diverse organizations catering to different regions. Companies that face very little global logic in terms of industry, competition, or size will find considerably less need to integrate international marketing operations. This situation leads to a more regional, or even country-specific, organization. Firms facing considerable global logic and a strong need to respond to that logic are typically forced to use different organizational forms leading to higher levels of integration.

COMPANY INTERNAL FORCES

Company specific factors often affect global marketing organizations. In this section, we examine these factors, including the size of a company's international business, its commitment to international business, the availability of human resources, and flexibility within the company.

Figure 16.2: Time Zones of the World

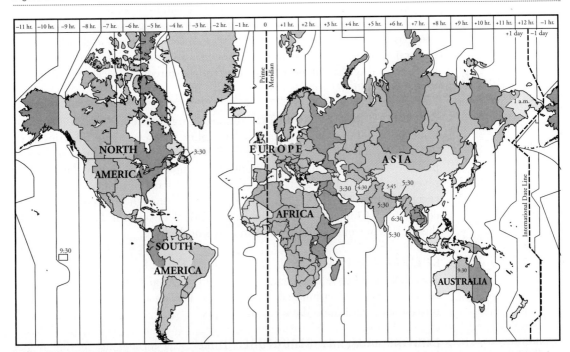

Source: From *The 1996 Information Please® Almanac,* p. 497. Copyright 1995 by Information Please. Reprinted by permission of Family Education Network. All rights reserved.

EXTENT OF INTERNATIONAL SALES. If only a small percentage of its sales (1 to 10 percent) are international, a company usually has a simple organizational structure with an export department. As the proportion of international sales increases relative to total sales, a company is more likely to change from an export department to an international division, and then to a global organization.

LEVEL OF INTERNATIONAL COMMITMENT. A company unwilling or unable to allocate adequate financial resources to its international efforts cannot sustain a complex or costly international structure. The less expansive organizational approaches to global marketing usually result in less control by the company at the local level. It is extremely important to build an organization that can provide the flexibility and resources necessary for achieving the corporation's long-term goals for global markets.

ACCESS TO HUMAN RESOURCES. Available and capable personnel are just as vital to a firm as financial resources. Some companies send top domestic executives to foreign operations and then find that these exported executives do not understand the host nation's culture. The hiring of local executives is also difficult because competition for such people is intense in many countries. Because people are such an important resource in global organizations, many companies base their organizational structure on the availability of globally trained executive talent. Also, many companies are developing cross-cultural training programs to help prepare executives for new environments.

   A current trend favors the hiring of local nationals among many international companies. This trend is driven by the understanding that hiring local marketing talent is the best way to build a local presence.[3] To create a global organization, General Electric believes in transplanting its universal corporate culture and nurturing local managerial talent, who will eventually direct the local organization to the best opportunities.[4]

ORGANIZATIONAL FLEXIBILITY. Although a rigid structure gives a firm more control over operations, it also restricts adaptability. When a company devises an organizational structure, it must build in some flexibility, especially because of the need for possible future reorganization. A study of the implementation of a global strategy for seventeen different products found that organizational flexibility was one of the key success factors. The structure needs to be flexible enough to respond to the needs of consumers.[5] Companies that establish a perfect design for the present only find themselves in trouble later if the firm grows or declines.

COMPANY MANAGERIAL STYLE AND GOALS

The managerial style of a company can be described in terms of its organizational structure and its decision-making processes. These factors influence the type of international organization the company adopts.

EXISTING COMPANY STRUCTURE. Three basic forms exist for the managerial structure of an organization: functional, market-based, or matrix. These options provide the foundation on which to design an organization. Figure 16.3 depicts the options a company has once it decides on the basic framework. When a company begins

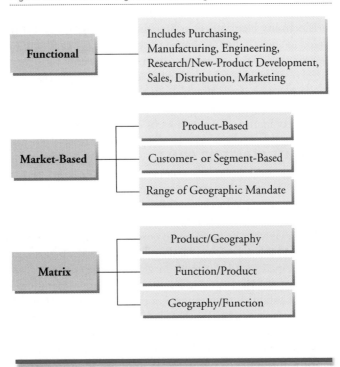

to expand its marketing organization internationally, the existing organization is the starting point for any global marketing effort.

The prospects of an integrated Europe gave several firms the impetus to change their traditional organizational structures. ICI, British Petroleum (BP), Unilever, Procter & Gamble, Electrolux, Philips, United Distillers, and many others reorganized to improve their abilities to respond to the needs of the European markets. For these firms, the international business became so important that the overall organizational structure was subjected to the global and regional demands. For many firms, however, the first or initial steps in global marketing will require an adjustment, not a wholesale change, until the international business becomes more important.

ALLOCATION OF DECISION-MAKING AUTHORITY. Who should make what decision guides any organizational design. If all decision-making responsibility is in the hands of headquarters, then the global marketing operation should reflect this setup. There are many layers, or types, of decisions to be made, from the purchasing of paper clips to the acquisition of a product line or a company. We will focus only on the most important decisions in this section.

Over a ten-year period, Electrolux made over one hundred acquisitions and thus became one of the leading manufacturers of large appliances, vacuum cleaners, chain saws, and garden appliances. Because the company grew so rapidly, it experienced pressure to develop a more formal and centralized decision-making process.

Electrolux adopted a multifaceted organization that both preserved local decision making where it was needed and allowed for global control over key product lines. At the Electrolux head office in Stockholm, Sweden, several product categories were created to cover major appliance areas: "Hot" (cookers, ranges), "Cold" (refrigerators, freezers), and "Wet" (washers, dryers). The product-category managers maintained control over design and coordinated local plant networks. Separate marketing groups coordinated the marketing activities for Europe and overseas. And local country managers were in charge of coordinating product divisions (plants) and local marketing sales companies. No single locus of decision making was selected.[6]

CORPORATE STRATEGIC GOALS. A company's mission—the values that drive the company and the belief the company has in itself—is part of the framework for its business. The glue that holds the company together, the mission statement, answers four questions: (1) Why do we exist? (2) Where are we going? (3) What do we believe in? and (4) What is our distinctive competence?[7]

After reviewing its mission, no company should begin establishing a global organization until it has reviewed and established its strategies and objectives. If the company anticipates future growth in global markets, it must establish a structure that can evolve effectively and efficiently into a large operation. Too often, shortsighted executives establish international operations that do not enable the managers to grow with the company when markets begin to expand. These managers are not equipped to take on any additional responsibility. Headquarters can also fail to communicate short-term goals, long-range objectives, and sometimes even the total mission of the company. Inadequate communications result in an ambiguous corporate image and the inability to facilitate coordination of all marketing elements.

STRATEGIC INTENT. Some authors go beyond the need for goals and objectives and call for "strategic intent." They argue that some companies that have risen to global leadership did so with a ten- to twenty-year quest for winning. If the head of a company can develop this sense of winning throughout the company, it will stretch the organization to excel and achieve far greater goals.[8] Although firms may express their strategic intent differently, many companies specifically aspire to a leading global position in a business segment, category, or sector. For firms where the announced intent is to lead globally in a business, the organizational structure and the basis for growing the marketing operation globally will be quite different than that of a company where the intent is to establish a market position based on a single (domestic) market.

CRITICAL MASS OR GLOBAL SCALE. An important consideration for the building of a global presence is the requirement for critical mass. Companies are extremely sensitive to achieving sufficient global scale to be able to fill a large enough organization for the strategic intent. Critical mass may be defined around a minimum sales level, a minimum plant size, or another element of the business as an IT infrastructure. Any firm falling below the required critical mass would be at an inherent disadvantage competitively. A company's global marketing organization needs to take into consideration the firm's strategic intent. Many of the current mergers around the world have to do with achieving sufficient critical mass to be able to compete on a global scale.

PROTOTYPE GLOBAL ORGANIZATIONS

To take advantage of the many opportunities in the global marketplace, a company must evaluate the options, develop a strategy, and establish an organization to implement the strategy. The organization should take into account all the factors that affect organizational design (refer again to Figure 16.1). In this section, we review the various types of international and global organizational structures.

COMPANIES WITHOUT GLOBAL MARKETING SPECIALISTS

When they begin marketing to foreign markets, many companies lack a separate international organization or global marketing specialists. A domestically oriented company may begin to receive inquiries from foreign buyers who saw an advertisement in a trade magazine or attended a trade show. The domestic salespeople will respond to the inquiry the same way that they do for other inquiries. Brochures will be sent to the potential buyer for review. If sufficient interest exists on the part of both buyer and seller, then more communication (email, airmail, faxes, telephone calls, personal visits) may transpire. Without an individual designated to handle international business, all this communication may be directed to a sales manager, an internal salesperson, a product manager, or an outside salesperson.

Companies without a formalized international organization will obviously have limited expenses. Of course, with no one responsible for international business, it will probably provide little sales effort. Also, when the firm attempts to respond to the occasional inquiry from a foreign buyer, none of the firm's employees will understand the difficulties of translation into another language, the particular needs of the customer, the transfer of funds, fluctuating exchange rates, shipping, legal liabilities, or the other many differences between domestic and international business. As the number of international inquiries grows or management recognizes the potential in global markets, global specialists may be added to the domestic organization.

ADDING GLOBAL MARKETING SPECIALISTS AND EXPORT DEPARTMENTS

The complexities of selling a product to different countries prompt most domestically oriented firms to establish a global expertise. The extent of this expertise can vary from retaining a part-time global specialist to having a full staff of specialists organized into an export department or international department. Figure 16.4 illustrates an organization operating with a global specialist (export manager).

Global specialists and export departments fulfill primarily a sales function. They respond to inquiries; exhibit at international trade shows; and handle export documentation, shipping, insurance, and financial matters. Also, the global specialist maintains contact with embassies, export financing agencies, and the U.S. Department of Commerce. All of these groups regularly publish requests for bid quotations from other countries. The global specialist or export department may use the services of an export agent, an export management company, or import intermediaries to assist in the process (see Chapter 15). Hiring global specialists gives firms the ability to respond to, bid for, and process foreign business. The size of this type of organization is directly related to the amount of international business handled. The costs should be minor when compared with the potential.

Figure 16.4: Organization with a Global Specialist (Export Manager)

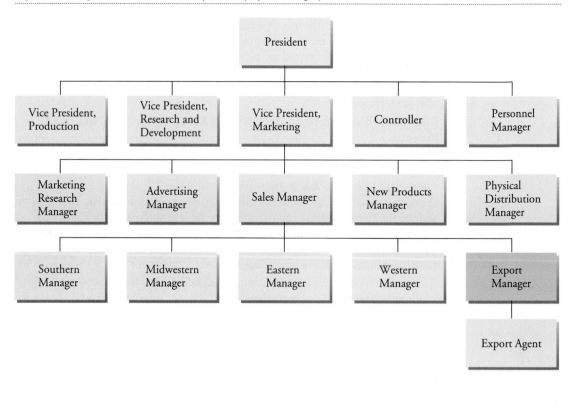

Global specialists and/or export departments are often reactive rather than proactive in nature. These specialists do not usually evaluate the worldwide demand for a product or service, identify pockets of opportunities, develop a strategy to infiltrate these opportunities, or reap the rewards; they usually respond to inquiries. Also, because international sales are so small, the global specialist may have little opportunity to modify the current products or services to meet global market needs. In most cases, the products are sold as is, with no modification.

CREATING AN INTERNATIONAL DIVISION

As sales to foreign markets become more important to the company and the complexity of coordinating the global effort extends beyond a specialist or a single department, a company may establish an international division. The international division normally reports to the president and thus has an equal status with other functions such as marketing, finance, and production. Figure 16.5 illustrates the organizational design of a firm maintaining an international division.

The international division is directly involved in the development and implementation of a global strategy. Heads of international divisions have marketing, sales, and possibly production managers reporting to them. These individuals focus their entire efforts on the global markets. It has been suggested that the international division is the best organizational alternative when international business represents a small percentage of the total business.

An international division focuses on the global market at a high enough level in the organization to influence strategy directly. Also, the international division begins actively to seek out market opportunities in foreign companies. The sales and marketing efforts in each country are supported through a regional or local office. These offices can understand the local environment, including legal requirements, customer needs, competition, and so on. This close contact with the market improves the organization's ability to perform successfully.

The use of international divisions is most common among large multinational corporations (MNCs) with many different product lines or businesses. This organizational structure has been typical in the United States, where many U.S. MNCs operate several separate product divisions for the large domestic market. Because the product divisions don't have extensive global experience, all international business is often combined into the international division, which is responsible for marketing in all overseas markets. IBM created its separate IBM World Trade

Figure 16.5: Organization with an International Division

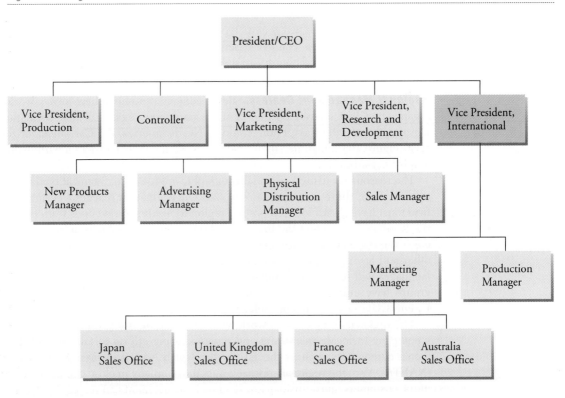

Organization, which became the focus for its global operations and control of international country subsidiaries. Alcon, a $1.5 billion U.S.-based company owned by Nestlé of Switzerland and active in the ophthalmic area, operated four major domestic divisions for equipment, pharmaceuticals, professional materials for surgeons, and over-the-counter eye-care products. Its international business was combined under an international division with operating responsibility for conducting its foreign business through its many subsidiaries.[9]

CREATING WORLDWIDE OR GLOBAL ORGANIZATIONAL UNITS

As a firm recognizes the potential size of the global market, it begins to change from a domestic company doing some business overseas to a worldwide company doing business in several countries. A worldwide focus will normally result in a worldwide organizational design. A company can choose to organize around four dimensions: geography, function, product, and strategic business unit. The matrix organization, another possible type of worldwide organization, combines two or more of the four dimensions. We will discuss and illustrate each organizational alternative.

GEOGRAPHY-BASED ORGANIZATIONAL STRUCTURES. Geographic organizational designs focus on the need for an intimate knowledge of the company's customers and their environment. A geographic organization gives a company the opportunity to understand local culture, economy, politics, law, and the competitive situation. There are two general types of geographic organizations: a regional management center and a country-based organization. In many cases, the regional management center and country-based organizations are combined.

Regional Management Centers. Regional management centers form a worldwide organization that focuses on one or more particular regions of the world, such as Europe, the Middle East, Latin America, North America, the Caribbean, or the Far East. Figure 16.6 illustrates the regional management structure of a worldwide geographic organization.

The reasons for using a regional geographic approach to organizational design are twofold. First, there is the pressure of size. Once a market reaches a certain size, the firm must have a staff focused on that region to maximize revenues from that area of the world and to protect the firm's assets there. The second reason for a regional focus is the regional nature of markets. A group of countries in close proximity to each other and having similar social and cultural histories, climates, resources, and often languages will have many similar needs for products. Often, these regional country groups have unified themselves for political and economic reasons. The European Union (EU) is an example of such a regional grouping.

The regional approach to a worldwide organization has several benefits. It allows a company to locate marketing and manufacturing efforts to take advantage of regional agreements such as the EU or the North American Free Trade Agreement (NAFTA). Also, the regional approach puts the company in close contact with distributors, customers, and subsidiaries. Regional management can respond to local conditions and react faster than a totally centralized organization in which all decisions are made at headquarters.

Figure 16.6: Geographic Organization by Regional Management Centers

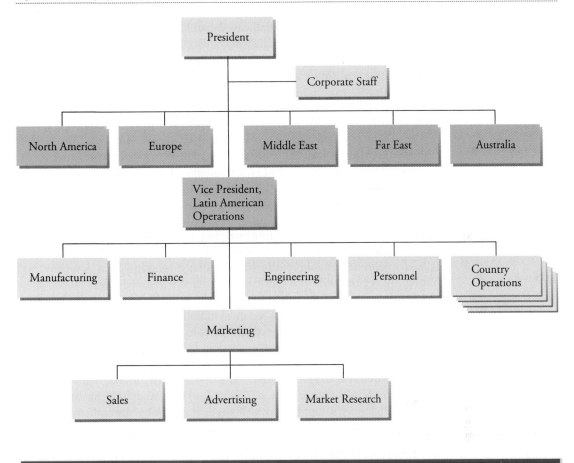

In Europe, many large international companies were organized on a national basis. The national organizations, including those in France, Germany, Italy, and the United Kingdom, were often coordinated through a regional management center, or the European headquarters. The development of a single European market prompted companies to rethink their European organization, often reducing the role of the national organization in favor of a stronger pan-European management. A study of twenty multinational companies found that one of the benefits of a regional or pan-European structure was reduced finance and accounting costs. The study showed that, by sharing accounting services such as accounts payable, billing, accounts receivable, and general ledger accounting, firms could save 35 to 45 percent of finance function costs.[10]

Restructuring of manufacturing and logistics in Europe proceeded at a rapid pace as companies centralized production to lower costs and increase flexibility. For example, Anglo-Dutch Unilever, one of the world's largest manufacturers of consumer products, set up a new organization in 1990 called Lever Europe. This change was a major one for Unilever, a company that had always been decentralized, with each national organization having full autonomy to modify and market products as dictated by local conditions. This decentralization had led to a large number of brands, resulting in the same liquid household cleaner being called Cif, Jif, Vif, or Viss, depending on the country organization. By centralizing both marketing and manufacturing, Unilever reduced the decision-making authority of its country managers, and it attempted to balance the need for centralized requirements in research, finance, and packaging with the need to stay close to the markets.[11] Coca-Cola Company organizes its business globally around five major operating units, each geographically defined around the regions of North America, Latin America, Africa, Asia, and Europe/the Middle East. This organizational structure is believed to give sufficient attention to the specific regional requirements. Marketing, however, is a global function at the head office.[12]

Regional organizations have disadvantages, too. First, regional organization implies that many functions are duplicated, either at regional head offices or in the countries themselves. Such duplication, together with the need to rent local offices, tends to add significantly to costs. A second and more serious disadvantage is that regional organizations inherently divide global authority. In a company organized purely by region, only the CEO has true global responsibility. Developing global marketing strategies for products or services is difficult because the key drivers are regional executives who tend to see most initiatives primarily from their regional perspective. It is difficult for such organizations to develop managers with a global marketing perspective.

Country-Focused Organizations. The second type of geographic organization is the country-based organization, which utilizes a separate unit for each country. Figure 16.7 illustrates a simple, country-based geographic organization.

Figure 16.7: Country-Based Geographic Organization

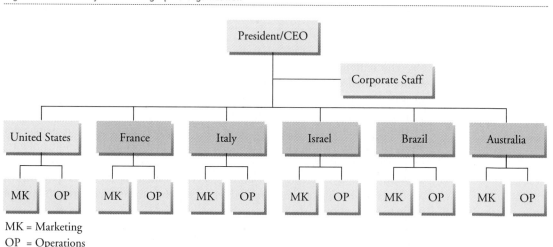

MK = Marketing
OP = Operations

A country-based organization resembles a regional management center, except that the focus is on individual countries rather than on a group of countries. For example, instead of having a regional management center in Brussels that oversees all European sales and operations, the company has an organizational unit in each country. The country-based organization can be extremely sensitive to local customs, laws, and needs, which may be different even though the countries participate in a regional organization, such as the EU. With the integration of Europe came the acceptance of European-wide product standards, the elimination of border restrictions, and the moves to financial unity. These changes have prompted many companies to look at Europe as a single market.

A major drawback of a country-based organization is its higher costs. Therefore, the benefit derived from a local organization must be sufficient to offset its cost. A second difficulty involves the coordination with headquarters. If a company is involved in forty countries, it is difficult and cumbersome to have all forty country-based organizational units reporting to one or more people in the company's headquarters. A third problem is that the country-based organization may not take advantage of regional groupings of countries (see Chapter 5). Regional trading agreements such as the EU make it valuable to coordinate activities in member countries. Also, regional media, such as television and print, often transcend country boundaries and require coordination.

As a result, country-based organizations are being phased out or reduced as pan-European organizations emerge. The experience of companies operating across Europe has demonstrated substantial cost savings from sharing services among organizations that were previously country-based. Annual cost savings of 30 percent, employee reductions of 60 percent, and a substantial cut in required working capital are the main benefits.[13]

In response to the creation of NAFTA, many firms began to integrate their separate organizations for Canada, the United States, and Mexico. Among those firms was Lego, the Danish toy maker with major U.S. operations. Lego reduced the responsibility of its Canadian operation and combined some executive positions at its U.S. operation. At the same time, it decided to build up its Mexican operation by using the U.S. location as a base. Other firms have chosen the same path: integrating their Canadian subsidiaries with their U.S. companies and developing the Mexican market from a U.S. base instead of building a separate Mexican company, as they might have done in the past.

To deal with the shortcomings of a country-based organization, many firms combine the concepts of a regional management center and a country-based unit, as shown in Figure 16.8. Combining regional and country approaches minimizes many of the limitations of both designs, but it also adds another layer of management. Some executives think that the additional layer at the regional headquarters reduces the country-level implementation of the strategy rather than improves it. To reap the benefits from a regional center in such a combined approach, there must be value in a regional strategy. Each company must reach its own decision regarding the organization design, its cost, and its benefits.

FUNCTIONAL ORGANIZATIONAL STRUCTURES. A second way of organizing a worldwide business is by function. In such an organization, the top executives in marketing, finance, production, accounting, and research and development all have

Figure 16.8: Organization Using Both Country-Based Units and Regional Management Centers

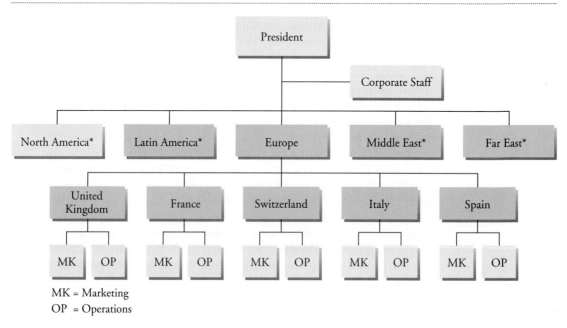

MK = Marketing
OP = Operations

*Under these regional offices would be country organization similar to those shown for the European center.

global responsibilities. For international companies, this type of organization is best suited for business units with narrow or homogeneous product lines, with little variation among geographic markets. As shown in Figure 16.9, the functional organization is a simple structure. Each functional manager has global responsibility for that function. Usually, the manager supervises people responsible for the function in different regions or countries around the world.

Coca-Cola Company reorganized its marketing function from a country-based organization to a functional global organization in the early 1990s. In the transition, market research and marketing operations that previously reported to a senior vice president of marketing in the United States were transferred to a newly created global marketing division. With the majority of its earnings growth coming from overseas markets, Coca-Cola decided to shift the focus away from a U.S.-dominated structure to a global one.[14] Ford adopted a functional global organization to eliminate the duplication of functions among regional organizations in the United States, Europe, Asia, and Latin America. Ford is expected to save $2 to $3 billion per year, as well as to speed up development of new models.[15]

PRODUCT-BASED ORGANIZATIONAL STRUCTURES. A global marketing organization may be based around a product line. The product group, which incorporates marketing, sales, planning, and in some cases production, becomes responsible for the performance of the organizational units. Other functions, such as legal, accounting, and finance, can be attached to the product group or may be performed by the corporate staff.

Structuring by product line is common for companies with several unrelated product lines. The rationale for selecting a product focus versus a regional focus is that the differences between the marketing of the products are greater than the differences between the geographic markets. In the 1970s and 1980s, many global companies used a dual structure referred to as a matrix, which we discuss below. During the 1990s, several companies such as Philips and ICI switched from geography-based to global product divisions. Typically, the customers for a product organization vary by product line, which creates little advantage to having a single group handling the marketing for the different product lines. The product line is the type of organizational structure shown in Figure 16.10.

A global product organization concentrates management around the product line, which is an advantage when the product line evolves constantly due to advances in technology. A product focus also provides the organization with flexibility. Within a product group, management can control the product life cycle, adding and deleting product line variations with a marginal effect on overall operations. Also, the firm can add new product groups as it adds new, unrelated products through an acquisition. When Monsanto adopted a global product organization, the transition was accompanied by a shift of the resins staff from St. Louis to Brussels, Belgium. The previous organization forced the company to focus primarily on North America—at the expense of product and market opportunities elsewhere.[16]

A product-focused organization has its limitations. Knowledge of specific functions may be limited because each product group cannot afford a fully developed local organization. This lack of knowledge may cause the company to miss some market opportunities. The managers of global product divisions can also create problems.

Figure 16.9: Functional Global Organization

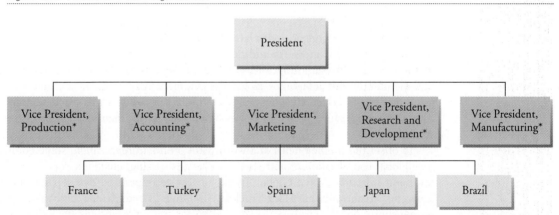

*Each functional vice president has managers of that function in the countries served reporting to him or her, as illustrated with the vice president, marketing.

Figure 16.10: Global Product Organization

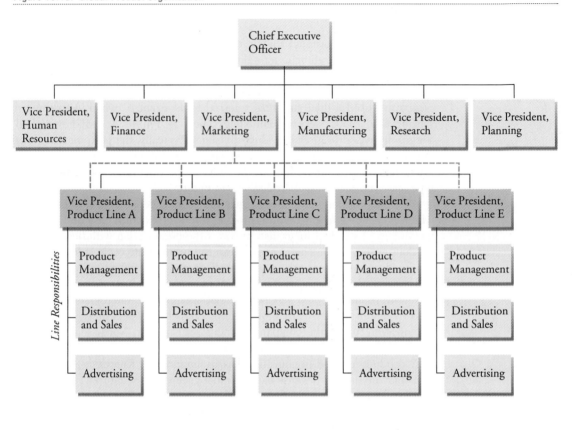

They may be ethnocentric and relatively disinterested in or uneasy with the international side of the business. An additional limitation of a product-focused organization is the lack of coordination in international markets. If each product group functions independently, the company's global development may result in inefficiencies. For example, two product divisions may be purchasing advertising space separately in the same magazine, which will be more expensive than if the purchases are combined.

To offset the inefficiencies of a worldwide product organization, some companies use global coordination of activities such as advertising, customer service, and government relations. Volvo Global Trucks of Sweden operated two separate business units for North America: Mack Truck in Allentown, Pennsylvania, and Volvo Truck in Greensboro, North Carolina. To achieve better synergies and greater efficiency, the company shared key activities, such as legal, customer engineering, dealer development, parts sales, and marketing, while keeping manufacturing separate for each unit.[17] Many companies are adopting such a hybrid model to combine the best of both situations.

MATRIX ORGANIZATIONAL STRUCTURES. Some companies have become disenchanted with the limitations of the one-dimensional geographic, product, and functional organizational structures. To overcome these limitations, the matrix organization was adopted. A matrix organization can include product, segment, functional, and geographic management components. Product managers have worldwide responsibility for a specific product line, whereas geographic managers are responsible for all product lines in a specific geographic area. These management structures overlap at the national product/market level. The matrix organization shown in Figure 16.11 allows for two dimensions of equal weight (here, geographic and product dimensions) in the organization structure and in decision-making responsibility. A matrix organization structure has a dual rather than a single chain of command, which means that many individuals have two superiors. Firms often adopt matrix organizations when they

Figure 16.11: Matrix Organization

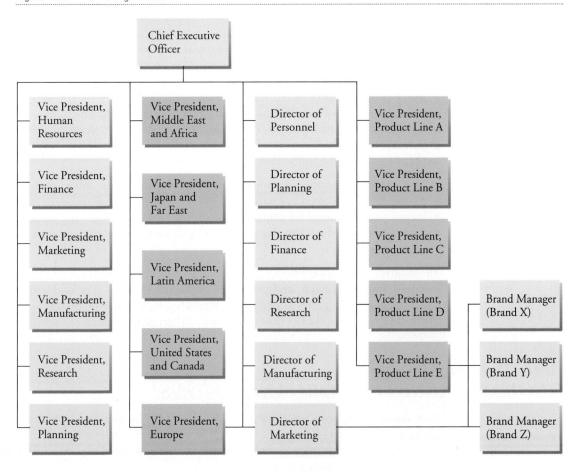

need to be highly responsive to two dimensions (for example, product and geography), when there are stringent constraints on financial or human resources, and when uncertainties generate high information-processing requirements.

The combination of different organizational objectives and dual reporting relationships fosters conflict and complexity. Tensions resulting from dual reporting relationships are common problems with matrix organizations. The authority limits of the two relationships are tested as each side attempts to identify its place in the organization. One of the most extensive global matrix organizations is employed by ABB, a Swedish-Swiss company with several major businesses in electric power generation, railways, industry automation, and environmental equipment. Formed in 1987 as a merger between Swedish-based Asea and Swiss-based Brown Boveri, the company operates approximately sixty business areas worldwide. Each business area has global responsibility for strategy and is measured on the basis of its own profit-and-loss account. On the other side of the matrix are numerous country organizations responsible for delivering the global strategy in their assigned territory. Each local manager reports to a regional manager and to the assigned global business area manager. For the matrix to work, both the regional and the business area managers must agree on the local strategy, budget, and business approach. The company has been structured into more than three thousand units with dual reporting. ABB has also promoted managerial behavioral patterns among its managers to make the best of the matrix organization.[18]

The key to successful matrix management is the degree to which managers in an organization can resolve conflict and achieve the successful implementation of plans and programs. The matrix organization requires a change in management behavior from traditional authority to an influence system based on technical competence, interpersonal sensitivity, and leadership. In addition, it

- permits an organization to function better in an uncertain and changing environment.
- increases the potential for control and coordination.
- gives more individuals the chance to develop from technical or functional specialists to generalists.

The matrix organization requires a substantial investment in dual budgeting, accounting, transfer pricing, and personnel evaluation systems. The additional complexity and cost of a matrix organization should be offset, however, by the benefits of the dual focus, increased flexibility and sales, and greater economies of scale.

EMERGING TRENDS IN GLOBAL MARKETING ORGANIZATIONS

International companies are continually challenged by the need to adapt their organizations to the needs of the marketplace. When companies compete on a worldwide basis, they need to develop global economies of scale. Instead of supporting manufacturing plants in each major market, products or components are standardized. Electrolux, Black & Decker, Unilever, and many other firms have rationalized their manufacturing to yield economies of scale. Although the washing machine or power tool may vary from country to country, the motors can be standardized and manufactured in large volumes to reduce costs. The organizational structure needs to encourage this trend toward efficiency, which is why, as part of its complex matrix organization, Electrolux created three product categories to cover major appliance areas—"Hot," for cookers and ranges; "Cold," for refrigerators and freezers; and "Wet," for washers and dryers. The product-category managers for each of these appliance areas coordinate the manufacturing and marketing of their product lines across all markets.[19]

ASSIGNING GLOBAL MANDATES

When companies are concerned with globalizing their marketing organizations, the issue of who, or which units, should receive global mandates becomes an important aspect of the discussion. Under the term *global mandate,* we understand that the expressed assignment or task must be completed on a global scale. Global mandates can be assigned to individual managers, such as a global brand manager, or to company teams, such as a global brand team. In both cases, the responsibility would be executed across all geographic areas, and the teams or marketing managers would be able to make decisions for all geographic areas. Global mandates can also be temporary. In this case, executives are named to a task force that deals with a particular global marketing issue and then the task force is dissolved when the issue is resolved. The decision about who should receive a global mandate is an important one for all globally active firms. It would be difficult to act on a required global marketing strategy if the company did not endow key marketing executives with global mandates.[20] We will describe several forms of global mandates below and describe the type of organizations in more detail.

STRATEGIC BUSINESS UNITS WITH GLOBAL RESPONSIBILITIES. One of the most recent forms of organizational design is the *strategic business unit (SBU)*. The SBU is an organizational group supporting products and technologies that serve an identified market and compete with identified competitors. The SBU may be either a separate organizational design, similar to a product organization, or an organizational unit used only for the purpose of developing a business strategy for many products in a geographic area.

The increase in global competition has forced many firms to set up SBUs to address the global markets and assess competition in developing a global business strategy. The SBU structure goes beyond the divisional structure. An SBU is organized as a self-contained unit, typically with its own associated production and technological resources. In some of the newer types of organizations, SBUs have been set up as legally incorporated firms, with the parent organization adopting the role of the key strategist, owning all the shares of its SBUs, and maintaining close involvement in the SBUs' strategy formulation.

Scandinavian firms pioneered the SBU organizational structure. Atlas-Copco, producer of compressors, and Alfa-Laval, manufacturer of industrial equipment (today part of Tetra Laval), are two examples. The establishment of SBUs as separate legal units has also been adopted by ABB and Novartis, a Swiss-based pharmaceutical firm. Shell organized its separately incorporated catalyst supply unit, CRI Catalyst Company, as a global SBU to supply catalysts used in various chemical processes to customers around the world. CRI maintains its own laboratories, development facilities, manufacturing plants, and marketing organization.[21]

When a business unit receives a global mandate to develop its business around the world, marketing is immediately given a global mandate too. These SBUs tend to have many executive positions with global mandates, although it is up to the SBU managers to decide how to organize. All of the organizational options described earlier in this chapter apply, and any one of them may be found given the business and industry environment. For example, a global SBU may be organized around a matrix, may be either geographically or product-focused, or may be organized along global functional lines.

For SBU structures to be successful, the individual business units must be self-contained, with different customer groups and different technologies and production units sharing relatively little of their daily operations. Critics of this type of organization charge that the resulting small units, each trying to build its own global structure in major global markets, can often be under critical mass.

Some companies believe that they cannot build a sufficiently strong global business unit. In this situation, they elect to retrench and sell out to another firm that can combine the acquired unit into a larger and stronger business. ABB, the Swiss/Swedish engineering firm, sold its air-handling equipment business to Global Air Movement. Together with the ABB business, Global Air Movement is in a position to build a globally focused business in a narrowly defined industry.[22] Sometimes, a firm spins off an entire unit to allow it to grow independently. IBM sold its printer business in 1991; the printer business later became Lexmark, an independent company listed on the stock market. Lexmark grew to sales of $3 billion with global operations.[23]

GLOBAL SEGMENT ORGANIZATIONS. Within individual product divisions or newly formed SBUs, companies often target different customer groups. To focus on these customer groups, global segment units are formed, and they are charged with marketing toward one particular segment only. Global segment units were formed by several chemical companies. ICI Explosives markets explosives to various types of mining firms. ICI created segment teams for different mining applications, such as deep mines, quarries, and surface mines.[24] Huntsman Chemicals' polyurethane unit created segment teams for marketing to athletic shoe firms and major appliance manufacturers, among others. In both situations, the segment units were responsible for marketing a full product line with respect to a homogeneous customer segment. These segment units were not full-fledged SBUs because they shared the same production units and technology base all over the world. Global segment organizations have also been recently adopted by some pharmaceutical companies. Organized around therapeutic areas, they comprise the marketing and development functions and allow firms to focus on specific patient groups or disease types. Each segment is given a global mandate and often has its own sales force. Manufacturing and several other corporate functions remain centrally coordinated.[25] Global segment organizations are of particular importance to firms pursuing global strategies from the same asset base but serving market segments with substantially different customer needs.

GLOBAL CATEGORY ORGANIZATIONS. Firms with several different but related products often find it advantageous to create category units that allow them to organize and coordinate global marketing. Many of the world's best-known consumer goods firms, such as Colgate, Nestlé, Procter & Gamble, and Unilever, have recently moved toward the adoption of global product categories. Nestlé has several such units for beverage, dairy, and similar categories. Each category contains numerous brands or products, which makes loose coordination across customer groups or technologies possible. Global categories typically contain separate global brand units with their own separate manufacturing, a setup that facilitates the coordination of new technologies. The global category organization allows for better transfer of learning across countries.

Procter & Gamble (P&G) adopted a global category organization along seven product-related groups, ranging from baby care (Pampers and related products) to food (Pringles potato chips and other products).[26] Previously, P&G operated largely from four major geographic units.[27] Dubbed "Organization 2005," this reorganization was expected to allow P&G to introduce new products more quickly overseas than it could with a regionally focused organization.[28] The reorganization replaced the many separate country organizations with global business units tied to product categories, such as paper goods and beauty care. This organizational change brought about changes in reporting relationships for thousands of managers and created a substantial upheaval. Eventually, P&G partly reinstated its geographic focus.[29] Unilever, a major competitor of P&G, has itself moved closer to a global category organization by grouping its brands into two major categories, one for personal care and the second for food. Both will have a global mandate.[30] And finally, Nestlé, the third of the leading global fast-moving consumer goods firms with extensive global marketing experience, grouped its brands into several broad product categories for better focus.[31] To develop its global strategy category by category, Nestlé acquired Ralston Purina (to strengthen its global position specifically in the pet food category). The company had slowly expanded its pet food business through several acquisitions starting in 1985 and achieved global leadership. Similar strategies are pursued in other Nestlé categories, such as bottled water and ice cream.[32]

GLOBAL CUSTOMER ORGANIZATIONS. As we explained in Chapter 11, some firms are creating global customer organizations intended to coordinate a firm's business with individual worldwide customers. Such organizations are useful if a company has a substantial amount of business distributed all over the world and organized in one worldwide account. Typically, these units are part of either a global business structure or are SBUs and do not have full independence with respect to production or technology. Sun Microsystems created a separate group of global account managers focused on its largest accounts. The managers had global responsibility for their assigned accounts and played the role of coordinators.

Over the past few years, companies have developed several different ways to organize their business globally. The trend has been toward the creation of increasingly global forms of organization and away from the traditional approach of divided responsibility for domestic and international business. This trend has created many opportunities for executives with global mindsets at ever lower levels of organizational management. Which type of organization a company selects should also reflect the type of global logic the company faces (see Chapter 7).

FORD: THE TRANSFORMATION INTO A GLOBAL ORGANIZATION. Ford Motor Company has undergone a major transformation in its organization. Once operating on a more or less regional structure, Ford had created major operating units in North America, Europe, Latin America, Africa, and Asia. Each regional unit was responsible for its own operations, developing and producing cars for its regional markets. Ford faced strong competition, however, from its bigger rival, General Motors, and the more efficient Japanese companies, especially Toyota. Ford realized that, under the regional setup, it incurred a massive penalty for unnecessary duplication of key functions and efforts. Even though it served what amounted to almost identical customer needs in many countries, the company developed separate power trains and engines and purchased different component parts, all at a cost of $3 billion, astronomical compared with what an integrated operation would spend.[33]

Ford had tried global integration before but usually on a project basis, not by integrating the entire organization. In the late 1970s, Ford created a subcompact car (Fiesta) that it hoped would be marketed in Europe and the United States. The resulting company infighting prevented a true world car from being developed, however, and Ford ended up with two similar cars that were developed separately in Europe and North America. In the 1990s, Ford spent about $6 billion to develop midsize cars for both Europe and North America. Successful in Europe, the cars did not fare well in the United States, where they were launched late.[34]

Ford began its reorganization by merging its North American operation with its European car operation, creating an integrated firm under the "Ford 2000" banner.[35] The new organization of Ford Automotive called for four major functions, each to be headed by one executive with global responsibility. The most important function was vehicle development, structured around five vehicle centers in the United States and in Europe. The other global functions were marketing and sales, manufacturing, and purchasing.[36] The development center for small cars was in Europe, with locations in both Germany and the United Kingdom. The development centers for rear-wheel-drive cars and commercial trucks, all with global development responsibility, were located in the United States.[37] The company hoped to cut development costs by using fewer components, engines, and power trains, and by speeding up development cycles. As a result of this reorganization, about twenty-five thousand Ford managers were believed to have been either relocated or reassigned to new supervisors. Ford continues to pursue an aggressive marketing strategy, both at home and abroad. This strategy culminated in the acquisition of Volvo Cars of Sweden.

PHASES IN THE DEVELOPMENT CYCLE OF GLOBAL MARKETING ORGANIZATIONS

Company organization evolves over time. As international involvement expands, the degree of organizational complexity increases, and firms reorganize accordingly. As a firm moves from exporting a few goods to being a worldwide organization, it finds itself going through organizational changes with differing structures and focus.

Organizations change to reflect the importance of different markets and the needs of the customer. As the amount of international business increases and the needs of the customers become more complex, the organization changes to reflect the market. Figure 16.12 depicts the typical progression in the evolution of a global organization. Because this process is dynamic and integrative, most companies do not follow this phased approach exactly, but the framework provides a method by which to evaluate the degree of focus and responsibility.

PHASE ONE: EXPORTING

When the domestic market becomes saturated or a need is identified in foreign markets, companies begin exporting their products or services. The export department is still a function of the domestic company, normally reports to the company, and follows company procedures and strategies. Often, companies first begin to receive inquiries from foreign companies about their products. At that point, an export person or department is established to process and respond to these inquiries.

Figure 16.12: Development Cycle of Global Marketing Organizations

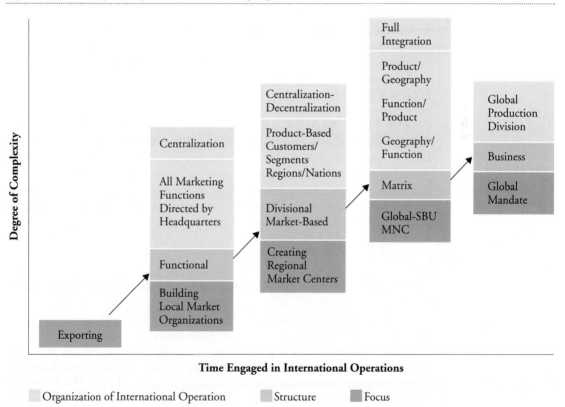

PHASE TWO: BUILDING LOCAL MARKET ORGANIZATIONS

When the demand for the product increases and an overseas office is needed to ease administrative procedures, to investigate new markets, or to refine old markets, a company normally establishes an office in a foreign country. Usually, this office is under the control of headquarters and acts according to home office directions.

PHASE THREE: CREATING REGIONAL MARKET CENTERS

Regional market centers act as filters between company headquarters and various country organizations. Regional market centers coordinate the marketing function of the branches so that they remain in line with corporate objectives. Regional market centers are normally organized along geographic lines; however, they may be organized along product groups or similar target markets.

PHASE FOUR: BALANCE THROUGH MATRIX ORGANIZATIONS

The matrix organization is the most complex and sophisticated structure. It requires a firm to be fully competent in the following areas:

1. Geographic knowledge
2. Product knowledge
3. Functional aspects, such as finance, production, and marketing
4. Customer and industry knowledge

Instead of focusing on one area—geographic or product organization—the matrix organization incorporates both and each operates as a profit center. Matrix organizations allow low levels to have substantial authority; however, they require an open and flexible corporate culture and company orientation for successful implementation.

PHASE FIVE: ASSIGNING GLOBAL MANDATES

Fully advanced global companies with complete integration have begun to establish strategic business units (SBUs). An SBU acts as a separate business and contains a group of products or technologies directed at a specific target market. SBUs are part of a formal structure but act primarily to determine strategies. As mentioned earlier in the chapter, several companies have moved from the geography/product division matrix to a global product division structure.

CONCLUSIONS

As we have seen in this chapter, organizing the global marketing efforts across a large number of countries is a difficult process. When the scope of a company's global business changes, its organizational structure must be modified in accordance with the internal and external environments. An organization must adapt as the number of countries with marketing activities increases, product lines expand, and objectives change. In this chapter, we have reviewed the various organizational structures commonly used and showed the benefits and disadvantages of each. The dynamic nature of business requires a constant reevaluation of organizational structure and the implementation of the necessary modifications to meet the objectives of the firm. The task of molding an organization to respond to the needs of a global marketplace involves building a shared vision and developing human resources. A clear vision of the purpose of the company that is shared by all employees gives meaning and direction to each manager.

Managers are a company's scarcest resource. The process of recruiting, selecting, training, and managing human resources must help build a common vision and values. The emerging global marketing organizations with well-articulated global mandates increase the number of managerial positions with global content. As a direct consequence, many companies find themselves searching for managerial talent who possess a global mindset and can step up to this challenge. As companies push global responsibilities further and further down in the organizational structure, the time it will take for a marketing manager starting out in his or her career to receive the first global mandate has been rapidly compressed. This trend has great implications for all aspiring global marketing practitioners now studying this text.

Questions for Discussion

1. What aspects of the external environment cause the structures of multicountry marketing organizations to be different from those of single-country marketing organizations?

2. What effect will the marketing strategy have on an international marketing organization? For example, if the key aspect of a computer manufacturer's strategy is to focus on three industries worldwide—banks, stockbrokers, and educational institutions—will the organization be different from that of another company that decides to focus on end users who require mainframe computers?

3. How does a single-country organization evolve into an international organization? What type of international organization is likely to develop first? Second? Why?

4. What prompts a company to develop an international marketing organization?

5. What are the pros and cons of a regional management center versus a product organization?

6. A country-based geographic structure responds well to the local culture and marketing. What will cause a company to switch from a country-based structure to a worldwide product organization?

7. Matrix organizations can be costly and complex. What advantages do they offer to offset these problems?

8. In addition to the formal organization structure, how does the global company ensure that it is responding to the market and achieving efficiency, local responsiveness, and global learning?

For Further Reading

Barnevik, Percy. "The Logic of Global Business: An Interview with Percy Barnevik." *Harvard Business Review*, March 1991, pp. 91–105.

Bartlett, Christopher A. "MNCs: Get Off the Reorganization Merry-Go-Round." *Harvard Business Review*, March–April 1983, pp. 138–146.

Bartlett, Christopher A., and Sumantra Ghoshal. *Managing Across Borders: The Transnational Solution.* Boston: Harvard Business School Press, 1989.

Brabeck, Peter, and Suzy Wetlaufer. "The Business Case Against Revolution: An Interview with Nestle's Peter Brabeck." *Harvard Business Review*, February 2001.

Doyle, Peter, John Saunders, and Veronica Wong. "Competition in Global Markets: A Case Study of American and Japanese Competition in the British Market." *Journal of International Business Studies*, 3rd Quarter 1992, pp. 419–426.

Handy, Charles. *The Age of Unreason.* London: Hutchinson, 1989.

——. *Inside Organizations*. London: BBC Books, 1990.

Howard, Robert. "The Designer Organization: Italy's GFT Goes Global." *Harvard Business Review,* September–October 1991, pp. 28–44.

Jeannet, Jean-Pierre. *Managing with a Global Mindset.* London: Financial Times/Prentice Hall, 2000.

Kets de Vries, Manfred F. R. "Charisma in Action: The Transformation Abilities of Virgin's Richard Branson and ABB's Percy Barnevik." *Organizational Dynamics,* vol. 26, no. 3, January 1, 1998.

Laabs, Jennifer. "Building a Global Management Team." *Personnel Journal,* 1993, vol. 72, no. 8, p. 75.

Lei, David, John W. Slocum, and Robert A. Pitts. "Designing Organizations for Competitive Advantage: The Power of Unlearning and Learning." *Organizational Dynamics,* January 1, 1999, vol. 27, no. 3, pp. 24–28.

Maruca, Regina Fazio. "The Right Way to Go Global: An Interview with Whirlpool CEO David Whitwam." *Harvard Business Review,* March–April 1994, pp. 135–145.

Ohmae, Kenichi. *The Borderless World.* London: Collins, 1990.

Rosenzweig, Philip, Xavier Gilbert, Thomas Malnight, and Vladimir Pucik. *Accelerating International Growth.* Chichester, England: Wiley, 2001.

Endnotes

1. Alfred D. Chandler, *Strategy and Structure* (Cambridge, Mass.: MIT Press, 1962).

2. Sumantra Ghoshal and Nitin Nohria, "Horses for Courses: Organizational Forms for Multinational Corporations," *Sloan Management Review,* Winter 1993, p. 27.

3. "U.S.-Based Companies Rely on Local Talent," *Workforce,* September 1999, vol. 78, no. 9, p. 28.

4. "GE Digs into Asia," *Fortune,* October 2, 2000, p. 164.

5. Kamran Kashani, "Why Does Global Marketing Work—or Not Work?" *European Management Journal,* June 1990, p. 154.

6. Christopher Lorenz, "The Birth of a Transnational," *McKinsey Quarterly,* Autumn 1989, p. 72.

7. Andrew Campbell, Marion Devine, and David Young, *A Sense of Mission* (London: Economist Books, 1990), pp. 19–41.

8. Gary Hamel and C. K. Prahalad, "Strategic Intent," *Harvard Business Review,* May–June 1989, pp. 63–68.

9. Jean-Pierre Jeannet, and Sam Perkins, "Alcon Laboratories, Inc." Case (Lausanne, Switzerland: IMD Institute, 1998).

10. "European Study Finds Companies Can Save 35–45% by Moving to Financial Shared Services," A. T. Kearney news release, December 16, 1993, p. 1.

11. Floris A. Maljers, "Inside Unilever: The Evolving Transnational Company," *Harvard Business Review,* September–October 1992, p. 48.

12. "Coke Shares Drop Following Resignation of No. 2 Executive," *Asian Wall Street Journal,* March 7, 2001, p. N5.

13. "Competitive Weapon," *CMA Management,* February 1999, p. 39.

14. "Coke's Zyman Fires Marketing Blitzkrieg," *Advertising Age,* August 30, 1993, p. 1.

15. "A Global Tune-up for Ford," *Business Week,* May 2, 1994, p. 38.

16. "When Head Office Goes Native," *Financial Times,* December 2, 1992, p. 11.

17. "Mack, Volvo Reorganize, Autocar Expends," *Waste Age,* January 2002, p. 20.

18. Christopher A. Bartlett, "ABB's Relays Business: Building and Managing a Global Matrix," Harvard Business School Case, 1993.

19. "An Impossible Organization, but the Only One That Works," *Financial Times,* June 21, 1989, p. 14.

20. Jean-Pierre Jeannet, Managing with a Global Mindset (London: Financial Times Pitman, 2000), Chapter 13, p. 171.

21. "Got Problems, We Have Answers," *Chemical Week,* March 13, 2002, p. S8.

22. "ABB Divests to Compass," *European Venture Capital Journal,* February 1, 2002, p. 73.

23. "Leveraging Europe into an Era of Higher Growth," *Wall Street Journal,* June 15, 1999, p. 12.

24. ICI has since sold its explosives business unit.

25. "Mergers Can't Save the Drug Industry," *Wall Street Journal,* May 27, 2002, p. A11.

26. "Can Procter & Gamble Make the Tide Turn?" *Los Angeles Times,* June 13, 1999, p. C1.

27. "P&G Jump-Starts Corporate Change," *Internetweek,* November 1, 1999, p. 30.

28. "Can P&G Recover Its Lost Ground?" *Marketing,* May 4, 2000, p. 19.

29. "Division Problem—Place vs. Product," *Wall Street Journal,* June 27, 2001, p. A1.

30. "Unilever Denies Split," *Marketing,* August 10, 2000, p. 7.

31. "Nestlé Won't Crunch Its Brands—Food Giant Points to Reorganization," *Wall Street Journal,* September 24, 1999, p. 8.

32. "Nestlé Nears Purchase of Chow Maker," *Asian Wall Street Journal,* January 16, 2001, p. 2.

33. "Ford Maps Out a Global Ambition," *Financial Times,* April 3, 1995, p. 9.

34. "Ford's Really Big Leap at the Future," *Fortune,* September 18, 1995, p. 134.

35. "Ford: Alex Trotman's Daring Global Strategy," *Business Week,* April 3, 1995, p. 94.

36. "The World That Changed the Machine," *Economist,* March 30, 1996, p. 63.

37. "Ford: Alex Trotman's Daring Global Strategy," *Business Week,* April 3, 1995, p. 94.

Chapter 17

Planning and Controlling Global Marketing

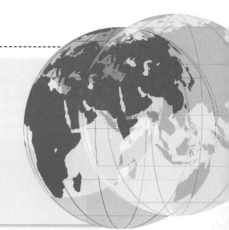

T he process of global marketing would not be able to function in a complex organization without the necessary attention to planning and controlling. In this chapter, we focus on the particular challenges faced by managers during the planning process when it is carried out in the global environment. Beginning with some of the traditional strategic planning approaches, we point out the difficulties in extending them across multiple markets. In particular, we argue that planning needs to occur with the full global opportunity in mind, and that global marketing is difficult, if not impossible, to plan on a country-by-country basis only. This chapter makes the distinction between corporate and business unit planning, covers the necessary control processes, and revisits the perennial debate between central versus local control. The chapter introduces you to the new developments of assigning global mandates to separate business units, and the challenge of making organizations learn globally rather than just locally. An overview of the chapter topics is provided in Figure 17.1.

THE GLOBAL PLANNING PROCESS

Planning in the global environment is challenging because of the added complexity caused by the number of external factors. Table 17.1 lists the differences between planning in a domestic setting and planning in a global one. As shown in the table, numerous factors, such as language, political differences, currencies, and insufficient market data, increase the complexity of global planning. These differences make developing and implementing global plans more difficult.

Strategic planning is a widely accepted practice of corporate business. The issue of globalization demands strategic research and thought in addressing increasingly

Figure 17.1: Planning and Controlling Global Marketing

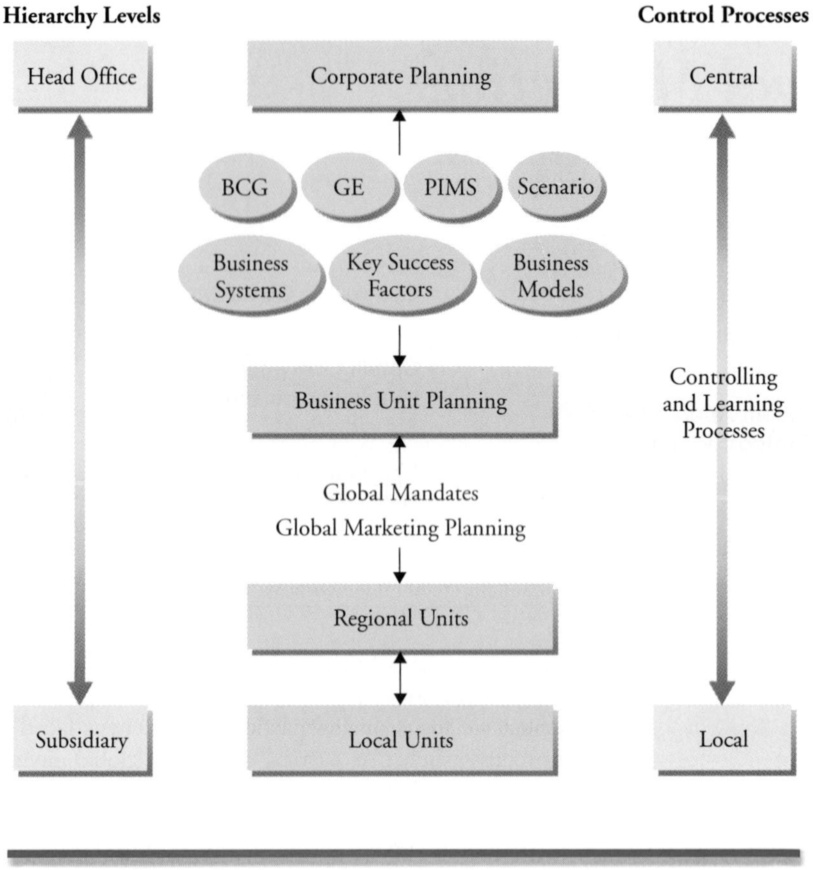

Hierarchy Levels

Head Office

BCG   GE   PIMS   Scenario

Business Systems   Key Success Factors   Business Models

Control Processes

Corporate Planning

Central

Business Unit Planning

Global Mandates
Global Marketing Planning

Regional Units

Controlling and Learning Processes

Subsidiary

Local Units

Local

complex and competitive world markets.[1] Global strategic planning often takes place at the highest levels of a company. Relatively young, well-trained executives commonly provide the information and analysis for these high-level discussions and decisions. It is important to understand the process that the board or executive committee follows when making a strategic decision because you may be the marketing manager implementing that decision.

CORPORATE VERSUS BUSINESS PLANNING

Global planning can take place at two levels. First, at the corporate level, a company decides which businesses it wants to engage in. This choice between different businesses has traditionally been the occupation of corporate planners. At a lower level, the business level, planning is undertaken to determine resource allocations and

Table 17.1 Domestic Versus Global Planning Factors

Domestic Planning	Global Planning
1. Single language and nationality	1. Multilingual/multinational/multicultural factors
2. Relatively homogeneous market	2. Fragmented and diverse markets
3. Market data is available, it is usually accurate, and collection is easy	3. Market data collection a formidable task, requiring significantly higher budgets and personnel allocation
4. Political factors relatively unimportant	4. Political factors frequently vital
5. Relative freedom from government interference	5. Involvement in national economic plans; government influences affect business decisions
6. Individual corporation has little effect on environment	6. "Gravitational" distortion by large companies
7. Chauvinism helps	7. Chauvinism hinders
8. Relatively stable business environment	8. Multiple environments, many of which are highly unstable (but may be highly profitable)
9. Uniform financial climate	9. Variety of financial climates ranging from overconservative to wildly inflationary
10. Single currency	10. Currencies differing in stability and real value
11. Business "rules of the game" mature and understood	11. Rules diverse, changeable, and unclear
12. Management generally accustomed to sharing responsibilities and using financial controls	12. Management frequently autonomous and unfamiliar with budgets and controls

Source: William W. Cain, "International Planning: Mission Impossible?" *Columbia Journal of World Business,* July–August 1970, p. 58. Reprinted by permission.

strategies within a particular business. Here, the issue is how to distribute resources across functional activities, product lines, segments, or geographic markets.

For the purpose of this text, we are more interested in planning at the business level and less in corporate planning activities. We cover some of the approaches for corporate level planning because they are frequently practiced at international firms. At the same time, we point out the weaknesses of those approaches when it comes to planning business activities, such as marketing, on a global basis within a particular business.

TRADITIONAL CORPORATE PLANNING MODELS

In this section of the chapter, we review the various types of planning processes currently being used, their application to the global market environment, and the advantages and disadvantages of each procedure when used for planning the global marketing effort. The most widely used approaches to planning are the following:[2]

- Boston Consulting Group (BCG) approach
- General Electric/McKinsey (GE) approach
- Profit impact of market strategy (PIMS)
- Scenario planning

Numerous articles and papers review and compare the various planning models as they apply to domestic markets. Using these domestic systems as a base, we will examine each approach as it is used for global markets.

Many companies consist of several different businesses. When initially established, each of these businesses is expected to grow. The company encourages growth by expanding research and development, advertising, and promotional budgets for all but declining products. In recent years, the cost and availability of capital have prompted corporations to be much more selective in the financing of their businesses. Firms look at their individual businesses and decide which ones to build, maintain, phase out, divest, or close down. Therefore, the job of corporate planning has become one of evaluating current businesses and searching for new opportunities so that the mixture of businesses within the firm will provide the necessary growth and cash flow for growth. Once the firm is subdivided into strategic business units (SBUs), the company needs to use the planning process to determine each SBU's expected future potential and the long-term opportunity for each business. Although the concept of an SBU is widely accepted, it does have its limitations. For example, vertically integrated businesses might share facilities, and performance may be interrelated; both factors make it difficult to separate business units into neat components.[3]

THE BOSTON CONSULTING GROUP APPROACH.   The Boston Consulting Group (BCG) approach classifies current strategic business units into a business portfolio matrix, as shown in Figure 17.2. The matrix includes both current SBUs and potential or proposed opportunities. The proposed opportunities are normally an extension of the current business via expansion into a new country or new product variation. BCG's methodology classifies these businesses by market growth and market share. Market growth is the expected total market growth per year. Market share is the company's relative share compared with that of the largest competitor. For example, a rating of 1.0 means that the SBU has the same size share as the largest competitor, a 0.5 rating means that it has one-half the share of the largest competitor, and a 3.0 rating means that it has a share three times larger than the largest competitor.

A firm's SBUs are evaluated and classified based on this approach. Market growth rate relates to the stage of the product life cycle, and relative market share is based on the concept of market dominance. To survive in the long term, a firm needs the proper balance of business in each area of the matrix. The different areas are dubbed stars, cash cows, dogs, and problem children.

Over time, businesses will change their positions. Many SBUs start as problem children, then become stars, then cash cows, and finally dogs. The corporate planning function must work with the managers of each SBU to forecast the future mix of businesses in each area. Then resources must be allocated based on this forecast as well as on the corporate objectives.

The BCG approach in global planning has the following major advantages:

- Requires a global view of the firm's businesses and its competition
- Provides a framework for analysis and comparison of each business

Figure 17.2: Boston Consulting Group Matrix

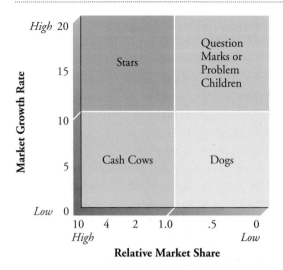

Source: PERSPECTIVES, no. 135, "The Experience Curve-Reviewed, 14.
The Growth Share Matrix or The Product Portfolio." Adapted by permission
from The Boston Consulting Group, Inc., 1973.

- Provides a solid basis for the formulation of marketing objectives for global markets
- Uses a convenient graphic format that is easily understood by executives

An individual firm may have other objectives besides cash generation, such as gaining technical information, preventing competition, or establishing good relations with a local government. For example, both Philips and Siemens, two European global firms, have argued for years that they must keep their unprofitable semiconductor businesses. Philips and Siemens executives maintained that, without proprietary access to semiconductor know-how, their companies' ability to keep up with Japanese competitors in consumer and industrial electronics would be fatally undermined. Both have since divested important parts of those businesses, and Siemens has spun off its semiconductor business under the name of Infineon, which was the spinoff of the tenth largest semiconductor business in the world, with sales of $3.8 billion in 1998.[4]

THE GENERAL ELECTRIC/MCKINSEY APPROACH. General Electric and McKinsey management consultants worked together to develop the GE business screen, a multifactor assessment based on an analysis of factors relating to profitability. The approach is an extension of the BCG approach.[5]

The GE screen uses the following factors to evaluate SBUs:

Industry Attractiveness	Business Strength
Market size	Relative market share
Market growth	Price competitiveness
Market diversity	Size, growth
Profit margins	Product quality
Competitive structure	Profitability
Technical role	Technological position
Cyclicality	Strengths and weaknesses
Environment	Knowledge of customers and the market
Legal and social environment	Image, pollution, people

The GE approach rates each SBU, on the basis of these factors, for industry attractiveness and business strength. Each factor is given a certain weight. A procedure of aggregating various executives' opinions on these weights results in high, medium, or low attractiveness and business strength ratings.[6] Each SBU is then located on GE's nine-cell business screen, which is shown in Figure 17.3.

The GE approach has the same limitations as the BCG method. However, the GE method is more adaptable to global markets. Each firm can determine which factors are important to its success in a global market and can evaluate SBUs based on these factors. Little empirical work has been done, however, on either approach in the global context. The GE approach remains two-dimensional only, using only factors of industry attractiveness and business strength. This approach ignores the form of entry, and the importance of political stability (an attractiveness element) varies greatly, depending on whether a firm is exporting or involved in a direct foreign investment. The GE approach is useful for international companies because it provides more flexibility than the BCG approach, but its limitations should not be ignored.

PROFIT IMPACT OF MARKETING STRATEGY (PIMS). The PIMS project was started at General Electric. The model was further refined over the years at the Harvard Business School, the Marketing Science Institute, and finally at the Strategic Planning Institute. The PIMS model database includes the history and performance of over 450 companies and 3,000 businesses. The model includes a computer-based regression model that utilizes the experience of the database to determine what explains (or drives) profitability.[7] Each business is described in terms of thirty-seven factors, such as growth rate, market share, product quality, and investment intensity. The PIMS model uses multivariate regression equations to establish relationships among these different factors and also uses two separate measures of performance: return on investment (ROI) and cash flow. PIMS research indicates that these performance measures are explained by general factors such as the following:

- Market growth rate
- Market share of business

Figure 17.3: GE's Business Screen for Evaluating SBUs

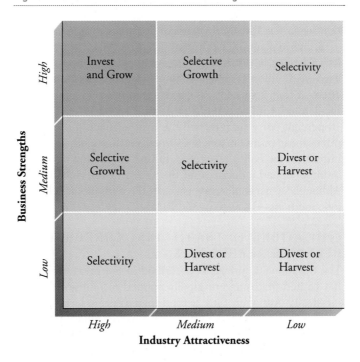

- Market share divided by the share of the three largest competitors
- Degree of vertical integration
- Working capital requirements per dollar of sales
- Plant and equipment requirements per dollar of sales
- Relative product quality

The PIMS model uses many more variables than either the BCG or GE approach. Using the thirty-seven factors, the model explains over 80 percent of the observed variation in profitability of the three thousand businesses in the database. The PIMS model may become one of the key strategic planning models in the future. With the utilization of a multinational database, the PIMS model will be able to assist planners in deciding how to allocate resources to meet corporate objectives.[8]

SCENARIO PLANNING. The three strategic planning models discussed so far are referred to as portfolio models. These models do not consider the impact of various external factors such as economic growth, energy costs, inflation, international relations, war, and economic fluctuations.[9] Scenario planning is a unique approach to strategic planning in which the multinational company's business is broken down into business/country segments. A central or most probable scenario is developed regarding significant external variables such as energy costs, world politics, and inflation. Possible variations of this central scenario are also developed. Then the business/country segments are evaluated based on the central scenario and the variation scenarios. Ideally, investment decisions can be based on this analysis.

Scenario planning has limitations. First, the development of a central scenario and its variations is difficult. There will be many inputs to this scenario, with limited agreement among managers about which inputs to include. Second, analysis of the effect of each scenario will also be complex. For example, if a firm is selling pipe to the United Kingdom and the central scenario predicts that oil prices will go up 10 percent per year, how will the firm evaluate the U.K. pipe market? Increased oil prices mean more tax revenues from North Sea oil, an increase in exports, a favorable impact on the balance of trade, the strengthening of the pound sterling, an increase in imports, and a decrease in the ability of the remaining U.K. industries to export. Although scenario planning is a useful technique, it is best used to augment the portfolio methods—BCG, GE, and PIMS.

LIMITATIONS TO TRADITIONAL CORPORATE PLANNING APPROACHES

The traditional approaches described in the previous sections were all conceived in the United States and originally applied to multiproduct companies competing domestically. Although they helped managers understand which businesses might be emphasized over others in terms of resource allocations, they did not help in allocating resources within a business once it was selected for additional investment.

To overcome the limitations of the data, some companies treated each country, or market, as a distinctly different business and analyzed each foreign market in the same way as the domestic division. The disadvantage of this approach stems from the fact that the firm treats each country as a separate investment decision, selecting those countries that "fit the approach" and eliminating others that do not compare favorably with the database. As we pointed out earlier in Chapters 7 and 8, however, a firm must consider the entire set of data on its chessboard on a global basis, and not evaluate opportunities on a country-by-country basis only. The former technique would preclude a firm from treating each country as a separate entry decision. Rather, the company would have to support an entire business, with all of its implications, and only later determine resource allocations within the business.

To make these approaches more helpful in planning at the corporate, multiproduct level, the entire database needs to consist of global data, not just U.S. or single-country data. Whether using a BCG, GE, or PIMS approach, the data must be drawn from the entire global market of each business. That is, only if a company were to complete a BCG analysis for each of its separate SBUs, each based on a complete and globalized data set, would the allocation or priority-setting process be relevant for the planning of global operations.

RECENT APPROACHES TO STRATEGIC PLANNING

Several new approaches to strategic planning have emerged in recent years. Most of these approaches focus on a single business rather than a portfolio of businesses. These more recent planning tools emphasize the competitiveness of a single business.

Figure 17.4: Macro Business Systems

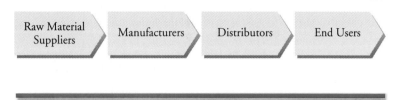

BUSINESS SYSTEM APPROACH

Initially developed by McKinsey, a U.S.-based consulting firm, the business system approach became most popular through the writing of Michael Porter.[10] Also known as the Porter model, this approach was adopted by global companies all over the world. A firm's business system consists of the value chain, as the products move from raw materials through the final stages of production, all the way to the end users and customers (see Figure 17.4).[11] For analysis purposes, a business needs to document each stage of the value chain; determine the value added at each level; and probe for the interaction at each stage of the chain among suppliers, manufacturers, and downstream end users or customers. The dynamics of the interaction, including the pressure from substitutes, is considered a major determinant of competitive intensity and will give managers some guidance about where to concentrate the firm's resources.

The business system can be divided into two major components. The macro business system deals with the overall industry structure and groups the types of participants that make up an industry. Typical participants are raw material or component suppliers, manufacturers, distributors, and retailers, as well as end-users or customers. Depending on the type of industry, there may be many more participant groups. The second component of a business system consists of the micro business systems. Each micro business system lists the internal value chain of a given participant group. The micro business system, sometimes called the internal business system, lists all the value-creating functions of a firm (see Figure 17.5).

This analysis yields understanding of the competitive forces as they affect a particular group. Different generic strategies, or strategic groups, might become apparent and can thus become prototype strategies that predict how to compete. The analysis helps managers understand how value is created in an industry and therefore helps them to allocate resources effectively. Although this type of competitive and industry analysis can be performed on a single-country industry, it is valuable to a global marketing operation because it gathers corresponding data from around the world and completes it with a global data set. The issues raised concern the industry structure in other countries, and a company needs this information to understand if it is facing the same or a different industry and competitive structure.

KEY SUCCESS FACTORS

Key success factors (KSFs) are the basic requirements for competing in an industry. Some examples are shown in Table 17.2. Any firm competing in the same industry is faced with the same requirements to compete. Without these key success factors,

Figure 17.5: Micro Business System

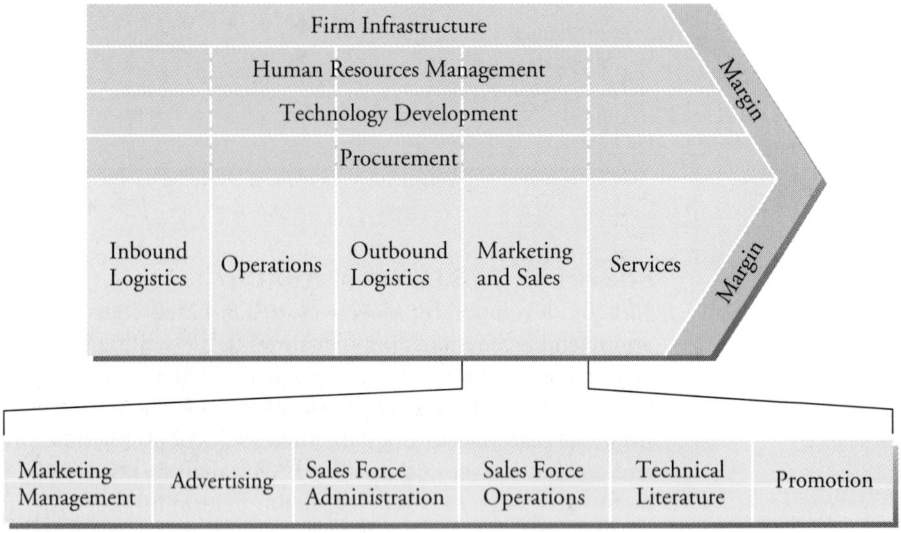

Source: Reprinted with the permission of The Free Press, a Division of Simon & Schuster Adult Publishing Group, from COMPETITIVE ADVANTAGE: Creating and Sustaining Superior Performance by Michael E. Porter. Copyright © 1985, 1998 by Michael E. Porter. pp. 46–47.

a company would suffer negative competitive consequences because these factors are essentially industry imperatives.[12] Through analysis, the company must not only identify these KSFs, but also learn how to apply the best mix of resources to get the maximum benefit relative to the competition.

KSFs are relevant to a given industry or to a sector of that industry. The factors are tangible and can be identified in the macro business system, as explained above. For application of the KSFs to be effective, managers must have a clear idea of the business system. KSFs come in two types. First are those KSFs that are required of all industry competitors (they are often referred to as qualifiers). A company needs to deliver on the qualifiers just to compete. Beyond the qualifiers are KSFs that differentiate various industry players. These KSFs are referred to as differentiators. Finally, all KSFs can be defined at the general industry, sector, or segment level and should relate to the space where a company has decided to compete. A company must isolate and understand KSFs to be able to allocate scarce resources effectively.

A global company needs to understand whether its defined KSFs are unique to a given country or region, or if they are in fact so similar that they apply easily everywhere. From a global marketing point of view, this distinction is of great importance. If we have a considerable degree of similarity among KSFs, we can speak of a high degree of global industry logic, as we discussed in Chapter 7. Companies finding a high industry logic gain from leveraging around those KSFs worldwide. Although they may have less to do with customers and much more to do with processes, globalizing around the marketing process may be very important to the success of a firm.

Table 17.2 Key Success Factors by Industry		
	Specimen Industries	
Key Factor or Function . . .	**. . . To Increase Profit**	**. . . To Gain Share**
Upstream — Raw materials sourcing	Uranium	Petroleum
Production facilities (economies of scale)	Shipbuilding, steelmaking	Shipbuilding, steelmaking
Design	Aircraft	Aircraft, Hi-Fi
Production technology	Soda, semiconductors	Semiconductors
Product range/variety	Department stores	Components
Application engineering/engineers	Minicomputers	LSI, microprocessors
Sales force (quality × quantity)	ECR	Automobiles
Downstream — Distribution network	Beer	Films, home appliances
Servicing	Elevators	Commercial vehicles, e.g., taxis

Source: Kenichi Ohmae, *The Mind of the Strategist.* Copyright © 1982 McGraw-Hill Companies, Inc. Used with permission.

A company would therefore leverage its branding expertise, rather than its brands, and build upon its ability to do positioning, rather than exploit a given position for a single product on a global basis.

BUSINESS MODELS

The practice of analyzing business in terms of business models was adopted during the ebusiness craze that followed the upsurge in Internet-based businesses. However, the business model approach is of value to any business, whether it is Internet-based or not, and the approach is a useful addition to the planning and control tools of a firm. Business models are essentially an outline of the configuration of a business. Business models describe what companies get paid for, how the revenue composition is created, and what a company must do to obtain that revenue flow. The same applies to the cost structure or asset structure of a firm. In that sense, business models are different from strategies. However, they are essential complements to traditional strategies, which are much more focused on the direction of a business, rather than on its configuration.[13]

In traditional industries, little attention was paid to the business model because all companies operated under the same one. The situation changed when several new industry players in many sectors competed successfully on the basis of a new business model. Initially, Dell Computer used a different business model (direct) than did its competitors. Wal-Mart operated under an existing business model (discounting) but applied it to a different segment (rural customers). Amazon.com changed the business model for buying books. In all these cases, the basic composition of the business, the flow of revenues, and the structure of assets was substantially different from traditional competition.

From a global perspective, business models are relevant to global marketing. Most companies become comfortable competing with a given business model and do not adopt another one easily. Whether or not a company can compete around the world with its own business model is therefore crucial. Perhaps the company wants to redesign its business model, or build its business from the beginning with a global model. A company might want to find out if it has to master more than one business model when its business grows globally. Because it may be difficult to master several business models simultaneously, companies may even want to consider staying out of a market where their own business models are not applicable.

CORPORATE PLANNING IN THE GLOBAL AGE: ASSIGNING GLOBAL MANDATES

Companies looking at the entire global opportunity frequently find that they must look at their business in a global context. Achieving global leadership is therefore considered a prize, a first competitive priority. With this goal as a company's priority, global market share in a sector, segment, or business is viewed as the ultimate aim. Business units, divisions, or SBUs are thus asked, even instructed, to maximize their opportunity globally, a situation we call *receiving a global mandate*. (See Chapter 16 for more information about global mandates.) Therefore, a major question to answer at the corporate level is, "Who should receive a global mandate?" Businesses that develop on a global basis typically need a larger resource base than those competing on a domestic basis only. Greater claims for resources make it more difficult for corporations to support all their businesses in the drive to achieve global leadership status. Corporate planning will thus have to assist in the selection of resources and in the resource allocation process.

First, corporate planners will initiate a thorough analysis of the need to assign global mandates to SBUs. Only businesses that face significant global logic should receive such global mandates. (Refer to Chapter 7 for more information about global logics.) For many firms, however, that criterion applies to several of their businesses. In the case of General Electric, in fact, global mandates apply to *all* of its major businesses, ranging from plastics to transportation, energy generation, medical technology, and more. At Siemens of Germany, all of its more than two hundred separate strategic planning units have global mandates. The same is true for the independent chemical businesses of ICI of the United Kingdom.

The resources required to make a global business out of one that isn't yet global are considerable. At one large European firm, the corporate planning staff determined that the company's cash-generating resources would never meet all the needs of the globalizing SBUs. Consequently, the company had to make resource allocations and set priorities. ICI was faced with enormous resource demands from both its chemical fibers and acrylics divisions. Neither had achieved global leadership status, and both were thus weak competitively. Making them leaders globally would have required substantial investments around the world. Rather than maintain two subcritical businesses or attempt to expand both not quite enough, the company found a partner to trade. ICI divested its fibers business, selling it to DuPont of the United States. In return, DuPont sold its acrylics business to ICI. This trade allowed ICI to become the global leader in the acrylics category. In return, DuPont strengthened its presence in the European fibers business and in the textile sector. Both parties obtained a business that became a global leader.

Another firm that has made substantial resource allocation by focusing on a few global opportunities is Nokia of Finland. Originally active in forestry and paper production, the company diversified successfully into machinery, electronics, and telecommunications in the 1980s. The demands of its growing telecommunications businesses became so important, however, that Nokia began to divest itself of several of its original businesses, including the paper business, the computer business, and the consumer electronics business. This restructuring left Nokia with essentially two businesses: cellular infrastructure and cellular handsets. Both are now in a leading position in the race for global market dominance. For Nokia, fewer businesses that were well positioned globally were far preferable to a wide range of regional businesses.

The substantial resource commitments demanded of companies that want to expand their SBUs globally has also taken its toll among large U.S.-based multinational firms. PepsiCo is involved in a very difficult fight with Coca-Cola Company for global market leadership in the soft-drink sector, and it has had to contend with a competitor that has a soft-drink business only. PepsiCo has a large snacks business (Frito-Lay) and several large, internationally active, fast food restaurant chains (Pizza Hut, Taco Bell, KFC), in addition to soft drinks. The company has announced its intention to divest itself of the restaurant business and to reinvest the proceeds into the soft-drink business, particularly for market expansion in countries such as China, India, and eastern Europe, where Coca-Cola's position is not yet entrenched. Pepsi will not expand into Japan and Germany, where it sees little chance to dethrone Coke.[14] It appears that the main efforts in the area of global corporate planning for all companies lie in selecting, supporting, and guiding businesses that have a realistic chance of achieving global leadership in selective niches.

GLOBAL BUSINESS STRATEGY PLANNING

When planning at the business unit level, the issues are different from those raised at the corporate level. In particular, when a business has been assigned a global mandate from the company's head office, the planning focus must turn toward the approach to be taken to build a globally competitive business that can attain a leading position. The pertinent issue turns from which business to support to which actions the business must undertake to achieve the required competitive position. The starting point again is the entire global opportunity for the business, or the relevant global chessboard that best depicts the potential around the world. In business planning, the business must allocate resources across various functions, and marketing is only one among others such as research and development (R&D) and production. Furthermore, the business unit needs to plan these resource allocations across the relevant geography and determine the nature of the business focus, whether it is narrow or broad.

The following questions must be addressed in global business planning:

1. What is the relevant global opportunity for the business?
   Description of the global chessboard, determination of the relevant metrics that describe the opportunity set on a worldwide or global basis. This question will have to be analyzed by company and industry sectors.

2. What are the future developments of the global chessboard?

   Determination of the trends in volume and future volume developments. This question will also have to be analyzed by industry sector and according to a company's relevant competition.

3. What are the global logics facing the business?

   Clear understanding of global logics (customer, purchasing, industry, competitor, size or scale, regulatory, competitive—as described in Chapter 7) and a sense of the "footprint" faced by a company. This analysis must be done by industry sector.

4. What are the imperatives of the global logics?

   Refers to the markets or countries where a company with a global mandate has to compete, the markets it must win, the segments to do business in, and the like. All of these elements are required for winning a global competitive position that could lead to market leadership. Each industry sector faces its own specific set of global imperatives.

5. How are resources to be allocated on a global basis?

   Resource allocations occur across numerous countries, segments, and business functions. Marketing is but one core function, although in global battles it is a key weapon. Other functions are R&D, production, logistics, etc.

6. What are the strategic objectives for the business or the marketing function?

   Setting measurable objectives, such as market share, volume, or profitability, that become guideposts for the business and the individual functions, such as marketing, in their own planning cycles.

For a business-to-business unit that operates under a global mandate, these planning issues are different than planning issues for domestic units. We argue that it is best to answer these questions *first* from a global point of view. If each country operation submits plans to be integrated later (a bottom-up approach), the achievement of a single, unified global strategy is questionable. A single, unified global strategy has a much better chance at success, however, if local country or regional units plan their activities in line with an overall global business strategy, an approach that follows more of a top-down approach.

THE GLOBAL MARKETING PLANNING PROCESS

The complexity of global markets requires a structured approach to the planning process. Research into the practices of multinational companies has revealed several problems regarding the planning process; among them are the following:

- Too much inaccurate information and a lack of useful information for planning
- A neglect of strategic or long-term planning
- Overemphasis on the plan as a control device instead of as a means for achieving the objectives
- A belief that forecasting and budgeting were market planning
- A separation of long-term and short-term plans, which precluded operational management from considering more desirable alternatives[15]

The heterogeneous nature of global markets and the difficulty of data collection require that the marketer take an organized approach to evaluating opportunities and

Figure 17.6: Global Marketing Planning Matrix

Global Decisions	Marketing Planning Variables					
	Situation Analysis	Problems-Opportunity Analysis	Objectives	Marketing Program	Marketing Budgets	Sales Volume Cost/Profit Estimate
A. Commitment Decision						
B. Country Selection						
C. Mode of Entry						
D. Marketing Strategy						
E. Marketing Organization						

Source: Reprinted with permission from Helmut Becker and Hans B. Thorelli: *International Marketing Strategy.* Copyright © 1980, Pergamon Press PLC.

preparing plans. Figure 17.6 illustrates a global marketing planning matrix. The planning matrix is an organized approach to evaluating global opportunities. The matrix requires that the marketer evaluate the marketing planning variables at each level of decision making. Levels of decision making, which are located on the vertical axis, begin with the commitment decision. This first decision, whether or not to enter foreign markets, is based on the firm's objectives, its resources, and the opportunities available in international versus domestic markets. After making the commitment decision, a company selects the country it wishes to enter. The country decision is based on an evaluation of the environment, the demand, the corporate resources, and the financial projections. The mode of entering the selected country will be based on the firm's commitment decision, the country selection, and the cost/benefit evaluation of different modes of entry.

As we discussed in Chapter 9, the mode of entry is itself affected by several other factors, such as risk assessment and laws of foreign ownership. The marketing strategy flows logically from the firm's objective in a market, which includes the marketing mix required to differentiate products in that environment. The market organization decision is related to the objective and strategy for each market. The organizational structure determines which employees will be where, how decisions will be made, what information and services will move back and forth between the organizational unit and headquarters, and the budgeting control process.

COORDINATING THE GLOBAL PLANNING PROCESS

Coordinating the strategic planning process between the product marketing functions and the country managers is a challenging process. A natural tendency to emphasize the product dimension at the same time de-emphasizes the geographic dimension. To improve the coordination of product management and country management while utilizing the expertise of each, many companies have each *country* executive develop a comprehensive country opportunity plan that covers all products and strategies. The country executive's plan is compared to the plans of the individual strategic business units for that market. The combination of the two different plans provides a rich pool of information on tactics and opportunities. The final plan integrates the product and country points of view, with conflicts identified and solutions proposed.

Hoechst, a leading global chemical company based in Germany, used a multilevel planning system to coordinate the different layers of management and to get the full benefit of managers' knowledge, and to coordinate strategy from different parts of the company. The Hoechst planning system is illustrated in Figure 17.7. The top layer is strategic planning covering a ten-year horizon for products and regions. For example, what is Hoechst planning over the next ten years for agricultural operations and pharmaceuticals? In addition, what are the plans for Japan or France? Note that the

Figure 17.7: Hoechst Planning System

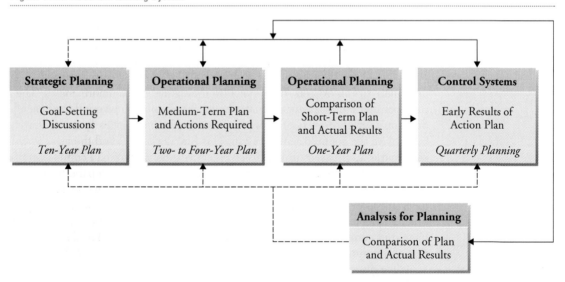

Source: Reprinted from *Long Range Planning*, vol. 23, no. 3, p. 18. Copyright 1990, with kind permission from Elsevier Science Ltd., The Boulevard, Langford Lane, Kidlington, OX5 IGB, UK.

strategic goals match for products and regions. Strategic planning at Hoechst involves the following four steps:

1. Gathering internal data about markets, competitors, and capacities
2. Gathering and analyzing external data on world economics, industry dynamics, market trends, and key success factors
3. Developing strategic options and selecting a preferred solution
4. Developing an implementation plan, with milestones identified and target dates set

The middle layers of Hoechst's system concern operational planning. This process covers the next four years on a rolling forecast, which is revised each year. The first year is in detail, and the second to fourth years are outlined roughly. The bottom layer is a control system for following up and monitoring the progress of the operational plans on a quarterly basis. This system allows deviations to be tracked and plans adjusted to deal with shocks, such as currency fluctuations. The planning system has proved successful, with Hoechst achieving a 1988 profit of 2.0 billion deutsche marks, the largest in its 125-year history.[16]

Siemens, a large electrical and electronics equipment manufacturer, has a formalized communication phase between the product groups and the geographic structures. During this formalized communication phase of the planning process, the product and country managers meet to establish an understanding of each other's position. Eaton Corporation is organized around a worldwide product structure, and the corporation found it necessary to inform managers of methods for responding to common environmental issues such as political conditions, taxes, inflation, and joint ownership.

CENTRALIZED VERSUS LOCALIZED MARKETING

The arguments about centralized versus localized decision making in planning have been around for a long time. Although differences exist between companies and industries, some widespread trends have emerged. Originally, when international firms had little experience with planning, much of the planning and decision making was centralized around headquarters. As companies became more mature and hired more managers with planning experience, and as managers around the world became more familiar with modern planning approaches, companies began to decentralize the planning process. Nevertheless, each company has to find the appropriate equilibrium between a desire to plan locally and the desire to retain home office control.

The central versus local argument centers around two separate decision areas. First is the location issue, ranging from head office, to regional office if applicable, to local subsidiary. Second are the decision areas themselves—issues such as segmentation, positioning, distribution, pricing, and other crucial marketing decisions. Who should make these decisions, and who should be responsible for planning them? See Figure 17.8 for a decision-making responsibility grid. Figure 17.9 shows typical patterns for global marketing responsibility.

The type of global marketing strategy selected by a firm greatly influences the type of organizational charter awarded to individual units. Companies subscribing to a multidomestic strategy (see Chapter 8) are more likely to favor local decision making because their business thinking rewards such an approach. Companies with a

Figure 17.8: Decision-Making Responsibility Grid

Marketing Decision Area	Head Office Control	Regional Control	Local Control
Marketing Planning			
Marketing Strategy			
Segment Selection			
Product Development			
Positioning			
Communications			
Pricing			
Sales Management			
Distribution Channel			

global marketing mix strategy, in which much of the marketing strategy is part of an integrated global marketing plan, are not inclined to let local affiliates make many decisions. A company that practices a global segment strategy is not in a position to let local management select target segments according to local requirements. Thus, the responsibility allocation matrix has to be consistent with the type of global marketing strategy adopted.

In global marketing, companies can distinguish between centralized or decentralized marketing parameters. Marketing parameters are decision areas, such as pricing, distribution, advertising, or positioning. Most companies can identify several such parameters in their marketing operations. The marketing parameters that make the list depend on the company and type of industry. For each firm, the key global marketing decision with respect to coordination centers on the selection of the appropriate parameters for centralized versus decentralized approaches. Given our earlier discussions on global logics in Chapter 7, marketing parameters subject to a high degree of global logic should be coordinated more centrally, whereas those subject to weak global logic can be left to local operations.

For firms subject to a high degree of global purchasing logic (that is, customers buy globally and are very much aware of differing offers around the world), pricing must be much more centrally coordinated than in an industry with little global pur-

Figure 17.9: Patterns of Global Marketing Responsibility

Marketing Decision Area	Head Office Control	Regional Control	Local Control	Head Office Control	Regional Control	Local Control	Head Office Control	Regional Control	Local Control
Marketing Planning	X			X			X		
Marketing Strategy	X					X	X		
Segment Selection	X					X		X	
Product Development	X					X		X	
Positioning	X					X		X	
Communications			X			X			X
Pricing			X			X			X
Sales Management			X			X			X
Distribution Channel			X			X			X

Marketing Decision Area	Head Office Control	Regional Control	Local Control	Head Office Control	Regional Control	Local Control	Head Office Control	Regional Control	Local Control
Marketing Planning	X			X					X
Marketing Strategy	X			X					X
Segment Selection		X		X					X
Product Development		X		X					X
Positioning		X		X					X
Communications		X		X					X
Pricing		X		X					X
Sales Management		X		X					X
Distribution Channel		X		X					X

chasing logic. Companies subject to considerable global information logic find it necessary to subject advertising to a much higher degree of coordination than those companies that do not experience such forces. Finally, firms confronted with a high degree of customer logic find it necessary to engage in the coordination of global positioning, or segmentation.

The fact that dynamic markets shift the predominant global logic forces constantly in many industries underscores the need to reevaluate the key marketing parameters regularly. This situation also means that the marketing parameters may shift from central to local, or vice versa, as the global logic forces affecting a company and industry change over time.

CONTROLLING GLOBAL MARKETING OPERATIONS

Maintaining control of global operations is a growing concern in light of the increasing trend toward globalization. As a company becomes larger, it faces more critical decisions, and control over operations tends to dissipate. A company's planning process is usually based on several assumptions about country environments, competitors, pricing, government regulations, and so on. As a plan is implemented, the company must monitor the plan's success, as well as the variables used to develop the plan. As the environment changes, so will the plan; therefore, a critical part of planning is control. Establishment of a system to control marketing activities in numerous markets is not easy. But if companies expect to achieve the goals they have set, they must establish a control system to regulate the activities for achieving the desired goals.

SELECTING A CONTROL METRIC

For a control strategy to be effective, it must measure the elements that are relevant to the business on a global scale. Because measurements used to control global marketing operations also affect managerial behavior and the motivation that drives organizations, companies need to be careful about selecting metrics that are useful and actually tell a strong story about the competitive position of a company's business. For an effective control strategy, a company needs to clarify not only what to measure or control (and the unit of measurement), but also the geographic delineation of the data, which might be on a country level, a regional level, or even a global level. Both choices are strategic, and both are important to the development of an effective control strategy. For the purpose of this section, we highlight three possible metrics that can be used alone or in combination. Each offers a different indication of the competitive health of a business.

PERFORMANCE AGAINST GLOBAL MARKET POTENTIAL. For a company to track its global market performance, it can compare a business against the global potential. This comparison requires the company to be knowledgeable about the true potential, not just the current market size, around the world and in key markets. A company should be able to document the current and the future global chessboard of its business with volume indicators against future growth. Comparing the firm's business allows the firm to measure progress and to see if it has taken advantage of the entire opportunity.

GLOBAL MARKET COVERAGE. The global market comprises about two hundred countries and territories, and few companies can afford to be present in all of them. Consequently, choices have to be made, and more important countries will need to be selected. This prioritizing of countries on the basis of "must win" markets was described in Chapter 8. Invariably, companies are confronted with the need to select the number of countries necessary to achieve their strategic objective. A company's control strategy therefore includes the choice about how many markets a firm needs to enter to be successful. Clearly, if a company has an aspiration to be a global leader, both in terms of position and market share, such a goal would be difficult to attain if only a fraction of the total global opportunity was covered. Figure 17.10 shows that two very different scenarios are possible when it comes to global market coverage.

First, a firm may encounter a highly concentrated market where the vast majority of the global opportunity is contained in a few markets. Once these few markets are covered, entering additional markets adds very little incremental volume to the business. This situation allows a firm to pick only the largest markets and still cover sufficient opportunity to have a good chance at reaching its strategic objectives, measured in terms of global market share. A second scenario consists of the opposite pattern, where many markets account for a large volume of sales. In this second scenario, a company may have to enter many more markets to reach a global share of sufficient size to reach its objectives.

GLOBAL VERSUS LOCAL SHARE OF MARKET. A recurring theme in global marketing control is the nature of the market share data to be collected. Everyone is familiar with the concept of market share, but the unit of analysis—country, region, or global—is not always clear. And this unit of analysis is also complicated by the fact that it must be computed by segment or by the total business. Figure 17.11 depicts the choices to be made in the form of a grid. Let us assume that a company is in six different business lines, or segments, and is active across a wide range of regions (and thus countries). When reviewing the company's performance, management needs to reflect on the most relevant share data because these data have great implications for the conduct of marketing operations.

Figure 17.10: Selection of "Must Win" Markets

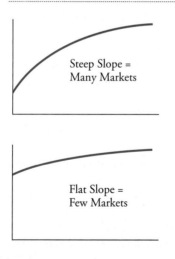
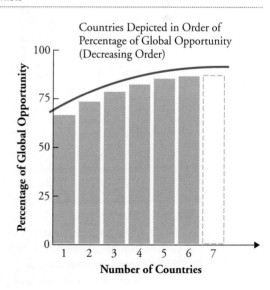

Figure 17.11: Relevant Global Rankings

Segments	Regions			
	North America	Europe	Asia/ Pacific Area	Worldwide
S_1	Local Rank			
S_2				
S_3				Global Segment Rank
S_4				
Company Rankings		Composite Regional Rank		Composite Global Rank

If a company measures its share, and corresponding competitive rank, on a country-by-country basis, the company implies that its performance in one country does not affect its performance in a second country. This situation is true when the competitive games logic, or global industry logic, is so low that little leverage can be obtained from combining businesses across multiple markets. Country-based market shares, or rankings, indicate a series of local battles with possibly different outcomes and no cross-relationships.

When a company measures its performance across several countries comprising a single region, such as Europe or Asia, the global chess game consists of regional battles, and what counts is the regional share, regardless of the outcome of individual country share. A company might want to be first in Europe, and it may not matter much what the outcome of the competition is in Germany, Italy, or Spain, as long as the company wins the overall European race. With such a strong regional logic, there are several regional battles to be waged, but share is measured independently by region.

A third scenario consolidates performance data across a series of segments, with the assumption that the overall global segment market share is most important. In this scenario, the firm operates under the assumption that the business is different from segment to segment, with limited leverage opportunities. In addition, it does not matter much what the segment positions are in each country, as long as the company attains global segment leadership.

Our fourth and final scenario takes us to the overall business volume and share, or the combined share across regions and segments. A company focusing on this measurement as its key control metric believes that it matters little what position it obtains geographically and in each segment, as long as the total across both results in a leading position.

The choice of the appropriate measurement depends greatly on the nature of the industry, and whether the method of competing varies substantially from country to country, from region to region, or from segment to segment. The presence or absence of these differences affects the leverage opportunities of the firm, and thus results in a different metric for global marketing control.

ELEMENTS OF A CONTROL STRATEGY

Control is the cornerstone of marketing management. Control provides the means to direct, regulate, and manage global marketing operations. The implementation of a marketing program requires a significant amount of interaction among the individual areas of marketing (product development, advertising, sales), as well as the other functional areas (production, research and development, finance). The control system is used to measure these business activities, in addition to competitive reaction and market reaction. Deviations from planned activities and actual results are analyzed and reported so that corrections can be made.

Many companies need to improve their control processes continuously. Without some type of control system, strategies are never implemented. Most strategies are long-term and can often take a back seat to the short-term tactical decisions needed for quarterly results. Through interviews with over fifty companies regarding their control systems, Goold assessed control systems on two dimensions: the number of performance criteria and the formality of the strategic control process. Figure 17.12 summarizes the control systems of eighteen multinational companies.[17] The research on these companies found that strategic control systems add value by:

- Forcing greater clarity and realism in planning
- Encouraging higher standards of performance
- Providing more motivation for business managers
- Permitting timely intervention by corporate management
- Ensuring that financial objectives do not overwhelm strategic objectives
- Defining responsibilities more clearly, making decentralization function better

A control system has three basic elements: (1) the establishment of standards, (2) the measurement of performance against standards, and (3) the analysis and correction of any deviations from the standards. Although control seems like a simple aspect of the management process, a wide variety of problems arises in international situations, resulting in inefficiencies and intracompany conflicts.

Companies have found many inefficiencies and redundancies in the way business is done. Thus, many are looking for ways to improve performance as well as to reduce costs. Business process reengineering is typically defined as the fundamental rethinking and radical design of business processes to achieve dramatic improvements in critical, contemporary measures of performance, such as costs, quality, service, and speed.[18] When Rank Xerox developed a set of seven uniform basic processes to be applied across all functional departments in Europe, the company

Figure 17.12: Strategic Control Processes
of Eighteen Multinationals

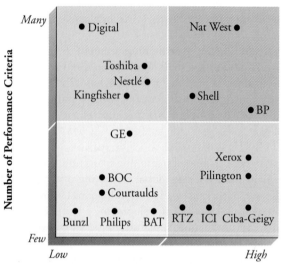

Source: Michael Goold, *Strategic Control* (London: Economist Books, 1990),
p. 33. Reprinted by permission.

was expected to cut overhead by $200 million per year while at the same time improve productivity.[19]

DEVELOPING STANDARDS.   Setting standards is an extremely important part of the control process because standards direct the efforts of individual managers. To influence the behavior of the managers who direct the global marketing programs, the standards must be clearly defined, accepted, and understood by these managers. Standard setting is driven by the corporate goals. Corporate goals are achieved through the effective and efficient implementation of a marketing strategy on a local-country level. The standards should be related to the sources of long-term competitive advantage. In companies where the strategies are decentralized to a business, only four to six key objectives are recommended. Fewer objectives focus management's efforts without causing confusion about priorities.[20] The standards should be set through a joint process with corporate headquarters and the local marketing organization. Normally, standard setting is done annually, when the operational business plan is established.

Control standards must be tied specifically to the strategy and based on the desired behavior of the local marketing personnel. The desired behavior should reflect the actions to be taken to implement the strategy, as well as the performance standards that indicate the success of the strategy, such as increased market share or sales. Examples of *behavioral standards* include the type and amount of advertising, the distribution coverage, market research to be performed, and expected price levels. *Performance standards* include trial rates by customers or sales by product line. A trend in the 1990s broadened the measures of business performance beyond financial data. More and more companies now measure quality, customer satisfaction, innovation, and market share.[21]

MEASURING AND EVALUATING PERFORMANCE. After standards are set, a process is required for monitoring performance. To monitor performance against standards, management must be able to observe current performance. Observation in the international environment is often impersonal because it is usually done through mail, cable, or fax, but it can also be done through more personal methods, like telephone, travel, or meetings. Much of the numerical information, such as sales and expenses, are reported through the accounting system. Other data, such as the implementation of an advertising program, are communicated through a report. The reporting system may be weekly, monthly, or quarterly.

ANALYZING AND CORRECTING DEVIATIONS FROM THE STANDARDS. The purpose of establishing standards and reporting performance is to ensure achievement of the corporate goals. To achieve these goals, management must evaluate performance versus standards and initiate actions when performance is below the standards set. Because of distance, communication, and cultural differences, the control process can be difficult in the international setting.

Control strategy can be related to the principle of the carrot and the stick, or using both positive and negative incentives. On the positive side, outstanding performance may result in increased independence, more marketing dollars, and salary increases or bonuses for the managers. On the negative side, unsatisfactory performance can lead to the reduction of all the rewards associated with a satisfactory performance, as well as the threat of firing the managers responsible. The key to correcting noncompliance with company standards is getting the managers to understand and agree with the standards, then giving them the ability to correct the deficiencies. This strategy often means that the managers are given some flexibility with resources. For example, if sales are down 10 percent, managers may need the authority to increase advertising or reduce prices to offset the sales decline.

MAKING STRATEGIC CONTROL WORK. Most companies do not have a formal strategic control system. Few define and monitor their strategic objectives as systematically as they monitor their budgets. Although most managers can tell you within pennies how much the advertising expenditures are over or under the budget, few can tell you the six milestones to implementing the 1998 strategy and the company's progress on each. To establish and get full value from a formal strategic control system, Goold offers several practical recommendations, which are summarized in Table 17.3.

GLOBALIZING THE CONTROL PROCESS. Many of the fundamental control processes we have described in this section apply to single-market, or domestic marketing, as much as they apply to multicountry, or global marketing. If we were to focus only on those characteristics that are due to the additional complexity of

Table 17.3 Making Formal Strategic Control Work

Issues	Recommendations
Selecting the right objectives	Based on analysis of competitive advantage
	Few in number
	Milestones that measure short-term progress
	Leading indicators of future performance
	Projects or action programs only if important for competitive advantage
Setting suitable targets	Precise and objectively measurable, if possible
	Proposed by business managers but stretched by the center
	Competitively benchmarked
	Consistent with budget targets: tradeoffs openly confronted and resolved
Creating pressure for strategic performance	Systematic progress monitoring and reviews
	Personal rewards indirectly tied to achievement of strategic targets
	Performance against strategic targets matters to top management and is the basis for corporate interventions
Strategic planning and strategic control	High-quality strategic planning needed as basis for strategic controls
	Strategic planning process used to review strategic progress
Formality without bureaucracy	Avoid large staff departments and lengthy reports
	Avoid specially gathered data
	Conduct reviews face to face
	Supplement formal reviews with informal contacts
	Be prepared to short-circuit formal process if necessary

Source: Michael Goold, *Strategic Control* (London: Economist Books, 1990), p. 199. Reprinted by permission.

controlling simultaneously across several markets or countries, the globalized control tools stand out. By that we mean tools, or approaches, that are or can be handled equally by all operations of a globally acting firm. A company with global operations that leaves each local organization to select its own control procedures discovers quickly that controlling and directing the entire global marketing program becomes much more difficult. When managers from different country organizations meet for coordination sessions, they need to be able to speak the same "control language"; otherwise, inherent conflicts are magnified.

Lego, the Danish toy maker, developed a highly standardized marketing control procedure that allowed senior management to determine the status of each market quickly. For years, Lego maintained a list of key charts that contained the key marketing parameters for each of its main segments, such as preschool, early school, or late-school, tied to its brands of Duplo, Lego, and Technics, respectively. These charts were maintained regularly for each country market and had the same look and feel. The entire marketing organization was used to apply these charts for control, and senior management could quickly establish if a given market was making progress. Communications to the regional offices and the central head office was also greatly aided by this system. Companies must find a set of charts or other standardized method of organizing data that captures the essential marketing information in each market.

The existing information technology (IT) environment that dominates current businesses around the world is a great help in developing standardized control tools. Many global firms have adopted standardized IT software, such as those developed by SAP or Oracle, that allow them to maintain the exact same type of information in a large number of local organizations. Globally standardized IT systems are therefore a prerequisite to effective control of global marketing operations.

CONFLICT BETWEEN HEADQUARTERS AND SUBSIDIARIES

A universal problem facing global marketing executives is internal conflict between headquarters and subsidiaries. A study of large U.S. and European multinationals and their worldwide subsidiaries found that this conflict was a bigger problem than competition, political instability, or any of the other challenges of global marketing. Table 17.4 summarizes the results of the study.

Conflicts between headquarters and subsidiaries are inevitable given the natural differences in orientation and perception between the two groups. The subsidiary manager usually wants less control from headquarters, more authority, and more local

Table 17.4 Key Problems Identified by Large U.S. and European Multinationals
Key Problems Identified by Executives at Headquarters
Lack of qualified personnel
Lack of strategic thinking and long-range planning at subsidiary level
Lack of marketing expertise at the subsidiary level
Too little relevant communication between headquarters and subsidiaries
Insufficient utilization of multinational marketing experience
Restricted control of the subsidiaries by headquarters
Key Problems Identified by Executives in Subsidiaries
Excessive control procedures from headquarters
Excessive financial and marketing constraints
Insufficient participation of subsidiaries in product decisions
Insensitivity of headquarters to local market differences
Shortage of useful information from headquarters
Lack of multinational orientation at headquarters

Source: Adapted and reprinted by permission of the *Harvard Business Review.* From "Problems That Plague Multinational Marketers," by Ulrich E. Wiechmann and Lewis G. Pringle (July–August 1979). Copyright © 1979 by Harvard Business School Publishing Corporation. All rights reserved.

differentiation, whereas headquarters wants more detailed reporting and greater unification of geographically dispersed operations. This expected conflict is not always a disadvantage. In fact, the conflict causes constant dialogue between different organizational levels during the planning and implementation of strategies. This dialogue can result in a balance between headquarters and subsidiary authority, between a global and local perspective, and between standardization and differentiation of the global marketing mix. Some of the problems in planning and controlling global marketing operations can be reduced or eliminated. Common problems, such as defi-

Figure 17.13: Global Learning on a Cross-Border Basis

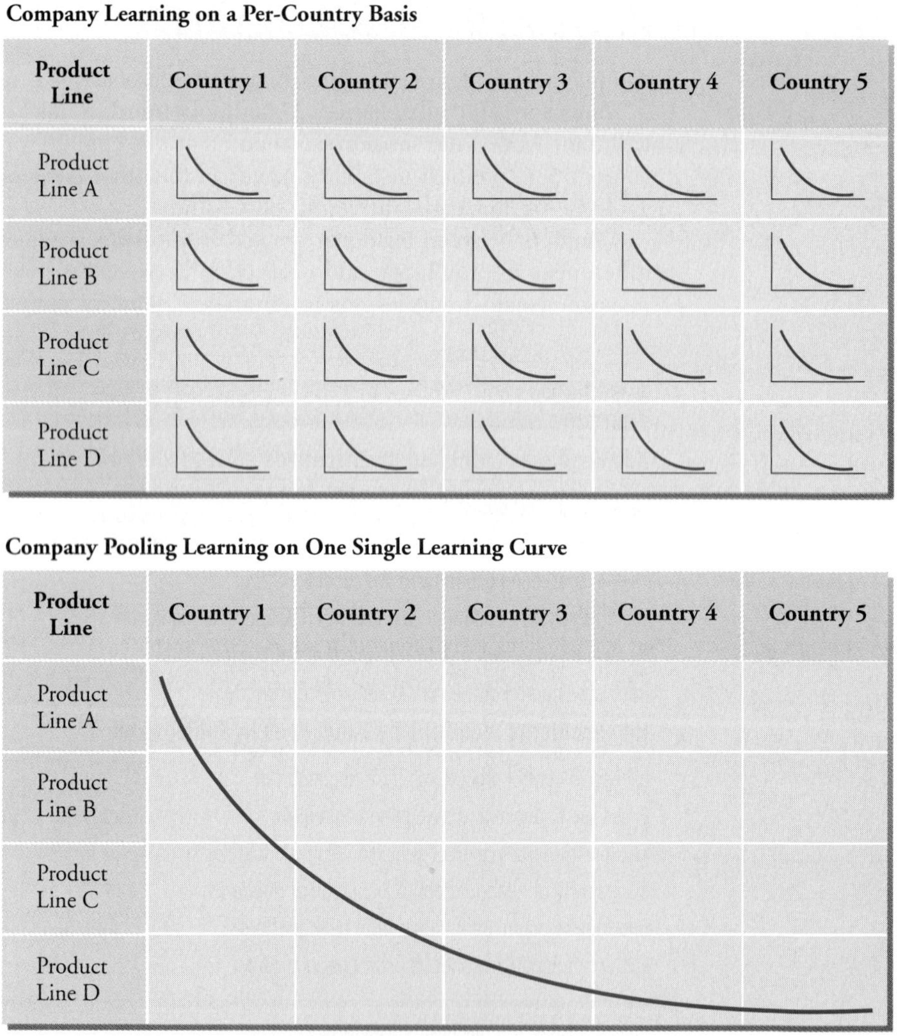
Company Learning on a Per-Country Basis
Product Line
Country 1
Country 2
Country 3
Country 4
Country 5
Product Line A
Product Line B
Product Line C
Product Line D
Company Pooling Learning on One Single Learning Curve
Product Line
Country 1
Country 2
Country 3
Country 4
Country 5
Product Line A
Product Line B
Product Line C
Product Line D

ciencies in the communications process, overemphasis on short-term issues, and failure to take full advantage of an organization's global experience, require open discussions between headquarters and subsidiary executives.

CREATING A GLOBAL LEARNING ORGANIZATION

Global companies with operations in many countries need to move beyond the traditional planning and controlling processes. One of the major problems that companies face is to assure that relevant knowledge learned from experience in one part of the world is transferred directly and put to use elsewhere. In conventional marketing responsibility, local managers accumulate local experiences and mature on a local learning curve. On that local learning curve, they accumulate new trends spotted locally, create ways to compete against other firms, and might even develop particular approaches to marketing practices.

In the globally learning company, all of these events are accumulated on a single learning curve, relevant for all local operations. This setup allows the firm to learn more quickly and to move along this experience curve more rapidly than if each local unit relied only on its own narrow experience (see Figure 17.13).[22] A firm that accomplishes this kind of learning can truly be called global, and its managers will develop global mindsets as a result. To achieve such global learning, both the planning and control processes must be shaped so that they facilitate cross-border learning.

CONCLUSIONS

The processes of planning global marketing programs and controlling their implementation are the first and last steps in global marketing. Marketers must first evaluate the global environment and select opportunities, using one of several planning approaches. This process leads to a strategy that is implemented by the organization. Sometimes, the organization's structure is changed to implement the strategy effectively. Finally, a system must be put in place to evaluate the implementation and measure progress toward the desired effect of the strategy.

The planning and controlling processes are critical parts of the global marketing process and require communication and agreement from different parts of the organization. And coordination of all this activity is difficult. It is no surprise that the planning and controlling processes lead to conflict. However, they also promote a firm's understanding of the world market, its development of effective strategies, and its successful implementation of those strategies with excellent results.

Questions for Discussion

1. You have recently been transferred from a domestic marketing division to the international marketing staff. Part of your new job is to review the planning process of each geographic marketing group in Europe, Asia, and South America. What differences between planning for these geographic marketing divisions and domestic planning can you expect?

2. What are the advantages and disadvantages of the Boston Consulting Group planning method when it is applied to global markets?

3. What are the advantages and disadvantages of the PIMS model over other planning methods that can be used for global planning?

4. What types of marketing decisions are usually left to local management? Why?

5. What is the purpose of a control system? How do you differentiate an effective control system from a poor one?

6. Recent feedback for sales, profit, and market share indicates that your subsidiary in Japan has not implemented the strategy that was developed. How will you influence the managers in Japan to focus more effort on successful strategy implementation?

7. You have recently lost four key international marketing people to other companies. You suspect that these losses indicate that the morale of your international executives is low. What can you do to improve morale?

For Further Reading

Ansoff, H. Igor, and Edward J. McDonnell. *Implanting Strategic Management*, 2nd ed. Englewood Cliffs, N.J.: Prentice Hall, 1990.

Bartness, Andrew, and Keith Cerny. "Building Competitive Advantage Through a Global Network of Capabilities." *California Management Review*, Winter 1993, pp. 78–103.

Cerny, Keith. "Making Local Knowledge Global." *Harvard Business Review*, May–June 1996, p. 22.

Day, George S. *Market Driven Strategy*. New York: Free Press, 1990.

Hamel, Gary. "Strategy as Revolution." *Harvard Business Review*, July–August 1996, p. 69.

Hamel, Gary, and C. K. Prahalad. "Strategic Intent." *Harvard Business Review*, May–June 1989, pp. 63–76.

Hax, Arnaldo, and Nicolas Majluf. *Strategy Concept and Process: A Pragmatic Approach*. Englewood Cliffs, NJ: Prentice Hall, 1996.

Jeannet, Jean-Pierre. M*anaging with a Global Mindset*. London: Financial Times/Prentice Hall, 2000.

Marchand, Donald. "Balancing Business Flexibility and Global IT." *Australian Financial Review*, September 30, 1998, p. 6.

Ohmae, Keniche. *The Mind of the Strategist*. New York: McGraw-Hill, 1982.

Porter, Michael, ed. *Competition in Global Industries*. Boston: Harvard Business School Press, 1986.

Porter, Michael. *Competitive Advantage*. New York: Free Press, 1985.

Porter, Michael E. "What Is Strategy?" *Harvard Business Review*, November–December 1996, p. 61.

Roth, Kendall, and Allen J. Morrison. "Implementing Global Strategy: Characteristics of Global Subsidiary Mandates." *Journal of International Business Studies*, 4th Quarter 1992, pp. 715–735.

Strebel, Paul. *Breakpoints*. Boston: Harvard Business School Press, 1992.

Endnotes

1. George Rabstejnek, "Let's Get Back to the Basics of Global Strategy," *Journal of Business Strategy*, September–October 1989, p. 34.

2. Richard G. Hamermesh, "Making Planning Strategy," *Harvard Business Review*, July–August 1986, p. 115.

3. Rael T. Hussein, "A Critical Review of Strategic Planning Models," *Quarterly Review of Marketing*, Spring–Summer 1987, p. 17.

4. "Siemens AG Names New Semi Division Infineon Technologies," *Electronic News*, March 22, 1999.

5. Information in this section is drawn from Managing Strategies for the Future Through Current Crises (Fairfield, Conn.: General Electric Company, 1975).

6. Peter Turnbull, "A Review of Portfolio Planning Models for Industrial Marketing and Purchasing Management," *European Journal of Marketing*, 1990, vol. 24, no. 3, pp. 7–10.

7. Robert D. Buzzell and Bradley T. Gale, *The PIMS Principles: Linking Strategy to Performance* (New York: Free Press, 1987).

8. Mark Drexler, and Thomas Reedy, "Managing Customers Profitably," *Canadian Insurance*, July 1, 1999, vol. 104, no. 8, p. 26.

9. Kerry Tucker, "Scenario Planning," *Association Management*, April 1, 1999, vol. 51, no. 4, p. 70.

10. Michael E. Porter, *Competitive Advantage* (New York: Free Press, 1985).

11. Ibid., p. 35.

12. Kenichi Ohmae, *The Mind of the Strategist* (New York: McGraw Hill, 1982), p. 42.

13. Joan Magretta, "Why Business Models Matter," *Harvard Business Review*, May 2002, p. 86.

14. "PepsiCo Loses Its Taste for Fast Food Chains," *Financial Times*, January 27, 1997, p. 19; "PepsiCo's New Formula," *Business Week*, April 10, 2000, p. 172.

15. Tom Griffin, "Marketing Planning: Observations on Current Practices and Recent Studies," *European Journal of Marketing*, 1989, vol. 24, no. 12, pp. 21–22.

16. Carol Kennedy, "Hoechst: Re-positioning for a Global Market," *Long Range Planning*, 1990, vol. 23, no. 3, pp. 16–22.

17. Michael Goold, Strategic Control (London: Economist Books, 1990), p. 125.

18. Michael Hammer and James Champy, *Reengineering the Corporation* (New York: HarperCollins, 1993), p. 32.

19. "Time to Get Serious," *Financial Times*, June 25, 1993, p. 9.

20. Michael Goold, *Strategic Control* (London: Economist Books, 1990), p. 120.

21. Ibid.

22. Jean-Pierre Jeannet, *Managing with a Global Mindset* (London: Financial Times/Prentice Hall, 2000), pp. 212–213.

Name and Company Index

Subject Index

for market entry, 308
regulation of, 124
Mexico
corruption in, 123
imports of, 35
joint ventures in, 502
NAFTA and, 4
MFN, *see* Most favored nation
(MFN) status
Micro business systems, 553, 554*f*
Microindicators, of market size, 143*t*,
143–144
Microlevel variables, in foreign market selection, 141–142
Middle East
global economy and, 59
market agreements in, 157*t*,
161–162
political risk in, 114–115
Mindscape, in global negotiating,
373
Mindsets
domestic, 217–218
global, 217*f*, 220–225, 246–249
international, 218–219
multinational, 219
panregional, 219–220
Mitbestimmung (Germany), 106
Mittelstände (Germany), 19
MNCs, *see* Multinational corporations (MNCs)
Mobile data transmission, 248
Mobile devices, Internet capabilities
of, 416
Modularized approach, for global
products, 467
Monetary union, European Union as,
58
Money market, covering foreign exchange risk through, 337, 338
Monopolies, telephone, 236
Most favored nation (MFN) status, 55
Multicountry issues
barriers to communication and,
365*f*, 365–366
marketing, 7*f*
personal selling through sales
force, 369–373
research, 208
Multidomestic strategies, 3, 274–283
Multinational corporations (MNCs),
12–13, 261

international divisions in, 527*f*,
527–528
investments by, 13
multidomestic marketing strategies and, 274–283
problems identified by, 571*t*
resource commitments by, 557
role in global marketing, 13
worldwide number of, 13
Multinational marketing, 3–4
use of term, 2
Multinational mindset, 219
Multiple-factor indexes, in marketing
research, 200
Multiregional strategies, 258–259,
274–276, 275*f*
Multivariate regression, in PIMS
model, 550
Murabaha process, 70
Music retail market, global, 5
Muslims, *see* Islam
"Must win" markets, targeting,
268–271
Mutual book credits, 48
Myanmar, Massachusetts contracts
and, 112

NAFTA, *see* North American Free
Trade Agreement (NAFTA)
Names, *see* Brands and branding
National economies, interdependence
of, 36
National income
accounting systems for, 43
prosperity and, 100
National interest, 98
Nationalistic countries, marketing in,
170–172
Nationalization, takeovers and,
109–110
Nationals, hiring of, 522
National security, *see* Security
National sovereignty, self-
preservation and, 99–100
National Technical Information
Services, data from, 191
NATO, *see* North Atlantic Treaty
Organization (NATO)
NATO-Russia Council, 159
Need(s)
felt, 197
global, 228

measuring, 196
satisfying through product function, 463–464
Needs hierarchy (Maslow), 165–166
Negotiations, in global selling
through multicountry sales
force, 372–373
Networks, global advertising,
420–422
New Construction Market Access
Pact (U.S.-Japan, 1994), 105
New-product development, 462–481
through acquisitions, 474–475
alliances for, 475
consortium approach to, 475–476
globalization of process, 476–478
idea sources for, 477–478
introducing to global markets,
478–481
joint ventures for, 475
market research and, 179–180
processes for global markets,
470–476
product introduction and,
478–481
product strategies in, 462–470,
463*f*
sources of, 463
News media, *see* Media; Promotion
Nigeria, data from, 189
NIH, *see* Not-invented-here (NIH)
syndrome
Noise, levels of, 365, 366
Noncash pricing, 351–356
Nondiscrimination, GATT and, 55
Nonrecourse financing, 348
Nontariff trade barriers, 52, 105
formal and administrative, 54–55
national prosperity and, 101
Nonverbal communication, 68
Nonverbal component, of Japanese
advertising, 402–403
Norms
buying motives and, 166
cultural, 373
North America
investment in, 263
market groups in, 159, 161
multidomestic marketing strategies in, 275–276
panregional marketing in, 4
as trading region, 243

Economy

Economy	GNI $ millions 2000	GNI per capita $ 2000	GNI per capita PPP $ 2000	GDP per capita average annual real growth % 1990–00	Agriculture % of GDP 2000	Gross capital formation % of GDP 2000	Average annual inflation rate % 1990–00	Current account balance % of GDP 2000	Total external debt $ millions 2000
Afghanistan	..	..c	..	..	..	..	..	..	..
Albania	3,833	1,120	3,600	2.7	51	19	39.2	-4.2	784
Algeria	47,897	1,580	5,040d	-0.1	9	24	18.1	..	25,002
American Samoa	..	..	..	..	..	..	..	..	..
Andorra	..	..e	..	..	..	..	..	..	..
Angola	3,847	290	1,180d	-1.8	6	28	740.6	0.0	10,146
Antigua and Barbuda	642	9,440k	10,000	2.8	4	30	2.5	-11.5	..
Argentina	276,228	7,460	12,050	3.0	5	16	5.2	-3.1	146,172
Armenia	1,991	520	2,580	-2.5	25	19	212.5	-14.6	898
Aruba	..	..	..	..	..	..	..	-1.1	..
Australia	388,252	20,240	24,970	2.9	3	24	1.5	-3.9	..
Austria	204,525	25,220	26,330	1.7	2	24	2.0	-2.8	..
Azerbaijan	4,851	600	2,740	-7.3	19	26	199.1	-2.8	1,184
Bahamas, The	4,533	14,960	16,400	0.1	..	..	2.7	-9.1	..
Bahrain	..	..e	..	1.7	§	17	-0.1	1.4	..
Bangladesh	47,864	370	1,590	3.0	25	23	4.0	0.0	15,609
Barbados	2,469	9,250h	15,020	1.7	6	18	3.1	-5.6	..
Belarus	28,735	2,870	7,550	-1.4	15	23	355.1	-0.5	851
Belgium	251,583	24,540	27,470	1.8	2	22	1.9	5.2	..
Belize	746	3,110i	5,240	1.6	21	32	2.7	-16.0	499
Benin	2,345	370	980	1.8	38	20	8.3	-7.7	1,599
Bermuda	..	..	..	..	..	..	3.5	..	..
Bhutan	479	590	1,440	3.4	33	49	9.5	-26.0	198
Bolivia	8,206	990	2,360	1.6	22	18	8.5	-5.6	5,762
Bosnia and Herzegovina	4,899	1,230	..	..	12	20	2.3	..	2,828
Botswana	5,280	3,300	7,170	2.3	4	20	9.7	10.2	413
Brazil	610,058	3,580	7,300	1.5	7	21	207.7	-4.1	237,953
Brunei	..	..e	..	-0.7	3	..	1.1	..	..
Bulgaria	12,391	1,520	5,560	-1.5	15	17	102.8	-5.8	10,026
Burkina Faso	2,422	210	970d	2.4	35	28	3.8	-3.0	1,332
Burundi	732	110	580d	-4.7	51	9	12.3	-7.1	1,100
Cambodia	3,150	260	1,440	2.0	37	15	24.6	-0.6	2,357
Cameroon	8,644	580	1,590	-0.8	44	16	5.1	-1.7	9,241
Canada	649,829	21,130	27,170	1.9	§	20	1.4	2.6	..
Cape Verde	588	1,330	4,760d	3.3	12	19	4.9	-11.6	327
Cayman Islands	..	..	..	..	..	..	..	..	..
Central African Republic	1,031	280	1,160d	-0.5	55	11	4.6	0.0	872
Chad	1,541	200	870d	-0.8	39	17	7.1	-11.2	1,116
Channel Islands	..	..	..	..	..	..	..	..	..
Chile	69,850	4,590	9,100	5.2	11	23	7.3	-1.4	36,978
China	1,062,919	840	3,920	9.2	16	37	7.1	1.9	149,800
Hong Kong, China	176,157	25,920	25,590	1.9	0	28	4.1	5.4	..
Macao, China	6,385	14,580	18,190	0.4	..	12	3.8	..	..
Colombia	85,279	2,020	6,060	1.1	14	12	21.1	0.4	34,081
Comoros	212	380	1,590d	-2.4	41	10	4.9	..	232
Congo, Dem. Rep.	..	..c	..	-8.2	§	§	1,423.1	-10.4	11,645
Congo, Rep.	1,735	570	570	-3.4	5	24	10.6	..	4,887
Costa Rica	14,510	3,810	7,980	3.0	9	17	17.2	-4.1	4,466
Côte d'Ivoire	9,591	600	1,500	0.4	29	12	7.5	-0.1	12,138
Croatia	20,240	4,620	7,960	1.8	9	22	86.2	-2.1	12,120
Cuba	..	..j	..	3.7	7	10	1.1	..	..
Cyprus	9,361	12,370	20,780d	3.1	§	19	3.5	-5.2	..
Czech Republic	53,925	5,250	13,780	1.0	4	30	11.5	-4.4	21,299
Denmark	172,238	32,280	27,250	2.1	3	22	2.2	1.5	..
Djibouti	553	880	..	-3.9	4	13	3.7	..	262
Dominica	..	..	..	3.0	17	29	3.0	-25.5	108
Dominican Republic	17,847	2,130	5,710	4.2	11	24	9.4	-5.2	4,598
Ecuador	15,256	1,210	2,910	-0.3	10	17	37.1	6.8	13,281
Egypt, Arab Rep.	95,380	1,490	3,670	2.5	17	24	8.2	-1.2	28,957
El Salvador	12,569	2,000	4,410	2.6	10	17	7.4	-3.2	4,023
Equatorial Guinea	363	800	5,600	18.9	7	38	14.9	..	248
Eritrea	696	170	960	1.1	17	38	9.4	-34.2	311
Estonia	4,894	3,580	9,340	1.0	6	26	53.1	-6.3	3,280
Ethiopia	6,737	100	660	2.4	52	14	7.0	-5.2	5,481
Faeroe Islands	..	..f	..	..	..	..	..	..	..
Fiji	1,480	1,820	4,480	0.7	18	13	3.3	1.1	136
Finland	130,106	25,130	24,570	2.4	4	20	1.9	7.3	..
France	1,438,293	24,090	24,420	1.3	3	21	1.5	1.6	..
French Polynesia	4,064	17,290	23,340	0.1	5	..	1.2	..	..
Gabon	3,928	3,190	5,360	0.1	6	26	6.2	7.8	3,995
Gambia, The	440	340	1,620d	-0.3	38	17	4.1	-11.5	471
Georgia	3,183	630	2,680	-12.4	32	15	387.5	-5.3	1,633
Germany	2,063,734	25,120	24,920	1.2	1	23	2.0	-1.0	..
Ghana	6,594	340	1,910d	1.8	35	24	26.7	-7.9	6,657
Greece	126,269	11,960	16,860	1.8	8	22	9.2	-8.7	..
Greenland	..	..	..	..	..	..	..	..	..
Grenada	370	3,770	6,960	2.9	8	39	2.5	-19.3	207
Guam	..	..e	..	..	..	..	..	..	..
Guatemala	19,164	1,680	3,770	1.4	23	17	10.3	-5.5	4,622
Guinea	3,303	450	1,930	1.7	24	22	5.1	-5.5	3,388
Guinea-Bissau	217	180	710	-1.1	59	18	32.5	..	942
Guyana	652	860	3,670	5.0	35	22	13.1	..	1,455
Haiti	4,059	510	1,470d	-2.7	28	11	20.3	-1.0	1,169
Honduras	5,517	860	2,400	0.4	18	35	18.8	-3.4	5,487
Hungary	47,249	4,710	11,990	1.9	6	31	19.3	-3.3	29,415
Iceland	8,540	30,390	28,710	1.8	9	23	3.2	-10.0	..
India	454,800	450	2,340	4.1	25	24	8.0	-0.6	99,062
Indonesia	119,871	570	2,830	2.5	17	18	15.5	5.2	141,803
Iran, Islamic Rep.	106,707	1,680	5,910	1.9	19	20	26.2	12.1	7,953
Iraq	..	..e	..	..	..	..	..	..	..
Ireland	85,979	22,660	25,520	6.5	4	23	3.5	-0.6	..
Isle of Man	..	..e	..	..	..	..	..	..	..
Israel	104,128	16,710	19,330	2.2	..	19	10.0	-1.3	..
Italy	1,163,211	20,160	23,470	1.4	3	20	3.8	-0.5	..
Jamaica	6,883	2,610	3,440	-0.4	6	27	24.1	-3.7	4,287
Japan	4,519,067	35,620	27,080	1.1	1	26	0.1	2.4	..
Jordan	8,360	1,710	3,950	1.0	2	20	3.2	0.7	8,226
Kazakhstan	18,773	1,260	5,490	-3.1	9	14	204.7	5.9	6,664
Kenya	10,610	350	1,010	-0.5	20	13	13.9	-2.3	6,295
Kiribati	86	950	..	0.5	21	..	3.8	..	..
Korea, Dem. Rep.	..	..e	..	..	..	..	..	..	..
Korea, Rep.	421,069	8,910	17,300	4.7	5	29	5.0	2.5	134,417
Kuwait	35,771	18,030	18,690	-1.4	§	11	3.0	39.3	..
Kyrgyz Republic	1,345	270	2,540	-5.1	39	16	110.2	-5.9	1,829
Lao PDR	1,519	290	1,540d	-3.9	53	20	27.0	6.2	2,499
Latvia	6,925	2,920	7,070	-2.3	4	27	49.2	-6.9	3,379
Lebanon	17,355	4,010	4,550	4.2	12	18	17.4	-18.6	10,311
Lesotho	1,181	580	2,590d	2.1	17	40	9.9	-16.8	716
Liberia	..	..c	..	..	..	..	..	..	..
Libya	..	..e	..	..	..	..	..	..	..
Liechtenstein	..	..	..	..	..	..	..	..	..
Lithuania	10,809	2,930	6,980	-2.9	8	21	75.2	-6.0	4,855
Luxembourg	18,439	42,060	45,470	4.1	1	21	2.2	8.2	..
Macedonia, FYR	3,696	1,820	5,020	-1.5	12	17	79.3	-3.0	1,465